Clearing OTC Derivatives in Europe

OXFORD EU FINANCIAL REGULATION SERIES

The *Oxford EU Financial Regulation Series* provides rigorous analysis of all aspects of EU Financial Regulation and covers the regulation of banks, capital markets, insurance undertakings, asset managers, payment institutions, and financial infrastructures. The series considers Brexit and third-country relations.

The aim of the series is to provide high-quality dissection of and comment on EU Regulations and Directives, and the EU financial regulation framework as a whole. Titles in the series consider the elements of both theory and practice necessary for proper understanding, analysing the legal framework in the context of its practical, political, and economic background, and offering a sound basis for interpretation.

Series Editors:

DANNY BUSCH

*Professor of Financial Law and founding Director of the Financial Law Centre (FLC),
Radboud University Nijmegen
Research Fellow at Harris Manchester College, and Fellow at the Commercial Law Centre,
University of Oxford
Visiting Professor at Università Cattolica del Sacro Cuore di Milano*

*Visiting Professor at Université de Nice Côte d'Azur
Member of the Academic Board of the European Banking Institute (EBI), Frankfurt
Member of the Appeals Committee of the Financial Services Complaints Tribunal
(Klachteninstituut Financiële Dienstverlening or KiFiD)*

GUIDO FERRARINI

*Emeritus Professor of Business Law, University of Genoa
Member of the Academic Board of the European Banking Institute (EBI), Frankfurt
Founder and fellow of the European Corporate Governance Institute (ECGI), Brussels
Former member of the Board of Trustees, International Accounting Standards Committee
(IASC), London*

VEERLE COLAERT

*Financial Law Professor and co-director of the Jan Ronse Institute for Company and Financial Law,
KU Leuven University
Chair of the Securities and Markets Stakeholder Group (SMSG) advising ESMA, Paris
Member of the Belgian Resolution Board, Brussels
Member of the Academic Board of the European Banking Institute (EBI), Frankfurt
Member of the Board of Directors of the European Association for Banking and Financial Law,
Belgian Branch (AEDBF Belgium), Brussels*

VOLUMES IN THE SERIES:

Busch and DeMott (eds): *Liability of Asset Managers* (published in 2012)
Van Setten and Busch (eds): *Alternative Investment Funds in Europe: Law & Practice* (published in 2014)
Busch and Ferrarini (eds): *European Banking Union* (published in 2015)
Busch and Ferrarini (eds): *Regulation of the EU Financial Markets: MiFID II & MiFIR* (published in 2017)
Busch, Avgouleas, and Ferrarini (eds): *Capital Markets Union in Europe* (published in 2018)
Busch, Ferrarini, and Solinge (eds): *Governance of Financial Institutions* (published in 2019)
Busch and Ferrarini (eds): *European Banking Union 2nd edn* (published in 2020)
Busch, Ferrarini, and Franx (eds): *Prospectus Regulation and Prospectus Liability* (published in 2020)
Ortolani and Louisse (eds): *The EU Crowdfunding Regulation* (published in 2021)
Binder and Saguato (eds): *Financial Market Infrastructures: Law and Regulation* (published in 2021)
Ventoruzzo and Mock (eds): *Market Abuse Regulation: Commentary and Annotated Guide 2nd edn*
(published in 2022)
Joosen, Lamandini, and Tröger (eds): *Capital and Liquidity Requirements for European Banks*
(published in 2022)
Busch, Gortsos, and McMeel (eds): *Liability of Financial Supervisors and Resolution Authorities*
(published in 2022)

Clearing OTC Derivatives in Europe

Edited by

BAS ZEBREGS, VICTOR DE SERIÈRE,
PATRICK PEARSON, AND REZAH STEGEMAN

OXFORD
UNIVERSITY PRESS

OXFORD
UNIVERSITY PRESS

Great Clarendon Street, Oxford, OX2 6DP,
United Kingdom

Oxford University Press is a department of the University of Oxford.
It furthers the University's objective of excellence in research, scholarship,
and education by publishing worldwide. Oxford is a registered trade mark of
Oxford University Press in the UK and in certain other countries

Published in the United States of America by Oxford University Press
198 Madison Avenue, New York, NY 10016, United States of America

British Library Cataloguing in Publication Data
Data available

Library of Congress Control Number: 2023943119

ISBN 978–0–19–286872–5

DOI: 10.1093/law/9780192868725.001.0001

Printed and bound by
CPI Group (UK) Ltd, Croydon, CR0 4YY

Preface by the Series Editors

The present volume offers in-depth analysis of another important area of European Union (EU) financial regulation: the law, regulation, and practice of over-the-counter (OTC) derivatives clearing. The authors—an outstanding group of practitioners and academics—focus on the gradual global development of a mandatory OTC derivatives clearing regime after the relevant deliberations of the G20 Pittsburgh Summit in 2009, and especially on the European Market Infrastructure Regulation (EMIR), which implemented a detailed regime in the EU through successive revisions and secondary legislation.

The volume complements two other titles in our series: *Regulation of the EU Financial Markets*, which includes the treatment of securities and derivatives trading under the Markets in Financial Instruments Directive (MiFID) and the Markets in Financial Instruments Regulation (MiFIR), and *Financial Market Infrastructures*, which offers the general framework for trading and post-trading infrastructures in the EU, the United States, and internationally. The resulting trilogy gives a sense of the impact and extent of financial market reform which has taken place in Europe and globally since the 2008 financial crisis and helps understanding of the theoretical and practical implications of the new EU measures from a comprehensive and interdisciplinary perspective. As the present volume shows, the reform is still in the making, and its impact still needs to be tested through practical experience and scholarly analysis. This creates a fascinating challenge to researchers in financial law and economics but also practical difficulties and uncertainties to clearing houses, intermediaries, and investors, which the present volume aims to reduce and possibly dissipate.

In particular, the fact that the United Kingdom, with London as the main financial centre within Europe, has left the EU adds complications, given that, from an EU perspective, some of the largest central counterparties (CCPs) are now located in 'third countries'. The effects of Brexit have been provisionally mitigated by the European regulators 'temporarily' recognizing UK CCPs. Moreover, EMIR was amended in 2019 (EMIR 2.2) with measures designed to enhance the supervision of third-country CCPs and make the supervision of EU CCPs more coherent. However, as the volume's editors argue, it is unclear how all this will play out in the end due to far wider political considerations, which may make it increasingly burdensome for market participants to remain globally active. In any case, Brexit adds another layer of uncertainty and complexity to the derivatives clearing markets, which the volume carefully analyses.

The Series Editors are very pleased to include the work in the Oxford EU Financial Regulation Series.

Danny Busch
Nijmegen, the Netherlands

Veerle Colaert
Leuven, Belgium

Guido Ferrarini
Genoa, Italy

Preface

This book aims to provide a comprehensive and practical guide to the legal, regulatory, and operational aspects of the over-the-counter (OTC) derivatives clearing industry in Europe. Clearing OTC derivatives is an essential element of the financial market infrastructure supporting the global financial services industry catering for the need of market participants to hedge various risks or create exposure through derivative contracts.

As a consequence of the way in which central counterparties (CCPs) managed to mitigate the impact of the Lehman Brothers' bankruptcy in 2008 and the financial crisis that followed, political leaders, legislators, and regulators quickly and unanimously concluded not only (i) that OTC derivatives clearing reduces systemic risk and enhances financial stability but also (ii) that CCPs themselves are systemically important institutions that can potentially raise issues of systemic risk. Until 2008, clearing OTC derivatives was largely unregulated and was mainly carried out 'bilaterally' between broker dealers. This has changed dramatically. In the European Union, the European Market Infrastructure Regulation (EMIR), which require clearing of designated OTC derivatives, has forced many end users into the clearing space. Consequently, the volume of cleared OTC derivatives has increased exponentially and CCPs are now recognized as being critically important for the effective and continuous functioning of the European financial system. This development means that all relevant stakeholders, including CCPs, clearing members (CMs), end users, and their respective regulators, need a thorough practical understanding of all aspects of the regulatory framework governing these infrastructures. Also, European legislators themselves need to be aware of certain inherent weaknesses and shortcomings in the regulatory regime and of possible ways to address them in the future. The editors hope that this book will help all stakeholders to improve their understanding of clearing and its intricacies and provide useful analyses to assist legislators and regulators in their own important ongoing efforts to maximize the effectiveness and practical workability of the legal framework applicable to these stakeholders.

Although OTC derivatives clearing has enjoyed a certain amount of academic attention in the aftermath of the financial crisis, authoritative publications on this complex subject matter remain scarce and narrowly focused on specific issues. This book intends to fill this gap by covering all relevant aspects of OTC derivatives clearing in Europe. It is written by a prominent group of authors who are widely recognized as authorities on the subject matters covered by this book. As OTC derivatives clearing is, by definition, multidisciplinary in nature, this book is not confined to strictly legal analyses. While acknowledging the fact that OTC derivatives clearing has important legal considerations as it is based on directly applicable law in the European Union Member

States' legal systems, a thorough understanding of the equally important wider dimensions of clearing, such as risk, commercial aspects, and the interconnectedness with trading and settlement platforms, as well as European politics, is crucial. This book accordingly aims to include, for the first time, a unique and comprehensive analysis of all relevant dimensions of this important segment of the European financial markets infrastructure.

The manuscript was completed end 2022. No account could be taken of developments since that date.

Bas Zebregs
Victor de Serière
Patrick Pearson
Rezah Stegeman
Amsterdam,
The Netherlands

Acknowledgements

It has been a great pleasure and privilege for the editors of this book to work with an outstanding group of authors, many of whom have been involved in shaping the European OTC derivatives clearing markets from the very beginning. We are grateful to all twenty-three authors for their enthusiasm, commitment, and willingness to bring this project to a successful close.

We would also like to thank the editors of the Oxford EU Financial Regulation Series, Professor Danny Busch, Professor Veerle Colaert and Professor Guido Ferrarini, for their positive and encouraging support. Finally, we are indebted to Rachel Mullaly and her team at the Oxford University Press for providing us with the necessary assistance during the editorial and publication process.

Contents

I. INTRODUCTION TO OTC DERIVATIVES CLEARING IN EUROPE

II. STRUCTURAL ELEMENTS OF CLEARING

III. DEFAULT MANAGEMENT

IV. THE TRANSACTION CHAIN

V. CROSS-BORDER ISSUES

VI. THE FUTURE OF OTC DERIVATIVES
CLEARING IN EUROPE

List of Figures

List of Tables

Table of Cases

Table of Legislation

Decisions

List of Abbreviations

AANA	average aggregate notional amount
AIG	American International Group
AIFMD	Alternative Investment Fund Managers Directive
ASX	Australian Stock Exchange
BaFin	Bundesanstalt für Finanzdienstleistungsaufsicht
BAU porting	business-as-usual porting
BBVA	Banco Bilbao Vizcaya Argentaria
BCBS	Basel Committee on Banking Supervision
BIS	Bank for International Settlements
BNY	Bank of New York
BoE	Bank of England
BRRD	Bank Recovery and Resolution Directive
BTC Network	Bitcoin Network
BU	Banking Union
CASS	Client Asset Sourcebook
CBI	central bank of issue
CBLC	Câmara Brasileira de Liquidação e Custódia
CBOT	Chicago Board of Trade
CCP	central counterparty
CCP SC	Central Counterparties Supervisory Committee
CCPR&R	CCP Recovery and Resolution Regulation
CCR	counterparty credit risk
CDM	common domain model
CDO	collateralized debt obligations
CDR	Commission Delegated Regulation
CDS	credit default swap
CEA	Commodity Exchange Act
CEBS	Committee of European Banking Supervisors
CEIOPS	Committee of European Insurance and Occupational Pensions Supervisors
CEO	chief executive officer
CEPS	Centre for European Policy Studies
CESR	Committee of European Securities Regulators
CFMA	Commodity Futures Modernisation Act
CFTC	Commodity Futures Trading Commission
CGFS	Committee on the Global Financial System
CLAM	Caisse de Liquidation des Affaires en Marchandises
CM	clearing member
CME	Chicago Mercantile Exchange
CMG	crisis management group
CMU	Capital Markets Union
COREPER	Committee of Permanent Representatives
CPMI	Committee on Payments and Market Infrastructures

CPSS	Committee on Payment and Settlement Systems
CRD	Capital Requirements Directive
CRR	Capital Requirements Regulation
CRO	chief risk officer
CSA	credit support annex
CSD	central securities depositary
CSDR	Central Securities Depositaries Regulation
CSFI	Centre for the Study of Financial Innovation
CSP	cloud service provider
CTM	collateralized to market
CVA	credit valuation adjustment
CVR	collateral valuation report
DAT	Derivatives Assessment Team
DC	Disclosed Client
DCM	direct clearing membership
DCO	Derivatives Clearing Organization
DCV	Depósito Central de Valores
DDoS	distributed denial of service
DG FISMA	Directorate-General for Financial Stability, Financial Services and Capital Markets Union
DLT	distributed ledger technology
DMG	default management group
DMP	debt management plan
DNO	declaration of no objectives
DORA	Digital Operational Resilience Act
DTCC	Depository Trust and Clearing Corporation
EACH	European Association of Clearing Houses
EAD	exposure at default
EBA	European Banking Agency
EBRD	European Bank for Reconstruction and Development
EC	European Commission
ECB	European Central Bank
ECDSA	Elliptical Curve Digital Signature Algorithm
ECJ	European Court of Justice
ECM	elementary clearing model
ECMI	European Capital Markets Institute
ECOFIN	Economic and Financial Affairs Council
ECON	European Parliament's Committee on Economic and Monetary Affairs
ECSDA	European Central Securities Depositories Association
EDIS	European Deposit Insurance Scheme
EEA	European Economic Area
EGMI	Expert Group on Market Infrastructures
EIOPA	European Insurance and Occupational Pensions Authority
ELA	emergency liquidity assistance
EMA	European Medicines Agency
EMIR	European Market Infrastructure Regulation
EP	European Parliament
EPE	expected positive exposure

EPTF	European Post Trade Forum
ESA	European Supervisory Authority
ESC	European Securities Council
ESCB	European System of Central Banks
ESMA	European Securities and Markets Authority
ESRB	European Systemic Risk Board
ETH	Ethereum
ETD	exchange-traded derivative
FC	financial counterparty
FCA	Financial Conduct Authority
FCM	futures commission merchant
FESE	Federation of European Securities Exchanges
FIA	Futures Industry Association
FICC	Fixed Income Clearing Corporation
FMI	financial market infrastructure
FINRA	Financial Industry Regulatory Authority
FOLTF	failing or likely to fail
FRA	forward rate agreement
FRANDT	fair, reasonable, non-discriminatory and transparent
FSA	Financial Services Authority
FSA 2021	Financial Services Act 2021
FSAP	Financial Services Action Plan
FSB	Financial Stability Board
FSOB	Financial Stability Oversight Board
FSMA	Financial Services and Markets Authority
FX	foreign exchange
GAAP	Generally Accepted Accounting Principles
GAO	General Accounting Committee
GCM	general clearing member
GDP	gross domestic product
GDPR	General Data Protection Regulation
GFC	global financial crisis
GOSA	gross omnibus segregated account
G-SIB	global systemically important bank
GSIM	gross standardized initial margin
HMT	His Majesty's Treasury
IAIS	International Association of Insurance Supervisors
ICCH	International Commodities Clearing House
ICEU	ICE Clear Europe Ltd
ICSD	international central securities depository
IDCM	ISA Direct clearing member
IFRS	International Financial Reporting Standards
IIF	Institute of International Finance
IM	initial margin
IMF	International Monetary Fund
IMM	internal models methodology
IOSCO	International Organization of Securities Commissions
IRD	interest rate derivatives

IRRD	Insurance Recovery and Resolution Directive
IRS	interest rate swaps
ISA	individually segregated account
ISDA	International Swaps and Derivatives Association
ISRB	Interactive Single Rulebook
JSCC	Japan Securities Clearing Corporation
KYC	know your customer
LCH	London Clearing House
LCR	Liquidity Coverage Ratio
LEI	Legal Entity Identifier
LSEG	London Stock Exchange Group
LSOC	legally segregated operationally commingled
LSV	legally segregated value
LTCM	Long-Term Capital Management
MAS	Monetary Authority of Singapore
MBS	mortgage-backed securities
MEP	Member of the European Parliament
MiFID	Markets in Financial Instruments Directive
MiFIR	Markets in Financial Instruments Regulation
MMoU	multilateral memorandum of understanding
MoU	memorandum of understanding
MPOR	margin period of risk
MSP	merchant services provider
MTF	multilateral trading facility
NASDAQ	National Association of Securities Dealers Automated Quotations
NCA	National Competent Authority
NCB	national central bank
NCD	non-cleared derivative
NCWO	no creditor worse off
New York Fed	New York Federal Reserve Bank
NFC	non-financial counterparty
NGFS	Network for Greening the Financial System
NGR	net-to-gross ratio
NICA	net independent collateral amount
NIS	network and information systems
NOSA	net omnibus segregated account
NQCCP	non-qualifying central counterparty
NRA	National Resolution Authority
NSIM	net standardized initial margin
NYSDFS	New York State Department of Financial Services
OATS	order audit trail system
OECD	Organisation for Economic Co-operation and Development
OIS	overnight index swaps
OSA	omnibus segregated account
O-SIB	other systematically important bank
OTC	over-the-counter
OTF	organized trading facility
P&L	profit and loss

PFMIs	Principles for Financial Market Infrastructures
P.R.I.M.E.	Panel of Recognised International Market Experts
PS	payment system
PSA	pension scheme arrangement
PWG	Presidential Working Group
QCCP	qualifying central counterparty
QE	quantitative easing
RTO	recovery time objective
RTS	regulatory technical standard
RWA	risk-weighted asset
SA–CCR	standardized approach for counterparty credit risk
SEB	Seaboard Corporate Common Stock
SEC	Securities Exchange Commission
SEF	swap execution facility
SFD	Settlement Finality Directive
SFT	security financing transaction
SFTR	Securities Financing Transactions Regulation
SI	systemically important
SIFI	systemically important financial institutions
SITG	skin in the game
SME	small and medium enterprises
SOFR	secured overnight financing rate
SoP	Statement of Policy
SRB	Single Resolution Board
SRMR	Single Resolution Mechanism Regulation
SRP	supervisory review process
SSS	securities settlement system
STIR	short-term interest rates
STM	settlement to market
STO	security token offering
STP	straight-through processing
SWIFT	Society for Worldwide Interbank Financial Telecommunications
T2S	TARGET2-Securities
TCA	Trade and Cooperation Agreement
TFEU	Treaty on the Functioning of the European Union
TLPT	threat-led penetration testing
TR	trade repository
TRR	temporary recognition regime
UBI	United Business Institutes
UCITS	Undertakings for Collective Investment in Transferable Securities
VaR	value at risk
VM	variation margin
VMGH	variation margin gains haircutting
V-SIFI	very systematically important financial institution
WA	European Union Withdrawal Agreement
WFE	World Federation of Exchanges

List of Contributors

Evariest Callens is a Manager in the financial regulatory team of EY Belgium and a Postdoctoral Researcher at the Financial Law Institute of Ghent University. His research focuses on the regulation and supervision of financial market infrastructures (FMIs). He has recently published the book *Regulation of Central Counterparties (CCPs) in Light of Systemic Risk* (Cambridge, 2022). Evariest holds a Master in Law, a Complementary Master of Science in Economics, and a PhD in Law, all from Ghent University.

Christian Chamorro-Courtland is an Assistant Professor in Law at the University of Dubai College of Law (UAE) and is an active member of the New York State Bar. He has a Bachelors (LLB) (2007) and Masters of Law (LLM) (2008) from King's College London (specialized in Commercial and Financial Law), and he completed his doctoral studies in Commercial, Financial, and Banking Law at Osgoode Hall Law School, York University (Canada) in 2012. His PhD thesis analysed the legal aspects and operations of central counterparty (CCP) clearing systems. He has fifteen years of university teaching experience in both law schools and business schools around the world, with a particular focus on business law subjects. He has published various peer-reviewed articles and book chapters and presented his research at various conferences around the world. He has special interests in CCPs and clearing and settlements systems, payment systems, fintech, consumer protection, financial regulation, and legal issues concerning the international financial markets.

Emma Dwyer is a partner in Allen & Overy's derivatives and structured finance team in London and advises on a broad range of issues relating to derivatives and structured finance transactions. Emma has been heavily involved in the evolving market infrastructure built to address the OTC derivatives regulation, including advising the International Swaps and Derivatives Association (ISDA) on the ISDA/Futures Industry Association (FIA) Cleared Derivatives Execution Agreement, the ISDA/FIA Client Cleared OTC Derivatives Addendum, the Markets in Financial Industries Directive II (MiFID II) and the Markets in Financial Instruments Regulation (MiFIR) Model Provisions for the Addendum, and related legal opinions. Emma has also advised the FIA on the impact of fair, reasonable, non-discriminatory, and transparent (FRANDT) clearing services. As a key market educator, Emma continues to speak at many industry events around the world on OTC derivatives regulation and is a Panel of Recognised International Market Experts (P.R.I.M.E.) Finance expert.

Tina Hasenpusch has more than twenty years of experience in derivatives and central clearing. She works for the CME Group, where she has been a managing director and member of the Clearing House Management Team since 2013. She is responsible for managing operations and risk of the Clearing House across its various global locations and for all OTC and exchange-traded products across the CME's multiple-asset classes. She also heads the area of banking and collateral management, responsible for administering the Clearing House's cash and non-cash collateral on deposit. Prior to this, she was the chief executive officer (CEO) for CME Clearing Europe. Tina has held various other senior leadership positions within the CME Group, following earlier roles at Barclays Investment Bank and Eurex. She has published academic articles and a book on the economics of central clearing. She is currently also a member of the ISDA's Board of Directors.

David Horner is the Chief Risk Officer of LCH Ltd, the UK clearing house. At LCH, he led the transition from LIBOR to risk-free rates, including the design and execution of USD discounting risk auction, and was part of the team responsible for liquidating the cleared portfolio of VTB Capital plc. Before joining LCH in 2014, David spent twelve years in various credit and market risk roles based in London, Hong Kong, and New York.

Julien Jardelot is Head of Europe, Government Relations & Regulatory Strategy at the London Stock Exchange Group (LSEG), supporting LSEG business developments on regulatory matters in Europe. Prior to that, Julien worked in the legal and regulatory and international affairs departments of the Autorité des Marchés Financiers on fund management and post-trade issues contributing to the French position on the UCTIS, the EMIR, the CSDR, the MIFIR, etc. He then joined the European Commission's Financial Markets Infrastructure Unit, where he worked on a wide variety of European Union and international post-trade issues. Julien Jardelot holds a law degree from the University Paris I Pantheon–Sorbonne and an MBA in Finance.

Ulrich Karl is Head of Clearing Services at the ISDA. Before that, he worked in various CCP and risk-related roles at HSBC. He holds an MSc in electrical engineering from Technische Universität Darmstadt.

Emma Lancelott is a professional support lawyer (PSL) Counsel at international law firm Allen & Overy. She has extensive experience of both derivatives and structured finance transactions, advising some of Allen & Overy's key sell-side and buy-side clients as well as trade associations. A key focus is advising on the regulatory developments affecting these markets such as EMIR, MiFIR, the Securities Financing Transactions Regulation (SFTR), bank recovery and resolution, sustainability, and the impact of Brexit.

Karel Lannoo is Chief Executive of the Centre for European Policy Studies (CEPS), Europe's leading independent European think tank, ranked among the top ten think tanks in the world. He is specialized in financial regulation, economic governance, and single market issues, while his recent publications cover European Union health-care sector policy, anti-money laundering, and crypto-currency regulation.

Rebecca Lewis is an associate at Sidley Austin L.L.P. She received her JD from Yale Law School in 2021. Prior to law school, Rebecca worked at the Federal Reserve Bank of Chicago as a financial markets analyst, where her work focused on derivatives regulation and financial market infrastructures.

Klaus Löber is the Chair of the CCP Supervisory Committee (CCP SC) and Director for CCPs at the European Securities Markets Authority (ESMA). He also chairs the ESMA CCP Policy Committee. Prior to joining ESMA, Klaus was Head of Oversight of the European Central Bank, in charge of the oversight of financial market infrastructures, payment instruments, and payment schemes. Earlier positions include the Committee on Payments and Market Infrastructures, the European Commission, Deutsche Bundesbank, and private practice.

David Murphy is a Visiting Professor in Practice in the Law School at the London School of Economics and Political Science. His practice focuses on derivatives regulation, central clearing, and prudential policy. He has published extensively in these areas and worked in both bank and CCP policy at national and international levels. His latest book, *Derivatives Regulation: Rules and Reasoning from Lehman to Covid* appeared from OUP in March 2022.

Patrick Pearson has spent more than three decades in financial services regulation at the European Commission, where he was responsible for European Union banking regulation until 2010 and for derivatives clearing and post-trade regulation until 2021. He has represented the European Commission in the Basel Committee on Banking Supervision and Committee on

Payments and Market Infrastructure–International Organization of Securities Commissions (CPMI–IOSCO) and co-chaired the G20 Financial Stability Board (FSB) Working Group on cross-border derivative issues. Patrick has been a frequent speaker representing the European Commission in public events and has lectured at a number of universities. He has a law degree from Leiden University and lives in the Netherlands, where he also works for various charitable organizations.

Marc Peters works for the European Commission Directorate-General for Financial Stability, Financial Services and Capital Markets Union (DG FISMA). He was previously advisor in the prudential policy and supervision areas at the National Bank of Belgium. He is a research fellow at CEBRIG, Université Libre de Bruxelles, Belgium.

Corentine Poilvet-Clediere is Head of the Repo Clearing, Collateral and Liquidity within LCH S.A. and, as such, heads the global pool of Euro-denominated cleared repos. Corentine is a group leader at the London Stock Exchange, which she joined ten years ago. During this period, she held various positions, including Global Head of Regulatory Strategy, and participated in the creation of the credit default swaps clearing business for LCH. Prior to this, she worked in investment banking in New York City. Corentine holds three masters degrees in France (Science Po), the United Kingdom (University of Bristol), and the United States (Harvard Business School).

Randy Priem is an adjunct professor of finance at UBI Business School (in partnership with Middlesex University) in Brussels, guest professor at Antwerp Management School, and research associate at the Katholieke Universiteit Leuven and Université Saint-Louis Brussels. He teaches financial management and financial markets courses as well as a FinTech and blockchain course. In addition, he is the coordinator of the markets and post-trading unit at the FSMA. In this respect, besides supervising trading and post-trading financial market infrastructures, he represents the FSMA at the ESMA markets standing committee, the post-trading working group, the distributed ledger technology working group, the data standing committee, and the CCP policy committee. Randy Priem is also a member of six colleges of supervisors monitoring CCPs and he was closely involved as a financial expert when EMIR and the CCP Recovery and Resolution Regulation were drafted. He often represents Belgium at the European Council when trade and post-trade regulations are being drafted or reviewed. He holds a PhD in Business Economics from the Katholieke Universiteit Leuven and worked as a visiting researcher at the Schulich School of Business in Toronto.

Christina Sell has been working for Deutsche Börse Group for more than twenty years. Before her promotion as Chief Sustainability Officer Trading & Clearing in 2021, she headed different teams in the exchange and clearing organization, with a strong focus on regulatory topics and client services. She studied German literature, political science, and history at the Goethe University of Frankfurt am Main with a degree Magister Artium.

Victor de Serière is an attorney at law working with the Amsterdam offices of Allen & Overy, of which he was a partner until 2009, and a Professor of Securities Law (civil law aspects) at Radboud University of Nijmegen, the Netherlands. His practice and university lecturing focus on financial regulatory work. He has published books and numerous papers on financial legal issues, and he is the author of the leading handbook on Dutch securities law (*Asser Effectenrecht* (Deventer, 2018)).

Manmohan Singh is with the IMF and writes extensively on topical issues including collateral velocity (a term he coined), monetary policy and collateral, and (recently) digital money and central bank operations and stablecoins. His new book, *Collateral Markets and Financial Plumbing* (3rd edn, London, 2020), staples together his decade-long research in this area, and his short policy articles can be found on his website, https://sites.google.com/view/msinghdc/home.

Rezah Stegeman works at the international law firm Simmons & Simmons (Amsterdam), where he has been a partner since 2013. He specializes in financial services regulation, derivatives, and clearing, advising both buy-side and sell-side clients. Rezah is a returning guest lecturer at two universities (the Vrije Universiteit Amsterdam and the Radboud Universiteit Nijmegen), the Law Firm School for trainee lawyers, and the Grotius Post-Graduate Financial Law Academy Regulatory for lawyers and in-house counsels. Furthermore, he established the Amsterdam Derivatives Academy in 2014, a four-monthly symposium which is the leading industry event for derivatives practitioners in the Netherlands.

Apostolos Thomadakis, PhD, is Research Fellow at the European Capital Markets Institute (ECMI). His work focuses on issues related to capital markets, financial markets and services, and market infrastructure. He has managed, coordinated, and contributed to various research projects on capital markets union (CMU), derivatives, small and medium enterprises (SMEs) financing, financial instruments, financial services, and regulation for European institutions and other organizations.

Dermot Turing worked for the Government Legal Service and then the international law firm Clifford Chance, where he was a partner until 2014. His specialism was financial sector regulation, financial market infrastructure, and bank failures. Dermot is a trustee of the Turing Trust and a Visiting Fellow at Kellogg College, Oxford.

Bas Zebregs is head of the financial markets team within the legal department of APG Asset Management with a primary focus on derivatives, clearing, custody, and settlement. Before joining APG in 2009, he worked at the legal department of Euroclear S.A. He teaches on clearing and settlement at the Grotius Post-Graduate Financial Law Academy, a fellow at the Financial Law Institute of the University of Nijmegen and the author of several publications on clearing and settlement-related topics.

I
INTRODUCTION TO OTC DERIVATIVES CLEARING IN EUROPE

1

After the Dust Has Settled

Clearing OTC Derivatives in Europe after a Decade of Regulation

Bas Zebregs, Victor de Serière, Patrick Pearson, and Rezah Stegeman

1 General

Following the financial crisis of 2007/2008 lawmakers, regulators, and practitioners have become acutely aware of the need to have a clearing infrastructure in place that is effective, dependable, and with a guaranteed continuity to the furthest extent practically feasible. This applies in particular to the global derivatives markets, which, until a decade-and-a-half ago, could best be described as fragmented in terms of liquidity, law, and supervision. Those dealing with over-the-counter (OTC) derivatives will immediately recognize the unambiguous statement of the G20 at the Pittsburgh Summit in 2009, which was the clearest, although as Chapter 3 'Development of the Regulatory Regime for OTC Derivatives Clearing' by Patrick Pearson in this volume explains not the first, wake-up call for lawmakers and regulators to act:[1]

All standardised OTC derivative contracts should be traded on exchanges or electronic trading platforms, where appropriate, and cleared through central counterparties by end-2012 at the latest. OTC derivative contracts should be reported to

---

[1] G20, 'Leaders' Statement', the Pittsburgh Summit (24–25 September 2009), p. 9, https://www.oecd.org (accessed 23 March 2023).

trade repositories. Non centrally cleared contracts should be subject to higher capital requirements.

This statement set in motion the global development of a mandatory OTC derivatives clearing regime. The G20 statement essentially required all OTC derivatives to be traded—as much as possible—on regular trading venues and cleared by central counterparties (CCPs), as such resembling traditional exchange-traded derivatives (ETDs), to the effect that the OTC derivatives markets (and its inherent risks) reduce systemic risk and become more transparent. Although many European market participants initially remained to be persuaded by means of such a mandatory regulatory clearing regime, sometimes preferring the traditional bilateral arrangements but at the cost of untransparent and often under-collateralized trades, markets have now become more accustomed to the use of central clearing facilities. Consequently, although the volume of non-centrally traded and cleared derivatives remains substantial (see section 2 below), it is undeniable that there has been a significant push towards trading venues and central clearing (see Chapter 13 'Clearing and Trading and Settlement' by Apostolos Thomadakis and Karel Lannoo in this volume). However, as explained below, central clearing of OTC derivatives is relatively new, and there is still a significant amount of work in progress.

1.1 A Developing Market

One should appreciate that the centrally cleared OTC derivatives markets are a relatively recent phenomenon. Although this development is described in more detail in Chapter 3 'Development of the Regulatory Regime for OTC Derivatives Clearing' by Patrick Pearson in this volume, the following milestone dates give an idea of the relative infancy of this market:

- In 2008, Lehman defaulted, followed by the G20 summit response calling for regulation in 2009.
- In 2009, SwapClear was the first European CCP to offer client clearing.[2] Until then, the OTC derivatives clearing activities had taken place mainly bilaterally, between dealer banks or on an intra-group basis.
- In 2012, EMIR was adopted, introducing mandatory clearing of designated OTC derivatives, regulatory requirements for CCPs, stricter rules for uncleared OTC derivatives, and a reporting obligation for derivatives to central trade repositories.[3]
- The first clearing obligation for designated interest rate derivatives entered into force between June 2016 and December 2018, followed by a second clearing

---

[2] The term 'client', as defined in Art. 2(15) of the European Market Infrastructure Regulation (EMIR), refers to market participants who access the CCP via a clearing member (CM).

[3] Regulation (EU) No. 648/2012 of the European Parliament and of the Council of 4 July 2012 on OTC derivatives, central counterparties and trade repositories, [2012] OJ L201/1 (27 July 2012) (EMIR).

obligation for designated index credit default swaps, which entered into force between February 2017 and May 2019.[4]

- On 12 August 2022, most provisions of a new Regulation on the recovery and resolution of CCPs entered into force.[5]

These milestones indeed suggest that the markets for central clearing of OTC derivatives markets are potentially immature in some aspects. In reality, it has taken years to fully implement EMIR, which is a directly applicable 'regulation' that does not require national transposition laws, and its second layer of required technical rules and regulations. CCPs and CMs are still in the process of developing their offerings. Many regulatory features remain untested, including important aspects like a default of major CMs or a CCP (see Chapters 10 'Segregation and Portability of Cleared OTC Derivatives in Europe' by Bas Zebregs and 12 'Recovery and Resolution of CCPs' by Victor de Serière in this volume).

1.2 Brexit

Although this book focuses on Europe, the markets for cleared OTC derivatives have always been global in nature. However, the fact that the United Kingdom, with London as the main financial centre within Europe, has left the European Union (EU) will certainly add complications as it places some of the largest CCPs outside of the boundaries of the EU. The effects of Brexit have—in the words of the European Commission—been 'temporarily' mitigated as the European regulators have 'temporarily' recognized UK CCPs (see Chapters 3 'Development of the Regulatory Regime for OTC Derivatives Clearing' by Patrick Pearson, 15 'Cross-Border Clearing' by Ulrich Karl, and 16 'Brexit: Equivalence; Location Policy' by Dermot Turing in this volume). It is unclear, though, how this will play out in the end due to far wider political considerations, but it may lead to further bifurcation of global trading blocks, making it increasingly burdensome for market participants to remain globally active. In any case, Brexit will add another layer of uncertainty and complexity to these markets and may even potentially make Europe less attractive as a whole.[6]

In this respect, it is noteworthy that on 7 December 2022 the European Commission issued a proposal to amend (dubbed: EMIR 3.0) which includes a controversial

---

[4] Regulation (EU) No. 2015/2205 contains a clearing obligation for certain interest rate derivatives in EUR/USD/GBP and was phased-in depending on the type and size of the relevant market participants, starting with CMs. Regulation (EU) No. 2016/5092 contains a similar clearing obligation for iTraxx credit default swap (CDS) transactions and has a similar phased-in approach.

[5] Regulation (EU) No. 2021/23 of the European Parliament and of the Council of 16 December 2020 on a framework for the recovery and resolution of central counterparties, [2021] OJ L22/1 (22 January 2021).

[6] UK CCPs benefit from a temporary equivalence until 30 June 2025. Brexit also resulted in a major overhaul of the EMIR recognition requirements for third-country CCPs. See Regulation (EU) No. 2019/2099 of the European Parliament and of the Council of 23 October 2019 amending Regulation (EU) No. 648/2012 as regards the procedures and authorities involved for the authorisation of CCPs and requirements for the recognition of third-country CCPs, [2019] OJ L322/1 (22 December 2019), (usually called EMIR 2.2).

proposal to introduce an obligation for EU market participants to clear a proportion of systemically important derivatives within the EU (active account obligation).[7] This can be regarded as the implementation of a partial location policy, which may lead to market fragmentation and further friction between the EU and other countries, in particular the United Kingdom and the United States, as this is another sign that the EU is moving away from the international practice of mutual recognition and deference. However, this is still a proposal and it is too early to say how this will play out.

Before briefly describing the approach and contents of this book, some market data is provided on the OTC derivatives clearing markets in Europe to illustrate the scope and scale of the sector (see also Chapter 13 'Clearing and Trading and Settlement' by Apostolos Thomadakis and Karel Lannoo in this volume).

2 Market Data

2.1 Market Size (Post Brexit)

In December 2021, the European Securities and Markets Authority (ESMA), issued its annual statistical report on the EU's derivatives markets, stating that, at the end of 2020, this market had reached an outstanding notional amount of EUR 244 trillion.[8] This is two-thirds less than at the end of 2019, when a notional amount of EUR 681 trillion was reported. This difference is almost entirely caused by the fact that the United Kingdom has left the EU, which underlines the enormous impact that this departure has had on the European OTC derivatives markets. Furthermore, about half of the contracts reported involved a counterparty from the United Kingdom.

2.2 Trading

About 8% of the total outstanding notional amount of EUR 244 trillion concerns ETDs, which means that the OTC derivatives markets were about twelve times the size of the ETD markets. However, it has to be taken into account that EMIR defines OTC derivatives as all derivatives contracts executed outside of a regulated market and therefore

---

[7] Proposal for a Regulation of the European Parliament and of the Council amending Regulations (EU) No. 648/2012, (EU) No. 575/2013, and (EU) 2017/1131 as regards measures to mitigate excessive exposures to third-country central counterparties and improve the efficiency of Union clearing markets, 7 December 2022, COM(2022) 697 final (usually called EMIR 3.0). The EMIR 3.0 proposal is accompanied by a Proposal for a Directive of the European Parliament and of the Council amending Directives 2009/65/EU, 2013/36/EU, and (EU) 2019/2034 as regards the treatment of concentration risk towards central counterparties and the counterparty risk on centrally cleared derivative transactions, 7 December 2022, COM(2022) 698 final. As the final manuscript for this book was already completed, these proposals have not been discussed in depth.

[8] ESMA, 'EU Derivatives Markets, ESMA Annual Statistical Report 2021' (17 December 2021), ESMA 50-165-2001, https://www.esma.europa.eu (accessed 23 March 2023) (ESMA Statistical Report 2021).

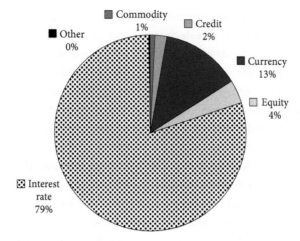

Figure 1.1 Types of OTC derivatives (EU)
Source: ESMA Statistical Report 2021

includes OTC derivatives executed on other trading venues including multilateral trading facilities (MTFs) and organized trading facilities (OTFs).[9]

ESMA also reported that, in 2020, of the 92% OTC derivatives, 16% were executed on trading venues while 76% of 'traditional' OTC derivatives were executed bilaterally between counterparts. In the previous year, only 10% of OTC derivatives were traded on venue, and it is expected that the volume of OTC derivatives traded on trading venues will further increase in the coming years.

2.3 Types of OTC Derivatives

Although many OTC derivatives are fairly bespoke in nature, the general types of OTC derivatives referred to in Figure 1.1 can be distinguished. Based on outstanding notional amounts, 79% of the EUR 244 trillion consist of interest rate derivatives and provide for the greater part of contracts in the market.[10]

2.4 Clearing Rates

As mentioned above, whereas OTC derivatives were traditionally largely unregulated, the regulatory obligation to clear designated OTC derivatives via CCPs has resulted in an enormous growth of the cleared OTC derivatives markets. At the beginning of 2017,

---

[9] EMIR (n 3), Art. 2(7).

[10] Derived from the ESMA Statistical Report 2021 (n 8), pp. 9 and 11. Interest rate derivatives have, by their nature, higher notional amounts. Based on outstanding amount of transactions, the picture is very different, with 41% of outstanding transactions being equity derivatives, 30% currency derivatives, and only 16% interest rate derivatives.

when the first clearing obligation requirements began to take effect, these percentages amounted to 49% for interest rate derivatives and 22% for credit derivatives.[11] Since then, the clearing rates have steadily increased. By the end of 2020, approximately 71% of all interest rate derivatives and 41% of all credit derivatives in the EU were cleared through CCPs.[12] The clearing rates for OTC derivatives classes subject to the clearing obligation are obviously much higher, that is, more than 90% for both designated interest rate and credit derivatives. These figures indicate that voluntary clearing has also increased significantly.

Although additional clearing exemptions have been introduced in order to exempt smaller market participants from the clearing obligation,[13] the main trend is unmistakably towards clearing. This has been incentivized by a wide range of developments, including higher capital requirements for uncleared derivatives as well as the fact that more and more (larger) counterparties must also exchange initial margin for uncleared OTC derivatives.[14] Furthermore, the expiration, in June 2023, of the clearing exemption for pension arrangements, which are significant players in the OTC derivatives markets, is likely to give another impetus to central clearing. In addition, the fact that more and more market participants have become accustomed to clearing OTC derivatives and have taken measures to put the relevant infrastructure in place means that liquidity in the uncleared markets will decrease and that clearing OTC derivatives is inexorably becoming market practice.

2.5   Access to Clearing

Against this background, the question whether clients have sufficient access to clearing remains critical. The entry barrier set by CMs is fairly high, which is understandable from a risk management perspective. However, the downside is that the number of available CMs is fairly limited as compared to the amount of available counterparties in bilateral OTC markets. This causes concerns because the clearing obligation, which is deemed beneficial from a systemic risk perspective, can only be effective if sufficient CCPs and CMs are available in the market. This is relevant not only in good times but also during periods of market stress, when a CM may default. It is doubtful whether

[11] ESMA, 'EU Derivatives Markets, ESMA Annual Statistical Report 2018' (18 October 2018), ESMA 50-165-670, https://www.esma.europa.eu (accessed 23 March 2023) (ESMA Statistical Report 2018).

[12] At the end of 2019, these percentages were 68% and 38%, respectively, and these clearing rates will be steadily rising. According to Bank for International Settlements (BIS) OTC Derivatives Statistics, 12 May 2022 (worldwide), by the end of 2021, the clearing rates were 78% for interest rate derivatives (IRD) and 62% for credit derivatives, https://www.bis.org (accessed 23 March 2023).

[13] Regulation (EU) No. 2019/834 of the European Parliament and of the Council of 20 May 2019 amending Regulation (EU) No. 648/2012 as regards the clearing obligation, the suspension of the clearing obligation, the reporting requirements, the risk-mitigation techniques for OTC derivative contracts not cleared by a central counterparty, the registration and supervision of trade repositories and the requirements for trade repositories, [2019] OJ L141/42 (28 May 2019) (usually called EMIR REFIT).

[14] Commission Delegated Regulation (CDR) EU/2016/2251 of 4 October 2016 supplementing Regulation (EU) No. 648/2012 of the European Parliament and of the Council on OTC derivatives, central counterparties and trade repositories with regard to regulatory technical standards for risk-mitigation techniques for OTC derivative contracts not cleared by a central counterparty, [2016] OJ L340/9 (15 December 2016).

sufficient clearing capacity and a willingness to accept new clients will be available in a situation of financial distress. CCP access structures and the potential for porting client positions are dealt with in Chapters 4 'CCP Access Structures' by Christina Sell and 10 'Segregation and Portability of Cleared OTC Derivatives in Europe' by Bas Zebregs in this volume.

In section 3, we provide a short outline of the book.

3 Outline of the Book

This book aims to offer a comprehensive and practical guide to the legal, regulatory, and operational aspects of the OTC derivatives clearing industry in Europe. Clearing OTC derivatives is an essential part of the financial market infrastructure supporting the global financial services industry. Importantly, OTC derivatives clearing performs a critical function catering for the need of market participants to hedge risks. As a response to the financial crisis, central clearing has also added greater safety and transparency in the financial sector. Nevertheless, although the main risks have been addressed, they have not disappeared altogether.

This book consists of six parts, which provide an in-depth analysis of all relevant aspects of the entire operation of clearing OTC derivatives. Each part may be referred to in itself by the reader as guidance for the specific issues addressed in that part.

3.1 Part I: Introduction to OTC Derivatives Clearing in Europe

This introductory chapter (Chapter 1 'After the Dust Has Settled: Clearing OTC Derivatives in Europe after a Decade of Regulation' by Bas Zebregs, Victor de Serière, Patrick Pearson, and Rezah Stegeman) is followed by a general description of the concept of OTC derivatives clearing (Chapter 2 'OTC Derivatives Clearing Explained' by Tina Hasenpusch and Rezah Stegeman).

Chapter 3 'Development of the Regulatory Regime for OTC Derivatives Clearing' by Patrick Pearson examines the many efforts by public authorities to regulate OTC derivatives since the 1980s. The global, US, and particularly the EU's regulatory regime and its subsequent revisions and CCP recovery and resolution are explained. The difficulties of EU supervision of the sector and, later, the difficulties caused by Brexit are discussed to provide a holistic perspective of how and why OTC derivative regulation came about in the EU. It explains that, although the EU's regulatory framework and most of its details are in place, work continues on technical interpretation questions, practical implementation issues, and, importantly, the uncertainty of the ramifications of Brexit and the EU's stated determination to reduce its dependency on, and exposure to, financial instability caused by critical clearing infrastructure located outside of the EU.

3.2 Part II: Structural Elements of Clearing

Chapter 4 'CCP Access Structures' by Christina Sell considers CCP membership structures where end users (may) have an option to become a direct CM or access the CCP
through a CM (client clearing) or through another intermediary (indirect clearing). In
addition, interesting alternative structures that have been developed by CCPs and CMs
are described.

The different methods used by CCPs to effect 'counterparty substitution' between
the CCP and its CMs are described in Chapter 5 'Clearing Mechanics' by Christian
Chamorro-Courtland. CCPs are able to interpose themselves between the CMs of the
clearing system and assume their obligations through the contractual mechanisms of
novation and open offer.

Chapter 6 'OTC Derivatives Clearing and Collateral Management' by Manmohan
Singh examines the important role of collateral in the OTC derivatives market and the
associated drawbacks in the regulatory initiatives moving these contracts to CCPs. As
cross-border issues continue to unfold, this chapter notes that these issues remain topical, mainly attributable to the absence of legal certainty and the inability to effectively
deal with certain key aspects, including shortage of collateral in the eurozone and the
consequences of Brexit.

The various political controversies relating to the ownership structure and the functioning and governance of CCPs are analysed in Chapter 7 ('What Kind of a Thing Is a
Central Counterparty? The Role of Clearing Houses as a Source of Policy Controversy'
by Rebecca Lewis and David Murphy) based on three stylized CCP models: utilities,
for-profit corporations under shareholder primacy, and clubs. The authors suggest
that, ultimately, stakeholder theories may provide a way forward to resolve these
conflicts.

Chapter 8 'OTC Derivatives Clearing Documentation' by Emma Dwyer and Emma
Lancelott provides an in-depth introduction to OTC derivatives clearing documentation, in particular between the CMs and their clients. Various standardization developments, including those of the International Swaps and Derivatives Association/
Futures Industry Association (ISDA/FIA), are described, and various regulatory obligations as to contract documentation, including EMIR requirements that clearing
services are to be 'fair, reasonable, non-discriminatory and transparent' (FRANDT),
are analysed.

The final chapter in Part II, Chapter 9 'Capital Requirements for Bank Exposures
to CCPs' by Marc Peters, provides an overview of the bank capital requirements that
apply to exposures to central clearing counterparties, in particular in the context of the
central clearing mandate of OTC derivatives. Although both sets of regulation, central
clearing and bank capital requirements, were developed separately by different global
standard setters (Committee on Payments and Market Infrastructure–International
Organization of Securities Commissions (CPMI–IOSCO) and the Basel Committee),
the incentive for central clearing binds the two regulatory regimes. The chapter

therefore also reviews the margin requirements for non-centrally cleared derivatives and illustrates the regulatory and supervisory incentives to central clearing that have been implemented through the past decade. Some of the challenges lying ahead are also identified.

3.3 Part III: Default Management

The third part of this book focuses on the regulatory efforts to prevent, and ultimately reduce, the costs of default in the clearing space. Chapter 10 'Segregation and Portability of Cleared OTC Derivatives in Europe' by Bas Zebregs deals with the segregation and portability of client positions and associated collateral in case a CM defaults. This chapter describes the segregation models as imposed by EMIR as well as the models that are actually offered in practice, including private omnibus models, value segregation models and different margin models. This is followed by a description of the portability framework as well as the main hurdles—including any potential insolvency complications—that may prevent or complicate porting or the return of assets.

Chapter 11 'Default Management' by David Horner considers default management from the CCP's perspective. This chapter seeks to understand how a modern CCP prepares itself to be successful in this discipline. Important default management logistics and tools are critically examined, including default decision-making processes, fire drills, hedging, auctions, client porting, and loss allocation principles and requirements. Historic examples of CCP default management illustrate the main issues involved.

Finally, Chapter 12 'Recovery and Resolution of CCPs' by Victor de Serière concludes with the unlikely, but potentially catastrophic, financial and economic consequences of a (potential or real) CCP default. CCP recovery and resolution is topical since the EU adopted the first regulation in the world in 2020 to comprehensively cover this subject. The new Regulation is critically assessed in this chapter.

3.4 Part IV: The Transaction Chain

Part IV of this book takes a closer look at the various regulatory aspects relating to the transaction chain.[15] Chapter 13 'Clearing and Trading and Settlement' by Apostolos Thomadakis and Karel Lannoo highlights that a few global financial centres have specialized, and are now clearing the lion's share of global trades. This is especially relevant to London, which currently clears over 90% of the global market in currencies such as

---

[15] There are a number of regulations impacting on clearing and settlement in Europe. While this book covers the transaction chain, it does not reflect on the legal issues concerning settlement and finality, which are currently the subject of substantial revision by the European Commission.

euros and dollars. Concerns about the concentration of risk in third-country CCPs and foreign currency exposure has been an issue among EU policymakers and supervisors for the past two decades. This chapter calls for a long-term vision for the future of the European clearing market by taking financial stability, efficiency, and market development objectives into account.

Chapter 14 'Open Access for OTC Derivatives: Concept and Implications' by Corentine Poilvet-Clediere and Julien Jardelot explores the concept of open access for OTC derivatives introduced under EMIR and MiFID II[16] requirements, as opposed to the regime applicable to exchange-traded derivatives, equities, and other asset classes. In this chapter, the origins of the concept, its implications, and how it works in practice are described as well as the expected benefits in terms of transparency, efficiency, innovation, settlement, and competition.

3.5 Part V: Cross-Border Issues

As mentioned above, the OTC-derivative market is inherently global in nature. Chapter 15 'Cross-Border Clearing' by Ulrich Karl focuses on issues relating to cross-border transactions. It describes the regulatory treatment of third-country (non-EU) CCPs and operational aspects of cross-border clearing, including the management of risks to which CCPs and CMs are exposed in a cross-border setting. The global OTC derivatives market will typically involve multiple jurisdictions. This will give rise not only to operational challenges but also to potential conflicts of laws. Different jurisdictions may govern different parts of the clearing process, and stakeholders in the clearing process must be aware of, and be able to effectively deal with, the complexities and risks involved. Chapter 15 aims to provide practical guidance to prepare for any potential pitfalls.

The consequences of Brexit for the OTC derivatives clearing industry are considered in Chapter 16 'Brexit: Equivalence; Location Policy' by Dermot Turing. At present (2023), the clearing of OTC derivatives remains to a large extent concentrated in the City of London, while the United Kingdom benefits from temporary transitional arrangements. The United Kingdom is still subject to a UK replication of EMIR, but this is likely to change over time. Brexit raises the question of regulatory 'equivalence' between the EU and the UK regulatory regimes and gives rise to political considerations of '(re-) location' policies. The applicable rules, possible steps, procedures, and timelines for decisions to be taken by the various actors involved are described, providing guidance as to how to achieve continuity of the operations of the London-based clearing houses as providers of clearing services to CMs and clients in the EU.

---

[16] Directive 2014/65/EU of the European Parliament and of the Council of 15 May 2014 on markets in financial instruments and amending Directive 2002/92/EC and Directive 2011/61/EU, [2014] OJ L173/349 (12 June 2014) (MiFID II).

3.6 Part VI: The Future of OTC Derivatives Clearing in Europe

The final part of this book looks ahead to future challenges for the sector. Chapter 17 'Potential Impact of the Distributed Ledger Technology on OTC Derivatives Markets' by Randy Priem focuses on the potential impact of the distributed ledger technology (DLT) on OTC derivatives markets. The chapter first explains the detailed operation of DLT and/or blockchains. After clarifying the basic concepts, the current trading life cycle is documented, followed by a discussion on how DLT could make the existing life cycle more efficient. This chapter focuses not only on the potential advantages of DLT but also on new risks that this technology might create. The chapter ends with a description of the evolution of regulatory approaches in this area.

The concluding chapter of this book (Chapter 18 'The Future of Centrally Cleared OTC Derivatives Markets' by Evariest Callens and Klaus Löber) discusses the future of OTC derivatives clearing in a wider perspective. Reflections are structured around the following elements: four emerging areas of risk (cyber risk, environmental risk, risk associated with new technologies, and legal risk) and the friction between the cross-border nature of centrally cleared OTC derivatives markets and the primarily domestic or regional regulatory and supervisory approach towards CCPs as well as CCP governance.

4 Conclusion

As a consequence of the way in which CCPs responded to the bankruptcy of Lehman Brothers in 2008 and enabled financial markets to continue to operate during the financial crisis, legislators and regulators immediately and unanimously concluded not only (i) that OTC derivatives clearing reduces systemic risk and enhances financial stability but also (ii) that CCPs themselves are systemically important institutions that can potentially raise issues of systemic risk.

This has led to a detailed European regulatory regime covering the clearing and trading of OTC derivatives. The mandatory clearing requirement for specific OTC derivatives has forced many end users into the clearing space. The volume of centrally cleared OTC derivatives has increased exponentially. In turn, the (systemic) importance of CCPs for the financial system has grown: the risk has not disappeared but has been moved into a relatively small number of financial infrastructures that have now become major nodes of systemic risk. This means that all relevant stakeholders, including CCPs, CMs, end users, and their respective regulators, need a thorough practical understanding of all legal and operational aspects of the regulatory framework governing these infrastructures, including any inherent weaknesses and how to mitigate any challenges and shortcomings.

It must be recognized that the current regulatory regime addressing the various complexities and challenges identified in this book is a work in progress and remains largely untested. The editors hope and expect that this book will enhance the practical understanding of the regime as it has evolved into its present state and that this book may provide insights and guidance to legislators and regulators as to how the regulatory regime could be improved going forward. Finally, it is also hoped that the book will serve as a useful practical guide for all those who are directly or indirectly involved in the clearing and settlement of OTC derivative transactions.

2

OTC Derivatives Clearing Explained

Tina Hasenpusch and Rezah Stegeman*

1 Introduction

The life cycle of a trade consists of trading, clearing, and settlement. Clearing and settlement are commonly referred to as post-trade services. Whilst settlement refers to the fulfilment of the legal obligation (e.g. delivery of an underlying), clearing is the process that occurs in between execution and settlement. While financial instruments such as securities (e.g. shares and bonds) and exchange-traded derivatives (ETDs, e.g. options and futures) have been cleared by central counterparties (CCPs) for more than a century,[1] over-the-counter (OTC) derivatives are the latest to the game, being cleared only since 1999.[2] However, OTC derivatives clearing was given a tremendous boost in 2009 when, following the global financial crisis of 2007–2008, the G20 leaders called for mandatory central clearing of standardized derivatives in recognition of the risk management benefits offered by CCPs.[3] Since then, the percentage of cleared interest rate derivatives has quadrupled to 78% of the notional amount in interest rate derivatives.[4] This percentage is likely to increase even further through the voluntary adoption of clearing and should more products become subject to a clearing obligation and once certain exemptions expire, for example, the pension scheme arrangement exemption under the European Market Infrastructure Regulation (EMIR).[5] Evidently, central

---

* The views expressed within the content of this chapter are our own and do not necessarily reflect the views or position of the CME Group or Simmons & Simmons.

[1] Futures have been cleared by CME Clearing since 1919.

[2] SwapClear, a service for clearing interest rate swaps, was launched by the London Clearing House (LCH) in 1999.

[3] Paragraph 13 of the G20 'Leader Statement', the Pittsburgh Summit (24–25 September 2009).

[4] Bank for International Settlement (BIS) statistical release, OTC derivatives statistics at end-June 2022 (30 November 2022). At end-June 2022, the notional value of outstanding OTC derivatives contracts globally was around $630 trillion (EUR 590 trillion), of which 80% regards interest rate derivatives. Although slightly more dated, the European Securities Markets Authority (ESMA) Annual Statistical Report on EU Derivatives Markets of 17 December 2021 (ESMA-50-165-2001) offers a wealth of information on the EU derivatives markets; see pp. 15–16 on central clearing.

[5] Please refer to Chapter 3 ('Development of the Regulatory Regime for OTC Derivatives Clearing' by Patrick Pearson) in this volume for a further discussion of EMIR.

clearing has become a key feature of global OTC derivatives markets. This development over the last decade or so conforms with the enormous growth of CCPs that serve
global clearing needs.

This is clearly ample reason to pay some (closer) attention to the phenomenon of
OTC derivatives clearing. Those doing so fit in with a general trend of growing interest
for this topic. While clearing used to be regarded as less glamorous than the creative
and headline-grabbing business of trading, it currently enjoys an unprecedented popu-
larity as people are realizing that it constitutes the core of modern financial infrastructure. It is no longer regarded as merely an operational thing. Furthermore, because of
its importance, it currently draws political attention, in particular where clearing occurs on a European Union (EU)/non-EU cross-border basis.[6]

The purpose of this chapter is to set the stage for the more detailed features of clearing
discussed in the other chapters of this book.[7] It should therefore not come as a complete
surprise that we kick off with a key term in this context: 'clearing'.

2 Definition of Clearing

The precise definition of 'clearing', including the composition of the value chain and the
related services, has been a matter of considerable debate among market participants,
regulators, and policymakers.[8] The term 'clearing' originates from the expression 'to
clear' (lat. *clarus*), which refers to the balancing of accounts with another party, that
is, clearing one's debts. In reality, however, clearing usually comprises a much greater
scope of services. Similarly, EMIR defines the term, for its purposes, as 'the process of
establishing positions, including the calculation of net obligations, and ensuring that
financial instruments, cash, or both, are available to secure the exposures arising from
those positions'.[9] Again, this only captures the central clearing part, as we will discuss in
more detail in section 2.2.2 on the 'unique' CCP services. In this chapter, we present a
definition[10] according to three different perspectives:

- the *process view* refers to clearing as a process that constitutes a vital part of the life
  cycle of a trade (section 2.1);

---

[6] Please refer to Chapters 13 ('Clearing and Trading and Settlement' by Apostolos Thomadakis and Karel
Lannoo), 15 ('Cross-Border Clearing' by Ulrich Karl), and 16 ('Brexit: Equivalence; Location Policy' by Dermot
Turing) in this volume for a further discussion of this topic.

[7] This chapter is an adaptation of a chapter in *Clearing Services for Global Markets* by Tina P. Hasenpusch
(Cambridge: Cambridge University Press, 2009).

[8] Cf. 'Securities Trading, Clearing, Central Counterparties and Settlement in EU 25—An Overview of Current
Arrangements', report commissioned by the Competition Directorate-General of the European Commission
(London, 2005), p. 3 and 'Report on Definitions', CESAME Group Meeting, 24 October (Brussels, 2005), p. 5
(CESAME, 'Report on Definitions').

[9] Regulation (EU) No. 648/2012 of the European Parliament and of the Council of 4 July 2012 on OTC derivatives, central counterparties and trade repositories (text with EEA relevance), [2012] OJ L201 (27 July 2021), Art.
2(3) (EMIR).

[10] The provided definition is consistent with, and builds upon, the view of important industry bodies and policy-
makers, as expressed in EACH's 'Functional Definition of a Central Counterparty Clearing House', Position Paper
(Zurich, 2004) (EACH, 'Functional Definition of a Central Counterparty Clearing House'); CESAME, 'Report on
Definitions' (n 9); and 'Update on Definitions', CESAME Group Meeting, 12 June (Brussels, 2006).

- the *functional view* focuses on clearing as a service and details the various value chain components (section 2.2);
- the *product view* concentrates on the peculiarity of clearing OTC derivatives (section 2.3).

In the context of financial services, clearing can refer to the processing of payment instruments or financial instruments. Because this book focuses on the clearing of OTC derivatives (rather than ETDs or securities), the definition of clearing used here refers exclusively to that subset of financial instruments. The following paragraphs provide a definition of OTC derivatives clearing according to each of the views outlined above.

2.1 Process View

Clearing constitutes a vital part of the life cycle of a trade. This life cycle consists of execution, clearing, and settlement.[11] By executing a trade, be it on a trading platform or over the counter, buyers and sellers enter into a specific legal obligation to buy or sell an underlying. Settlement refers to the fulfilment of the legal obligation. For example, in the trading of OTC derivatives, the legal obligation is fulfilled when the duration of a contract expires or when a close-out of the position occurs.

The process that takes place between execution and settlement (i.e. during the respective time lag) is referred to as clearing (see Figure 2.1). Whereas, in the context of

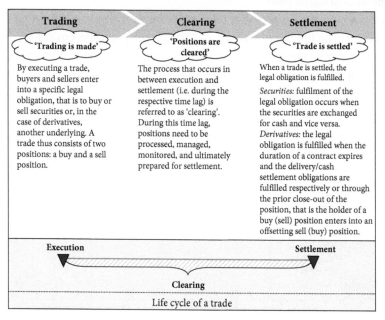

Figure 2.1 Process view on clearing
Source: authors.

---

[11] Please refer to Chapter 17 ('Potential Impact of the Distributed Ledger Technology on OTC Derivatives Markets' by Randy Priem) in this volume for a discussion of how this may be impacted by using distributed ledger technology.

trading securities, this time lag is usually minimal (between one and five days), it can be substantially longer in OTC derivatives trading (from one day up to several decades). During this time lag, trades need to be processed, managed, monitored, and ultimately prepared for settlement.

2.2 Functional View

The functional view focuses on clearing as a service and details the various value-chain components. The number of services offered within the clearing value chain generally depends on the characteristics of the cleared market and product and the provider offering these services. The scope and type of clearing services available can be classified as follows (see Figure 2.2):

- basic clearing services (section 2.2.1);
- value-added clearing services in general, with unique CCP services in particular (section 2.2.2);
- complementary clearing services (section 2.2.3).

Each of these clearing service levels has a different scope and comprises different functions, which are detailed in the next paragraphs.

2.2.1 Basic clearing services

Clearing refers to the process that takes place between the execution of a trade and its settlement. The linking of trading and settlement processes creates the need for a number of essential clearing services including cleared trade confirmation, transaction/position management, and delivery management. These services are categorized as basic clearing services.

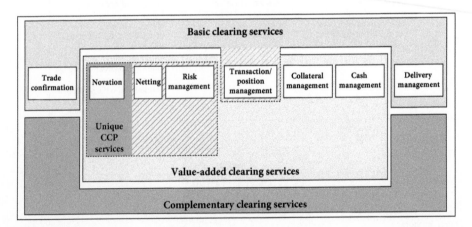

Figure 2.2 Functional view on clearing
Source: authors.

Trade confirmation

Trading entails a specific legal obligation between a seller and a buyer. Once this obligation has been entered into (through the execution of a trade), the trade proceeds to the clearing process. The first step in the clearing process is to assess the consistency of the buyer's and seller's terms of trade in order to prevent any unintentional errors. This service is referred to as cleared trade confirmation. Providing cleared trade confirmation means comparing the trade details of the selling and buying instructions in order to identify and link the related transactions. This commonly includes identifying the underlying; price; and the settlement, delivery, or expiry date.

Transaction/position management

Positions need to be processed and managed until the respective legal obligations are successfully fulfilled. The need for, and intensity of, this management strongly depends on the type of asset class. For this reason, transaction/position management can either be classified as a basic clearing service or as a value-added clearing service—depending on the scope of managerial services offered.

As outlined earlier, in the context of securities transactions, the legal obligation is usually fulfilled within a very short time frame (i.e. the standard settlement period), which is a pre-determined date as close as possible to the trade day (T + 1, T + 2, T + 3, etc.).[12] Fulfilment of the legal obligation for OTC derivatives positions may require much longer time frames.

Important managerial services provided between the execution and fulfilment of the legal obligation include corporate action services during this period[13] as well as any previously announced transfer of pending obligations to another counterparty, for example, position transfers, give-up, and take-up services.[14] A counterpart or counterparty is the contracting party in a trade.

Delivery management

Delivery management constitutes the final service within the clearing cycle. It is the process of preparing the settlement instructions for an underlying. Settlement instructions are then sent to the respective settlement institutions. It should be taken into account that settlement instructions only result from OTC derivatives transactions if a position has not been closed out prior to the expiry of the contract. Delivery can take the form of exchange of cash or so-called physical delivery, by which the respective underlying is exchanged.

---

[12] T = the day on which the trade is made. 1, 2, 3, etc. stand for the number of elapsed business days before the legal obligation is fulfilled.

[13] Cf. EACH, 'Functional Definition of a Central Counterparty Clearing House' (n 10), p. 4.

[14] When a so-called 'give-up' occurs, the counterparty A executing a trade relinquishes the trade to another counterparty, B. Reasons for this might vary and can be related to market access, customer relationships, etc. For example, counterparty A is executing an order on behalf of a client whilst the client utilizes counterparty B as a clearing member to the clearing house. The term 'take-up' refers to the reverse process on the part of B; whereas A gives up the trade to B, counterparty B takes up the trade from counterparty A.

2.2.2 Value-added clearing services

In addition to the basic clearing services described earlier, clearing often comprises a much greater spectrum of services. Whereas these additional services are not essential to the life cycle of a trade, they offer important value-added to the trade's counterparties. These services are therefore referred to as value-added clearing services. These comprise unique CCP services, such as novation, netting, and risk management, as well as transaction/position management, collateral management, and cash management. The scope of netting and risk management services a CCP can offer is unique.

Unique CCP services

Due to the nature of derivatives products (especially the leverage effect)[15] and the potentially significant time lag between execution and settlement of derivatives (which can lead to a build-up of large, unsettled exposures between market participants),[16] the evolution of derivatives clearing services have been shaped by the counterparties' desire to control their risk of losses from non-performance.[17] This desire led to the introduction of the so-called central counterparty (CCP), '[a]n entity that interposes itself between the counterparties to trades, acting as the buyer to every seller and the seller to every buyer'.[18]

Compared to the market structure of bilateral relationships between counterparties, CCPs offer a number of important clearing services. Some of these services are unique to the CCP structure in terms of their scope and nature. CCP clearing has become an integral part of modern clearing services[19] and forms a core part of the financial market infrastructure in most developed economies.[20]

Novation

Novation is a crucial unique CCP service.[21] It refers to the legal process of replacing the original counterparties to a trade with a single (thus central) counterparty to both sides of the transaction.

---

[15] The leverage effect of derivatives signifies the effect to which the value of a derivative position is greater than the value of the underlying. Cf. Udo Rettberg and Dietrich Zwätz, *Das kleine Terminhandels-Lexikon* (Düsseldorf: Wirtschaft Und Finanzen, 1995), p. 101.

[16] Cf. Raymond Knott and Alastair Mills, 'Modelling Risk in Central Counterparty Clearing Houses: A Review' (London: Financial Stability Review, Bank of England, No. 12 (2002), p. 162 (Knott and Mills, 'Modelling Risk').

[17] Cf. James Moser, 'Contracting Innovations and the Evolution of Clearing and Settlement Methods at Futures Exchanges', Federal Reserve Bank of Chicago, Working Paper Series, No. 26 (Chicago: Federal Reserve Bank of Chicago, 1998), p. 7, (Moser, 'Contracting Innovations'); Knott and Mills, 'Modelling Risk' (n 16), p. 162; Kirsi Ripatti, 'Central Counterparty Clearing: Constructing a Framework for Evaluation of Risks and Benefits', Bank of Finland, Discussion Paper, No. 1 (Helsinki, 2004), p. 4 (Ripatti, 'Central Counterparty Clearing').

[18] Bank for International Settlements, 'Recommendations for Securities Settlement Systems', report in co-operation with the Committee on Payment and Settlement Systems and the Technical Committee of the International Organization of Securities Commissions (Basel, 2001), p. 45 (Bank for International Settlements, 'Recommendations for Securities Settlement Systems').

[19] Cf. Ripatti, 'Central Counterparty Clearing' (n 17), p. 4.

[20] Cf. Knott and Mills, 'Modelling Risk' (n 16), p. 162.

[21] Please refer to Chapter 5 ('Clearing Mechanics' by Christian Chamorro-Courtland) in this volume for a further discussion of novation.

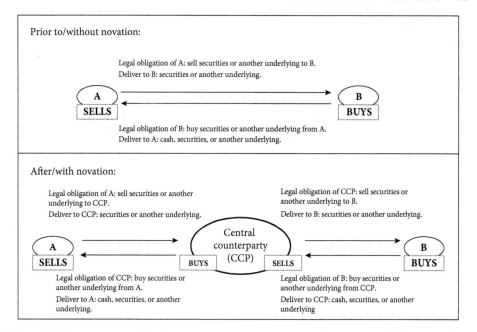

Figure 2.3 Legal relationship between counterparties to a trade prior to and after novation
Source: authors.

Figure 2.3 illustrates the process by which the CCP interposes itself between counterparties A and B to assume their rights and legal obligations, thereby becoming the buyer to every seller and vice versa.[22] The process of novation replaces the original bilateral contractual obligations by new obligations with the CCP. Novation entails that the CCP assumes the associated risks of counterparty default.[23] As a result, bilateral counterparty risk (of variable quality) is replaced with a (high-quality) counterparty risk against the CCP.

Netting
When a CCP is involved in the clearing process, novation is usually followed by netting. This is possible because market participants commonly maintain a number of offsetting positions with the same underlying and the same attributes. When many counterparties are replaced by one central counterparty by means of novation, these offsetting positions can be netted off against each other, thereby reducing the overall number of positions.

---

[22] Central clearing can be 'direct' in the sense that the counterparties to the trade are clearing members of the CCP through which the trade is cleared. It can also be 'indirect' in the sense that a counterparty to the trade is not a clearing member but employs a clearing member to clear the trade. This means that not only the CCP but also the clearing member is interposed between the original counterparties. Please refer to Chapter 4 ('CCP Access Structures' by Christina Sell) and Chapter 8 ('OTC Derivatives Clearing Documentation' by Emma Dwyer and Emma Lancelott) in this volume for a further discussion of EMIR.
[23] A default is the failure to satisfy an obligation on time.

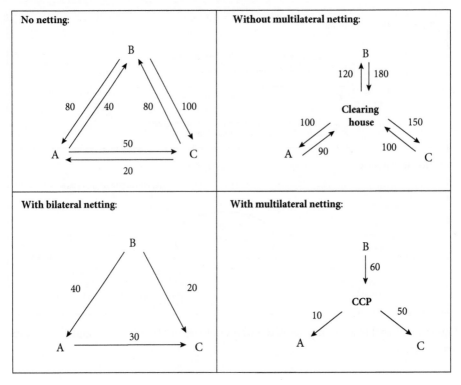

Figure 2.4 Exchange of payments arising from financial transactions
Source: authors.

There are two types of netting services: simple bilateral and more sophisticated multilateral netting (see Figure 2.4). *Bilateral netting* allows amounts owed between two counterparties to be combined into a single net amount payable from one party to the other. Bilateral netting therefore consolidates the flows between each pair of counterparties into one single net obligation.

Multilateral netting means that the CCP nets all offsetting exposures of its counterparties and reduces all outstanding residuals to a single debit/credit between itself and each counterparty rather than a multiplicity of bilateral exposures between the original counterparties to a trade. This multilateral net exposure encompasses the bilateral net position between each clearing member and the clearing house. The scope for multilateral netting is greatest in markets where multiple firms trade intensively among themselves, with each firm both extending and receiving credit, creating a web of bilateral exposures. The value of being able to net all positions into a single position naturally becomes more pronounced as volumes grow.[24]

---

[24] Cf. Albert Bressand and Catherine Distler, 'When Clearing Matters; CCPs and the Modern Securities Industry's Value Chain', in Promethee (ed.), *The Central Counterparties Dialogue* (Paris, 2001), p. 5 (Bressand and Distler, 'When Clearing Matters').

An additional classification further distinguishes two netting levels according to their varying degrees of legal enforceability. Unfortunately, no universal definition has yet emerged for either netting level: 'This is due, in part, to the fact that terms tend to be used loosely in the markets and various forms have been developed to accommodate specific types of transactions.'[25] We will refer to these two netting levels as 'type 1 netting' and 'type 2 netting'. Whereas type 1 netting signifies the legally enforceable dissolution of gross positions into one single net obligation, type 2 netting neither satisfies nor discharges the original individual obligations.[26] Whereas both netting levels provide significant efficiency gains to users, the legal enforceability of netting levels is of crucial importance in the event of counterparty (i.e. member of a CCP) default. Type 1 netting, as distinct from type 2 netting, must therefore provide for 'contract liquidation procedures in the event that one of the parties defaults under a contract or becomes bankrupt'.[27] The most prominent form of type 1 netting is close-out netting.[28] Close-out netting signifies the legally enforceable consolidation of individual trades into net amounts of securities, cash, or other underlyings. The offsetting positions with the same underlying and the same attributes (such as a contracting party, security, or trading currency) are thus dissolved into one single net obligation in either cash, or cash and securities, or another underlying.[29]

Important efficiency gains can also be realized through type 2 netting. During the time a derivatives position is open at the clearing house, the value of the positions is constantly recalculated and adapted to market movements, which can result in certain payment obligations.[30] Position netting then reduces collateral requirements by taking offsetting positions into account;[31] it is an agreement that nets payments across multiple contracts[32] but keeps each contract distinct.[33] Without such netting, total

[25] Jiabin Huang, *Legal Aspects of the Role and Functions of Central Counterparties* (London: King's College London, 2006), p. 62.

[26] The type of netting arrangement that neither satisfies nor discharges the original individual obligations is often also referred to as 'position netting' or 'payment netting', again depending on the type of transaction and the type of clearing service provider: 'Payment netting takes place during the normal business of a solvent firm, and involves combining offsetting cash flow obligations between two parties on a given day in a given currency into a single net payable or receivable; payment netting is essentially the same as set-off', according to David Mengle in 'The Importance of Close-Out Netting', International Swaps and Derivatives Association (ISDA) research notes (2010), p. 2.

[27] New York Foreign Exchange Committee (ed.), *Guidelines for Foreign Exchange Settlement Netting* (New York: New York Foreign Exchange Committee, 1997), p. 4.

[28] Other forms of a legally enforceable dissolution of gross positions into one single net obligation are exposure netting, trade netting, or obligation netting; depending on the type of transaction and the type of clearing service provider. Cf. Bank for International Settlements (ed.), 'OTC Derivatives: Settlement Procedures and Counterparty Risk Management', report by the Committee on Payment and Settlement Systems and the Euro-Currency Standing Committee of the Central Banks of the Group of Ten Countries (Basel, 1998), pp. 21, 41 (Bank for International Settlements, 'OTC Derivatives'); Bank for International Settlements, 'Recommendations for Securities Settlement Systems' (n 18), p. 38.

[29] Cf. EACH, 'Functional Definition of a Central Counterparty Clearing House' (n 10), p. 5.

[30] For more details, refer to the explanation of risk management services.

[31] Cf. OM Group (ed.), 'Electricity Market Settlement Solutions to Meet Rapidly Changing Market Requirements with Lower Risk', White Paper (Stockholm, 2002), p. 1.

[32] Cf. Bank for International Settlements, 'OTC Derivatives' (n 28), p. 43.

[33] Cf. George Tsetsekos and Panos Varangis, 'The Structure of Derivatives Exchanges: Lessons from Developed and Emerging Markets', Working Paper (Drexel/Washington DC: World Bank, 1997), p. 9. Position netting reduces

credit risk exposures[34] would grow in proportion to the respective counterparty's gross number of trades.[35]

Risk management

The information about the full portfolio of positions provided by transaction/position management is also required for risk management processes. Risk management is a crucial part of the clearing services value chain.[36] Positions managed and processed by a clearing house are associated with specific risks inherent to the different product types. The exact risks a CCP must manage depend on the product types it processes and the specific terms of its contracts with participants as well as the scope of services offered.[37]

CCPs typically incorporate the following tiers of safeguards to mitigate counterparty risks:[38]

- Members of a CCP (clearing members) must comply with the various membership and due diligence requirements set by the clearing house regarding minimum net capital, regulatory authorization requirements, fulfilment of additional operational and technological requirements, etc. They are subject to minimum financial and capital adequacy requirements as well as daily monitoring and periodic reviews of their risk management practices, policies, and operations.[39] Exercising selectivity and imposing risk-based membership requirements is one important feature of the framework with which clearing houses protect and mitigate the consequences in case of a clearing member default event.

collateral requirements because the clearing house often only charges margin on the net (and not gross) positions of a clearing member. The term 'margin' is explained in more detail below.

[34] Exposure is the maximum loss from default by a counterparty.

[35] Cf. Robert Bliss and George Kaufman, 'Derivatives and Systemic Risk: Netting, Collateral, and Closeout', Federal Reserve Bank of Chicago, Working Paper No. 3 (Chicago, IL, 2005), p. 10 (Bliss and Kaufman, 'Derivatives and Systemic Risk').

[36] Cf. Edward Green, 'Clearing and Settling Financial Transactions, Circa 2000', paper presented at The Federal Reserve Bank of Atlanta '2000 Financial Markets Conference', 15–17 October (Chicago, IL, 2000), p. 12.

[37] Nonetheless, all CCPs are exposed to a common set of risks, which have to be managed effectively. There is, for example, the risk that participants will not settle the full value of their obligations at any time (counterparty credit risk). Cf. Charles Kahn, James McAndrews and William Roberds, 'Settlement Risk under Gross and Net Settlement', Federal Reserve Bank of Atlanta, Working Paper No. 10a (Atlanta, GA, 1999), p. 3. Another risk is that participants will settle obligations late (liquidity risk). For more details and further types of risks to which a CCP is exposed, refer to Bank for International Settlements (ed.), 'Recommendations for Central Counterparties', consultative report by the Committee on Payment and Settlement Systems and the Technical Committee of the International Organization of Securities Commissions (Basel, 2004), p. 8; Ripatti, 'Central Counterparty Clearing' (n 17), p. 15.

[38] Cf. Richard Dale, 'Risk Management in US Derivative Clearing Houses', London Institute of International Banking, Finance and Development Law, Essays in International Financial and Economic Law No. 14 (London: London Institute of International Banking, Finance & Development Law, 1998), pp. 9–12; EACH, 'Functional Definition of a Central Counterparty Clearing House' (n 10), p. 5; David Loader, *Clearing, Settlement and Custody* (3rd edn) (Oxford: Butterworth-Heinemann, 2020), p. 21 (Loader, *Clearing, Settlement and Custody*).

[39] By imposing rules on the quality of its membership, the clearing house achieves an important degree of risk control.

- The clearing house imposes a margining regime to ensure that the obligations of clearing members, as well as their customers, are adequately collateralized. Margining regimes are designed to reflect anticipated close-out costs of a portfolio of positions in normal market conditions.
- There are clearly defined and transparent rules and procedures as well as financial back-up arrangements to address a situation of default[40] by a clearing member. These measures include the instalment of supplemental clearing house resources (e.g. set-up of a default fund to which the CCP contributes its own capital and which may include the instalment of supplemental insurance policies) and the collection of mutualizable contributions by its clearing members. A CCP's total resources should be sufficient to cover a default that occurs in abnormal (extreme but plausible) market conditions.[41]

'Margin' generally refers to the cash and collateral used to secure an obligation, either realized or potential. Although margins alone are typically not designed to protect CCPs from rare extreme but plausible events,[42] they constitute an integral element of a CCP's risk management function.

Margining encompasses the entire process of measuring, calculating, and administering the cash and collateral that must be put up to cover open positions. The provision of margin is intended to ensure that all financial commitments related to the open positions of a clearing member can be liquidated within a very short period of time once default has occurred.[43] The margin system effectively acts as an ex-ante risk-based tool to cover potential future exposures.[44] Margin levels are usually designed to protect against losses resulting from typical price movements over one or more days.[45] Clearing houses differentiate and calculate various margin types, most importantly the so-called 'initial margin' and the 'variation margin'.

Initial margin is the primary layer of protection, intended to mitigate the risk of non-performance as well as the possibility that shifting market prices will leave the

---

[40] A default is the failure to satisfy an obligation on time. A clearing house may specify certain other events (e.g. insolvency) as constituting default for the purpose of triggering its default procedures. Please refer to Chapter 11 ('Default Management' by David Horner) in this volume for a further discussion of such procedures.

[41] So-called systemically important European and US CCPs are subject to the 'cover 2' regulatory standard, requiring its total financial resources to cover their two largest clearing member defaults.

[42] Cf. Knott and Mills, 'Modelling Risk' (n 16), p. 162.

[43] In case of 'client-clearing' or 'indirect-clearing', arrangements (see n 22) are in place to ensure that the client's margin is segregated from that of its clearing member to facilitate transfer of that margin and the related positions to another clearing member in case of the default of its clearing member. Please refer to Chapter 10 ('Segregation and Portability of Cleared OTC Derivatives in Europe' by Bas Zebregs) in this volume for a further discussion of margin segregation.

[44] Cf. CME Group, *CME Clearing Risk Management and Financial Safeguards* (Chicago: CME Group, 2022), p. 11.

[45] The definitions of normal markets can vary; one possibility is to define normal market conditions as those observed 99 out of 100 days. The appropriate amount of data used to determine that level will vary from market to market and over time and potentially be subject to regulatory requirements.

counterparty with a credit risk.[46] Initial margin can be thought of as a good faith deposit that guarantees market participants' financial performance by collateralizing their potential future exposure.[47] Common practice is to collect initial margin at least once a day and more often (intra-day), as defined by the clearing house's risk management standards and certain regulatory requirements.[48] Margin requirements can generally be collected based on either net positions or gross positions.[49] CCPs commonly calculate margin requirements across a portfolio of positions, taking correlations into account. This approach is referred to as portfolio margining. Portfolio margining is based on the concept that CCPs can offset or reduce the required margin across products which they clear if the price of one product is significantly and reliably correlated to the price of another product. A CCP's ability to offer portfolio margining (i.e. the calculation of margin required across a market participant's trading portfolio rather than an evaluation of exposures at the individual position level) is a key benefit of centralized clearing.[50]

Variation margin is a payment determined by changes to the market price of a product[51] and the composition of market participants' cleared portfolios.[52] It is therefore a risk management tool to cover the latest exposure. Variation margin is called for when positions are revalued using the marking-to-market procedure.[53] This revaluation of positions occurs daily or intra-daily. Margin calls are then issued.[54] Due to this continuous marking-to-market of positions, variation margin payments are, in effect, a settlement of unrealized profit or loss and are, as such, designed to limit the accumulation of debt in the system.[55]

As explained earlier, the employment of margins is but one component in a CCP's risk management framework. CCPs need to assess the losses they could face on

---

[46] Cf. CME Group, *Stability in Times of Stress: CME Clearing's Anti-Procyclical Margining Regime* (Chicago: CME Group, 2021), p. 2 (CME Group, *Stability in Times of Stress*).

[47] Cf. Anuszka Mogford, 'The Road Ahead' (2005) 4 Futures and OTC World 34–37 (Mogford, 'The Road Ahead').

[48] By increasing the initial margin, excesses in risk accumulation in the market can be avoided and the impact of potential defaults can be reduced. Cf. Mogford, 'The Road Ahead' (n 47), pp. 34–37.

[49] Under a net margin system, margin is charged for net long or net short positions.

[50] Cf. EACH, *Views on Portfolio Margining* (Brussels: EACH, 2015), p. 4 (EACH, *Views on Portfolio Margining*).

[51] Cf. Ben Bernanke, 'Clearing and Settlement during the Crash', (1990) 3(1) Review of Financial Studies 137; Knott and Mills, 'Modelling Risk' (n 16), p. 163; Loader, *Clearing, Settlement and Custody* (n 38), p. 211.

[52] Cf. CME Group, *Stability in Times of Stress* (n 46), p. 10.

[53] Cf. Ripatti, 'Central Counterparty Clearing' (n 17), p. 5. The expression 'mark-to-market' refers to the process of revaluing positions on a continuous basis, at least once a day or intra-daily. Its value is the difference between the previous price (i.e. from the previous day or the previous mark-to-market) and the current price. Increases in settlement prices produce gains for long positions and losses for short positions. Conversely, decreases in settlement price result in losses to long positions and gains to short positions. The respective profits or losses can then be settled accordingly. Cf. Raymond Fishe and Lawrence Goldberg, 'The Effects of Margins on Trading in Futures Markets' (1986) 6(2) Journal of Futures Markets 262; David Weiss, *After the Trade is Made: Processing Securities Transactions* (2nd edn) (New York: Penguin Random House, 1993), p. 336; John Hull, *Einführung in Futures- und Optionsmärkte* (3rd edn) (Munich/Vienna/Oldenbourg: Oldenbourg Wissenschaftsverlag, 2001), pp. 33–34.

[54] Cf. EACH, 'Functional Definition of a Central Counterparty Clearing House' (n 10), p. 5. Note that collateral is deposited as initial margin payment; variation margin is usually deposited in cash only. For methodologies to calculate collateral value (haircuts), refer to Alejandro García and Ramo Gençay, 'Valuation of Collateral in Securities Settlement Systems for Extreme Market Events', Discussion Paper (Ottawa/Burnaby: Federal Reserve Bank of Chicago, 2006). For details on the legal aspects concerning collateralization, refer to Michael Clarke and Dean Naumowicz, *An Introduction to the Legal Aspects of Collateralization* (London/New York, 1999).

[55] Cf. CME Group, *Stability in Times of Stress* (n 46), p. 10.

occasions when margin proves insufficient and ensure that they can meet these losses from extreme but plausible events by other means.[56]

Collateral management

The term 'collateral' refers to cash and non-cash assets that are delivered to the clearing house by clearing members to secure their positions and for the purposes of margin requirements, delivery obligations, and default fund contributions. On a daily basis, collateral management is the process performed by clearing houses used to control counterparty assets against all exposures and obligations calculated as part of the risk management process.[57] Most importantly, collateral management ensures that margin requirements are covered by available collateral. If there is a collateral shortfall, a collateral call is generated. If there is collateral excess, a collateral release is generated (automated or upon clearing member request). Depending on the level of sophistication, a clearing house might offer certain functionalities and services to enable optimization of clearing members' collateral utilization.

It further involves the functions of processing new collateral, management of collateral on deposit, substitutions of cash for non-cash collateral, and evaluating the value on a daily or ongoing basis. Collateral needs to be evaluated on an ongoing basis to ensure adequate coverage of risk exposure.[58] In line with risk management requirements, CCPs define the scope of acceptable collateral beyond cash. CCPs need to comply with strict regulatory requirements regarding the holding, depositing, and investment of clearing members' collateral.

Cash management

Cash management, in addition to the broader collateral management function, provides important services for the smooth functioning of the clearing house, which is highly relevant for appropriate risk management. Cash management comprises operational and treasury management. Operational cash management includes the processing of cash instructions from netting, premium payments, realized profit and loss (P&L) cash instructions, fines and fees, unrealized P&L, income events, or margin calls. Sources can be regular trading and clearing activities, corporate actions, P&L adjustments, or margins. Treasury management may include the following services: realignment of the CCP's cash positions, interest payments on cash collateral deposited by users, or investment activity and liquidity management.

---

[56] Cf. Knott and Mills, 'Modelling Risk' (n 16), p. 162. Effective risk management therefore requires CCPs to have access to additional default resources. Best practice typically involves CCPs setting up a default fund (also referred to as compensation or guarantee fund) that serves as financial back-up once a default by a clearing member has occurred. CCPs and clearing members typically contribute to the default fund. A clearing house might have one default fund across all cleared asset classes or it might set up various default funds for different cleared asset classes.

[57] Please refer to Chapter 6 ('OTC Derivatives Clearing and Collateral Management' by Manmohan Singh) in this volume for a further discussion of collateral management

[58] Cf. EACH, 'Functional Definition of a Central Counterparty Clearing House' (n 10), p. 5.

2.2.3 Complementary clearing services

The final category of clearing services is complementary clearing services. Whereas these services are not required to maintain the life cycle of a trade, they constitute an important additional value provision. Despite the fact that there is a value-added inherent to these services, only some CCPs engage in the provision of these services (or only to a limited extent). Therefore, and due to their status as 'add-on features', they are classified as complementary clearing services. Complementary clearing services can comprise a number of different services, such as:

- margin services enabling market participants to calculate margin requirements, possibly including the service of modelling portfolio margin savings;
- single interface and access to many markets and various CCPs, including centralized collateral and cash management services;
- technical and operational support;
- risk management and services across multiple asset classes and CCPs;
- accounting and regulatory information provision;
- regulatory reporting services;
- bookkeeping services;
- sophisticated and flexible customer account structure and management solutions, that is, establishment of customized sub-account structures;
- provision of enhanced risk management tools;
- multiple account reporting and consolidation levels.

2.3 Product View

Trades executed in securities versus derivatives markets possess different particularities and dynamics; the markets themselves also have unique characteristics.

As outlined earlier, CCPs have traditionally played a more significant role in OTC derivatives than in securities markets due to the demands for efficient risk reduction. Securities transactions are processed and settled as fast as technological, legal, and regulatory restrictions will allow; the time frame usually consists of a few days. Because these transactions only remain with the clearing house for a relatively short period of time, the need for risk management, transaction monitoring, and management is relatively modest. Once a securities trade has been executed, the primary objective is to fulfil the legal obligations as quickly, efficiently, and securely as possible, optimizing the use of collateral required for securing the trade. The focus has therefore traditionally been on settlement rather than on clearing.

By contrast, the fulfilment of the legal obligation in OTC derivatives trading can be a matter of a much longer time frame—months and years rather than days. Large unsettled exposures may consequently build up between counterparties, which underscores the need for enhanced risk management. CCPs were therefore originally established to protect market participants from counterparty risk in ETD markets. The elimination of counterparty risk through novation, as well as the benefits of multilateral netting, margining, sophisticated risk management, and position management through a CCP, is thus highly advantageous.

3 Benefits of CCP Clearing

This paragraph outlines why CCP clearing has become such an integral part of modern financial market structures; exchange-traded and OTC clearing now forms a core part of the financial market infrastructure in most developed economies. Reasons for this are described from two vantage points. From a microeconomic perspective, CCPs provide benefits and value-added for individual market participants. In macroeconomic terms, CCPs are key infrastructures playing a vital role by facilitating the smooth and frictionless functioning of financial markets, thus increasing their efficiency, supporting financial stability, and reducing systemic risks.

3.1 Microeconomic View

The services offered by CCPs translate into several benefits to market participants:[59]

- trading benefits;
- risk reduction;
- capital efficiency;
- balance sheet benefits;
- operational efficiency;
- settlement benefits.

First, due to the reallocation of counterparty risk to the CCP, market participants can trade without having to assess the creditworthiness of the original counterparty to a trade. Through the process of novation, the introduction of a CCP effectively allows market participants to face a market-risk neutral, creditworthy counterparty.[60] As novation entails exposure to a standard credit risk, the associated credit monitoring and

---

[59] Cf. Deutsche Börse Group (ed.), 'Zentraler Kontrahent für Aktien startet am 27. März', press release, 10 February (Frankfurt a.M., 2003); Chris Wright, 'Central Counterparty Clearing and Settlement: Implications for Financial Statistics and the Balance of Payments', Bank of England, paper for the 17th Meeting of the IMF Committee on Balance of Payments Statistics, 26–29 October (Pretoria, 2004); SWX Swiss Exchange (ed.), 'SWX Swiss Exchange Introduces a Central Counterparty Service', press release, 3 March (Zurich, 2006); Randall Kroszner, 'Central Counterparty Clearing: History, Innovation, and Regulation' and Gertrude Tumpel-Gugerell, 'Issues Related to Central Counterparty Clearing', both speeches at the Joint Conference of the European Central Bank and the Federal Reserve Bank of Chicago on Issues related to Central Counterparty Clearing, 3–4 April (Frankfurt a.M., 2006).
[60] Cf. CME Group, *Stability in Times of Stress* (n 46), p. 2.

collateral management processes become less complex, which, in turn, reduces legal as well as operational costs.[61]

Multilateral netting and risk management services also furnish trading benefits by reducing the amount of capital that is tied up for the management of a specific portfolio of positions. These services free up resources, credit lines, and cash flow and increase the volume of business that can be supported on a given capital base.[62] Netting enables the efficient use of capital because each outstanding position generates a need for capital, margin, or collateral. Reducing the number of outstanding positions thus translates into diminished costs of capital.[63] The offsetting of all gross positions against each other so that all outstanding positions are converted into a single debit or credit between the CCP and another party[64] also offers higher levels of automation, which helps to minimize operational costs.[65] Since the introduction of clearing mandates for OTC derivatives transactions following the financial crisis of 2008, regulatory capital requirements typically have also provided for a more favourable treatment of cleared versus uncleared exposures.[66]

The risk management services performed by a CCP offer a number of benefits such as the mitigation of all or part of the risk of default,[67] centralized and transparent risk management and continuous exposure monitoring, and delivering transparency into risk exposures. The daily settlement of variation margin serves the important function of enabling market participants to settle their P&L on at least a daily basis (or intradaily, if offered by the CCP). Posting margin on a portfolio of positions, which were originally executed with various different counterparties, reduces opportunity costs to market participants and entails balance-sheet benefits by enabling a more efficient use of collateral. Mark-to-market and collateralization disciplines also create savings at the operational level, free up credit lines, and reduce collateral requirements. Through the use of a central pool of collateral against a cleared portfolio of trades, the amount of tied-up collateral can be optimized.

Additional benefits result through sophisticated transaction/position management, which allows for continuous centralized position records, monitoring, and control as well as an up-to-date, transparent, and consistent view of the cleared portfolio. Simplified, standardized, and rationalized back-office processes result from the use of a central collateral/cash pool and the calculation, collection, and custodial management of margin and collateral payment; delivery management services offer many of

[61] Cf. Carsten Murawski, 'The Impact of Clearing on the Credit Risk of a Derivatives Portfolio', Working Paper (Zurich, 2002), NCCR FINRISK (financial support: https://papers.ssrn.com/sol3/papers.cfm?abstract_id=339660) p. 3; LCH.Clearnet (ed.), *Creating the Central Counterparty of Choice* (Amsterdam/Brussels/London/Paris, 2003), p. 31 (LCH.Clearnet, *Creating the Central Counterparty of Choice*).

[62] Cf. LCH.Clearnet, *Creating the Central Counterparty of Choice* (n 61), p. 29; Bliss and Kaufman, 'Derivatives and Systemic Risk' (n 35), p. 11.

[63] Cf. David Hardy, 'The Future of Clearing', in Patrick L. Young (ed.), *An Intangible Commodity* (Derivatives Publishing: Petts Wood, 2004), p. 58 (Hardy, 'The Future of Clearing').

[64] Cf. Patrick van Cayseele and Christophe Wuyts, 'Cost Efficiency in the Securities Settlement and Safekeeping Industry', Discussion Paper (Leuven/Amsterdam, 2005), p. 3.

[65] Cf. Bressand and Distler, 'When Clearing Matters' (n 24), p. 4.

[66] Please refer to Chapter 9 ('Capital Requirements for Bank Exposures to CCPs' by Marc Peters) in this volume for a further discussion of capital requirements.

[67] Cf. Michael Moskow, 'Public Policy and Central Counterparty Clearing', speech at the Joint Conference of the European Central Bank and the Federal Reserve Bank of Chicago on Issues related to Central Counterparty Clearing, 3–4 April (Frankfurt a.M., 2006) (Moskow, 'Public Policy').

the same benefits. By standardizing processes, documentation, and systems as well as processing trades through a single channel, straight-through-processing (STP) can be increased and operational errors reduced.

Finally, CCP services result in settlement benefits. A considerable reduction in the value and volume of trades eligible for settlement can be achieved by netting.[68] The reduced number of delivery/payment instructions translates into lower settlement costs[69] and a reduced administrative burden.[70]

Not all markets are necessarily suitable for central counterparty clearing. Its potential benefits come at a cost, and it is simply not available in some markets.[71] The trade-off between potential costs and benefits to market participants determines the suitability of a CCP for a given market.[72] This balance depends on factors such as the volume and value of transactions, trading patterns among counterparties, the characteristics of the traded products, the composition of market participants, and the availability of reliable prices for traded products.

3.2 Macroeconomic View

Central counterparty clearing creates value-added not only for individual market participants but also for wider markets as a whole. This paragraph explains how the efficiency of capital markets can be enhanced through the introduction of central clearing.[73] CCPs enhance the allocation of risk and capital and can positively influence market liquidity.[74] The main reason that policymakers around the globe have mandated central clearing for a broad scope of OTC products and asset classes following the 2008 crisis is its contribution to supporting financial stability and reducing systemic risk.[75] During the financial crisis, the value of central clearing was demonstrated through the benefits of CCPs' default management processes and the resulting prevention of contagion between market participants.[76]

---

[68] Cf. Alistair Milne, 'Competition and the Rationalisation of European Securities Clearing and Settlement', Working Paper (London, 2002), p. 6.

[69] Cf. Bressand and Distler, 'When Clearing Matters' (n 24), p. 4 and Hardy, 'The Future of Clearing' (n 63), p. 58.

[70] Cf. LCH.Clearnet, *Creating the Central Counterparty of Choice* (n 61), p. 29.

[71] Cf. Ruben Lee, *What is an Exchange?: The Automation, Management, and Regulation of Financial Markets* (Oxford: Oxford University Press, 2000), p. 35; Bank for International Settlements, 'OTC Derivatives' (n 18), p. 11; Ripatti, 'Central Counterparty Clearing' (n 17), p. 8; Moskow, 'Public Policy' (n 67).

[72] Cf. DTCC (ed.), *Central Counterparties: Development, Cooperation and Consolidation, a White Paper to the Industry on the Future of CCPs* (London/New York, 2000), p. 1.

[73] Efficient capital markets are both allocationally and operationally efficient. In an allocationally efficient market, scarce savings are optimally allocated to productive investments in a way that benefits the market as a whole. Operational efficiency is achieved if the costs for transferring funds are minimized. Cf. Thomas Copeland and John Fred Weston, *Financial Theory and Corporate policy* (3rd edn) (New York: Pearson Education (US), 1998), pp. 330–331.

[74] Also refer to John McPartland, 'Clearing and Settlement Demystified', Federal Reserve Bank of Chicago, Chicago Federal Letter, January, No. 210 (Chicago, IL, 2005) regarding the question of how clearing systems support a sound financial system.

[75] Whilst simultaneously ensuring supervision of CCPs and their recovery and resolution, for which we refer to Chapter 3 ('Development of the Regulatory Regime for OTC Derivatives Clearing' by Patrick Pearson) and Chapter 12 ('Recovery and Resolution of CCPs' by Victor de Serière), respectively, in this volume.

[76] Cf. EACH, *Views on Portfolio Margining* (n 50), p. 3.

Whereas the central counterparty structure offers significant benefits and risk-reducing attributes,[77] the funnelling of market activity through one institution[78] also means that CCPs have the responsibility for continuously improving their risk management frameworks for the benefit of the wider market.[79]

A CCP does not remove credit risk; rather, it reallocates and mitigates counterparty risk, replacing a firm's exposure to bilateral credit risk (of variable quality) with the standard credit risk of the CCP. As outlined earlier, market participants can trade without the limitations of having to worry about the creditworthiness of individual counterparties. With novation, CCPs can manage and redistribute counterparty credit risk more efficiently than individual market participants can.[80] CCPs can substantially reduce the potential losses in the event of a participant default,[81] and this permits the size of the credit risk exposures to grow at lower rates than the market as a whole.[82] Further efficiencies are created through the specialization effect of pooling risk management facilities at the CCP.[83]

The effectiveness and prudence of a CCP's risk management framework and sufficient levels of financial resources are therefore crucial for the stability of the markets it serves. It is thus essential that a CCP has sophisticated tools, procedures, and frameworks in place to monitor and control the credit, liquidity, and legal and operational risks it incurs as well as a robust financial safeguards package to absorb losses under various market conditions.

Central clearing can also positively impact the allocation of capital within markets. Through multilateral netting and portfolio margining, a CCP can minimize the amount of collateral that has to be deposited for risk management purposes. This can result in an increased return on capital via cost reduction and improved credit standing and thus also balance sheet benefits. Ultimately, it leads to more capital being available for trading.[84]

CCPs can contribute to a market's liquidity by reducing the cost of trade and risks[85] and providing multilateral netting.[86] Through novation, a CCP creates more

---

[77] Cf. Competition Commission (ed.), 'Working Paper on Exchanges and Post-Trade Services: An Overview', June (London: Competition Commission, 2005), p. 27.

[78] Where this occurs within a structure of a trading venue that is part of the same group as the relevant clearing house, this touches on the concept of 'open access', for which we refer to Chapter 14 ('Open Access for OTC Derivatives: Concept and Implications' by Corentine Poilvet-Clediere and Julien Jardelot) in this volume.

[79] Cf. EACH, *Views on Portfolio Margining* (n 50), p. 3. Please refer to Chapter 7 ('What Kind of a Thing Is a Central Counterparty? The Role of Clearing Houses as a Source of Policy Controversy' by Rebecca Lewis and David Murphy) in this volume for a further discussion of risk bearing.

[80] Cf. Ripatti, 'Central Counterparty Clearing' (n 17), p. 12.

[81] Cf. Bank for International Settlements, 'Recommendations for Securities Settlement Systems' (n 18), p. 11.

[82] Cf. Bliss and Kaufman, 'Derivatives and Systemic Risk' (n 35), p. 11.

[83] Cf. Richard Dale, 'Derivatives Clearing Houses: The Regulatory Challenge', in Ferrarini, Guido A. (ed.), *European Securities Markets: The Investment Services Directive and Beyond* (London/The Hague/Boston, MA: Kluwer Law International, 1998), p. 296.

[84] Cf. Bliss and Kaufman, 'Derivatives and Systemic Risk' (n 35), pp. 10–11.

[85] Cf. Randall Kroszner, 'The Supply and Demand for Financial Regulation: Public and Private Competition around the Globe', paper presented at the Federal Reserve Bank of Kansas City Symposium on 'A Global Economic Integration: Opportunities and Challenges', 25 August (Chicago, IL/Jackson Hole, WY, 2000), p. 6.

[86] Cf. Citigroup (ed.), 'CCPs: A User's Perspective', Discussion Paper for the Joint Conference of the European Central Bank and the Federal Reserve Bank of Chicago on Issues related to Central Counterparty Clearing, 3–4 April (Frankfurt a.M., 2006), p. 1.

certainty in trading.[87] With lower counterparty risk and an optimized level of capital created by netting, market participants may have the ability to more optimally manage their risk management needs through the use of cleared derivatives.[88] The effects on liquidity can be substantial, especially if the size of the counterparty exposures is actually a limiting factor for trade, although this need not always be the case.[89] The positive effects of risk redistribution become more evident when the market is turbulent and risks increase.[90] In volatile markets, and in the absence of a known and secure counterparty to trade with, market participants might stop trading· A CCP can thus contribute to more stable market liquidity by providing that function of an established and trusted CCP.

Given the important impact CCPs have on enhancing market liquidity, in particular in times of crisis, it is crucial that clearing houses operate governed by a solid risk management framework to ensure that all risk management parameters are adequately set to support financial stability and reduce systemic risk and that the financial integrity of a clearing house is never called in question.

Similar principles apply to the margin methodology used by a CCP. Empirical evidence suggests that exorbitant margins can have a negative effect on market activity.[91] CCP good practice means to set the margin at a risk-appropriate level sufficient to provide protection against all but the most extreme price moves but not so high as to damage market liquidity or discourage the use of the CCP.

4 Conclusion

We hope that you found this introductory chapter helpful in understanding the general concept of clearing. As you will have realized, it entails far more than one might derive from statutory definitions such as that of EMIR. Moreover, as mentioned in the outset of the chapter, the vast size of the growing clearing market makes it deserving of a wider understanding of its intricacies. We have touched upon many features of clearing that will be picked up in more detail in the following chapters of this book.

As a final remark we should note that, as with all processes, especially those subject to a continuing quest for financial efficiencies and risk mitigation, clearing is still developing and so will its definition.[92]

---

[87] Cf. Moser, 'Contracting Innovations' (n 17), p. 7; Ripatti, 'Central Counterparty Clearing' (n 17), p. 5.

[88] As a result of established practice or, in some cases, regulations, market participants will limit their trading volumes to a certain percentage of their balance sheet. In these cases, the netting effect increases the participants' scope for action. Cf. Riksbank (ed.), 'Central Counterparty Clearing for the Securities Market', financial stability report, Central Bank of Sweden, No. 2 (2002), p. 50 (Riksbank, 'Central Counterparty Clearing').

[89] Cf. Riksbank, 'Central Counterparty Clearing' (n 88), p. 52.

[90] Cf. Riksbank, 'Central Counterparty Clearing' (n 88), p. 51.

[91] Cf. Knott and Mills, 'Modelling Risk' (n 16), p. 166.

[92] Please refer to Chapter 18 ('The Future of Centrally Cleared OTC Derivatives Markets' by Evariest Callens and Klaus Löber) in this volume for a further discussion on possible developments.

3

Development of the Regulatory Regime for OTC Derivatives Clearing

Patrick Pearson

1 Introduction

This chapter describes the efforts to regulate the over-the-counter (OTC) derivatives sector. The business of clearing OTC derivatives is inherently global. The need to regulate the sector started with efforts in the United States and became a global regulatory goal after the financial crisis. The main part of this chapter focuses on the efforts in the European Union (EU) (where this chapter refers to 'Europe' in general, it means the European Union) over the past fifteen years. They reflect wider international work to make the business safer and more transparent through global standards, which are also discussed. The chapter is divided into four parts. After the introduction, Part 2 describes the earliest efforts to regulate the sector starting in the United States in 1987, global standard setters' first discussions in 1997, increasing concerns after the Long-Term Capital Management (LTCM) default, the EU's first non-legislative measures in 2006, and the watershed moment in 2008 after the Lehman Brothers' default unleashed the financial crisis resulting in a strong call from G20 leaders to introduce tighter, global regulation of the sector. Part 3 is devoted to the preparation and adoption of the EU's regulatory response: the European Market Infrastructure Regulation (EMIR). It is a textbook case for those seeking a better understanding of the dynamics and checks and balances driving regulation in the EU. It looks at the earliest indications for legislative intent and explains how European Commission speeches, statements, 'Communications', and 'working papers' interacted with Council 'conclusions' and European Parliament 'resolutions' and, almost inexorably, led to regulation of the OTC sector. Some of the necessary political and economic compromises that led to the final text of EMIR are also explained to understand the challenging process of aligning twenty-eight (now twenty-seven) Member States and the European Parliament (EP) to unanimously agree on a legislative proposal that is key to the financial stability of the Union. Part C of this chapter describes the first material amendment to EMIR: the EMIR Regulatory Fitness and Performance (EMIR REFIT) Regulation. This is a first example of checking whether an original regulation was still fit for purpose—after a few years—and to make any necessary revisions. Part 4 discusses probably the most politically contentious revision of EMIR: 'EMIR 2.2', which contains the EU's response to Brexit in particular and shows the institutional difficulties in reaching agreement between Member States to give more supervisory powers at the EU level to the European Securities Markets Authority (ESMA). The European Commission's proposal of December 2022 to amend EMIR and strengthen the EU's clearing system is also briefly discussed. Finally, Part 5 considers the central counterparties (CCP) Recovery and Resolution Regulation, which is the final piece of prudential legislation for CCPs, regulating the way in which a financial collapse of these new nodes of financial risk can be mitigated.

2 Early Efforts to Regulate OTC Derivatives Clearing

2.1 US Regulatory Efforts

Although derivative-type products have been traded for centuries, for instance in the English wool trade or tulip bulbs in the seventeenth century in Holland, 'modern' derivatives trading took off in the United States with the Chicago Board of Trade (CBOT) in 1849 for futures and options on agricultural commodities. The financial world entered the world of derivatives at the end of the 1970s to manage exchange rate volatility, followed by interest rate options and futures. The first groundbreaking swap between IBM and the World Bank took place in 1981. In 1984, the total volume of currency and interest rate derivatives amounted to $80 billion.[1]

In 1985, the banking industry itself took the first step to install a degree of discipline in the swaps business by setting up an industry body to survey the market and agree on standards for swaps deals: the International Swap Dealers Association (ISDA).[2]

Although the market in various derivatives soared, regulators were relatively late to step in. Concerns were initially focused on acquiring a better understanding of the type of financial product that had entered the financial market and that had become increasingly popular. Although commodities derivatives traded on the CBOT and equities traded on the New Stock Exchange or National Association of Securities Dealers Automated Quotations (NASDAQ) were regulated and supervised by the US Commodities Futures Trading Commission (CFTC) and the Securities Exchange Commission (SEC), respectively, most derivatives were traded OTC, directly between parties. The lack of data meant that regulators encountered difficulties in estimating the risks involved in the business.

The first proposals to regulate OTC derivatives came from the CFTC in 1987,[3] which sought to regulate interest rate and currency swaps in the same way it regulated commodities derivatives.[4] In 1992, the notional value of interest rate and credit derivatives had increased to $4 trillion according to the Bank for International Settlements (BIS). In January 1992, the Chairman of the New York Federal Reserve Bank, Gerald

---

[1] In the absence of formal reporting requirements, estimates of the market tended to vary. See Jan G. Loeys, 'Interest Rate Swaps: A New Tool for Managing Risk' (1985) Federal Reserve Bank of Philadelphia, Business Review May/June, p. 21. Also: 'Recent Developments in the Swap Market' (February1987) Bank of England Quarterly Bulletin, p. 66.

[2] The name was subsequently changed from 'Swap Dealers' to 'Swaps and Derivatives Association' to reflect a wider suite of trades beyond interest rate derivatives.

[3] In 1987, the CFTC published for comment an advance notice of proposed rule-making in which it asserted jurisdiction over virtually all hybrid instruments, with only limited exclusions or exemptions for hybrid instruments having 'de minimis' or 'incidental' futures or commodity option features.

[4] Alan Schick, 'A Review and Analysis of the Changing Financial Environment and the Need for Regulatory Realignment' (1988) 44(1) Business Lawyer 43–64, http://www.jstor.org/stable/40687164 (accessed 23 March 2023).

Corrigan, delivered a landmark speech explicitly warning about possible regulation of the industry.[5] What made derivatives different was that, being neither loans nor securities, they were largely unaccounted for in the existing legal structure of finance. Corrigan's concerns as a central banker and Chairman of the Basel Committee on Banking Supervision (BCBS) were driven by concerns about low-probability, high-impact events that could undermine financial stability.

An important G30 report published in 1993 was the first attempt to set out a number of principles for banks' derivatives trading activities, including the use of value-at-risk (VaR) tools and marking-to-market their daily derivatives exposures.[6] However, to the disappointment of some regulators, the report did not recommend public regulation of the activity.[7]

At the request of Congress, in 1994 the US General Accounting Office (GAO) was the next body to review financial derivative products, focusing on their nature and risks, firms' and regulators' attempts to control these risks, and the possible need for regulation. The GAO report delivered crystal clear and, for some, uncomfortable recommendations. The report recommended that 'given the weaknesses and gaps that impede regulatory preparedness for dealing with a crisis associated with derivatives, Congress should require federal regulation of the safety and soundness of all major U.S. over-the-counter (OTC) derivatives dealers'.[8] The US government did not follow up on the GAO's recommendations, although, as discussed below, key elements of the GAO's recommendations found their way into CFTC proposals six years later.

During the 1980s and 1990s, regulatory attention in the United States mostly focused on the need for legal certainty as to the scope of the Commodity Exchange Act (CEA) and the CFTC's powers. The debate whether the CEA, which did not generally exclude financial derivatives, and therefore the CFTC were empowered to regulate 'swaps' occupied the best part of a decade. The discussion contained the familiar elements of those seeking regulation versus those who felt that these innovative markets should be unregulated or, at most, self-regulated. Jurisdictional quarrels between regulators

---

[5] Gerald Corrigan, 'Remarks before the 64th annual mid-Winter meeting of the New York State Bankers Association, January 30 1992', Waldorf-Astoria, Federal Reserve Bank of New York. For an interesting and prescient industry response to Corrigan's speech, see 'Why Derivatives Rattle the Regulators' (September 1992) Institutional Investor.

[6] Group of Thirty, 'Derivatives: Practices and Principles' (July 1993), https://group30.org/images/uploads/publications/G30_Derivatives-PracticesandPrinciples.pdf

[7] In the foreword to the report, the working group's Chairman, Paul Volcker, wrote:

The general attitude of the Study towards regulation is plain: derivatives by their nature do not introduce risks of a fundamentally different kind or of a greater scale than those already present in the financial markets. Hence, systemic risks are not appreciably aggravated, and supervisory concerns can be addressed within present regulatory structures and approaches. Where the official priority should be placed, in the view of the Study, is in clarifying legal uncertainties, and resolving legal inconsistencies between countries, that may impede risk-reduction procedures such as 'netting'.

[8] General Accounting Office, 'Financial Derivatives: Actions Needed to Protect the Financial System' (18 May 1994), GGD-94-133

preferring capital rules and those seeking a functional, wider, market-based approach were also prevalent.

2.2 First Steps toward International Standards: Basel and International Organization of Securities Commissions (IOSCO) 1995

By 1995, the notional value of derivatives had increased further to $8.5 trillion.[9] Wider international efforts focusing on the development of the derivatives sector initially focused on cooperation between regulators. The BCBS, chaired by Gerald Corrigan, as part of a broader move to create uniform capital standards, BIS, and the International Organization of Securities Commissions (IOSCO) set up a joint committee to work on ways to account for derivatives and require that capital be held against them. This seemingly technical process was fraught with political agendas as various countries and regulators jockeyed for competitive advantage. It was clear that any agreement between bank regulators and between securities supervisors amongst themselves, and then between the two of them, meant that a consensus would only ever be possible on the lowest common denominator.

In 1995, the BCBS, IOSCO, and the recently established International Association of Assurance Supervisors (IAIS) agreed to collaborate in the Joint Forum and to share experience on, inter alia, derivatives.[10] Although the Joint Forum made little headway beyond exchanging information about the use of derivatives in the three financial sectors involved, the Basel Committee was intent on progressing in earnest with international regulatory standards for the banking sector. The Basel Committee had been working hard on improving the old, so-called 'Basel I' framework from 1988 to align regulatory capital requirements more closely to banks' underlying risks and to encourage banks to better identify those risks and improve their risk management. After long discussions, 'Basel II' was agreed in 2004,[11] but even on the date of its publication, banking regulators agreed that 'immediate work' was required in a number of areas to keep up with market developments, including the treatment of counterparty credit risk for OTC derivatives and the treatment of cross-product netting arrangements. The Basel II rules had introduced methods for measuring risk for margined OTC derivatives and netting but required further

---

[9] See Kim Pernell, 'Market Governance, Financial Innovation, and Financial Instability: Lessons from Banks' "Adoption of Shareholder Value Management"' (2020) 49 Theory and Society 282, also for understanding how financial innovations, deregulation, and market governance arrangements combine to shape instability.

[10] Charles A.E. Goodhart, The Basel Committee on Banking Supervision: A History of the Early Years 1974–1997 (Cambridge: Cambridge University Press, 2011), p. 511ff.

[11] Basel Committee on Banking Supervision, 'International Convergence of Capital Measurement and Capital Standards: A Revised Framework' (Basel, June 2004).

clarification and consistency in a number of areas.[12] The Basel Committee acknowledged that its work would also be of interest to securities firms, over which it had no say, but was keen to press ahead with rules for banks in view of the expected delays and difficulties a common project with IOSCO would incur. Previous experience with securities regulators had shown that very different approaches to regulation and its objectives existed.

2.3 LTCM

In September 1998, Long-Term Capital Management (LTCM), the largest hedge fund in the United States, nearly collapsed when Russia defaulted on its sovereign debt, from the loss over a period of weeks of $4.6 billion (or about 90% of its capital) on losses from, inter alia, OTC derivatives positions.[13] Regulators feared that LCTM's failure would cause the failure of many of its counterparties which were the hedge fund's OTC derivative counterparties and creditors, including some of the world's largest financial institutions. Under the auspices of the New York Federal Reserve Bank, on 23 September 1998, fourteen of those institutions contributed a total of $3.6 billion to buy out the fund to keep it from failing. In April 1997, a subsequent report by the President's Working Group on the LTCM failure recommended that the SEC, the CFTC, and the Treasury receive expanded authority to require OTC derivative counterparties to provide credit risk information; record keeping; and reporting and data on concentrations, trading strategies, and risk models as well as the ability to inspect risk management models.[14]

2.4 Further US Attempts to Regulate: 2000–2005

In order to end the controversy over how swaps and other OTC derivatives related to the CEA, a Presidential Working Group (PWG) on Financial Markets was established. The PWG Report was published in November 1999.[15] It provided the basis for the Commodities Futures Modernisation Act (CFMA) of 21 December 2000.[16]

---

[12] Basel Committee on Banking Supervision, 'The Application of Basel II to Trading Activities and the Treatment of Double Default Effects', Consultative Document (April 2005).

[13] LTCM's highly leveraged trading strategies included trades in interest rate swaps.

[14] 'Report of the President's Working Group on Financial Markets, 'Hedge Funds, Leverage, and the Lessons of Long-Term Capital Management' (April 1997). Note that Federal Chairman Greenspan declined to endorse this set of recommendations but deferred to those regulators with supervisory authority.

[15] Report of the President's Working Group on Financial Markets, 'Over-the-Counter Derivatives Markets and the Commodity Exchange Act' (November 1999).

[16] H.R.5660 Commodities Futures Modernisation Act (CFMA) of 21 December 2000 was incorporated by reference in the conference report to H.R.4577 Consolidated Appropriations Act 2001 and became Public Law 106-554 on 21 December 2000.

This was the first substantive revision of the CEA in more than twenty years and the last serious attempt to regulate OTC derivatives before the financial crisis erupted. The CFMA ensured that OTC derivatives remained unregulated, at that time amounting to $80 trillion notional value. Specifically, the CFMA provided legal certainty that most OTC derivative transactions between 'sophisticated parties' would not be regulated as 'futures' under the CEA or as 'securities' under the federal securities laws. Instead, the banks and securities firms would continue to have their dealings in OTC derivatives supervised by their federal regulators. Thus, the OTC derivatives market was exempt from the CEA's capital adequacy requirements; reporting and disclosure; regulation of intermediaries; self-regulation; any bars on fraud, manipulation, and excessive speculation; and requirements for clearing. The Securities Exchange Commission (SEC) was similarly barred from OTC derivatives oversight except for the limited fraud jurisdiction it maintained over securities-based swaps.

In hindsight, the CFMA's treatment of OTC derivatives such as credit default swaps (CDS) has become controversial in view of their major role in the financial crisis of 2008 and the subsequent 2008–2012 global recession.[17] The view that the CFMA 'deregulated' the OTC derivatives market is, however, incorrect: it did not remove any existing restrictions to practices that would have prevented the financial crisis but merely codified the status quo.

Regulators' concerns nevertheless continued. End-2005, New York Federal Reserve Bank President Timothy Geithner urged the fourteen world's largest banks to clear up the substantial backlogs in the documentation of credit derivatives. In a Basel Committee meeting in which Geithner cogently argued his case, regulators gave universal support to his argument that the backlog of legal confirmations would become an operational nightmare if credit markets were rocked by, for example, a series of corporate defaults. The banks rapidly erased the backlog. However, Geithner's request to the banks to establish a clearing house for complicated derivatives contracts fell on deaf ears.

2.5 EU Tentative First Steps: Code of Conduct 2006

The EU was subject to similar pressures as the United States. First discussions about regulating OTC derivatives in earnest in the EU took place in July 2006 after ideas had been recommended by an important industry group created by the European Commission to provide expert industry advice on clearing and settlement issues

---

[17] See, e.g. Michael Greenberger, 'The Role of Derivatives in the Financial Crisis', testimony to the Financial Crisis Inquiry Commission (30 June 2010); Ranajoy Ray Chaudhuri, *The Changing Face of American Banking: Deregulation, Reregulation, and the Global Financial System* (Newyork: Palgrave Macmillan, 2014), pp. 120ff.; Paul G. Mahoney, 'Deregulation and the Subprime Crisis' (April 2018) 104(2) Virginia Law Review 235–300.

in the EU.[18] After having considered the advantages and disadvantages of a legislative solution, the European Commission, led by the Irish Commissioner Charlie
McCreevy, who was responsible for financial services and harboured doubts about
regulating the sector, decided not to propose any new legislation in the area of post-
trading and CCPs. Instead, the Commission opted for a two-pronged approach. In
order to increase efficiency and integration in the market for post-trading services, it
called on the industry itself to provide a self-regulatory solution. In November 2006,
the industry responded by adopting a Code of Conduct on Clearing and Settlement
that addressed three main issues: transparency of prices and services, access and
interoperability, and unbundling of services and accounting separation. Its scope was
limited to cash equities.[19]

After more than twenty-five years, no jurisdiction had successfully succeeded in
regulating the OTC derivatives market. This would become acutely clear when the financial crisis erupted in 2008.

2.6 Financial Crisis of 2008

Much has been written about this financial crisis, which found its origins in the
subprime mortgage sector. This chapter is limited to the part that OTC derivatives played. As at end-2008, they had reached USD 598 trillion (EUR 430 trillion)
measured by notional value and USD 35 trillion (EUR 25 trillion) by gross market
value.[20] It is now almost universally accepted by the global regulatory community that the unregulated multi-trillion-dollar OTC CDS market did not cause but
certainly helped foment a mortgage crisis, the problems of Lehman Brothers and
American International Group (AIG), then a credit crisis, and finally a systemic financial crisis.[21]

In brief, the securitization of subprime mortgage loans evolved to embed simple
mortgage-backed securities (MBS) within highly complex collateralized debt obligations (CDOs). These CDOs pulled together and dissected large numbers of

---

[18] See the 'Giovannini Reports' named after the working groups' chairman, Alberto Giovannini, which con-
tinued to influence the Commission's policy for many years: The Giovannini Group, 'Cross-Border Clearing and
Settlement Arrangements in the European Union' (Brussels, November 2001); 'Second Report on EU Clearing and
Settlement Arrangements' (Brussels, April 2003).

[19] Code of Conduct: https://www.eesc.europa.eu/en/policies/policy-areas/enterprise/database-self-and-co-reg
ulation-initiatives/76 (accessed 23 March 2023).

[20] Included within that amount was estimated to somewhere between $35 and 65 trillion in credit default
swaps: Bank for International Settlements (BIS) semi-annual OTC derivatives survey data (September 2008).

[21] See Remarks of Chairman Gary Gensler, OTC Derivatives Reform, Chatham House, London (18 March
2010); testimony of Alan Greenspan, Committee of Government Oversight and Reform (23 October 2008). In
November 2008, two months after the collapse of Lehman Brothers, the Washington G20 summit listed 'increasingly complex and opaque financial products, and consequent excessive leverage' as one of the root causes of
the global financial crisis; see for the declaration http://www.g20.utoronto.ca/2008/2008declaration1115.html
(accessed 23 March 2023).

MBSs into tranches. The tranches were, theoretically, designed to diversify and offer gradations of risk to those who wished to invest in subprime mortgages. However, investors became unmoored from the essential risk underlying loans to non-creditworthy individuals by the continuous reframing of the form of risk (e.g. from subprime mortgages to MBS to CDOs); the false assurances given by credit rating agencies that were misleadingly high evaluations of the CDOs; and, most important-ly, by the purported 'insurance' offered on CDOs in the form of CDSs as a safety net to these risky investments.[22] The CDS swaps exchanged the financial viability of a CDO between counterparties paying respectively a premium and a guarantee. CDSs were deemed to be so risk-free (and so much in demand) that financial insti-tutions began to write 'naked' CDSs, that is, offering the guarantee against default to investors who had no risk at all in any underlying mortgage-backed instruments or CDOs. Naked CDSs provided a method to short the mortgage lending market (i.e. bet that that those who could not afford mortgages would not pay them off) without any exposure to its risks.

The lack of swaps regulation, in any jurisdiction, meant that there were no clearing requirements to ensure that CDS commitments were adequately capitalized, so under-writers of CDSs did not have adequate capital to pay off guarantees when housing prices plummeted; there were no exchange trading requirements, which would have allowed the market to regularly and transparently price these assets rather than leaving such pricing to the highly contentious mathematical algorithms that constitute the dis-putatious mark-to-model system of pricing; and there were no record-keeping and re-porting requirements.

To be clear, and as can be seen from the Lehman bankruptcy proceedings, Lehman Brothers itself did not engage in the one-sided selling of credit protection on mort-gages like the AAA-rated AIG. Lehman was a counterparty or guarantor of over 930,000 OTC derivatives. To the extent that these contracts did not involve CDS, they did involve unregulated interest rate, currency, foreign exchange, and energy swaps.[23]

---

[22] While CDSs enjoy the hallmarks of insurance, 'monoline' insurance issuers of CDSs refrained from refer-ring to it as 'insurance' out of fear that CDSs would be subject to insurance regulation and strict capital adequacy requirements. By using the term 'swaps', CDSs fell into the regulatory blackhole afforded by the CFMA's swaps exclusion because no federal agency had direct supervision over, or even advance knowledge of, what went on in the private, bilateral world of swaps. See 'The Role of Financial Derivatives in the Current Financial Crisis', hearing before the Senate Agricultural Committee, 110th Congress (14 October 2008) (opening statement of Eric Dinallo, Superintendent, and New York State Insurance Dept.) stating:

> We engaged in the ultimate moral hazard [...] no one owned the downside of their underwriting de-cisions, because the banks passed it to the Wall Street, that securitized it; then investors bought it in the form of CDOs; and then they took out CDSs. And nowhere in that chain did anyone say, you must own that risk.
> https://www.govinfo.gov/content/pkg/CHRG-110shrg49574/pdf/CHRG-110shrg49574.pdf (accessed 23 March 2023).

[23] Guy Laine Charles, 'OTC Derivative Contracts in Bankruptcy: The Lehman Experience' (Spring 2009) 1 New York Business Law Journal 14 ; Kimberly Summe, 'Misconceptions about Lehman Brothers' Bankruptcy and the Role Derivatives Played' (2011) 64 Stanford Law Review Online 16, 17, https://www.stanfordlawreview.org/online/misconceptions-about-lehman-brothers-bankruptcy-and-the-role-derivatives-played (accessed 23 March 2023).

Lehman's OTC derivative counterparties' significant margin calls on those derivatives were a key factor in its bankruptcy, together with consistently ignoring its own risk thresholds through its commercial real estate investments, an extremely low liquidity ratio, and temporarily lowering its leverage ratio by moving certain assets off its balance sheet.

As further evidence of the interconnectedness of OTC derivative counterparties, on 3 April 2008, New York Fed President Timothy Geithner offered an explanation after the Bear Stearns collapse. In short, the sudden discovery by Bear's derivative counterparties that important financial positions they had put in place to protect themselves from financial risk were no longer operative would have triggered substantial further dislocations in markets. This would have precipitated a rush by Bear's counterparties to liquidate the collateral they held against those positions and to attempt to replicate those positions in already fragile markets.[24]

Of course, it was the very failure of Lehman, and the cascading adverse and substantial impacts its bankruptcy has caused, that led the Federal Reserve and the Treasury to alter course on the day after Lehman's failure and to prevent AIG's bankruptcy and then to recommend a bail out. Those actions revealed to the world the correlation between interconnectedness of unregulated OTC swaps transactions and the 'too-big-to-fail' doctrine.[25]

2.7 G20 Summit, Pittsburgh, September 2009

The watershed moment for the regulation of OTC derivatives arrived at the Pittsburgh summit in September 2009, where G20 leaders committed to increase the resilience and transparency of OTC derivatives markets and 'to reach agreement on an international framework of reform'. This would include:

> Improving over-the-counter derivatives markets: All standardized OTC derivative contracts should be traded on exchanges or electronic trading platforms, where appropriate, and cleared through central counterparties by end-2012 at the latest. OTC derivative contracts should be reported to trade repositories. Non-centrally cleared contracts should be subject to higher capital requirements. We ask the FSB and its relevant members to assess regularly implementation and whether it is sufficient to improve transparency in the derivatives markets, mitigate systemic risk, and protect against market abuse.[26]

---

[24] 'Actions by the New York Fed in Response to Liquidity Pressures in Financial Markets', testimony before the U.S. Senate Committee on Banking, Housing and Urban Affairs, Washington, D.C. (3 April 2008).

[25] Congressional Oversight Panel, 'June Oversight Report: The AIG Rescue, Its Impact on Markets, and the Government's Exit Strategy' (10 June 2010), 286, https://www.govinfo.gov/content/pkg/CPRT-111JPRT56698/pdf/CPRT-111JPRT56698.pdf (accessed 23 March 2023).

[26] G20 'Leader Statement', the Pittsburgh Summit (24–25 September 2009), pp. 8–9.

The G20 summits in Cannes (November 2011) and St Petersburg (September 2013) added additional aspects to the OTC derivative reform agenda, notably margining requirements for non-centrally cleared derivatives in the case of the former and the agreement that jurisdictions should defer to the CCP rules of other jurisdictions in the case of the latter. As will be discussed below, the reference to 'deference' was the consequence of the disagreement between the EU and the United States, led by the European Commission and the CFTC. The implementation of the aforementioned four sentences in the Pittsburgh commitment on OTC derivatives resulted in an unprecedented wave of new standards and regulations at the global level and in individual jurisdictions, with the ultimate aim of improving transparency, avoiding market abuse, and reducing systemic risks of OTC derivatives markets.

2.8 The Financial Stability Board (FSB)

The G20 meeting in Pittsburgh also took the opportunity to establish and mandate work for the recently established Financial Stability Board (FSB), the successor to the Financial Stability Forum. The G20 endorsed the FSB's objectives, mandate, and organizational structure. The FSB has since assumed a key role in promoting the reform of international financial regulation and supervision. At the initiative of the FSB,[27] in April 2010, and reflecting the need to address regulatory issues from a global perspective, a working group was set up comprised of international standard setters and authorities responsible for translating the G20 commitments into standards and implementing regulations and to make recommendations on the implementation of the G20 objectives.[28] The working group had three co-chairs representing the Committee on Payment and Settlement Systems (CPSS), IOSCO, and the European Commission. The working group was focused on common approaches to OTC derivatives market reforms to achieve consistency in implementation across jurisdictions, while promoting greater use of OTC derivatives products in standardized form and minimizing the potential for regulatory arbitrage. The working group continued to make regular reports on progress in implementing reforms to the FSB. The first report was issued in March 2011; recent reports have been published on an annual basis.[29] Particularly, the first reports indicated the problems arising from diverging approaches to regulation across jurisdictions. Besides monitoring the progress of reform, the key issue for discussion during the first years of the working group was potential cross-border conflicts. The EU and the United States used the working group and the FSB to comment on shortcomings in each others' regulatory approaches. The differences in opinion and the EU's opposition to the US extraterritorial application of its

---

[27] The FSB's decisions are not legally binding on its members—instead, the organization operates by moral suasion and peer pressure in order to set internationally agreed policies and minimum standards that its members commit to implementing at national level.

[28] See https://www.fsb.org/wp-content/uploads/r_101025.pdf (accessed 23 March 2023).

[29] For the most recent report of November 2022, see https://www.fsb.org/2022/11/otc-derivatives-market-refo rms-implementation-progress-in-2022/ (accessed 23 March 2023).

rules resulted in the refusal of the European Commission to grant the CFTC 'equivalence' under EMIR until 2016, as explained in 3.5.

2.9 Dodd–Frank Act 2009

The United States was the first major jurisdiction to comprehensively legislate the OTC derivatives area. On 11 August 2009, the Treasury Department sent to Congress proposed legislation titled the 'Over-the-Counter Derivatives Markets Act of 2009'. To accomplish this 'comprehensive regulation', the proposed legislation would repeal many of the provisions of the CFMA. The proposed legislation established new requirements for parties dealing in non-'standardized' OTC derivatives and would require that 'standardized' OTC derivatives be traded through a regulated trading facility and cleared through regulated central clearing. The proposed legislation would also repeal the CFMA's limits on SEC authority over 'security-based swaps'.[30] In late April 2010, debate began on the floor of the Senate over their version of the reform legislation and on 21 July 2010, H.R.4173 passed in the Senate and was signed into law as the 'Dodd–Frank Wall Street Reform and Consumer Protection Act'.[31]

2.10 Global Standards: Committee on Payments and Market Infrastructures (CPMI)–IOSCO Principles 2012

As part of a global regulatory response to the crisis, work started on enhanced global standards for financial market infrastructures (FMIs). In February 2010, the Committee on Payment and Settlement Systems (CPSS), later renamed the Committee on Payments and Market Infrastructures (CPMI) and IOSCO launched a comprehensive review of three existing sets of standards for systemically important payment systems, securities settlement systems, and CCPs.[32] The discussion and framing of the principles offered a good occasion to compare jurisdictions' legislative efforts as each jurisdiction sought to have its own rules reflected in the international principles. Many of the EU's regulatory approaches and requirements were brought to the table of the international standard setter as EMIR was being negotiated in parallel in Brussels. At the same time, the US and Asian regulators sought to see their own national regulatory preferences reflected in the rules that were being discussed.

---

[30] For a comprehensive legal analysis and explanation of the division of jurisdiction and powers between the SEC and the CFTC, see US Regulation of the International Securities and Derivatives Markets, § 12.01, SECURITIES. ISDM, 12th edition. For an overview of how the Dodd–Frank Act expanded the CFTC's powers, see Clifford Chance, *Guide to United States and United Kingdom Derivative and Commodity Market Enforcement Regimes* (Clifford Chance, 2019).

[31] H.R.4173—Dodd–Frank Wall Street Reform and Consumer Protection Act, https://www.congress.gov/bill/111th-congress/house-bill/4173/text/pp (accessed 23 March 2023).

[32] In 2014, the CPSS was renamed the Committee on Payments and Market Infrastructures (CPMI). See https://www.bis.org/cpmi/publ/d94.htm (accessed 23 March 2023).

Published in April 2012, the Principles for Financial Market Infrastructures (PFMIs) reflect the lessons learned from the financial crisis. This applies in particular to the need to mitigate risks arising from centrally cleared OTC derivatives.[33] The PFMIs set strong risk management standards for CCPs.[34] To increase the resilience of CCPs, the PFMIs set stronger requirements for CCPs' credit and liquidity risk management as well as their investment and custody risk. CCPs need to cover credit exposures to their members for all products through an effective margin system that is risk-based and regularly reviewed and tested[35] and also maintain financial resources sufficient to cover the default of the largest member (or, in the case of globally active CCPs, the two largest members) in extreme but plausible market conditions.[36] This discussion about financial resources reflects a difference between the United States and the EU in the CPMI–IOSCO discussions about appropriate standards for FMIs, where the former was of the view that the default of the single largest member ('cover 1') should be the yardstick and the EU held the position that the default of the two largest members should be reflected ('cover 2'). Indeed, all CCPs regulated in the EU, regardless of size or whether they operate locally or internationally, are subject to the 'cover 2' requirement in EMIR (see below). A final compromise was reached in the meeting between the CPMI and IOSCO in Venice in 2011, and co-chaired by Bill Dudley from the New Federal Reserve Bank representing CPMI and Masamichi Kono from the Japanese Financial Services Authority, to limit the 'cover 2' principle to 'globally active CCPs', effectively excluding US clearing organizations that do not operate internationally. In addition to the discussion between the United States and the EU about the extraterritoriality of CFTC regulations, this divergence of views that first appeared in the CPMI–IOSCO discussions was a further reason for the European Commission to examine CFTC 'equivalence' under EMIR (see below). Importantly, for the first time, the PFMIs also introduced a framework for trade repositories. The PFMIs also outline responsibilities for central banks, market regulators, and other relevant authorities responsible for FMIs in implementing the standards. The PFMIs are not legally binding, although the FSB, IOSCO, and CPMI member jurisdictions have committed to implement them, while CPMI and IOSCO continue to monitor progress in this respect.

3 EMIR: The EU Regulation on OTC Derivatives Clearing

3.1 Preparing for Regulation in the EU, 2006

In Europe, a large part of the Pittsburgh reform initiative was formalized in 2012 in the European Market Infrastructure Regulation (EMIR).[37] Work on regulating OTC

---

[33] See https://www.bis.org/cpmi/publ/d101a.pdf (accessed 23 March 2023).
[34] See Principles 4, 6, 7, 13, 14, and 20.
[35] See Principle 6.
[36] See Principle 4.
[37] Regulation (EU) No. 648/2012 of the European Parliament and of the Council of 4 July 2012 on OTC derivatives, central counterparties and trade repositories, OJ L201/1 (27 July 2012). The working title European Market

derivatives commenced in parallel with the United States and that of CPMI–IOSCO but was subject to the longer lead times for final adoption by the European institutions. EMIR also implements the PFMIs but in far greater detail and providing a legally binding framework that is directly applicable in the legal orders of the EU Member States. This means that no national transposition laws are required.[38] EMIR entered into force in August 2012 and, for the first time, introduced a common EU regulatory and supervisory framework for CCPs and trade repositories. The preparatory work for regulation in the EU took more than four years.[39]

3.1.1 The European Commission's regulatory process starts with 'Public Communications'

The European legislative process to adopt EMIR is a good example of the general way in which legislation is prepared in Brussels. EMIR offers some clear insights as to how the Commission will often, at an early stage, indicate its intention to legislate and how that process will often develop and involve other EU institutions, such as the Council, Parliament, and, in this case, the European Central Bank (ECB), to a proposal and final legal text. As usual, the European Commission started its legislative process with a public announcement in the form of a 'Communication' to outline its broad ideas and seek a response from the Member States and the industry. At the end of 2008, the Commission staff had already started to review the OTC derivatives market as it stood in the second half of 2008, and early signals were that regulation was high on the agenda: a speech by the European Commissioner responsible for the financial sector was employed to announce its regulatory intentions.[40] Initially, the Commission services' attention focused solely on the CDS market, which was at the centre of attention with Bear Stearns and Lehman's. In order to facilitate the monitoring of the major dealers' commitment in this area, the Commission established the Derivatives Working Group (DWG). The DWG included representatives from the financial institutions that committed to clear European-referenced CDS by July 2009 and representatives from CCPs, trade repositories, and other relevant market participants and from relevant European (ECB, the Committee of European Securities Regulators (CESR), the Committee of European Banking Supervisors (CEBS) and the Committee of European Insurance and Occupational Pension Supervisors (CEIOPS)[41]) and national supervisory (Autorité

Infrastructure Regulation (EMIR) was coined in 2010 when Commission staff originally dubbed the draft proposal European Market Infrastructure Legislation (EMIL), referencing the Christian name of a senior manager in the Commission who was involved in the legislative project and who immediately and personally renamed the draft proposal as 'EMIR'.

[38] In June 2013, the Governing Council of the ECB adopted the PFMIs as Eurosystem 'oversight standards' for all FMIs in the euro area under Eurosystem responsibility.

[39] Note that the adoption of EMIR still required the preparation and adoption of many technical details in further regulations for the key principles in EMIR to enter into force, as will be discussed below.

[40] In October 2008, European Commissioner, Charlie McCreevy, called for concrete proposals as to how the risks from credit derivatives can be mitigated. Charles McCreevy, 'Time for Regulators to Get a Better View of Derivatives', SPEECH/08/538 (17 October 2008).

[41] The Committee of European Securities Regulators (CESR), Committee of European Banking Supervisors (CEBS), and Committee of European Insurance and Occupational Pension Supervisors (CEIOPS) were the

des Marchés Financiers (AMF), Federal Financial Supervisory Authority (BaFin), and Financial Services Authority (FSA)) authorities. In view of the OTC market structure and discussions in the DWG, it soon became clear to the Commission that it needed to look beyond CDS and consider also other sectors, such as interest rate derivatives.[42] At the end of 2008, the Commission made a series of public announcements over a twelve-month period. As the financial crisis had evolved into a global depression, policymakers from within and outside the EU needed to be involved and committed to financial sector reform.

This started with a report from a 'High Level Group' set up in 2008, chaired by Jacques de Larosière, which proposed recommendations for financial sector reform in response to the financial crisis, with a particular focus on the institutional aspects of supervision and how supervisors and regulators interacted and cooperated. The High Level Group reported on 25 February 2009, offering an analysis of the causes of the financial crisis and thirty-one recommendations for regulatory, supervisory, and global repair action.[43] The report, which is the basis for establishing the various supervisory 'committees' in the EU (including ESMA for financial markets, the European Banking Agency (EBA) for banking, and the European Insurance and Occupational Pensions Authority (EIOPA) for insurance and pensions) is surprisingly short on OTC derivatives, offering three brief recommendations to simplify and standardize OTC derivatives; introduce and require the use of at least one well-capitalized central clearing house for CDSs in the EU; and guarantee that issuers of securitised products retain on their books, for the life of the instrument, a meaningful amount of the (non-hedged) underlying risk.

Three weeks later, a Commission Communication of 4 March 2009 to the European Council contained an ambitious reform programme, referring to the High Level Group and including the first indication of a commitment to OTC derivatives regulation in the EU by promising 'a report on derivatives and other complex structured products'.[44] The wide-ranging agenda of regulatory reform required separate Communications for the various areas of the programme, which included banking, credit rating agencies, hedge funds, and financial stability as well as financial markets.

Meanwhile, at global level, discussions between the Commission, certain Member States and the US authorities ensured that the G20 Summit in London in April remained committed to regulatory reform. The G20 continued to promote the standardization

---

predecessors of the later European supervisory authorities ESMA, CEBS, and EIOPA, respectively. See below for a discussion of these authorities.

[42] The size of the EU OTC derivatives market in terms of notional outstanding was around EUR 460 trillion according to the EMIR public data for end-June 2016. By far the largest asset class, reaching 85% of the notional outstanding at end-June, were interest rate derivatives, followed by foreign exchange (FX) derivatives (9%), while credit, commodity, and equity-linked derivatives together made up around 6%. See https://www.ecb.europa.eu/pub/pdf/other/eb201608_article02.en.pdf (accessed 23 March 2023), p. 10.

[43] Report from the High Level Group on Financial Supervision in the EU (Brussels, 25 February 2009).

[44] European Commission, 'Driving European Recovery, Communication for the Spring European Council' (Brussels, 4 March 2009) COM(2009) 114 final.

and resilience of credit derivatives markets, in particular through the establishment of central clearing counterparties subject to effective regulation and supervision.[45]

The Commission's ideas and intentions also required specific political endorsement by EU leaders. Without political endorsement by Member States' heads of state and government, the progress of legislative proposals would be difficult. The Commission, working with the presidency of the Council and the Member States, put the need for regulatory reform of the financial sector on the agenda of the July meeting of the European Council. When it met in London in June 2009, the European Council provided the necessary political backing to the Commission's proposed reform agenda calling for further progress to be made in the regulation of financial markets, 'notably on the transparency and stability of derivatives markets'.[46]

The details of the Commission services' preliminary work that had been underway since mid-2008 became public in its Communication of 3 July 2009, called 'Ensuring Efficient, Safe and Sound Derivatives Markets'.[47] In this Communication, the Commission assessed in greater detail the role of derivatives in the financial crisis and prepared the ground for its forthcoming regulation of the sector to address the problems identified.[48] Importantly, for the very first time, the Commission announced its views about the need to locate CCP clearing in Europe for 'regulatory, supervisory and monetary policy concerns'.[49] The Communication was very clear that if a CCP is located in Europe, it is subject to European rules and supervision. Supervisors accordingly have undisputed and unfettered access to the information held by CCPs. It is also easier for European authorities to intervene in case of a problem at a European CCP.' For example, central banks do not provide direct access to their liquidity facilities to financial institutions located outside their currency areas'.[50] Of course, the discussion about 'CCP location' remains with the EU until today. The Commission's Communication included two further papers; a 'staff working paper', with a detailed analysis of the derivatives sector, and a public Consultation Document on possible regulatory measures. The response time for the public consultation was extremely short: two months.[51]

Following a conference on derivatives markets in Brussels on 25 September 2009,[52] the Commission finally presented a further Communication on 20 October 2009 outlining, for the first time, the specific actions it intended to take to reduce the risks

[45] G20 'Leader Statement' (London, 2 April 2009), https://www.imf.org/external/np/sec/pr/2009/pdf/g20_040 209.pdf (accessed 23 March 2023).

[46] Presidency Conclusions, Brussels European Council (18–19 June 2009), paras 15–24 concluded on the need for 'a new order in financial markets', https://www.consilium.europa.eu/uedocs/cms_data/docs/pressdata/en/ec/108622.pdf (accessed 23 March 2023).

[47] Communication from the Commission, 'Ensuring Efficient, Safe and Sound Derivatives Markets' (Brussels, 3 July 2009) COM(2009) 332 final.

[48] The Communication was a reference point for the Commission to announce the preparation of a legislative proposal on the derivatives market in its work programme for 2010, https://commission.europa.eu/system/files/2016-10/cwp2010_en.pdf (accessed 23 March 2023).

[49] See p. 4.

[50] See p. 10.

[51] See https://eur-lex.europa.eu/LexUriServ/LexUriServ.do?uri=COM:2009:0332:FIN:EN:PDF (accessed 23 March 2023). Under current Commission rules, a public consultation would require a longer feedback period.

[52] The conference's recordings and documents are available on the Commission's website https://eur-lex.europa.eu/LexUriServ/LexUriServ.do?uri=COM:2009:0563:FIN:EN:PDF (accessed 23 March 2023).

associated with derivatives.[53] These included standardization of products, trade re-porting, and incentives for central clearing and trade execution. The Commission also made it clear that it was already in regular contact with international regulators to ensure a coherent implementation of its policies across the globe 'and in particular with the US, which is also in the process of designing a new approach for derivatives markets'.[54] As we will see below, these discussions were, first and foremost, about the need for regulations in the EU and the United States that promoted global business and avoided cross-border regulatory friction. Still, the Communication did not contain a great amount of detail about the possible content of legislative proposals, but it did clarify the timeline for those proposals:'mid-2010'.[55]

3.1.2 EU Member States get involved in the Council

On 2 December 2009, the Economic and Financial Affairs Council (ECOFIN) of EU finance ministers discussed the Commission's intentions to legislate and endorsed the broad approach suggested by the Commission.[56] The Council had already committed itself to a 'roadmap' at a meeting in October including CCP clearing of standardized OTC derivative contracts, higher capital requirements for uncleared trades, and re-porting non-standardized derivative contracts to trade repositories. One important comment in the ECOFIN conclusions should be stressed. ECOFIN welcomed

> the paradigm shift in the approach towards derivatives markets suggested by the Commission, namely moving from so-called 'light-handed regulation' to a more am-bitious and comprehensive regulatory policy, that is aimed at reducing counterparty and operational risks, increasing transparency of the derivatives market and strength-ening market integrity and oversight and, operationally, is expected to shift derivatives trading and clearing from predominantly OTC bilateral transactions towards central-ised trading and clearing infrastructures.[57]

The Commission's intention to work on a comprehensive regulation of OTC deriva-tives, similar to the United States, had now been fully endorsed by all Member States.

3.1.3 First contours of legislation: Commission 'working papers'

This was the starting sign for the Commission to call together the Member States to dis-cuss in a working group the forthcoming legislation.[58] The working group was chaired by the Commission's services and was constituted of experts from Member States'

---

[53] Communication from the Commission to the European Commission to the European Parliament, the Council, the European Economic and Social Committee, the Committee of the Regional and the European Central Bank, 'Ensuring Efficient, Safe and Sound Derivatives Markets: Future Policy Actions' (Brussels, 20 October 2009) COM(2009) 563 final.

[54] See p. 3.

[55] See pp. 10–11.

[56] See http://www.consilium.europa.eu/ueDocs/cms_Data/docs/pressdata/en/ecofin/111706.pdf (accessed 23 March 2023).

[57] See para. 5.

[58] Member States Working Group on Derivatives and Market Infrastructures.

market supervisory authorities, central banks, and finance ministries. Representatives from Member States' Permanent Representations and the ECB also participated. The working group considered discussion papers prepared by the Commission's services focusing on a wide number of specific topics and policy options such as scope, clearing incentives, decision-making procedures, trade repositories, etc. The working group did not discuss the draft legal text itself as this could potentially pose legal problems for the Commission when it adopted its final text. The Commission did, however, present outlines of legal texts on individual subjects where possible. The value of the meetings of the working group cannot be overstated. The discussion papers also found their way to the industry, which took the opportunity to make its own views known to the Commission, in writing and in meetings. Member States' experts groups allowed the Commission to 'road-test' the technical and political feasibility and support for its legislation. At least as important, the participants in the discussions were often the same individuals who participated in the next steps of the legislative negotiations in the Council's working groups. Many of the participants also met in the international forums, such as the FSB OTC derivatives working group, CPMI–IOSCO meetings, etc. In short, participants knew each other personally, which contributed to a strong sense of common purpose.

During the spring of 2010, the internal drafting of the draft legislation was well underway in the Commission. However, as the drafting of the legal text progressed, it became clear from discussions in the Member States' working group that further consultation of the sector was required on a number of issues. The need for further consultation can be explained by the fact that this was a completely new area of financial sector regulation for the Commission. Unlike the banking or insurance sectors, which could build on legislation dating back to the 1970s, legislation on OTC derivatives clearing was a blank sheet. The only existing regulatory requirements were in the field of bank regulatory capital (see below for the bank Committee's 'trading book review'), and only a minority of Member States had relevant national rules in place for the Commission as a point of reference.

This explains why a further public consultation was initiated by the Commission from 14 June to 10 July 2010 to get feedback from interested stakeholders on the contours of the legislative measures.[59] This time, the details of the Commission's thinking had become clearer. The consultation document, noting that the Commission was in the process of finalizing its draft legislative proposals, said that it needed to finalize its views on four specific issues: clearing and risk mitigation of OTC derivatives, CCP requirements, interoperability, and reporting to trade repositories. The internal drafting process of the legislation had also made it clear that a number of technical standards and guidelines would not be included in the legislation itself but would need to be developed by the newly established ESMA, in some instances with the cooperation of either its new banking counterpart, the EBA, or the European System of Central Banks (ESCB). This reliance on 'level 2' measures was a clear departure from the old style of

---

[59] European Commission, Public Consultation on Derivatives and Market Infrastructures, https://ec.europa.eu/finance/consultations/2010/derivatives/docs/100614_derivatives_en.pdf (accessed 23 March 2023).

financial sector legislation in the EU and followed up from the High Level Group's report in February 2008 and the Commission's Communication of March 2008.

3.1.4 The European Parliament expresses its views

The EP also became increasingly involved in OTC derivatives. A small number of Members of the EP (MEPs) from the EP's Committee on Economic and Monetary Affairs worked hard to prepare the EP's input on the forthcoming legislation.[60] During the June 2010 plenary session, the EP adopted a Resolution that:

> [w]elcomes the Commission's initiative for better regulation of derivatives, and in particular OTC derivatives with a view to reducing the impact of the risks in the OTC derivatives markets for the stability of financial markets as a whole, and backs the calls for legal standardisation of derivatives contracts [...], the use of trade repositories and centralised data storage, [and] the use and strengthening of central clearing houses.[61]

3.2 Commission's Proposal for Regulating OTC Derivatives in the EU: EMIR 2010

On 15 September 2010, the European Commission finally adopted its legislative proposal.[62] The proposal for a regulation was accompanied by an impact assessment analysing the options to reduce systemic risk by increasing the safety and efficiency of the OTC derivatives market.[63]

EMIR is an interesting first example of major financial services legislation in the form of a regulation. Until the financial crisis, almost all legislation took the form of a directive, which is binding on Member States in so far as achieving its objectives is concerned. A 'directive' is a legislative act that sets out a goal that all EU countries must achieve. However, it is up to the individual countries to devise their own laws on how to reach these goals.[64] Regulations, on the other hand, are directly applicable in Member States' legal orders and do not need national laws to transpose the European legislation. One of the key drivers to choose regulations as the preferred instrument in the financial

---

[60] The ECON rapporteur W. Langen and ECON members K. Swinburne and P. Beres in particular showed a keen interest and contributed significantly to improving the Commission's proposal in substance and in creating a conducive process for agreement in the Parliament.

[61] 'Report on Derivatives Markets: Future Policy Actions' ('Langen Report') https://eur-lex.europa.eu/legal-cont ent/EN/TXT/?uri=CELEX:52010IP0206 (accessed 23 March 2023).

[62] Proposal for a Regulation of the European Parliament and of the Council on OTC Derivatives, Central Counterparts and Trade Repositories (Brussels, 15 September 2010) COM(2010) 484 final. Although the text had been finalized before the summer, the Commission's internal adoption procedures requiring consultation of associated Commission services, translation requirements (the original text had been drafted in English), and preparatory discussions between the cabinets of the Commissioners added, as usual, around three months to the final adoption of the proposal.

[63] The impact assessment report can be found on https://eur-lex.europa.eu/legal-content/EN/TXT/PDF/?uri= CELEX:52010SC1058&from=EN (accessed 23 March 2023).

[64] Treaty on the Functioning of the European Union (TFEU), Art. 288.

services sector was the unhappy experience with the Capital Requirements Directive implementing Basel II in 2004.[65] Compared to the first series of banking legislation at the beginning of the 1980s,[66] the rules had become increasingly complex and technical. This reflected the increasing sophistication of the banking sector to develop more complex financial products and risk management systems. As supervisors needed to keep up with the pace of market developments, so did the regulatory framework. Inserting a significant amount of technical detail in directives was necessary for two reasons: first to ensure that Member States did not enjoy too much latitude to diverge from the requirements in national laws (although it was possible to go further with even stricter 'goldplated' rules at national level); second, details in those directives could not be revised quickly to align with rapid market developments: the full and lengthy institutional procedures needed easily took around eighteen months to complete.

For these reasons, the Commission decided to base EMIR on Art. 114 of the Treaty on the Functioning of the European Union (TFEU). A Regulation was considered to be the most appropriate legal instrument to introduce a mandatory requirement for all actors to clear standardized OTC derivatives through CCPs and to ensure that CCPs (that will, as a consequence, assume and concentrate significant risk) are subject to uniform prudential standards in the EU. Furthermore, a Regulation was considered to be the appropriate legal instrument to confer new powers on ESMA as the sole authority with the responsibility to register and exercise surveillance of trade repositories in the EU.

The Commission' proposal was discussed and revised in a number of places during the inter-institutional negotiations in the Council and the EP. After almost two years of intensive negotiations, the structure and content of the final legislative text did not depart significantly from the Commission's original proposal—the most evident difference being the supervisory powers allocated to ESMA. To a large extent, this was the result of Commission's extensive preparatory discussions with the Member States and the industry during the period 2008–2009. The preparatory work in the Commission's Member States' experts working group also contributed. As usual, further detail, precision, and clarification was added by the Council working group in particular. Many of the clarifications of the text were necessary to make sure that the text was unambiguous and could be applied directly by the Member States without discretion and the need for interpretation. This was a necessary and reasonable price to pay for Member States accepting a regulation rather than a directive in this area. As not all Member States were in favour of a regulation and preferred a directive, the additional detail of a regulation was also a means to alleviate some of their concerns.

---

[65] Directive 2006/48/EC of the European Parliament and of the Council of 14 June 2006 relating to the taking up and pursuit of the business of credit institutions (recast) OJ L177, 30.6.2006 p.1; Directive 2006/49/EC of the European Parliament and of the Council of 14 June 2006 on the capital adequacy of investment firms and credit institutions (recast) OJ L177 (30 June 2006), p. 217.

[66] Second Council Directive 89/646/EEC of 15 December 1989 on the coordination of laws, regulations and administrative provisions relating to the taking up and pursuit of the business of credit institutions and amending Directive 77/780/EEC, OJ L386 (30 December 1989), p. 1.

3.3 Final Adoption by Council and EP EMIR 2012

3.3.1 Scope and definitions

The Regulation consists of a number of 'titles', subdivided into 'chapters'. Title I provides for the scope and definitions of EMIR. The scope of the Regulation is wide and lays down uniform requirements covering financial counterparties, non-financial counterparties (exceeding certain thresholds), and all categories of OTC derivative contracts. Its prudential parts apply to CCPs as a result of the clearing obligation and, for the reporting requirement, to trade repositories. It is important to note, however, that the authorization and supervision requirements for CCPs apply irrespective of the financial instrument the CCPs clear: OTC or other. This approach reflected the development in the Commission's thinking after 2008, when it originally focused only on CDS trades. Exemptions are explicitly foreseen for the members of the ESCB (and certain other central banks), public bodies charged with or intervening in the management of the public debt, and to multilateral development banks, in order to avoid limiting their powers to intervene to stabilize the market if and when required. The Council and the EP added an important exemption from the clearing obligation for intra-group transactions, reflecting industry requests to take into account the way in which derivative transactions are booked in practice in subsidiaries across the world through intra-group transactions.

3.3.2 EMIR: Clearing obligation

Title II is central to implementing the obligation to clear all designated 'standardised OTC derivatives' as agreed in the G20. It regulates the clearing, reporting, and risk mitigation of OTC derivatives (see also Chapter 4 'CCP Access Structures' by Christina Sell in this volume). In order to implement the G20 commitment into legislative obligations, the Commission originally approached 'standardized' contracts, meaning those contracts that are eligible for clearing by CCPs. with a process that will take into account the risk aspects connected to mandatory clearing. The Council and the EP revised and expanded the proposal and introduced a far more detailed procedure and mandate for ESMA, including establishing a public register of OTC contracts subject to the clearing obligation.

To establish a process that ensures that as many OTC contracts as possible will be cleared, EMIR includes two approaches to determine which contracts must be cleared:

(1) a 'bottom-up' approach, according to which a CCP decides to clear certain contracts and is authorized to do so by its competent authority, who is then obliged to inform ESMA once it approves the CCP to clear those contracts. ESMA will then have the powers to decide whether a clearing obligation should apply to all of those contracts in the EU. ESMA will need to base that decision on certain objective criteria;

(2) a 'top-down' approach, according to which ESMA, together with the European Systemic Risk Board (ESRB), will determine which contracts should potentially be subject to the clearing obligation. This process is important to identify and capture those contracts in the market that are not yet being cleared by a CCP.

Non-financial (corporate) counterparties are, in principle, not subject to the rules of the Regulation unless their OTC derivatives positions reach a threshold and are considered to be systemically important. Because their derivatives activities are generally assumed to cover those derivatives that are directly linked to their commercial activity rather than speculation, those derivatives positions have been exempted from EMIR's clearing obligation. Other transactions, such as certain foreign exchange transactions and risks hedged by pension funds, were also exempted from the clearing obligation (see below).

In concrete terms, this means that the clearing obligation only applies to those OTC contracts of non-financial counterparties that are particularly active in the OTC derivatives market and if the contracts are not directly linked to their commercial activity. For example, this may be the case for energy suppliers that sell future production, agricultural firms fixing the price at which they are going to sell their crops, airlines fixing the price of their future fuel purchases, or any other commercial company that must legitimately hedge the risk arising from their specific activity. There are, however, reasons for not granting non-financial counterparties a full exemption from EMIR's scope.

First, non-financial counterparties are active participants in the OTC derivatives market and often transact with financial counterparties. Excluding them entirely would diminish the effectiveness of the clearing obligation. Second, some non-financial counterparties may take systemically important positions in OTC derivatives. Leaving systemically relevant non-financial counterparties, whose failure may have a significant negative effect on the market, completely outside the scope of regulatory attention would not be an acceptable course of action. Third, a full exclusion of non-financial counterparties could lead to regulatory arbitrage. A financial counterparty could easily circumvent the obligations set out in the Regulation by establishing a new non-financial entity and direct its OTC derivative business through it. Finally, their inclusion in the scope of application is also necessary to ensure global convergence with third countries. US legislation does not provide a complete exemption of non-financial counterparties from the reporting and the clearing obligations.

In view of the above, EMIR sets out a process that helps to identify the non-financial institutions with systemically important positions in OTC derivatives and subjects them to certain obligations specified under the Regulation. The process is based on the definition of two thresholds:

(1) an information threshold;
(2) a clearing threshold.

These thresholds have been specified by the European Commission at 'level 2' on the basis of draft regulatory standards proposed by ESMA. The information threshold will allow financial authorities to identify non-financial counterparties that have accumulated significant positions in OTC derivatives. The clearing threshold, on the other hand, is used to establish whether a non-financial counterparty will become subject to the clearing obligation. Both thresholds are defined taking into account the systemic relevance of the sum of net positions and exposures of a counterparty per class of derivatives. However, and importantly, and as clarified and confirmed above, in calculating the positions for the clearing threshold, derivative contracts should not be taken into account if they have been entered into to cover the risks arising from an objectively measurable commercial activity.[67]

As not all OTC derivatives will be considered eligible for central clearing, there remains a need to improve arrangements and the safety of those contracts that will continue to be managed on a so-called 'bilateral' basis. Non-standardized OTC derivative contracts that are not considered suitable for CCP clearing entail counterparty credit and operational risk, and, therefore, rules are established to manage that risk. To mitigate counterparty credit risk, market participants that are subject to the clearing obligation should have risk management procedures that require the timely, accurate, and appropriately segregated exchange of collateral.[68]

'CCP access' was heavily debated in the EP and the Council working group. In the final stage of Council negotiations in the ECOFIN meeting in Luxembourg on 5 October, it was one of two remaining political obstacles preventing agreement between finance ministers (the second issue was CCP authorization, see Chapter 3.3.4). The dominance of certain exchanged-owned clearing structures (e.g. Deutsche Börse) could be challenged by EMIR breaking open such 'vertical silo' structures by allowing open access to clearing. EMIR's attempts to open access to vertical silos had already been diminished by limiting its scope to OTC derivatives and excluding exchange traded derivatives as well as the removal of a draft provision guaranteeing access to trade feeds. The final text of EMIR contains no reference to trade feeds at all; it is limited to a general reference that access to a CCP may only be refused if it would threaten the smooth and orderly functioning of the markets or would adversely affect systemic risk.[69]

---

[67] Commission Delegated Regulation (EU) No. 149/2013 of 19 December 2012 supplementing Regulation (EU) No. 648/2012 of the European Parliament and of the Council with regard to regulatory technical standards on indirect clearing arrangements, the clearing obligation, the public register, access to a trading venue, non-financial counterparties, and risk mitigation techniques for OTC derivatives contracts not cleared by a CCP, OJ L 052 (23 February 2013), p. 11.

[68] Commission Delegated Regulation (EU) No. 2016/2251 of 4 October 2016 supplementing Regulation (EU) No. 648/2012 of the European Parliament and of the Council on OTC derivatives, central counterparties and trade repositories with regard to regulatory technical standards for risk-mitigation techniques for OTC derivative contracts not cleared by a central counterparty, OJ L340 (15 December 2016), p. 9.

[69] See also Chapters 7 ('What Kind of Thing Is a Central Counterparty? The Role of Clearing Houses as a Source of Policy Controversy' by Rebecca Lewis and David Murphy) and 14 ('Open Access for OTC Derivatives: Concept and Implications' by Corentine Poilvet-Clediere and Julien Jardelot) in this volume for a further discussion of these issues.

3.3.3 Initial margins

On 1 September 2019, phase four of the initial margin (IM) rules for non-cleared derivatives (NCDs) under the ESMA and the EBA's joint margin regulatory technical standards (RTS) was implemented. This 'phase' obliged counterparties to NCDs to exchange IM (subject to any available exemptions) where both counterparties (or their groups) each had an 'average aggregate notional amount' (AANA) of NCDs above EUR 750 billion, calculated across the last business day of March, April, and May in the year of implementation. The various 'phases' and quantums were negotiated at international level between IOSCO and the Basel Committee.

Under the Margin RTS, phase five, with an AANA threshold of EUR 8 billion, was due to come into effect on 1 September 2020. However, it was agreed that no IM need to be exchanged if the amount of IM between two counterparties (exceeding the AANA) was less than EUR 50 billion. This threshold was increased following industry pressure over the sheer number of groups that would be required to comply at once. Further, in April 2020, due to the coronavirus pandemic, the BCBS and the ISOC recommended that implementation of the final two phases be delayed a further year.[70] The Margin RTS Amending Regulation provides for a formal implementation of these recommendations in the EU so that regulatory enforcement of phase five was delayed until 1 September 2021. Phase six, using the original phase five AANA threshold of EUR 8 billion, was postponed until 1 September 2022.

3.3.4 EMIR CCP supervision and prudential requirements

The authorization and supervision of CCPs is provided for by Title III. It reflects the reality that a large majority of Member States was of the view that the time was not ripe to give ESMA direct supervisory powers over CCPs, nor that ESMA would bear any responsibility for the financial and fiscal implications of the failure of a CCP. The final text of EMIR followed the Commission's proposal so that *national* authorities should retain the responsibility for authorizing (including withdrawal) and supervising CCPs.[71] Nevertheless, and given the systemic importance of CCPs and the cross-border nature of their activities, a central role is played by ESMA in the authorization process.

This reflects the final, and most controversial issue for EU finance ministers in the ECOFIN meeting in Luxembourg in October 2011. The authorization process faced fierce opposition by the United Kingdom. At stake were still the concerns among certain EU Member States and the ECB about clearing derivatives contracts denominated in euros. All EU CCPs would need to be authorized under EMIR and the authorization procedure is complicated, involving the college of supervisors, who should reach a 'Joint Opinion by Mutual Agreement'.[72] The final procedure in EMIR reflects the result of the October 2011 ECOFIN meeting, which reached a compromise to alleviate the United Kingdom's concerns that its CCPs might not be authorized in view of the voting

---

[70] BCBS and IOSCO statement (3 April 2020), https://www.iosco.org/news/pdf/IOSCONEWS560.pdf (accessed 23 March 2023).
[71] See Recitals (51) and (52).
[72] EMIR (n 37), Art. 17(4).

arrangements in the college of supervisors. Voting requires a mutual agreement in the college, but if two-thirds of its members vote against with a simple majority (depending on the size of the college for each specific CCP, which was the basis for the compromise in the ECOFIN meeting),[73] the matter can be referred to ESMA for a decision under its dispute settlement procedure according to which ESMA can take a binding decision.[74] The final text of the authorization procedure in Arts 17 and 19 has often been viewed as extremely complicated or even contradictory and can only be understood in the context of the difficult ECOFIN negotiations between finance ministers. It also explains why the final text of Art. 19 has two duplicative provisions which have never been rectified because of the sensitivity attached to the text.[75]

ESMA's powers were limited to the direct responsibility of recognizing CCPs from third countries. (As discussed below, those powers have been increased over time.). Recognition requires that the Commission has ascertained the legal and supervisory framework of that third country as 'equivalent' to EMIR, that the CCP is authorized and subject to effective supervision in that third country, and that ESMA has established cooperation arrangements with the third country competent authorities. A CCP of a third country will not be allowed to perform activities and services in the Union if these conditions are not met. As will be discussed below, a further revision of EMIR (EMIR 2.2) returned to this subject.

EMIR also lays the ground for the recovery and resolution of CCPs, which would be the subject of a specific regulation a few years later (see below and Chapter 12 'Recovery and Resolution of CCPs' by Victor de Serière in this volume). EMIR already included a number of important elements relating to the 'recovery' phase of CCPs, including the default waterfall,[76] 'skin in the game', and cooperation arrangements and contingency plans between authorities in CCP colleges (see below on CCP Recovery and Resolution).

The prudential requirements for CCPs are covered by Title IV and closely follow the PFMIs. As EMIR introduces a mandatory clearing obligation for OTC derivatives, the robustness and regulation of CCPs is important. EMIR contains strong governance arrangements to address potential conflicts of interest between owners, management, clearing members (CMs), and indirect participants. EMIR sets out clear roles and responsibilities of the risk committee. The Regulation also requires governance arrangements to be publicly disclosed. In addition, a CCP should have adequate internal systems and operational and administrative procedures and should be subject to independent audits.

As a CCP will be a counterparty to every position, it bears the risk that one of its CMs might fail. Similarly, any CM, as well as its clients, bear the risk that the CCP itself

---

[73] EMIR (n 37), Art. 17, paras 1 and 3.

[74] EMIR (n 37), Art. 17(4); ESMA's dispute settlement procedure can be found in Art. 19 of the ESMA founding Regulation (EU) No. 1095/2010.

[75] Article 17(4), subparas 3 and 6 are duplicative as they were included in the final text signed off by ministers after extremely difficult negotiations, they have never been rectified.

[76] EMIR (n 37), Art. 45(4).

might fail. By virtue of its central role, a CCP is a critical component of the market it serves. Consequently, the failure of a CCP would, in almost all cases, become a potential systemic event for the financial system. In view of their systemically important role and in view of the proposed legislative requirement to clear all 'standardized' OTC derivatives through CCPs, the need to subject them to strict prudential regulation at EU level cannot be overemphasized. EMIR provides that a CCP must mitigate its counterparty credit risk exposure through a number of reinforcing mechanisms. These include stringent but non-discriminatory participation requirements, financial resources, and other guarantees. Outsourcing of functions by a CCP will only be allowed, if it does not impact on the proper operation of the CCP and on its ability to manage risks, including those arising from the outsourced functions. Thus, CCPs must always monitor, and have full control of, the outsourced functions and continuously manage the risks they face. In practical terms, no risk management functions will be allowed to be outsourced.

A minimum quantum of capital[77] must be required for authorization to exercise the activities of a CCP (see also Chapter 9 'Capital Requirements for Bank Exposures to CCPs' by Marc Peters in this volume). A CCP's own capital is also its last line of defence in the event of the default of one or more members, after the margins collected from the defaulting member(s), the default fund, and any other financial resources have been exhausted. If a CCP decides to use part of its capital as an additional financial resource to be used for risk management purposes, then this portion must be in addition to the capital needed to perform the services and activities of a CCP on an ongoing basis. The CCP's investment policy also follows international standards and is limited to highly liquid instruments.[78] Note that the other side of the coin also applies as counterparties to CCPs banks themselves are also subject to capital requirements reflecting the riskiness of their exposure.[79]

EMIR requires a CCP to have a mutualized default fund to which members of the CCP will have to contribute.[80] A default fund enables loss-mutualization and thus represents an additional line of defence that a CCP can use in case of the insolvency of one or more of its members.

The Regulation also provides for important rules on segregation and portability of positions and corresponding collateral (see Chapter 10 'Segregation and Portability of Cleared OTC Derivatives in Europe' by Bas Zebregs in this volume).[81] These are critical to effectively reduce counterparty credit risk through the use of CCPs, to achieve a level playing field among European CCPs, and to protect the legitimate interests of clients

---

[77] EMIR (n 37), Art. 16.

[78] ESMA consulted stakeholders on the potential extension of the list of financial instruments eligible for investments by CCPs under EMIR, including EU Money Market Funds, in November 2021. See https://www.esma.eur opa.eu/press-news/consultations/consultation-highly-liquid-financial-instruments-regards-investment-policy (accessed 23 March 2023).

[79] This is discussed in detail in Chapter 9, 'Capital Requirements for Bank Exposures to CCPs' by Marc Peters in this volume.

[80] EMIR (n 37), Art. 42.

[81] EMIR (n 37), Art. 39.

of CMs. This responds to a call by CMs and their clients for greater harmonization and protection in this field. It also responds to the issues highlighted by Lehman's demise.

3.3.5 EMIR interoperability

The shortest part of EMIR is Title V: interoperability.[82] Although interoperability is an essential tool to achieve an effective integration of the post-trading market in Europe, it can expose CCPs to additional risks. For this reason, regulatory approval is required before entering into an interoperable arrangement. CCPs should carefully consider and manage the extra risks that interoperability entails and satisfy the competent authorities about the soundness of the systems and procedures adopted. In view of the complexity of derivatives markets and the early stage of development of CCP clearing for OTC derivatives, it is not appropriate to extend the provisions on interoperability to instruments other than securities and money-market instruments at this point in time. However, this exclusion should not limit the possibility of CCPs to enter into such arrangements in a safe manner, subject to the conditions provided in the Regulation.

3.3.6 EMIR trade repositories

Trade repositories are regulated in Title VI, which looks at the registration and surveillance of trade repositories, and Title VII, setting out the requirements for trade repositories. EMIR's reporting requirement of OTC and exchange-traded derivatives (ETD) derivative transactions to trade repositories increases market transparency. EMIR gives ESMA the powers to register trade repositories, withdraw registration, and perform the surveillance of trade repositories.[83] This is the only area where ESMA has been given direct supervisory powers. As there are no fiscal responsibilities implications connected to the surveillance of trade repositories, a national supervisory approach is not necessary. EMIR also contains provisions for trade repositories to guarantee their compliance with a set of standards.[84] These are designed to ensure that the information that trade repositories maintain for regulatory purposes is reliable, secured, and protected. In particular, trade repositories will be subject to organizational and operational requirements and ensure appropriate safeguarding and transparency of data.

In order to be registered, trade repositories must be established in the EU. However, a trade repository established in a third country can be recognized by ESMA if it meets a number of requirements designed to establish that such trade repository is subject to equivalent rules and appropriate surveillance in that third country. In order to ensure that there are no legal obstacles in place that would prevent an effective mutual exchange of information and unfettered access to data maintained in a trade repository located in a third country, EMIR envisages the need to negotiate and conclude an 'international agreement' to that effect.[85] EMIR stipulates that if such an agreement is not in place, a trade repository established in that third country would not be recognized by

---

[82] EMIR (n 37), Arts 51–54.
[83] EMIR (n 37), Arts 55 et seq.
[84] EMIR (n 37), Art. 78.
[85] EMIR (n 37), Art. 75.

ESMA. The requirement to conclude an 'international agreement' raised an issue with the United States because, under US law, such agreement would need to be concluded by an executive act of the President, which would pose insurmountable difficulties. This legal problem was resolved in the later amendments in EMIR REFIT (see below).

3.3.7 Delegated acts and implementing acts

As discussed, many technical details are not regulated directly in EMIR but have been set out in legally binding 'level 2' acts by the Commission. EMIR contains two types of law-making powers for the European Commission: 'delegated acts' and 'implementing acts'. Both powers need to be specifically conferred on the Commission in the basic legal act—in this case, EMIR.

Delegated acts

Under Art. 290 of the Treaty, the Council and the EP may grant powers to the Commission, through specific rules, the basic act to adopt '*delegated acts*'. These are legal acts adopted by the European Commission to amend or supplement the 'non-essential' core elements of the legislation. The Commission's powers to adopt delegated acts are subject to strict conditions: the basic act must define the objectives, content, scope, and duration of the delegation of power; a delegated act cannot change the essential elements of the basic act; and these delegated acts can only be of general application, that is, they cannot address individual situations.[86] EMIR not only gives the Commission the power to adopt those acts but also requires the Commission to base them on advice provided by ESMA in so-called 'regulatory technical standards' (RTS). The requirements for ESMA to develop, draft, and adopt RTS is laid down in great detail in the Regulation establishing the three European Supervisory Authorities ESMA, the EBA, and EIOPA.[87] The most noteworthy requirement for ESMA (and the other authorities) is that RTS must be technical, shall not imply strategic decisions or policy choices, and their content shall be delimited by the legislative acts on which they are based.[88] ESMA's powers are restrained by the so-called 'Meroni' doctrine in which the Court ruled on the extent to which EU institutions may delegate their tasks to regulatory agencies.[89] The Meroni judgment of 1956 was broadly upheld, but with some additional comments, by the Court in 2014 in the Short-Selling Case.[90]

---

[86] See Art. 82 for the (indeterminate) duration to adopt certain acts.

[87] Regulation (EU) No. 2019/2175 of the European Parliament and of the Council of 18 December 2019 amending Regulation (EU) No. 1093/2010 establishing a European Supervisory Authority (European Banking Authority), Regulation (EU) No. 1094/2010 establishing a European Supervisory Authority (European Insurance and Occupational Pensions Authority), Regulation (EU) No. 1095/2010 establishing a European Supervisory Authority (European Securities and Markets Authority), Regulation (EU) No. 600/2014 on markets in financial instruments, Regulation (EU) No. 2016/1011 on indices used as benchmarks in financial instruments and financial contracts or to measure the performance of investment funds, and Regulation (EU) No. 2015/847 on information accompanying transfers of funds, OJ L334 (27 December 2019), p. 1.

[88] See Arts 10–14 for the procedure to present a draft RTS.

[89] Cases C-9/56 and C-10/56 (*Meroni v High Authority* [1957/1958] ECR 133).

[90] Case C-270/12 (*United Kingdom v Parliament and Council*) [check] ECR. See also M. van Rijsbergen and M. Scholten, 'The ESMA Short-Selling Case: Erecting a New Delegation Doctrine in the EU upon the Meroni–Romano Remnants' (2014) 41(4) Legal Issues of Economic Integration 389–406.

The Commission can adopt the draft RTS in part only, or with amendments, 'where the Union's interests so require'. This reflects the European Commission's right of legislative initiative under the Treaty and the 'Meroni' limitations on agencies. In practice, the Commission will seldom reject part or the whole of a draft RTS: the cooperation between the Commission and the agency is sufficiently close and cooperative to prevent such incidents. The excellent management and steering of ESMA's responsibilities under EMIR by its first Chairman, the experienced Dutchman Steven Maijoor and his colleagues responsible for post-trade matters, were key to an efficient and fruitful cooperation, often facing fierce deadlines. However, the Commission will sometimes see a need to revise a draft RTS submitted by ESMA simply to improve its legal drafting—in the end, the RTS is published as Commission 'delegated regulation'. The Commission's practice of 'improving' ESMA's draft texts will result in a discussion between the institution and the agency as to what extent the Commission has changed the substance of a draft standard and, if possible, to find agreement on the changes. If this cannot be achieved, a complicated and time-consuming procedure applies.[91] Finally, a delegated act adopted by the Commission can only enter into force if no objection is raised by the Council or the EP within the deadline set in the basic act, which is three months, with a further three-month extension if required.[92]

EMIR contains a long list of well-defined areas where the Commissions is required to adopt delegated acts to supplement it with further technical details. These standards cover, among many, CCP colleges, general and prudential requirements for CCPs, the clearing obligation, risk mitigation techniques, non-financial counterparties (NFCs), details of the data to be reported to trade repositories (TR), details of the application for registration as a TR, and data to be published by trade TRs and operational standards.[93] In all cases, ESMA's involvement is invaluable to ensure the appropriate technical input.[94] Over the years, a strong cooperation has developed between the Commission and ESMA.

Implementing acts

These legal acts are different from 'delegated acts'. The power for the Commission to adopt implementing acts under Art. 291 of the Treaty must also be provided by the EP and the Council in the basic legal act, that is, EMIR. Implementing acts are adopted

[91] Where the Commission intends not to adopt a draft RTS or to adopt it in part or with amendments, it must send the draft RTS back to ESMA, explaining why it does not adopt it or explaining the reasons for its amendments. The Commission must copy its letter to the EP and to the Council, and, within six weeks, ESMA can amend the draft RTS in line with the Commission's proposed amendments and resubmit it to the Commission with a copy to the EP and to the Council.
[92] Regulation No. 2019/2175, Art. 13.
[93] For a full overview of delegated and implementing acts, see https://ec.europa.eu/info/law/derivatives-emir-regulation-eu-no-648-2012/amending-and-supplementary-acts/implementing-and-delegated-acts_en (accessed 23 March 2023).
[94] ESMA has issued Q&As; Regulatory/implementing technical standards for CCPs (on EMIR's general and capital requirements, colleges, and CCP records); reports on procyclicality and margining requirements and on segregation and portability, and interoperability. For a complete overview of the regulatory standards and supervisory convergence guidance developed by ESMA and the Commission, see the Interactive Single Rulebook (ISRB) on EMIR, https://www.esma.europa.eu/publications-and-data/interactive-single-rulebook/emir (accessed 23 March 2023).

in areas where uniform conditions for implementation are needed.[95] Equivalence decisions are a good example of implementing acts. Before the Commission can adopt an implementing act, it must consult a committee, chaired by the Commission, in which the EU Member States are represented to oversee the Commission's work. The Commission has been specifically empowered by the Council and the EP to adopt such acts in EMIR after consulting the European Securities Committee (ESC).[96] These consultative committees, comprising representatives from the Member States,[97] are subject to specific procedural rules and general principles to be followed (referred to in EU jargon as 'comitology'), which are provided for in a specific regulation.[98] These procedures differ in their voting rules and in the way their votes influence the Commission's possibilities to adopt the implementing act in question. The choice of procedure for a given act is made by the EU legislator.[99] Unlike delegated acts, the Council and the EP have far less power to object or block the adoption of implementing acts. For this reason, discussions are not unknown in the negotiating process in the EP and Council to change the Commission's proposals to confer powers to adopt implementing acts into delegated acts. Because the legal definition of both acts is sufficiently clear those attempts have not been successful. Nevertheless, for both types of act, the Commissions' delegated powers are limited in time and subject to review by the co-legislators, the Council and the Parliament.

3.3.8 CCP 'location requirement'

The Commission's proposal did not include a requirement for a systemically relevant CCP to be established in a Member State of the EU. The concept of such a 'location requirement' had been floated in particular by the ECB. In the aftermath of the global financial crisis, concerns in the central bank community had increased about the potentially negative impact of derivatives clearing on financial stability. The ECB's Governing Council on 18 December 2008 opined for the first time that, although currency swaps agreements may exist between central banks, because of the absence of direct access to liquidity facilities there was a strong preference for the CCP to be located in the euro area.[100] As discussed above, recommending the use of CCPs located in Europe was also reflected on the Commission's Communication of March 2009. The ECB raised its concerns again with the ECOFIN Council on 2 December 2009, where, in its conclusions, the ECOFIN Council recognized 'that there are strong reasons for some CCPs being located in Europe, relating to regulatory, supervisory and monetary

---

[95] Taxation, agriculture, health and food safety, the internal market, etc.

[96] For an up-to-date overview of its meetings, see https://ec.europa.eu/transparency/expert-groups-register/scr een/expert-groups/consult?do=groupDetail.groupDetail&groupID=2553&Lang=EN (accessed 23 March 2023).

[97] Note that after an inter-institutional agreement on the subject, the EP was also represented in these committee meetings.

[98] Regulation (EU) No. 182/2011 of the European parliament and of the Council of 16 February 2011 laying down the rules and general principles concerning mechanisms for control by Member States of the Commission's exercise of implementing powers, OJ L55 (28 February 2011), p. 13.

[99] EMIR (n 37), Art. 86 provides that the ESC's proceedings are governed by Art. 5 of the Regulation.

[100] ECB, 'Decisions Taken by the Governing Council' (18 December 2008), http://www.ecb.europa.eu/press/ govcdec/otherdec/2008/html/gc081219.en.html (accessed 23 March 2023).

policy concerns'.[101] As the Commission had not included a 'location requirement' in its legislative proposal, the ECB decided to pursue its policy aim through other means, as will be discussed in section 3.4.

3.4 UK–ECB Court Case on the ECB's 'Location Requirement'

In its Policy Framework published on 5 July 2011, six months after the Commission had adopted its proposal for EMIR without a 'location requirement', the ECB stated that it had 'major concerns' about the development of a major euro FMI outside the euro area, 'since this could potentially place in question the Eurosystem's control over the euro'.[102] According to the ECB, it had led to a growing importance of financial market infrastructures that settle in euro or clear euro-denominated transactions outside the eurozone ('off-shore infrastructures'). The ECB noted, in particular, that the Eurosystem's 'ability to influence off-shore infrastructures is, in practical terms, restricted. This may have serious consequences for the smooth functioning of market infrastructures operating in euro and, more generally, for financial stability in the euro area.'[103]

The Policy Framework set forth the contested statement that 'As a matter of principle, infrastructures that settle euro-denominated payment transactions should settle these transactions in central bank money and be legally incorporated in the euro area with full managerial and operational control and responsibility over all core functions for processing euro denominated transactions, exercised from within the euro area.' It underpinned the principle with clear thresholds. A 'location requirement' should apply to 'offshore' CCPs with:

- an average daily net credit exposure of more than €5 billion in one of the main euro-denominated product categories and
- all CCPs that hold on average more than 5% of the aggregated daily net credit exposure of all CCPs for one of the main euro-denominated product categories."[104]

The ECB's concerns were not alleviated by difficult behind-the-scenes discussions with the Bank of England about the exchange of information to contribute to the ECB's 'Blue Book', providing an annual comprehensive description of the main payment and securities settlement systems in EU Member States. The information provided formed the basis of the Eurosystem's oversight process. The paucity of information on UK clearing houses compared to that provided by other central banks is indeed noticeable.

---

[101] See n 49, para. 7c.

[102] Eurosystem Oversight Policy Framework, published on the website of the ECB (5 July 2011), https://www.ecb.europa.eu/pub/pdf/other/eurosystemoversightpolicyframework2011en.pdf (accessed 23 March 2023).

[103] The reference to 'crisis situations' is important as it returns in the EU's later regulatory discussions about EMIR 2.2 and CCP Recovery and Resolution.

[104] Section 6 of the Policy Framework.

Only two months after the ECB published its Policy Framework, the United Kingdom started a case before the European Court of Justice ('the Court') to annul the Policy Framework in so far as it set out a location policy for CCPs established in Member States that are not part of the Eurosystem. France, Spain, and Italy intervened in support of the ECB.[105] Sweden intervened in support of the United Kingdom. The European Commission did not intervene in this important case involving fundamental Treaty principles.

The United Kingdom relied on five legal arguments to annul the ECB's Policy Framework. First, it submitted that the ECB lacked competence to lay down a location requirement for CCPs. Second, the ECB's location policy infringed the Treaty provisions on the freedoms of establishment, services, and the free movement of capital. Third, the Policy Framework breached Arts 101 and 102 of the Treaty. Fourth, the ECB\s location requirement infringed the principle of non-discrimination, and, finally, the location requirement would be disproportional.

The Court delivered its judgment on 4 March 2015.[106] In brief, the Court settled the case on the United Kingdom's first line of defence.[107] The Court did not need to scrutinize the legal argument put forward by the United Kingdom that the ECB was discriminating against a member country as it concluded that the ECB did not have the power to make a decision in the first place: 'The ECB lacks the competence necessary to regulate the activity of securities clearing systems as its competence is limited to payment systems alone.'[108]

In reaching its decision, the Court went to some lengths to delineate the institutional powers of the ECB to regulate CCP clearing activities. The ECB's reasoning and the Court's response are insightful as they provide a clear perspective of the ECB's concerns about the securities clearing system, the risks it presents for financial stability, and why and which measures are required to mitigate those risks.

Concerning its *legal and institutional competence* to promulgate measures for securities clearing and CCPs, the ECB argued that the Policy Framework used the term 'payment, clearing and settlement systems' in a 'generic' manner. Furthermore, its 'oversight' powers under Art. 127(2) TFEU and Art. 22 of the Statute of the ESCB and of the ECB ('the Statute') assigned to the ESCB the basic task of promoting the smooth operation of payment systems and powers for the ECB to make regulations to ensure efficient and sound clearing and payment systems.[109] The ECB added that those legal bases should be interpreted in their historical context and that the lack of an explicit

---

[105] Italy withdrew its intervention a few months later.

[106] Judgment of 4 March 2015 in *United Kingdom of Great Britain and Northern Ireland v European Central Bank (ECB)*, T-496/11, ECR, EU:T:2015:133.

[107] The Court ruled that the case was admissible for an action for annulment as the Policy Framework had legally binding effects and that the United Kingdom as a Member State had standing to bring the case before the Court, regardless of the fact that it was not a member of the eurozone.

[108] Paragraph 110. Note that the Court considered 'securities clearing' to include the clearing of OTC derivative contracts.

[109] Article 22 of the Statute provides that '[t]he ECB and national central banks may provide facilities, and the ECB may make regulations, to ensure efficient and sound clearing and payment systems within the Union and with other countries'.

reference to a task of 'oversight' could be explained by the fact that, at the time when the Treaty on the European Union was signed, such a function was not yet perceived as constituting an independent competence, and at that time, cross-border transactions were less relevant for settlement and clearing systems.[110]

The Court rejected the ECB's arguments. It ruled that the Eurosystem's task of promoting the smooth operation of 'payment systems' in Art. 127(2) TFEU and 'clearing and payment systems' in Art. 22 of the Statute, for which the ECB has competence to adopt regulations, could not be regarded as including, not even implicitly, *securities clearing* systems and, therefore, the activity of CCPs.[111] The Court also made it clear that if the ECB wished to have such regulatory powers, Art. 129(3) of the Treaty already provided for a simplified mechanism to amend the Statute and that it would be for the ECB, to request the EU legislature to amend Art. 22 of the Statute by the addition of an explicit reference to securities clearing systems.[112] As we will see below, a few years later, the ECB indeed presented a proposal to amend Art. 22 of the Statute but withdrew its proposal in light of Member State opposition to granting the ECB those far-reaching powers.

Regarding *the need for a location policy*, in its arguments, the ECB paid particular attention to the negative impact on financial stability of the failure of a clearing system, and particularly a CCP, as a justification for its location requirement. The ECB argued that as CCPs are a focal point for credit and liquidity risk, the malfunctioning 'of non-Eurozone CCPs could have adverse effects on payment systems located in the euro area, whilst the euro area has no direct influence on such infrastructures.'[113] In the ECB's opinion, 'the development of major market infrastructures outside the euro area is worrying.'[114] The ECB continued by noting that international cooperation was, in itself, insufficient as it did not provide 'direct influence' and that further-reaching regulatory powers were necessary. Those regulatory powers should be employed, as recalled in the Policy Framework, in the case of OTC credit derivatives, to have 'at least one European CCP for credit derivatives' but also that 'given the potential systemic importance of securities clearing and settlement systems, this infrastructure should be located within the euro area.'[115] To be more precise, and 'as a matter of principle, infrastructures that settle euro-denominated payment transactions should settle these transactions in "central bank money" and be legally incorporated in the euro area with full managerial and operational control and responsibility, over all core functions, exercised from within that area.'[116]

It is clear from the Policy Framework and the argumentation before the Court that the ECB was extremely concerned about CCPs located in the United Kingdom. The reference to the need to locate in the eurozone can leave no doubt in this regard. Nor

---

[110] Paragraphs 5 and 6.
[111] Paragraphs 99, 106–107.
[112] Paragraphs 108–109.
[113] Paragraph 11.
[114] Paragraphs 10 and 11.
[115] Paragraph 13.
[116] Paragraph 12.

can the reference to CCPs' clearing OTC credit derivatives leave any doubt that the ECB was concerned about one CCP in the United Kingdom in particular: the London Clearing House (LCH) and its interest rate clearing business.

The Court's judgment of 4 March 2015 was important and would have consequences for the EU's future regulation of OTC derivatives clearing, in particular the role and powers of the ECB. The Court case had already had a bearing on the EMIR negotiations in the Council. Three years before the Court handed down its decision, Member States' finance ministries and market authorities had their own exchange of views about the powers of the ECB. After long discussions in the Council working group, a recital was added to EMIR to explain where the Council believed regulatory powers for CCPs and OTC derivatives rested: with the Council and the EP. The recital notes that although EMIR was without prejudice to 'the responsibilities of the ECB and the national central banks (NCBs) to ensure efficient and sound clearing and payment systems, in order to prevent the possible creation of parallel sets of rules, ESMA and the ESCB should cooperate closely when preparing the relevant draft technical standards'. Taking into account the ECB's arguments that had been presented to the Court, there was a real concern that the ESCB would want to adopt its own potentially different and conflicting rules in this area.[117] The Court's judgment in 2015 should have given the Council solace.

As we will see further on in this chapter, the powers and role of the ECB would once again become key points of attention in the discussions about EMIR 2.2 and CCP Recovery and Resolution.

3.5 EU–US 'Cross-Border' Discussions

EMIR also had an impact on trans-Atlantic discussions. The different regulatory efforts across the globe had a number of challenges; the most difficult and publicly debated became the cross-border impact of national legislation. The importance of an internationally coordinated approach cannot be overstated. Given the global nature of the OTC derivatives market, the lack of internationally coordinated action would only lead to regulatory arbitrage. This would severely curtail the effectiveness of measures to increase the safety of the financial system in any individual jurisdiction. The need of a coordinated approach had therefore been recognized by the G20[118] as well as by the Council[119] and the EP.[120] The Commission had inserted a legal provision in EMIR to avoid duplicative or conflicting rules applying to counterparties, of which one was established outside the EU and subject to regulation there.[121]

---

[117] EMIR (n 37), Recital (11).
[118] See para. 12 of the Pittsburgh Summit statement.
[119] See para. 2 of the Council conclusions of 2 December 2009.
[120] See Langen Report (n 61), Recital U.
[121] EMIR (n 37), Art. 13.

Discussions between the EU and the United States—particularly between the European Commission and the CFTC—concentrated on two specific areas. The first involved concerns about the prudential requirements for US CCPs.[122] The Commission was particularly concerned about the financial soundness of US CCPs which, in the Commission's view, in a number of areas were subject to lower requirements than under EMIR. Those lower requirements would give US CCPs a potentially competitive advantage in the European clearing space. As the perceived lower US requirements all related to financial resources, the calculation of initial margin requirements competition was only one of the issues at stake. At least as important as level competitive playing fields was the need to ensure financial stability. The three areas of concern were the required minimum amount of financial resources of a CCP (which had already been raised during the negotiations on the global CPMI–IOSCO principles, see above); minimum liquidation periods applied to margin calculations; and pro-cyclicality requirements for margin calculations. Three years of discussion were required before the European Commission was able to determine that the CFTC's legal and supervisory arrangements were equivalent to EMIR.[123] Bilateral technical discussions between the European Commission and the US CCP Chicago Mercantile Exchange (CME) started in 2011 and formed a sound basis to better understand the way in which US CCPs managed their financial resilience. These discussions paved the way for the European Commission to grant 'equivalence' to the CFTC in 2016 and to the SEC in 2021 (see section 3.6).

However, an equally important—and most publicly visible—obstacle to equivalence could be found in a different area of regulation: the perceived extraterritoriality of US rules. The global OTC derivatives space was in need of rules that worked not only for regulators and market participants in a national jurisdiction but also in a cross-border environment and between jurisdictions. OTC derivative reforms that are consistent and coherent within a single jurisdiction can have adverse impacts when they apply to cross-border transactions. This is so even where the different jurisdictions involved have apparently similar rules. Cross-border application of multiple rules will inhibit the execution and risk management of cross-border transactions and a European Commission comparison of US and EU rules had identified numerous potential conflicts, inconsistencies, and gaps between the rules that needed to be addressed. The problem of inconsistent cross-border rules was raised tirelessly by the European Commission in almost every international meeting. The FSB particularly insisted on international coordination on the cross-border scope of regulations and cooperation on implementation in order to avoid unnecessary overlap, conflicting regulations, and regulatory arbitrage.[124]

---

[122] CCPs are referred to as 'Derivatives Clearing Organisations' under CFTC regulations and 'Clearing Agencies' under SEC regulations.

[123] EMIR (n 37), Art. 25, para. 6.

[124] See, e.g. the FSB's Twelfth Progress Report on Implementation of OTC Derivatives Market Reforms of 29 June 2017, stating that 'Further progress on cross-border issues, some of which could be addressed through deference when it is justified, in line with the St Petersburg G20 Leaders' Declaration, remains important to achieve the intended objectives of the reforms', 2, https://www.fsb.org/wp-content/uploads/P290617-2.pdf (accessed 23 March 2023).

Discussions between the EU and the United States became public by the end of 2012, when the European Commission decided to raise its concerns in the US Congress in Washington.[125] Its testimony in the House of Representatives Agricultural Committee provided the Commission with a unique opportunity to explain in greater detail where problems arose in its view.

Its first practical example was that it was possible that two parties to a transaction may be required to trade in different venues, clear on different CCPs, or report to different trade repositories. Trades would nevertheless be subject to mandatory clearing in one jurisdiction and to margining requirements in another jurisdiction—this was particularly relevant for corporate end users. 'Scope' was the root cause of many cross-border problems and particularly proposals from the CFTC that would extend the territorial reach of its rules to counterparties outside the United States. This would create conflicts and undue burdens for market participants.

According to the European Commission, this would be best resolved by ensuring comparability of rules than by over-extending the reach of national rules. What ultimately matters, according to the Commission, was where the counterparties to a transaction are established, not the location where that transaction is concluded, as was the CFTC's approach.

A further difficulty was the different terminology used in Brussels and Washington: the principles of 'recognition', 'equivalence', or 'substituted compliance'. The CFTC's approach of 'substituted compliance' avoids the application of multiple rules to the same entity or the same transaction. But it continues to apply US law, which can be complied with through similar foreign laws. In short, two sets of rules applied. Although the CFTC had proposed to rely on substituted compliance in the application of its OTC derivative rules, the European Commission believed that where different requirements achieved the same objectives, market participants should be subject to a single set of rules for their cross-border activity and that the CFTC should apply 'deference' to those rules, like the EU, rather than continue to apply its own rules with substituted compliance as an exception.[126] The Commission looked at three problems in the CFTC's approach.

First, the CFTC was asked to apply substituted compliance between a domestic and a third-country counterparty established in a jurisdiction with comparable and consistent requirements. The CFTC, however, restricted substituted compliance to transactions between two non-domestic counterparties. Practice showed that the situation explained by the Commission reflected the area where the large majority of conflicts and inconsistencies existed. Applying one set of rules to those transactions would ensure legal certainty for cross-border transactions.

---

[125] See https://www.govinfo.gov/content/pkg/CHRG-112hhrg77833/pdf/CHRG-112hhrg77833.pdf (accessed 23 March 2023).

[126] For a more detailed perspective on the US CFTC's policy on 'substitutive compliance' and its contrast with the EU's 'equivalence' approach, see Paulo Saguato, Guido Ferrarini, and Eric Pan, 'Financial Market Infrastructures: The International Approach and the Current Challenges', in *Financial Market Infrastructures: Law and Regulation* (Oxford: Oxford University Press, 2022), chapter 4.

Second, the Commission requested that substituted compliance should apply to the more material 'transaction level' requirements between counterparties in different jurisdictions and not just to 'entity-level' requirements, as the CFTC had suggested.[127] Where transaction-level requirements were comparable, counterparties should be able to discharge their obligations by complying with one set of requirements. The CFTC had used its statutory powers to do this in the past in other areas of its rulemaking.

The Commission furthermore pointed out that foreign infrastructure, which is subject to comparable requirements in the EU jurisdiction, should not be required to comply with domestic requirements in the United States in order to service the domestic market. Agreement on this was essential to ensuring that clearing obligations can be complied with in respect of cross-border transactions.

The CFTC's registration process was also criticized because foreign swap dealers would be required to register without knowing with sufficient certainty the complete set of rules that would bind them as a consequence and how those rules will be applied in an international context—including how substituted compliance would work. Although a possible waiver or 'no action letter', as offered by the CFTC, could provide solace, this would only delay, not eliminate, the problem. In addition, even if registration only triggered certain trade reporting requirements, lack of substituted compliance could immediately create issues in terms of conflicting requirements, for example, conflicts with data privacy and data protection considerations in national and European law. The Commission argued that the lack of international consistency would put firms in the impossible position where they were forced to choose between breaching either US law or EU law.

Bilateral discussions between the European Commission and the CFTC, and in particular between European Commissioner Michel Barnier, who was responsible for financial services, and CFTC Chairman Gary Gensler, continued for three years in an extraordinary friendly and cooperative relationship, despite their disagreement on the best policy approach. The differences were, however, so wide-ranging that it was not until 2016 that they had been worked through and an agreement was reached. By that time, Michel Barnier had been replaced by Jonathan Hill as European Commissioner and Tim Massad had become the new CFTC Chairman. The agreement was important as it permitted the Commission to adopt an 'equivalence' decision for the CFTC under EMIR. The Decision explains in some detail how agreement was reached on three key prudential areas of divergence or CCPs regulated by the CFTC.

---

[127] *Entity-level* requirements apply to a swap dealer or major swap participant as a whole, including requirements related to: capital adequacy, chief compliance officer, risk management, swap data record keeping, swap data repository reporting ('SDR reporting') and record keeping, and physical commodity large swaps trader reporting ('large trader reporting'). *Transaction-level* requirements apply to an individual swap transaction or trading relationship or on a transaction-by-transaction basis. *Transaction-level* requirements include, in particular, required clearing and swap processing, margining (and segregation) for uncleared swaps, mandatory trade execution, swap trading relationship documentation, portfolio reconciliation and compression, real-time public reporting, trade confirmation, and daily trading records.

3.6 CFTC Conditional Equivalence Decision 2016

The Decision[128] is the first equivalence finding that is conditional on ESMA checking that its details are applied. The three areas subject to ESMA's checking compliance were those on which Commission staff and US counterparts had spent years discussing. The outcome of those discussions is clearly explained in the equivalence decision itself.

- *Minimum liquidation period for margins.* EMIR requires margins take into account minimum liquidation periods of two days for non-OTC derivative contracts and five days for OTC derivative contracts, typically with margin collected on a net basis. However, the CFTC rules differ in that for the initial margin applied to CM's proprietary positions the primary rules provide for a minimum liquidation period of one day for non-OTC derivative contracts, with margin collected on a net basis. This means that EU CCPs collect more margin. However, for initial margins collected for the positions of clients of CMs, the CFTC requires margin to be collected on a gross basis for all classes of derivative contracts. EMIR has no such requirement. Detailed discussions between the CFTC and the Commission and calculations of the difference between net and gross margin collections demonstrated to the satisfaction of the Commission that there was nevertheless a broadly equivalent outcome, which compensated for the difference in the liquidation period.
- *Margin pro-cyclicality.* EMIR requires in the case of all derivative contracts, at least one of three measures designed to limit pro-cyclicality:
    (i) measures applying a margin buffer at least equal to 25% of the calculated margins which the CCP allows to be temporarily exhausted in periods where calculated margin requirements are rising significantly;
    (ii) measures assigning at least 25% weight to stressed observations in the look-back period;
    (iii) measures ensuring that margin requirements are not lower than those that would be calculated using volatility estimated over a 10 year historical look-back period.

None of these requirements, or equivalent measures are applied by US CCPs. As a condition for ESMA registration it must confirm that the rulebooks of US CCPs seeking registration with ESMA to clear trades in the EU include these risk management principles:

- 'Cover 2 financial resources'. EMIR requires all EU CCPs to have sufficient prefunded and freely available financial resources that can 'at all times enable the

---

[128] COMMISSION IMPLEMENTING DECISION (EU) No. 2016/377 of 15 March 2016 on the equivalence of the regulatory framework of the United States of America for central counterparties that are authorised and supervised by the Commodity Futures Trading Commission to the requirements of Regulation (EU) No. 648/2012 of the European Parliament and of the Council, OJ L70 (16 March 2016), p. 32.

CCP to withstand the default of at least the *two* clearing members to which it has the largest exposures under extreme but plausible market conditions' ('cover 2').[129] The Decision confirms that although the CFTC's rules with respect to liquidity risks do not require all CCPs (only those designated as systemically important in multiple jurisdictions or where they are involved in activities with a more complex risk profile) to apply cover 2 rules, they are nevertheless required to set up procedures to cover any uncovered liquidity shortfall, ensuring that committed resources are available where losses exceed the default of the CM to which it has the largest exposure. Although this is a different approach than the 'cover 2 principle' contained in EMIR, according to the Commission it delivers equivalent outcomes.

The cross-border access issues had also been resolved. Although the equivalence decision does not describe in any detail the long and intensive discussions that took place between the Commission and the CFTC, the latter had satisfactorily resolved the Commission's concerns. The CFTC's statutory authority[130] to provide for 'substituted compliance' in respect of third-country CCPs to the extent that it has determined comparability between its own requirements for derivatives clearing organizations (DCOs) (CCPs) and the requirements of the EU's regulatory regime was deemed to be satisfactory and sufficient. Bilateral technical discussions had already compared those areas where the EMIR and CFTC requirements were sufficiently comparable and where the CFTC had undertaken to provide substituted compliance.

Finally, and of importance to the United States, the Commission concluded that listed agricultural derivatives would be excluded from the scope of the decision. After analysing the US market, the Commission concluded that these derivatives that were executed on regulated markets in the United States and cleared by US CCPs posed a 'negligible' risk the Union and that the equivalence assessment was not substantially affected by those derivative contracts.[131] This is a clear example of the application of the principle of proportionality in the field of equivalence.

A number of observations can be made about this important equivalence decision. First, the European Commission took into account the different legislative and regulatory approaches adopted in a third country. This reflects the fact that in the EU's unique legal order, EMIR is a directly applicable regulation in all of its Member States, requiring a particular mode of detail which cannot be expected to be applied in any other jurisdiction. The Commission therefore did not limit itself to a basic comparison of the CFTC's primary legislation (as, for instance, ESMA had done in its technical advice comparing the CFTC's rules to EMIR in 2013) but adopted a holistic and outcomes-based view and also took into consideration the interaction between the CFTC rules

---

[129] EMIR (n 37), Art. 43.
[130] 7 U.S.C. 2(i).
[131] Article 2 of the Decision.

and the CCPs internal rulebooks. Furthermore, the degree of detail and analysis in the US CFTC's decision contrasts with that in many other jurisdictions that are deemed of less systemic importance for the EU, where the Commission applies the proportionality principle in its assessments.

3.7 EMIR Equivalence for Other Third Countries

Two years before the Commission adopted its equivalence decision for the CFTC, it had already issued equivalence findings for a number of other countries. It is important to note that the concept of 'equivalence' was entirely new to EU legislation. EMIR was the first legal act to introduce the approach. It was driven by the need to find a regulatory consent that could apply to a global industry facing heavy regulation in numerous jurisdictions after the financial crisis. In 2009, the Commission's draftspersons were extremely conscious of the potential of overlapping and conflicting rules between different jurisdictions. Although various concepts were discussed by staff, 'equivalence' was the only approach that could meet the needs of competing global regulatory efforts. It builds on the principle of 'comity' under international law and reflects the principle that one sovereign nation voluntarily adopts or enforces the laws of another sovereign nation out of deference, mutuality, and respect. The European Commission did not seek to review decisions by domestic authorities from other jurisdictions *de novo* but to show deference to their decisions.[132]

The practical process of establishing equivalence is relatively straightforward.[133] European Commission staff will contact the authorities in a third country—at the Commission's initiative, or at the request of the third country, or sometimes even at the request of EU industry—and send them a questionnaire. A questionnaire is usually based on a standard format but may be adapted in certain areas to allow the Commission to have a better understanding of the regulatory approach of a third country. The reply to a questionnaire will often be followed up with further specific questions. A draft equivalence decision will always be submitted to the authorities of the third country concerned to ascertain that it reflects a correct understanding of, and reference to, the rules in force. This dialogue between Commission staff and regulators in that third country is also important to develop mutual trust.

The equivalence decisions are so-called 'implementing acts' (see section 3.3.7 for the difference between 'implementing acts' and 'delegated acts'). Implementing acts

---

[132] For further reading, see, e.g. Adrian Briggs, 'The Principle of Comity in Private International Law', in *Collected Courses of the Hague Academy of International Law*, Vol. 354 (The Hague: Brill, 2012); James Edelman and Madeleine Salinger, 'Comity in Private International Law and Fundamental Principles of Justice', in Andrew Dickinson and Edwin Peel (eds), *A Conflict of Laws Companion* (Oxford: OUP, 2021) p. 325; Joel R. Paul, 'The Transformation of International Comity' (2008) 71 Law and Contemporary Problems 19.

[133] For a comprehensive description and overview of the Commission's equivalence process in the financial services sector, see the Commission Staff working document on 'EU Equivalence Decisions in Financial Services Policy: An Assessment' (Brussels, 27 February 2017) SWD(2017) 102 final, https://ec.europa.eu/info/sites/default/files/eu-equivalence-decisions-assessment-27022017_en.pdf (accessed 23 March 2023).

are adopted in areas where uniform conditions for implementation are needed.[134] The Commission will usually seek to adopt a 'batch' of equivalence decisions at the same time. This is done for reasons of internal procedural efficiency, taking into account the intensive and lengthy internal decision-making process involving different Commission services (e.g. the Commission's Legal Service, the Competition, Economic and Finance, and Trade Directorate Generals), consulting the ESC, and the need to adopt the legal acts translated into the official EU languages. Although ESMA is not required to offer its opinion on draft equivalence decisions, it may do so voluntarily and has done so on a number of occasions, offering valuable technical advice and comparing the legal requirements of a third country with EMIR.

Equivalence has both political and market practice relevance. The consequence of being granted equivalence was that CCPs registered with the CFTC would then be able to obtain recognition by ESMA in the EU. Market participants would be able to use those CCPs to clear standardized OTC derivative trades as required by EU legislation, while the CCPs remained subject solely to the regulation and supervision of their home jurisdictions. CCPs that had been recognized by ESMA under the EMIR process would also obtain 'qualifying CCP' (QCCP) status across the EU under the Capital Requirements Regulation (CRR). This meant that EU banks' exposures to these CCPs would be subject to a lower risk weight in calculating their regulatory capital.[135]

The first EMIR CCP-equivalence decisions were issued by the Commission in October 2014 for: Australia, Singapore, Japan, Hong Kong, Canada, Switzerland, South Africa, Mexico, and the Republic of Korea. Since then, Dubai, the United Arab Emirates, Mexico, Brazil, New Zealand, and India have also been granted equivalence.[136] The US CFTC was granted equivalence in 2016, US SEC in 2021.

3.7.1 US SEC conditional equivalence 2021

The negotiations on the equivalence decision for the US SEC adopted a slower pace than for the CFTC, but a decision was eventually adopted in January 2021.[137] The reasons for this were the more limited scope of activities, which is limited to CCPs clearing securities or security-based derivatives ('security-based swaps'), and the different way the SEC regulates those entities (referred to as 'clearing agencies'). The discussions between the Commission and the SEC clearly benefited from those with the CFTC.[138]

The result of the Commission's holistic, outcomes-based view developed during the discussions with the CFTC is clearly reflected in a number of areas in the SEC

---

[134] Taxation, agriculture, health and food safety, the internal market, etc.

[135] Regulation(EU) No. 575/2013 of the European Parliament and of the Council of 26 June 2013 on prudential requirements for credit institutions and investment firms and amending Regulation (EU) No. 648/2012, OJ L176/ (27 June 2013).

[136] For a complete overview, see https://ec.europa.eu/info/sites/default/files/business_economy_euro/banking_and_finance/documents/emir-equivalence-decisions_en.pdf (accessed 23 March 2023).

[137] Commission Implementing Decision (EU) No. 2021/85 of 27 January 2021 on the equivalence to the requirements of Regulation (EU) No. 648/2012 of the European Parliament and of the Council of the regulatory framework of the United States of America for central counterparties that are authorised and supervised by the U.S. Securities and Exchange Commission, OJ L29 (28 January 2021), p. 27.

[138] See Recital (3) of the Decision.

equivalence decision, which also contains conditions. First, the Commission took into account the specific regulatory approach for clearing agencies which does not prescribe specific tools or arrangements on how to achieve its requirements.[139] Clearing agencies must themselves, in their own rulebooks, provide prescriptive detail on the way in which it will meet the requirements laid down in the Exchange Act. This permits those CCPs to consider their specific characteristics and circumstances and particularly the markets served and the risks inherent in products cleared. Once registered by the SEC, the rules, policies, and procedures approved by the SEC become legally binding on the CCP as a 'self-regulatory organisation'. As was the case for the CFTC, the SEC also diverged from EMIR's key prudential requirements in a number of areas. The 'cover 2 principle' is not required for clearing agencies in primary legislation.[140] After detailed discussions and comparative calculations and examples with the SEC, the Commission accepted that the SEC's approach, requiring clearing agencies to set up procedures to cover any uncovered liquidity shortfall so that committed resources are actually available if losses exceed the default of the CM to which it has the largest exposure, delivers substantive equivalent outcomes to EMIR's 'cover 2' principle. Segregation and portability of positions and collateral of clients of CMs for cash securities and listed options also required attention because the regulations apply at the level of the CMs rather than the CCP.[141] After establishing that those rules already ensure the appropriate level of segregation and portability and adequately protect client positions and collateral, the Commission could determine that this 'different approach' to segregation and portability resulted in similar outcomes.

The Commission also encountered similar differences as with the CFTC for the minimum margin liquidation period and for margin anti-pro cyclicality but was able to establish that these requirements are covered and achieve equivalent effects in the rulebooks of clearing agencies.[142] As was the case for the CFTC, ESMA was entrusted with checking that clearing agencies that registered with ESMA continued to meet these requirements on an ongoing basis.

3.7.2 UK conditional equivalence decisions 2018–2022

The recent equivalence decisions for the United Kingdom are a special case. After leaving the EU, the United Kingdom has been granted temporary equivalence four times. The main reason for this is because the market for central clearing of OTC derivatives is highly concentrated, in particular the market for central clearing of euro-denominated OTC interest rate derivatives. In 2018, more than 90% of these contracts were cleared in one CCP—LCH, established in the United Kingdom.[143] The importance of London, and LCH in particular, required the Commission to adopt an equivalent decision in its

---

[139] A combination of the Exchange Act, the Dodd–Frank Act, and the SEC's regulations.

[140] Primary rules only require CCPs qualified as covered clearing agencies to apply the 'cover 2 principle' if they clear security-based derivatives.

[141] Segregation and portability of security-based derivatives is regulated similarly to EMIR, see Recital (19).

[142] See Recitals (17) and (18).

[143] In each of the four temporary equivalence decisions, the Commission refers to the amount of euro-denominated OTC interest rate derivatives cleared by LCH in London.

own interests to avoid EU CMs and clients being left without a good alternative clearing venue in the EU to fall back on (see also Chapter 16 'Brexit: Equivalence; Location Policy' by Dermot Turing in this chapter). The Commission went to some length to make it clear that it was in its own interests to grant equivalence, putting the potential disruption of the markets for EU CMs and clients before any trade-related interests with the United Kingdom. These comments reflected the difficult political relationship between the EU and the United Kingdom during the withdrawal negotiations.

The first temporary equivalence decision was adopted very late, in December 2018, despite extremely heavy industry lobbying during the year for the Commission to speed up and provide certainty to the sector. The decision took place against the backdrop of potential disagreement between the EU and the United Kingdom on a Brexit withdrawal agreement and the United Kingdom opting for a 'hard Brexit'.[144]

The temporary decision needed to be extended in a second decision by a further year after the EU and the United Kingdom agreed to extend the date on which the Treaties would cease to apply to 31 January 2020.[145] This meant that there would be insufficient time, predictability, and legal certainty for EU CMs and clients to act in the case that the United Kingdom would still decide to leave the EU without an agreement. However, this second decision made it very clear that the reasons for a limited duration persisted, in particular as regards the uncertainties surrounding the future relationship between the EU and the United Kingdom as well as the potential impact on the financial stability of the Union and its Member States and on the integrity of the single market. The latter part of the sentence is a clear reference to the concerns harboured by the EU since the ECB's first discussions ten years earlier in 2008, as discussed above.

The third temporary equivalence decision was adopted by the Commission in September 2020, after the EU and the United Kingdom had been able to reach agreement on the United Kingdom's withdrawal from the EU on 17 October 2019.[146] The United Kingdom had formally become a third country on 1 February 2020 and Union law ceased to apply to and in the United Kingdom on 31 December 2020. During 2020, the Commission had already been engaging with the financial sector to prepare for Brexit. For instance, a technical working group set by the European Banking Federation had been examining the legal and technical obstacles to moving contracts from the United Kingdom to EU CCPs. The Commission had also issued several communications from the Commission to the EP, the Council, and ECB, including a Contingency

---

[144] Commission Implementing Decision (EU) No. 2018/2031 of 19 December 2018 determining, for a limited period of time, that the regulatory framework applicable to central counterparties in the United Kingdom of Great Britain and Northern Ireland is equivalent, in accordance with Regulation (EU) No. 648/2012 of the European Parliament and of the Council, OJ L 325 (20 December 2018), p. 50.

[145] Commission Implementing Decision (EU) No. 2019/2211 of 19 December 2019 amending Implementing Decision (EU) No. 2018/2031 determining, for a limited period of time, that the regulatory framework applicable to central counterparties in the United Kingdom of Great Britain and Northern Ireland is equivalent, in accordance with Regulation (EU) No. 648/2012 of the European Parliament and of the Council, OJ L332 (23 December 2019), p. 157.

[146] Commission Implementing Decision (EU) No. 2020/1308 of 21 September 2020 determining, for a limited period of time, that the regulatory framework applicable to central counterparties in the United Kingdom of Great Britain and Northern Ireland is equivalent, in accordance with Regulation (EU) No. 648/2012 of the European Parliament and of the Council, OJ L306 (21 September 2020), p. 1.

Action Plan urging preparedness and readiness on the part of market participants.[147] This third equivalence decision is of interest for a number of reasons.

In the first place, it is the first substantive and detailed equivalence decision for the United Kingdom. This contrasts with the first two equivalence decisions of 2018 and 2019, which were intended to prevent the cliff effects of a sudden UK withdrawal without an agreement. However, in 2020, for the first time, the Commission analysed UK rules against the EMIR CCP-equivalence requirements. The United Kingdom's legal and supervisory arrangements were considered to be equivalent to these of EMIR, its legal and supervisory arrangements ensured effective supervision and enforcement on an ongoing basis, and it provided for an effective equivalent system for the recognition of CCPs. This is not surprising as UK law still incorporated EMIR, and nothing had changed in terms of the Bank of England's responsibilities for CCP supervision. The equivalence decision noted some uncertainty about the United Kingdom's new 'Temporary Recognition Regime', which gave the Bank of England wide discretionary powers to withdraw temporary recognition but considered this to be acceptable 'at this point in time'.

In the second place, the Commission's decision is conditional in two important respects. First, the United Kingdom's rules will only be considered equivalent if they are maintained and continue to be effectively applied and enforced. The Commission's Decision expressed concern about the possible consequence of the United Kingdom changing its regulatory and supervisory framework that could lead to an unlevel playing field between Union and UK CCPs or to financial stability risks for the Union.

The second condition is of an entirely different nature and focuses in detail on the right of immediate access in all situations, on an ongoing basis, to all relevant information by ESMA, the ECB, and the other members of the ESCB at the Bank of England, requiring the latter to conclude comprehensive cooperation arrangements to pro-actively share all relevant information.[148] The objective is for the EU authorities to be able to assess any material risks posed directly or indirectly by UK CCPs to the EU. Such detailed information requirements cannot be found in any other Commission equivalence decision for any other third country. They can only be understood in terms of the

---

[147] Communication from the Commission to the European Parliament, the Council, the European Economic and Social Committee and the Committee of the Regions of 9 July 2020, 'Getting Ready for Changes—Communication on Readiness at the End of the Transition Period between the EU and the United Kingdom', COM(2020) 324 final; Communication from the Commission to the European Parliament, the Council and the European Central Bank of 4 May 2017, 'Responding to Challenges for Critical Financial Market Infrastructures and Further Developing the Capital Markets Union', COM (2017) 225 final; Communication from the Commission to the European Parliament, the European Council, the Council, The European Central Bank, the European Economic and Social Committee, the Committee of the Regions and the European Investment Bank of 19 July 2018, 'Preparing for the Withdrawal of the United Kingdom from the European Union on 30 March 2019', COM(2018) 556 final; Communication from the Commission to the European Parliament, the European Council, the Council, The European Central Bank, the European Economic and Social Committee, the Committee of the Regions and the European Investment Bank of 13 November 2018, 'Preparing for the Withdrawal of the United Kingdom from the European Union on 30 March 2019: A Contingency Action Plan', COM(2018) 880 final.

[148] The detailed list includes information on financial instruments denominated in Union currencies, trading venues, and clearing participants as well as subsidiaries of Union credit institutions and investment firms; interoperability arrangements with other CCPs; own resources; default funds composition and calibration; margins, liquid resources, and collateral portfolios, including haircut calibrations; and stress tests: Recitals (14) and (15).

Commission's continuing concerns—and those of ESMA and the E(S)CB—about the potentially negative impact on EU financial stability of operations in London.

Finally, the Decision contains two instructive references about the Commission's thinking of the future of OTC derivatives clearing. It refers to the need for EU CMs to reduce their exposure to UK CCPs and for EU CCPs to develop further their clearing capacity as an alternative to UK CCPs. Once again, explicit reference is made to the possible impact on the EU's financial stability and on the conduct and transmission of the Union's monetary policy.[149] Furthermore, the decision expects ESMA to review and report on the systemic importance of UK CCPs and the need to 'relocate' trades to the EU.[150] This is the first clear reference to the Commission's power to legally require such a 'relocation' under EMIR 2.2 (see section 5 below).

Following the Commission's Communication in early 2021, and making it clear that it was seriously concerned about the EU's exposure to LCH in particular, it established a working group to consider if and how (systemically important) derivatives clearing could be transferred from the United Kingdom to the Union. The working group looked at the same challenges that the European Banking Federation has examined in 2020. After considerable analysis of the market, positions taken by EU CMs and clients, the capacity of EU CCPs to assume those positions, and the costs involved, the working group concluded that some transactions cleared in UK CCPs 'simply cannot be cleared elsewhere at this point in time and that a combination of different measures will be needed to develop the Union's own clearing capacity and reduce Union market participants' excessive exposures to systematically important UK CCPs in the years to come'.[151]

In addition to the working group's analysis, ESMA also presented a report required by EMIR on systemically important CCPs in December 2021, which concluded that the costs of de-recognizing specific UK clearing services by London Clearing House (LCH) and Intercontinental Exchange (ICE) Clear Europe would outweigh the benefits.[152]

ESMA's assessment identified three clearing services—one provided by LCH SwapClear (clearing EURO and Polish Zloty interest rate derivatives) and two by ICE Clear Europe (clearing EURO-denominated CDS and short-term interest rate derivatives)—as being of substantial systemic importance for the EU's financial stability and posing risks that may not be fully mitigated under EMIR.[153] ESMA notes the significant dependencies of the EU on LCH and ICE EU's activities at the time that arise from

[149] Recitals (17) and (19).
[150] Recital (18).
[151] Commission Implementing Decision (EU) No. 2022/17 of 8 February 2022 of 8 February 2022 determining, for a limited period of time, that the regulatory framework applicable to central counterparties in the United Kingdom of Great Britain and Northern Ireland is equivalent, in accordance with Regulation (EU) No. 648/2012 of the European Parliament and of the Council, OJ L28 (9 February 2022), Recital (8) (Commission Implementing Decision (EU) No. 2022/17).
[152] ESMA, 'Assessment Report under Article 25(2c) of EMIR', https://www.esma.europa.eu/sites/default/files/library/esma91-372-1913_statement_uk_ccp_article25_2c_assessment_2021.pdf (accessed 23 March 2023).
[153] ESMA concludes that the following clearing services are of substantial systemic importance for the financial stability of the Union or one or more of its Member States: LCH Ltd SwapClear for products denominated in EUR and PLN; ICE Clear Europe Ltd Credit Default Swaps (ICEU CDS) for products denominated in EUR, and ICEU Short-Term Interest Rate (STIR) for products denominated in EUR.

the size of the clearing services, in combination with their interconnectedness with EU CMs and clients (EU banks, investment funds, insurance companies, pension funds, and corporates), in number of Member States, their dominant nature, and the current lack of viable alternatives. Nevertheless, and in line with the Commission's working group, ESMA also concluded that, 'at this point in time, the costs of de-recognising those clearing services would outweigh the benefits', in particular, the long-standing costs involving the legal transfer costs, broken netting sets, competitive disadvantages for EU CMs, and the risk that contracts would not move to the EU but to another third country instead, for instance the United States.

The working group's conclusions and ESMA's report provided the basis for the Commission's fourth equivalence decision of February 2022, as the third, and latest, temporary extension of UK equivalence, until June 2025.[154] Once again, it is important to pay attention to the explanation of the Commission's equivalence decisions in its recitals and to compare them to previous versions. Because the legal provisions are necessarily succinct, the explanation contained in the recitals, which will usually go through various internal drafting processes, is key to understanding the direction of policymaking. The decision confirms, once again, the major challenges for EU financial stability posed by the significant amount of clearing by LCH London of euro-denominated OTC interest rate derivatives.[155] However, it also confirms in the clearest manner so far the Commission's view that the extension of equivalence with a further three years is only intended to provide sufficient time to increase the clearing capacity and services of EU CCPs and to explore ways to enhance their liquidity. For the first time, the Commission mentions that it is prepared to adopt 'regulatory measures' to significantly reduce EU CMs' exposures to LCH and ICE EU.[156] In other words, the Commission places priority on a policy approach that is in the EU's own interests. It is also the first time that the Commission indicates that it will use the coming period to review the EU's supervisory framework for CCPs. The most recent development on this subject comes from the Commission's policy regarding the temporary derogation for pension fund arrangements from EMIR's clearing obligation: a decision to extend that derogation until 2023 has been linked to the need to give EU CCPs sufficient time to build their clearing capacity to absorb clearing business that would be transferred from the United Kingdom to the EU (see section 5 on EMIR 2.2 below).

3.7.3 Equivalence decisions in other areas

Although most attention tends to focus on the CCP equivalence decisions under EMIR, Art. 25, it also requires equivalence decisions under Art. 13(2) for the existence of clearing and reporting obligations in a third country and for operational risk mitigation measures for uncleared derivative trades (contractual confirmation, portfolio compression and reconciliation, and the exchange of margins). The objective of

---

154 Commission Implementing Decision (EU) No. 2022/17 (n 151), p. 40.
155 See Recital (3).
156 See Recital (20).

these equivalence decisions is to avoid any duplication of conflicting rules if one of the counterparties is established outside the EU and to ensure an internationally consistent application of the international principles and standards. The mechanism, building on deference to a third country's regulatory system, is simple. If one of the counterparties is established in a third country, it is deemed to have fulfilled EMIR's requirements by complying with the requirements set out in that third country's legal regime. The Commission has adopted seven equivalence decisions to date: the first was adopted in 2017 for the US CFTC, then Japan (2019), Canada, US banking regulators,[157] Brazil, Australia, Singapore, and Hong Kong (2021).[158]

Although EMIR also requires equivalence decisions for trade repositories established in a third country, a detailed discussion goes beyond the scope of this chapter.

4 'EMIR REFIT' 2019

EMIR was materially amended twice after its adoption. The first amendment, 'EMIR REFIT', was based on a requirement in EMIR for the Commission to make an assessment, review, and report to the EP and the Council, together with any appropriate proposals, in a number of areas.[159] Mostly, these were issues that had been too difficult to reach agreement on during the original negotiations. It was the first time that the European Commission engaged on such an extensive review of a key piece of financial market legislation before all of its provisions were fully applicable. The Commission undertook an extensive assessment of EMIR between 2015 and 2016.

These areas included the need for measures to facilitate the access of CCPs to central bank liquidity facilities. This question arose during the original negotiations about those CCPs that enjoyed such liquidity access because they—for historical reasons— were authorized under a banking licence,[160] while a further question of continued discussion was to what extent, and under which circumstances, central banks would provide liquidity access to CCPs in general.[161] The lengthy discussions about the systemic importance of the transactions of non-financial firms in OTC derivatives and, in particular, the impact of EMIR on the use of OTC derivatives by non-financial firms

---

[157] A separate decisions was required for the US bank regulators because the CFTC Regulations only apply to swap dealers and major swap participants that are not subject to a prudential regulator. The CEA definition of 'prudential regulator' includes the Board of Governors of the Federal Reserve System, the Office of the Comptroller of the Currency, the Federal Deposit Insurance Corporation, the Farm Credit Administration, and the Federal Housing Finance Agency. The equivalence decision was adopted in July 2021.

[158] See, for a full and up-to-date list, https://ec.europa.eu/info/sites/default/files/business_economy_euro/banking_and_finance/documents/emir-equivalence-decisions_en.pdf (accessed 23 March 2023).

[159] Article 85, para. 1. The Commission was instructed to report by 17 August 2015.

[160] This is the case for CCPs authorized in France and Germany.

[161] Access to central bank liquidity under EMIR (n 37), Art. 44(1) and Recital (71)—to be distinguished from central bank deposits under EMIR (n 37), Art. 47(4)—is important for financial stability. A recent overview conducted by the European Association of Clearing Houses (EACH) shows the lack of a common approach across the EU. Calls for a harmonized approach continue, but the central bank community is wary about potential 'moral hazard' implications. See EACH Paper 'CCP access to Central Banks' Facilities' (December 2021), https://www.eachccp.eu/wp-content/uploads/2021/12/EACH-Note-on-CCP-access-to-Central-Banks-deposits-and-liquidity-December-2021.pdf (accessed 23 March 2023).

also required further analysis in the light of practical experience. The effectiveness of supervisory colleges, EMIR's voting modalities, and ESMA's role during the authorization process for CCPs, which had been a key political issue for the United Kingdom in the final stage of negotiations, also required further analysis. The need to assess the efficiency of margining requirements to limit procyclicality and CCP policies on collateral margining were also areas that required further attention. With the exception of non-financial companies, none of these points were picked up in the EMIR REFIT review.

4.1 Public Consultation

The Commission's ambitious review started with a public consultation and a public hearing on EMIR so that the Commission could get feedback from stakeholders on their experiences in the implementation of EMIR.[162] More than 170 contributions from a broad range of stakeholders were received. A second and wider form of input came from a broad evaluation of EMIR rules as part of the call for evidence on the overall EU regulatory framework for financial services. The latter input allowed the Commission to get a clearer understanding of the interaction across sectors and different legislative acts and of the individual rules and cumulative impact of the legislation as a whole, including potential overlaps, inconsistencies, and gaps. In particular, EMIR's reporting requirements and its potential overlaps with reporting under the Markets in Financial Instruments Directive (MIFID) would prove to be of interest.

The Commission adopted its report in November 2016.[163] On the one hand, the report indicated that no fundamental change should be made to the nature of the core requirements of EMIR, which are integral to ensuring transparency and mitigating systemic risks in the derivatives market and for which there is general support from authorities and market participants. Although a comprehensive review of the impact of EMIR was not yet possible since certain core requirements provided for under EMIR had yet to be implemented or completed, the report pointed to the possibility of amending EMIR in some specific areas so as to eliminate disproportionate costs and burdens on certain derivatives counterparties—especially NFCs—and to simplify rules without compromising the objectives of the legislation.

In the course of the review exercise, the Commission decided to apply the framework of its Regulatory Fitness and Performance Program (REFIT), which also required the publication of an inception impact assessment on possible amendments to EMIR. One of the reasons to use the Commission's REFIT approach was because its timing coincided perfectly with the Commission's 2016 REFIT, which was all about eliminating

---

[162] The consultation can be found at http://ec.europa.eu/finance/consultations/2015/financial-regulatory-framework-review/index_en.htm (accessed 23 March 2023).

[163] European Commission, Report from the Commission to the European Parliament and the Council under Article 85(1) of Regulation (EU) No. 648/2012 of the European Parliament and of the Council of 4 July 2012 on OTC derivatives, central counterparties and trade repositories, COM(2016) 857.

disproportionate costs and burdens to small companies and simplifying rules and cutting red tape. The 'REFIT' label was important for the process as it did not permit broad changes to the fundamental elements of the regulation.

4.2 Commission's Legislative REFIT Proposal 2017

The Commission adopted its proposal to amend EMIR on 4 May 2017.[164] It set out a series of targeted amendments to EMIR, simplifying its reporting and clearing requirements and relying heavily on the accompanying impact assessment analysing the costs and benefits of areas of EMIR where targeted action could provide more proportionate, efficient, and effective rules. The impact assessment estimated that the combined effect amounted to cost reductions ranging from EUR 2.3 billion to EUR 6.9 billion in fixed (one-off) costs and from EUR 1.1 billion to EUR 2.66 billion in operational costs.

The proposal gained broad support in the Council and the EP and proceeded fairly rapidly in the co-legislator.[165] On 12 June, the trilogue negotiations started between the three institutions. After just over half a year of negotiations, on 5 February 2019, the EP and Council[166] reached a political agreement in a first reading on the Regulation.[167] Although neither the EP nor the Council introduced fundamental changes to the Commission's original proposal, the co-legislator did clarify and improve EMIR REFIT in a number of important areas. The most important changes to EMIR are described below.

4.3 Financial Counterparties

EMIR's definition of 'financial counterparty' (FC) was amended. (i) It was expanded to include alternative investment funds (AIFs) established in the EU (even those with a non-EU manager) and central securities depositaries. This brought more entities within the scope of EMIR's clearing requirements and margining provisions

---

[164] Proposal for a Regulation of the European Parliament and of the Council amending Regulation (EU) No. 648/2012 as regards the clearing obligation, the suspension of the clearing obligation, the reporting requirements, the risk-mitigation techniques for OTC derivatives contracts not cleared by a central counterparty, the registration and supervision of trade repositories and the requirements for trade repositories (Brussels, 4 May 2017) COM(2017) 208 final.

[165] Work by the EP was led by the ECON Committee, which appointed Werner Langen as its rapporteur for the proposal. On 26 January 2018, the ECON Committee published its draft report. On 5 March 2018, amendments were tabled to the draft proposal, and the final report was adopted in Committee on 16 May 2018. The ECON Committee's report was discussed and adopted in Parliament's plenary session on 11 June 2018.

[166] On 1 March 2018, the Council of the EU published an 'I' item note with an accompanying addendum, setting out the final compromise text of the proposed Regulation to amend the European Market Infrastructure Regulation (EMIR REFIT Regulation), inviting its Committee of Permanent Representatives (COREPER) to approve the final compromise text of the EMIR REFIT Regulation with a view to reaching an agreement at first reading with the EP.

[167] On 21 March, the Parliament's ECON committee approved the agreed text. On 18 April, the text was approved in plenary. EMIR REFIT was adopted by the Council on 14 May 2019 and signed on 20 May 2019.

for non-cleared derivatives (NCDs). (ii) Securitization special-purpose entities and employee share purchase plans were excluded from the definition of an AIF (the result of industry lobbying, supported by France in particular), meaning that these entities are treated as NFCs for EMIR purposes. 'Employee share purchase plans' are an undertaking for collective investment in transferable securities (UCITS) or an AIF, set up exclusively for the purpose of serving one or more employee share purchase plans.

4.4 Thresholds for Clearing and Margining

EMIR REFIT implemented clearing thresholds for FCs and NFCs. In order to take into account any development of financial markets, the clearing threshold will be periodically reviewed by ESMA and, if necessary, updated.[168]

(1) Small FCs with such a low OTC derivatives activity that central clearing is not economically viable and does not pose systemic risk for the financial system are exempted from the clearing obligation. However, FCs will be required to clear all asset classes if they exceed the clearing threshold for at least one class of OTC derivatives calculated at the group level.[169] This is because of the interconnectedness between financial counterparties and possible systemic risk to the financial system if those contracts were not centrally cleared (and are required to follow margining rules regardless).

(2) NFCs will only be required to clear asset classes for which they exceed the threshold (but are subject to margin obligations in all asset classes if they exceed the clearing threshold for any asset class).[170]

4.5 Removal of Frontloading

This provision aimed to ease the administrative burden imposed on market participants at the time of EMIR's introduction and removed the obligation to clear OTC derivative contracts entered into after a CCP has been authorized under EMIR and before the date of application of the clearing obligation. In practice, the 'frontloading' requirement implied that contracts concluded on a bilateral basis following the authorization of a CCP might become subject to the clearing obligation before their expiration date.

---

[168] ESMA sought feedback from stakeholders on the effectiveness and proportionality of the clearing thresholds and EMIR generally by comparing it to similar third-country regimes in November 2021.

[169] The financial counterparty may, at any time, demonstrate that its position no longer exceeds the clearing threshold, in which case the clearing obligation ceases to apply.

[170] The calculation for threshold purposes is made by reference to the aggregate average month-end position in OTC derivatives contracts over the past twelve months.

This practice created legal uncertainty and operational complications for limited supervisory benefits. Only contracts entered into after the clearing obligation took effect are required to be cleared under EMIR REFIT. This decision would also bring the EU in line with approach adopted in other jurisdictions such as the United States.

4.6 Streamlined Reporting Requirements

(1) Transactions between counterparties within a group where at least one of the counterparties is an NFC are exempted from the reporting obligation (regardless of the place of establishment of the NFC) because this relatively small number of intra-group transactions are used primarily for internal hedging within groups and does not significantly contribute to systemic risk and interconnectedness, although the reporting obligation is costly and burdensome.

(2) Single-sided reporting by CCPs for exchange-traded derivatives transactions (ETDs) is required.

(3) FCs are responsible and legally liable for reporting on behalf of both themselves and an NFC that is not subject to the clearing obligation for OTC contracts entered into by those counterparties as well as for ensuring the correctness of the reported details. This significantly reduces the reporting burden for NFCs. The NFC must provide the details of the OTC derivative transactions that the financial counterparty cannot be reasonably expected to possess so that the FC has the data needed to fulfil its reporting obligation.[171] EMIR REFIT clarifies that the responsibility and legal liability for reporting OTC derivative contracts falls on the management company of a UCITS or AIFs.

4.7 Trade Repository (TR) Data Reconciliation and Access

EMIR REFIT also provides for (i) reconciliation of trade data between TRs and (ii) access by non-EU regulators to EU TR data. In the latter case, cooperation arrangements are required between ESMA and such non-EU regulators, guaranteeing the treatment of that data by the third country, and the third country must provide for a legally binding and enforceable obligation granting Union authorities direct reciprocal access to data reported to trade repositories in that third country. This latter arrangement resolves a long-standing problem with the United States which was unable to meet EMIR's requirement for an 'international agreement'; according to US law, such an agreement would need to be signed by the President, which would have been unachievable.

---

[171] Optionally, an NFC can choose to report its OTC derivative contracts.

4.8 FRANDT Requirements

Counterparties with a limited volume of activity in the OTC derivatives markets face difficulties in accessing central clearing, either as a client of a CM or through indirect clearing arrangements (see Chapter 4 'CCP Access Structures' by Christina Sell in this volume). CMs and clients of CMs that provide clearing services directly to other counterparties or indirectly by allowing their own clients to provide those services to other counterparties are therefore required to do so under fair, reasonable, non-discriminatory, and transparent commercial terms (FRANDT).[172] While this requirement should not result in price regulation or an obligation to contract (the biggest concern of industry during the negotiations), CMs and clients should be permitted to control the risks connected to the clearing services offered, for example, counterparty risks. FRANDT regulatory standards came into force on 18 June 2021. A delegated act from the Commission setting out the details for FRANDT was adopted with a delay only on 2 June 2021.[173] To ensure legal certainty and to give clearing service providers sufficient time to prepare for the application of FRANDT requirements, a transitional period was granted until 9 September 2022 to review and modify contracts agreed before 9 September 2021.

4.9 Suspension of the Clearing and Trading Obligations

In exceptional situations, ESMA can request the European Commission to suspend the clearing obligation for up to three months,[174] for specific asset classes or types of counterparty, where necessary due to changes in clearing suitability or availability or to maintain financial stability. This could be the case, for example, if classes of OTC derivatives become unsuitable for mandatory central clearing or if a CCP ceases to offer a clearing service for specific classes of OTC derivatives or for a specific type of counterparty and other CCPs cannot step in fast enough to take over those clearing services. The suspension of the clearing obligation should also be possible where it is deemed necessary to avoid a serious threat to financial stability in the Union.[175] In view of the link between EMIR and MiFIR,[176] requiring counterparties to trade

---

[172] The Commission's proposal referred to FRAND; the need for 'transparency was added in the Council working group and resulted in 'FRANDT' requirement.

[173] A Commission delegated act provides for the details of FRANDT, see Commission Delegated Regulation (EU) No. 2021/1456, supplementing Regulation (EU) No. 648/2012 of the European Parliament and of the Council by specifying the conditions under which the commercial terms for clearing services for OTC derivatives are to be considered to be fair, reasonable, non-discriminatory and transparent (2 June 2021).

[174] Renewable in three-month periods up to a total of twelve months.

[175] The necessary implementing powers are conferred on the Commission.

[176] Regulation (EU) No. 600/2014 (n 87).

derivatives subject to the clearing obligation on trading venues, the suspension of the clearing obligation might prevent counterparties from being able to comply with the trading obligation. Therefore, ESMA can propose the concurrent suspension of the trading obligation under MiFIR.[177]

4.10 Insolvency Risk

Although EMIR did not harmonize Member States' insolvency laws as this went beyond its scope and legal basis, EMIR REFIT attempts to bring greater clarity to its provision on insolvency (see Chapter 10 'Segregation and Portability of Cleared OTC Derivatives in Europe' by Bas Zebregs in this volume).[178] Member States' national insolvency laws should not prevent CCPs from being able to perform with sufficient legal certainty the transfer of client positions or to pay the proceeds of a liquidation directly to clients in case of insolvency of a CM with regard to assets held in omnibus or individually segregated client accounts.

4.11 Post-Trade Risk Reduction Services

These include services such as portfolio compression. During the EMIR negotiations, some (smaller) Member States wanted regulatory acknowledgement and treatment of these services, which could reduce the clearing requirement.[179] Other Member States were more concerned about the potential to circumvent the clearing obligation as well as the extent to which post-trade risk reduction services mitigate or reduce risks. To a certain extent, this reflected regulators' cautious approach to agreeing on industry-devised algorithms and models after the weaknesses of VaR-based risk models in the banking sector. In a typical compromise, EMIR REFIT does not introduce a regulatory acceptance of these services but asks the Commission, in cooperation with ESMA and the ESRB, to assess which, if any, trades resulting from post-trade risk reduction services should be granted an exemption from the clearing obligation. This could provide the basis for regulatory acceptance of such techniques, which could also be of assistance in other areas of risk management such as posting collateral during periods of collateral paucity.

---

[177] Note the link with the CCP Recovery and Resolution Regulation, discussed further under Chapter 12, 'Recovery and Resolution of CCPs' by Victor de Serière in this volume.

[178] EMIR (n 37), Art. 39.

[179] MiFIR does include an exemption from the trading obligation for trades that have been subject to these techniques.

4.12 Treatment of Physically Settled Foreign Exchange (FX) Forwards and Physically Settled FX Swaps

These needed to be aligned with requirements in other jurisdictions, in particular the United States. The mandatory exchange of variation margins on physically settled foreign exchange (FX) forwards and physically settled FX swaps to transactions is restricted to transactions between the most systemic counterparties in order to limit the build-up of systemic risk and to avoid international regulatory divergence. Small FCs are excluded and subject to special risk management procedures.

4.13 Pension Scheme Arrangements

The longest and most difficult negotiations in EMIR REFIT were about extending EMIR's temporary clearing exemption for pension scheme arrangements (PSAs).[180] The enormous difficulties that mandatory clearing would pose in respect of PSAs were obvious from the beginning of discussions about EMIR in 2010. The three key Member States for PSAs in the EU (Germany, Ireland, and the Netherlands—the United Kingdom was also heavily engaged until it left the EU) spearheaded the need for a temporary exemption. PSAs in these Member States provide an important and long-standing social and economic function in providing old-age retirement. In contrast, other Member States rely more on insurance-based solutions provided by private undertakings. The discussions were not only influenced by industry lobbying from the insurance sector but also by certain CCPs,[181] which saw an opportunity to increase their market share if the exemption for PSA clearing was terminated.

However, requiring such entities to clear OTC derivative contracts would lead to their divesting a significant proportion of their assets for cash in order to meet the ongoing margin requirements of CCPs which require cash for variation margin (VM) postings. They must meet the ongoing margin requirements of CCPs that require cash to deposit VM. This contrasts with investment preferences of many PSAs. In the present situation, cash holdings are obviously not the preferred investment category. The liabilities of EU PSAs are long dated: fifty years or longer with an average maturity at around twenty-five to thirty years (longer than US pension funds for instance), linked to interest rates and/or inflation. To hedge their liability risks, PSAs typically invest in high-quality government bonds. PSAs use OTC derivatives by PSAs to manage interest rate risk, mostly because of the lack of scale of issuance of long-dated, high-quality sovereign and corporate bonds. Meeting CCP variation margin cash calls would be particularly challenging for PSAs in periods of market stress and the high volatility of cash calls which must be met immediately.

---

[180] EMIR (n 37), Art. 89(1).
[181] Eurex and LCH Ltd offer interest rate swap clearing services.

A series of consecutive exemptions have been required to provide further time for CCPs to develop viable technical solutions to allow PSAs to meet the cash variation margin calls of CCPs.

EMIR's temporary PSA clearing exemption expired in August 2018. For reasons of legal certainty, and to avoid any discontinuity, it is necessary to retroactively apply the exemption for PSAs introduced by this Regulation to OTC derivative contracts entered into by PSAs between 17 August 2018 and 2021.

In 2017, the Commission had already decided to set up an informal working group of PSA representatives from the Netherlands, Germany, and Ireland (and the United Kingdom until it left the EU), CCPs, CMs, central banks, and ESMA in order to ana-lyse the issue and discuss possible solutions. The group discussed a number of pos-sible options, including (i) requiring CCPs to accept non-cash collateral for VM, (ii) collateral transformation by CMs, (iii) market-based repo solutions, or (iv) PSA ac-cess to central bank liquidity facilities. All of the options proved problematic and in-volved either potential liquidity issues for CCPs, determining appropriate haircuts for non-cash collateral, or relying on repo-markets, which had proven to be unstable in stressed market conditions and a moral hazard issues for central banks. The discus-sions informed the Commission's position in the EMIR negotiations in the Council and the EP.

The negotiations in the Council and the EP on the PSA derogation were difficult. The three Member States with funded PSAs were intent on avoiding the social and economic problems at home that ending the derogation without a solution would cause, while those that had no interest in such schemes wanted the clearing obliga-tion to apply as soon as possible.[182] The co-legislators finally agreed in EMIR REFIT to extend the exemption until June 2021, which could then be extended twice by one year through two Commission-delegated acts, depending on the progress made in finding a solution. EMIR REFIT also transformed the Commission's informal working group into a formal expert group, comprising the same members, but ex-panded to representatives from the EP's Committee on Economic and Monetary Affairs (ECON Committee) secretariat, the Council Presidency, EIOPA, and the EBA.[183] The Commission, after consulting ESMA, EIOPA, and the EBA was required, to report annually on progress.

The Commission adopted its first report in September 2020.[184] ESMA published its first report months later in December 2020. Both reports reached the same conclu-sion: efforts to make progress had been made, while some PSAs had started clearing a portion of their derivatives on a voluntary basis in CCPs, but no viable technical

---

[182] The Commission had proposed a further extension of three years in its EMIR REFIT proposal.

[183] EMIR (n 37), Art. 1(24), replacing Art. 85, paras 2 and 3.

[184] Report from the Commission to the European Parliament and the Council under Article 85(2) of Regulation (EU) No. 648/2012 of the European Parliament and of the Council of 4 July 2012 on OTC derivatives, central coun-terparties and trade repositories, as amended by Regulation (EU) No. 834/2019, assessing whether viable technical solutions have been developed for the transfer by pension scheme arrangements of cash and non-cash collateral as variation margins and the need for any measures to facilitate those viable technical solutions (23 September 2020) COM(2020) 574 final.

solution had been reached. The Commission therefore adopted a delegated act on 6 May 2021 to extend the derogation for one year until 18 June 2022.[185]

The third possible extension of the clearing derogation by one final year was the subject of an ESMA, EIOPA, and EBA report to the Commission of January 2022, in which it concluded that PSAs were largely operationally ready.[186] A number of solutions was now available to PSAs, including sponsored, cleared repo models, for PSAs to source cash to meet variation margin calls in all possible scenarios, in particular in stressed market conditions. Two relevant CCPs (Eurex in Germany and LCH in the United Kingdom) were offering sponsored clearing repo models and adding further collateral transformation capacity to the system.

The report advised that, although there was less reason to extend the derogation by one more year, further time is required for two reasons. The first is technical: market participants need time to finalize their clearing and collateral management arrangements in order to absorb the important additional cleared volume corresponding to PSAs' OTC interest rate derivative trading activity that is not yet voluntarily cleared. The second reason is political: the start of the clearing obligation for PSAs should be considered in the context of the broader plan to build clearing capacity in the EU and reduce reliance on UK CCPs. The derogation could be held in this context. The report therefore recommended a final one-year extension of the derogation until 19 June 2023. On 9 June 2022, the European Commission indeed published a Delegated Regulation that will extend by one year, until 18 June 2023, the temporary exemption from the EU EMIR clearing obligation applicable to pension scheme arrangements.[187]

5 'EMIR 2.2' 2017

EMIR 2.2 was proposed in June 2017,[188] adopted by the EP and the Council in 2019,[189] and came into effect on 1 January 2020.[190] In contrast to almost all of its

---

[185] Commission Delegated Regulation of 6 May 2021 extending the transitional period referred to in Article 89(1), first subparagraph, of Regulation (EU) No. 648/2012 of the European Parliament and of the Council (Brussels, 6 May 2021) COM(2021) 3114 final.

[186] See the report, in the form of a letter, https://www.esma.europa.eu/sites/default/files/library/esma70-451-110_letter_to_the_ec_-_clearing_obligation_for_psas.pdf (accessed 23 March 2023).

[187] Commission Delegated Regulation of 9 June 2022 extending the transitional period referred to in Article 89(1), first subparagraph, of Regulation (EU) No. 648/2012 of the European Parliament and of the Council (Brussels 9 June 2022) COM(2022) 3114 final.

[188] Proposal for a Regulation of the European Parliament and to the Council amending Regulation (EU) No. 1095/2010 establishing a European Supervisory Authority (European Securities and Markets Authority) and amending Regulation (EU) No. 648/2012 as regards the procedures and authorities involved for the authorisation of CCPs and requirements for the recognition of third-country CCPs (13 June 2017) COM(2017) 331 final.

[189] The EP's ECON Committee appointed Danuta Hübner as rapporteur for this file. The rapporteur presented her draft report on 31 January 2018. The report was voted in Committee on 16 May 2018 and the decision was taken the same day to open interinstitutional negotiations. On 27 November 2018, the Council mandate for negotiations with the EP was published. On 13 March 2019, Parliament and Council reached a political agreement on this proposal. On 1 April, the ECON committee of the EP approved the text of the agreement. On 18 April, the text was adopted in plenary. Because of the tight timeline for finalization before the end of the parliamentary term, linguistic corrections to the voted text were needed. That is why, at its plenary from 9–10 October 2019, the EP approved a corrigendum to its position at first reading. The act was adopted by the Council on 15 October and it was signed on 23 October.

[190] Regulation (EU) No. 2019/2099 of the European Parliament and of the Council of 23 October 2019 amending Regulation (EU) No. 648/2012 as regards the procedures and authorities involved for the authorisation of CCPs

other proposals for financial services legislation, the Commission did not organize a working group of Member States' experts to discuss its intended policy, draft text, and policy options to sound out views.[191] This indicates the urgency of the proposal for the Commission.

The Commission motivated its proposal by considering the relatively small number of CCPs facing the increased scale and scope of centrally cleared transactions due to successful global regulatory efforts. This concentration of risk makes the failure of a CCP a low-probability but potentially extremely high-impact event. Given the centrality of CCPs to the financial system, the increasing systemic importance of CCPs gives rise to concerns. CCPs have themselves become a source of macro-prudential risk as their failure could cause significant disruption to the financial system and would have systemic effects. A CCP failure due to increased concentration of risk would be amplified by a growing interconnectedness between CCPs both directly and indirectly via their members (usually large global banks) and clients.[192] Finally, the proposal was a response to the United Kingdom's Brexit referendum less than a year earlier, noting explicitly that the substantial volume of euro-denominated derivatives transactions (and other transactions subject to the EU clearing obligation) was currently cleared in UK CCPs located in the United Kingdom, outside the EU's jurisdiction, and raising significant challenges for EU financial stability.

The Commission's proposal for a Regulation on CCP Recovery and Resolution of November 2016 (see above) was under negotiation in the EP and the Council when the Commission adopted its proposal for EMIR 2.2 and had refocused attention on the shortcomings of the supervisory arrangements for EU and third-country CCPs in EMIR. Negotiations in the Council on CCP Recovery and Resolution were therefore put on hold until EMIR 2.2 had been finished.

5.1 Perceived Shortcomings of the Existing EMIR Regulation

According to the Commission, the three shortcomings in the current supervisory system for CCPs in EMIR were that (i) the concentration of clearing in a limited number of CCPs in a few Member States meant that 'host-countries' needed a greater role in the home-country authorities' exclusive decision making powers; (ii) in 2012, EMIR side-stepped the politically sensitive division of supervisory powers in the EU, but this was causing diverging supervisory practices for CCPs by individual Member States and creating risks of regulatory and supervisory arbitrage for CCPs and their

---

and requirements for the recognition of third country CCPs, OJ L322 (12 December 2019), p. 1. The '2.2' reference was an internal working title by the Commission's services: 'EMIR 2.1' referred to the REFIT amendments, and 'EMIR 2.2' to the third-country amendments.

[191] The only other financial services proposal that was not discussed by Member States' experts before its adoption was the proposal for European Deposit Insurance Scheme (EDIS) in November 2015.

[192] The Commission's impact assessment accompanying the proposal provides a detailed perspective of these risks.

CMs or clients;[193] (iii) the role of central banks—as issuers of currency—was not adequately reflected in CCP colleges, in particular their key responsibilities with respect to monetary policy and payment systems. The Commission's response was twofold: to provide ESMA with more supervisory powers over CCPs and to fine-tune the recognition process for third-country CCPs. The new powers for ESMA proved to be the most contentious for Member States.

5.2 ESMA's New Supervisory Powers

The Commission had three options to improve the supervision of EU CCPs: set up a new agency, give the task to an existing agency, or give the responsibility to the ECB. The first option would be politically complicated as Brexit had caused complicated negotiations about transferring existing agencies in the United Kingdom—the European Banking Authority (EBA) and the European Medicines Agency (EMA)—to EU Member States. Creating a new CCP supervisory agency would only further complicate this process.[194] Giving CCP supervisory powers to the ECB made more sense in view of its monetary policy and payment systems functions, but, in 2017, it was in the process of acquiring new banking supervisory powers over systemically important EU banks and investment firms.[195] Adding CCPs to these powers would complicate the discussions and add questions about the extent of the ECB's reach. In this light, the option of enhancing the powers of an existing agency, ESMA, which was already involved in technical work under EMIR and providing invaluable and high-quality input into the EU's regulatory process, made practical and political sense.

5.3 Governance

The Commission proposed to create a specific and separate body for CCP supervision within ESMA, alongside the financial market part of the agency: an independent 'CCP Executive Session' would be created 'within' the Board of Supervisors of ESMA to handle tasks related to CCPs in general and supervise Union and third-country CCPs in particular.[196] This was required, according to the Commission, in view of the specific prudential requirements for CCP supervision, experts that ESMA did not have in

---

[193] The Commission had drawn attention to these risks and the need for more supervisory convergence. See Commission Communication on the 'State of the Union 2016: Completing the Capital Market Union—Commission Accelerates Reform' (14 September 2016) IP/16/3001.

[194] The EU27 ministers voted to relocate the UK-based EU agencies on 20 November 2017. The EMA moved to Amsterdam, and the EBA to Paris, https://www.consilium.europa.eu/en/policies/relocation-london-agencies-brexit (accessed 23 March 2023).

[195] For a description of the ECB Single Supervisory Mechanism powers, see https://www.bankingsupervision.europa.eu/ecb/pub/pdf/ssmguidebankingsupervision201411.en.pdf (accessed 23 March 2023).

[196] See, for an explanation of the governance of the CCP Executive Session, Recitals (10)–(16) of the Commission's proposal.

abundance as its main focus had always been predicated towards financial markets rather than financial institutions. The governance challenge was to create an independent body with the necessary expertise without creating the post of a 'second chairman' in ESMA, which could be confusing and a potential source of organizational tension.

Although the co-legislator supported the need for a specific CCP governance in ESMA, after long discussions, it created a 'unique', independent permanent internal committee for CCPs ('CCP Supervisory Committee') to handle tasks related to EU and third-country CCPs. The co-legislator faced the same challenge as the Commission in finding something organizationally separate but within the existing ESMA structure.[197] To make things even more complicated, amendments to the ESA founding regulations took place at the same time as the negotiations on EMIR 2.2.

The composition of the CCP Supervisory Committee reflects the cross-border activities of CCPs and the interconnectedness of the financial markets through CM and client participation. It is composed of a Chair, two independent members, and representatives of the competent authorities of Member States with an authorized CCP. Central banks participate in meetings concerning their issues of competence as non-voting members. The Chair can also invite members of CCP colleges as observers.[198]

The important weight attached to the Committee is reflected by the fact that its Chair and two independent members can only be appointed with the approval of the EP and that they are directly accountable to the EP and to the Council for any decisions taken on the basis of EMIR 2.2.[199] They are required to act independently and objectively in the interest of the Union.[200] Although the EU institutions did not create a second chairmanship in ESMA, the requirements for the CCP Committee members and their institutional position are strikingly similar to such a post.

5.4 Supervisory Powers: From Prior Consent to Comply or Explain

The biggest area of contention and key discussion point by far in the EP and the Council concerned the extent of supervisory powers over EU CCPs by ESMA and the ECB. The Commission had proposed an extensive list of powers under EMIR that should be transferred from national level to the CCP Supervisory Committee at EU level. This proved unacceptable to some, but certainly not all, of those Member States with CCPs that would have been required to forego their national powers.

The disagreement between Member States is best illustrated by comparing the powers proposed by the Commission[201] and those finally accepted by the Council and

---

[197] See ESMA's founding regulation: Regulation (EU) No. 1095/2010 of the European Parliament and of the Council of 24 November 2010 establishing a European Supervisory Authority (European Securities and Markets Authority), amending Decision No. 716/2009/EC and repealing Commission Decision 2009/77/EC, OJ L 331 (15 December 2010), p. 84.

[198] Article 24a sets out the composition of the CCP Supervisory Committee.

[199] Article 24a(5).

[200] Article 24a(6).

[201] Article 44b of the Commission's proposal.

the EP. The Commission had proposed a system of prior consent by ESMA for many national decisions in order to promote consistency in EU CCP supervision and prior consent by the central banks for those issues concerning monetary policy and payment systems.[202] The Commission did not go so far as to actually transfer supervisors powers from national authorities because the agency does not have the power to respond to any financial and monetary consequences of its decisions. A specific voting procedure and mechanism was proposed for cases of disagreement between ESMA and the national competent authorities.

EMIR 2.2's final text was a compromise that had been worked on by intensive and informal discussions behind the scenes, and was far less ambitious than originally proposed by the Commission. Instead of a system of prior consent by ESMA for draft national supervisory decisions, the co-legislator decided on a 'comply-or-explain' mechanism as the maximum on which Member States in the Council could reach a compromise.

As usual, EMIR 2.2 highlights the contentious specific negotiating areas by requiring the Commission to prepare reports and any appropriate legislative proposals on those issues to the Council. By 2 January 2023, the Commission therefore needed to prepare reports on the effectiveness of ESMA in fostering supervisory convergence; the recognition and supervision of third-country CCPs; level playing fields among EU CCPs authorized and third-country CCPs; and the division of responsibilities between ESMA, national authorities, and central banks.[203]

5.5 Role and Powers of the ECB

The increased role of the ECB in CCP supervision was heavily debated in the institutions. The limits to the ECB's competencies over CCP supervision had already been clearly spelled out by the Court of Justice in its decision of 2015. In order to acquire legal competence in this area, the ECB needed to amend Art. 22 of its Statute so that it would also explicitly include a reference to 'securities clearing systems' (see above section 3.4).

The Commission's proposal already appeared to have taken into account the prospect of a change to the ECB's Statute and increased CCP regulatory powers for the ECB.[204] On 17 June 2017, the ECB indeed sent to the EP and the Council for adoption

---

[202] Article 21a of the proposal required national authorities to prepare and submit draft decisions in areas covered by the following articles in EMIR (n 37): Arts 7, 8, 14, 15, 16, 20, 21, 30, 31, 35, 49, and 54 and Arts 35 and 36 of Regulation (EU) No. 600/2014 and decisions adopted in the carrying out of their duties resulting from the requirements set out in Art. 16 and Titles IV and V. Article 21b, including draft decisions, would have to be submitted to the central banks of issue for any decision pursuant to Arts 14, 15, 20, 44, 46, 50, and 54.

[203] See new Art. 85(7) inserted by EMIR 2.2.

[204] Recital (7) of the Commission's proposal correctly states that 'The basic tasks to be carried out through the ESCB include the definition and implementation of the monetary policy of the Union and the promotion of the smooth operation of payment systems'. However, it continues that 'Safe and efficient financial market infrastructures, in particular clearing systems, are essential for the fulfilment of these basic tasks, and the pursuit of the ESCB's primary objective of maintaining price stability'. For this to be the case, the ECB's Statute needed to be amended first.

a recommendation to amend Art. 22 of its Statute in line with the Court's judgment of 2015.[205] The ECB announced that 'the amendment would provide the ECB with a clear legal competence in the area of central clearing, which would pave the way for the Eurosystem to exercise the powers that are foreseen for central banks in EMIR 2.2 as proposed by the European Commission'.[206]

The Commission issued a favourable opinion on the ECB's Recommendation.[207] However, the EP and the Council had concerns about the lack of legal clarity and reached an agreement in March 2019.[208] The co-legislator made far-reaching revisions to the ECB's Recommendation to amend the Statute and inserted an exhaustive list of specific and circumscribed regulatory powers for the ECB.[209] Furthermore, in order to prevent any conflicting rules and inconsistencies between the internal market and monetary policy, the EP and the Council inserted a requirement for the ECB to exercise any new regulatory powers 'having due regard to the general framework for the internal market established by the co-legislators and in a manner which is fully consistent with the legal acts of the European Parliament and the Council as well as measures adopted under such acts'.[210]

Less than two years later, in March 2019, the ECB withdrew its Recommendation to amend Art. 22 extending its legal competence over clearing and payment systems to CCPs.[211] In the ECB's view, the draft amendment to Art. 22 of the Statute no longer met the objectives of its proposal. In particular, the ECB objected against the limited list of regulations it could adopt which would deprive it of discretion to adopt measures which are necessary to carry out the Eurosystem's basic tasks and would thus violate the ECB's Treaty-based independence. Furthermore, the ECB objected against the de facto creation of a hierarchy between measures pursuing the EU's internal market and those establishing an economic and monetary union.

---

[205] The revised Art. 22 would read as follows: 'The ECB and national central banks may provide facilities, and the ECB may make regulations, to ensure efficient and sound clearing and payment systems, and clearing systems for financial instruments, within the Union and with other countries.'

[206] OJ, C 212 (1 July .2017), p. 14. See also the ECB's announcement, https://www.ecb.europa.eu/press/pr/date/2017/html/ecb.pr170623.en.html (accessed 23 March 2023).

[207] Commission Opinion on the Recommendation of the European Central Bank for a Decision of the European Parliament and of the Council amending Article 22 of the Statute of the European System of Central Banks and of the European Central Bank (3 October 2017) COM(2017) 6810 final. The Commission recommended adding to the ECB's text that the ECB's regulations should be 'consistent with acts adopted by the European Parliament and the Council and with measures adopted under such acts'.

[208] The European Parliament's ECON Committee and its AFCO Committee adopted their report on 19 June 2018, which was adopted in Parliament's plenary session on 4 July 2018.

[209] These were specifically limited to CCP reporting to and cooperation with the ECB to assess the resilience of the system to adverse market developments; opening an overnight deposit account with the ESCB; and to address situations in which a clearing system for financial instruments posed an imminent risk of substantial harm to the EU such as liquidity risk controls, settlement arrangements, margins, or collateral or interoperability arrangements.

[210] See Amendments adopted by the European Parliament on 4 July 2018 on the draft decision of the European Parliament and of the Council amending Article 22 of the Statute of the European System of Central Banks and of the European Central Bank, https://www.europarl.europa.eu/doceo/document/TA-8-2018-0288_EN.html (accessed 23 March 2023).

[211] Letter from the President of the ECB to the European Parliament and the Council, https://eur-lex.europa.eu/legal-content/EN/TXT/PDF/?uri=IMMC:LET/2019/03201&from=EN (accessed 23 March 2023).

5.6 Third-Country CCPs

The Commission's Communication of May 2017 on responding to challenges for critical financial market infrastructures and further developing the Capital Markets Union (CMU) already indicated that 'further changes [to EMIR] will be necessary to improve the current framework that ensures financial stability and supports the further development and deepening of the Capital Markets Union (CMU)'[212]

The term 'location policy' is used for the first time in EU legislation in the Commission's explanatory memorandum for EMIR 2.2, where it explicitly refers to the need for proportionality:

> In addition, a location policy that would not be tailored to the systemic risk of the third-country CCP, defined according to objective criteria, could have an impact on the costs of clearing, the access to indirect clearing for clients of CMs (including non-financial counterparties and small financial counterparties) and therefore generally in the ability to hedge risks for EU counterparties.[213]

As discussed above, the argument of determining the EU's own best interests (i.e. economic costs and benefits) remains key in whether or not to give the United Kingdom equivalence under EMIR and played a major role in the decision to provide temporary equivalence until June 2025.

5.7 Tiering Procedure

The principle of introducing a new structure in EMIR's equivalence process and the possibility to apply stricter requirements to systemically important third-country CCPs was never heavily contested in the Council and the EP, nor was the possibility for the Commission to deny recognition to a 'super systemic' third-country CCP and only allow it to provide its clearing services from within the EU.

The EU's new policy approach takes place through a detailed procedure and is essentially the same as proposed by the Commission, with further details added by the Council and the EP. After the Commission grants equivalence to a third country, EMIR 2.2's new procedure applies for the recognition of individual CCPs from that country. The procedure is relatively straightforward. After the Commission has determined that the rules and supervision in a third country are equivalent to those of EMIR, a (new) process applies for ESMA's recognition of CCPs from that third country to determine

---

[212] Communication from the Commission to the European Parliament, the Council, and the European Central Bank on Responding to challenges for critical financial market infrastructures and further developing the Capital Markets Union (Brussels, 4 May 2017) COM(2017) 225 final.

[213] EMIR 2.2 Explanatory memorandum, p. 14.

the risks those CCPs present for the financial stability of the Union or of one or more of its Member States. The degree of risk will classify CCPs from a third country into two tiers: non-systemically important ('Tier 1') CCPs or systemically important for the EU ('Tier 2') CCPs (see also Chapter 16 'Brexit: Equivalence; Location Policy' by Dermot Turing in this volume).

ESMA's assessment of systemic risk that the CCP could present to the financial stability of the Union or of one or more of its Member States is based on five objective and transparent criteria:

(1) its nature, size and complexity in terms of:
  – the aggregate value of each Union currency of transactions cleared by the CCP or the aggregate exposure of the CCP to its CMs and, where possible, their clients and indirect clients;
  – its risk profile, including operational risks, such as fraud, criminal activity, IT- and cyber-risk;
(2) the effect of its failure or a disruption on the financial system, markets, and institutions;
(3) its clearing membership structure, including, if possible, EU clients and indirect clients;
(4) the availability of alternative clearing services for OTC derivatives denominated in Union currencies for CMs and, where possible, their EU clients and indirect clients. This criterion was added by the Council in order to ensure that any decision would take into account the EU's own interests;
(5) its wider relationships, interdependencies, or other interactions with other CCPs, financial institutions, and the broader financial system.

None of the criteria are determinative on their own and they should give a holistic perspective of the risk to the financial stability of the EU or one of its Member States. If ESMA determines that a third-country CCP is not systemically important for the EU's financial stability, EMIR's existing recognition conditions simply continue for that CCP. However, if ESMA determines that a third-country CCP is systemically important, specific requirements are be imposed on that CCP, and it can only be recognized if that CCP complies with those requirements. It is therefore immensely important for a third-country CCP to know the results of its tiering assessment. A crucial Commission delegated regulation was adopted in July 2021 to further specify the five criteria.[214] Importantly, the Commission's Delegated Regulation contains risk quantifications as objective thresholds ('indicators') to determine the tiering process. ESMA

---

[214] Commission Delegated Regulation (EU) No. 2020/1303 of 14 July 2020 supplementing Regulation (EU) No. 648/2012 of the European Parliament and of the Council with regard to the criteria that ESMA should take into account to determine whether a central counterparty established in a third country is systemically important or likely to become systemically important for the financial stability of the Union or of one or more of its Member States, OJ L305 (21 September 2020), p. 7.

can only determine that a third-country CCP is a Tier 2 CCP if it meets at least one of the following quantitative indicators.[215]

(a) The maximum open interest—the total number of outstanding derivative contracts, such as options or futures that have not been settled—of securities transactions, including securities financing transactions, or exchange traded derivatives in Union currencies cleared by the CCP over a period of one year prior to the assessment or intended to be cleared by the CCP over a period of one year following the assessment is more than EUR 1 000 billion;

(b) the maximum notional outstanding of OTC derivatives transactions in Union currencies cleared by the CCP over a period of one year prior to the assessment or intended to be cleared by the CCP over a period of one year following the assessment is more than EUR 1 000 billion;

(c) the average aggregated margin requirement and default fund contributions for accounts held at the CCP by EU-CMs (or part of a group subject to consolidated supervision), calculated by the CCP on a net basis at CM account level over a period of two years prior to the assessment is more than EUR 25 billion;

(d) the estimated largest payment obligation committed by EU-entities (or part of a group subject to consolidated supervision), of aggregated EU-currencies, and computed over a period of one year prior to the assessment, that would result from the default of at least the two largest single CMs and their affiliates, in extreme but plausible market conditions is more than EUR 3 billion.

Consistent with the Commission's equivalence decision for the CFTC (see section 3.6), certain listed agricultural derivative contracts executed on regulated markets in third countries that largely serve domestic non-financial counterparties in that third country are excluded from the assessment as it had already been established that they have a low degree of systemic interconnectedness with the rest of the financial system and pose a negligible risk to the Union.[216] Furthermore, ESMA should take into account to what extent a third country has in force a framework for the recovery and resolution of CCPs; this will have an effect on any impact an applicant CCP from that third country could have on the EU's financial stability.[217]

5.8 Requirements for Tier 2 CCPs

Third-country CCPs in the systemically important Tier 2 category are now subject to stricter supervision. They can only be recognized by ESMA if they meet three types of requirements.

---

[215] Commission Delegated Regulation (EU) No. 2020/1303 (n 214), Art. 6.
[216] See Commission Delegated Regulation (EU) No. 2020/1303 (n 214), Recital (2).
[217] Commission Delegated Regulation (EU) No. 2020/1303, Art. 2 refers to the existence of recovery and/or resolution plans in a third country.

First, EMIR's core prudential requirements for EU CCPs will also apply to Tier 2 CCPs on an ongoing basis. These include inter alia EMIR's capital requirements, organization, record keeping, business conduct, outsourcing, risk management, liquidity, margins, default fund, and interoperability.[218] When it applies these requirements to a third-country CCP, ESMA will take into account the extent to which it already complies with comparable requirements in the third country.[219]

Second, the third-country CCP must comply with any specific requirements that the central banks may have imposed in carrying out their monetary policy tasks. Those requirements should relate to providing information, cooperating in stress-testing exercises, opening an overnight deposit account,[220] and requirements 'in exceptional situations'[221] that the central bank can impose to address temporary systemic liquidity risks affecting the transmission of monetary policy or the smooth operation of payment systems and relating to liquidity risk control, margin requirements, collateral, settlement arrangements, or interoperability arrangements.[222]

The central bank measures are subject to clear limitations involving a prior information and justification procedure with other regulators, central banks, and the college third-country CCP college and an opinion by ESMA and other central banks about the effects on the efficiency, soundness, and resilience of the CCP.[223] The central bank of must 'duly consider' any amendments proposed in the opinions of ESMA or the central banks. This procedure clearly reflects the discussion about the powers of the ECB discussed above,[224] and seeks to avoid any duplicating or conflicting requirements for prudential reasons by ESMA and monetary policy requirements set by a central bank. The co-legislator attempted to determine the dividing line between 'monetary policy' considerations and the prudential framework of CCP supervision under EMIR. This is an extremely difficult exercise as the boundaries of both can never be determined with precision.

Third, the CCP must provide ESMA with legally enforceable guarantees to provide ESMA with access to any documents, records, information and data, and the right to on-site inspections.[225] These requirements enable ESMA to carry out full and

---

[218] The CCP must comply with EMIR's requirements in Art. 16 and Titles IV and V.

[219] Article 25 (2b). See Art. 25a for comparable compliance, which must be initiated at the request of the CCP itself. The Commission has adopted an implementing act with further details on comparable compliance: Commission Delegated Regulation of 14 July 2020 supplementing Regulation (EU) No. 648/2012 of the European Parliament and of the Council with regard to the minimum elements to be assessed by ESMA when assessing third-country CCPs' requests for comparable compliance and the modalities and conditions of that assessment, OJ L305 (21 September 2020), p. 13.

[220] This should not amount to an obligation to relocate all or part of the clearing services of the CCP.

[221] See Recital (34). Exceptional situations may arise in centrally cleared markets in situations such as stressed money and repurchase markets on which the CCP relies to obtain liquidity, situations where CCPs' operations contribute to the drying up of liquidity in the market, or serious malfunctions of payment or settlement arrangements that impede the CCP's ability to meet its payment obligations or increase its liquidity needs.

[222] The requirements in exceptional situations can apply for six months and can be extended for a further six months.

[223] A special short procedure applies in an emergency situation.

[224] Recital (34) notes that these measures can be taken by central banks 'to the extent allowed under their respective institutional frameworks'. As discussed above, the co-legislator (successfully) sought to limit the ECB's powers in the context of Art. 22 of the ECB' Statute.

[225] Article 25(2b)(c).

effective supervision of a CCP.[226] They were motivated by past problems encountered by ESMA in accessing information about CCPs regulated by the US CFTC because EMIR's original wording did not legally guarantee such access. This resulted in the unbalanced situation that US regulators had full and unfettered access to data on EU CCPs while ESMA had access to almost no information at all about US CFTCs. This was finally resolved by new bilateral cooperation arrangements in 2021.[227] In addition to data access, EMIR 2.2 contains provisions and procedures concerning on-site inspection by ESMA.[228] The procedures follow the normal international cooperation arrangements, including sufficient advance notice to the home regulator of the CCP and the arrangements agreed with that regulator in bilateral supervisory cooperation agreements.[229]

The calibration of the quantitative thresholds was done with great care by the Commission, together with ESMA and the ECB, measuring each individual threshold against the situation of individual CCPs that had already been recognized by ESMA and those third-country CCPs that were expected to be requesting recognition in the future. Informal discussions also took place with third-country regulators in a close and collaborative setting to avoid any misunderstandings and miscommunication in this sensitive area.[230]

5.9 Requirements for Substantially Systemically Important CCPs

The degree of risk posed by a systemically important Tier 2 CCP to the financial system and stability of the Union varies. The Commission and the EP therefore sought a way to apply the requirements for systemically important CCPs proportionate to the risks that a systemic CCP might present to the Union.[231] Therefore, if a non-EU Tier 2 CCP cannot be adequately supervised, the Commission may require that it establishes an entity in the EU and seeks authorization from the relevant national competent authority to continue providing its services. Those Tier 2 CCPs are referred to as 'substantially systemically important CCPs'.[232]

---

[226] Article 25f sets out detailed requirements for ESMA to requests for information to third-country CCPs.

[227] ESMA and the CFTC eventually worked out a way to share information, although the imbalance remained until 2021. An enhanced memorandum of understanding (MoU) was signed between ESMA and the CFTC in January 2021 which governs ESMA's access to information for tier 2 CCPs regulated by the CFTC. https://www.cftc.gov/sites/default/files/idc/groups/public/@internationalaffairs/documents/file/cftc-esma-clearingmou060216.pdf

[228] Article 25h.

[229] Article 25(7) requires ESMA to conclude bilateral cooperation arrangements with third-country regulators on information exchange, on-site inspections, and notifications. These bilateral MoUs usually follow the standardized format established by IOSCO referred to as the Multilateral Memorandum of Understanding Concerning Consultation and Cooperation and the Exchange of Information (MMoU). See https://www.iosco.org (accessed 23 March 2023) for details.

[230] For example, CFTC Chairman Heath Tarbert and his staff were instrumental in these discussions, fostering a mutually respectful cooperation and understanding of each other's perspectives, which was crucial to reaching a positive result for both sides and demonstrated the benefits of the good relationship between the authorities.

[231] See the reference to proportionality in Recital (38).

[232] See also Chapter 16, 'Brexit: Equivalence, Location Policy' by Dermot Turing in this volume.

A Commission decision requiring a third-country CCP to 'relocate' the provision of certain services to the EU could have important consequences for cross-border clearing. The Council therefore made it clear that it should only be applied as 'last resort', and the co-legislator made sure to require following a rigorous procedure to determine the need and effects of such a decision.

The procedure is lengthy and includes a number of checks and balances.

(1) The first step is a general review[233] by ESMA of all recognized third-country CCPs at least every five years.[234] If ESMA determines that a third-country CCP that has been classified as a Tier 1 CCP should be (re-)classified as a Tier 2 CCP, within eighteen months, that CCP must comply with the requirements for Tier 2 CCPs.[235]

(2) On the basis of its assessment, if ESMA concludes that a third-country CCP 'with or without prior classification or some of its clearing services'[236] are of such systemic importance that compliance with EMIR would not sufficiently address the financial stability risk for the Union or for one or more of its Member States, and in the event that other measures are deemed insufficient to address financial stability risks, ESMA must recommend to the Commission that that CCP or some of its clearing services not be recognized. ESMA's assessment must be fully reasoned and include a quantitative technical cost–benefit assessment. ESMA's recommendation must include:

– a consultation of the ESRB and

– the agreement of the central banks of issue of all Union currencies of the financial instruments cleared or to be cleared by a third-country CCP or some of its services. It is important for central banks of issue to be individually consulted by ESMA and express their agreement with a recommendation to deny recognition to a third-country CCP, given the impact that such a decision could have on the currency that they issue. The agreement or concerns that a central bank of issue may raise should only relate to the currency that it issues and not to the recommendation as a whole or to the report as a whole.

(3) On the basis of that recommendation, the Commission has the power to adopt, as a measure of last resort, an implementing act specifying that the third-country CCP in question should not be able to provide some or all of its clearing services to CMs and trading venues established in the Union unless that CCP

---

[233] An updated list of third-country CCPs and their tiering status is available on ESMA's website, https://www.esma.europa.eu/sites/default/files/library/third-country_ccps_recognised_under_emir.pdf (accessed 23 March 2023).

[234] ESMA has adopted a detailed methodology for assessing a third-country CCP under article 25(2c), https://www.esma.europa.eu/sites/default/files/library/methodology_for_assessing_a_tc_ccp_under_article_252c_of_emir_.pdf (accessed 23 March 2023).

[235] Article 25(5); in exceptional circumstances the adaptation period can be extended by a further six months.

[236] This covers new CCPs and the UK CCPs that did not require recognition when the United Kingdom was still a member of the EU.

is authorized in any Member State to do so in accordance with EMIR. The Commission must include an 'appropriate' adaptation period of up to two years (which might be extended once by six months) and the conditions under which that CCP can continue to provide certain clearing services or activities during the adaptation period. The Commission must also consider any measures that should be taken during that period in order to limit the potential costs to CMs and their clients, in particular clients established in the Union.

In December 2021, ESMA published a further report on UK CCPs, in advance of the Commission's decision to temporarily extend the United Kingdom's equivalence decision.[237] The report identifies three clearing services—one provided by LCH Ltd and two by ICE Clear Europe Ltd—as being of substantial systemic importance for the EU's financial stability and posing risks that may not be fully mitigated under the current EMIR regulatory framework. However, it also concludes that the costs and risks of de-recognizing these services would outweigh the benefits to the EU at this time. It suggested four sets of policy measures as a response to identified risks and vulnerabilities relating to systemically important UK CCPs serving European market participants:

(1) considering appropriate incentives for reducing the size of EU exposures to Tier 2 CCPs;
(2) revising the comparable compliance framework;
(3) expanding ESMA's supervisory and crisis management toolbox; and
(4) enhancing cooperation with UK authorities on CCP Recovery and Resolution.

The existing colleges of national supervisors established under EMIR for each EU CCP will continue to act as bodies fostering cooperation. The role of the ECB is strengthened through its permanent membership in the CCP Executive Session and in the supervisory colleges.

5.10 Commission 2022 Proposal to Amend EMIR and Strengthen the EU Clearing System

As discussed in section 4 above, the Commission's intentions to continue to revise EMIR cannot come as a surprise and follow the well-known steps to prepare the ground for legislative initiatives. The Commission's deeply rooted concern about the financial stability risk posed by over-reliance on UK-based CCPs remained a key motive for action. In 2021, the Commission had already established a Working Group (with the ECB, the European Supervisory Authorities, and the ESRB) to explore the opportunities and

---

[237] 'Assessment Report under Article 25(2c) of EMIR', Assessment of LCH Ltd and ICE Clear Europe Ltd (16 December 2021). The report can be found in a redacted version at https://www.esma.europa.eu/press-news/esma-news/esma-publishes-results-its-assessment-systemically-important-uk-central (accessed 23 March 2023).

challenges involved in transferring derivatives from the United Kingdom to the EU. The working group had indicated that a combination of different measures to improve the attractiveness of clearing, to encourage infrastructure development, and to reform supervisory arrangements were needed to build a strong and attractive central clearing capacity in the EU in the years to come. In November 2021, and following that advice when explaining the temporary and conditional extension of the EMIR equivalence decision for UK CCPs, European Commissioner McGuinness had publicly announced the Commission's intention to revisit EMIR. The United Kingdom's temporary equivalence decision was explained as a necessary step to buy more time to put 'a more permanent solution in place to develop and expand the clearing capacity of EU-based CCPs as a means to reduce over-reliance on UK CCPs'.[238] As usual, in the course of 2022, the Commission's proposal was preceded by a variety of stakeholder consultations, including a public 'Call for Evidence' (February 2022), stakeholder meetings and meetings with Member State Experts (Spring 2022), and discussions with MEPs and industry.[239] At the end of December 2022, the Commission finally published its proposal for a further revision of EMIR to respond to three challenges:[240]

(1) improving the attractiveness of EU CCPs. Proposed measures inter alia simplify procedures for launching products and changing models, standardized CCP application documents, and an ex-post approval/non-objection procedure for certain changes. Furthermore, the need for an equivalence decision for intra-group transactions would be replaced by a simple list of jurisdictions with a high anti-money laundering and counter terrorist financing risk for which an exemption cannot be granted;

(2) strengthening the EU supervisory framework. This would also respond to challenges posed by the energy crisis, and covers inter alia hedging and liquidity planning of energy derivatives and margin models. Joint supervisory teams, monitoring cross-border risks to the EU throughout the clearing chain by EU authorities, and allowing the CCP Supervisory Committee to co-ordinate common responses to emergency situations on the basis of up-to-date information are envisaged;

(3) incisive measures referring to the need for the EU to reduce its 'excessive exposures' to systemic infrastructures located in particular in the United Kingdom by increasing clearing capacity in EU CCPs. Taking account of EMIR's history,

---

[238] 'Commissioner McGuinness Announces Proposed Way Forward for Central Clearing Statement', (Brussels, 10 November 2021), https://ec.europa.eu/commission/presscorner/detail/en/STATEMENT_21_5905 (accessed 23 March 2023).

[239] For a full overview of stakeholder meetings, see Annex 2, Commission Staff working document, 'Impact Assessment Report' (Brussels, 7 December 2022) SWD(2022) 697 final, https://eur-lex.europa.eu/legal-content/EN/TXT/?uri=CELEX:52022SC0697 (accessed 23 March 2023).

[240] Proposal for a Regulation of the European Parliament and of the Council amending Regulations (EU) No. 648/2012, (EU) No. 575/2013 and (EU) No. 2017/1131 as regards measures to mitigate excessive exposures to third-country central counterparties and improve the efficiency of Union clearing markets (Brussels, 7 December 2022) COM(2022) 697 final, https://eur-lex.europa.eu/legal-content/EN/TXT/PDF/?uri=CELEX:52022PC0 697&from=EN (accessed 23 March 2023).

the EU's strategic autonomy can be said to be the most important driver of the proposal. The Commission notes that the United Kingdom continues to plays a key role as a hub for central clearing (in the first half of 2021, 91% of all euro-denominated interest-rate swaps trades were still cleared in the United Kingdom). Repeating its long-standing concern, in case of stress, excessive reliance of EU market participants on CCPs established in third countries would therefore make it difficult for EU regulators and supervisors to address the financial stability risks for the EU. In line with its calls on market participants to reduce their exposure to UK CPs, the Proposal now requires market participants subject to a clearing obligation to clear a portion of the products that have been identified[241] as of substantial systemic importance through 'active accounts' at EU CCPs.[242] The level set should reduce clearing in those derivatives at substantially systemically important Tier 2 UK CCPs to such an extent that those activities are no longer of substantial systemic importance.

The United Kingdom's current temporary equivalence decision for CCPs expires on 30 June 2025. It remains to be seen whether the Commission's proposals will be enacted in time. The proposal is part of a wider, holistic policy and is complemented by separate legislative proposals for some limited changes to the bank Capital Requirements Directive (CRD), the Investment Firms Directive (IFD) and the UCITS Directive.[243] These limited changes were necessary to improve the coherence of the treatment of concentration risk towards CCPs and the counterparty risk on centrally cleared derivative transactions.

6 CCP Recovery and Resolution 2020

6.1 Background

If the EU was behind the United States in regulating OTC derivatives, it was the first jurisdiction to have a comprehensive recovery and resolution framework in place, setting the benchmark at a global level. The EU's CCP Recovery and Resolution Regulation (CCPR&R) is the natural pendant for EMIR. Where EMIR regulates the going-concern situation of a CCP, CCPR&R regulates a situation of potential financial

---

[241] Article 7A (new): interest rate derivatives denominated in euro and Polish zloty, short-term interest rate futures and credit default swaps denominated in euro.

[242] In a new Art. 7A, ESMA would establish the details of the calibration of the activity to be maintained in these active accounts and the reporting requirements of transactions cleared at such active accounts. The Commission could adopt a delegated act to amend the list of categories of derivative contracts which are subject to the active account requirement.

[243] Proposal for a Directive of the European Parliament and of the Council amending Directives 2009/65/EU No. 2013/36/EU and (EU) No. 2019/2034 as regards the treatment of concentration risk towards central counterparties and the counterparty risk on centrally cleared derivative transactions, COM/2022/698 final, https://eur-lex.europa.eu/legal-content/EN/TXT/?uri=CELEX:52022PC069 (accessed 23 March 2023).

default and winding down. The European Commission, in a 2010 Communication, already promised to investigate 'what crisis management and resolution arrangements, if any, are necessary and appropriate for [...] financial institutions' other than banks.[244] Following that communication, the Commission launched a consultation on a possible framework for recovery and resolution of non-bank financial institutions in 2012.

It soon became generally accepted that the G20's global regulatory reform of OTC derivatives after the 2008 financial crisis had resulted in widespread regulatory requirements for standardized OTC derivatives to be centrally cleared by a CCP. The upside of this was that the pre-existing web of opaque bilateral, often under-collateralized OTC transactions had largely been replaced by transparent, centrally cleared, and collateralized trades. However, as the obligation to centrally clear OTC derivatives came into effect, the volume and range of CCP-cleared trades increased significantly. CCPs have evolved from primarily serving domestic needs and markets to constituting 'critical nodes' in financial markets. At a global level, the FSB concerning CCP resolution, and CPMI–IOSCO concerning CCP recovery, updated the global standards on financial markets infrastructures in 2014 and 2017 to enhance CCPs' resilience, recovery planning, and resolvability.[245] At the international level, the FSB is also still active in the discussion around financial resources to support CCP resolution and the treatment of CCP equity in resolution. The FSB published its report in November 2020 and will continue to work with other international standard-setting bodies on the adequacy of CCPs' equity in resolution in the following years (see below).

Not only had CCPs become 'critical nodes', but it has also been accepted that, while some CCPs remain focused on domestic EU markets, a significant amount of the financial risk of the EU's financial system and internal market is processed by, and concentrated in, CCPs on behalf of CMs and their clients. Furthermore, all CCPs are systemically important, at least in their home markets. This statement is important as it contrasts with, for example, the United States, where only CCPs that have been designated as such by the Financial Stability Oversight Board (FSOB) are considered to be of systemic importance to the United States.

The history of failing CCPs is short,[246] although it is generally accepted that a CCP failure is a low probability but a high-impact event. International discussions between regulators showed that, similar to banks, there was a lack of adequate tools to

---

[244] European Commission, Communication on an EU Framework for Crisis Management in the Financial Sector, COM(2010) 0579.

[245] Key Attributes of Effective Resolution Regimes for Financial Institutions, Financial Stability Board (November 2011), http://www.financialstabilityboard.org/publications/r_111104cc.pdf (accessed 23 March 2023). Updated in 2017 with sector-specific annexes, https://www.fsb.org/wp-content/uploads/P050717-1.pdf (accessed 23 March 2023).

[246] Caisse de Liquidation des Affaires en Marchandises in France in 1974, the Kuala Lumpur Commodities Clearing House in 1984, the Hong Kong Futures Exchange in 1987, and also the Commodities Clearing House in New Zealand in 1989. See, e.g. D. McLaughlin and R. Berndsen, 'Why Is a CCP Failure Very Unlikely?', CentER Discussion Paper, Vol. 2021-002, CentER, Center for Economic Research.

preserve the critical functions provided by failing CCPs. Furthermore, unlike banking supervisors meeting in the Basel Committee, CCP regulators lacked cooperation and coordination frameworks, in particular those located in different Member States or jurisdictions, to allow swift and decisive action. The experience in the banking sector had not been encouraging. Without such tools and in the absence of cooperation and co-ordination frameworks, EU Member States were compelled to rescue financial institutions using taxpayer money to stem contagion and reduce panic. While CCPs were not direct recipients of extraordinary public financial support in the 2008 financial crisis, they were protected from the effects that banks failing to perform their obligations would otherwise have had on them.

CCPR&R therefore closely follows and 'complements' its counterpart in the banking sector, the Bank Recovery and Resolution Directive (BRRD). This is logical because recovery and resolution of CCPs cannot be considered in isolation from the recovery and resolution regimes of CMs operating under a banking license. The BRRD materially reduces the risk and the potential scale of a CCP's CM default. If a bank's CCP liabilities are not subject to bail-in, then the CCP would also have the absolute benefit of the member's own recovery and resolution plan and resources prior to the beginning of the CCP's own waterfall.

The policy objective of CCPR&R is clear: to maintain a CCP's critical functions and its ability to serve the real economy when a CCP is failing or likely to fail, while minimizing the cost to taxpayers of a CCP failure. The choice of a regulation as a legal act is also straightforward. As it complements and builds on EMIR, which is also a regulation providing for uniform prudential requirements for CCPs. Setting recovery and resolution requirements in a directive would create inconsistencies by the adoption of potentially different national rules in an area otherwise governed by directly applicable Union law.

6.2   EP and Council Support for Work

From the beginning, the Council and the EP strongly supported work in this field. In a 2013 own-initiative report, the EP called on the Commission to prioritize the recovery and resolution of CCPs and of central securities depositories (CSDs) exposed to credit risk.[247] The EP reiterated its request in a 2015 resolution on building a CMU.[248] In the following September, the ECB tabled a favourable opinion, focusing on the involvement of central banks in recovery and resolution.[249] Against this background, the Commission published its proposal for a regulation on the recovery and resolution

---

[247] European Parliament Legislative Observatory, Procedure file on Initiative Report Recovery and Resolution framework for non-bank institutions, 2013/2047(INI).

[248] European Parliament, Resolution of 9 July 2015 on Building a Capital Markets Union, 2015/2634(RSP).

[249] Opinion of the European Central Bank on a proposal for a regulation of the European Parliament and of the Council on a framework for the recovery and resolution of central counterparties and amending Regulations (EU) No. 1095/2010, (EU) No. 648/2012, and (EU) No. 2015/2365, CON/2017/38. The ESRB and ESMA also delivered opinions.

of CCPs on 28 November 2016.[250] It was adopted by the EP and the Council on 16 December 2020 and entered into force on 11 February 2021.[251]

The EP's Committee on Economic and Monetary Affairs (ECON) appointed three co-rapporteurs for this file. They presented their draft report on 25 September 2017. The ECON Committee adopted its final report on 24 January 2018. The institutional negotiations in the Council and the EP were delayed in 2018 and 2019 because of the priority given to the negotiations on EMIR 2.2. The conclusion of that proposal would impact the CCP Recovery and Resolution proposal, in particular where it concerned the role of ESMA: if ESMA had been given supervisory powers over EU CCPs in EMIR 2.2, large parts of the CCP Recovery and Resolution text would have needed to be revised to reflect those powers. Ultimately, as discussed above, ESMA's supervisory powers were limited to third-country CCPs. The negotiations in the institutions were concluded fairly quickly afterwards.

6.3 Scope

The scope of the CCPR&R covers all EU CCPs that are subject to authorization and the prudential requirements of EMIR. This is regardless of whether they have a banking licence.[252] The latter is important in view of the fact that two EU CCPs (EUREX in Germany and LCH SA in France), for historical reasons, operate under a banking licence.[253]

A further area of attention concerns CCPs that are part of a wider corporate group. Similar to the banking sector and the BRRD, the Commission proposed that specific powers could apply to the parent companies of CCPs, for example, an option for authorities to decide, on a case-by-case basis, that recovery plans should cover parent companies[254]. The Commission's proposal contained a specific provision requiring a parent undertaking to submit a recovery plan for the group.[255] This encountered opposition from Germany in the Council working group, as EUREX is part of the Deutsche Börse group, which would give rise to difficult legal and political discussions about the extent to which parental support could be provided. This discussion was only resolved at the end of the trilogue negotiations, when a compromise was reached to explicitly state that the group of which a CCP forms part does not need to be subject to CCPR&R but that the group dimension should be taken into account in the CCP's recovery and

---

[250] European Commission, Proposal for a Regulation of the European Parliament and of the Council on a framework for the recovery and resolution of central counterparties and amending Regulations (EU) No. 1095/2010, (EU) No. 648/2012, and (EU) No. 2015/2365, COM(2016) 856.

[251] Regulation (EU) No. 2021/23 of the European parliament and of the Council of 16 December 2020 on a framework for the recovery and resolution of central counterparties and amending Regulations (EU) No. 1095/2010, (EU) No. 648/2012, (EU) No. 600/2014, (EU) No. 806/2014 and (EU) No. 2015/2365 and Directives 2002/47/EC, 2004/25/EC, 2007/36/EC, 2014/59/EU and (EU) No. 2017/1132, OJ L 22 (22 January 2021), p. 1.

[252] Article 2(1).

[253] See also Chapter 12, 'Recovery and Resolution of CCPs' by Victor de Serière in this volume for and in-depth analysis of the Regulation

[254] Article 2(24) of the Commission proposal defined a 'group' as a parent undertaking and its subsidiaries.

[255] Article 11 of the Commission proposal.

resolution planning.[256] When assessing the recovery plan, the competent authority may take parental support agreements into consideration as valid parts of the recovery plan only where those agreements are contractually binding.[257] Furthermore, if a CCP is part of a group and contractual parental or group support agreements are part of the recovery plan, the plan must include scenarios in which those agreements cannot be honoured.[258] The recovery and resolution process is broadly similar to the BRRD for the banking sector.

6.4 Prevention and Preparation: Recovery Plans

CCPs are required to prepare recovery plans to overcome any form of financial distress which would exceed their default management resources and other requirements under EMIR.[259] The scenarios applied must be more severe than those used for the regular stress tests under EMIR, Art. 49 while remaining plausible. The recovery plans also should clearly distinguish between losses arising from a CM default (default losses) and losses due to other reasons (non-default losses) such as CCP operational failures. The CCP's capital should bear first losses, in both cases, before any other recovery tools can be activated. CCPs can determine the appropriate range of options and recovery tools, including tools to rematch the CCP's book through tearing up contracts, establishing voluntary agreements such as auctions with the remaining CMs such that they voluntarily take on positions, or to arrange for additional resources by capped 'cash calls' on CMs and haircutting payments to clearing participants as a result of an economic gain in a derivatives contract ('variation margin haircutting'). Although 'haircuts' of IM had originally been discussed, this was not explicitly included in the Regulation. The potential for increased volatility in an already stressed financial situation by introducing IM haircuts, which would cause clearing members to rush to the exit, was considered to be an unacceptable downside of such measures. Contrary to resolution plans (see below) the CCP is required to provide quantitative triggers for recovery measures 'if possible', otherwise the indicators must be qualitative.[260] The CCPR&R list of possible measures is open-ended in this respect.

The recovery plan must form part of the CCP's internal rulebook, which should contain operating rules agreed contractually with CMs. An important reason for this is the possibility to enforce the recovery plan against CMs in a third country because these CMs will be subject to the local laws and enforcement by the courts in that third country. This avoids any extra-territorial effect of the Regulation.[261]

---

[256] See Recital 12 CCPR&R.
[257] Article 10(4). Also Annex A(21) requires the CCP to take into account a range of scenarios that would severely affect the financial soundness or operational viability of the CCP and be relevant to the CCP's specific conditions such as events specific to the legal entity and any group to which it belongs.
[258] CCPR&R (n 256), Art. 9(13).
[259] CCPR&R (n 256), Art. 9.
[260] CCPR&R (n 256), Art. 9(3).
[261] See CCPR&R (n 256), Recital (25).

Great consideration was given to the position of clients in the discussions in Council and the EP, including compensating non-defaulting CMs' clients if recovery was successful thanks to the application of variation margin gain haircuts to their assets (see Chapter 12 'Recovery and Resolution of CCPs' by Victor de Serière in this volume).

Recovery plans must be assessed and approved by the Resolution Authorities, who can require a CCP to take 'appropriate measures'[262] if they identify obstacles to resolvability in the course of the planning process.[263]

6.5 CCP Recovery Measures

The recovery phase starts when there is a significant deterioration in the CCP's financial situation or risk of breach of its prudential requirements under EMIR that could lead to the infringement of its authorization requirements that would justify the withdrawal of its authorization, according to certain viability indicators and based on the prepared recovery plan. These include cash calls to non-defaulting CMs, the reduction in value of the collateral provided daily to the CCP (so-called variation margin gains haircutting), and the use of the CCP's own resources. If A CCP decides to activate a recovery measure, it must immediately inform its competent authority, who can block the CCP from taking that measure if it could cause significant adverse effects to the financial system or is unlikely to be effective.[264] Furthermore, supervisory authorities will have the possibility to intervene at an early stage, that is, before the problems become critical and the financial situation deteriorates irreparably. For example, they will be able to require the CCP to undertake specific actions in its recovery plan or to make changes to its business strategy or legal or operational structure.

6.6 Second Skin in the Game (SIG)

The most heavily discussed issue in the negotiations in the Council and the EP was the introduction of a new, second contribution by the CCP in a recovery scenario. EMIR already included a skin-in-the-game (SIG) contribution to create sound risk management incentives in a CCP. EMIR's default waterfall is to use, first, the defaulting CM's margin, then its default fund contribution, then a tranche of capital of the CCP (SIG), and finally the rest of the default fund.[265]

International standards do not refer to or specify a minimum amount of SIG for a CCP: they only 'require FMIs to maintain sufficient financial resources to cover their credit exposure to each participant fully with a high degree of confidence, and

---

[262] Article 10(10) sets out the objectives of those measures, but does not specify which particular measures should be taken, leaving necessary flexibility to the authorities.

[263] CCPR&R (n 256), Art. 10.

[264] CCPR&R (n 256), Art. 10(7).

[265] EMIR (n 37), Art. 45(4).

encourages systemically important CCPs to maintain additional financial resources sufficient to cover a wide range of potential stress scenarios'.[266] The co-legislator, particularly after insistence by the European Parliament, nevertheless went further and introduced a *second* SIG requirement 'to further reduce the risks of losses for the taxpayer'.[267] The discussion focused on the need to introduce a second tranche of CCP capital in view of the increasingly systemically important role of a CCP.[268] Nevertheless, it was agreed at the final trilogue meeting in Brussels in the Spring of 2020 that a CCP must use a portion of its pre-funded, dedicated own resources under EMIR.[269] That second SIG can include any capital it holds in addition to its minimum capital requirements to comply with the 'notification threshold'[270] as a recovery measure before resorting to other recovery measures requiring financial contributions from CMs. The second SIG should not be lower than 10% nor higher than 25% of EMIR's risk based capital requirements.[271] The EU is the first jurisdiction to require such a quantitative first and second SIG; indeed, some jurisdictions do not even require a 'first' CCP capital contribution in recovery scenarios. Singapore appears to be the only other jurisdiction with a quantitative SIG requirement.[272] The United States does not specify an amount of required own resources for CCPs and leaves it to the CCP's 'reasonable discretion'.[273] Canadian, Japanese, Hong Kong, and Australian regulators describe in a qualitative manner that they expect SIG to apply to ensure that a CCP has appropriate incentives to set robust risk management standards.[274]

Taking into account the fact that EU CCPs will be subject to new and stringent standards that do not apply in any other jurisdiction, and in order to allow EU CCPs to prepare and adapt to the new requirement, implementation depends on the necessary 'level 2' regulatory technical standards being in place, which have been deferred until 12 February 2023.

As usual, a review clause requires the Commission to present a report and proposals for amendment on the amount of own resources to be used by a CCP by February 2026.[275]

---

[266] See Principle 4 of the PFMIs. The Report 'Resilience of Central Counterparties (CCPs): Further Guidance on the PFMI' of July 2017 also leaves it to national legislation to regulate on the amount of a CCP's own resources. See https://www.bis.org/cpmi/publ/d163.pdf (accessed 23 March 2023).

[267] CCPR&R (n 256), Art. 9(14).

[268] See Chapter 6, 'OTC Derivatives Clearing and Collateral Management' by Manmohan Singh in this volume.

[269] EMIR (n 37), Art. 43.

[270] The notification threshold is if a CCP's capital is lower than 110% of the capital requirements or lower than 110% of EUR 7,5 million. Article 4 of Commission Delegated Regulation (EU) No. 152/2013 of 19 December 2012 supplementing Regulation (EU) No. 648/2012 of the European Parliament and of the Council with regard to regulatory technical standards on capital requirements for central counterparties, OJ L52 (23 February 2013), p. 13.

[271] EMIR (n 37), Art. 16(2).

[272] An internal regulatory directive from the Monetary Authority of Singapore (MAS) requires each Singapore CCP to contribute an amount that is at least 25% of the default fund and that 15% of this SIG must constitute a first layer.

[273] See 'Financial Resources' of the Derivatives Clearing Organization General Provisions and Core Principles section 39.11, para. (a)(1), https://www.federalregister.gov/documents/2020/01/27/2020-01065/derivatives-clearing-organization-general-provisions-and-core-principles (accessed 23 March 2023).

[274] See https://www.rba.gov.au/payments-and-infrastructure/financial-market-infrastructure/clearing-and-settlement-facilities/standards/201212-new-fss-ris/pdf/attachment-2.pdf (accessed 23 March 2023).

[275] CCPR&R (n 256), Art. 96.

6.7 Early Intervention

In order to preserve financial stability, competent authorities can remedy the deterioration of a CCP's financial and economic situation before that CCP reaches a point at which authorities have no other alternative but to resolve it or to direct the CCP to change its recovery measures where they could be detrimental for overall financial stability.[276] The authorities are granted 'early intervention' powers to avoid or minimize adverse effects on financial stability or on the interests of clients that could result from the CCP's implementation of certain measures.

6.8 Resolution Plans

Contrary to recovery plans which are drawn up by the CCP, detailed resolution plans are prepared by the resolution authorities and jointly agreed in the resolution college.[277] To avoid any moral hazard, resolution plans cannot assume any extraordinary public support from the government or the central bank.[278] Resolution authorities are required to assess the 'resolvability' of a CCP and can use that assessment to require changes to the legal or operational structure and organization of a CCP to reduce or remove material impediments to the application of resolution tools.

Normal corporate insolvency procedures may not always ensure sufficient speed of intervention or adequately prioritize the continuity of the critical functions of financial institutions for the sake of preserving financial stability. As CCPs are systemically important financial entities, the continuity of their services is essential for maintaining financial stability. For that reason, it was necessary to create a special resolution framework for CCPs: a CCP will not enter into formal bankruptcy proceedings but, instead, will be subject to 'resolution' procedures. Similar to banks, national authorities acting in the public interest should also have powers to resolve a CCP if these measures fail or could damage financial stability. Resolution measures constitute extraordinary steps which authorities would be able to take to swiftly restructure CCPs and secure the continuity of their functions that are critical to the economy, thereby mitigating the damage to the financial system and the broader economy while placing the residual parts of the CCP in insolvency, ensuring market efficiency. In the process, costs and losses are imposed as far as possible on the CCP's owners and creditors, not the taxpayer, in line with how they would be treated if the CCP had entered insolvency. Resolution does not aim to prevent the failure of inefficient institutions; rather, it aims to maintain the critical functions of an institution while allowing the remaining parts to be wound down in an orderly manner.

---

[276] CCPR&R (n 256), Art. 18.
[277] CCPR&R (n 256), Art. 12(1). See para. 7 for the issues that need to be covered in the resolution plan.
[278] CCPR&R (n 256), Art. 12(4).

6.9 Triggering Resolution

The procedure for CCP resolution was initially dominated by the need for quantifiable 'triggers' as to when to enter into resolution. On the one hand, prescriptive triggers for resolution, such as the breach of specific requirements, would bring transparency to the resolution framework by making clear *ex ante* to all stakeholders when a possible public intervention might be prompted. On the other hand, prescriptive triggers would not be suitable as it would be difficult to identify single or compound indicators that can clearly predict future events compromising financial stability. Prescriptive triggers could also leave undue room for entities to 'game the system', that is, take measures around the triggers that would compromise the trigger's validity. Furthermore, CCPs could fail in a way that may not meet specific prescriptive conditions, and therefore resolution would not be available as an option to achieve an orderly restructuring or wind down. For these reasons, the Commission, Council, and the EP decided that more flexible triggers that leave the decision on entry into resolution to authorities would avoid these problems and allow quick and decisive action. This meant that authorities can only use resolution tools if a CCP is close to failure and no other measures can restore its viability and ensure overall financial stability and, most importantly, that it would be in the public interest to place the CCP into resolution rather than subjecting it to normal winding up or insolvency proceedings. The degree of flexibility increased considerably, which meant that the definition of 'failing or likely to fail' is critical.

A CCP is considered to be failing or likely to fail if it infringes, or is likely in the near future to infringe, the requirements for continuing authorization; when its recovery has failed or is likely to fail to restore its viability; when the CCP is unable, or is likely to be unable, to provide a critical function; when the assets of the CCP are likely, or are likely in the near future, to be less than its liabilities; when the CCP is likely, or is likely in the near future, to be unable to pay its debts or other liabilities as they fall due; or when the CCP requires extraordinary public financial support. However, the fact that a CCP does not comply with all the requirements for authorization would not justify by itself the entry into resolution.[279]

6.10 Resolution Tools

Resolution authorities are equipped with a harmonized but *not exhaustive and prescriptive* resolution toolkit that affords authorities the necessary discretion to take into

---

[279] The provision of emergency liquidity assistance from a central bank, where such a facility is available, should not be a condition that demonstrates that a CCP is, or will be in the near future, unable to pay its liabilities as they fall due. In order to preserve financial stability, in particular in the case of a systemic liquidity shortage, state guarantees on liquidity facilities provided by central banks or state guarantees of newly issued liabilities to remedy a serious disturbance in the economy of a Member State should not trigger entry into resolution, provided that a number of conditions are met.

account the circumstances of a potential crisis. The prime objectives of resolution are to ensure the continuity of critical functions, to avoid adverse effects on financial stability, and to protect public funds.[280] The alternative option of equipping authorities with a comprehensive, exhaustive toolkit and setting out the order in which the tools should be used was rejected as it could risk the effectiveness of resolution by limiting authorities' ability to respond in a flexible way to the specific circumstances of an evolving crisis situation. It was considered unlikely that perfectly matched resolution tools and a hierarchy of their use could be developed to address all conceivable crisis scenarios, which would risk that envisaged resolution measures would not be appropriate to deal with the concrete problems at stake. Resolution tools include the (partial) termination of the CCP's contracts, variation margin gains haircutting, the write-down of CCP capital, a cash-call to CMs, the sale of the CCP or parts of its business, or the creation of a bridge CCP. While, in certain limited cases, extraordinary public support may be provided as a last resort, the purpose of resolution actions is to minimize the extent to which the cost of a CCP's failure is borne by taxpayers, while ensuring that shareholders bear an appropriate part of the losses and that taxpayer funds are recouped to the extent possible.

If a resolution authority takes resolution actions, it must follow the measures provided for in the resolution plans drawn up within the resolution college unless it considers, taking into account the circumstances of the case, that the resolution objectives can be achieved more effectively by taking other actions. The resolution authority will be engaged in a balancing act with the interests of the CCP's stakeholders and those of the (relevant authorities of) Member States where the action could have implications for the financial stability or fiscal resources. In particular, the resolution authority should inform the resolution college of the planned resolution actions, including where such actions deviate from the resolution plan (see Chapter 12 'Recovery and Resolution of CCPs' by Victor de Serière in this volume for a discussion of the Resolution College).

6.11 No creditor worse off (NCWO)

Similar to the BRRD, the framework for CCPs is fully compatible with the Charter of Fundamental Rights. While resolution action may entail changes to the assets and rights of CCPs' owners and clearing participants, in accordance with Art. 52 of the Charter, limitations on some rights and freedoms are allowed. As required by the Charter, such limitations on the exercise of these rights and freedoms are provided for by CCPR&R, they respect the essence of these rights and freedoms, and they are only applied where genuinely necessary to meet the objectives of general interest recognized by the Union. The protection of financial stability has been recognized by the Court of Justice as a 'general interest', justifying restrictions to fundamental rights and freedoms under the

---

[280] CCPR&R (n 256), Recital (4).

Treaty provided that they are proportionate and suitable to reach the objectives they pursue.

Importantly, the legal position of the resolution authority is clear when it takes a decision to accelerate a move from recovery to resolution. Resolution authorities may take a resolution action which deviates from the general no creditor worse off (NCWO) principles set out in CCPR&R, Arts 23 and 60 if it is justified in the public interest to achieve the resolution objectives and is proportionate to the risk addressed. However, and although a deviation from the NCWO principle can be acceptable under strict conditions, if it results in a shareholder, a CM, or any other creditor incurring greater losses than it would have incurred under the NCWO principle, they are entitled to payment of the difference.[281]

Therefore, and similar to the BRRD, the NCWO principle applies: affected shareholders, CMs, and other creditors of the CCP should not incur losses greater than those which they would have incurred if the resolution authority had not taken resolution action in relation to the CCP and they had instead been subject to all applicable outstanding obligations pursuant to the CCP's default rules or other contractual arrangements in its rulebook, and the CCP had been wound up in normal insolvency proceedings.[282]

Affected stakeholders can also appeal specific elements of resolution decisions which impact them and are entitled to compensation in case they are left worse off than they would have been if the CCP had not been resolved but they would have been subject to further possible actions under the CCP's operating rules for allocating losses or the CCP had entered insolvency.

If the CCP is under resolution and the business has been sold, any net proceeds from the transfer of assets or liabilities should benefit the entity left in its winding-up proceedings. This implies compensation of the shareholders with any net proceeds from the transfer of instruments of ownership issued by the CCP. Any consideration paid by the purchaser of the business should also benefit any non-defaulting CMs that have suffered losses.

6.12 Equity in Resolution

The treatment of equity in resolution remains, to a certain extent, unresolved. The CPMI–IOSCO report on recovery of financial market infrastructures (CPMI–IOSCO Recovery Guidance) calls for a CCP to have comprehensive loss allocation arrangements for any general business risk (e.g. custody and investment losses) the CCP incurs as a result of its clearing and settlement activity. Other standards apply with respect to other non-default losses.

---

[281] CCPR&R (n 256), Arts 23(2) and 62.
[282] In the event of a partial transfer of assets of a CCP under resolution to a private purchaser or to a bridge CCP, the residual part of the CCP under resolution should be wound up under normal insolvency proceedings.

At the same time, the FSB principles for effective resolution regimes for financial institutions also require equity holders of a CCP to absorb losses in resolution first.

The problem then arises that, if CCP equity would need to absorb any uncovered losses arising from the materialization of general business risk, in an extreme case it is possible that a CCP's recovery plan is not sufficient to fully cover potential non-default losses, orderly wind-down of the service may not be appropriate, and resolution may be required.

This problem was raised first by EU members of the FSB in its working group, which started a public consultation process in 2018 and issued guidance at the end of 2020.[283] The FSB Guidance provides options to resolution authorities—depending on their powers—to consider requiring CCPs to change their capital structures, rules, or other governance documents in a manner that subordinates shareholders to other creditors or sets out the point at which equity legally absorbs losses. If these powers are not available to resolution authorities, they may 'need to accept any limitations on CCP equity fully bearing losses and include a statement in the resolvability assessment why such limitations exist (which may include a lack of legal authority)'. Any available alternative measures to achieve as similar an economic outcome as possible in a reasonable range of resolution scenarios to support an orderly resolution must also be considered. The guidance will be considered by the Commission and will be part of the general CCPR&R review by 2025 at the latest.

6.13 Resolution Colleges

A great deal of discussion was spent in the Council on the composition of the new resolution colleges for public authorities.[284] On the one hand, they needed to be as inclusive as possible in view of the cross-border nature and impact of CCP activities and the need to protect financial stability in the Member States where the CCP provides services. On the other hand, a resolution of CCPs should strike the balance between the need, on the one hand, for procedures that take into account the urgency of the situation and, on the other, allow for efficient, fair, and timely solutions. It goes without saying that (some) Member States with a large systemic CCP were keen to avoid an extensive resolution college with a large number of members with different mandates—monetary policy, supervision, fiscal responsibility—that could hinder the required rapid decision-making in a time of serious financial market stress. The final result was the creation of an inclusive college structure, with authorities whose areas of competence would be affected by the failure of a CCP based on their assessment, but with a justification to the resolution authority of the impact that the CCP's resolution could have on financial stability in their respective Member

---

[283] FSB Guidance on Financial Resources to Support CCP Resolution and on the Treatment of CCP Equity in Resolution, Final Report (16 November 2020), https://www.fsb.org/wp-content/uploads/P161120-1.pdf (accessed 23 March 2023).

[284] CCPR&R (n 256), Art. 4.

State.[285] In other words an attempt was made to make sure that everybody who should have a seat at the table should be represented, but avoiding an unworkable forum. Practice will show if the chosen format indeed works as intended. Importantly, relevant third-country authorities, can also be invited to participate in resolution colleges as observers, where necessary, to ensure a regular exchange of views and coordination with the EU college members. This reflects the global nature of the derivatives sector (see also Chapter 12 'Recovery and Resolution of CCPs' by Victor de Serière in this volume).

6.14 ESMA's Role

ESMA has been given new coordinating powers under the Regulation, including the creation of a new 'ESMA Resolution Committee' to prepare various decisions, promote the drawing up and coordination of resolution plans, and develop methods for the resolution of failing CCPs.[286]

As has become customary, many technical regulatory details will be left to 'level 2' legislation. The EP and the Council have empowered the Commission to adopt the necessary delegated and implementing acts. An important role has been given to ESMA to develop draft regulatory technical standards and guidelines. Of particular importance is its work on the NCWO counterfactual and the second SIG. ESMA's work involves all areas of the CCPR&R.[287]

7 Conclusion

Regulating the OTC Derivatives sector has taken a quarter of a century, and regulators' work still continues, as does that of participants and stakeholders in the clearing and settlement space. After a decade-and-a-half of an absence of regulation or, at best, 'self-regulation by the industry', it took a global financial crisis in 2008 to spur a global response and commitment to install regulatory discipline in the business. The experience revealed deep-rooted concerns about lack of transparency, price-risk mismatches, lack

---

[285] Member States should have the possibility to be represented in the resolution college by the competent authorities and resolution authorities of clearing members. Member States which are not represented by clearing members' authorities should be able to participate by choosing between participation in the college of the competent authority of clearing members' clients and of the resolution authority of clearing members' clients.

[286] CCPR&R (n 256), Art. 5.

[287] For recovery measures: RTS on factors for assessing CCP recovery plans (Art. 10(12)), RTS on the methodology for calculation and maintenance of the additional amount of pre-funded dedicated own resources (Art. 9(15)), RTS on order of compensation (Art. 20(2)), Guidelines on triggers for the use of early intervention measures (Art. 18(8), Guidelines on circumstances for temporary restrictions in the case of a significant non-default event (CCPR&R (n 251), Art. 87(8)—EMIR (n 37), Art. 45a(3)), Guidelines on CCP recovery plan scenarios (Art. 9(12)), and Guidelines on CCP recovery plan indicators (Art. 9(5)). For resolution measures: RTS on resolution colleges (CCPR&R (n 251), Art. 4), RTS on the content of CCP resolution plans (CCPR&R (n 251), Art. 12(9)), RTS on the valuation of CCPs assets and liabilities in resolution (CCPR&R (n 251), Arts 25(6), 26(4), and 61(5)), RTS on safeguards for clients and indirect clients (CCPR&R (n 251) Art. 63(2)), Guidelines for the methodology to value each contract prior to termination (CCPR&R (n 251), Art. 29(7)), Guidelines on the application of the circumstances under which a CCP is deemed to be failing or likely to fail (CCPR&R (n 251), Art. 22(4)).

of data, under-collateralization, off-shore risks that rebounded, perceived cross-border extra-territoriality, suspicion of potential mercantile advantages, regulatory turf battles, legal proceedings, and the need to explore unknown regulatory paths and adopt innovative solutions. Although jurisdictions have adopted different, and sometimes diverging, regulatory approaches because of different regulatory histories and backgrounds, the key elements and objectives are strikingly similar. This is largely due to the leading roles adopted by the global standard-setters: CPMI–IOSCO, the Basel Committee, and the coordinating role played by the FSB. Work continues as regulators attempt to achieve even greater consistency and to settle some of the technical details left open in their regulatory frameworks.

II
STRUCTURAL ELEMENTS
OF CLEARING

4

CCP Access Structures

Christina Sell

1 Introduction

To enter into the world of over-the-counter (OTC) derivatives clearing, it is helpful to understand the configuration of central counterparty (CCP) access options.

Thus, this chapter is dedicated to CCP access structures, which were briefly outlined in Chapter 1 'After the Dust Has Settled: Clearing OTC Derivatives in Europe after a Decade of Regulation' by Bas Zebregs, Victor de Serière, Patrick Pearson, and Rezah Stegeman in this volume. It aims to facilitate an easy as well as systematic introduction into the complex network of players and explains how OTC derivatives clearing regulations translate into practice and form structural elements.

This system will be illustrated through a concrete case study, that is, the (OTC) access structures of Eurex Clearing AG (Eurex Clearing). As one of the world's leading and largest European Union (EU) clearing houses, Eurex Clearing is well suited as an example. Eurex Clearing is a wholly owned subsidiary of Eurex Frankfurt AG—which is part of Deutsche Börse Group. It was founded in 1998, serving as the clearing house for Eurex Exchange. Today, a broad range of listed and OTC-traded business, including equities, bonds, and foreign exchange as well as secured funding and financing business, is cleared.

It was authorized as a CCP under the European Market Infrastructure Regulation (EMIR) in 2014 and as a derivatives clearing organization (DCO) for the clearing of swaps in relation to entities located in the United States by the US Commodity Futures Trading Commission (CFTC) in 2016, serving around 200 clearing members and more than 4,000 clients around the globe.

The chapter starts with the illustration of Eurex Clearing's membership types and structures and their main characteristics.

A detailed description of access structures at other CCPs that are relevant in the European context is waived here. Given their status as authorized European CCPs (e.g. National Association of Securities Dealers Automated Quotations (NASDAQ) OMX Clearing AB: a complete list of CCPs authorized to offer services and activities in the Union in accordance with Regulation (EU) No. 648/2012 of the European Parliament and of the Council of 4 July 2012 on OTC derivatives, central counterparties and trade repositories (EMIR) can be found on ESMA's website[1]), recognized third-country CCPs (e.g. London Clearing House (LCH) Limited: a complete list of CCPs established in a third country recognized to offer services and activities in the Union in accordance with Regulation (EU) No. 648/2012 of the European Parliament and of the Council of 4 July 2012 on OTC derivatives, central counterparties and trade repositories (EMIR) can be found on ESMA's website[2]) or DCOs, their access structures are subject to the same regulations which were just mentioned and are thus similar. In general, dedicated clearing member (CM) licences for proprietary clearing and client clearing are offered. In terms of client segregation models, at least one omnibus and one individual clearing model is facilitated whereby it must be considered that numerous variants of client segregation offerings under EMIR exist complemented by the legally segregated operationally commingled (LSOC)-style model offerings.

In accordance with the requirement under EMIR, Art. 39(7), a CCP has to disclose publicly certain information in relation to the levels of protection and account segregation. Respective disclosure statements can be found easily on each CCP's website for further information with regards to client clearing.

The in-depth explanation of Eurex Clearing's access structures is followed by a reflection of their market take-up and related developments. Moreover, direct comparisons between OTC patterns and other market structures, such as those existing for Eurex Clearing's listed derivates and repo markets as well as other CCPs, are drawn in this chapter to put the subject into a broader context. Finally, an outlook is provided that defines requirements for a future access structure approach to benefit from a most efficient clearing ecosystem.

2 Membership Types

Based on international standards[3] and legislation,[4] Eurex Clearing has established objective, risk-based, and publicly disclosed criteria for participation which permit fair and open access.

---

[1] See https://www.esma.europa.eu/sites/default/files/library/ccps_authorised_under_emir.pdf (accessed 20 December 2021).

[2] See https://www.esma.europa.eu/sites/default/files/library/third-country_ccps_recognised_under_emir.pdf (accessed 20 December 2021).

[3] Bank for International Settlements and International Organization of Securities Commissions, 'Principles for Financial Market Infrastructures', Principle 18 (2012), https://www.iosco.org/library/pubdocs/pdf/IOSCOPD 377-PFMI.pdf (accessed 11 June 2022).

[4] Regulation (EU) No. 648/2012 of the European Parliament and of the Council of 4 July 2012 on OTC derivatives, central counterparties and trade repositories (text with EEA relevance), [2012] OJ L201 (27 July 2021), Art. 37 (EMIR).

Furthermore, Eurex Clearing has to ensure, like all other CCPs, that it holds all required licences, fulfils all notification obligations, and verifies the enforceability of its clearing conditions before services to customers are offered in a certain jurisdiction. The offering of certain member types, products, or marketing activities can be restricted in some jurisdictions by the local regulations and authorities.

Market participants can access the CCP in two categories: clearing members and clients. Only legal entities can apply for both categories; natural persons are not permissible.

Multiple factors have to be considered when making the choice of the best membership type. Apart from complying with legal obligations, choosing the right membership type is a trade-off between costs, complexity, and, first and foremost, risk considerations such as margin requirements, collateral mechanisms, mitigation of insolvency and fellow customer risks (portability), and transparency.

2.1 Clearing Members

Clearing members (CMs) are direct participants with a principal relationship to the clearing house. They apply for a clearing licence, dependent on the role and market in which they want to be active. Eurex Clearing offers clearing member licences for the following markets: Eurex Exchange, Eurex OTC Interest Rate Derivatives, Deutsche Börse Cash Market, and Eurex Repo.

The following CM types are available that are relevant for OTC derivatives:

(1) General clearing membership (GCM): GCMs are entitled to clear their own business and those of clients. They can also act as clearing agents for ISA Direct members; credit institutions and investment firms are generally eligible for this licence.

(2) Direct clearing membership (DCM): DCMs are entitled to clear their own OTC derivatives transactions and have a limited scope of client business with regards to other markets; insurance companies, financial institutions, pension funds, and investment funds are generally eligible for this licence.

(3) ISA Direct clearing membership (IDCM): IDCMs are entitled to clear their own transactions but require the support of a clearing agent; insurance companies, financial institutions, pension funds, and investment funds are generally eligible for this licence. The licence is limited to the clearing of OTC interest rate transactions and repo transactions.

(4) OTC interest rate swaps (IRS) US clearing member/futures commission merchant (FCM) clearing member (FCM CM): OTC IRS US. CMs may only clear own business and transactions for FCM clients. Only companies that are registered as FCMs with the CFTC are eligible for the FCM licence. The OTC IRS US CM and FCM CM licences are limited to the clearing of a subset of OTC swaps products.

As mentioned above, admission criteria for all CM types do not limit access on grounds other than risks and consist of legal, financial, and operational requirements. The most relevant ones are listed in the following sections.

2.1.1 Legal requirements

The applicant must provide evidence of the registration of the applicant's principal office and/or branch office in a permissible jurisdiction, evidence of required tax declarations, and a confirmation of the respective home Member State supervisory authority that the firm is supervised. CMs that intend to offer client clearing must be permitted to provide credit to customers in relation to OTC transactions and receive collateral in the form of cash or securities. CMs shall also conclude a legal Clearing Member Agreement with Eurex Clearing (FCM CMs shall conclude an FCM Clearing Agreement) and provide know-your-customer (KYC) documentation for identification and verification purposes.

2.1.2 Financial requirements

As a precondition to receive a clearing licence, the applying institution needs to demonstrate sufficient own funds or equivalent regulatory capital as defined by Eurex Clearing. The amount depends on the product and the type of clearing membership the new member applies for. A minimum requirement is defined for admission, and Eurex Clearing additionally employs a dynamic component for own funds or equivalent regulatory capital requirements in the course of the CM's life cycle. The dynamic component ensures that the own funds or equivalent regulatory capital requirements are scaled to represent the risk of the individual CM. The dynamic component is calculated as a percentage of each CM's margin requirement.

The different minimum requirements for the own funds or equivalent regulatory capital are as follows for OTC interest rate derivatives and currency transactions:

- GCM: EUR 30 mn
- DCM: EUR 7.5 mm/EUR 100 mn (EUR 100 mn applies for investment funds, pension funds, and insurance pools)
- IDCM: EUR 7.5 mm/EUR 100 mn (EUR 100 mn applies for investment funds, pension funds, and insurance pools)
- FCM CM: EUR 30 mn.

Furthermore, different minimum requirements for default fund contributions are applicable depending on the type of clearing membership. At admission, a CM's contribution to the Default Fund is as follows:

- GCM: EUR 5mn
- DCM: EUR 1mn/0.1 mn (EUR 0.1 mn applies for investment funds, pension funds, and insurance pools)

- IDCM: EUR 1mn/0.1 mn (EUR 0.1 mn applies for investment funds, pension funds, and insurance pools)
- FCM CM: EUR 5mn.

In case of an ISA Direct clearing membership the IDCM appoints a clearing agent to provide its contribution to the default fund. After admission, the default fund contributions are recalculated on a monthly basis (at the end of each month to ensure that the default fund is calibrated accurately to cover all losses resulting from a simultaneous default of Eurex Clearing two largest CMs with a confidence level of 99.9%). In addition, Eurex Clearing undertakes an initial (and later ongoing) credit risk assessment, where internal and external credit ratings, market indications like share prices, and similar factors relating to the applicant are considered.

2.1.3 Operational requirements

Eurex Clearing assesses the applicant's operational capability. Members must provide proof of technical and functional connections, the use of appropriate technical equipment (back-office facilities), and sufficiently qualified back-office personnel. Evidence is also necessary with regards to required account infrastructure for cash and securities depending on the respective licence and individual product coverage. CMs also have mandatory bidding obligations in the event of default auction. Thus, each applicant has to nominate a default management process coordinator. The default management process (DMP) coordinator is contacted by Eurex Clearing in the case of a default situation. It is the responsibility of the DMP coordinator to distribute all DMP-related information to the relevant persons within his or her organization. In case of an ISA Direct membership, a clearing agent takes over the bidding obligation on behalf of its IDCM.

2.2 Clients

Clients do not clear directly at Eurex Clearing but have their transactions cleared via a CM on their behalf. They can be either undisclosed or disclosed as well as direct or indirect from a CCP perspective, that is, clients are divided into further subcategories:

(1) undisclosed direct client: direct client of a CM not known to Eurex Clearing;
(2) disclosed direct client: direct client of a CM known to Eurex Clearing; disclosed direct clients are subject to a simplified on-boarding process in general, that is, only mandatory pieces of information are required such as name of the company, legal form, address, Legal Entity Identifier (LEI). A more detailed compliance check during on-boarding is only required for disclosed direct clients requesting post-trade management activities with respect to transactions relating to them. Three alternatives are available for the set-up:

- basic disclosed clients (basic DCs): basic DCs are disclosed direct clients that do not conduct post-trade management activities with respect to transactions relating to them. From a functional point of view, basic DCs can be set up in the systems of Eurex Clearing either with or without a member ID;
- disclosed clients with system access (DCs with system access): DCs with system access are disclosed direct clients (other than DC market participants) that have access to the systems of Eurex Clearing and can conduct post-trade management activities with respect to the transactions relating to them; and
- disclosed client market participants (DC market participants): DC market participants are disclosed direct clients that are trading participants on one or more markets in relation to which Eurex Clearing offers its clearing services and which conduct post-trade management activities with respect to the transactions relating to them. DC market participants are not relevant for the OTC interest rate derivatives and OTC currency markets but are mentioned here for the sake of completeness;

(3) indirect clients: clients of a direct client;

(4) FCM clients: FCM clients are disclosed clients whose transactions are cleared via an FCM CM. FCM clients can be either US persons or clients of the FCM located in other jurisdictions. From a functional point of view, they are comparable with basic DCs. An overview of the different client types can be found in Figure 4.1.

2.3 Client Clearing Models

Depending on the client type, varying levels of position and asset protection can be achieved. This section only addresses the key information with regards to position and asset protection. Additional insights with regards to segregation and portability are

Undisclosed clients	Disclosed direct client (DC)		
Direct/indirect client	Basic DC	DC with system access	DC market participation
• Relationship remains solely between CM and client • No onboarding requirements with Eurex Clearing • Available for direct as well as indirect clients	• No, or limited, contractual relationship with Eurex Clearing • Known via name, legal form, address of it's statutory seats, contact details (for DMP), and LEI • Available for omnibus segregation (GOSA) and individual segregation (SA)		
	• No trading licence • Optional reporting available	• No trading licence • Access to post-trade management	• Executes own transactions on the exchange • Access to post-trade management

Figure 4.1 Overview of client types, Eurex Clearing

Source: Eurex Clearing AG, https://www.eurex.com/resource/blob/32876/3ed46527cd5f64b99dfab461edaaf941/data/brochure_cap.pdf (accessed 23 March 2023).

provided in Chapter 9 'Capital Requirements for Bank Exposures to CCPs' by Marc Peters in this volume.

Eurex Clearing offers the following client clearing models under the Clearing Conditions of Eurex Clearing AG (Clearing Conditions) and the FCM Clearing Conditions of Eurex Clearing AG (FCM Clearing Conditions):

- elementary clearing model (ECM);
- individual segregated account (ISA);
- LSOC without excess model;
- LSOC with excess model.

ECM and ISA are regulated in the Clearing Conditions in accordance with EMIR and operated as so-called 'principal-to-principal' models. This means that Eurex Clearing only looks to the CM as a principal in respect of cleared transactions and corresponding margin (even where the relevant transactions are cleared for the account of a client). Under ECM and ISA, the client does not have a direct contractual relationship with Eurex Clearing.

The LSOC without excess model and the LSOC with excess model are regulated in the FCM Clearing Conditions and operate as a so-called 'agency clearing' model. The FCM CM will act in its capacity as an agent and on behalf and for the account of its FCM clients, and the entire clearing relationship is administered and settled through the FCM CM so that the FCM CM is directly bound by the FCM Clearing Conditions and responsible for all payment and delivery obligations in relation to all its FCM clients. Eurex Clearing treats the FCM CM as principal for purposes of the rights and obligations arising from all FCM client transactions. The FCM client does not have any direct contractual relationship with Eurex Clearing.

The most important characteristics of the client clearing models are described below.

The ECM is an omnibus client segregation model within the meaning of EMIR, Art. 39(2). It ensures the segregation of proprietary positions and assets of a CM from its client-related positions and assets. At least two collateral pools are required. Collateral in an omnibus structure will always be shared across multiple clients and leads to fellow customer risk for any potential shortfall in a collateral pool in case of a CM default. Under ECM, Eurex Clearing offers the following omnibus client segregation options:

(1) 'Net omnibus client segregation' (NOSA), where positions of multiple undisclosed direct clients are held in one position account and margin is posted by the CM to Eurex Clearing on a net basis across transactions relating to all such undisclosed direct clients. Porting is available with fellow customers.

(2) 'Gross omnibus client segregation' (GOSA), where a position account of a disclosed direct client is held separately from other clients and margin is posted by the CM to Eurex Clearing on a gross basis across transactions relating to a particular direct client. Porting is available on an individual basis.

Furthermore, Eurex Clearing supports CMs domiciled in the United Kingdom to clear certain Eurex transactions or OTC interest rate derivative transactions in accordance with the rules of the Client Asset Sourcebook (CASS) of the United Kingdom Financial Conduct Authority (CASS Rules) for the benefit of their clients with regards to ECM. Positions and assets forming part of a CASS client account are legally segregated from any non-CASS transactions and assets. It is the responsibility of the CM to comply with the CASS Rules.

The ISA is an individual client segregation model within the meaning of EMIR, Art. 39(3), segregating client-related positions and specific assets of each disclosed direct client.

Maximum protection is achieved for disclosed direct clients which opt for this segregation model. Positions and margin collateral of an individually segregated client are held in dedicated, individual accounts at CCP level and hence are completely ring-fenced from the CM's or other client's positions and margin collateral. Portability of client positions and margin collateral is available for each client.

Also with regards to ISA, Eurex Clearing supports CMs domiciled in the United Kingdom to clear ISA transactions in accordance with the CASS Rules for the benefit of their clients. If a CM chooses to deliver assets in the form of securities under the CASS Rules, the securities collateral may only be provided under a pledge arrangement to Eurex Clearing. It is the responsibility of the CM to comply with the CASS Rules.

2.3.1 Indirect clearing

Since 2018, Eurex Clearing facilitates also indirect clearing arrangements for derivatives transactions in accordance with two separate Delegated Regulations—one supplementing EMIR and one supplementing the Markets in Financial Instruments Regulation (MiFIR).

CMs offering clearing services to indirect clients are required to open and maintain the following accounts, on the level of CCP, in accordance with the request of the client:

(1) an omnibus account with the assets and positions held by that direct client for the account of its indirect clients (NOSA);

(2) an omnibus account with the assets and positions held by that direct client for the account of its indirect clients, in which the CM has to ensure that the positions of an indirect client do not offset the positions of another indirect client and that the assets of an indirect client cannot be used to cover the positions of another indirect client (GOSA).

Thus, CMs are able to select different levels of segregation and set up multiple collateral pools providing enhanced protection in the event of a direct client default. Porting is available in the event of a CM default, and the porting of an indirect client will be facilitated alongside the porting of its direct client. Figure 4.2 below visualizes the structural layers of indirect clearing.

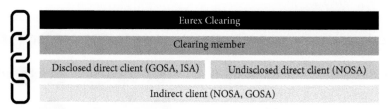

Figure 4.2 Indirect clearing, Eurex Clearing

Source: Eurex Clearing AG, https://www.eurex.com/resource/blob/32876/3ed46527cd5f64b99dfab461edaaf941/data/brochure_cap.pdf (accessed 23 March 2023).

The LSOC models are only offered to CMs that are registered as FCMs in compliance with the CFTC Regulation Part 22 under US law. The FCM CM has the choice to provide clearing services to FCM clients under the LSOC without excess model and the LSOC with excess model:

- The LSOC *without excess model* is the basic LSOC model, under which the portion of the FCM client margin account reserved for a particular client (legally segregated value—LSV) is equal to the FCM client margin requirement and the legally segregated value cannot exceed the FCM client margin requirement on a day-to-day basis.
- The LSOC *with excess model* provides the FCM CM the option to assign specific portions of the FCM client margin account to specific FCM clients, including excess margin. This requires the FCM CM to deliver a collateral value report (CVR) to Eurex Clearing in which the LSVs for all its FCM clients are determined.

The LSOC structure shows certain similarities to the GOSA model but differs finally and significantly because the value of collateral associated with every individual FCM client is legally segregated and protected, although collateral related to all FCM clients is operationally commingled in one account. The value of assets assigned to one FCM client can never be utilized to meet the obligations of another FCM client.

Any action Eurex Clearing may take regarding porting of FCM client transactions will be taken in compliance with the Commodities Exchange Act, CFTC Regulations, and (as applicable) the US Bankruptcy Code and related CFTC Part 190 Regulations. Figure 4.3 provides a complete overview of the client segregation options that are offered by Eurex Clearing.

2.4 Innovative Direct Clearing Access: ISA Direct

At this point, it is worthwhile to explicitly focus on the specifics of the ISA Direct clearing membership, which have not been explained so far. ISA Direct, also called

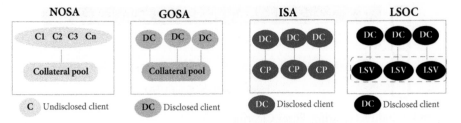

Figure 4.3 Eurex Clearing client segregation options including LSOC

Source: Eurex Clearing AG, https://www.eurex.com/resource/blob/2432592/183affc43a2ff2d4b1e355e04c7e848f/data/Cheat-Sheet-Segregation-Model.pdf (accessed 23 March 2023).

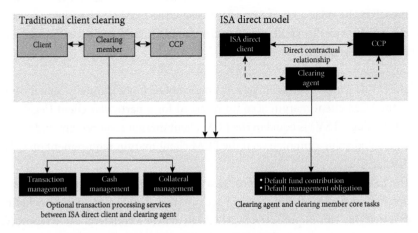

Figure 4.4 Comparison of traditional client clearing vs ISA Direct

Source: Eurex Clearing AG, https://www.eurex.com/resource/blob/244226/3206550879234fe2bbf38bc1277fee02/data/factsheet-eurex-clearing-isa-direct.pdf (accessed 23 March 2023).

a 'Direct Access Model', combines elements of a direct clearing membership and the traditional service relationship in client clearing.

It is a "hybrid" model, in which the IDCM is the undertaking which directly participates in the clearing with Eurex Clearing and bears the full responsibility to discharge all the financial obligations vis-à-vis Eurex Clearing following from its participation. Accordingly, the IDCM has to meet all admission criteria, equivalent to regular CMs, and a direct contractual relationship exists between the IDCM (de facto CM for proprietary business and ultimate responsible party) and the CCP. A GCM acting as an agent provides extended servicing functions. It is also appointed by the IDCM to provide default fund contributions and carry out default management obligation as mandatory functions of the clearing agent. Further, the clearing agent may, in alignment with the IDCM, take over extended service functions like transaction, cash, and collateral management (cf. Figure 4.4). To reflect the IDCM/clearing agent relationship and allow the agent to perform appropriate risk management functions for its obligations taken over vis-à-vis Eurex Clearing, the agent is provided with transaction-, collateral-, and cash-related data of the IDCM. The ISA Direct clearing membership type was explicitly designed for buy-side clients based on the situation that buy-side clients must cope with a shrinking number of client clearing providers.

> Since the early 2000s, we've seen concentration and consolidation in client clearing markets across the globe. Over the past two decades or so, a steady number of clearing members have exited the industry while few new players have entered the space [...] For instance, five clearing members (all bank-affiliated) account for more than 80 per-cent of total client margin for cleared interest rate swaps in the United States, the United Kingdom, and Japan.[5]

The reasons for the concentration and consolidation within the clearing industry are multi-fold. Market observers have argued that changes in business models, a low-interest rate environment, and shifting changing customer preferences may be key fac-tors.[6] Increased regulatory pressure that substantially increases costs for participants in offering client clearing services contributes to this development: Basel III raised capital requirements significantly based on risk-weighted assets (RWAs) and a new leverage ratio requirement against unweighted on- and off-balance sheet exposure. The Basel Committee on Banking Supervision and the International Organization for Securities Commissions (BCBS–IOSCO), Liquidity Coverage Requirements (LCR), EMIR, and other regulations increased margin, haircut, and collateral requirements whilst limiting re-use of collateral, particularly for bilateral transactions, with new Basel III liquidity rules putting additional strain on global collateral balances.[7] It was also noted that 'the risk management requirements of OTC Derivatives client clearing are "substantially more burdensome" as compared to futures client clearing, requiring significantly more trading capacity to manage a client default'.[8]

A limited offering from clearing firms regarding CCP client clearing services and segregation offerings, higher service fees, and wider bid-ask spreads is the consequence.

Additionally, the concentration of clearing firms raises concerns with regards to counterparty risk and porting in a CM default scenario. This major development not only affects single clients but is also relevant for the stability of the whole market.

On the other hand, self-clearing (i.e. direct clearing) is most often not an op-tion because regulatory restrictions make it almost impossible to obtain a traditional CCP member licence for a buy-side entity. Complex and uncommon operational

---

[5] Nahiomy Alvarez and John McPartland, 'The Concentration of Cleared Derivatives: Can Access to Direct CCP Clearing for End-Users Address the Challenge?', Working Paper (June 2019), https://www.chicagofed.org/publications/working-papers/2019/2019-06 (accessed 20 December 2022) (Alvarez and McPartland, 'The Concentration of Cleared Derivatives').

[6] Alvarez and McPartland, 'The Concentration of Cleared Derivatives' (n 5).

[7] Eurex Clearing AG, 'OTC Derivatives: Balancing Regulatory Obligations with Efficiency' (2019), https://www.eurex.com/resource/blob/1647134/ce00f507c54a12cdc706d1e5d1fc44bb/data/otc-derivatives-balancing-regulatory-obligations.pdf (accessed 11 June 2022).

[8] Bank for International Settlements and International Organization of Securities Commissions, 'A Discussion Paper on Client Clearing: Access and Portability' (November 2021), https://www.bis.org/cpmi/publ/d200.pdf (accessed 20 December 2021) (Bank for International Settlements and International Organization of Securities Commissions, 'Discussion Paper on Client Clearing').

requirements, high capital requirements, and expensive membership fees, but especially legal restrictions to contribute to risk mutualizing default funds are insurmountable hurdles.

The dilemma is addressed and solved by the ISA Direct model. By making the buy-side organization a direct legal counterpart of the CCP, the capital and balance sheet impact is significantly reduced in terms of RWA and leverage ratio for a traditional clearing broker which is acting as a clearing agent. The changed treatment (reduction of capital costs) is based on the legal structure of the model in which the clearing agent is not exposed to the counterparty risk of its buy-side client anymore because the clearing agent is not guaranteeing the performance of the IDCM (in contrast to the traditional client model) whilst being able to retain the client relationship providing mandatory and voluntary services. This mechanism enables the IDCM to overcome the above-mentioned regulatory and operational obstacles and leads to more favourable clearing and price conditions for the IDCM. Moreover, the likelihood of porting increases based on two factors. First, the ISA Direct model provides for greater independence in the IDCM—agent relationship in comparison to a traditional client clearing relationship. Second, the structure of the ISA Direct model increases the willingness of clearing brokers to on-board clients in a CM default crisis, which is not only driven by the quality of the client but also by the additional capital necessary to cover the additional capital requirements caused by the additional exposure.

Finally, the safety of the CCP for the good of the entire market benefits from the direct access model. As an intermediating risk management mechanism, a CCP and its participants benefit most from a broad and diverse membership for several reasons: (i) efficiencies of a CCP in terms of multilateral netting and mutualization of tail-risk are greatest for large markets, (ii) default scenarios decorrelate the more different members are, and (iii) the general reduction of concentration risk for positions across proprietary and agent accounts improve the overall risk profile.

In this context, it is worth noting that client clearing has been going through a general transformational phase for years: Not only Eurex Clearing but also many other CCPs have developed, and are still developing, new solutions to overcome the shortcomings of traditional client clearing. The bandwidth of these innovative types varies from tackling specific pain points to comprehensive sponsored or direct access models (mainly offered for repo markets); that is, they alternate between a closer tendency towards a traditional individual client segregation model and a closer affinity towards a full clearing membership. The following two examples demonstrate the different shades.

The first one, the 'CustodialSeg Model',[9] was launched by LCH in 2017. The specifics of this model can be compared with Eurex Clearing's 'direct transfer option' that forms part of the ISA model and can be used to avoid the double-transfer mechanism of collateral from the client via the clearing member to the clearing house.

The core of LCH's offering is the so called 'CustodialSeg' client account type that allows buy-side clients to deliver collateral directly to the CCP and retain beneficial title.

---

[9] London Clearing House, 'CustodialSeg A Higher Level of Protection' (2021), https://www.lch.com/sites/defa ult/files/media/files/CustodialSeg_1.pdf (accessed 11 June 2022).

The transfer is designed as a triparty process: first, the client or their custodian instructs the international central securities depository (ICSD) where the account is held to deliver the securities collateral to an LCH account. As a next step, LCH seeks affirmation from the clearing broker before accepting a specific value of collateral to move the collateral to the LCH account. Finally, LCH matches the client instruction and securities move from the client account at the ICSD to the LCH account via a triparty transaction.

The great advantage of this procedure lies—in addition to the general benefits of an individual segregation like individual porting of ring-fenced positions and collateral—in the fact that transit risk associated with moving securities to and from the CCP via a clearing member is removed. In addition, the client has the possibility to continue to deliver securities post clearing broker default during a transition period. Hence the grade of client asset protection is further improved in comparison to the standard individual segregation. However, it is debatable, from a customer perspective, whether this process also increases operational efficiency. It certainly requires a deeper involvement in clearing processes and more sophisticated back-office capabilities for the buy-side client in case they want to execute the process themselves.

The next case, ICE Clear Europe's 'Individual segregation through Sponsored Principal Account'[10] for repo transactions, has been available since 2015 but goes one considerable step further. In this model, the buy-side client becomes a direct counterparty of the clearing house, a fact that is a significant deviation from the example previously described. However, the client does not enter autonomously into this relationship but rather as a sponsored principal. The legal conditions require that the 'relevant Sponsored Principal and Sponsor shall each be jointly and severally liable, with one another, in each case as principal and without limitation, to the Clearing House in respect of all obligations and liabilities arising in connection with the Individually Segregated Sponsored Account and all Contracts recorded in it'.[11] Thus, the basic legal structure of this sponsored model does not move completely away from the traditional client clearing concept in which the clearing member guarantees the performance of the client. While this is the major difference in comparison to the ISA Direct model, other characteristics are comparable; for example, becoming a sponsor (clearing agent in the ISA Direct model) requires a qualification as CM and operational processes can be transferred from the sponsored principal to the sponsor (clearing agent in the ISA Direct model), who will also provide the guaranty fund contribution. Also a better starting position in a sponsor's respectively clearing agent's default scenario can be reasonably expected thanks to the greater independence of the sponsored principal. But this should not conceal the point that the joint liability might be less appealing for a clearing broker and hence a barrier for take-up. From this perspective, Eurex Clearing's ISA Direct model appears more attractive. It remains the only direct access model for cleared OTC derivatives that establishes a 'full' contractual relationship between a 'former client' as ISA Direct CM and the CCP without involvement of the clearing

---

[10] ICE Clear Europe, 'Client Clearing' https://www.theice.com/clear-europe/client-clearing (accessed 1 April 2022).
[11] ICE Clear Europe, 'ICE Clear Europe[sm] Clearing Rules, Rule 1902' (updated 12 December 2022), https://www.theice.com/publicdocs/clear_europe/rulebooks/rules/Clearing_Rules.pdf (accessed 1 April 2022).

broker who can benefit from substantial balance sheet and capital efficiencies, as mentioned previously.

If one would want to include further direct or sponsored access patterns into the analysis, one last point should be mentioned as noteworthy: all these models:

> share one key feature: they shift the responsibility for contributing to the CCP's default fund away from the participant. In the majority of cases, this obligation is fulfilled by a 'sponsor', which guarantees that the risk exposure created by the transactions of the new, direct participants to the CCP is covered. However, in a few cases, the CCP waives the default fund contribution and it is not paid by anyone. In these cases, the relevant CCPs justify the exemption because of the perceived low credit risk of the new, direct participants (e.g. public pension funds. Other CCPs collect a multiplied margin requirement that is equivalent to either full collateralization or to a figure that accounts for both margin and the default fund contributions of direct clearing members.[12]

This finding indicates that the inability of some buy-side clients to contribute to the default fund is a major structural problem to simplify clearing access.

3 Development and Market Take-Up of Cleared OTC Services at Eurex Clearing

Eurex Clearing launched its OTC clearing services in November 2012. Since then, Eurex Clearing has admitted around 100 CMs and more than 4,000 clients (counted on an LEI basis) for the clearing of OTC transactions. As explained, the on-boarding options are manifold and require different financial and operational levels of maturity. Thus, it is interesting to have a closer look at the development and the market take-up.

3.1 Developments Regarding Clearing Members

With regard to clearing member types, Eurex Clearing initially offered a (general) clearing member licence only.

This was followed by the launch of the innovative OTC and Repo ISA Direct clearing membership offering in June 2016. In the meantime, the number of OTC IDCMs account for around 5% of all OTC clearing member licences.

In January 2017, the DCM licence for OTC clearing, with lower admission requirements in comparison to a GCM licence by means minimum default fund contribution

---

[12] Bank for International Settlements and International Organization of Securities Commissions, 'Discussion Paper on Client Clearing' (n 8).

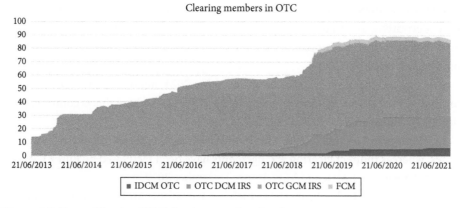

Figure 4.5 Eurex Clearing OTC clearing member development
Source: Eurex Clearing AG.

and own funds requirements, was introduced. This addition aimed to further harmonize the direct access framework from a cross-market perspective and to bridge the gap on the OTC side between an ISA Direct membership and a GCM, targeting applicants that were only interested in conducting proprietary business and seeking full independence from clearing service providers. These applicants were equipped with the required operational capability and were not impacted by legal restrictions with regards to the default fund contribution.

In December 2018, as the most recent undertaking to further extend its CCP access framework for the time being, Eurex Clearing published new FCM rules based on its refined LSOC client clearing framework to achieve high market acceptance.

Figure 4.5 shows a steadily increasing total number of GCMs until 2021, which corresponds with the constantly higher market share of Eurex Clearing since the launch of its OTC derivatives clearing offering. The highest increase of new CMs was recorded during the time period 2018–2019. GCMs are the biggest group, followed by DCMs, but it should be noted that the number of GCMs has slightly decreased since 2020, whereas the number of DCMs and IDCMs is further growing moderately. The number of FCMs is low and steady.

A comparison with the listed derivates side shows that here also, GCM licences outweigh DCM licences (FCM and IDCM licences are not offered), whereas at the repo market, where client clearing is practically non-existent, the DCM membership is the predominant category, followed by IDCM (FCM licences are not offered).

3.2 Developments Regarding Clients

The development on the DC side reveals certain similarities to the development on the CM side. The total number of clients has been constantly growing, with onboarding spikes during 2019–2020.

Figure 4.6 shows that ISA is the clearly preferred EMIR client segregation model for OTC derivatives and that this preference has not changed over time. Approximately 70% of disclosed clients opted for ISA and approximately 30% of disclosed clients for omnibus segregation (ECM).

Also remarkable is the fact that, as of December 2021, not one single NOSA account for undisclosed direct clients was set up on the OTC side, where this is common practice for exchange-traded derivatives (ETDs).

In addition, not a single account for indirect clients was set up for cleared OTC derivates, whereas indirect clearing arrangements have been facilitated by Eurex Clearing in compliance with EMIR and MiFIR since December 2017.

With regards to the LSOC model (which is not available for listed business), the figures show that on-boardings have far exceeded ISA since the launch in December 2018. More than twice as many LSOC clients as ISA clients exist.

Quite interestingly, a closer look at the listed derivates market shows a reversed and even more extreme pattern; that is, more than 85% of disclosed clients are set up under the ECM model (Figure 4.7).

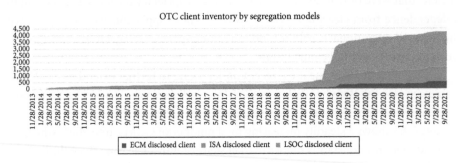

Figure 4.6 Eurex Clearing OTC client development
Source: Eurex Clearing AG.

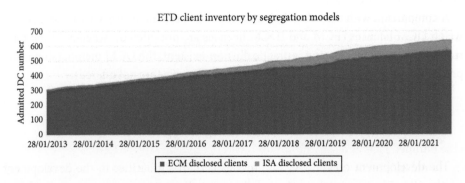

Figure 4.7 Eurex Clearing ETD client development
Source: Eurex Clearing AG.

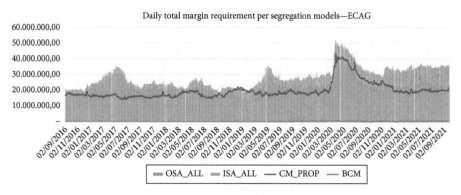

Figure 4.8 Total margin requirement per segregation model
Source: Eurex Clearing AG.

3.3 Margin Perspective

From a total margin perspective, Figure 4.8 illustrates that the CM proprietary business is similar to the omnibus segregation (OSA) client business. The proportion of the IDCM (BCM) is significantly lower than the proportion of clients. As Eurex Clearing uses a cross-margining method, the figures below reflect the margin requirements across all markets and are not limited to OTC derivatives.

The overall ratio of the client segregation models is as follows:

- the *elementary clearing model* (omnibus segregation—OSA) is approximately two-thirds of overall client margin (net omnibus segregation deriving mainly from listed derivates; gross omnibus segregation);
- the *individual segregated account* (individual segregated account—ISA) is approximately one-third of overall client margin but seems to be an increasing portion;
- the *LSOC model* is below 0.1% of overall client margin, that is, not visible in the chart.

In comparison, Figure 4.9 shows that LSOC is the preferred client clearing model at LCH. The total numbers (based on end-of-quarter snapshot data) are only conditionally comparable with the Eurex Clearing figure but prove a general difference.

3.4 Conclusions

The outlined facts above allow the summary of the following most important observations and interpretations.

The development of the Brexit negotiations and the growing importance of the clearing obligation applicable to standardized classes of OTC derivative contracts in

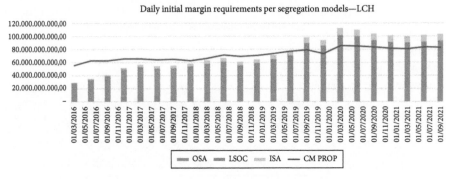

Figure 4.9 LCH initial margin requirement per segregation model
Source: Eurex Clearing AG based on data published by LCH Group CCP Disclosures/LCH Group.

accordance with EMIR, Art. 5(2) between 2018 and 2019 have obviously influenced the course of the curve, that is, the on-boarding peaks at this point in time.

Furthermore, the proprietary business of GCMs and DCMs account generally for the largest proportion of cleared transactions at Eurex Clearing. The market take-up of ISA Direct is slower than expected, given the continuing high interest from the client side. However, this status may change soon. According to customer surveys, the attractiveness of direct access models seems to be generally high, especially with regards to the repo market, 'due to balance sheet offsets that such models afford and the resulting decrease in capital charges when compared to similar activity not carried out via a CCP'.[13] However, this is currently not mirrored in the participants statistics of Eurex Clearing. At present, statistic figures show nearly equal numbers of IDCMs admitted for cleared OTC derivatives and repo. What is remarkable is that banks make up the majority of OTC IDCMs. The ISA Direct model is obviously an efficient solution for small and medium-sized credit institutions to transfer operational procedures to an agent. Buy-side firms are more hesitant due to several reasons. First, the change to a direct access model is a really fundamental shift for buy-side firms in terms of structures and operational demands. Second, other challenges, such as mastering Brexit, MiFID II or the COVID pandemic, had priority and obviously sufficient clearing brokers are still available despite the downward trend. Third, risk considerations 'particularly regarding the unlikely but real possibility of a default is unpalatable in terms of the size of the risk and exposure'[14] may have led to a more general wait-and-see attitude towards central clearing, particularly after the default of the direct member Einar Aas at NASDAQ Clearing AB in Sweden in 2018 (see also Chapter 7 'What Kind of Thing is a Central Counterparty? The Role of Clearing Houses as a Source of Policy Controversy' by Rebecca Lewis and David Murphy in this volume), when a loss of EUR 108 m was mutualized via the default fund. Last but not least, direct access models face

---

[13] Bank for International Settlements and International Organization of Securities Commissions, 'Discussion Paper on Client Clearing' (n 8).
[14] Lynn Strongin Dodds, 'Direct Clearing: Why Has Uptake Been Slow?' (15 November 2018), https://www.derivsource.com/2018/11/15/direct-clearing-why-has-uptake-been-slow (accessed 20 December 2021).

legal impediments. Although many CCPs have developed such structures over the past years, they are not sufficiently reflected in current regulations to ensure legal certainty in all aspects. In addition, the absence of uniform laws across different jurisdictions complicates the offering.

The ratio CMs/disclosed clients is also disproportional and reflects the global trend of a high concentration of clearing firms that offer client clearing.

Furthermore, the diametrically opposed client structure of the cleared OTC derivatives (mainly individually segregated disclosed clients) and listed derivates (mainly undisclosed clients) implies that the patterns of both segments has evolved fundamentally differently for many decades and has not assimilated immediately after the complete integration in central clearing. This is caused by the different levels of product standardization: 'The contract specifications for Listed Derivates are typically standardized to a relatively high degree, which facilitates trading and enhances liquidity. At the same time, execution through an exchange facilitates price discovery and transparency and affords anonymity of trade counterparties.'[15] In contrast to that, and caused by the lower degree of standardization, cleared OTC transactions are bilaterally negotiated involving an executing broker before being booked with a CCP; that is, anonymity is not a relevant criterion feature of the OTC client clearing workflow.

The non-existence of any indirect client accounts for cleared OTC transactions more than three years after the implementation of the regulatory requirement to facilitate indirect OTC client clearing shows that the regulations do not correspond to the real situation of the market.

Finally, it may be assumed that the extraordinarily high number of LSOC clients derives from the situation that US fund managers represent one of the largest investor groups in the EURO-denominated IRS market and that the majority of US fund managers are obliged to clear swaps at a US-regulated DCO and utilize LSOC segregation. However, the small margin requirements assigned to LSOC clients indicate that they are already prepared but not very active at Eurex Clearing yet. This hypothesis is substantiated by the large LSOC proportion at LCH, where the US client clearing model was established in 2014 and had more time to build a solid client base.

4   Outlook

After having described the as-is situation, the question arises how the future of access structures with regards to cleared OTC derivatives will develop in the next few years. Again, there cannot be an isolated answer. The broader financial ecosystem needs to be considered.

---

[15] Richard Heckinger and David Mengle, 'Understanding Derivatives: Markets and Infrastructure' (2013), https://www.chicagofed.org/publications/understanding-derivatives/index (accessed 20 December 2021).

In this context, it is noteworthy that there are no signs that the regulatory and political environment in Europe will change significantly on a short-term basis. A scenario
where buy-side clients can attain traditional CM licences appears highly unlikely. In
addition, causal chains will remain on a short-term basis, which have created higher
capital and margin obligations, higher leverage ratio requirements, greater transparency, and increased standardization in the OTC derivatives market and beyond, whilst
volumes in cleared derivatives are expected to rise further.[16] Thus, market players will
further strive for solutions as to how they can navigate not only safely but also most efficiently and commercially successfully through this landscape.

Various scenarios can be envisaged, which can be only partially reflected in this
chapter. For a broader context, it is recommended to read the closing chapter of this
book, Chapter 18 'The Future of Centrally Cleared OTC Derivatives Markets' by
Evariest Callens and Klaus Löber in this volume.

With regard to access structures, a noteworthy development which has slowly
started to emerge is the conversion of systems, processes, and structures of the previously separated OTC and exchange-traded derivatives markets in line with the need
for modernization and innovation in the trading and clearing workflow.[17] This trend
manifests itself in diverse ways. A good example is the futurization trend of swaps.
Another variant is that multi-asset clients are working on the consolidation of their
clearing relationships to create in-house synergies and save costs. A consequence
might be a higher number of disclosed participants on the listed derivates side in the
future. In order to benefit from improved porting options in a CM default scenario
and Eurex Clearing's efficient portfolio-based risk management methodology (Eurex
Clearing Prisma) applied to each member's entire portfolio across all markets, it is a
functional prerequisite to on-board or streamline the member set-up in accordance
with one disclosed access type.

Aside from that, Eurex Clearing will continue to work on efficient solutions that
encourage the widest possible CCP access to not only cleared OTC derivatives but
also all centrally cleared asset classes under strict adherence to the risk management standards of the CCP, thus ensuring the resilience and stability of the clearing
house. Enhancements of the ISA Direct model are in development, and support of
an industry-led design of a 'European Agent Trust Model' broadly replicating the US
FCM agency structure is underway.

As set out at the beginning of this chapter, membership criteria are determined by
risk considerations. It remains to be seen whether the economic disputes and political
crises can be viewed as moderate in the years ahead.

Instead, the removal of cross-border barriers and legal uncertainties as well as a balanced recalibration of the capital framework should be the focus to further facilitate
access to the advantages of central clearing. New challenges, such as disrupting new

---

[16] Futures Industry Association (FIA), 'FIA Survey Shows Strong Outlook for Cleared Derivatives Markets' (16
March 2021), https://www.fia.org/articles/fia-survey-shows-strong-outlook-cleared-derivatives-markets (accessed 20 December 2021) (FIA, 'FIA Survey').

[17] FIA, 'FIA Survey' (n 16).

technologies or the green transformation, must also be tackled, which will certainly influence access structures in the future.

It needs a strong collaboration between regulators, policymakers, CCPs, and clearing and trading firms to master these challenges and to preserve and improve a clearing ecosystem of stability and resilience.

5

Clearing Mechanics

Christian Chamorro-Courtland*

1 Introduction

In the broad sense, a central counterparty (CCP) is a *sui generis* financial market infrastructure that operates by interposing itself between a group of merchants, known as clearing members, who have contractually entered into the CCP arrangement in order to clear transactions they have entered into, which gives rise to rights and obligations between the clearing members and the CCP. Through either (i) *novation* or (ii) *open offer*, the CCP assumes the contractual rights and obligations of the parties in order to guarantee the performance of each and every clearing member, thereby eliminating counterparty risk.[1]

A 'novation' involves the termination of an earlier contractual agreement that was entered into between two counterparties (i.e. a buyer and a seller) and a substitution with a new agreement and a new counterparty (i.e. the CCP). Conversely, in an 'open offer', a contractual agreement is created between each counterparty and the CCP at the moment that the counterparties (i.e. a buyer and a seller) agree to enter into a particular transaction so that there is never a contract between the two counterparties. These two mechanisms are known as the counterparty substitution process, which, in essence, involves the CCP

* This chapter is based on two previous publications by the same author: Christian Chamorro-Courtland, 'Contemporary Substitution in Central Counterparty (CCP) Systems' (2010) 26(3) Banking and Finance Law Review 519–542 and Christian Chamorro-Courtland, 'The Legal Aspects of Non-financial Market Central Counterparties (CCP)' (2012) 27(4) Banking and Finance Law Review 553. I would like to thank Randy Priem for his helpful comments.

[1] 'Counterparty risk', which is also known as 'credit risk', is the risk that a counterparty to a financial transaction will default on its contractual obligations due to an intervening insolvency or other related reasons.

becoming 'the buyer to every seller and the seller to every buyer'.[2] This process is critical as it permits the CCP to guarantee the termination of any position in fungible contracts with standardized terms according to the clearing rules set by the CCP clearing system.

The counterparty substitution mechanism is supposed to ensure that a CCP is able to guarantee the outstanding contractual obligations of the system's participants as the main principal to every transaction that it assumes. Therefore, the counterparty substitution process is critical because it ensures that the CCP is able to neutralize counterparty credit risk with its arsenal of collateral resources (known as the 'default waterfall'). The guarantee from the CCP also has the potential to dampen the effects of systemic risk[3] during a financial crisis.

In addition to the counterparty substitution process, CCPs perform multilateral netting to reduce exposures and to facilitate the settlement of obligations between the CCP and the system's participants. The processes of counterparty substitution and multilateral netting are collectively referred to as the 'clearing' mechanism.

A CCP's main operations involve (i) risk management, (ii) clearing and settlement, and (iii) collateral arrangements. Initially used in derivatives exchanges, CCPs have increasingly been introduced into securities exchanges, over-the-counter (OTC) markets (which is the focus of this chapter), and repurchase agreement markets due to the significant benefits they confer. In the context of the cleared OTC derivatives markets (also known as 'cleared swaps'), the CCP interposes itself between a group of merchants that have entered into a derivatives contract (e.g. an interest rate swap, a credit default swap, or a foreign-exchange (FX) swap) with each other on a bilateral basis. The CCP then clears those contracts multilaterally in a process called multilateral netting.

The legal and economic benefits have proven to decrease certain risks[4] inherent in clearing systems and have provided efficiency gains by lowering costs. CCPs are relatively new and increasingly important financial market infrastructures with respect to the clearing of OTC derivatives. Hence, the goal of this chapter is to provide some legal clarity with respect to the clearing mechanics. A crucial requirement for the operations of a CCP is 'a well founded, *transparent* and *enforceable* legal framework for each aspect of its activities in all relevant jurisdictions',[5] thereby providing *legal certainty*[6] to the system operators and participants.

---

[2] Committee on Payment and Settlement Systems–International Organization of Securities Commissions (CPSS–IOSCO), 'Recommendations for Central Counterparties, Bank for International Settlements (2004)', Committee on Payment and Settlement Systems Publications No. 64 (November 2004), Annex 3, Glossary, 64 (CPSS–IOSCO, 'Recommendations for Central Counterparties').

[3] Systemic risk is the risk that the failure of one or more participants in a particular financial market to meet their required contractual obligations will cause other participants or financial institutions to be unable to meet their obligations (including settlement obligations) when due. Such a failure may cause significant liquidity or credit problems for several market participants and, as a result, might threaten the stability of financial markets.

[4] These risks are counterparty credit risk, systemic risk, settlement bank risk, custody risk, liquidity risk, investment risk, legal risk, and operational risk.

[5] Recommendation 1 of CPSS–IOSCO, 'Recommendations for Central Counterparties' (n 2). This recommendation originates from the Report of the Committee on Interbank Netting Schemes of the Central Banks of the Group of Ten Countries, Bank for International Settlements, Committee on Payment and Settlement Systems Publications (November 1990) (Lamfalussy Report), which outlines the six minimum standards for netting schemes. The first requirement is for netting arrangements to have a *well-founded legal basis* under all relevant jurisdictions.

[6] 'The [systemically important payment] system should have a well-founded legal basis under all relevant jurisdictions.' See CPSS–IOSCO, 'Core Principles for Systemically Important Payment Systems', Bank for International

First, it is important for the purpose of legal clarity to establish a clear definition of a CCP system. It is important to note that the terms 'clearing house' and 'CCP' are legally distinct and should not be used interchangeably, as is often the case in the literature in this area. An ordinary clearing house operates as the 'agent' of the clearing members in the clearing process, and it does not perform counterparty substitution.[7] The type of clearing performed by an ordinary clearing house is known as 'position netting,'[8] which does not involve a substitution of any kind. Therefore, an ordinary clearing house does not assume liability for any of the transactions that it clears for the system's participants. Conversely, a CCP operates as the 'principal' to every transaction entered into by the clearing members so that it can assume the counterparty risk of the parties and guarantee performance.

This chapter analyses the clearing mechanism from a legal perspective and focuses mainly on common law jurisdictions as many of the large CCPs are based in the United Kingdom,[9] including London Clearing House (LCH) Ltd SwapClear—the largest CCP for OTC interest rate swaps.[10] Although civil law jurisdictions have their own legal requirements that may differ from the laws in common law jurisdictions, some consideration will be had to CCPs based in civil law jurisdictions, in particular those based in the European Union (EU). In the EU, many of the differences between common law and civil law jurisdictions have narrowed (or even disappeared) with the passing of regulations (i.e. statutes) for CCPs located in the EU. Nevertheless, the principle is the same for CCPs operating in both types of legal regime: legal certainty can help to reduce losses, avoid unnecessary delays during litigation, and prevent systemic risk during a financial crisis.

2 Clearing Mandate

Before 2012, it was common for OTC derivative contracts to be executed between market participants on a bilateral basis. As the name suggests, 'OTC' meant that these were contractual arrangements that were entered into by market participants on a private and bilateral basis, that is, not via a centralized and regulated derivatives exchange.

Settlements, Committee on Payment and Settlement Systems Publications No. 43 (January 2001), Core Principle 1 (CCPS–IOSCO, 'Core Principles'). In order to avoid legal risk, 'a CCP should have a well founded, transparent and enforceable legal framework for each aspect of its activities in all relevant jurisdictions'. See CPSS–IOSCO, 'Core Principles' (above).

[7] An example of this would be a clearing house for cheques.

[8] Professor Geva has stated that in 'position netting, there is no substitution'; that is to say, there is no counterparty substitution in ordinary clearing house arrangements, and the clearing house does not guarantee the transactions of the system's participants. Benjamin Geva, 'The Clearing House Arrangement' (1991) 19 Canadian Business Law Journal 138, 147 (Geva, 'The Clearing House Arrangement').

[9] It is possible in a post-Brexit world that some of the CCPs currently based in the United Kingdom may move their operations to an EU Member State (such as Ireland) in the future.

[10] 'SwapClear clears more than 50% of all OTC interest rate swaps and more than 90% of the overall cleared OTC interest rate swap market. [They] regularly clear in excess of $3 trillion notional per day and have more than 2 million cleared trades outstanding', https://www.lch.com/services/swapclear/volumes (accessed 23 March 2023).

In order to facilitate the settlement of contractual obligations, the counterparties would use contractual netting arrangements, typically under the International Swaps and Derivatives Association (ISDA) Master Agreement, which would allow the parties to set off their obligations on a bilateral basis.

Bilateral set-off means that the party owing the larger obligation deducts (i.e. sets off) the amount that they are owed by their counterparty and merely pays the difference. However, the parties to these bilateral arrangements experienced significant counter-party credit risk as there was no guarantee that a counterparty to a derivative contract would be able to perform all their outstanding contractual obligations in the future, as happened in the cases of Lehman Brothers and American International Group (AIG) in 2008.

In 2009, the leaders of the G20 countries produced a joint statement at the Pittsburgh Summit[11] that would require all standardized OTC derivatives to be cleared through a CCP ('the clearing mandate'). This policy was introduced in response to the global financial crisis (GFC) in 2008 as it was perceived by policymakers that the global OTC derivatives market—which was mainly comprised of bilateral contracts entered into by counterparties that were not registered and were not cleared—was an unregulated and opaque market that could be the source of future systemic risk to the global financial system. It was also perceived that some OTC derivatives products such as credit default swaps (CDSs) were particularly risky and were partially to blame for causing the GFC. Therefore, the clearing mandate was pursued as an option for mitigating any potential risk in the OTC markets as CCPs neutralize risk through their clearing mechanism by providing a type of insurance function.

After the Pittsburgh Summit, various jurisdictions around the world with developed derivatives markets gave effect to the clearing mandate for certain OTC derivatives by passing domestic legislation. In 2012, the Parliament and Commission of the EU passed the European Market Infrastructure Regulation (EMIR)[12] and implemented the clearing mandate in Arts 4 and 5 for certain 'standardized' OTC derivatives that were being traded by market participants based in EU Member States.[13] The goal of this EU-wide legislation was to mitigate the spread of systemic risk to avoid another financial crisis.[14]

---

[11] G20 Pittsburgh Summit Press Room, https://www.oecd.org/g20/summits/pittsburgh/ (accessed 23 March 2023).

[12] Regulation (EU) No. 648/2012 of the European Parliament and of the Council of 4 July 2012 on OTC derivatives, central counterparties and trade repositories (text with EEA relevance), [2012] OJ L201 (27 July 2021), Art. 1 (EMIR).

[13] The latest amendment to EMIR affecting the clearing mandate was passed in 2019: Regulation (EU) No. 2019/834 of the European Parliament and of the Council of 20 May 2019 amending Regulation (EU) No. 648/2012 as regards the clearing obligation, the suspension of the clearing obligation, the reporting requirements, the risk-mitigation techniques for OTC derivative contracts not cleared by a central counterparty, the registration and supervision of trade repositories and the requirements for trade repositories.

[14] Preamble, at para. 21, EMIR (n 12):

> In determining whether a class of OTC derivative contract is to be subject to clearing requirements, ESMA should aim for a reduction in systemic risk. This includes taking into account in the assessment factors such as the level of contractual and operational standardisation of contracts, the volume and the liquidity of the relevant class of OTC derivative contract as well as the availability of fair, reliable and generally accepted pricing information in the relevant class of OTC derivative contract.

Since the introduction of the clearing mandate in various jurisdictions, the percentage of OTC derivatives that were cleared increased from 21.3% in 2007 to over 88.5% in 2017.[15] Consequently, the clearing mandate has led to an increased concentration of risk in CCPs, which means that now, more than ever, there needs to be legal certainty in the event that a system participant defaults on their obligations to the CCP. CCPs are responsible for drafting clearing rules that provide legally certain outcomes to the system's participants, in particular with respect to the operation of the clearing mechanism.

3 Legal Aspects of a CCP

3.1 Importance of Avoiding Legal Risk

Legal risk is the most important risk for lawyers to manage. It is the risk that a party will suffer a loss because laws or regulations do not support the rules and contracts of the CCP or the property rights and other interests held through the CCP. Legal risk has the potential to decrease confidence in the CCP system and to substantially increase losses associated with a default for the CCP, its participants, and even the wider financial community (in the form of systemic risk).

The most significant legal risk is that insolvency liquidators may challenge a CCP's right to close out positions and liquidate a defaulting counterparty's assets. In order to avoid this type of legal risk, the laws and regulations governing a CCP, its rules (i.e. the clearing rules), procedures, contractual arrangements, and the *time* of counterparty substitution should be clearly stated, internally coherent, and readily accessible to participants and the public. If the legal framework is underdeveloped, opaque, and inconsistent, the resulting risk will undermine a CCP's ability to operate effectively, which could lead to counterparty risk and potentially systemic risk.

Some jurisdictions have avoided legal risk by implementing specific legislation[16] for protecting CCP arrangements and their operations. These statutes, often known as

---

[15] ISDA, 'Non-Cleared OTC Derivatives: Their Importance to the Global Economy' (2013), https://www.isda.org (accessed 23 March 2023); ISDA, 'Swaps Info Second Quarter 2017 Review' (2017), https://www.isda.org (accessed 23 March 2023).

[16] The main statutes protecting netting arrangements (often referred to as 'carve-out statutes' since they exempt some financial arrangements from the effects of domestic corporate insolvency laws) are: European Union: EC, Directive 98/26/EC of the European Parliament and of the Council of 19 May 1998 on settlement finality in payment and securities settlement systems, [1998] OJ L 166 (SFD); England: Companies Act 1989, c. 40, Part VII, ss 154–191 (supports netting in insolvency situations); Financial Services and Markets Act 2000, c. 8, Part XVIII, ss 285–324. The SFD was implemented as the Financial Markets and Insolvency (Settlement Finality) Regulations 1999, SI 1999/2979; United States: Bankruptcy Code 1978, ss 362, 546–548, 553, 556, 560 ('Bankruptcy Code'); Federal Deposit Insurance Corporation Act; Canada: Budget Implementation Act, RSC, 2007, c. 29 (exempts 'eligible financial contracts' from corporate insolvency laws); Bankruptcy and Insolvency Act, RSC, 1985, c. B-3, s. 65.1 (7)–(9) (BIA); Payment Clearing and Settlement Act, 1996, c. 6, Sch., ss 8, 13, 13.1; Canada Deposit Insurance Corporation Act, RSC, 1985, c. C-3, s. 39.15(7); Winding-Up and Restructuring Act, RSC, 1985, c. W-11, s. 22; and Companies' Creditors Arrangement Act, RSC, 1985, c. C-36; Australia: Payment Systems and Netting Act 1998 (Cth.), s. 5 and Parts 3 and 4.

'carve-outs', protect certain financial market operations (such as counterparty substitution and multilateral netting) from the burdensome effects that domestic corporate
insolvency laws[17] can have on them in an insolvency scenario.

However, these statutes have not all been specifically drafted for the exclusive protection of CCP systems, and they tend to apply to a wider spectrum of financial institutions. This means that many of the terms and concepts have not been properly
explained in the relevant statutes. For example, Recommendation 4 of the Committee
on Payment and Settlement Systems–International Organization of Securities
Commissions (CPSS–IOSCO) Recommendations for Central Counterparties 2004[18]
requires a particular legal system to support 'novation' or 'open offer' as mechanisms
for counterparty substitution:

> In most jurisdictions, the legal concept that enables a CCP to become the counter-
> party is either novation or open offer. Through novation, the original contract be-
> tween the buyer and seller is extinguished and replaced by two new contracts, one
> between the CCP and the buyer and the other between the CCP and the seller. In an
> open offer system, a CCP is automatically and immediately interposed in a transac-
> tion at the moment the buyer and seller agree on the terms. If all pre-agreed condi-
> tions are met, there is never a contractual relationship between the buyer and seller
> in an open offer system. Both novation and open offer give market participants legal
> certainty that a CCP is obligated to effect settlement if the legal framework is sup-
> portive of the method used.[19]

Although 'novation' is mentioned in EMIR, Art. 4(1)(b), the concept is not explained.
Furthermore, none of the carve-out statutes examined by the author mentioned the
concept of 'open offer'.[20] This has the potential to cause legal uncertainty for CCPs operating in the EU. Thus, the CCPs will be responsible for creating legal certainty by
drafting clearing rules that are crystal clear.

3.2 CCP Clearing Rules

The rules of the CCP system are contractually binding on the system participants,
and the members are bound to obey the system's rules and membership agreement.
The members are prevented from arguing that the clearing rules, which will have the
effect of altering the rights and obligations of the members, are void. Since a CCP will

---

[17] For example, the carve-out statutes (listed n 16) were passed to protect the operations of CCPs from the
following domestic corporate insolvency statutes: England: Insolvency Rules 1986, SI 1986/1925, rule 4.90;
Australia: Corporations Act 2001, Act No. 50 of 2001.

[18] CPSS–IOSCO, 'Recommendations for Central Counterparties' (n 2).

[19] Recommendation 4.1.2, CPSS–IOSCO, 'Recommendations for Central Counterparties' (n 2).

[20] For example, open offer was not mentioned in EMIR nor in the relevant US legislation: Dodd–Frank
Wall Street Reform and Consumer Protection Act, Pub L 111–203, 124 Stat. 1376, H.R.4173 (enacted 21
July 2010).

have the power to draft the clearing rules 'as to its mode of business',[21] a CCP should be clear when drafting important rules such as the method and time of counterparty substitution with the CCP. This will ensure that all the system participants will have a clear understanding of when the CCP becomes the principal to every transaction and, in cases where novation is used as the main method for counterparty substitution, at what point in time the mutuality requirement is satisfied, as explained below.

The 'mutuality' requirement, which was the main issue litigated in the cases of *British Eagle International Air Lines Ltd v Cie Nationale Air France*[22] and *International Air Transport Association v Ansett Australia*,[23] has been a necessary ingredient for performing an effective insolvency set-off (also known as 'close-out' netting in the context of CCPs that clear derivatives) in most common law jurisdictions. Non-satisfaction of the mutuality requirement on the insolvency of a clearing member may require the solvent member to pay their obligations to the liquidator of the insolvent member without being allowed to set off any corresponding amount owed.

Insolvency set-off is a critical tool for CCPs to mitigate counterparty risk when a system participant defaults on their obligations. CCPs operating in common law jurisdictions use contractual netting clauses (which expressly provide for open offer or novation) to ensure that counterparty substitution takes place immediately after trades have been executed between the system's participants. This is crucial to ensure that there is always mutuality between the CCP and the system's members for transactions executed by the members. Hence, open offer and novation are supposed to create *mutuality* between each counterparty and the CCP to eliminate the risk that the corporate insolvency laws of a particular jurisdiction will block an insolvency set-off from taking effect.

3.3 Insolvency Set-Off

Insolvency set-off is a type of set-off arising where one of the debtor-creditors is insolvent.[24] Professor Roderick J. Wood describes insolvency set-off as the '*extinguishing*' of the insolvent debtor's claim against the solvent creditor and the '*reduction*' of the solvent creditor's claim against the insolvent debtor.[25] Since insolvency set-off is mandatory and automatic for corporate insolvencies in many common law jurisdictions, the risk arises that if all the requirements (e.g. the mutuality requirement) for set-off are not satisfied *before* the insolvency of one of the parties, the use of the set-off facility will not be permitted.

---

[21] In *Cunliffe-Owen v Teather & Greenwood* [1967] 1 WLR 1421; [1967] 3 All ER 561 (Eng. Ch. Div.) [1439], it was held that the stock exchange has power to make rules 'as to its mode of business'. By analogy, this reasoning applies to CCP clearing arrangements.

[22] [1975] 2 All ER 390; [1975] 1 WLR 758 (UKHL).

[23] 82 ALJR 419; 242 ALR 47; 65 ACSR 1; 26 ACLC 38; 2008 WL 307972; [2008] HCA 3; [2008] ALMD 2248; [2008] ALMD 2043 (HCA 2008).

[24] Philip R. Wood, *Set-Off and Netting, Derivatives, Clearing Systems*, 2nd edn (London: Sweet & Maxwell, 2007), p. 5 (Wood, *Set-Off*).

[25] Roderick Wood, *Bankruptcy & Insolvency Law* (Toronto: Irwin Law Inc., 2009), p. 91.

The insolvency law requirements for insolvency set-off in common law jurisdictions are 'mutuality' 'capacity',[26] and 'maturity',[27] with mutuality being the most important requirement. The fulfilment of these requirements and the availability of insolvency set-off is crucial for risk reduction in a CCP system so that the net creditors[28] will be paid notwithstanding the insolvency of any net debtors. Failure to meet these requirements may carry serious consequences; for example, a scenario may arise where a net creditor becomes an *unsecured creditor* in the bankruptcy ladder of priorities and has to pay the gross amount of their outstanding claims to the estate of the insolvent net debtor without (i) being paid what they are owed and (ii) being able to set off the corresponding amount owed.

3.4 Mutuality Requirement

Historically, the function of the mutuality requirement was to determine the circumstances in which set-off should operate in an insolvency situation. Therefore, the counterparty substitution stage in a CCP system is important because it represents the point at which mutuality is created between the clearing members and the CCP. The clearing members require counterparty substitution in order for the CCP to become the principal and assume liability for all the transactions entered into by the clearing members. As mentioned above, mutuality is also necessary so that the CCP can use close-out netting to minimize counterparty risk when a clearing member defaults on their obligations.

Professor Philip R. Wood has written[29] that the doctrine of mutuality[30] requires that (i) there must only be *two counterparty claimants* in the capacity of debtor-creditor *prior* to an insolvency; (ii) each claimant is the *beneficial/economic owner* (not the legal owner) of the claim owed to it or a clear partitioned share of it; and (iii) each claimant is *personally liable* on the claim owed by it and is not liable in some representative capacity, such as trustee or agent. The reciprocal claims do not have to arise under the same transaction, connected transactions, or transactions of the same type.

Therefore, the CCP must ensure that it creates mutuality between it and all of the clearing members to ensure that insolvency set-off is permitted upon the default of one or more of the clearing members.[31] As will be seen below, novation and open

---

[26] A CCP must always act in the same capacity, that is, as a principal.

[27] The claims must be mature debts; that is, they must no longer be executory contracts.

[28] The net creditors, who are more correctly known as the 'net net' creditors, are the clearing members who are owed obligations by the CCP after the clearing cycle is completed (i.e. before the settlement stage), whereas the net debtors, or 'net net' debtors, are the clearing members who owe the CCP obligations after the clearing cycle is completed.

[29] Wood, *Set-Off* (n 24), 2-006 and 4-001.

[30] Also known as the doctrine of 'privity' and 'reciprocity'. See *Gye v McIntyre* [1991] HCA 60; 171 CLR 609 [623]; 65 ALJR 221; 98 ALR 393; 1991 WL 1121056. Philip Wood calls it 'connexity': Wood, *Set-Off* (n 24), 4-001.

[31] *Air Canada, Re*, 2003 CarswellOnt 4016, [2003] OJ No 6058, 45 CBR (4th) 13, 39 BLR (3d) 153 (Ont SCJ [Commercial List]).

offer, which are both forms of contractual netting arrangements found in CCP arrangements, have been drafted specifically to ensure that the mutuality requirement is satisfied.

Whereas solvent parties have free disposition over their claims as proprietary interest owners, the mutuality doctrine requires that 'one [person's claim] shall not be used to pay another [person's] debt'[32] when one of the parties is insolvent because 'a non-mutual set-off involves a divestment of the claim owned by it which should be available to [the insolvent party's] creditors and is therefore a post-insolvency forfeiture contrary to insolvency laws'.[33] In other words, the policy behind the mutuality requirement in insolvency set-off is the intention of protecting other unsecured creditors of the insolvent debtor so that set-off does not confer an unfair advantage on the creditor exercising it.[34]

Consequently, the role of the CCP has been to create mutuality between the CCP and all of the clearing members of the system so that insolvency set-off is available on a multilateral basis if one or several of the clearing members become insolvent. It is crucial that mutuality be created between the CCP and all of the counterparties *before* the initiation of insolvency proceedings or else the insolvency laws of the jurisdiction where the CCP is established may divert the remaining assets of the insolvent clearing member to the insolvency administrator. In these cases, the risk is that the CCP would be treated as a general creditor of the insolvent clearing member. This could be problematic because general creditors usually only receive a small fraction[35] of what they were owed by their debtor in an insolvency situation as the insolvent clearing member's assets are first used to pay creditors with a higher priority, for example, creditors with a security interest in the insolvent company's assets. Furthermore, even if the CCP recovered some of the debt owed by an insolvent clearing member, this could be several months or years later in a situation where there is litigation, as was the case in the insolvency of Lehman Brothers.

Therefore, it is crucial for a CCP to expressly mention in the clearing rules of the system the exact time of counterparty substitution in order to ensure that there is mutuality between the clearing members and the CCP for every transaction that is executed by the clearing members. It is important to note that in order for the CCP to be able to assume the contractual positions of the parties and create mutuality, there must be a clear way for the parties to be able to communicate (i.e. notify) their positions to the CCP.

---

[32] *Jones v Mossop* (1844) 67 ER 506; 3 Hare 568 (Eng. Ch. Div.), *per* Wigram VC.

[33] Wood, *Set-Off* (n 24), 4-002.

[34] Sheelagh McCracken, *The Banker's Remedy of Set-Off*, 2nd edn (London: LexisNexis, 1998), p. 180.

[35] Rizwaan J. Mokal, *Priority as Pathology: The Pari Passu Myth* (2001) 60(3) CLJ 581.

3.5 Creation of Contractual Netting

Professor Roy Goode has stated that:

> netting arrangements are designed (1) to ensure as far as possible either that all set-offs are completed before the relevant date, so that there is no need to resort to insolvency set-off, or (2) that the contractual rights on both sides will have undergone such conversion (if any) as may be necessary to satisfy the requirements of the [insolvency laws] as to mutuality of claims and parties.[36]

It is the second function of netting which is relevant for CCP arrangements, which allows the CCP to contractually decide the point in time for counterparty substitution and the creation of mutuality.

The main question for lawyers is whether contractual netting survives an insolvency situation. The legislatures in many jurisdictions with large financial markets have introduced financial market carve-out statutes[37] to exempt and protect the operations of CCPs operating in the financial markets and to enable them to enforce netting agreements in post-insolvency scenarios.

3.6 Super-Priority Creditors

Several jurisdictions have passed financial markets 'carve-out' statutes to ensure that the clearing arrangements of CCPs operating in the financial markets are exempted from certain domestic corporate insolvency laws. These CCPs and their clearing members are provided with 'super-priority' creditor status[38] so that they can carry out their operations unhindered from any burdensome corporate insolvency laws. The carve-out statutes[39] reflect a policy for protecting the clearing arrangements of CCPs operating in

---

[36] Roy M. Goode, *Principles of Corporate Insolvency Law* (London: Sweet & Maxwell, 2003) pp. 178–179 (Goode, *Corporate Insolvency Law*).

[37] For example, the zero-hour rule and retroactivity could lead to the unwinding of settled transactions; the mutuality requirement could prohibit multilateral insolvency set-off or netting if unfulfilled; *pari passu* distribution could affect the ladder of priorities; and insolvency freezes could cause legal uncertainty and enhance liquidity or systemic risk.

[38] These are a special class of creditor who are paid before all the other creditors of the insolvent counterparty. They include secured creditors, title finance creditors, creditors with a set-off, and beneficiaries under a trust.

[39] The main statutes exempting CCP arrangements from the effects of domestic corporate insolvency laws are: England: the Companies Act 1989, Part VII, c. 40, ss 154–191; the Financial Services and Markets Act 2000, c. 8, Part XVIII, ss 285–324; the Financial Markets and Insolvency (Settlement Finality) Regulations 1999, No. 2979; Canada: the Budget Implementation Act, SC, 2007, c. 29; the Bankruptcy & Insolvency Act, RS, 1985, c. B-3., s. 65.1 (7)–(9); the Payment Clearing and Settlement Act 1996, c. 6, Sch., ss 8, 13, 13.1; the Canada Deposit Insurance Corporation Act, RS, 1985, c. C-3, s. 39.15(7); the Winding-Up and Restructuring Act, RS, 1985, c. W-11, s. 22; and the Companies Creditors Arrangement Act, RS, 1985, c. C-36; Australia: the Payment Systems and Netting Act 1998, No. 83 (Cth.) s. 5 and Parts 3 and 4; the Bankruptcy Code (n 16), ss 362, 546–548, 553, 556, 560; the Federal Deposit Insurance Corporation Act, 12 U.S. Code Chapter 16; the Dodd–Frank Wall Street Reform and Consumer Protection Act, Pub. L 111–203, 124 Stat. 1376, H.R.4173 (enacted 21 July 2010); European Union: Directive 98/26/EC, Settlement Finality Directive 1998; EMIR (n 12), Art. 1.

the financial markets (including those that clear OTC derivatives) and their clearing members.

There are several observations that can be made. First, CCPs have evolved from being ordinary corporations into *sui generis* financial market infrastructures, which, in many jurisdictions, fall outside the scope of corporate insolvency laws altogether. CCPs, like banks, 'have distinct characteristics that justify a separate bankruptcy regime, allowing greater regulatory intervention [...] In most jurisdictions, bank bankruptcy is dealt with either by separate legislation from corporate bankruptcy or within the same legislative framework with modifications.'[40] As a result of the important role that CCPs play in mitigating risk in the financial system, the carve-out statutes have been enacted in several jurisdictions to provide CCPs operating in the financial markets with their own separate bankruptcy regime. The legislation protects their netting agreements and the CCP rules against invalidation by corporate insolvency laws.

Professor Goode has stated that the carve-outs are designed to 'insulate' the relevant transactions from the corporate insolvency laws and 'replace them with the approved rules of the exchange or clearing house'.[41] Furthermore, he suggests that 'the broad effect is to substitute the approved rules of [...] the clearing house for the insolvency distribution rules, thus in effect creating a *self-contained mini-insolvency distribution system* for [... the relevant] contracts and charges'.[42]

Second, the *sui generis* nature is evident in the 'risk-neutral' role that CCPs perform. Unlike ordinary corporations, CCPs provide a form of insurance protection to their clearing members with their risk management functions, for example, with multilateral close-out netting. They concentrate risk and neutralize it through the clearing process.

Third, the *sui generis* nature of the CCPs is evident in the special relationship of the participants, which is a principal-to-principal relationship between the clearing members vis-à-vis the CCP, as opposed to a principal-to-agent relationship. Consequently, modern-day CCPs operating in the financial markets have become *sui generis* financial market infrastructures with super-priority creditor status. They are able to confer this status on their members, and they are able to guarantee multilateral insolvency set-off if one of their members defaults on their obligations.

However, since the legislation defers to the clearing arrangement in determining the measures that will be taken when a clearing member defaults on their obligations, it is crucial for the clearing rules to be crystal clear. Moreover, CCPs have developed mechanisms to ensure that there is always mutuality between the CCP and its clearing members for all transactions executed by the system's participants. CCPs are able to provide for the immediate and instantaneous creation of mutuality between the CCP and the clearing members by combining contractual devices such as novation and open offer with their clearing operations, for example, multilateral netting. The following sections examine the mechanics of these processes.

---

[40] Stephanie Ben-Ishai, *Bank Bankruptcy in Canada: A Comparative Perspective* (2009) 24(3) Business and Finance Law Review 59.

[41] Goode, *Corporate Insolvency Law* (n 36), pp. 1–28.

[42] Goode, *Corporate Insolvency Law* (n 36), pp. 1–29 (emphasis added).

4 Novation

A 'novation' involves the termination of an earlier contractual agreement that was entered into between two clearing members and a substitution with a new agreement and a new counterparty (the CCP). When the novation process is combined with netting and is conducted between the CCP and all of the clearing members on a multilateral basis, this process is known as 'multilateral novation netting'.[43] This clearing method is used at LCH Ltd and Eurex AG,[44] which are two of the largest CCPs in Europe that clear OTC derivatives.

The term 'multilateral novating netting' is often generically referred to as the 'clearing' process of a CCP system.[45] It is a process that can be used for (i) *substituting* counterparties (the counterparty substitution stage) and (ii) *calculating* claims (the multilateral netting stage). Each stage performs a separate novation. The CCP can choose, in its method for clearing, whether to perform the counterparty substitution and the multilateral netting stages together[46] or whether to bypass the counterparty substitution stage and to perform the netting stage on its own.[47]

4.1 Counterparty Substitution Stage: Multilateral Netting by Novation and Substitution

If the CCP chooses to use novation as a method for counterparty substitution, the entire clearing process is typically called 'multilateral netting by novation and substitution'.[48] The *counterparty substitution stage* involves a novation of the counterparties (the first novation) so that the position of a clearing member in a debtor–creditor relationship with another clearing member is substituted for a relationship with the CCP, which becomes the principal.

4.2 Multilateral Netting Stage

Subsequently, the multilateral netting stage involves a *calculation* (the netting leg) and a *discharge* (the second novation) of the gross bilateral contractual claims between a

---

[43] Also known as obligation netting or contractual consolidation; Goode, *Corporate Insolvency Law* (n 36), p. 179.

[44] 'OTC Interest Rate Derivative Transactions, OTC Currency Transactions and OTC NDF Transactions pursuant to this Chapter VIII are concluded by way of novation': Condition 1.2, Clearing Conditions of Eurex Clearing AG (13 December 2021).

[45] As is seen below, 'novation netting' is often referred to as 'multilateral novation netting'. This chapter uses the terms interchangeably.

[46] This involves two separate novations.

[47] This involves only one novation.

[48] BIS, *Report on Netting Schemes*, CPSS Publications (February 1989), at para 6.18, http://www.bis.org/publ/cps s02.pdf (accessed 23 March 2023) (Angell Report).

clearing member and the CCP in order to produce a new 'net net' contractual claim owing one way or the other. The netting and the second novation are 'multilateral' from the perspective of the CCP, which takes into consideration the claims of all the clearing members when calculating what the CCP owes each clearing member and what each clearing member owes the CCP. This is known as the 'multilateral netting stage'.

Since the CCP factors in all the net claims of all the clearing members when calculating the final claims, the new net obligations that are created are referred to as 'net net' obligations. Consequently, a clearing member that owes the CCP obligations after multilateral netting is a 'net net debtor', and a clearing member that is owed obligations by the CCP is a 'net net creditor'. The 'net net' claim is subsequently discharged by a settlement[49] from the 'net net' debtor to the 'net net' creditor.

4.3 Practical Implications

It should be noted that although the 'counterparty substitution' stage and the 'multilateral netting' stage are two different stages from a legal perspective, from a practical perspective, the two stages will often occur immediately one after the other.[50] This chapter analyses the two stages separately as a practical guide for lawyers who may have to deal with the situation of an insolvent clearing member, or even worse, of an insolvent CCP.

4.4 The Two Novations in Multilateral Netting by Novation and Substitution

As mentioned above, CCPs which use multilateral netting by novation and substitution perform two separate and independent novations. There is a first novation[51] of the original bilateral contractual obligations[52] entered into between the clearing members and a substitution with the CCP (the counterparty substitution stage). The second novation[53] occurs in the multilateral netting stage, which nets and novates the bilateral obligations between the clearing members vis-à-vis the CCP in order to produce a new 'net net' obligation (the multilateral netting stage).

---

[49] Settlement can involve a payment and/or a delivery of an asset, depending on the nature of the transaction which the CCP is involved in and depending which type of market the CCP operates in. A CCP can operate in securities, exchange traded derivative, and OTC derivative markets.

[50] 'Straight-through processing' (STP) means that all the transactions are processed automatically and electronically. CCPs will generally not review individual transactions that satisfy certain predetermined criteria. All the transactions that fit a certain profile will be instantaneously and immediately processed and cleared.

[51] See Figure 5.2.

[52] The bilateral obligations represent the contractual obligations which were created when the two counterparties to an OTC derivative contract initially entered into the agreement. See Figure 5.1.

[53] See Figure 5.3.

In support of this argument, Professor Dalhuisen has stated that 'the [first] *novation* itself could then be seen as not being a part of the clearing, but rather a *prelude* to it'.[54] Consequently, 'open offer' (described in section 5) was developed as a contractual legal tool to avoid the need for the first novation stage altogether, thereby providing more legal certainty and efficiency for CCP operations.

4.5 Purpose of Netting by Novation and Substitution

The aim of novation netting is to ensure *instantaneous* and *continuous* mutuality[55] between the CCP and clearing members for all trades. Professor Goode has described this process as the following:

> Each new contract is automatically consolidated with existing contracts to produce a new contract (novation) involving a single net indebtedness. It has *immediate* contractual force and produces a single new indebtedness that does not fall due for payment until an agreed future date between the parties. When payment falls due, only a single sum is involved on one side or the other.[56]

Therefore, immediate and continuous novation netting, as a species of novation,[57] is a theoretical construct[58] aiming to increase efficiency and protect against counterparty risk by reducing exposures in clearing and settlement systems that inherently have prolonged clearing cycles; for example, an OTC derivative contract will typically remain executory (open) for several months or years. This creates mutuality between the clearing members and the CCP and guarantees insolvency set-off if a system participant or the CCP defaults.

4.6 The Steps Involved in Multilateral Netting by Novation and Substitution

4.6.1 Stage 1
First, in the context of CCPs operating in the financial markets, the first *novation* stage (which is the main counterparty substitution stage) involves the termination[59] of an earlier contractual agreement that was executed between two counterparties on an

---

[54] Jan Dalhuisen, *Transnational and Comparative Commercial, Financial and Trade Law*, 3rd edn (Oxford: Hart Publishing, 2007), pp. 1046–1047 (emphasis added) (Dalhuisen, *Transnational and Comparative Commercial, Financial and Trade Law*).

[55] Dalhuisen, *Transnational and Comparative Commercial, Financial and Trade Law* (n 54), p. 1039.

[56] Goode, *Corporate Insolvency Law* (n 36), p. 472.

[57] Geva, 'The Clearing House Arrangement' (n 8), 141.

[58] This may be invalidated by the courts in some jurisdictions.

[59] The terms 'extinguishing' (Geva, 'The Clearing House Arrangement (n 8)) and 'rescission' (Joseph Chitty and Anthony Guest, eds, *Chitty on Contracts: General Principles*, 27th edn (London: Sweet & Maxwell, 1994) (Chitty, *Chitty on Contracts*) have been used interchangeably for the term 'termination'.

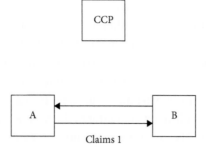

Figure 5.1 Pre-novation stage

Note: The arrows point in the direction that the obligations are owed. The clearing numbers are represented by 'A' and 'B' in the figures.

Source: author.

exchange or OTC (the pre-novation stage) and substitution[60] with a new agreement[61] and a new counterparty.[62] In effect, consenting counterparties immediately transfer[63] their full contractual positions[64] between themselves to the CCP and are substituted by it. This is the stage where the CCP becomes the buyer to every seller and the seller to every buyer.

The first novation becomes legally effective from the moment the CCP 'accepts' to assume responsibility as principal for a particular transaction. Therefore, it is crucial that the clearing rules of a CCP specify the exact time that it 'accepts'[65] a particular set of transactions in order for the novation and counterparty substitution to occur or else the clearing members will continue to be exposed to each other's counterparty risk. CCP systems must avoid confirmation backlogs in order for this stage to work properly. The longer the delay in accepting, the longer that the parties to an original transaction are exposed to each other's counterparty risk.

In the case of exchange traded derivatives, novation and substitution (i.e. the 'acceptance') will generally occur as soon as the original transactions between the transacting parties are executed and matched on an exchange as a part of the back-office or post-trade services. CCPs use software and STP to automate this procedure. The

---

[60] This term is used by both Geva, 'The Clearing House Arrangement' (n 8), 148, and Chitty, *Chitty on Contracts* (n 59), p. 1083.

[61] The discharge of the old contract is considered sufficient '*consideration*'; Chitty, *Chitty on Contracts* (n 59), p. 1083. The *consent* of the clearing members to enter into a novation is expressly or implicitly provided by contractually entering into the CCP arrangement.

[62] 'Counterparty substitution' results in there being a new counterparty— the CCP; Geva, 'The Clearing House Arrangement' (n 8), 148.

[63] 'Novation is a species of transfer', although the legal effect is to 'extinguish and replace (substitute) existing rights and duties with identical new ones', and there is no actual assignment or transfer of rights or liabilities; Chitty, *Chitty on Contracts* (n 59).

[64] The contractual positions transferred consist of rights (assets) and duties (liabilities/obligations).

[65] Clearing Condition 1.2.2, Clearing Conditions for Eurex Clearing AG (14 March 2021):

The novation becomes legally effective at the point in time when Eurex Clearing AG accepts the relevant Original OTC Transaction for Clearing by making the relevant OTC Trade Novation Report available to the relevant Clearing Member or, if applicable, to the relevant Basic Clearing Member electronically via Eurex Clearing AG's system.

novation process involves the immediate termination of the original contracts between the clearing members after their creation and a replacement by two new mirroring contracts between each clearing member and the CCP.[66] In practice, there may not be much of a delay between the time that the parties enter into the original transactions on the exchange and the time when the CCP is substituted as the main principal for those particular transactions. This means that counterparty risk is significantly reduced as the CCP quickly becomes the main guarantor of the transactions that it assumes.

In the case of cleared OTC derivatives, the novation and substitution process may also be automated and take effect in a similar manner to the one that takes place on an exchange. The parties that have entered into OTC transactions will have to use an electronic communications platform to notify the CCP about their transactions so that the CCP can either accept or reject each transaction for novation. A CCP system should ensure that it is quick to assume as the principal any eligible transactions that are entered into between the system's participants in order to minimize the window of counterparty risk that the original parties may face vis-à-vis one another (and possibly systemic risk where there are multiple member defaults).

As an example of the substitution process, Eurex AG has specified in its clearing rules the time that counterparty substitution will take place:

> The novation and clearing process will be carried out on each Business Day ('Daily Novation') for each Original OTC Transaction which has been submitted to Eurex Clearing AG via an [Approved Trade Source System] and which fulfils the applicable novation criteria.

Furthermore, in the case of cleared OTC derivatives, it may be the responsibility of the parties to the original OTC transaction to agree, on a bilateral basis, that the original OTC transaction shall be cancelled vis-à-vis each other upon an effective novation.[67]

4.6.2 Stage 2

Second, the *multilateral netting stage* involves the bilateral *calculation* and subsequent *discharge* of two mutual gross obligations[68] between each clearing member and the CCP and the *replacement* (the second novation) through the creation of a new single 'net net' obligation. The netting stage takes place during the clearing process, and the specific time of this process will be included in the clearing rules.

---

[66] For example, Regulation 12(a) of the LCH General Regulations (February 2022), states that the original contracts are replaced by 'novation' upon 'registration':

> Upon registration of an original contract by the Clearing House, such contract shall be replaced by novation […] by two open contracts, one between the seller and the Clearing House as buyer, as principals to such contract, and one between the buyer and the Clearing House as seller, as principals to such contract. Following such novation the original contract shall be extinguished.

[67] Clearing Condition 1.2.1(5), Clearing Conditions for Eurex Clearing AG (14 March 2021).

[68] The new novated contracts between each clearing member and the CCP produce gross obligations (Figure 5.2), which are discharged in the course of netting (Figure 5.3) to produce a new 'net' obligation (Figure 5.4); Geva, 'The Clearing House Arrangement' (n 8), 145.

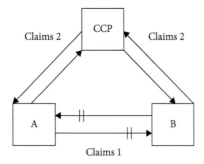

Figure 5.2 Stage 1: First novation
Source: author.

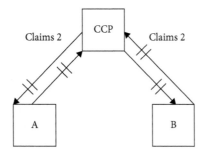

Figure 5.3 Stage 2: Netting and second novation
Source: author.

In practice, stages 1 and 2 will normally occur instantaneously and simultaneously in most CCP systems.[69] Alternatively, stage 2 may occur at specific points throughout the day (intra-day), at the end of the day,[70] or at any other time specified in the clearing rules.

4.6.3 Stage 3

The *settlement* stage[71] requires the 'net net' debtors to pay or deliver their obligations to the 'net net' creditors after multilateral novation netting is completed. The new 'net net' obligations are discharged upon payment or delivery by the respective 'net net' debtors.[72] In the example below (Figure 5.4), clearing member A is the 'net net' creditor, whereas clearing member B is the 'net net' debtor.

---

[69] This involves continuous novation netting on a real-time basis of all the claims which the CCP assumes as principal. This process is automated using computer software.

[70] For example, under the Eurex clearing house rules, 'same-day netting' means that claims from transactions of one trading day shall be netted on that trading day. Clearing Condition 2.5.4, Clearing Conditions for Eurex Clearing AG (14 March 2021): 'The netting shall generally take place in the system of Eurex Clearing AG on each business day with the daily end processing.'

[71] See Figure 5.4.

[72] In this case, B and the CCP are the 'net net' debtors. B will pay the CCP, and the CCP will pay A the net amount owed.

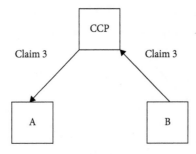

Figure 5.4 Stage 3: Settlement stage upon the completion of novation netting
Source: author.

In practice, instantaneous and continuous multilateral novation netting means that each new transaction is automatically, instantaneously, and continuously consolidated with all other transactions with the CCP. This normally occurs as soon as the transacting parties report (notify) their outstanding claims to the CCP and the CCP registers the transactions in their accounts, even if payment is deferred, 'so that theoretically there is always one netted outstanding amount between each participant and the system'.[73] Therefore, it is necessary for parties entering into OTC derivative contracts to report their trades as soon as possible to the relevant CCP in order to minimize counterparty risk.

4.7 Effect of an Intervening Bankruptcy

The counterparty substitution stage, which is achieved with the first novation, remains crucial as part of a CCP's risk management function. It is an important method for achieving mutuality instantaneously upon the execution of a transaction, thereby guaranteeing insolvency set-off to the CCP and its participants upon a clearing member default. The parties to a transaction will not receive a guarantee from the CCP system if one of the parties becomes insolvent before the CCP has novated the transactions.

Therefore, it is important to ensure that there is only a small window between the time when the parties enter into the original derivatives transactions and the time when the CCP accepts those transactions as the principal, as this will minimize the amount of time that the parties are exposed to each other's counterparty risk. The CCP will not be able to guarantee the transactions until it has been substituted as the main counterparty.

In the case of CCPs that clear derivatives (both exchange-traded and OTC) in the EU, there are carve-out statutes which prioritize the clearing rules of a CCP in order to ensure that the clearing procedure takes precedence over any conflicting corporate insolvency laws. However, in order for the clearing rules to take precedence over the

---

[73] Dalhuisen, *Transnational and Comparative Commercial, Financial and Trade Law* (n 54), p. 479.

corporate insolvency laws, it must be clear that the counterparty substitution has taken place at some point during the day. In order to create legal certainty, it is crucial for CCPs that use novation as the main method for counterparty substitution to specify in their clearing rules the exact time that this substitution takes place.

5 Open Offer

Open offer provides an alternative method for counterparty substitution. Open offer is a process where the CCP assumes obligations and becomes the principal to every transaction by means other than novation. Open offer is a contractual innovation that was created in order to avoid the requirements of 'notice' and 'consent', which are legal requirements for performing a valid novation.

A CCP using open offer automatically and immediately interposes itself in a transaction at the moment the buyer and seller of a derivative contract execute the contract. If all pre-agreed conditions are met, there is never a bilateral contractual relationship between the buyer and the seller.[74] In this sense, 'the CCP is the party to any contract concluded on an exchange'.[75]

Open offer is a unilateral contract[76] in the form of an *offer* by the CCP (i.e. the offeror) to enter into a contractual relation which is *open* to a clearing member (i.e. the offeree), which the clearing member can *accept* by conduct. The CCP (the promisor) undertakes to assume the rights and obligations of a clearing member (the promisee) as the principal if the clearing member accepts the CCP's offer by entering into a transaction of the kind stipulated in the clearing arrangement.

Hence, open offer is legally distinct from novation. The first novation stage is bypassed altogether with the effect of creating instantaneous mutuality between all the clearing members and the CCP through connecting all the transactions into one single transaction. Although the novation and open offer processes are legally distinct, from a practical perspective, they both serve the same function of *substituting* the clearing members for the CCP as principal.

The CCP's open offer will generally be subject to a *condition subsequent*.[77] This means that the contracts entered into between the CCP and the clearing members

---

[74] An older version of the clearing rules of SIX x-clear Ltd, a CCP based in Switzerland, provided that 'an open offer implicates that solely contracts between the CCP and its clearing members result from the order matching process in the trading system—there is *no bilateral contract between the trading counterparties*'; Provision 7.2, SIX x-clear Ltd, 'Service Description' (October 2009) (emphasis added), on file with the author.

[75] Robert Bliss and Chryssa Papathanassiou, 'Derivatives Clearing, Central Counterparties and Novation: The Economic Implications' (2006) 30(4), Fourth Quarter 20, http://ssrn.com/abstract=948769 (accessed 23 March 2023) (Bliss and Papathanassiou, 'Derivatives Clearing, Central Counterparties and Novation').

[76] A '*unilateral contract*' is 'a contract in which one party (the promisor) undertakes to do or refrain from doing something if the other party (the promisee) does or refrains from doing something, but the promisee does not undertake to do or refrain from doing that thing': Elizabeth A Martin, *The Oxford Dictionary of Law* (Oxford: Oxford University Press, 2003).

[77] For example, the old rule for the SIX Swiss Exchange provided that the open offer was subject to a *condition subsequent*: Swiss Exchange, Condition 1.2.1, the old Directive 24 on Clearing and Settlement (7 September 2007) (emphasis added).

can be cancelled by the CCP in specified circumstances as outlined in the particular system's clearing rules. Further, the *acceptance* must be in the form of objectively identifiable conduct, such as through the 'performance' of a service for a clearing member and a concurrent 'receipt' of a service by a clearing member or through the 'matching' of order book trades of two trading participants.[78]

Furthermore, Bliss and Papathanassiou have stated that 'the open offer has a binding character on the CCP […] and the CCP cannot reject these contracts'.[79] This can be interpreted as meaning (i) that a CCP cannot reject *any* contracts which are accepted for open offer by the clearing members or (ii) that the CCP cannot reject contracts which satisfy the conditions provided in the clearing rules but can reject contracts which do not satisfy such conditions. It is submitted that the latter interpretation is preferred and was likely intended since the CCP needs to have control over which contracts it clears.

The implications of being able to cancel a contract unless it meets the clearing criteria is to create legal certainty and to not bind the CCP to a contract which could burden the system. Legally speaking, the breach of a condition as a major term (express or implied) of a contract constitutes a fundamental breach of the contract and entitles the injured party to treat it as discharged.

Open offer can be expressly included as a term in the clearing rules of a CCP as the main method for counterparty substitution or it can exist in the form of an implied term if it is evident from the language used in the clearing rules that the CCP is using this method for counterparty substitution. For example, open offer is described in an older version of the SIX Swiss Exchange clearing rules, which accurately describes the legal process for performing a valid open offer:

> When an on order book trade arises as a result of matched orders between two trading participants, the *matching* is deemed to be an *acceptance* by the trading participant of CCP's Open Offer. *The Open Offer is a concept as defined in the CCP rules.* The Open Offer is an expression of *willingness to contract*, made with the intention that it is to become binding upon the person making it as soon as it is accepted by the person to whom it is addressed […] The *acceptance* of the Open Offer made by the CCP gives rise to contracts between the CCP and its clearing members which are subject to a *condition subsequent*. The rejection by the CCP of contracts arising from the Open Offer will result in their *cancellation*.[80]

---

[78] This occurs in the CCP operated by the Eurex derivatives exchange and clearing system.
[79] Bliss and Papathanassiou, 'Derivatives Clearing, Central Counterparties and Novation' (n 75), 20:

> Legally, the CCP makes an open offer to eligible clearing members following which two contracts are immediately concluded as soon as the parties have agreed on the details of the trade during the process of 'matching'. The open offer has a *binding character* on the CCP so that a contract between each trading participant and the CCP is concluded and *the CCP cannot reject these contracts*. In the open offer system, there is no bilateral contract between trading participants and therefore no obligations ever arise between the trading participants. Should for any reason the CCP not become party to the contract with each trading partner, *there is no contract*.

The same reasoning should apply to CCPs that clear OTC derivatives.
[80] Swiss Exchange, Condition 1.2.1, the old Directive 24 on Clearing and Settlement (n 77) (emphasis added).

After the CCP becomes the main principal to a particular set of transactions through the mechanism of open offer, the CCP will perform a multilateral netting of the executory transactions on a daily or intra-daily basis in the same manner as if it had assumed the obligations using novation. Therefore, the CCP will use multilateral novation netting to ensure that there is always a single net amount owing to the CCP or owed by the CCP to the clearing members.

6 Legal Distinction between Novation and Open Offer

Although there is no functional or practical distinction between open offer and novation, since both, in effect, substitute the clearing members for each other with the CCP, there is a clear legal distinction. Whilst there is a *legal substitution* of the counterparties with the CCP in an open offer, there is no *actual substitution* of anything at all because there is never a contract created between the members for a service performed or received under the clearing arrangement, and therefore no rights or obligations are ever created between them. The word 'substitution' is used, for lack of a better word, since there is only a *de jure* substitution of the counterparties when open offer is used.

Open offer, however, clearly provides an important benefit that novation does not. It guarantees that a counterparty will always have a contractual relationship with the CCP, notwithstanding a major disruption to a CCP's clearing operations. This significantly reduces counterparty risk vis-à-vis the other clearing members.

Furthermore, whereas novation requires *consent* (notification) of all the relevant claims to be effective, open offer does not. Novation requires some 'positive act' of informing the new counterparty (i.e. the CCP) of the specifics of the contractual obligations that they are going to assume. A CCP will generally receive communication of any transactions entered into between the counterparties via a designated electronic messaging platform.[81] The act of notification is not necessary when open offer is used because there is no intention to involve a new counterparty in the agreement. Therefore, from a legal perspective, open offer is a less burdensome process than novation for performing counterparty substitution.

However, it has been observed that CCPs that use novation for counterparty substitution will often ignore the notification requirement altogether. Ledrut and Upper have argued, in the context of OTC derivatives that are novated to a CCP, that the lack of consent and confirmation does not impede an effective novation from occurring as a

---

[81] For instance, in the case of SwapClear, the counterparties will communicate the information via an 'Approved Trade Source System'; Rule 1.1.1, LCH Ltd, Procedures Section 2 C, SwapClear Clearing Service (February 2022). In the case of Eurex, 'Eurex Clearing AG accepts such Original OTC Transaction for inclusion in the Clearing Procedures by making an OTC Trade Novation Report available to the Clearing Member or, if applicable, the Basic Clearing Member electronically via its system': Clearing Condition 1.2.1. (2)(c), Clearing Conditions of Eurex Clearing AG (n 44).

matter of market practice.[82] Whether or not this would work as an argument in court is yet to be determined.[83]

The main problem with using novation as a method for counterparty substitution is that there still remains the theoretical possibility for the disruption of the clearing process between stages 1 and 2 (as noted in section 4.6), especially if there are backlogs in the system or if the system goes offline due to a cyber-attack. Conversely, counterparty risk is fully eliminated if open offer is used as this contractual device bypasses stage 1 altogether.

Nevertheless, despite the huge benefit provided by open offer, it has been observed that this method of counterparty substitution has only been used for exchange-traded derivatives. From a legal point of view, there is nothing preventing a clearing system from using open offer as a method of counterparty substitution for cleared OTC derivatives. Yet, CCPs have preferred to use the novation method of counterparty substitution in the case of OTC derivatives for risk management purposes.[84]

From a legal perspective, it is possible for the CCP to make a unilateral 'offer' to any authorized counterparty to clear any standardized OTC derivative contract that is executed between a pair of counterparties. This 'offer' would be communicated to the OTC counterparties by way of the CCP's clearing rules. It would then be possible for the counterparties to 'accept' this offer by conduct or performance,[85] which occurs when the counterparties communicate with each other that they agree to execute a particular derivative contract. It is at this point that a contract is created between the CCP and each of the counterparties. Therefore, there is nothing hindering CCPs from using open offer for cleared OTC derivatives from a contract law perspective.

However, there is an important reason why CCPs are currently unwilling to use open offer and have preferred using novation as a method of counterparty substitution for cleared OTC derivatives.[86] In practice, the bilateral nature of OTC contracts means that

---

[82] Elisabeth Ledrut and Christian Upper, 'Changing Post-Trading Arrangements for OTC Derivatives', International Banking and Financial Market Developments, BIS Quarterly Review (December 2007), pp. 85–86, http://www.bis.org/publ/qtrpdf/r_qt0712.pdf (accessed 23 March 2023) Ledrut and Upper stated at p. 87 that:

> a confirmation describes all the details of the trade [... and] sets out the general terms and conditions related to [...] derivatives trades between [...] two counterparties. A confirmation proposal may either be prepared by both counterparties and then matched [...] or prepared by only one and affirmed by the other [...] While unconfirmed trades [resulting from confirmation backlogs] are legally binding in most jurisdictions, potential disagreement about their precise terms can result in lengthy and costly litigation. Similarly, knowledge of a firm's precise positions is a precondition for successful risk management.

and at p. 89, '[w]hile the ISDA master agreements have always required traders to seek the consent of their original counterparties before novating a trade, this was often not adhered to in practice' (emphasis added). It is interesting to note that the confirmation backlogs they describe have been eliminated through the combined regulatory efforts of financial market regulators in various jurisdictions.

[83] It should be noted that it is not possible for a CCP to perform *netting* without reporting or notifying the relevant claims or amounts to the CCP. Some information or data is necessary on the relevant claims to be able to know the value (cash) or volume (securities) of what is being calculated and discharged.

[84] Clearing Condition 1.2.3 (7), Clearing Conditions of Eurex Clearing AG (n 44) (emphasis added): 'The Original OTC Transaction that is transmitted to the system of Eurex Clearing AG in order to be *novated* into an OTC Interest Rate Derivative Transaction must be of a product type recognised by Eurex Clearing AG as published on the Eurex Clearing Website.'

[85] In the case of a unilateral contract, there is no need for the offeree to communicate acceptance of the offer because acceptance is achieved through performance; *Carlill v Carbolic Smoke Ball Company* [1893] 1 QB 256 CA.

[86] For example, Muqassa, the new CCP in Saudi Arabia, uses novation for the counterparty substitution of cleared OTC derivatives and open offer for clearing exchange-traded derivatives; Muqassa, Securities Clearing Centre Rules, Arts 26(a) and 28 (on file with author).

the counterparties negotiate the details of the contact with each other and reach an agreement in private. The CCP is not generally privy to these negotiations. The counterparties may not report the executed transactions to the CCP until later in the day. This can be problematic for a CCP as the CCP may become the main principal for the financial obligations resulting from several privately negotiated transactions at the moment they are executed by the system's participants, for which it might have no information for several hours.

Until the CCP is notified of the details of these newly executed transactions, there will be a period in the day where the CCP will be unaware of its total financial exposures. This would be unacceptable for a critical market infrastructure whose main task is to neutralize risk. Therefore, CCPs have demonstrated that they are unwilling to assume the contractual obligations of counterparties for transactions that they are fully unaware of. In the context of cleared OTC derivatives, CCPs prefer to use novation as the CCP then only assumes the contractual obligations of the counterparties at the moment that the details are communicated to the CCP. This keeps the CCP fully apprised of all the contractual obligations that it is responsible for and provides the CCP with an opportunity to reject any contracts where it is unwilling to assume the risk, that is, if they are non-standardized or considered to be too risky.

The case of exchange-traded derivatives is different as the CCP will be linked electronically to the derivatives exchange where all the trades are executed by the system's participants. Each of these positions will be instantly communicated to the CCP, and the CCP will at all times be fully aware of the contractual obligations and the full financial exposures that it has assumed through open offer.

It is possible that a CCP might be willing to use open offer for OTC derivatives in cases where it receives immediate notification of all the outstanding transactions executed by the counterparties. This would be possible, for example, if all the OTC counterparties used a common platform (i.e. an online platform that uses distributed ledger technology, DLT) to execute their privately negotiated transactions and the platform had a direct communication link with the relevant CCP. In these cases, the CCP would permit the use of open offer because the CCP would be fully apprised in real time of all the contracts it assumed for clearing. We may see a move in this direction in the future as there are various CCPs experimenting with and building new DLT platforms.

7 Summary and Conclusions

The distinction between open offer and novation in the context of CCP arrangements is artificial in practice since both 'open offer' and immediate and continuous 'novation' permit the clearing system to become the central counterparty at the moment that the parties enter into their respective derivatives transactions. However, in theory, open offer conveniently bypasses the notification requirement altogether, meaning that counterparty substitution will always occur immediately after a pair of counterparties enter into a transaction for derivatives. Therefore, open offer guarantees that there will always be mutuality between the system's participants and the CCP.

A court may find that substitution occurs at a different time than that intended by the CCP if the method or time of counterparty substitution is not specifically pinpointed in the clearing arrangement. Legal uncertainty can be avoided in a clearly drafted scheme or in one that expressly provides that it uses open offer as the main method for counterparty substitution. In order to provide legal certainty, CCPs should specify in their clearing rules and arrangements the precise moment of counterparty substitution.

It has been observed that CCPs that clear OTC derivatives in Europe have preferred to use novation over open offer as a method of counterparty substitution, despite the obvious benefits that open offer provides. This is because a CCP may not want to use open offer if the CCP is not going to find out the details of the obligations that it has assumed until a later time. It would be truly bizarre if a CCP were found to have assumed as the principal a particular set of OTC transactions that had been privately negotiated between counterparties and of which the CCP was unaware.

Therefore, a CCP may not want to assume responsibility for all the transactions entered into by the system's participants. A CCP will typically only want to assume the risk of transactions that it knows exist. Open offer will only be used by CCPs that have a direct communications link with the platform where particular trades are executed. This may be possible in the case of exchange traded derivatives, but it may not always be possible in the case of OTC derivatives that are privately negotiated between the counterparties. This may explain why SIX x-clear, which is a CCP based in Switzerland, uses open offer for trades executed on a formal exchange, whereas it uses novation for trades executed on multilateral trading facilities (MTFs), which are informal exchanges that permit the trading of OTC products and other exotic trading instruments.[87]

Finally, it is unfortunate that the relevant legislation dealing with the clearing mandate in the EU, which regulates the operations of CCPs that clear OTC derivatives, does not specifically recognize open offer or define novation under their definitions and does not distinguish between these two concepts. These two contractual mechanisms should clearly be defined in all legislation that applies to clearing and settlement systems in order to avoid any legal uncertainty in the future.

---

[87] SIX x-clear Ltd uses either open offer or novation for the counterparty substitution stage, depending on where the trades were originally executed by the parties. SIX, Service Description SIX x-clear Ltd, CCP Clearing Services for Equity Transactions for Members on SECOM, xcl-800 (4 December 2019), para. 6.0:

> "The Single Contracts between SIX x-clear and its Members arise either by way of acceptance of the Open Offer or Novation. In general, with the acceptance of the Open Offer SIX x-clear takes over the counterparty risk already upon trade matching in the trading system of the relevant exchange (as Liquidnet H2O, London Stock Exchange and SIX Swiss Exchange). In case of Novation SIX x-clear takes over the counterparty risk not before the entry of the matched trades from any MTF or Matching Service into SIX x-clear's clearing system.

6

OTC Derivatives Clearing and Collateral Management

Manmohan Singh

1 Introduction

As part of the extensive regulatory reform proposals, the new rules will warrant a significant increase in the use of collateral across the financial system. Estimates by markets and policy institutions suggest that the Dodd–Frank Act, Basel III (Dodd–Frank Wall Street Reform and Consumer Protection Act. Basel III: International Regulatory Framework for Banks. It is an internationally agreed set of measures developed by the Basel Committee on Banking Supervision in response to the financial crisis of 2007-09. The Directive 2009/138/EC of the European Parliament and of the Council of 25 November 2009 on the taking-up and pursuit of the business of Insurance and Reinsurance (Solvency II)), and the European Market Infrastructure Regulation (EMIR) may warrant US$2–$4 trillion in additional unencumbered collateral that will span margins for over-the-counter (OTC) derivatives at central counterparties (CCPs), liquidity ratio(s) under Basel III, and related needs stemming from parallel developments under the EMIR and Solvency II. At the same time, due to the global financial crisis and efforts at quantitative easing (QE) in the United States and Europe, significant amounts of collateral have been drained out of the financial system and siloed at central banks. In addition, due to counterparty risk in dealing with large banks and the risk aversion of clients, collateral reuse (or velocity) has also been decreased. In fact, the bilateral pledged market, which offers a genuine market clearing price for collateral, has shrunk from about US$10 trillion to about US$6.0 trillion at the end of 2016, now rebounding to US$9.6 trillion (end of 2021). More importantly, many of the proposed regulations (e.g. moving OTC derivatives to CCPs) have not yet been in force and some key start dates postponed on several fronts.

The financial crisis following Lehman Brothers' demise and the American International Group's (AIG) bailout provided the impetus to move the lightly regulated OTC derivative contracts from bilateral clearing to CCPs. The debate about the future of financial regulation has heated up as regulators in both the United States and the European Union (EU) seek legislative approval to mitigate systemic risk associated with systemically important financial institutions (SIFIs), which include large banks and non-banks. In order to mitigate systemic risk that is due to counterparty credit risks and failures, either the users of derivative contracts will have to hold more collateral (or equivalent capital) from bilateral counterparties or margin will have to be posted to CCPs. Almost a decade ago, studies showed that this US$600 trillion OTC derivatives market is seriously undercollateralized and thus contributes to systemic risk (see below). Also, research in this topic has shown that the associated demand for additional collateral to satisfy the envisaged regulatory efforts will be onerous.[1] A recent study suggests that a costs comparison between central clearing and bilateral clearing does not favour the move to CCPs if netting losses and default waterfall funds are calibrated more closely.[2]

2 Moving (Some) OTC Derivatives to CCPs

By way of background, prior to the momentum to move OTC derivatives from large banks books, CCPs were viewed under the rubric of payment systems. In the aftermath of the Lehman crisis, the G20 Pittsburgh meetings in 2009 decided that a critical mass of banks' derivative-related risks would be moved to CCPs. Regulators are forcing, en masse, considerable OTC derivatives to CCPs. This is a huge transition, primarily to move this risk outside the banking system. These new entities may also be viewed as 'derivative warehouses' or concentrated 'risk nodes' of global financial markets. There are many proposals on trying to unwind SIFIs; it is a difficult (if not an impossible) task. So creating new SIFIs such as CCPs should be backed by sound economics. Singh (2010) illustrates that in the past, on average, each of the top ten banks has carried, on average, about US$100 billion of derivative-related tail risk.[3] This is the cost to the financial system from the failure of

---

[1] International Swaps and Derivatives Association (ISDA) (2012). Indeed, the margins requirements (also due to netting losses) were not trivial. No wonder the clearing has been phased.

[2] Samim Ghamami and Paul Glasserman, 'Does OTC Derivatives Reform Incentivize Central Clearing?', Working Paper 16-7, Office of Financial Research, https://www.financialresearch.gov (accessed 23 March 2023) describes the total capital and collateral costs when banks transact fully bilaterally and when they clear all contracts through CCPs; they find the cost incentive may not favour central clearing—netting loss and guarantee fund burden are significant.

[3] Manmohan Singh, 'Collateral, Netting and Systemic Risk in OTC Derivatives Market', IMF Working Paper No. 10/99 (Washington: International Monetary Fund) (Singh, 'Collateral').

a large bank (where tail risk is measured by residual derivative liabilities at a large bank after netting and collateral); the underlying economics holds under both International Financial Reporting Standards (IFRS) and the Generally Accepted Accounting Principles (GAAP). For example, Barclays' recent annual report indicates derivative liabilities of US$527 billion; after netting of US$427, the risk is US$100 billion of contracts if Barclays fails. This is reflected in GAAP accounting but not under IFRS as it does not allow netting. However, the economics of US$100 billion residual risk to the market if Barclays fails holds true even under IFRS accounting.

Yet, instead of addressing the derivatives tail risk, the present regulatory agenda is focused on offloading most of the derivatives book to CCPs. Past and present market practices result in residual risk in the form of derivative liabilities (and derivative assets), based on ISDA netting agreements, because sovereigns, AAA insurers, corporates, medium–small banks, multilateral institutions (e.g. the European Bank for Reconstruction and Development, EBRD), and the Berkshire Hathaway types of firms do not post adequate collateral since they are viewed by banks and regulators as privileged and (presumably) safe clients.

It was envisaged that CCPs will require collateral to be posted from all members and thus offer a transparent ground for the regulatory overhaul. In essence, all parties should post collateral to CCPs; there should be no exceptions or exemptions. This is also called two-way credit support annexes (CSAs) under ISDA. However, this is not happening as envisaged. As stated above, there will be exemptions to some end users, and many central banks, sovereigns, and municipalities are not required to post collateral.

Not surprisingly, the regulatory efforts(s) are meeting resistance from the financial industry, including the large banks, asset managers (such as pension funds), and insurers. Another market that has lobbied to avoid posting collateral is the 'end users', such as airlines and non-financial corporates, who, presumably, are genuine hedgers but will nevertheless contribute towards the systemic risk stemming from the use of OTC derivatives if they pass the buck to their bank by not posting their share of collateral.

Some issues relevant for discussion under the proposed regulations are detailed below and include the onerous collateral requirements, a central bank backstop for CCPs, the fallacy of the utilities comparison, and reduced collateral reuse rate (velocity). There are still many other impediments to the successful implementation of the proposed reform agenda, lower overall netting, no interoperability between CCPs, demand for segregated collateral, and CCPs 'equivalence' across jurisdictions—especially after Brexit, extraterritoriality, and regulatory arbitrage.

3 Under-collateralization in the OTC Derivatives Market

While a much-cited figure, the notional value of contracts of about US$600 trillion overstates the importance of this market. More relevant are the 'in-the-money' (or gross-positive-value) and 'out-of-the money' (or gross-negative-value) derivative positions, which are further reduced by 'netting' of related positions. From a collateral demand–supply framework, undercollateralization is the more relevant metric for policy discussions. While, typically, collateral—both initial and variation-margin—is posted by hedge funds, asset managers, and other clients, large banks active in this space do not have a two-way margin agreement with some clients (e.g. sovereigns, quasi-sovereigns, large pensions and insurers, and AAA corporations), so collateral may not be forthcoming when due and, as a quid pro quo, the banks may not be posting collateral, either, to such clients. Interestingly, regulatory proposals also exempt foreign-exchange (FX) swaps from central clearing, and CLS Finance, the major FX settlement house, does not novate or inherit the original contracts, unlike CCPs, so this FX risk stays with banks. A key incentive for moving OTC derivatives to CCPs is higher multi-lateral netting, that is, offsetting exposures across all OTC products on banks' books—intuitively, the margin required to cover the exposure of the portfolio would be smaller in a CCP world. However, if there are multiple CCPs that are not linked, the benefits of netting are significantly reduced because across-product netting will not take place since almost all CCPs presently offer multilateral netting in the same asset class and not across products.

At present, there is undercollateralization within the OTC derivatives space that stems from several privileged investors within the financial system—sovereigns, sovereign wealth funds, central banks, corporate, multilateral institutions, etc. There has been reported undercollateralization since 2008 of about US$3–5 trillion, according to the Bank for International Settlements (BIS) semi-annual surveys.[4] However, these figures may not pick up the full extent of collateral shortfall. Even if we consider half of the total positions (i.e. when banks are out of the money) that are risks to taxpayers, these estimates are sizable. Therefore dedicated collateral may not be enough (only initial margin) as the variation margin is fungible and does not stay in a 'derivative silo', so additional collateral will be required to be posted (see Chapter 2 'OTC Derivatives Clearing Explained' by Tina Hasenpusch and Rezah Stegeman in this volume) and is reused as it is with 'title transfer'.

4 Interoperability

Interoperability, or linking of CCPs, will increase each CCP's clearing fund in line with the net open positions between them. So CCPa may hold or have access to collateral from CCPb, which may go bankrupt in the future so that losses involved in closing out CCPb's obligations to CCPa can be covered. However, legal and regulatory sources indicate that cross-border margin access is subordinate to national bankruptcy laws, such as the US Bankruptcy Code's 'Chapter 11'. It is unlikely that CCPa in one country would be allowed access to collateral posted by CCPb registered in another country. Nor is it in the interests of CCPs to change their business model and lose their niche market(s). The sheer collateral arithmetic to support interoperability is daunting.

---

[4] Cf. Singh, 'Collateral' (n 3), p. 8.

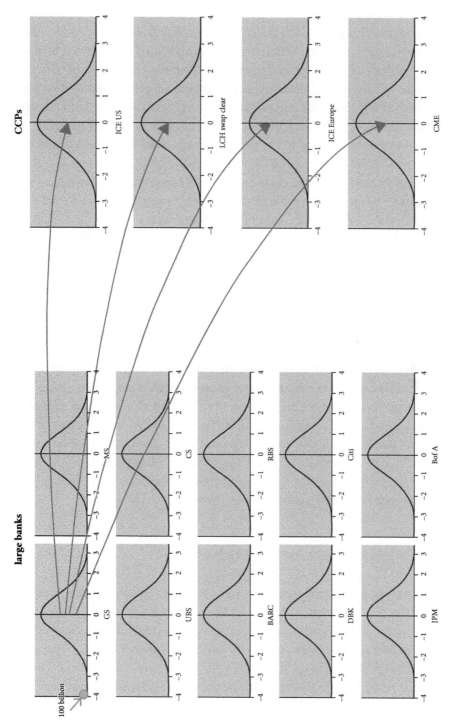

Figure 6.1 How SIFIs offload most of their OTC derivative book to CCPs

Source: author.

5 Sizeable Collateral Requirements

The ten largest banks will continue to keep systemic risk from OTC derivatives on their books since only standard OTC derivatives are mandated by regulation to move to CCPs. Regulatory efforts will introduce more new entities (i.e. CCPs) that will also hold systemic risk from OTC derivatives. This goes against the intuition that suggests the need to minimize the number of SIFIs (and benefit from additional netting) rather than increasing their number. Thus, collateral needs will be higher in the proposed world. Most of the major banks' derivatives books are largely concentrated in one 'business' (a legal entity) to run the derivatives clearing business so as to maximize global netting. Some clients, such as sovereigns and US municipalities, are presently not in a position to post collateral. Due to exemptions, a significant part of this market will not reach CCPs. Other research also finds considerable additional collateral needs. The ISDA has also acknowledged the significant collateral needs resulting from moving derivative positions to CCPs, despite their (earlier) margin surveys indicating that most of this market is collateralized. The considerable collateral needs, along with the exemptions, imply that CCPs may not inherit all the derivative positions from banks. As discussed above, interoperability of CCPs (on a cross-border basis) is unlikely, so overall global netting will not increase. Netting is the flipside of collateral needs. The large banks active in the OTC derivative space are reluctant to unbundle 'netted' positions on their books as this results in deadweight loss and increases collateral needs; however, punitive regulations, such as uncleared margin rules, may result in more unbundling. In late 2019, DekaBank moved sizeable positions from London Clearing House (LCH) Swapclear (UK) to Eurex, Frankfurt, perhaps motivated by Brexit. Since LCH (UK) and Eurex are not interoperable, such cross-border moves may entail loss of netting and new collateral needs. The recent Gilts saga in the United Kingdom and the unwinding of euro-swaps in the very near future should keep LCH's (UK) collateral team alert.

6 Central Bank Backstop

A CCP may face a pure liquidity crisis if it is suffering from a massive outflow of otherwise solvent clearing members, in which case the risk is that it will have to realize its investment portfolio at low prices. Assuming an external shock where everyone is trying to liquidate collateral simultaneously, this will lead to a problem if the CCP has repo'd out the collateral it has, cannot get it back, and, for whatever reason, does not want to pay cash to the members, effectively purchasing the securities at that price. In these circumstances, a central bank would be repo'ing whatever collateral the CCP would ultimately get back. In such instances, it would be more sensible to require the bank members (e.g. J.P. Morgan, Credit Suisse) of the CCP to access the central bank and then provide the CCP with liquidity. However, recent trends suggest a closer relationship, as CCPs in the United States are now allowed to deposit directly at central banks rather than at private banks, with no limits on such deposits—unlike what the Bank of England requires (as would be the case for the treasurers of corporates with large cash holdings, such as Apple and Microsoft).

The CCP may also need central bank support if it has suffered a series of member defaults and is subject to a run because of credit concerns. In this case, the CCP's book is not balanced (since the trades of the defaulting members have fallen away), and if the central bank provides liquidity support, it will be taking credit/solvency risk on whatever the net CCP position is. In this regard, the report 'Principles for Financial Market Infrastructures' from the Committee for Payments and Settlement Systems (CPSS) and the International Organisation of Securities Commissions (IOSCO) is a good background.

A CCP failure should not be ruled out. As CCPs begin to clear more complex, less liquid, and longer-term instruments, their potential need for funding support in extremis will rise.

In the most extreme scenario, where a temporary liquidity shortfall at a CCP has the potential to cause systemic disruption, or even threaten the solvency of a CCP, it is likely that a central bank will stand ready to give whatever support is necessary. However, such an arrangement would create moral hazard. For example, in the United States, under the Dodd–Frank Act, the Federal Reserve cannot bail out any derivatives dealer. More generally, there is no complete clarity on whether non-banks would have access to central bank liquidity. Sections 802–806 of Dodd–Frank generally authorize the Federal Reserve to provide liquidity support under unusual or exigent circumstances to CCPs that have been designated as systemically important (the EU has similar language). A taxpayer bailout is not ruled out but will be handled not by the Fed but by the US Treasury. Regulators are keen on avoiding a CCP bailout and, thus, the thrust to use recovery tools (e.g. variation-margin haircuts) before a CCP defaults—see Turing's 'magic relighting candles'.[5]

7 Central Bank Backstop with and without Interoperability

CCPs might need a central bank backstop, even if they take adequate collateral. Central bank support for interoperable CCPs that are in distress could well span several jurisdictions due to the associated contagion. Previous analytical work suggests that if a critical mass (about two-thirds) of OTC derivatives does move to CCPs, then about US$200 billion will need to be contributed to initial margin and default funds at CCPs.[6]

---

[5] Dermot Turing, 'Central Counterparties: Magic Relighting Candles?' (2019) 8(1) Journal of Financial Market Infrastructures 27–49. Suspension or cancellation: if clearing is a critical function that must be continued in the interests of financial stability, it is hard to see how suspension of clearing could ever satisfy a financial stability test. Something of a paradox has crept into the draft legislation. The answer to this conundrum, as with the problem of the self-relighting candle, should, surely, be to reduce the financial system's dependency on CCPs and their criticality. That means *cancelling, not suspending,* the requirement for all derivatives of a particular class to be cleared.

[6] Cf. Singh, 'Collateral' (n 3), p. 9. Since CCPs would require all standard positions to have collateral against them, offloading a significant portion of OTC derivatives transactions to CCPs would require large increases in

Augmenting default funds would imply that the four linked CCPs hold more than US$200 billion. In the context of this chapter, the focus is on CCPs relevant to OTC derivatives such as ICE Clear UK, ICE Trust US, LCH.Clearnet's Swapclear, the Chicago Mercantile Exchange (CME), and Eurex (some of the newer names are not included). If these four CCPs are linked, they will augment their default funds, and additional netting will result from consolidation of exposures by participants at their chosen CCP. A back-of-the-envelope calculation, assuming the four key CCPs are about equal in size (each with about US$50 billion in default funds), suggests that each default fund may need to be augmented by another US$75 billion, midway between the envisaged US$50 billion and the US$200 billion maximum.

Increased netting results in lower residual risk across all SIFIs' books. In an interoperable world, if international legal challenges are overcome, the increased netting benefits may exceed the extra funds needed to augment default funds at linked CCPs. In the more likely scenario (i.e. under 'no interoperability'), central bank support will presumably be limited to the failed CCP in one jurisdiction, assuming there is no contagion. However, the present non-linked CCP world (and a realistic scenario going forward) results in lower multilateral netting that will require much higher collateral costs for all users of derivatives.

8 CCPs and Utilities

The revenue and benefits from OTC derivatives come from three sources: the origination fee plus netting on books plus the clearing fee. Banks will still keep all of the origination fee plus some of the netting (from OTC derivatives that do not clear). A utility has two characteristics: (i) government backstop but (ii) at negotiated 'economic rents'. So, for CCPs to be utilities, all three revenue pieces mentioned above (which comprise the total economic rent) should be negotiable. But banks will never let go of the origination or structuring fee—this is the biggest piece. The negotiation between regulators and banks is such that this fee will remain undisclosed—especially since this fee straddles several items in their annual reports that fall under fixed income, currency, and commodities (FICC). The comparison of CCPs as utilities is not apt unless it spans the full spectrum of 'economic rents'.

9 Decrease in Collateral Velocity (or Reuse Rate)

The decrease in the 'churning' of collateral may be significant since there is demand from some banks and/or their clients (asset managers, hedge funds, and so forth) for

posted collateral, possibly requiring large banks to raise more capital. These costs suggest that most large banks will be reluctant to offload their positions to CCPs. This chapter proposes an appropriate capital levy on remaining positions to encourage the transition.

legally segregated/operationally commingled accounts (LSOCs) for the margin that they will post to CCPs. Also, the demand for bankruptcy-remote structures—another form of silo-ing collateral, which stems from the desire not to legally post collateral with CCPs in jurisdictions that may not have the central bank's lender-of-last-resort back-stop (i.e. liquidity and solvency support), will reduce rehypothecation. (Chapter 2 'OTC Derivatives Clearing Explained' by Tina Hasenpusch and Rezah Stegeman in this volume discussed collateral velocity, now much lower at 2.2 relative to 3.0 before Lehman; and unlikely to bounce back as dealer bank balance sheet are maxed.)

There are still other issues that may be important to consider. For example, regu-latory arbitrage is likely due to the staggered implementation of this ambitious inter-national agenda. Under Dodd–Frank, SIFIs' banking groups can keep relatively safe OTC derivatives such as interest-rate, FX, and investment-grade credit default swaps (CDSs) on the bank's book; the rest have be to be 'pushed' outside the banking entity, although this is not the case in Europe and Asia. Extraterritoriality issues that are being discussed in the United States and Europe may also lead to regulatory divisions and possibly to booking of OTC derivative books to another jurisdiction (such as Asia) to 'accommodate' and adhere to the final definition of extraterritoriality.

10 Case Study: Eurozone's 'Out-of-the-Money' Derivatives When Interest Rates Rise

The official sector has largely focused on appropriate haircuts (and risk weights) for the sovereign bonds; the flexibility allows for inconsistency (and thus overvaluation of the bonds) relative to other risk.[7] However, the rhetoric about cutting the umbilical cord between banks and sovereigns will not get full traction unless sovereigns post collateral on their derivatives contracts with banks.

Due to the sizable volume of business (and associated revenue), most banks do not force sovereigns to post collateral when the sovereigns are 'out of the money' on their derivative contracts (also called one-way CSA; a two-way CSA will entail both parties posting collateral when due). Estimates of 'out-of-collateral' positions are not trivial and thus cannot be ignored when discussing the sovereign–bank nexus. Market sources indicate that between 10 and 15% of a large dealer's assets that need to be hedged may stem from sovereigns, supranational, and agencies (SSAs); an equal fraction is from corporate clients, thus addressing the undercollateralization issues in the OTC deriva-tive market.

Typically, the 'street', or between fifteen and twenty large dealers active in the OTC derivative market, are often on the same side of a trade (a few of them may hold similar positions when dealing with a sovereign). For example, informal discussions with the official sector indicate that the street is 'in the money' on interest-rate-swap (IRS)

---

[7] Hervé Hannoun, 'Sovereign Risk in Bank Regulation and Supervision: Where Do We Stand?', Bank for International Settlements, Financial Stability Institute High-Level Meeting (n 1).

positions that have been written since in the mid-2000s. Most dealers took the floating-rate leg of an IRS, and the sovereign typically took the fixed leg. As global interest rates have remained low since the 2008 crisis (but are unlikely to remain low from 2022 onwards), many of the IRS positions are now substantial derivative assets on the books of the banks since sovereigns typically do not post collateral to the large banks and settle at maturity and IRSs can typically be thirty years in tenor. As ECB rates cycle will change, sovereign will be less 'out of the money' and may even become 'in the money' as many of these contracts expire around 2035.

A few sovereigns have started to post collateral now and signed two-way CSAs (e.g. Italy) but not all of them.[8] In the past, some treasurers of some peripheral sovereigns banks have occasionally been active in the OTC derivatives market to reduce their CDS spreads.[9] In one case, the treasury requested that large banks active in OTC derivatives market should not hedge their exposure to the sovereign since it would lead to an increase in the CDS spreads of the sovereign. By the assignment of OTC derivatives contracts from large global banks to the sovereign's local banks, the original derivatives contract is reassigned from the large global bank to the periphery's local bank (or another request of the treasury), but the out-of-the-money positions of the treasury are not due until maturity of the contract. On the other hand, novation would entail a 'tear-up' of the original contract, and the treasury would have to 'settle' the out-of-the-money positions and pay the accrued balance up to the date of the novation at the time of the novation. However, legacy 'out-of-the-money' positions remain at large, but if two-way CSAs are not signed and/or do not encompass the past positions, all this is 'book entry' until 2035.[10]

11 Case Study: Brexit Swaps Moving to Eurozone—Netting Fragmentation

If there was (close to) one global interest rate swap (IRS) CCP, then it would be LCH (UK). LCH (UK) has become the counterparty to most IRSs. This preserves the cross-currency nature of the IRS netting. In the present scenario, let us say $p = 1$; that is, LCH is the only IRS clearer. However, the status quo will not remain due to political, legal, and business model constraints. There will be multiple euro IRS CCPs—let us say $p > 1$. Thus, the netting sets (n) proliferated will become ($n \times p$). The unbundling of the original netting sets will create more sets (numerically), but smaller and less diversified in content, until a CCP can offer to clear all euro swaps (Eurex, LCH (SA), etc.) or can net euro/dollar/sterling swaps in a CCP that offers cross-currency IRS netting

---

[8] Risk Magazine, 'Sovereign Risk Manager of the Year: Italy's Ministry of Economy and Finance' (1 February 2011), http://www.risk.net (accessed 23 March 2023).

[9] Manmohan Singh and Mohsan Bilal, 'CDS Spreads in European Periphery, Some Technical Issues to Consider', IMF e-library (1 March 2012), https://www.imf.org/en/Publications/WP/Issues/2016/12/31/CDS-Spreads-in-European-Periphery-Some-Technical-Issues-to-Consider-25777.

[10] Stefania Perrucci, 'Sovereign Swaps Users Should Learn from Italy's Mistakes', Risk Magazine (18 April 2019), https://www.risk.net (accessed 23 March 2023).

somewhere else, for example, in the United States or Asia. Non-cleared trades, despite uncleared margin rules that require collateral to be posted, will continue to remain on the books of the banks, thus causing more fragmentation. It is like breaking a Ming vase by dropping it and then picking up one of the pieces and saying, 'Well at least this bit's not broken.'

The flip side of less netting (due to fragmentation) means more overall collateral. The literature on the additional collateral needs for moving euro IRS to the eurozone are sketchy, from £5 billion[11] to lower numbers by ESMA (2021);[12] the numbers are likely to be higher as the opportunity cost moves up in tandem with the European Central Bank (ECB) interest rate cycle (and the 'wake-up' call after the autumn Gilts saga in the United Kingdom).

Interestingly, despite regulatory reservations on high collateral velocity, collateral reuse is being encouraged by the official sector to alleviate collateral shortage. For example, securities-lending has been encouraged by the ECB in recent years; national central banks, such as Bundesbank, or Banca d' Italia, or Banque de France, lend the good collateral they hold (as part of the ECB's asset purchase programme) and lend out the German Bunds. French OATS are other good collateral. The returns from securities-lending such bonds are very attractive (often forty basis points for two weeks). There is a reason why Germany can issue debt at 0% coupon (as securities-lending this bond, often, can yield 3–5% or more per annum). See Figure 6.2,

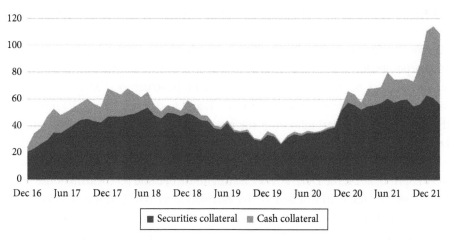

Figure 6.2 Usage of Eurosystem securities lending programme, monthly averages (Euro bn)
Source: ECB.

[11] Mark Carney, 'A Fine Balance', Bank of England (20 June 2017), https://www.bankofengland.co.uk/-/media/boe/files/speech/2017/a-fine-balance.pdf (accessed 23 March 2023).
[12] ESMA, 'ESMA Publishes Results of Its Assessment of Systematically Important UK Central Counterparties' (17 December 2021), https://www.esma.europa.eu/press-news/esma-news/esma-publishes-results-its-assessment-systemically-important-uk-central (accessed 23 March 2023).

which shows significant reuse since rules changed in January 2017, when cash for collateral swap was allowed.

Some issues will need to be addressed in the very near term:

- the eurozone may need to relax collateral requirements;
- there will need to be more clearing exemptions from eurozone entities (e.g. Dutch pension funds); and
- good collateral rates (e.g. Bund repo) may not align with the ECB policy rates that will be on the rise going forward.

12 The Case of Brazil's Brasil Bolsa Balcão S.a. or B3 (Formerly BM&FBovespa)

Emerging markets may take a cue from Brazil if they do not want to export their derivatives market to global financial centres; for example, South Africa is contemplating this decision. If local CCPs are linked (as in Brazil) and offer cross-product netting, the local cost to hedge will be lower than a global foreign CCP cost, for example, LCH, ICE, or CME. So when Brazil may face a low FX reserves position (e.g. a balance-of-payments difficulty), its corporates or banks, who may be also in an 'out-of-the-money' position on their derivatives, will not be asking FX from the central bank but will need to find local currency for their 'out-of-the-money' position.

CCP.B3 Clearinghouse performs the activities of registration, acceptance, clearing, settlement, and counterparty risk management of transactions executed in the financial, commodity, and equities derivatives markets; in the cash markets for gold, equities, and corporate debt (exchange-traded markets and OTC markets); and in the securities lending market, being the sole financial market infrastructure (FMI) in Brazil to perform securities settlement system (SSS), CCP, and trade repositary (TR) functions for these markets. B3 Clearinghouse is the result of two clearinghouses integrating—the Derivatives Clearinghouse, operated by BM&F, and Câmara Brasileira de Liquidação e Custódia (CBLC) (Brazilian Settlement and Custody Clearinghouse), operated by BOVESPA. In 2014, the Derivatives Clearinghouse became B3 Clearinghouse after replacing its clearing platform and its risk calculation model. This was the first phase of B3's post-trade integration project. The second phase of this project consisted of integrating, to B3 Clearinghouse, the markets then settled at CBLC—equity spot, derivatives, and lending markets and the corporate debt spot market.

There were several benefits of the clearinghouses integration for both B3 and participants, notably (i) improved liquidity management due to the unification of settlement windows, offsetting rights and obligations in markets previously settled in separate windows; (ii) more efficient capital allocation through the new integrated risk model (which assesses the risk of portfolios with different types of assets, contracts, and collateral jointly) and unification of the collateral pool, reducing the margin values without, however, reducing the level of clearing protection; (iii) cost reduction due to the standardization of rules, processes, time sheets, systems, and participant structure as well as the higher level of automation of operational routines; and (iv) reduction of technological and operational risks, given the modernization and simplification of technological infrastructure and the reduction of the number of registration, position management, settlement, and risk management systems, among others.

B3 Clearinghouse became, after integration in 2017, a multi-asset clearinghouse, returning to the market approximately BRL 35 billion deposited as collateral and increasing daily market liquidity by more than BRL 400 million. Its participant structure has about eighty clearing members, including banks and brokerage houses, all of them under the supervision of the Central Bank of Brazil, and more than 200,000 individual accounts under their responsibility.

Under Brazilian regulations, positions and collateral are segregated into individual investor-level accounts and, as such, B3 performs intra-day risk calculation and daily calculation of rights and obligations net values, both in cash and in assets, at all levels of the accounts (investor, brokerage house, and clearing member). This segregation model, while requiring large investments in information technology and business processes, contributes to reducing systemic risk and increasing investor protection as well as providing regulators with complete and consolidated information on a daily basis. Also in accordance with Brazilian regulations, financial settlement in local currency takes place in central bank money, through B3 Clearinghouse's own settlement account in the reserve transfer system is managed by the Central Bank of Brazil. In terms of custody of collateral assets, B3 Clearinghouse acts as its own custodian at the various central depositories (for emerging markets, this reduces FX reserves that are needed when their domestic clients need to post margins internationally with CME or ICE or LCH).

13 The Case of US Treasuries 'Clearing' CCP Route vs Taxpayer 'Put'

Does the safest asset in the world need to be made safer? That is the question regulators have set themselves as they consider reforming the US Treasury market in the wake of unprecedented volatility witnessed during the 2020–2021 coronavirus crisis—a move that could result in a shift to mandatory clearing. The off-and-on debate over US Treasury clearing took on fresh urgency in March 2020, when panic selling from funds desperate to raise cash as markets crashed saw dealers struggle to process the mass liquidation of huge off-the-run positions. As spreads blew out and liquidity stuttered, the Federal Reserve was forced to step in and shore up confidence in the basic functioning of the market.

One proposed answer—mandatory clearing of cash treasuries and repo trades—has spilt the market down the middle. In one camp are those who argue that central clearing would yield powerful netting and capital benefits and help alleviate balance-sheet constraints of the kind dealers claim crimped liquidity provision during huge-volume days, when the market needs it the most. Another group contends that US treasuries are already safe enough, and should be exempted from the leverage ratio in exceptional times, when the supply of money or collateral spikes so that dealer-banks have the capacity to maintain liquidity provision.

Recent work suggests that a clearing mandate may, in theory, unlock greater netting efficiencies, though a lack of complete data makes a comprehensive analysis impossible. Realizing those efficiencies in practice will be tricky for basic practical reasons: first and foremost, the infrastructure underpinning the US Treasury market is fragmented, with CME clearing all US Treasury futures, while cash and repo trades are cleared at the Fixed Income Clearing Corporation (FICC), a subsidiary of the Depository Trust & Clearing Corporation.

When CME bought the owner of BrokerTec, the largest interdealer treasuries trading platform, it triggered speculation in the market that the firm would look to offer clearing of cash instruments too, offering potentially significant margin offsets with its huge pool of open interest in futures. Three years on, that has yet to happen. Since 2004, FICC and CME have maintained a so-called two-pot, cross-margin agreement, which allows the CCPs to offer offsets between cash treasuries and treasury futures while still holding and managing members' positions and collateral separately. The netting benefits of this arrangement have been limited.

If clearing of US treasuries is mandated, a one-pot, cross-margin arrangement would be necessary to alleviate dealer balance-sheet constraints meaningfully. Under a one-pot system, offsetting positions would be placed into a separate account jointly overseen by both CCPs. FICC and CME would need to agree a single margin methodology, and US Treasury market participants might have to contribute additional initial margin and default resources.

Even within such an arrangement, clean netting would remain out of reach: there, basis risk would remain, given that futures and options cleared at CME will always be of long duration relative to the shorter-tenor settlement for cash and repos cleared at FICC. That residual duration would need to be margined at a gross level.

The underlying margin models of CME and FICC suggest that linking them may not be in the best interest of one, or even both, CCPs. They have different products and selling points, with some CME customers favouring the option of full asset segregation, which comes at the expense of less efficient netting, versus many FICC members preferring to commingle dealer and customer accounts to maximize netting opportunities. In short, do not expect much from enhanced 'clearing' proposals.

If a regulatory mandate forces this link to enhance netting (unlikely due to the regulatory overhang post Basle III and the Dodd–Frank Act), US treasuries clearing would simply replace capital requirements with margin requirements and default fund contributions. It would cram more of the most important bond market in the world into already too-big-to-fail institutions ultimately 'puttable' to the taxpayer. That would likely require greater scrutiny from the Federal Reserve and maybe the guarantee of further liquidity lines.

14 Policy Issues

Since the Lehman bankruptcy and AIG bailout, there has been increased momentum to move OTC derivatives from the books of large banks to clearing houses—or CCPs—in effect, moving the risk off large banks' balance sheets. But moving counterparty risk from banks to CCPs does not eliminate it. It means that risk will instead be shifted from individual banks to new institutions similar to concentrated 'risk nodes' in the financial system. This may work in normal times, but what happens during the next crisis?

Little progress has been made on crisis resolution frameworks for unwinding large banks, let alone huge new institutions called CCPs that would house trillions of dollars in financial derivatives. Thus, the underlying economics of having more 'too-big-to-fail' entities needs to be justified. Financial statements show that each of the large banks active in the OTC derivatives market in recent years carries an average of $100 billion of derivative-related tail risk; that is, the potential cost to the financial system from its collapse after all possible allowable 'netting' has been done within the bank's derivatives book and after subtracting any collateral posted on the contracts. Past research finds that the ten to fifteen largest players in the OTC derivatives market may have about $1.5 trillion in undercollateralized derivatives liabilities, a cost that taxpayers may have to bear unless some solution to the 'too-big-to-fail' question can be proffered.

Housing derivatives in one single global CCP backstopped and regulated by the leading central banks would have been an ideal 'first-best' solution as it would enhance netting, reduce collateral cost, and 'house' overall risk in one place. A 'second-best' solution would have involved a few linked CCPs scattered around the globe. However, local politics has resulted in the least-best outcome. A plethora of CCPs are being created because countries such as Australia and Singapore do not want to lose oversight to an overseas entity incorporated in a foreign country.

The proposals to create these institutions also have several exemptions for key derivative users that dilute the intended objectives of such a move and increase the overall collateral requirements for the financial system because of the fragmentation that will follow in this new CCP world. Even then, the large banks will keep the more complex derivatives on their books. At present, collateral is fungible and the large banks do an excellent job in reusing it.

In a CCP world, a decrease in the reuse of collateral may be significant as there is increasing demand from some derivative clients for 'legally segregating' margin that they will post to CCPs. The MF Global and Peregrine sagas have resulted in increased demand for segregation, so the collateral velocity or reuse within the OTC derivatives market will fall further and may lead to a cottage industry in 'collateral transformation' reminiscent of the mid-2000 securitization in the housing market. The result could be more, not less, moral hazard. In the most extreme scenario, a temporary liquidity short-fall at any of these CCPs would immediately cause systemic disruption. It is likely that central banks, and governments, would have to give whatever support was necessary at taxpayers' expense. In essence, this is a roundabout way for derivatives risk to be picked up by taxpayers.

What should be done instead? A levy on derivative liabilities is a more transparent approach, given that the costs to bail out CCPs will ultimately fall on taxpayers. If the levy is punitive enough, large banks will strive to minimize their derivative liabilities, which could eliminate the systemic risk in the derivatives market should a large bank fail. This proposal addresses the source of the problem—undercollateralization in this market—and does not bury it in technical jargon such as swap execution facilities (SEFs), futures commission merchants (FCMs), direct clearing membership (DCM), derivatives clearing organizations (DCOs), DCE, merchant services providers (MSPs), Legal Entity Identifiers (LEIs), portability, interoperability, non-cleared trades, and extraterritoriality. The levy will force banks to take (and give) collateral with clients when it is due on the derivatives.

Also, some by-products of the levy will be most welcome. First, a fund from levy revenues could be used to bail out banks that prefer to keep OTC derivatives on their books and thus pay the levy. Second, when all derivative users, including sovereigns, post their fair share of collateral, banks will not need to hedge positions where they are in the money but with default risk. Demand for hedging leads to higher CDS spreads that may increase the cost of debt issuance. The CCP proposal that regulators are so enamoured with is a sleight of hand that, instead of resolving the 'too-big-to-fail' problem, deflects it back to taxpayers.[13]

The only residual actor left in the financial system to bridge demand and supply will be the ten or fifteen banks that specialize and span the global pledged cross-border collateral market (although, digital and fintech advances can complement these traditional ten to fifteen 'pipes'). This would entail 'connecting' clients (such as a pension fund) that have good collateral to lend to clients (such as a hedge fund) that do not have good collateral but need to post collateral acceptable to a CCP. In general, central banks, sovereign wealth funds, and long-term asset managers desire collateral that is of low volatility but is not necessarily highly liquid—these entities should be net providers of liquidity in the financial system. On the other side are large hedge funds, mutual funds that have a dramatically shifting need for liquid and good collateral. So, in theory, the two sides should create a 'market'; but you need the banks to 'connect' the two sides and banks cannot do that in vacuum—they need balance-sheet space (on and off) to connect.

In a genuine 'mandatory clearing' world, there would have been no exempted clients and no arbitrage. But we have a bifurcated world now, with a cleared and non-cleared world that exist simultaneously (and also the legacy trades that will remain uncleared as they are not addressed by the new regulations). These are already leading to arbitrage as banks and clients will try to minimize their overall costs of using OTC derivatives—will clear some, may not clear some.

---

[13] Manmohan Singh, 'Taxpayers Should Not Be Made Accountable for CCPs', *Financial Times* (17 October 2012).

Derivatives are not banks—a point often lost in parallel studies, where bank reso-lution plans are supposed to fit CCPs also. Generally speaking, large losses stemming to a bank from its OTC derivative positions—if it leads to a bailout—will typically be picked up by the taxpayer from the jurisdiction in which the bank is located. Thus, derivative losses at a branch of a Canadian bank in London will become a Canadian taxpayer liability if the Canadian branch has to be bailed out. However, moving OTC derivative positions from, say, a Canadian bank to a foreign CCP that is owned/incorp-orated in, say, the United Kingdom, could shift some of the Canadian taxpayer liability related to cleared OTC contracts to a UK taxpayer liability if the United Kingdom had to bail out the CCP.

Looking ahead, if a large CCP is bailed out by taxpayers in the future, would the clearing agenda accept that the economics was not well thought through?

7

What Kind of Thing Is a
Central Counterparty?

The Role of Clearing Houses as a Source of Policy Controversy

Rebecca Lewis and David Murphy

1 Introduction

This chapter considers the related topics of central counterparty (CCP) risks, the mitigation of those risks, the parties who stand to profit from risk-taking in clearing, and CCP governance. These topics are linked through the idea that those responsible for bearing a risk, and those who could profit from taking it, should in equity have some say in how that risk is taken and managed.

In the prototypical for-profit corporation, shareholders support the corporation's risk-taking through their provision of equity capital, which provides both funding and loss absorption. Shareholders, as the beneficiaries of corporate success and bearers of the risk of corporate failure, have a good claim to a significant say over the operations of the corporation.[1] They are, in this model, the corporation's *principals*, and the corporation's governance exists to protect their interests.

CCPs differ in some important ways from this model. The central purpose of a clearing house is to stand between counterparties to cleared transactions, acting as a shock absorber if one of the parties fails. Thus, *taking and mitigating counterparty credit risk* is a core function of a CCP. One key feature in central clearing is the use of a *default waterfall* to manage this counterparty credit risk. Here, any loss created for a CCP by the default of one of its direct or *clearing members* is mitigated first though resources provided by the defaulter, then—if any loss remains—through a layer of CCP capital, then through resources provided collectively by the other clearing members.

Other risks are handled differently in central clearing. *Non-default* risks may either be taken by the CCP's shareholders, allocated to members, or perhaps mitigated by third parties.

CCPs generate profits through charging clearing fees (among other things), and these are often disbursed to shareholders. Clearing houses also create both positive and negative externalities for their clearing members and for the wider financial system.[2] Diverse benefits for financial markets and for individual market participants arise from CCP activities.

CCP loss allocation creates controversy, both over risk-bearing itself, and over which parties should have influence over different aspects of CCP governance in recognition of their risk-bearing. This chapter maps these disagreements, explaining how they arise from different conceptions of the role of CCPs and the identity of its key stakeholders. Different classes of stakeholder have diverse claims to a say over particular aspects of CCP operations and risk-taking. Many of these claims are at

---

[1] Corporations often hedge their risks, for instance through derivatives or insurance. The parties providing these risk transfer contracts often negotiate conditions which bind their counterparties: the terms of an insurance policy are an example of this. Thus, the risk bearer often imposes terms on the risk taker as a condition of the transfer.

[2] The positive externalities include multilateral netting benefits, an increase in confidence caused by the transparent and consistent pricing and margining of positions and by known default management practices, decreased cost of counterparty due diligence, and the increased likelihood of trade continuity despite the default of other clearing members. Negative externalities include the liquidity risk created by margin and the risk of CCP stress leading to losses for its clearing members and, possibly, the wider financial system.

least partially accepted by other classes of stakeholder. As a result, there is no single class of principals of a clearing house whose status justifies their complete control over the operations of the CCP. Rather, as we shall see, CCPs are a type of hybrid entity which balances, often imperfectly, different stakeholder interests in different situations. This balancing lies at the heart of many of the features of modern central clearing and explains the intractable nature of the key policy conflicts in it.

The remainder of the chapter is structured as follows. Our central claim is that disagreement about the nature of CCPs lies at the heart of many important conflicts in contemporary CCP policy, so section 2 presents three candidate models of the role of a clearing house. Whose interests an entity should serve—the entity's principals—and how these interests should be protected are two key questions that motivate and shape the governance of an entity. Section 3 discusses the governance approaches commonly found in each of our three models in order to throw light on these questions.

Section 4 turns to the risks in central clearing and who bears them, introducing the various stakeholders in CCP operations and the European Union (EU) regulatory requirements for CCP robustness.[3] Section 5 outlines the claim that each class of stakeholder has to a say in CCP governance, based on the risks they face, while section 6 discusses both key regulatory requirements for CCPs' treatment of stakeholders and CCP practice in this area.

The claims of different classes of stakeholder are irreconcilable: they cannot be simultaneously satisfied. As a result, disagreement arises. Section 7 sets out five important examples of stakeholder conflicts in contemporary CCP policy. Sections 8 and 9 synthesize what has come before, looking first at the evidence for each candidate model of the CCP from practice and from regulatory requirements and then at the consequences of taking each model seriously. The failure of any of the models to satisfactorily explain the main features of clearing houses suggests a synthesis whereby CCPs should be viewed as examples of stakeholder governance. Section 10 concludes with a summary and consideration of the implications of this proposal.

2 Potential Roles for Clearing Houses

Various accounts of central clearing present three stylized models for the CCP, each capturing key aspects of their nature.[4] None perfectly captures what a

---

[3] EU regulation is used as a baseline both because the EU is an important jurisdiction and because UK regulation after Brexit is based on it. See, however, the (at the time of writing open) consultation by His Majesty's Treasury on 'The Future Regulatory Framework for Central Counterparties and Central Securities Depositories' (updated 20 July 2022), https://www.gov.uk/government/consultations/future-regulatory-framework-review-central-counter parties-and-central-securities-depositories (accessed 23 March 2023).

[4] For a further discussion of the nature of CCPs and potential alternative designs, see F. Cerezetti, J. Cruz Lopez, M. Manning, and D. Murphy, 'Who Pays? Who Gains? Central Counterparty Resource Provision in the Post-Pittsburgh World' (2019) 7(3) Journal of Financial Market Infrastructures 21–44 (Cerezetti et al., 'Who Pays?'), and R. Cox and R. Steigerwald, 'A CCP Is a CCP Is a CCP', Federal Reserve Bank of Chicago, Policy Discussion Paper No. 2017-01 (2017) (Cox and Steigerwald, 'A CCP Is a CCP Is a CCP').

contemporary CCP is, but they are useful edge cases for delimiting its character. These models are:

(1) public *utilities*;
(2) shareholder-owned *for-profit corporations* under *shareholder primacy*; and
(3) member *clubs*.

2.1 CCPs as Utilities

The purpose of a public utility is to meet a general need or needs. Often these are needs that private providers are unlikely to meet in a manner or at a price that is acceptable, given public policy goals. Thus, in many countries, utilities provide essential services such as water, power, or postal services. Utilities are often either government owned, or privately owned but heavily regulated, not only for safety (as is the case for banks, say) but also often for price, non-discriminatory access,[5] and standards of service provision.[6] Utilities are often monopolies for a large part, or all, of their activities.

In the utility model of clearing, a CCP is seen as an essential component of financial markets. The public provision of clearing—or intense regulation of its private provision—is justified by market structure and by CCPs' central role. CCPs are natural monopolies,[7] which may create the potential for the abuse of market power. CCPs also have to be as robust as possible,[8] not least because their use is mandated and because the consequences of their failure would likely be very severe for confidence and financial stability. Finally, CCP actions can affect financial stability for good and ill. All of this recommends a utility model of clearing. The phrase 'CCP as systemic risk manager' has sometimes been used in this context.[9]

2.2 CCPs as For-Profit Corporations

The for-profit model sees a CCP as a financial services provider like most banks, insurance companies, or asset managers. We assume, in this case, that the CCP is owned

---

[5] See Regulation (EU) No. 648/2012 of the European Parliament and of the Council of 4 July 2012 on OTC derivatives, central counterparties and trade repositories (text with EEA relevance), [2012] OJ L201 (27 July 2021), Art. 7 (EMIR) and the EMIR REFIT, as Regulation (EU) No. 2019/834 of the European Parliament and of the Council of 20 May 2019 amending Regulation (EU) No. 648/2012 is known, for access requirements.

[6] See EMIR (n 5), Art. 34 and the EMIR regulatory technical standards, Commission Delegated Regulation (EU) No. 153/2013 of 19 December 2012, OJ L52, Arts 17–21 (EMIR RTS).

[7] See, e.g. F. Chang, 'The Systemic Risk Paradox: Banks and Clearinghouses under Regulation' (2014) 3 Columbia Business Law Review 747–816.

[8] Robustness here means not only low probability of failure but also highly robust service provision. As Baker suggests in C. Baker, 'Incomplete Clearinghouse Mandates' (2019) 56(3) American Business Law Journal 507 (Baker, 'Incomplete Clearinghouse Mandates'), 'the lights at the financial market infrastructures known as clearinghouses must always be on'.

[9] Baker, 'Incomplete Clearinghouse Mandates' (n 8), 507 and P. Tucker, 'Clearing Houses as System Risk Managers', speech at the Depository Trust & Clearing Corporation (DTCC)–Centre for the Study of Financial Innovation (CSFI) Post Trade Fellowship Launch (London, 1 June 2011) (Tucker, 'Clearing Houses as System Risk Managers').

and controlled by shareholders, for their benefit: in other words, for the purposes of this edge case, we assume *shareholder primacy* (discussed further in section 3). In this setting, the purpose of the CCP is to make a profit by providing clearing (and related) services.[10] The clearing house may be regulated, as many other financial institutions are, but this regulation would be aimed at mitigating the externalities of the CCP's failure rather than controlling what it does, who it does it for, and what it charges for its services.

2.3 CCPs as Clubs

Early CCPs (discussed further below in section 4.3) grew up under neither of these models. Rather, they were closer to clubs, set up by a group of financial institutions for their mutual benefit. These prototypical CCPs had membership requirements, rule books to define the behaviour expected from members, and governance committees made up of members. The focus of these CCPs was to serve the needs of members, not on the benefits or costs of clearing for the wider financial system.[11]

3 The Governance of Different Types of Entity

A stylized theory of entity governance is that governance arrangements exist to solve a principal-agent problem.[12] The managers of an entity determine its day-to-day operations. These operations are generally aimed at the interests of some other set of individuals. This separation of control—vested in management—from the right to have the entity governed in one's interests—vested in parties such as shareholders or workers—creates a potential problem. If the interests of the management and the parties with the right to have the entity act on their behalf diverge, the latter should prevail, but the former have control. Hence, the need for governance.

In order to be effective and equitable, the nature of the governance arrangements should reflect the nature of the entity being governed. In this section, we discuss the general issue in more detail, then turn to governance for each of the three stylized models of clearing houses discussed in section 2.

---

[10] A CCP may also be necessary to support other profit-making activities: for instance, nearly all derivatives exchanges have an associated CCP.

[11] An early conflict between the Liverpool cotton brokers and cotton spinners over access and risk management arrangements for futures are a good example of this. The spinners, as end users, wanted access to the exchange. The brokers, who profited from intermediating trades, did not want them to have it. The spinners also supported margin arrangements to reduce leverage and decrease speculation, while the brokers, who were typically poorly capitalized and without easy access to the substantial amounts of cash needed to pay margin, opposed them. The brokers controlled the infrastructure, so they refused to agree to the spinners' demands until the latter threatened to set up a rival exchange. See N. Hall, 'The Liverpool Cotton Market: Britain's First Futures Market' (2000) 149 Transactions of the Historical Society of Lancashire and Cheshire 112–114.

[12] See, e.g. M. Jensen and W. Meckling, 'Theory of the Firm' 1976 3(4) Journal of Financial Economics 305–360 (Jensen and Meckling, 'Theory of the Firm').

3.1 The Entity Governance Problem

There are many reasons to think that the interests of an entity's managers and its principals will, in practice, diverge. Managers may seek to expand the entity for the sake of increasing their personal power, they may seek to maximize their convenience or leisure, or they may simply have personal preferences or values that they seek to satisfy as they run the corporation. Depending on the type of entity and its stakeholders, these interests may stand in contrast to those of other parties. Shareholders, if present, are often thought (at least in the strong form of the anglophone tradition of capitalism) to desire that the entity maximizes profits; in contrast, employees of an entity may be most interested in the entity's stability and longevity, while members of a club may desire the provision of services at the lowest possible cost.

A question therefore arises: how do the parties with the right to have an entity managed in their interests ensure that the actions of an entity's management are, at least broadly, constrained by their wishes? Systems of entity or corporate *governance* exist to do just that.

The key questions for a governance system in this setting are:

(1) For whose interests will the entity operate?
(2) How will those interests be protected?

Different governance regimes suggest different answers to these questions depending on the type of entity concerned.[13] We will examine three different models matching the three edge cases introduced in section 2. These are the governance of utilities, the governance of corporations under shareholder primacy, and the governance of clubs.

3.2 Governing Utilities

As noted in section 2, utilities exist to serve a public purpose where the private market is unable to do so. This purpose provides a framing for the governance arrangements of utilities. A utility could be broadly based, as in the case of a postal service, which exists to directly serve all the residents of a country. Or it could be more narrowly tailored, as in the case of a utility CCP serving a particular financial market and aiming to enhance financial stability and confidence in financial markets.

---

[13] The literature in this area is vast: see, for instance, M. Becht, P. Bolton, and A. Röell, 'Corporate Governance and Control', in G. Constantinides, M. Harris, and R. Stulz (eds), *Handbook of the Economics of Finance* (Amsterdam: Elsevier, 2005); N. Fligstein and J. Choo, 'Law and Corporate Governance' (2005) 1 Annual Review of Law and Social Science (Fligstein and Choo, 'Law and Corporate Governance'); O. Hart, 'Corporate Governance: Some Theory and Implications' (1995) 105(430) The Economic Journal; or A. Shleifer and R. Vishny, 'A Survey of Corporate Governance' (2012) 52(2) Journal of Finance.

The different ways in which the public interest can be construed suggests that the specific ways in which a particular utility is to act in the service of its purpose should be made clear both to the public and to those in charge of operating the utility.[14] This will provide clarity to management: it is also a necessary element in their accountability. Thus, the utility's charter or other founding documents might establish the robust provision of particular services at a uniform cost to all who want them as the central purpose of the utility.

The Organisation for Economic Co-operation and Development's (OECD's) 2021 comprehensive review of national practices regarding the governance of state-owned enterprises proposes several additional mechanisms for ensuring that utility governance is carried out in a manner consistent with the utility's specified public purpose.[15] It suggests that there should be a single state entity tasked with the ownership of a given enterprise and that the entity must have 'the capacity and competencies to effectively carry out its duties'. Utilities can be organized similarly to shareholder-owned corporations: indeed, the OECD suggests the need for a board to act as 'an intermediary between the state as a shareholder, and the company and its executive management'. In this arrangement, ensuring that the board has members with the expertise and competence necessary to govern the enterprise is essential.[16]

3.3 Governing For-Profit Shareholder-Owned Corporations under the Shareholder Primacy Model

One of the most prominent governance models of for-profit shareholder-owned corporations is shareholder primacy. This model has historically been dominant in what we will loosely call the anglophone tradition, although it is also prominent elsewhere. It recognizes shareholders as the corporation's principals and thus requires that corporations be governed in the interests of those shareholders. In the past fifty years, the main interest of shareholders has generally been assumed to be profit maximization.[17] A board of directors protects shareholder interests by overseeing the corporation's executives on behalf of the shareholders. Shareholders elect the members of the board, and board members are subject to legal duties to act to diligently further the shareholders' interests.

A good example can be found in Delaware, the most prominent corporate law jurisdiction in the United States. Delaware corporate law requires that 'within the limits

---

[14] For a discussion, see V. Baumfield, 'The Governance of Monopolistic Government-Owned Businesses Supplying Necessary Goods: Lessons from Stakeholder Theory' (2016), p. 27, https://www.business.unsw.edu.au/About-Site/Schools-Site/Taxation-Business-Law-Site/Documents/V-Baumfield-CLTA-2016-The-Governance-of-Monopolistic-GOBS-and-Stakeholder-Theory-Final.pdf (accessed 23 March 2023).

[15] See Organisation for Economic Co-operation and Development (OECD), 'Ownership and Governance of State-Owned Enterprises: A Compendium of National Practices' (2021), p. 7, https://www.oecd.org/corporate/Ownership-and-Governance-of-State-Owned-Enterprises-A-Compendium-of-National-Practices-2021.pdf (accessed 23 March 2023) (OECD, 'Ownership and Governance').

[16] See OECD, 'Ownership and Governance' (n 15), p. 10.

[17] See, for instance, D. Gordon Smith, 'The Shareholder Primacy Norm' (1998) 23(2) Journal of Corporation Law 277–323.

of their discretion, directors must make stockholder welfare their sole end, and [...] other interests may be taken into consideration only as a means of promoting stockholder welfare'.[18]

A shareholder-primacy approach has been justified in several ways. Some commentators have treated shareholders as the 'owners' of the corporation.[19] An essential right of ownership is the right to determine what to do with one's property. Others argue that shareholder primacy is the best way to ensure that the company is run as well as possible: the interest upon which the shareholders can agree is to maximize the return on their investment, which means maximizing corporate profits. And, in a well-functioning market economy, maximizing corporate profits will occur when the corporation is run in the manner that most efficiently satisfies the demand from its customers or users.[20] A third justification for shareholder primacy arises from the difficulty of adjudicating between competing interests. This argument holds that if a governance system is to protect shareholder interests at all, they must be protected to the exclusion of other interests because a board of directors is ill placed to judge between competing claims.[21]

3.4 Governing Clubs

A club exists to serve the needs and interests of its members. Thus, the main purpose of the club CCP is to provide clearing for the benefit of clearing members. The benefit here may include facilitating the provision of client clearing and reducing members' exposure to each other. A club's broader impact is incidental to its main purpose, although the provision of member benefits will have various effects on the broader market.

Many of the institutions essential to modern financial markets, such as stock exchanges, began as clubs. Traditionally, a club's members exercise control over its operations through voting rights granted to each member. For example, when they operated as mutualized clubs, exchanges would give a 'seat' to each member: 'a seat entitled the

---

[18] See L. Strine, 'The Dangers of Denial: The Need for a Clear-Eyed Understanding of the Power and Accountability Structure Established by the Delaware General Corporation Law' (2015) 50 Wake Forest Law Review 761, 769. There is, of course, the question of whether stockholder welfare should be identified with profit maximization.

[19] See Jensen and Meckling, 'Theory of the Firm' (n 12), 312, but cf. L. Stout, 'The Shareholder Value Myth', Cornell Law Faculty Publications, Paper 771 (2013), p. 3, https://scholarship.law.cornell.edu/cgi/viewcontent.cgi?referer=&httpsredir=1&article=2311&context=facpub (accessed 23 March 2023) (arguing that 'corporations are legal entities that own themselves [...] What shareholders own are shares, a type of contract between the shareholder and the legal entity that gives shareholders limited legal rights').

[20] The 'intellectual foundation for the "shareholder value" revolution', as Hart and Zingales call it, was provided by Milton Friedman in a 1970 essay: see M. Friedman, 'The Social Responsibility of Business Is to Increase Its Profits', New York Times Magazine, The New York Times, September 13, 1970, Section SM, p. 17 1970 and O. Hart and L. Zingales, 'Companies Should Maximize Shareholder Welfare Not Market Value' (2017) 2 Journal of Law, Finance, and Accounting 247–274.

[21] See F. Brandt and K. Georgiou, 'Shareholders vs Stakeholders Capitalism' (2016) 27 Comparative Corporate Governance and Financial Regulation 36–37 (Brandt and Georgiou, 'Shareholders vs Stakeholders Capitalism').

owner to trade on the floor of the exchange [...] and each seat holder had an equal vote on the exchange's affairs'.[22]

Given the voting power assigned to members, clubs maintain conditions for entry that ensure that only candidates whose interests and standing are thought to be consistent with the interests of the existing members are allowed to join.[23] As previously noted, expectations of member behaviour consistent with the joint interest are often codified in club rule books. Clubs also often maintain disciplinary mechanisms to incentivize members to adhere to these rules.[24]

3.5 Approaching Governance at CCPs

As discussed above, a model of entity governance seeks to provide fair and broadly acceptable answers to two difficult questions:

(1) In whose interests will an entity operate?
(2) How will those interests be protected?

It is difficult to provide solutions to these problems in the context of a generic class of entity, as the governance literature and this section's brief discussions demonstrate. The unique nature of CCPs and their central position in the financial system makes agreeing upon answers for CCPs even more delicate: CCP governance is controversial. In order to map this controversy and the possible responses to it, we must first address the structure of CCPs, their stakeholders, and the risks borne by those stakeholders, so we turn to these questions next.

4. CCP Risks and Their Mitigation

There is a simple account of the parties responsible for bearing risks in each of the three edge cases discussed in sections 2 and 3. In a utility, the state is responsible. In a for-profit corporation, shareholders are. In a club, the members are. For a CCP, the situation is more complicated. Clearing houses have a variety of different techniques for mitigating the impact of different risks. As a result, different parties will suffer losses depending on how the loss arises and how big it is. Together, these different techniques should be comprehensive,[25] but they form something of a bricolage, with no single

---

[22] See J. Elliott, 'Demutualization of Securities Exchanges: A Regulatory Perspective', IMF Working Paper (2002), p. 4, https://www.imf.org/external/pubs/ft/wp/2002/wp02119.pdf (accessed 23 March 2023) (Elliott, 'Demutualization').

[23] See Elliott, 'Demutualization' (n 22), 4.

[24] See R. Cranston, 'Law in Practice: London and Liverpool Commodity Markets c.1820–1975', London School of Economics Law, Society and Economy Working Papers 14 (2007), pp. 5–8 (Cranston, 'Law in Practice'), for examples in the early history of clearing.

[25] The CCP Recovery and Resolution Regulation, Regulation (EU) No. 2021/23 of 16 December 2020, OJ L 22, Art. 9 (CCPR&R) requires that CCPs have a recovery plan which details the 'measures to be taken in the case

ultimate risk-taker. Moreover, approaches differ from CCP to CCP.[26] In this section, this patchwork is examined. We consider the risks created by central clearing and the parties who suffer losses if they crystallize.

4.1 The Risks in Central Clearing

The central purpose of a clearing house is to stand between counterparties to cleared transactions, acting as a shock absorber if one of the parties fails. Thus, as noted in section 1, taking and mitigating counterparty credit risk is a core function of a CCP.[27] This means that CCPs must have highly robust arrangements for absorbing any losses that might arise from the default of one of their clearing members.

Other risks naturally arise in the course of central clearing. The relationships between a CCP and its clearing members are defined contractually, largely through the CCP's rulebook. CCPs take margin, either in the form of securities or cash. Securities are typically held by *custodians*, and cash is invested. CCPs also make and take payments relating to cleared contracts and margin, among other things, and they generally use settlement banks for these activities. These activities are also governed by contractual arrangements. It is vital that all of these contractual arrangements are robust and enforceable.[28] Thus, *legal risk* is central to CCP operations.

CCPs make many payments: there are cashflows on cleared contracts, on margin, and on CCP investments. Default management may involve significant cash movements as the defaulter's portfolio is liquidated. For all these reasons, central clearing involves *liquidity risk*: CCPs need to have sufficient cash to make both expected and unexpected payments as they come due.

The successful operation of a clearing house is a highly active operation: the cleared portfolios of the most active CCP users change often; margin moves at least every day on most cleared accounts, and often more frequently; cash margin is invested. In addition, default management can involve a great deal of activity on a very compressed timetable. All of these activities generate *operational risk*.

---

of both default and non-default events and combinations of both, in order to restore their financial soundness, without any extraordinary public financial support'. These measures must 'comprehensively and effectively address all the risks identified in the different scenarios'.

[26] Notably over which non-default losses are allocated, and how, as discussed further below.

[27] For a detailed description of CCPs, their place in the financial system, and their regulation see D. Murphy, *Derivatives Regulation: Rules and Reasoning from Lehman to Covid* (Oxford: Oxford University Press, 2022).

[28] The key regulatory source is the Principles for Financial Market Infrastructures (PFMI), Board of the International Organization of Securities Commissions, Principles for Financial Market Infrastructures (2012). Legal risk is addressed in Principle 1. For an account of the legal risks in central clearing under English law, see J. Braithwaite and D. Murphy, 'Central Counterparties and the Law of Default Management' (2017) 17(2) Journal of Corporate Law Studies 291–325 (Braithwaite and Murphy, 'Central Counterparties').

Finally, many CCPs are businesses. As such, they generate *business risk*. A CCP can fail slowly by failing to gain or losing the confidence of current and potential clearing members, or simply by not charging enough for its services to cover its costs.

The subsections 4.2–4.4 explore the mitigation of these risks in more detail: sections 4.2 and 4.3 focus on the mitigation of counterparty credit risk, while 4.4 considers other risks CCPs face. In each case, the minimum regulatory standards for risk mitigation are also discussed.[29]

4.2 The Default Waterfall

Any loss due to the default of a clearing member crystallizes during the CCP's default management process.[30] For our purposes, we assume that the size of the loss (if any) after a default is known and discuss how it is absorbed. CCPs have a series of resources which are used sequentially for this. Collectively, they are known as the CCPs' *default waterfall.*

An important element of the waterfall is a fund of mutualized resources provided jointly by clearing members. This is known as the *default fund*. The typical structure of the default waterfall is:

- first, margin provided by the defaulter is used;
- then the defaulter's default fund contribution;
- then a tranche of capital contributed by the CCP[31] known as its *skin in the game*;
- finally, the rest of the default fund is available.

There may be additional loss absorption available too. For instance, some CCPs have a second layer of skin in the game at this point, and many have the right to call for additional default fund contributions from clearing members if the default fund is depleted.[32] CCPs may also have the right to reduce variation margin payments if default losses are sufficiently large.

---

[29] The key sources in European regulation are the regulation known as EMIR (n 5) and the EMIR regulatory technical standards (EMIR RTS (n 6)). Regulators review CCP compliance with the relevant regulations through various means including on-site visits, analysis of CCP returns and reporting, and market intelligence: see EMIR (n 5), Art. 21.

[30] See Braithwaite and Murphy, 'Central Counterparties' (n 28) for more details of CCP default management.

[31] CCPs are required to have minimum amounts of capital: these are defined in EMIR (n 5), Art. 16 and elaborated in Commission Delegated Regulation (EU) No. 152/2013 of 19 December 2012. This minimum capital is set as six months' gross operational expenses plus various other elements for operational, legal, business, and other risks, which are, for large CCPs, usually small.

[32] The CCPR&R (n 25) requires that CCPs 'should use a portion of its pre-funded dedicated own resources' as a recovery measure before 'resorting to other recovery measures requiring financial contributions from clearing members' and that these should 'not be lower than 10% nor higher than 25%' of the capital required by EMIR (n 5), Art. 16. See also EMIR (n 5), Art. 43 for regulatory requirements on other CCP financial resources and J.-H. Binder, 'Central Counterparties' Insolvency and Resolution—the New EU Regulation on CCP Recovery and Resolution', European Banking Institute Working Paper No. 82 (2021) for a further discussion. See also Chapter 12 ('Recovery and Resolution of CCPs' by Victor de Serière) in this volume.

4.3 The Size and Source of Contributions to the Default Waterfall

In order to understand stakeholders' relative contributions to loss absorption in the default waterfall, it is necessary to consider how the various elements are sized.

Variation margin is called each day—and sometimes intra-day—based on the current mark-to-market value of each cleared account.

Initial margin, or 'IM', is calculated using a *margin model*. This model is based on the idea that, in a default, a cleared portfolio will be liquidated over a fixed period known as the *margin period of risk* or 'MPOR'. Over this period, the potential changes in value of a given portfolio form a distribution: typically, relatively small changes in value are relatively likely and larger ones are less likely. The shape of this distribution depends on the risk factors the portfolio is exposed to, their volatility, and how they move together. A margin model typically estimates IM for a cleared portfolio as its potential fall in value over an MPOR to some degree of confidence.

Thus, a margin model might, for instance, *target* the ninety-ninth percentile of potential falls in value over a five-day MPOR. This would aim to ensure that initial margin is sufficient to absorb the loss on liquidating the portfolio over five days 99% of the time. Regulation constrains the choices here, setting minimum standards for IM model targets and MPORs.[33] It also requires that margin models are independently validated, regularly tested, and annually recalibrated.[34]

Skin in the game is a layer of resources provided by the CCP. In most clearing houses, it is small compared to both total IM and the default fund, and European regulation does not require it to be larger;[35] but it does require that it is used before non-defaulters' default fund contributions.[36]

CCP skin in the game provides an incentive for CCPs to ensure that initial margin (together with the—usually much smaller—defaulter's default fund contribution) is sufficient to cover to nearly all default losses, even absent regulatory requirements. Clearing members are incentivized to prefer CCPs whose margin models are prudent, too, as they are responsible for managing client defaults, and margin is typically the main resource they have available to absorb any losses created by the failure of a client to perform.[37] Thus, there are incentives for various parties to ensure that the resources

---

[33] EMIR (n 5), Art. 41 requires that initial margin 'shall also be sufficient to cover losses that result from at least 99% of the exposure movements'. The EMIR RTS (n 6) in Art. 24 adds additional requirements, setting the target at 99% for financial instruments other than OTC derivatives and 99.5% for OTC derivatives, and, in Art. 26, setting the minimum MPOR at five business days for OTC derivatives and two business days for other financial instruments. This 'two business day' standard was reduced to one day for client accounts in 2016: see European Securities Markets Authority (ESMA), 'Review of Article 26 of RTS No. 153/2013 with Respect to MPOR for Client Accounts' (2016).

[34] See EMIR RTS (n 6) Arts 24–28, 47–52, and 59–60 for more on regulatory requirements for CCP models and model testing and validation.

[35] See EMIR RTS (n 6), Art. 35, which sets it at 25% of the CCPs' minimum capital.

[36] See EMIR (n 5), Art. 45(4).

[37] Clearing members can impose higher margin on client accounts than CCPs require, but there is significant commercial pressure not to do so.

provided by the defaulter are sufficient to absorb most losses caused by counterparty default.

The default fund is sized based on the observation that the losses in excess of the target percentile of margin are possible and could, for some portfolios in some situations, be large. Thus, CCPs *stress test* cleared portfolios, examining the loss in excess of IM under various scenarios of *extreme but plausible* market events. Both historical and hypothetical scenarios must be included.[38] These losses are then aggregated to determine the loss caused by the default of a clearing member in the worst 'extreme but plausible' scenario.[39]

The default fund is sized to ensure that total financial resources are sufficient to *cover* the potential loss caused by default of the two largest clearing members in the worst extreme-but-plausible scenario.[40] For large CCPs, this typically results in a default fund that is substantially smaller than the total amount of initial margin held but still large in absolute terms.[41]

All clearing members jointly contribute to the default fund. Once its total size has been established by the stress testing process discussed above,[42] member contributions are calculated. This is usually based on risk so that a clearing member's contribution to the default fund might be the same fraction of the total fund that its initial margin is to the total IM.

Central clearing grew up over an extended period of time. For example, something recognizable as a CCP was present in both Chicago and Liverpool commodity markets in the late nineteenth century, and these early clearing houses, and others, have continued to improve their arrangements and adapt to market developments regularly since then.[43] The default waterfall described above is a result of these evolutionary developments: margin limits the leverage that market participants can take on and ensures that a participant is the first to bear any loss that arises from its own non-performance. However, it is inefficient to provide sufficient resources to protect the CCP through margin alone, and it is helpful to have an incentive for CCPs to design robust margin arrangements and for clearing members to contribute towards CCP governance and risk management. Skin in the game and the default fund arose to provide these incentives.

---

[38] EMIR RTS (n 6), Art. 30 requires 'a range of historical scenarios, including periods of extreme market movements observed over the past 30 years, or as long as reliable data have been available, that would have exposed the CCP to greatest financial risk' and 'a range of potential future scenarios [...] drawing on both quantitative and qualitative assessments of potential market conditions'.

[39] House and client accounts are aggregated: losses on client accounts in a given scenario can be offset by gains on the house account but not vice versa.

[40] See EMIR RTS (n 6), Art. 53: this requires that the CCPs' initial margin, skin-in-the-game, and default fund are 'sufficient to cover the default of at least the two clearing members to which it has the largest exposures under extreme but plausible market conditions'.

[41] Details on CCPs' financial resource levels can be found in the disclosures mandated by regulators discussed further below.

[42] This process is carried out regularly to ensure that the default fund remains adequate for current risk levels in cleared portfolios: monthly review is commonplace. See EMIR (n 5), Art. 42 and EMIR RTS (n 6), Arts 29–31 for further details of regulatory requirements for CCP default funds.

[43] For more on the history of clearing houses, see J. Moser, 'Origins of the Modern Exchange Clearinghouse: A History of Early Clearing', Federal Reserve Bank of Chicago Working Paper WP-94-3 (1994), pp. 38–46; Cranston, 'Law in Practice' (n 24), pp. 15–26.

Table 7.1 Key funded elements of the default waterfall

Resource	Provided by:	Sized to:	Approximate size for a large European derivatives CCP
Margin	Defaulter on each cleared account	Mark-to-market (VM) Initial margin model (IM)	€10–200 billion
Skin-in-the-game	CCP	Operating expenses	€20–120 million
Default fund	Clearing members	Cover largest two stressed losses over IM	€1–10 billion

Source: authors.

The incentive created by the default fund[44] is sharpened by default fund *juniorization*. This is an approach, codified in the CCP's rule book, where the default fund contributions of clearing members who do not provide good bids in a default management auction are used before those of clearing members who do bid well. It is a common, but not mandatory, feature of clearing.

Table 7.1 summarizes these layers of funded resources in the default waterfall. The size estimates in the table make it clear that large derivatives CCPs have very substantial amounts of resources available to absorb any losses caused by clearing member default. It is important—and difficult—to determine whether a CCP has sufficient resources, not least because there have been episodes of CCP stress in the past where the resources available proved inadequate for the situation.[45] A key element of a sufficiency analysis is to determine whether a given default waterfall is deep enough to cover the loss that might plausibly arise on the liquidation of any collection of cleared portfolios associated with two defaulting clearing members.[46]

4.4 Margin Models under Stress: The Case of Einar Aas

A particular challenge in the design of margin models comes from large or *concentrated* positions.[47] Liquidating concentrated positions will probably move the market, but the extent of this movement is difficult to estimate as it depends on the extent to which

---

[44] The incentives created by the default waterfall are discussed in A. Capponi, W. Cheng, and J. Sethuraman, 'Incentives Behind Clearinghouse Default Waterfalls' (2017) and R. Lewis and J. McPartland, 'The Goldilocks Problem: How to Get Incentives and Default Waterfalls "Just Right"' (2017) 1 Federal Reserve Bank of Chicago Economic Perspectives 5–7.

[45] See R. Cox, D. Murphy, and E. Budding, 'Central Counterparties in Crisis: the International Commodities Clearing House, the New Zealand Futures and Options Exchange and the Stephen Francis Affair' (2016) 4(3) Journal of Financial Market Infrastructure 65–92;R. Cox, 'Central Counterparties in Crisis: The Hong Kong Futures Exchange in the Crash of 1987' (2015) 4(2) Journal of Financial Market Infrastructures 73–98 for two of these episodes.

[46] 'Two' because the minimum standard is 'cover 2' and 'collection' because the assumption is that both house and client-cleared portfolios are liquidated.

[47] Such positions have been central to a number of episodes of CCP stress, such as the one described in Cox et al. 'Central Counterparties in Crisis' (n 45) as well as the Aas default, so this additional margin is important.

market participants will provide bids close to market values for large portfolios cleared by defaulters. CCPs often charge additional or *concentration* margin for this class of position to address this risk, sometimes by polling their members on the extra compensation they would require to take on a large position.

A recent episode of CCP stress provides some useful insights into the design of margin models, their safe operation, incentives for robust CCP risk management, and the problems created by concentrated cleared positions. This was the default of Einar Aas at the National Association of Securities Dealers Automated Quotations (NASDAQ) Clearing in 2018.

Einar Aas was an individual trader who had been very successful in the European energy and energy derivatives markets. His net worth in 2018 exceeded €1 billion, and he was one of Norway's largest individual taxpayers in that year. Aas was a self-clearing member of the commodity clearing service at NASDAQ Clearing Aktiebolag, a Swedish CCP which was part of the NASDAQ, Inc. group. In September 2018, he had a large position which depended, in large part, on the difference, or spread, between the price of German power futures and Norwegian ones.

German power at that time was largely fossil-fuel generated, and hence its price depended on the price of carbon credits. Norwegian power was largely hydroelectric. This meant that power prices fell after heavy rain. In a short period in the autumn of 2018, European carbon credit prices rose, and it rained at lot in Norway. This caused a large move in the spread between German and Norwegian power futures, which caused substantial losses for Mr Aas.

NASDAQ Clearing issued a margin call, which the trader was unable to meet. He was declared in default on the morning of 11 September 2018. The CCP began to default manage the position, holding an auction which hedged most of the risk in the position on 12 September. This resulted in a loss that exceeded the margin available on the position by €114 million. The skin in the game available was €7 million, so there was a loss to the default fund of €107 million, out of a total of €166 million available. The CCP called for additional default fund contributions from clearing members to replenish the default fund, and the CCP's parent injected additional capital into the CCP.

This episode caused significant disquiet amongst many clearing members and the wider community of stakeholders. Among the concerns raised immediately after the event and subsequently, as more information became available, were ones concerning the design and operation of the CCP's margin model, the selection of default fund sizing scenarios, and the size of the CCP's skin in the game.

For our purpose here, considering the sizing of CCP financial resources, this raises three issues: first, how to margin a position like Aas's; second, how to handle the residual risks after margin; and third, whether the relatively small skin in the game of €7 million was sufficient incentive for the CCP to arrange its affairs prudently. We consider the first two issues below and the third in section 7.1.

Criticism has been levelled at NASDAQ's margin model for, amongst other things, failing to impose concentration margin on Aas's position, despite it being large enough that it proved difficult to successfully auction, and failing to account for the possibility

that Norwegian and German power prices would move significantly in opposite directions at the same time. The reason this is important is that spread positions such as Aas's
can have a relatively low margin requirement if the probability of a large move in the
spread is estimated by the model to be beyond its target—but the loss, should this situation materialize, can be very high. Essentially, the tails of the return distribution for a
spread position are very fat. The question then arises whether ignoring all of the risk
beyond the target percentile of margin is prudent.

It is generally accepted among CCP risk professionals that if plausible and material
market risk is not handled in the margin model, then it should be handled in default
fund sizing scenarios. NASDAQ's scenarios did not include a scenario examining
decoupling of the German and Norwegian power markets to the extent experienced in
September 2018, and Aas's portfolio was not one of the ones which determined 'cover
2'. There was thus a meaningful market risk which was not captured in either margin or
the default fund.[48]

4.5 Non-default Losses and Their Mitigation

There is a linear order of loss absorption for default risk: first, margin; then skin in the
game; then the default fund. For *non-default losses*, the situation is more complex. The
resources used to mitigate non-default losses depends on their nature[49] and the contractual arrangements in place.

There are three main approaches:

- losses can be allocated to clearing members; or
- they can be absorbed by third parties under risk-transfer contracts such as insurance; or
- if nothing else is in place, they are absorbed by CCP capital.

In order to understand the rationale behind loss allocation, it is helpful to consider
how certain risks arise at the CCP. An important example is *investment risk*. This arises
through the payment of cash margin. CCPs typically take both cash and securities as
margin.[50] They typically pay (or, if the rate is negative, receive) interest on the former to
the poster. For initial margin, this interest is generated by an *investment strategy*. This
strategy requires that cash margin is invested: the CCP's *treasury* is responsible for this.

---

[48] For further details into NASDAQ Clearing's management of the Aas default and the events around it, see the
warning and administrative fine issued by their regulator, Finansinspektionen, in 2021.

[49] Our discussion previously has assumed that a loss can be unambiguously classified as a default or non-default
loss. This may not be true, especially if a defaulter has a number of relationships with the CCP such as clearing
member and settlement bank and investment counterparty. The situation becomes even more complex when distinctions are introduced between different classes of non-default loss.

[50] See R. Anderson and K. Karin Jõeveer, 'The Economics of Collateral', Financial Market Group Discussion
Papers No. 732, London School of Economics (2014).

The intent is typically that these investments should be very safe, so common choices are posting the cash at a central bank, buying government bonds, or investing in the government bond repo market.[51]

Three main risks arise in this process: the risk of loss due to a default on an investment; the risk of loss due to failure of repo counterparty; and the risk of loss caused by duration mismatch, so that cash is not available when required at the anticipated cost.[52] Finally, there are risks which arise both for margin posted in the form of securities and cash invested in securities: that of the failure of a custodian or sub-custodian, or of a deposit-taking bank involved in CCP payment flows.[53]

CCPs often argue that these risks arise due to clearing member or client choices: these parties decide on the form of margin, subject to the constraints of the CCP rule book; they participate in CCP risk governance (as described further below), and thus oversee the CCP's investment strategy; and they choose, or at least have a say in, the choice of custodian. Thus, supporters of non-default loss allocation suggest, it is reasonable for any losses that arise in the investment of margin to be shared by clearing members as financial responsibility for a loss 'should be shared among the parties whose decisions contributed to the loss'.[54] CCPs' rules differ on the details of loss allocation, with a common strategy being the requirement that, if there is a meaningful treasury loss, clearing members promptly compensate the CCP for their share of this loss after some initial deductible.[55]

Clearing members of some CCPs have (sometimes reluctantly) accepted allocation of some non-default risks that they have some control over. They are, however, unwilling to accept allocation of all of the risks of clearing, especially when the CCP has shareholders who profit from clearing.[56]

CCPs can transfer losses to third parties by the same means as any other entity: they can purchase insurance[57] or issue securities which can be written down if a pre-specified

---

[51] EMIR RTS (n 6), Art. 45 requires that 95% of CCPs' cash investments are secured. See EMIR (n 5), Art. 47 and EMIR RTS (n 6), Arts 43–45 for further rules relating to CCP investments.

[52] EMIR (n 5), Art. 44 addresses CCP liquidity risk, requiring that CCPs 'at all times have access to adequate liquidity to perform its services and activities'. See also EMIR RTS (n 6), Arts 32–34.

[53] These flows can arise from cleared contracts, from margin, from CCP investment activity, and/or from other forms of clearing house activity.

[54] This principle is articulated in R. Lewis and J. McPartland, 'Non-Default Loss Allocation at CCPs', Federal Reserve Bank of Chicago Working Paper PDP 2017-02 (2017), p. 1.

[55] For an example, see General Regulations of London Clearing House (LCH) Limited (October 2021), Regulation 46A. Here, the deductible, analogous to skin in the game in the default waterfall, is €15 million, and clearing members are allocated a pro rata share of any 'Solvency Threatening Treasury Default Loss', which must be paid within one hour. The pro rata allocation is determined by the clearing member's share of total initial margin. Relatedly, CCPs often disclaim liability for third-party custodial and banking risk. For an argument in support of this practice, see World Federation of Exchanges (WFE), *Guidance on Non-Default Loss* (WFE, 2020).

[56] See Futures Industry Association (FIA) and International Swaps and Derivatives Association (ISDA), *CCP Non-Default Losses* (FIA/ISDA, 2021) for a summary of clearing member objections to comprehensive allocation of CCP non-default losses.

[57] Insurance has also been used as a layer in CCP default waterfalls in the past. It was, for instance, present in the CCP involved in the Stephen Francis affair described in Cox et al. 'Central Counterparties in Crisis' (n 45), 67. It has fallen out of use for this purpose since the PFMIs were issued as these standards require that risk out to 'extreme but plausible' default losses is covered by funded resources.

risk crystalizes.[58] This gives them a range of techniques to hedge risks which they do not wish to bear and cannot allocate to members.

Finally, there are risks which are difficult or expensive to transfer to members or third parties and, hence, which are usually born by the CCP. These typically include legal, cyber-, and general business risk. Here, CCP equity is often the only loss absorbing resource.

5 Stakeholder Rights in the Governance of CCPs

CCPs' propensity to allocate losses away from their shareholders generates controversy over who should bear which risks and how much control risk bearers should have over the CCP as a consequence of their provision of loss absorption.[59] Therefore, determining the appropriate governance structure for a CCP requires understanding not only what sort of entity a CCP is, as discussed in sections 2 and 3, but also what risks surround a CCP and who bears those risks, as discussed in section 4.

Risk-taking, together with the clearing mandate,[60] gives four parties a strong claim to some say in CCP governance: shareholders, clearing members, clients, and regulators. The interests of these four parties cannot be fully reconciled, requiring some means of balancing or ranking their interests.[61] Understanding how to do so equitably requires first understanding what undergirds each group's claim: that is the subject of this section.

5.1 Shareholder Governance Rights

At shareholder-owned entities, shareholders generally have governance rights. This can be justified on both fairness and efficiency grounds. Shareholders are investors in a corporation; their investment is at risk if the corporation is managed poorly. Therefore, in exchange for granting the corporation the use of their capital, the shareholders demand oversight over how that capital is used. In the absence of such oversight power, investors may go elsewhere with their capital; this is particularly likely in the often low-margin business of clearing.[62] Another justification for shareholder rights is

---

[58] There has been continued interest in the possibility of CCPs issuing convertible securities either to absorb non-allocatable, non-default losses or to recapitalize the CCP before resolution, so there may be further developments in this area of CCP loss absorption technology.

[59] See nn. 46–48 for perspectives on non-default loss absorption and section 7.1 below for controversy over the size of CCP skin in the game.

[60] This is the requirement, first articulated by the G20 in their Pittsburgh summit communique in 2009, that all standardized OTC derivative contracts should be cleared through central counterparties, and subsequently implemented in EMIR (n 5), Art. 4.

[61] See P. Saguato, 'Financial Regulation, Corporate Governance, and the Hidden Costs of Clearinghouses' (2021) 82 Ohio State Law Journal 1071–1140 for an alternative discussion of CCP governance and governance policy.

[62] CCP legal entities typically have relatively small returns in absolute terms: over €1B in annual net revenue from clearing would be very unusual. However, they are typically relatively poorly capitalized entities, so their returns on shareholders' funds can be attractive, and clearing is necessary to support other, often more profitable parts of the business of financial market infrastructures, such as running a futures and options exchange. The low

efficiency.[63] This argument suggests that for-profit corporations in capitalist economies are most likely to make a profit when they are serving some societal need. Shareholders, as the parties ultimately entitled to corporate profits, are the parties most likely to demand that the corporation is run in a profit-maximizing manner and, therefore, are the parties that will best ensure that the corporation maximizes social welfare.

This argument can easily be taken too far; there are numerous examples of companies making a profit over long periods of time in a manner inconsistent with broader social welfare.[64] Nevertheless, *if* one accepts that there is some positive relationship between corporate profits and the corporation's contribution to social welfare, then it follows that empowering the group most active in the pursuit of profit can help to secure social benefits as a by-product of their activity.

5.2 Clearing Member Governance Rights

The governance rights of clearing members find their justification in the importance of clearing members to the safe and effective operations of a CCP as well as in the danger of moral hazard. A core function of a CCP is to effectively manage defaults and to ensure that, should a default occur, the CCP's book is rematched at a loss small enough that the defaulter's resources will cover it. As discussed in section 2, clearing members bear the majority of any default loss that exceeds the defaulter's resources. Therefore, if they are given a role in CCP governance, clearing members are incentivized to advocate for policies that reduce the risk of large losses in default.

Moreover, because clearing members bear substantial default risk, only vesting governance rights in shareholders risks excessive risk-taking. Decisions that increase profits but which also increase CCP risk would likely be attractive to shareholders since they would gain all of the potential profits but only face a portion of the potential costs.

The key role clearing members play in meeting public policy goals provides a further justification for assigning governance rights to them. The clearing mandate reflects the belief of policymakers that clearing increases the stability of the financial system. Clearing is only accessible to clients through clearing members. Thus, the ability of smaller parties to access CCPs on fair terms and the ability of a CCP to manage its portfolio during a crisis both depend upon the presence of a number of clearing members willing to take parties on as clients and to bid on the positions of a defaulter. If clearing members must take on significant financial risk and have little control over the

---

absolute return of CCPs, a fact which is often omitted from discussions about the economics of clearing, helps to explain CCP shareholder's reluctance to see higher capital requirements for clearing houses.

[63] As Fligstein and Choo, 'Law and Corporate Governance' (n 13) put it, 'at the heart of the literature on law and corporate governance is the question of whether or not some set of rules promotes economic efficiency more than others'.

[64] Consider, for example, a company that produces a significant amount of pollution. If the company is not charged for the social cost of pollution, as is often the case, it may make significant profits while having a net negative effect on social welfare.

decisions influencing the size and scope of that risk, the willingness of financial inter-mediaries to play that role will diminish.[65]

5.3 Client Governance Rights

The case for granting clients governance rights relies on the difficulty they face in transfer-ring risk without using a CCP. The clearing mandate forces clients to centrally clear rather than trade bilaterally.[66] This, combined with regulatory incentives to clear unmandated transactions,[67] provides a justification for granting clients input into CCPs' governance processes.

In this context, it should be noted that a single CCP often dominates a given asset class, at least in over-the-counter (OTC) derivatives.[68] Therefore, the clearing mandate effect-ively forces clients to clear through a particular CCP, giving that CCP significant market power.[69] Many clients cannot become clearing members themselves, either due to regula-tory constraints or because the cost of becoming a direct member of the CCP is prohibi-tive.[70] The clearing mandate thus forces clients to work with one of the limited number of clearing members at a single CCP, giving those clearing members substantial market power over clients. A governance role for clients, particularly regarding policies that af-fect the costs they face or the market power of clearing members, can help address these imbalances.

5.4 Public Interest and Governance Rights

The public interest in the stability of CCPs arises from their central-by-design role in the financial system. The failure of a systemically important CCP could lead to a finan-cial crisis. Such a crisis would likely have significant negative effects on the broader economy. There is also some risk that taxpayers might incur costs in CCP failure,

---

[65] In fact, there is already significant concentration of clearing activity among a diminishing number of clearing members: see Derivatives Assessment Team (DAT), *Incentives to Centrally Clear Over-the-Counter (OTC) Derivatives* (2018), pp. 21–24, 53–57 (DAT, *Incentives to Centrally Clear Over-the-Counter (OTC) Derivatives*).

[66] EMIR (n 5), Art. 10(3) does exempt the hedging activity of non-financial counterparties from the mandate.

[67] These incentives include capital and margin requirements which preference cleared over bilateral trades: see DAT, *Incentives to Clear Over-the-Counter (OTC) Derivatives* (n 65) for an extensive discussion.

[68] See the Basel Committee on Banking Supervision (BCBS), the Committee on Payments and Market Infrastructure (CPMI), the Financial Stability Board (FSB), and the International Organization of Securities Commissions (IOSCO), *Analysis of Central Clearing Interdependencies* (2018) and DAT, *Incentives to Clear Over-the-Counter Derivatives* (n 65) for a discussion of this and other features of CCP, clearing member, and client-clearing service provider concentration.

[69] In Europe, clients generally have a 'principal-to-principal' relationship with clearing members and do not dir-ectly interact with the CCP: see J. Braithwaite, 'The Dilemma of Client Clearing in the OTC Derivatives Markets' (2016) 17 European Business Organization Law Review 355–378, 364 (Braithwaite, 'Dilemma of Client Clearing'). Nevertheless, a CCP's market power will allow it to dictate terms to clearing members, which will, in turn, affect the terms that clearing members are willing to offer clients.

[70] This is discussed further in Part F of DAT, *Incentives to Clear Over-the-Counter (OTC) Derivatives* (n 65).

either in resolving the CCP or in mitigating the effects of its distress on the wider economy.[71]

An additional public interest arises from the clearing mandate, which enlisted clearing houses as policy tools for ensuring the stability of the broader financial system. Given this public role, and the regulatory bodies that exist to protect it, CCP governance policies must be consistent with the public interest. This does not necessarily mean that regulators should have a direct role in CCP governance but rather that the effect of CCP arrangements on the public interest, as understood by regulators, cannot be ignored.[72]

6 CCP Governance, Disclosure, and Access: Regulatory Requirements and Current Practice

This section summarizes the regulatory requirements relating to CCP governance and public disclosure. It also considers requirements for access to clearing. These topics are important in and of themselves and also because they shed additional light on where to place CCPs between the three possible edge-case roles of clearing houses discussed in section 2.

6.1 The Regulation of CCP Governance

EMIR requires that a CCP 'shall have robust governance arrangements'.[73] It must have a *board* including independent members with 'adequate expertise in financial services, risk management and clearing services'.[74]

A key governance mechanism by which CCP stakeholders influence its operations is the *risk committee*. This committee is composed of representatives of the CCP's clearing members, independent members of the board, and representatives of its clients, with none of these three classes of stakeholder having a majority. Its presence and composition are mandated by regulation, and regulators may request to attend the committee's meetings and be informed of its activities and decisions.[75]

The board is responsible for the CCP. This includes responsibility for risk management, for the availability of sufficient loss absorbing resources, and for stakeholder

---

[71] The CCPR&R (n 25) sets out the aim of resolution as being to '*minimize* the costs of the resolution of a failing CCP borne by the taxpayers' rather than to *eliminate* the risk of any cost being borne by taxpayers. Further, Arts 45–47 contemplate 'government financial stabilisation', 'public equity support', and 'temporary public ownership': the taxpayer is not off the hook and thus has an interest in CCP robustness.

[72] Thus, EMIR (n 5), Art. 49, as amended by EMIR 2.2, requires that when a CCP 'intends to adopt any significant change to its models and parameters [...] it shall apply to the competent authority and ESMA for validation of that change'. This gives regulators in the EU right of veto over significant changes to CCP models or business as incorporating a new product into the CCP's margin model—which is necessary to clear it—often counts as a significant change.

[73] See EMIR (n 5), Art. 26.

[74] See EMIR (n 5), Art. 27.

[75] See EMIR (n 5), Art. 28 and the EMIR RTS (n 6) Art. 3. See also EMIR RTS (n 6), Art. 7 for various requirements on segregation of duties and CCP organizational structure.

disclosure.[76] The role of the risk committee is to 'advise the board on any arrangements that may impact the risk management of the CCP, such as a significant change in its risk model, the default procedures, the criteria for accepting clearing members, the clearing of new classes of instruments, or the outsourcing of functions'.[77] It is therefore the principal mechanism by which stakeholders can influence the CCP's choice of membership criteria, margin model, default fund sizing procedures, and other loss allocation mechanisms.[78]

6.2 CCP Governance in Practice

Current governance practice at CCPs imperfectly reflects a delicate balancing of interests that prioritizes parties based upon the risk they bear in a particular situation. As discussed in section 5.1, shareholder-owned CCPs are generally run by executives who report to a board of directors. In so far as shareholders can vote for board resolutions, including those relating to board composition, they have their financial interests protected. However, decisions at CCPs are not made in the interests of shareholders alone: CCP risk committees provide input into key risk management decisions. This subsection summarizes the risk committee structures at four leading CCPs: ICE Clear Europe, London Clearing House (LCH) Limited, Eurex Clearing, and Chicago Merchant Exchange (CME) Clearing.

At ICE Clear Europe, the clearing house-level risk committees play an 'advisory role to the president' and work to protect the default fund, manage credit and market risk, consider membership applications, and review new cleared products. These risk committees include clearing member representatives, clearing house officers, and a non-executive director of ICE Clear Europe. ICE Clear Europe also maintains a client risk committee with both clearing member and customer representation.[79]

LCH Limited maintains a risk committee composed of independent directors, clearing members, and clients. The committee is tasked with considering and commenting on 'aspects of the Company's risk appetite, tolerance and strategy'.[80]

---

[76] The CPMI–IOSCO Resilience of Central Counterparties (CCPs): Further Guidance on the PFMI (2017), state, in section 2.2.1, that 'The board has ultimate responsibility for establishing a risk-management framework and for the effectiveness of its implementation' and, in section 2.2.8, for 'ensuring that the CCP maintains the required levels of financial resources on an ongoing basis'. Section 2.2.18 requires the board to establish 'a comprehensive disclosure and feedback mechanism for soliciting views from direct participants, indirect participants and other relevant stakeholders to inform the board's decision-making regarding the CCP's risk-management framework'.

[77] While the risk committee's role is advisory, EMIR (n 5), Art. 28 requires that the CCP promptly inform its regulator 'of any decision in which the board decides not to follow the advice of the risk committee'.

[78] Of course, this mechanism only works if stakeholders do actually participate in CCP governance. The burden of so doing can be large: detailed scrutiny of a new CCP initial margin model, for instance, requires substantial expertise. However, given that exposures to large CCPs are amongst some banks' largest, it is appropriate that they carefully scrutinize CCP risk management and financial resources.

[79] ICE Clear Europe, 'Risk Management', https://www.theice.com/clear-europe/risk-management (accessed 23 March 2023).

[80] See LCH Limited, 'Terms of Reference of the Risk Committee of the Board of Directors' (9 September 2020), https://www.lch.com/system/files/media_root/LCH%20Limited%20-%20RiskCo%20ToRs.pdf (accessed 23 March 2023).

Meanwhile, at Eurex Clearing, the risk committee is composed of members of the supervisory board, clearing members, and clients.[81] The Eurex risk committee advises the supervisory board on matters including significant changes to the risk model, changes to default procedures, changes to clearing membership requirements, and the introduction of new cleared products.[82] Finally, at CME Clearing, a board risk committee composed of members of the CME Group board oversees 'the operational risk posed by the Clearing House to CME Group on an enterprise-level basis'. Clearing house risk committees include members of the board as well as representatives from market participants. These committees review and approve changes to the default fund, review substantive changes to membership requirements, and review 'matters that would have a significant impact on the risk profile of the Clearing House'.[83] Thus, while practices across large CCPs differ in detail, they all include a measure of user representation, but none give users a final say in clearing house decision-making.

6.3 CCP Disclosures

Effective governance of a complex organization is very difficult without information. *Disclosures* allow stakeholders (including CCP participants, equity holders, and the wider market) to:

- 'compare different CCPs' risk controls, including their financial condition and financial resources';
- develop an 'understanding of the risks associated' with a particular CCP and with participating in it; and
- understand its systemic importance.

In order to facilitate this, regulators have set standards for CCP public quantitative and qualitative disclosures.[84]

6.4 Access to Clearing

The issue of access to clearing is a nuanced one. On the one hand, it is important that clearing members have the resources and operational capacity to carry out their

---

[81] See Eurex, 'EMIR Risk Committee', https://www.eurex.com/ec-en/find/corporate-overview/emir-risk-committee (accessed 23 March 2023).

[82] See Eurex, 'Statutes for the EMIR Risk Committee' (20 September 2021), https://www.eurex.com/resource/blob/253914/530cc1fc79a7eb3e63db639e50ec7855/data/04_01_statutes_emir-risk-committee_en_2021_09_20.pdf (accessed 23 March 2023).

[83] See Chicago Mercantile Exchange (CME) Group, 'Governance' (16 July 2020), https://www.cmegroup.com/education/articles-and-reports/governance.html# (accessed 23 March 2023).

[84] See CPMI–IOSCO. *Public Quantitative Disclosure Standards for Central Counterparties* (2015) for details. The quotes in the list above come from this document.

functions. But on the other, access to clearing could be used to defend an oligopoly in derivatives trading. European regulation addresses this by allowing clearing houses to establish criteria for clearing members but requiring that they are non-discriminatory, transparent, and objective and that they are 'permitted only to the extent that their objective is to control the risk for the CCP'.[85]

Access to client clearing is also required on fair, reasonable, non-discriminatory, and transparent commercial terms.[86] This helps with access, but it does not address the problem that the fixed costs of client clearing are high, both in terms of fees and the infrastructure required. A substantial number of clients have experienced issues in finding a client-clearing service provider, and those that do clear are often subject to caps on total margin or outstanding notional.[87] Derivatives clearing, in other words, is not provided on the open-access, uniform-cost basis typical of many utilities.

7 Conflicts in Central Clearing

At least four classes of party—shareholders, clearing members, clients, and regulators—have a claim to influence over CCP governance. The interests of these four classes cannot be fully reconciled.[88] This makes it difficult to design a governance system that appropriately and effectively empowers each group. We discuss these challenges further below. Before doing so, it is useful to consider some specific clashes between the different parties as this illustrates the challenge of reconciling the competing interests. We therefore now turn to a discussion of some of the most prominent issues in CCP policy.

This discussion is informed by interviews with a variety of stakeholders carried out by one of the authors in 2020 and 2021.[89] The interviews were anonymized and so participants are cited by their role in the clearing industry and the date of the interview.

---

[85] See EMIR (n 5), Art. 37.

[86] See the EMIR REFIT amendments to EMIR (n 5), Art. 4. These are discussed in J. Braithwaite and D. Murphy, 'Take on Me: OTC Derivatives Client Clearing in the EU', in P. Saguato, and J.-H. Binder (eds), *Financial Market Infrastructure: Law and Regulation* (Oxford: Oxford University Press, 2022), p. 461.

[87] See Part E of DAT, *Incentives to Clear Over-the-Counter (OTC) Derivatives* (n 65), for more details on these issues in client-clearing service provision.

[88] See Cerezetti et al., 'Who Pays?' (n 4) for a further discussion of the conflicts in central clearing and a discussion of how they arise as a result of a lack of clarity over the nature of CCPs.

[89] The first author carried out a series of twenty interviews on CCP governance during her JD studies at Yale Law School. The full methodology and results can be found in Rebecca Lewis, 'Public Purpose at For-Profit Corporations: A CCP Case Study', on file with the first author. Interview subjects included five regulators, seven CCP representatives, four clearing member representatives, two client representatives, two industry lawyers (participating together in a single interview), and one academic. The author conducted seventeen interviews as video conferences and three over the phone. Interviews lasted between thirty and sixty minutes and were semi-structured: each interview began with the same set of topics and a general list of questions but then developed in its own way, depending on the interests and knowledge of each subject.

7.1 Skin in the Game: Shareholders vs Clearing Members

As discussed in section 2, CCP skin in the game sits before the default fund contributions of non-defaulting clearing members in the default waterfall. CCP owners generally seek a lower level of skin in the game as it represents capital that cannot be deployed elsewhere, and it is at risk from defaults. In contrast, clearing members generally seek higher levels of skin in the game—and sometime much higher. They argue that skin in the game provides incentives for for-profit CCPs to prudently manage their business.[90] The Einar Aas incident, discussed in section 4.4, is sometimes used as evidence that current levels of skin in the game have not provided sufficient incentives. Increased skin-in-the-game would also provide a larger buffer above clearing member capital at risk during a default, something that advocates suggest would be more equitable than the current arrangement. This conflict therefore turns on who should bear counterparty credit risk once the defaulter's resources are exhausted and in what quantum.

7.2 The Treatment of CCP Equity in Resolution: Shareholders vs Clearing Members

Resolution powers enable public authorities, subject to legal constraints, to step in if they determine that a CCP is failing or likely to fail. Public intervention can help to ensure that a CCP's critical functions are preserved, while maintaining financial stability. It may also help to avoid the costs associated with the CCP's failure and potential restructuring from falling on taxpayers.

A key issue in resolution is the treatment of CCP equity. Should it absorb losses, as it does in ordinary corporate bankruptcy and in the resolution regime for banks?[91] Clearing members and CCP shareholders disagree over this. Clearing members argue that concentrating losses on market participants and sparing CCP shareholders will result in misaligning incentives and in moral hazard.[92] It is, they suggest, fundamentally unfair for clearing members to backstop the recapitalization of a clearing house when they do not own it. In contrast, CCPs argue that exposing CCP equity to losses

---

[90] For a flavour of the disagreements, see V. Albuquerque and C. Perkins, 'Central Counterparties Need Thicker Skins' (2016) 4 Journal of Financial Market Infrastructures 55–63; D. McLaughlin, 'Skin in the Game' (2018) 7(1) Journal of Financial Market Infrastructures 47–55. Berndsen identifies the size of skin in the game as one of the five fundamental contemporary questions about CCPs: see R. Berndsen, 'Five Fundamental Questions on Central Counterparties' CentER Discussion Paper, Vol. 2020-028 (2020).

[91] See J. Braithwaite and D. Murphy, 'Get the Balance Right: Private Rights and Public Policy in the Post-Crisis Regime for OTC Derivatives' (2017) 12(4) Capital Markets Law Journal 480–509 (Braithwaite and Murphy, 'Get the Balance Right') for a further discussion of this question and Financial Stability Board, *Guidance on Financial Resources to Support CCP Resolution and on the Treatment of CCP Equity in Resolution* (2020) for the authority view. Because the outcome in bankruptcy is a statutory safeguard to arbitrary authority action in resolution, the question of what would happen in a CCP bankruptcy is highly relevant to clearing house resolution.

[92] See, for instance, FIA, Institute of International Finance (IIF) and ISDA, Response to the FSB Consultation Paper 'Financial Resources to Support CCP Resolution and the Treatment of CCP Equity in Resolution' (2020).

in resolution could affect market participants' incentives to actively participate in re-covering the CCP and that resolution should not subvert the CCP's contractual loss allocation provisions.[93] This conflict therefore turns on the allocation of the risks and rewards of operating a CCP.

7.3 Membership Requirements: Shareholders, Clearing Members, Regulators vs Clients, Potential Clearing Members, Regulators

CCPs impose obligations on their clearing members. Some of these requirements are crucial to the CCP's stability: when one clearing member defaults, non-defaulting clearing members are obliged to help rebalance the CCP's book and, if necessary, to contribute resources to cover any shortfall beyond the defaulter's resources and skin in the game. It is important that members have the operational capacity and finan-cial strength to do this. Thus, as previously noted, CCPs set minimum membership standards.

CCP owners and CCP regulators generally will prefer more stringent requirements as these make it more likely that clearing members will perform when required to do so.[94] However, such requirements can also act as barriers to entry that can protect the current members' market share. Market and financial stability regulators may be more concerned with the accessibility of clearing and the dangers of CCP or clearing member concentration.[95] For clients, more competition among clearing members for their business would decrease the ability of clearing members to raise fees or dictate unfavourable terms. These concerns tend to create a preference among some regulators and clients for less stringent requirements that allow for more clearing members to enter the market.[96] The tension is thus between highly robust CCPs and CCPs for, if not all, at least as many as possible.

7.4 The Pursuit of Profit: Shareholders vs Clearing Members

Many CCPs are for-profit corporations. This creates a tension, if not an outright con-flict, between two parties. The shareholders of the CCP generally will want to maxi-mize the CCPs profits. Clearing members want to minimize the chance that instability at the CCP endangers their default fund contributions or otherwise exposes them to risk. Clearing members often argue that the desire to maximize profits can endanger a

---

[93] See, for instance, CCP12, Response to FSB consultative document entitled 'Guidance on Financial Resources to Support CCP Resolution and on the Treatment of CCP Equity in Resolution (2020).

[94] See Braithwaite, 'Dilemma of Client Clearing' (n 69), 362.

[95] For a further discussion, see D. Murphy, 'Too Much, Too Young: Improving the Client Clearing Mandate' (2020) 8(3) Journal of Financial Market Infrastructure 7–15 and N. Alvarez, and J. McPartland 'The Concentration of Cleared Derivatives' (2020) 8(3) Journal of Financial Market Infrastructures 15.

[96] See Braithwaite, 'Dilemma of Client Clearing' (n 69), 362–363.

CCP's stability, for example, by leading the CCP to introduce new products that are ill suited for clearing.[97] CCP owners, in contrast, argue that the long-term profitability of a CCP depends upon its ability to prudently manage risk, and so there is no incentive to pursue profit at the expense of risk management,[98] and that CCPs should be free to innovate. This conflict therefore turns on who should have a say in CCP business strategy.

7.5 The Responsibility for Systemic Liquidity Risk: Shareholders and Clearing Members vs Regulators and Clients

At least once a day, CCPs make margin calls on clearing members. It is essential for the CCP's risk management that clearing members meet these capital calls promptly. However, in times of stress, the size of these calls often increases—requiring clearing members to pay more to the CCP when it is most difficult for them to raise funds, a phenomenon known as the *procyclicality of margin*. This creates a systemic liquidity risk that concerns financial regulators.[99] Some regulators have sought to address procyclicality by mandating that CCPs 'adopt measures to prevent and control possible procyclical effects' of their risk management practices.[100] Such efforts may increase the stability of margin payers in times of systemic stress—but they do so at the expense of the ability of CCPs to fully control the behaviour of their margin models.[101]

Another issue relating to margin is its overall level. Clearing members generally prefer higher IM levels since IM protects their default fund contribution if another clearing member defaults and because margin protects them from the risk of default of their clients. Clients, in contrast, benefit from lower IM levels—IM increases the cost of holding a position, clients do not have any default fund contributions to protect, and the cost of funding margin is typically higher for clients than for clearing members.[102] Therefore, even absent procyclicality, clients and clearing members have different views on the optimal level of CCP margin.

[97] Video interview with clearing house representative (27 October 2020); video interview with clearing member representative (22 October 2020); phone interview with clearing member representative (17 November 2020); phone interview with clearing member representative (20 November 2020).
[98] Video interview with regulator (20 October 2020); video interview with clearing house representative (23 October 2020); video interview with clearing house representative (27 October 2020); phone interview with clearing house representative (30 October 2020); video interview with clearing house representative (6 November 2020); video interview with clearing house representative (17 November 2020); video interview with regulator (23 November 2020); video interview with academic (1 December 2020).
[99] See BCBS, CPMI, and IOSCO, Review of Margining Practices (2021) for a discussion of authority concerns.
[100] See ESMA, 'Guidelines on EMIR Anti-Procyclicality Margin Measures for Central Counterparties', Final Report (2018), p. 3, https://www.esma.europa.eu/sites/default/files/library/esma70-151-1293_final_report_on_guidelines_on_ccp_apc_margin_measures.pdf (accessed 23 March 2023).
[101] CCP margin procyclicality and the trade-offs involved in its mitigation are further discussed in D. Murphy and N. Vause, 'A Cost–Benefit Analysis of Anti-Procyclicality: Analyzing Approaches to Procyclicality Reduction in Central Counterparty Initial Margin Models' (2021) 9(4) Journal of Financial Market Infrastructure 27–50.
[102] See D. Murphy, 'I've Got You under My Skin: Large Central Counterparty Financial Resources and the Incentives They Create' (2017) 5(3) Journal of Financial Market Infrastructures 12–14.

7.6 The Persistence of Stakeholder Conflicts

The conflicts described above are profound and ongoing. For instance, clearing members have argued for higher levels of skin in the game for at least seven years. They continue to raise questions about the effect of the profit motive on the quality of risk management at for-profit CCPs. CCPs, meanwhile, argue that they should be free to allocate losses as they choose, that skin in the game should not be used to absorb default losses, and that higher levels of CCP capital should not be required.[103] These arguments, in turn, are used to advocate for or oppose policy change. Indeed, clearing member advocacy contributed to a December 2020 revision to EU regulations to increase skin-in-the-game requirements.[104] This change, however, did not create a new, stable equilibrium; after the change was announced, a market participant was still calling for skin in the game 'to be calculated using members' default fund contributions as the starting point, rather than existing CCP capital'.[105]

The procyclicality debate also continues. In January 2022, the European Securities Markets Authority (ESMA) launched a consultation to review EMIR's anti-procyclicality requirements, noting that while EU CCPs generally

performed well during the early stages of the COVID-19 crisis, the surge in initial margin has raised questions as to whether some of these increases acted in a procyclical manner, potentially causing, or even, amplifying liquidity stress in other parts of the financial system.[106]

In contrast, CCP representatives maintain the position that a CCP 'cannot do something different from what it's designed to be doing. The design of the CCP is to manage the risk of the clearing members that are directly related to it, not to manage systemic risk'.[107] One CCP representative has described a 'gradual mission creep' in which policymakers 'have tried to recharacterize CCPs' as systemic risk managers, a change that the interviewee characterized as 'extremely unhelpful'.[108]

This conflict stems, in part, from a disagreement about the role of CCPs. If clearing houses are utility-like systemic risk managers, it is evident that they should not create

---

[103] See, e.g. A. Kristofersson, 'These Are Both Sides in the CCP "Skin" Controversy', PostTrade360 (9 April 2021), https://posttrade360.com/news/infrastructure/these-are-both-sides-in-the-ccp-skin-controversy (accessed 23 March 2023); J. Reeves, 'FCMs, CCPs Debate "Skin in the Game" and Consolidation Concerns' (30 October 2019), https://www.fia.org/marketvoice/articles/fcms-ccps-debate-skin-game-and-consolidation-concerns (accessed 23 March 2023).

[104] See CCPR&R (n 35, Art. 9(14).

[105] See S. Wilkes, 'EU Hands CCP Members a Narrow Win on Skin in the Game' (19 August 2020), https://www.risk.net/regulation/7663321/eu-hands-ccp-members-a-narrow-win-on-skin-in-the-game (accessed 23 March 2023).

[106] See ESMA, 'Review of RTS No 153/2013 with Respect to Procyclicality of Margin', Consultation Paper (2022).

[107] Video interview with clearing member representative (22 October 2020); video interview with clearing house representative (6 November 2020).

[108] Video interview with clearing house representative (17 November 2020). Cf. Tucker, 'Clearing Houses as System Risk Managers' (n 9), p. 2.

burdensome liquidity drawdowns and thus should mutualize more default risk in stressed conditions. But clearing members are profoundly opposed to this solution: a CCP-as-clearing-member club would be highly unlikely to act this way.

These ongoing debates illustrate that, while the stakeholders negotiate their conflicts within the existing governance and regulatory framework, the status quo remains contested. A compromise satisfactory to most stakeholders is unlikely, and so disagreements are likely to persist.

8 The Roles of Clearing Houses

We have seen that a number of stakeholders, including clearing members, clients, market participants, and various types of regulator, have strong claims to a right to have their interests taken into account in CCP decision-making. These claims provide some evidence in support of each stylized model of CCP introduced in section 2, albeit that none are conclusive.

8.1 Evidence from the Purposes of CCPs

Modern CCPs serve a public policy purpose: clearing some products is mandatory. Partly as a result, some CCPs are systemically important to the financial system and, therefore, to the broader economy, and elements of the CCP regulatory framework reflect this. These features weigh in favour of the utility model of the CCP.

8.2 Evidence from CCP Governance, Disclosure, and Access Requirements

The regulation of CCP governance discussed in section 6 does not unequivocally support any of the 'edge-case' models of clearing.[109] The requirement to include a range of stakeholders in governance suggests that CCPs should not be thought of as pure for-profit corporations, but the ultimate responsibility of the CCP's board hints that they are somewhat like them. Both disclosure and access requirements suggest that CCPs are somewhat utility-like, but the absence of price regulation means that it is hard to make the case that they are pure utilities. The obligation to have a default fund and a risk committee—and the use of self-policed membership requirements—underline the club-like nature of CCPs.

---

[109] It has been argued that CCPs are unique and, hence, that care is needed in translating structures which work for other entities to clearing houses: see Cox and Steigerwald, 'A CCP Is a CCP Is a CCP' (n 4). The discussion here supports that view.

8.3 Evidence from CCP Risk Taking

Clearing members play a vital role in sustaining CCP operations. In particular, they are central to CCP default management, assisting the CCP in both managing defaulter's portfolios and by absorbing the vast majority of any losses over IM created in that process. CCP equity does not backstop much of this risk, and clearing members often take substantial amounts of non-default risk, too. Moreover, CCP governance arrangements must give users a significant say, as we have seen. These features argue instead in favour of the club model of clearing houses.

8.4 Evidence from CCP Ownership and Profit-Taking

Most globally systemic CCPs are for-profit, shareholder-owned corporations,[110] and the profits from clearing accrue to shareholders. Moreover, it could be suggested that many of the club-like features of CCPs are remnants of an earlier era, given that many large CCPs acquired their current status because they demutualized.[111] The fact that many CCPs are for-profit corporations suggests that this element of their nature cannot be ignored.

9 Taking the Role Seriously

Each of the three edge-case models of a CCP suggest an allocation of the benefits and costs of clearing. In this section, we consider the consequences of taking each edge case seriously. This analysis suggests that no edge case would equitably allocate rights and responsibilities. Instead, a stakeholder model best explains current CCP governance and operations.

9.1 The CCP as a Pure Utility

The central focus of the CCP-as-utility model in its purest form is the provision of clearing as a general good. It encourages the view that taxpayers should profit from the provision of clearing ordinarily, and the taxpayer should backstop the CCP against extraordinary losses.[112] It also suggests an explicit taxpayer backstop, in contrast to

---

[110] A counterexample is the DTCC, which is closer to a user-owned club.

[111] Cox and Steigerwald, 'A CCP Is a CCP Is a CCP' (n 4) insightfully suggest that 'incomplete' demutualization, 'wherein the benefit of ownership, but not the risk, was demutualized' is at the heart of much of the current tension between CCPs, clearing members, clients, and regulators. See R. Cox and R. Steigerwald, '"Incomplete Demutualization" and Financial Market Infrastructure: Central Counterparty Ownership and Governance after the Crisis of 2008–9' (2016) 4(3) Journal of Financial Market Infrastructures, 36.

[112] A case could also be made for the CCP providing clearing services at cost and allocating any losses back to the clearing member contractually or to the wider market via transaction taxes or other fees.

the (not widely viewed as wholly credible) official sector assurances that bailouts of financial firms are a thing of the past. For a utility CCP, skin in the game would simply be an incentive for CCP managers to perform well:[113] there would be no shareholders and, hence, no conflict between shareholder interests and clearing member interests. Similarly, the case for the default fund would rest on the need for an incentive for clearing members to assist in default management rather than on absorbing all extreme but plausible losses. Finally, the utility CCP would be run by the state, for the public good, so its primary purpose would be systemic risk reduction.[114]

9.2 The CCP as a Pure For-Profit Corporation under Shareholder Primacy

The purely for-profit model of clearing would suggest following the usual anglophone corporate model of operating the CCP for shareholders and shareholders being the providers of risk capital, with third party risk mitigation purchased as decided by the corporation's management. After all, it would be unusual to hear that diners 'bring risk' to a privately owned restaurant by eating there, even though more diners mean more ingredients and more preparation and, hence, all other things being equal, a bigger risk of food poisoning. Certainly, diners are not usually asked to bear the restaurant's financial loss if closure is necessary after a food hygiene violation (or if the restaurant's cash register is robbed[115]). The norm is that diners should not have to assess the food safety risk of a restaurant: rather, there is regulation of hygiene standards (and, often, disclosure of hygiene ratings). In the shareholder primacy model, then, the CCP's shareholders are the primary providers of risk capital and the primary beneficiaries of CCP risk-taking. Skin in the game and the default fund would both change in size under this model, with the former becoming the predominant source of loss absorption and the latter merely providing an incentive for auction participation. The case for non-default loss allocation in this model is weak.

9.3 The CCP as a Pure Club

In the club model of clearing, the CCP is operated by the club of members, for their benefit, so it is natural that the members bear the risks of CCP operations and profit

---

[113] Regardless of how and by whom CCPs are owned, there is a case for CCP managers to receive some of their compensation in a form which can be written down or clawed back in the event of CCP stress or failure.

[114] Relatedly, see S. Griffith, 'Governing Systemic Risk: Towards a Governance Structure for Derivatives Clearinghouses' (2012) 61 Emory Law Journal 1153–1240 for a discussion of how the model whereby 'CCPs are systemic risk managers' leads to implications for CCP loss allocation and governance.

[115] It is, however, common for securities custodians to disclaim liability for their use of third-party sub-custodians and not even to disclose the contracts in place with such entities. For a further discussion, see E. Micheler, 'Intermediated Securities from the Perspective of Investors: Problems, Quick Fixes and Long-Term Solutions', in Louise Gullifer and J. Payne, *Intermediation and Beyond* (Oxford: Hart Publishing, 2019) p. 237–258.

from them. There would be no need for skin in the game, except perhaps as means of incentivizing clearing house management. There would be no shareholders; clearing members would provide the capital not only for loss absorption but also for the CCP's ongoing operations. The members of the clearing club would jointly determine the CCP's arrangements based on their mutual interests.

9.4 Why the Question about the Role of the CCP Is Important

Much of the difficulty with finding an allocation of the costs and benefits of clearing that is acceptable to all parties is that each of these models apply to central clearing to some degree but, as noted above, they suggest quite different answers to loss allocation and governance. Wide agreement on the role of the CCP would also greatly assist the resolution of the conflicts described in section 7.

Unfortunately, none of the edge cases are persuasive as their consequences clearly disenfranchise one or more classes of stakeholder. So long as shareholders do, in fact, own CCPs, the utility and club models are impossible to fully adopt. But the public importance of CCPs and the prominent role of clearing members makes pure shareholder primacy untenable. A synthesis is necessary. CCPs are part mutualized club, part for-profit company, and part quasi-public actor. This means that CCP policy requires a delicate balancing of interests that prioritizes different stakeholder interests in different situations. Section 9.5 considers a model which supports this balancing.

9.5 The Stakeholder Model

Shareholder primacy is not the only model of the for-profit corporation.[116] Another prominent approach, *stakeholder governance*, considers interests beyond those of the corporation's shareholders. Under a stakeholder-oriented model, 'the goal of corporate activity should be to increase the welfare of all [or key] groups that closely interact with the firm and have an interest in its continuous well-being'.[117]

Germany provides one of the most prominent long-standing examples of a stakeholder-oriented corporate governance system.[118] In this system, governance policies protect a variety of interests. German companies have a two-tiered board structure: a management board that oversees the day-to-day operations of the corporation and a supervisory board that oversees the management board and approves significant

---

[116] As Kershaw and Schuster point out in D. Kershaw and E. Schuster, 'The Purposive Transformation of Corporate Law' (2021) 69(3) American Journal of Comparative Law 478–538, a prior question to 'Whose interests should the corporation act for?' is 'What is the purpose of the corporation?'. They suggest that an agreed purpose for an entity 'has the capacity to bond internal and external stakeholders': the flipside of this is that disagreement over an entity's purpose has the capacity to generate substantial inter-stakeholder conflict.

[117] See M. Gelter, 'Taming or Protecting the Modern Corporation' (2011) 7(2) Journal of Law & Business 5.

[118] See Brandt and Georgiou, 'Shareholders vs Stakeholders Capitalism' (n 21), 12.

decisions such as a major merger. Under what is known as codetermination, German companies with more than 500 employees must allow employee representation on the supervisory board. For companies with over 2,000 employees, workers and shareholders each elect half of the supervisory board.[119]

In recent years, there has been considerable interest in the stakeholder model across the political spectrum in jurisdictions which had hitherto been more supportive of shareholder primacy. For instance, in the United States, Senator Elizabeth Warren has argued that the shareholder primacy model has led to significant corporate profits but stagnant wages for workers, and she has proposed a bill that would require large US corporations to allow employees to elect at least 40% of board members, among other reforms,[120] while the Business Roundtable—an influential association of corporate chief executive officers—announced a revision of its conception of corporate purpose which included stakeholder concerns.[121] Subsequently, the World Economic Forum urged for-profit corporations to move away from shareholder primacy to a stakeholder model.[122]

Regardless of the merits of the stakeholder model generally,[123] it provides a compelling model for clearing houses, particularly systemically important ones where the public interest in CCP robustness is strongest. Existing regulation and current CCP practice are only fully explicable in the context of multi-stakeholder governance[124] where no single interest dominates and where we speak of the purposes of the clearing house.

In this view, conflicts will persist. There is no single argument that resolves them in a compelling fashion. These conflicts are intensified by the clearing mandate, which focuses attention on the acceptability of CCP arrangements for the parties who are mandated to use them, given that CCP shareholders extract profits arising partly from a public policy choice.[125]

---

[119] See Brandt and Georgiou, 'Shareholders vs Stakeholders Capitalism' (n 21), 16 and, for co-determination more broadly, L. Fulton, *Codetermination in Germany: A Beginner's Guide*, Mitbestimmungspraxis No. 32 (Düsseldorf: Hans-Böckler-Stiftung Institut für Mitbestimmung und Unternehmensführung, 2020).

[120] E. Warren, 'Accountable Capitalism Act', S.3348, 115th Congress (2017–2018).

[121] Business Roundtable, 'Statement on the Purpose of a Corporation' (2019), https://www.businessroundta ble.org/business-roundtable-redefines-the-purpose-of-a-corporation-to-promote-an-economy-that-serves-all-americans (accessed 23 March 2023). A key passage is: '[W]e share a fundamental commitment to all of our stakeholders […] Each of our stakeholders is essential. We commit to deliver value to all of them, for the future success of our companies, our communities and our country'.

[122] See World Economic Forum, 'Davos Manifesto 2020: The Universal Purpose of a Company in the Fourth Industrial Revolution' (2 December 2019), https://www.weforum.org/agenda/2019/12/davos-manifesto-2020-the-universal-purpose-of-a-company-in-the-fourth-industrial-revolution (accessed 23 March 2023).

[123] See L. Bebchuk and R. Tallarita, 'The Illusory Promise of Stakeholder Governance' (2020) 106 Cornell Law Review 91–177 for the case against stakeholder governance and C. Mayer, 'Shareholderism versus Stakeholderism—a Misconceived Contradiction', ECGI Working Paper No. 522 (2022) for a response to Bebchuk and Tallarita.

[124] See K. Johnson, 'Governing Financial Markets: Regulating Conflicts' (2013) 88(1) Washington Law Review 239 for a related discussion of stakeholder representation in CCP governance.

[125] For a further discussion of the choice to use largely private CCPs for public policy purposes, see Braithwaite and Murphy, 'Get the Balance Right' (n 91).

10 Conclusions

This chapter has made the case that a disagreement about the nature of CCPs lies at the heart of many important conflicts in contemporary CCP policy. The controversy has been illustrated through the use of three stylized models of clearing houses: utilities, for-profit corporations under shareholder primacy, and clubs. These models encapsulate different notions of whose interests a CCP should serve and, as a result, they have different governance arrangements.

Central clearing involves taking risk so fulfilling the purpose of a CCP requires some party or parties to provide loss absorption. The various risks of central clearing and the mechanisms for absorbing them in both the default waterfall and in non-default loss allocation have been set out. These mechanisms provide very substantial loss absorption capacity, and this often comes largely from clearing members.

The idea that risk-bearing should, in equity, imply some say in how that risk is taken and managed has been used to shed light on the claims of various parties for participation in CCP governance and on their current governance rights. It was seen that CCP loss allocation is complex, and there is no simple read-across from a party bearing a risk to that party having a say in clearing house governance when decisions about that risk are being taken. Rather, there is a general tendency for risk-bearing to be associated with a role in governance. Regulatory standards for governance, access, and disclosure, which support and frame the rights of various stakeholders, were discussed along with existing governance practices.

Notwithstanding regulation and arrangements that enfranchise key stakeholders, the diverse community of CCP stakeholders remain in conflict over fundamental aspects of CCP policy. Some of the key conflicts within the stakeholder community were outlined: this illustrated their persistent and intractable character.

The evidence for each of the stylized models of a clearing house has been considered. None of the three edges cases was found to be satisfactory or determinative. In particular, the resolution of the policy conflicts by choosing any of the models would entail an inequitable discrimination against one or more class of stakeholder.

Conflict in clearing policy has been seen to arise through the choice to use largely private entities—CCPs—to meet a public policy purpose—that derivatives be cleared. The evidence from CCP loss allocation, governance, and from an analysis of those who benefit from clearing suggests that CCPs must—and generally do—balance the rights and interests of stakeholders, including their owners, clearing members, clients, the wider financial system, and the public. This suggests that a stakeholder model best explains governance at CCPs, with all the potential for difficult trade-offs and dissatisfied parties that entails.

The picture that emerges is one of CCPs as hybrid entities, dynamically balancing competing interests within a slowly changing policy framework. Their bespoke arrangements reflect the complexity of this balancing act. Meanwhile, various stakeholders attempt to advance their interests at the CCP, in the community of stakeholders, and with policymakers. Thus, central clearing will remain a contested area where disputes will be resolved—perhaps only provisionally and temporarily—by negotiation, power, evidence, or advocacy rather than one where general agreement about role of the CCP acts as a lodestar leading to a stable compromise.

8

OTC Derivatives Clearing Documentation

Emma Dwyer and Emma Lancelott*

1 Introduction to OTC Derivatives Clearing Documentation

There are a number of different ways in which an over-the-counter (OTC) derivatives transaction can be centrally cleared. Certain entities (clearing members) can clear

---

* This chapter was completed on 1 July 2022.

transactions directly with a central counterparty (CCP). However, not all entities are able (or want) to meet the strict membership requirements that must be satisfied in order to become a clearing member, thus enabling them direct access to a CCP. In the case where an entity wishes, or is required, to clear an OTC derivatives transaction but is not a clearing member itself, that entity (a client) may approach a clearing member to clear a trade via a CCP either on a proprietary basis (so-called client clearing) or for one or more of its customers (so-called indirect clearing). When an OTC derivatives transaction is to be cleared, both counterparties must, therefore, be either (i) a clearing member or (ii) have a clearing arrangement in place with a clearing member or a client of a clearing member of the relevant CCP through which they agree to clear their OTC derivatives trades.

2 Clearing Models: Principal-to-Principal vs Agency

There are two different models that may be used to facilitate client and indirect clearing.

2.1 Principal-to-Principal Model

The principal-to-principal model (borne out of the futures markets in the European Union, EU) is the model predominantly used in the EU, the United Kingdom, and Asia. It involves two back-to-back transactions comprising:

(1) a principal-to-principal transaction between the client and its clearing member (a Client Transaction) and
(2) a principal-to-principal transaction between the clearing member (CM) and the relevant CCP (a CM/CCP Transaction). In this latter case, the positions and assets relating to the transaction will be held on the client's behalf in a client account in the name of the CM at the relevant CCP.

CCP clearing is a key method in respect of which counterparty credit risk of an OTC derivatives contract (i.e. the risk that a counterparty will default in its obligations under a contract) can be managed. Once a transaction is cleared, the credit risk which each counterparty has to the other under the original bilateral trade is replaced by the credit risk of the CCP. A key concept in the client-clearing structure is, therefore, that the CM acts as a 'riskless principal', in other words, that the CM is essentially an intermediary. This is critical to achieve the stated aim of clearing, which is to reduce or eliminate counterparty credit risk (and, therefore, systemic risk) by clearing via, and taking credit risk on, a CCP which is structured to withstand the default of one or more CMs rather than transacting with, and taking credit risk on, a bank, corporate, or other bilateral counterparty.

In the case of indirect clearing, there will be an additional back-to-back, principal-to-principal transaction entered into between the client and the customer. In the context of OTC derivatives, there is no industry standard documentation for the indirectly cleared (i.e. client vs customer) relationship. As such, we do not discuss indirect clearing any further in this chapter. However, we note that the concept of the 'riskless principal' in the indirectly cleared transaction (in this case, it will be the client acting as riskless principal) and the documentation implications discussed further below would apply equally in the context of an indirectly cleared transaction, albeit amended to provide for the indirect, back-to-back transaction.

2.2 Agency Model

The agency model[1] involves a client entering into a principal-to-principal transaction with the relevant CCP. However, in contrast to the principal-to-principal model, there is no separate transaction entered into between the client and its CM. The client's CM acts as its 'agent', and, in this regard, the CM generally:

- accepts derivatives transactions on behalf of the client for clearing at the relevant CCP;
- holds the assets and positions relating to the client's transactions on the client's behalf in a client account at the relevant CCP. Such positions and, to the extent transferred to the CCP, such assets, will generally be identified as client assets and positions on the books and records of the relevant CCP;
- intermediates the exchange of collateral between the client and the CCP; and
- guarantees[2] the performance of the client's obligations to the relevant CCP, although the CM does not guarantee the performance of the obligations owed by the CCP to the client.

In practice, however, the way that the client interacts with the CM in an agency model context is broadly the same as the principal-to-principal model.

The client-clearing arrangement that exists and is predominantly used in the United States is a type of agency model, commonly referred to as the 'FCM model'. Under this model, a client enters into a transaction with the relevant CCP through a futures commission merchant (FCM), which is a CM at the relevant CCP. Although there may be some differences between the 'FCM model' and the general agency model described above, two fundamental principles are consistent between the two models. First, the

---

[1] The phrase 'agency model' is commonplace in the cleared derivatives market to distinguish this type of arrangement from a back-to-back principal-to-principal model. However, it does not necessarily imply that there is a true agency relationship under applicable agency law between a client and its CM.

[2] The word 'guarantees' is used in the context of agency models of client clearing to identify the fact that the CM has an obligation to perform to the CCP if the client has failed to perform its obligations under its transaction with the CCP. However, the word should not be read to suggest that there is a conventional guarantee by the CM of a primary obligation of the client. Rather than the CM having a secondary obligation to perform to the CCP, there is typically an independent primary obligation on the CM to perform to the CCP in certain circumstances. The word 'guarantee' does not therefore imply that there is any relationship of surety, as would be the case under an English law guarantee, for example.

transaction is ultimately between the client and the relevant CCP. Second, the role of the FCM is broadly to carry out those functions identified above. Therefore, the general agency model and the 'FCM model' are substantially similar.

Like the 'riskless principal' concept, agency is another legal technique which can be employed to alleviate the credit risk of a CM in a client-clearing structure, with the CM acting as agent and, thus, ensuring that the legal relationship (and the credit risk) remains as between the client and the CCP.

2.3 Focus on the Principal-to-Principal Model

The focus of this chapter is the principal-to-principal model of client clearing as it is the model most widely used in the EU and the United Kingdom. Unless otherwise stated, we consider the law from an EU and a UK perspective only.

3 Role of the CCP: An Overview

As discussed in section 2.1, a key risk attached to OTC derivative transactions is counterparty credit risk—the risk that one party to a contract defaults and cannot meet its obligations under the contract leading to a loss for the other counterparty. If those losses are severe enough, they may cause the affected parties financial distress, which, in turn, can have a knock-on effect for their creditors. In this way, counterparty credit risk is an important channel for contagion and can be a potential source of systemic risk.

It is widely thought that CCP clearing was effective in reducing counterparty credit risk during the financial crisis in 2008/2009. Therefore, following the crisis, legislators sought to introduce regulation which incentivized CCP clearing in new markets, such as the mandatory clearing requirement for certain OTC derivatives transactions under the European Market Infrastructure Regulation (EU EMIR),[3] which aims to move certain bilateral OTC derivatives into the 'less risky' cleared world.

Broadly, the role of the CCP is to stand between two bilateral counterparties; to keep track of obligations via a matched book (the CCP will always enter into a back-to-back trade and so, in theory, its exposure will always be flat); to ensure that transactions are netted on a multilateral basis; and to ensure that parties provide enough collateral (principally in the form of variation margin (VM) covering current exposure and initial margin (IM) covering potential future exposure) to protect against any defaults. As a result of the systemic importance of CCPs, legislation sets out the organizational, conduct of business, and prudential requirements for CCPs. The rules include that a CCP must ensure it has resources in place to manage any counterparty defaults in an

---

[3] Regulation (EU) No. 648/2012 of the European Parliament and of the Council of 4 July 2012 on OTC derivatives, central counterparties and trade repositories, [2012] OJ L201/1 (27 July 2012) (EU EMIR). With effect from 1 January 2021, EU EMIR has been onshored in the United Kingdom (UK EMIR).

orderly way so that it is able to withstand, under extreme but plausible market conditions, either the default of the CM to which it has the largest exposures or of the second and third largest CMs if the sum of their exposures is larger (measured by reference to margin and to volume of trades).[4] In this way, the CCP allows counterparties to trade without concerning themselves with each other's creditworthiness. Instead, the concern for a CM is the credit risk of the CCP, which, in theory, cannot fail (although this has not yet been tested in practice[5]).

Therefore, if one CM defaults (e.g. it becomes insolvent), the CCP should be in a position to step in using the rules and resources it has in place to ensure all obligations owed by the defaulting CM to the CCP are met. To ensure this can be done, each CCP is mandated to have a default waterfall in place, which involves the CCP using its resources in the following order:[6] (i) margin posted by the defaulting CM; (ii) default fund contribution of the defaulting CM; (iii) pre-funded financial resources of the CCP; and (iv) default fund contributions of the non-defaulting CMs.

It is important to understand the way CCPs are structured and operate as this impacts OTC derivatives clearing documentation, as further discussed below.

Further discussion on CCPs (including a more detailed discussion of organizational, conduct of business, prudential, and recovery and resolution requirements) is set out in Chapter 12 'Recovery and Resolution of CCPs' by Victor de Serière in this volume.

4 The CM vs CCP Relationship

Pursuant to a CM/CCP Transaction, CMs enter into cleared OTC derivative transactions directly with the relevant CCP, either on a proprietary basis or for one of their clients.

The primary documentation governing a CM/CCP Transaction is the relevant CCP rules and procedures. Each CCP has its own bespoke rules and procedures, which are generally lengthy, complex, and updated on a regular basis. As each set of CCP rules is not standardized as between CCPs, CMs (and, in respect of rules which affect them, clients) will need to analyse each relevant rule set in detail to ensure that they fully understand the relationship and their obligations.

Typically, CMs are large, sophisticated financial institutions with a significant derivatives business. This is because CMs must be able to satisfy the strict membership criteria set by the relevant CCP (including substantial financial commitments such as contributing to the CCP's default fund to cover losses that exceed the losses to be covered by margin requirements[7]) and have the resources to carry out a comprehensive review of the CCP rules and procedures. Strict membership criteria and CCP rules are necessary to help ensure that the CCP remains sufficiently robust in a default scenario.

---

[4] See EU EMIR and UK EMIR (n 3), Art. 42.
[5] See further discussion on CCP recovery and resolution in Chapter 12 'Recovery and Resolution of CCPs' by Victor de Serière in this volume.
[6] See EU EMIR and UK EMIR (n 3), Art. 45.
[7] See further section 3 above.

Although each CCP rule set is different (and, consequently, we do not analyse each rule set in this chapter), CCP rules and procedures generally cover the same key themes, as follows:

- the criteria for becoming a CM (including costs and infrastructure requirements) and the process for termination of membership;
- how transactions are cleared and which transactions are eligible for clearing;
- account types offered by the CCP and rules relating to client clearing;
- arrangements for the provision and return of collateral;
- what happens in the event of a CM, CCP, or other default;
- the operation of the default fund and CMs' contributions thereto; and
- dispute resolution, governing law, and jurisdiction.

In the case of client clearing, many of these provisions are mirrored in the back-to-back Client Transaction to ensure that the CM remains a 'riskless principal' in the client-clearing structure, either by direct inclusion in the relevant client-clearing agreement or by the CM and client agreeing to be bound by the relevant CCP rules, see section 9.1 below.

Where a CCP clears multiple products, there may also be subsets of rules that relate to different product types.

In addition to reviewing and complying with the relevant CCP rules and procedures, a CM will need to have processes in place to assess (i) which of its OTC derivatives contracts are (or will be) required to be cleared (e.g. as a result of the mandatory clearing obligation under EU EMIR or UK EMIR[8]) or are to be voluntarily cleared; (ii) which CCP(s) can, and will, be used to clear those OTC derivatives contracts (which may be mandated by regulation[9]); and (iii) whether it will offer client clearing and, if so, how its client-clearing offering will be provided, including which CCPs will be used and what documentation and disclosure needs to be put in place, as to which see further below.

5 The CCP and CM Account Structures and Written Disclosure Requirements

5.1 The CCP and CM Requirements

A CCP is required to keep separate records and accounts that shall enable it, at any time and without delay, to distinguish in accounts with the CCP the assets and positions

---

[8] See Chapter 3 ('Development of the Regulatory Regime for OTC Derivatives Clearing' by Patrick Pearson) in this volume for further information on EU EMIR and UK EMIR (n 3) requirements.

[9] See Chapter 3 ('Development of the Regulatory Regime for OTC Derivatives Clearing' by Patrick Pearson) in this volume for further information on EU EMIR and UK EMIR (n 3) requirements.

held for the account of one CM from the assets and positions held for the account of any other CM and from its own assets.[10]

In addition, a CCP is required to keep separate records and accounts enabling each CM to distinguish in accounts with the CCP:

(1) the assets and positions of that CM from those held for the accounts of its clients (omnibus client segregation); and

(2) the assets and positions held for the account of a client from those held for the account of other clients (individual client segregation).

A CM is also required to keep separate records and accounts that enable it to distinguish, both in accounts held with the CCP and in its own accounts, its assets and positions from the assets and positions held for the account of its clients at the CCP. It is further required to offer its clients, at least, the choice between omnibus client segregation and individual client segregation and inform them of the costs and level of protection associated with each option.

The segregation of client assets should provide comfort to the client that its assets (or equivalent) will be returned upon a CM/CCP default.[11]

5.2 Omnibus Segregation Accounts

An omnibus segregated account is an account where the CCP and the CM provide a single account for multiple clients of the CM (although the account is distinct from the assets of the CCP and the CM). Clients may select from a net or gross omnibus structure.

In a net structure, margin requirements are determined based on the combined or 'net' position of all clients in the relevant account, meaning that less margin is required to be provided by each client. However, it is possible that there may not be sufficient assets to cover all clients' exposures upon a default.

In a gross structure, margin requirements are determined on a per client or 'gross' basis, meaning that a client may be required to provide more margin to cover its positions.

In both cases, the particular assets provided as margin are not allocated to a specific client in the CCP's books and so the client will only be entitled to receive assets of an equivalent value upon a default. However, an omnibus account is likely to be a cheaper option than an individually segregated account due to the fact that the protections that the client may benefit from are not as robust.

---

[10] See EU EMIR and UK EMIR (n 3), Art. 39. See also Chapters 4 ('CCP Access Structures' by Christina Sell) and 10 ('Segregation and Portability of Cleared OTC Derivatives in Europe' by Bas Zebregs) in this volume for further detail.

[11] See also EU EMIR and UK EMIR (n 3), Art. 48 relating to default procedures.

5.3 Individual Segregation Accounts

An individually segregated account is an account where the CCP and the CM provide a separate account for each client (as well as being distinct from the assets of the CCP and the CM). An individual account offers better protection for a client's assets than an omnibus account but will generally be a more expensive option.

5.4 Article 39(7) Disclosure

CCPs and CMs are required to publicly disclose the levels of protection and the costs associated with the different levels of segregation that they provide and must offer those services on reasonable commercial terms (so-called Art. 39(7) disclosure).[12] Details of the different levels of segregation include a description of the main legal implications of the respective levels of segregation offered, including information on the insolvency law applicable in the relevant jurisdictions.

CCP Art. 39(7) disclosure is available via the relevant CCP websites. CM Art. 39(7) disclosure is available via the relevant CM website and is often based on the International Swaps and Derivatives Association/Futures Industry Association (ISDA/FIA) Art. 39(7) Clearing Member Disclosure Document, which is designed to help facilitate CMs' compliance with their obligations.[13]

5.5 Client Considerations When Selecting an Account

The client of a CM is required to confirm its choice of account in writing. Considerations are set out in the ISDA/FIA Art. 39(7) Clearing Member Disclosure Document and may include (i) requirements that apply to a client under law and regulation (e.g. the UK Financial Conduct Authority (FCA) client money rules), (ii) cost,[14] (iii) amount of margin required to be provided, (iv) a client's appetite for porting and the likelihood of porting, and (v) whether there is exposure to other clients upon default.

6 The Client vs CM Relationship

As discussed above, client clearing allows entities which want (or are required) to clear an OTC derivatives transaction but cannot enter into a direct relationship with the CCP to clear a transaction (as they are not CMs themselves).

---

[12] See EU EMIR and UK EMIR (n 3), Art. 39(7).

[13] The disclosure document can be accessed at https://www.isda.org//2012/11/16/disclosures (accessed 23 March 2023).

[14] Pursuant to EU EMIR and UK EMIR (n 3), Art. 38, a CCP and its CMs are required to publicly disclose the prices and fees associated with the services provided.

As part of the preparation for clearing, a client will, therefore, need to have processes in place to assess (i) which of its OTC derivatives contracts are (or will be) required to be cleared (e.g. as a result of the mandatory clearing obligation under EU EMIR or UK EMIR[15]) or are to be voluntarily cleared, (ii) which CCP(s) can, and will, be used to clear those OTC derivatives contracts (which may be mandated by regulation[16]), (iii) which CM(s) can be, and have been, selected to be used to access the clearing services of such CCP(s), and (iv) what documentation needs to be put in place and is most suited to its needs. The relevant client-clearing documentation will then need to be negotiated and executed and relevant operational processes put in place in sufficient time (noting that this may take many months to complete and so should be started well ahead of the intended clearing date for a transaction). A counterparty will also need (or have an arrangement with a dealer who has) access to an electronic platform, which matches the trade data submitted by it and its execution counterparty and then communicates that data to the relevant CCP.

In addition, when negotiating a client-clearing agreement, both the CM and the client will need to be cognizant of the fact that the agreement will interrelate with the relevant CCP rules. It will not be enough to know the terms which are set out explicitly in the client-clearing agreement. Parties will need to be familiar with the relevant CCP rules in order to understand what processes need to be followed in some circumstances (e.g. pre-default porting) and what protections are available to the client and how they are delivered. As discussed in section 5, clients, in particular, will need to understand the different levels of protection offered by the relevant CCP in order that they can choose the most suitable type of segregated client account as well as (i) the fees for the client-clearing services they wish to use and how they are calculated, (ii) any relevant position limits and the consequences of exceeding those limits, and (iii) the availability of pre-funding margin or of single currency margin together with any associated charges.

A client will also need to establish how many CMs it needs. In most cases, a client will need at least two CMs with each relevant CCP so that it has a back-up CM for pre-default and post-default porting (see further sections 9.4 and 9.5 below).

In order to clear a trade, a client must put in place:

- *an execution/give-up agreement with an executing broker*: this agreement deals with the position just before clearing, prior to an OTC derivatives transaction being accepted by the relevant CCP into the clearing system and, in particular, what happens if a transaction is not accepted for clearing. An agreement may take the form of the ISDA/FIA Cleared Derivatives Execution Agreement (the CDEA)[17]—we discuss the CDEA further below;

---

[15] See Chapter 3 ('Development of the Regulatory Regime for OTC Derivatives Clearing' by Patrick Pearson) in this volume for further information on EU EMIR and UK EMIR (n 3) requirements.

[16] See Chapter 3 ('Development of the Regulatory Regime for OTC Derivatives Clearing' by Patrick Pearson) in this volume for further information on EU EMIR and UK EMIR (n 3) requirements.

[17] The CDEA can be used in conjunction with the Addendum and can be accessed at https://www.isda.org/book/isda-fia-cleared-derivatives-execution-agreement-eu-arrangements (accessed 23 March 2023). Please note that a French law-governed version of this agreement is also available via the ISDA website.

- *a master agreement with each relevant CM*: this agreement sets out the key terms of the derivatives relationship between the parties and typically (although not always) takes the form of the 1992 or 2002 ISDA Master Agreement,[18] the FIA 2018 Terms of Business,[19] or the FIA Professional Client Agreement.[20] Clients may choose whether they would prefer to use an ISDA or FIA master agreement and often base this decision on their previous derivatives trading history and relationship with the relevant CM. OTC market participants are likely to be more familiar with the ISDA Master Agreement, whereas futures industry participants will likely be more familiar with FIA documentation. However, the choice of master agreement may also be influenced by the way a client would like to undertake OTC derivatives clearing, which may determine which clearing agreement is used—we discuss this further below (although note that, in this chapter, we will not focus in detail on the ISDA or FIA master agreements themselves as, typically, they do not include the key OTC client-clearing provisions);
- *a client-clearing agreement with each relevant CM*: this agreement sets out the key clearing-related provisions that apply between the client and the CM, typically forms part of the relevant master agreement, and is typically based on the ISDA/FIA Client Cleared OTC Derivatives Addendum[21] (the Addendum), the FIA 2018 Terms of Business, or, in respect of the FIA Professional Client Agreement only, the FIA Clearing Module—we discuss client-clearing agreements in sections 8 and 9 below;[22]
- *a collateral arrangement with respect to cleared transactions with each relevant CM*: for example, a form of Paragraph 11 to the English law-governed ISDA 1995 Credit Support Annex (English CSA) and a form of Paragraph 13 to the New York law-governed 1994 ISDA Credit Support Annex (NY CSA) are available for use with the Addendum; and
- *documentation supporting operational processes*: for example, in respect of the opening of relevant accounts (as to which see further above).

In the context of OTC derivatives clearing, the market has aimed to align the documentation with existing bilateral OTC derivatives documentation as closely as possible to provide consistency for OTC derivatives market participants when OTC trades

[18] The ISDA Master Agreements can be accessed at https://www.isda.org/books/library (accessed 23 March 2023).
[19] The FIA 2018 Terms of Business can be accessed at https://www.fiadocumentation.org/fia/pages/new-fia-terms-of-business-2018-version-20 (accessed 23 March 2023) (member access only).
[20] The FIA Professional Client Agreement and FIA 2017 Regulatory Patch, which is designed to update the 2011 version of the FIA's Professional Client Agreement to reflect in-scope regulatory developments, can be accessed at https://www.fiadocumentation.org/fia/pre-fia-terms-of-business-2018 (accessed 23 March 2023) (member access only).
[21] The Addendum can be accessed at https://www.isda.org/book/isda-fia-client-cleared-otc-derivatives-addendum (accessed 23 March 2023). We note that there is also the ISDA/Fédération bancaire française (FBF) Annex to the Addendum, which is a template for use by cleared swaps market participants where the underlying master agreement is an AFB/FBF Master Agreement (available via the ISDA website). Other jurisdictions may also have domestic agreements that may be used, such as the German Clearing-Rahmenvereinbarung.
[22] The FIA Clearing Module (August 2015) can be accessed at https://www.fiadocumentation.org/fia/pre-fia-terms-of-business-2018 (accessed 23 March 2023) (member access only).

move into clearing whilst also ensuring that provisions in the back-to-back CM/CCP Transaction are mirrored to enable the CM to remain a 'riskless principal' in the client-clearing structure.

We discuss the different documentation requirements in turn below.

7 Execution Agreement: The CDEA

7.1 Purpose

The CDEA deals with the process of getting OTC derivatives transactions[23] into clearing (i.e. the position just before an OTC derivatives transaction is accepted by the relevant CCP into the clearing system) as well as the consequences of a transaction not being accepted for clearing. It is an industry standard template for use by market participants (an executing broker and a client) when negotiating execution-related agreements in respect of OTC derivatives transactions that are entered into with the intention of being centrally cleared outside of the United States. The CDEA is non-CCP specific and can be used in relation to the execution of any OTC derivatives transaction that is intended to be cleared on any non-US CCP. The CDEA's use has become less widespread due to the mandatory trading obligation resulting in more OTC cleared derivatives transactions being executed on venue.

7.2 Submission of OTC Derivatives Transactions to Clearing

The general process involved in getting a transaction into clearing that is entered into OTC and off venue, and on the basis that it will be cleared, involves the following stages:

(1) matching and submission of the relevant trade details (by the executing broker and the client);

(2) acceptance of the OTC derivatives transaction by a CM (whereby the executing broker 'gives up' the transaction to the CM); and

(3) acceptance of the OTC derivatives transaction for clearing by a CCP (stages (1), (2), and (3) together, the Process).

These steps are reflected in the CDEA, although the CDEA only expressly requires the parties (being the executing broker and the client) to carry out the first stage of the

---

[23] The CDEA is suitable for OTC derivatives transactions only and does not deal with exchange-trade derivatives, which are instead subject to the rules of the relevant exchange. The CDEA provides that it does not cover 'any futures and options on futures contracts and other Derivatives Transactions executed in anonymous markets or, markets operated as central limit order books or on trading venues (including, without limitation, multilateral trading facilities and organised trading facilities as defined in [EU Markets in Financial Instruments Directive II (MiFID II)])'.

Process—the matching and submission stage. The parties must electronically submit details of the relevant OTC derivatives transaction to an applicable 'Matching System',[24] as soon as practicable in the circumstances after execution of the OTC derivatives transaction to enable the relevant trade to be matched and submitted to the relevant CCP for clearing. This obligation is subject to an exception in relation to 'automatically matched transactions', where the OTC derivatives transaction will be automatically matched and submitted to the relevant CCP by the electronic facility on which the transaction was executed.

The remaining stages of the Process—acceptance by a CM and acceptance by a CCP—are addressed indirectly through (i) a general obligation on the parties to take 'reasonable steps' to enable an OTC derivatives transaction to be cleared and (ii) the concept of 'Relevant Events'.

A Relevant Event occurs when one of the stages of the Process is not completed by the relevant deadline or the relevant CCP otherwise rejects the OTC derivatives transaction at any time during the Process. EU MiFIR Art. 29(2),[25] EU Regulatory Technical Standards (RTS) 26,[26] and their UK equivalents set out the time frames for the transfer of information between the parties.[27] Relevant Events help signpost the key stages of the Process and if a Relevant Event occurs, the parties will either resolve the issue— the provision requiring the parties to take reasonable steps to clear a transaction includes an illustrative list of 'reasonable steps' linked to the various Relevant Events (e.g. seeking an alternative CM or CCP)—or take 'alternative action' (see further below).

Once an OTC derivatives transaction is cleared, then such transaction will be replaced by a cleared transaction pursuant to the rules of the applicable CCP and any relevant client-clearing agreement, and the parties will have no further rights or obligations against each other in respect of the original OTC derivatives transaction or under the CDEA.

7.3 Alternative Action

The CDEA incorporates two alternative courses of action where the parties are unable to clear an OTC derivatives transaction (i) accept the transaction as a bilateral transaction or (ii) terminate the transaction.

---

[24] A Matching System is defined as 'an electronic facility, trading system or platform that provides services for real-time or post-execution centralised matching of trade data in relation to Derivatives Transactions submitted by its participants and, in relation to a Derivatives Transaction, means such electronic facility, trading system or platform that is agreed between the parties'.

[25] Regulation (EU) No. 600/2014 of the European Parliament and of the Council of 15 May 2014 on markets in financial instruments and amending Regulation (EU) No. 648/2012, [2014] OJ L173/84 (12 June 2014) (EU MiFIR).

[26] Commission Delegated Regulation (EU) No. 2017/582 of 29 June 2016 supplementing Regulation (EU) No. 600/2014 of the European Parliament and of the Council with regard to regulatory technical standards specifying the obligation to clear derivatives traded on regulated markets and timing of acceptance for clearing, [2017] OJ L87/224 (31 March 2017) (EU RTS 26).

[27] The most recent version of the CDEA (published in 2017) has been amended to account for the timeframes under EU MiFIR (n 25) for the transfer of information in respect of cleared derivatives transactions concluded between counterparties on a bilateral basis.

If a transaction is not accepted for clearing, there is likely to be a pricing impact. If entities enter into a transaction and flag it for clearing in anticipation that it will be cleared, it will typically attract more favourable pricing than an uncleared trade due to the anticipated counterparty credit risk being on the relevant CCP as opposed to on a bilateral counterparty. This will, in turn, lower the price of a transaction.

Therefore, in respect of accepting an OTC derivatives transaction as a bilateral transaction, this can only be done by the mutual agreement of the parties if a Relevant Event occurs and, in particular, it is subject to the parties (i) agreeing the necessary amendments to the terms of the transaction, including pricing, collateral, and other credit terms; and (ii) having, or putting in place, the appropriate documentation for the bilateral transaction. This alternative action will only be available to the parties to the extent that the OTC derivatives transaction is not subject to a mandatory clearing obligation under EU EMIR, UK EMIR, or other applicable law.

In respect of termination, if a Relevant Event occurs, the executing broker may, at any time, elect to terminate the OTC derivatives transaction. The client's termination right, including the time from which it may elect to use it, are negotiable points in the Annex to the CDEA. If a party terminates an OTC derivatives transaction, then an Early Termination Amount, calculated in accordance with (and as defined in) a standard ISDA 2002 Master Agreement, will be determined by the executing broker (or the client if the executing broker delays in making such determination). The side of the market on which the Early Termination Amount will be determined depends on the nature of the event that led to the OTC derivatives transaction failing to be cleared— broadly, if one of the counterparties is 'at fault', then it will be determined on the side of the market of the other party; otherwise, it will be determined at mid-market.

The CDEA also includes an elective termination provision such that if a Relevant Event occurs and the relevant OTC derivatives transaction is not cleared within a time period specified by the parties in the Annex to the CDEA, then such transaction will automatically terminate. The parties can elect in the Annex to the CDEA whether or not this provision applies.

7.4 Representations

The CDEA contains a limited number of representations between the parties, including representations in respect of the relevant party's status, power, and authority; the binding nature of the obligations; and that the party either has a clearing agreement with a relevant CM or is itself a CM.

7.5 Breach of Agreement

If there is a breach of the CDEA, then there will be no event of default, termination event, or similar event under the CDEA or any other agreement, and the sole available remedy will be for a party to terminate the OTC derivatives transaction in accordance with the termination provisions that apply when a Relevant Event occurs (see above). However, if a party fails to make a payment under the CDEA and there is an applicable master agreement in place, then the CDEA will be deemed to be a Specified Transaction for the purposes of (and as defined in) the master agreement, and such payment failure should constitute a Default under Specified Transaction event of default under the master agreement.

7.6 Relationship with Clearing Agreement

If the executing broker is also acting as the client's CM, then the parties acknowledge that their relationship under the CDEA in respect of any OTC derivatives transaction is entirely separate from, and independent of, the relationship between the client and the executing broker in its CM role in respect of any corresponding cleared transaction. This is to avoid the risk of any implied waivers or amendments in respect of the clearing relationship being caused by the executing broker's actions under, or in connection with, the CDEA or any OTC derivatives transaction.

7.7 Limitation of Liability

There is a mutual limitation of liability provision that excludes liability for losses or damages incurred due to (i) error, negligence, or misconduct of any Matching System, CCP, or service provider or of the party who has suffered the loss or damage; (ii) transmission, communication, or electronic order failures; or (iii) causes beyond the control of the party.

7.8 General Right to Terminate

Each party has the general right to terminate the CDEA with effect from a specified time on a specified date by notice to the other party.

8 Client-Clearing Agreements: An Overview

8.1 Purpose and Common Themes in Client-Clearing Agreements

The client-clearing agreement sets out the key clearing-related provisions governing the relationship between the client and the CM; that is, it deals with transactions from the point of clearing—when the relevant transaction is registered in a client account at the relevant CCP. Although the form and legal structure may vary, there are a number of common themes which form the cornerstone of a client-clearing agreement:

- *CM as 'riskless principal'/an intermediary*: as discussed above, clients are required to approach a CM in order to access client clearing as this is the way that a non-CM accesses a CCP. Under the principal-to-principal model, absent any specific provisions to the contrary, the client takes credit risk on the CM (as its counterparty). However, the intention is for credit risk to be taken on the CCP via the back-to-back CM/CCP Transaction. Various contractual provisions are, therefore, included to ensure that the CM sits in the middle of two principal-to-principal and back-to-back transactions and, in this way, can be seen to be an 'intermediary' between the relevant CCP and the client. The role of the CM as an intermediary drives a number of provisions in the client-clearing agreement, including limitation of liability and indemnity provisions and provisions that allow the CM to make changes to the Client Transaction if changes are made to the CM/CCP Transaction. There are also legislative protections in place (see the above discussion of segregated account structures) which dictate that client assets must be segregated from the proprietary account of the CM with the relevant CCP to ensure that the client's assets are available notwithstanding any default of the CM.[28]
- *Early termination*: a detailed early termination provision is at the heart of most client-clearing agreements, ensuring that both the client and the CM are adequately protected in the event of a default of the other or of a default of the relevant CCP. It would be typical for any rights that the client would expect to have in a bilateral OTC derivative relationship to be severely curtailed such that the OTC cleared transactions will only terminate upon the declaration (or automatic occurrence) of default under the relevant CCP rules, with the timing and valuation in respect of such termination mirroring the provisions under the relevant CCP rules for the timing and valuation in respect of the termination or transfer of the corresponding transactions between the CM and the relevant CCP.
- *Pre-default porting*: this is a provision that allows a client to require its CM to transfer all its rights and obligations with respect to a Client Transaction(s) to a back-up CM, generally subject to certain conditions being satisfied.
- *Margin*: provisions that allow a CM to call margin with the frequency and in the amounts that are required by the relevant CCP in relation to the corresponding CM/CCP Transaction, including, where relevant, provisions that support separate calls for IM and VM broken down into currency portfolios.

---

[28] Prior to legislative protections being put in place under the EU EMIR (n 3) framework, parties used assignment by way of security, whereby the CM would assign to the client by way of security its rights to receive from the CCP anything that belonged to the client at the CCP as security for the obligations of the CM to the client in a Client Transaction.

We will discuss each of these themes in more detail in the context of the Addendum below.

8.2 Form and Legal Structure of Client-Clearing Agreements: A Short History

Although not entirely new, as exchange trading and related documentation were well established, the industry effectively went back to the drawing board to find a documentation solution for OTC derivatives client clearing. Over the years, various client-clearing agreements have been proposed including CCP-based initiatives and industry-based initiatives as well as some individual CM bespoke initiatives.

8.2.1 CCP-specific models

The first OTC client-clearing documentation models proposed were CCP-specific (and often CCP-service-specific, see Figure 8.1). Clients would typically approach a CM and request to clear particular product types. Different product types may be cleared at different CCPs or at the same CCP but via a different CCP service. Detailed CCP rules and procedures at the CM/CCP Transaction level supported these product types and services and for each CCP. Therefore, in the early 2010s, the initial thinking was that a client would potentially need to enter into multiple sets of bespoke OTC client-clearing documentation with a CM specific to each CCP and/or CCP service.

These client-clearing agreements often operated as standalone agreements for OTC client-cleared transactions that related to a single CCP or to a single CCP service only and did not additionally cater for uncleared OTC derivatives transactions.

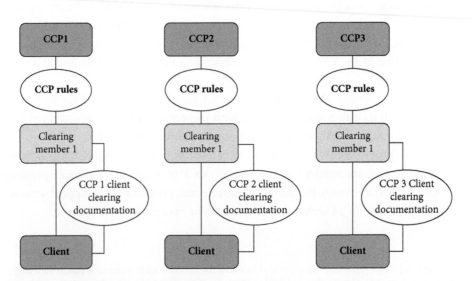

Figure 8.1 Client clearing: CCP-specific model, overview
Source: authors.

Such client-clearing agreements could be completely bespoke or, alternatively, leverage off master agreement technology. In the latter case, this involved creating a separate, standalone master agreement setting out the OTC client-clearing service for the relevant set of transactions that was then amended to accommodate, amongst other things, the common themes set out in section 8.1 above. The London Clearing House (LCH) SwapClear client-clearing agreement was an example of a client-clearing agreement developed to operate in this way by creating and tailoring an ISDA Master Agreement between the CM and the client that governs OTC derivatives transactions between them cleared through the LCH SwapClear service (see Figure 8.2). Whilst the LCH SwapClear client-clearing agreement covers OTC derivatives transactions cleared through the LCH SwapClear service, the master agreement did not cater for OTC derivatives transactions cleared through other CCP services or for uncleared OTC derivatives transactions, in each case entered into with the same CM. Uncleared OTC derivatives transactions would have needed to continue to be documented under a separate ISDA Master Agreement, meaning that there would have been, at a minimum, at least two different master agreements and netting sets (cleared and uncleared) for OTC derivative transactions entered into with the same CM, as well as further bespoke documentation required and netting sets created if products were cleared at one or more other CCPs.

In practice, this presented potential issues in the context of default. One of the key strengths of an industry master agreement (such as the ISDA Master Agreement) is that the parties understand, and can rely on, its standard terms in a default scenario to terminate and close out their derivatives transactions in the knowledge that the analysis is supported by industry standard netting and collateral legal opinions, thus reducing litigation risk, additional costs, and delays amongst other things. If parties are required to look at a proliferation of client-clearing agreements across the cleared and uncleared

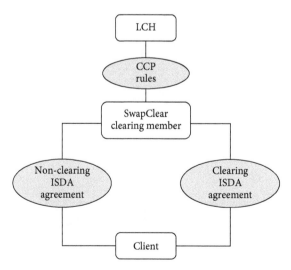

Figure 8.2 Client clearing: LCH SwapClear model
Source: authors.

space (as may be the case for a CM clearing high volumes for a proliferation of clients), the benefits of standardization are reduced.

Therefore, the market sought a more holistic approach which would reflect the overall derivatives relationship between a client and a CM and provide a scalable solution for CMs and clients to be used across multiple CCPs as the volume of OTC client clearing increased across products and platforms. The solution was a cross-CCP model in the form of the Addendum (and, subsequently, the FIA Clearing Module).

8.2.2 Cross-CCP models: ISDA and FIA

Some client-clearing agreements operate to form part of a wider master agreement that covers (or could cover) other transactions (e.g. uncleared OTC derivatives transactions or listed transactions) in addition to OTC client cleared transactions. Such client-clearing agreements are typically not CCP- (or CCP-service-) specific and are capable of operating on a cross-CCP basis. They supplement, and form part of, the master agreement to which they relate and include provisions that set out the OTC client-clearing service for the relevant sets of transactions. These provisions accommodate, amongst other things, the common themes set out in section 8.1 above and amend the terms of the relevant master agreement, where appropriate (i.e. for the purposes of the OTC client cleared transactions). The Addendum and the FIA Clearing Module both leverage off a form of master agreement and are examples of client-clearing agreements that operate in this way (see Figure 8.3).

Indeed, as a result of the ability to function cross-CCP, the market has now converged on the ISDA and FIA solutions to OTC client clearing and, as discussed above, an English law client-clearing agreement is now typically based on the Addendum or the FIA Clearing Module. The cross-CCP structure delivers increased standardization and flexibility.

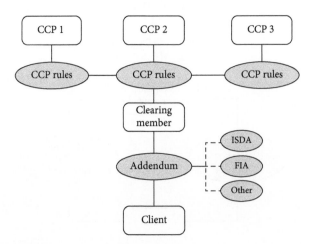

Figure 8.3 Client clearing: Cross-CCP model
Source: authors.

The Addendum (but not the FIA Clearing Module) can be used in conjunction with the ISDA Master Agreement to cover uncleared as well as cleared derivatives that are entered into between the counterparties. However, the ISDA Master Agreement is typically used for OTC derivatives only (and not exchange-traded derivatives).

The Addendum or the FIA Clearing Module can be used in conjunction with the FIA Professional Client Agreement to cover cleared derivatives transactions (either exchange-traded, OTC, or a combination). The FIA 2018 Terms of Business can also be used to cover cleared derivatives transactions (either exchange-traded, OTC, or a combination). However, if counterparties wish to document uncleared OTC derivatives under the same master agreement as cleared derivatives, the ISDA Master Agreement (rather than FIA master documentation) is typically used.

The content of the Addendum and the FIA Clearing Module are closely aligned and broadly cover the same content. However, the Addendum covers a slightly wider set of provisions (including those related to, for instance, Modification Events, limitation of liability, and indemnity). The reason for the discrepancy is largely that, in the case of the FIA Clearing Module, many of the wider provisions are already covered in the relevant FIA master agreement. The FIA Clearing Module also differs from the Addendum in that it includes additional provisions relating to collateral where particular areas have been identified as requiring modification (e.g. to allow for collateral to be transferred on a title transfer basis).

In terms of client-clearing agreements, this chapter focuses on the Addendum, which can be used with both the ISDA Master Agreement and the FIA Professional Client Agreement and covers the wider and more comprehensive set of provisions needed to support the client-clearing relationship.

9 The Addendum

9.1 Structure and Scope

The Addendum is a standard form agreement capable of supplementing and forming part of existing CM/client master agreements and, most commonly, the ISDA Master Agreement or the FIA Professional Client Agreement[29] (each a Master Agreement[30]). Each master agreement has the benefit of being widely adopted in the market with supporting netting and collateral insolvency analysis available via industry legal opinions.

It can be used to document the relationship between a CM and its client for the purposes of clearing OTC derivatives and/or exchange-traded derivatives transactions across CCPs that use the principal-to-principal client-clearing model, depending on whether the Addendum is used in conjunction with the ISDA Master Agreement or the

---

[29] Although there is also the potential for use with prime brokerage and other master agreements, to date, no specific provision has been developed.

[30] Note that the relevant master agreement is defined as the 'Agreement' in the Addendum (n 22).

FIA Professional Client Agreement (as to which see section 8.2.2 above). If the ISDA Master Agreement is used, it may also cover uncleared OTC derivatives that are entered into between the counterparties.

In respect of cleared transactions, it covers transactions capable of being cleared by the CM and which are of a type agreed between the parties (Clearing Eligible Trades[31]) from the point at which they are novated into a relevant CCP and become Client Transactions[32] (including any transactions that are transferred to the CM in its capacity as a back-up CM as a result of a pre-default or post-default porting).[33]

The main body of the Addendum (ss 1–20) includes the industry standard provisions. Any amendments to the provisions in the main body of the Addendum should be included in the Addendum Annex, which allows for elections and specifications to be made as well as for any customization of the client cleared relationship. The Appendices to the Addendum cover English CSA or New York CSA collateral terms (in Appendices 1 and 2), tax provisions (in Appendix 3) and New York CSA amendments to Addendum content (in Appendix 4).

The Addendum is CCP agnostic. In other words, it is designed to operate in conjunction with any non-US CCP that does not mandate its own form of CM/client-clearing agreement and that designs its client protections in a way that can be used with the Addendum. In Table A to the Addendum, the parties agree a list of CCPs and CCP services which may be used (Agreed CCPs and Agreed CCP Services) and set out a cross-reference to the applicable Core Provisions (i.e. the provisions of the relevant CCP rules which relate to Client Transactions, including the consequences of a CM default) and applicable Mandatory CCP Provisions (i.e. the provisions specified by the relevant CCP as being mandatory for inclusion in Client Transactions) which will apply to the relationship. The use of one client-clearing agreement across all CCPs provides simplicity and flexibility both operationally and in terms of default mechanics.

The relevant Core Provisions and Mandatory CCP Provisions are not set out in full in the Addendum as they are established and maintained by the relevant CCP, either in their rulebook or elsewhere. However, they are designed to facilitate simplicity of the Addendum by reducing the requirement for duplication of applicable provisions.

Core Provisions and Mandatory CCP Provisions are likely to include, amongst other things, provisions relating to (i) the segregation of collateral; (ii) the mechanic for close-out and the realized value, if any, to be returned to the client on CM default if default porting does not occur; (iii) the mechanism for porting transactions to the back-up CM on the default of the original CM and other consequences of CM default; and (iii) the exclusion of liability for the CCP.

---

[31] Clearing Eligible Trades are set out in Table A in the Addendum (n 22).

[32] Note, however, that the Addendum (n 22) does not deal with the execution and give-up stage of client clearing (as to which see section 7 above). In addition, note that nothing in the Addendum (other than the provisions relating to offsetting transactions—as to which see section 9.7 below) imposes any obligation on a CM to consent to the clearing of a Clearing Eligible Trade or to enter into Client Transactions or CM/CCP Transactions (see Section 3(g) of the Addendum (n 22)).

[33] See Section 3(a) and (b) of the Addendum (n 22).

It is important that there is a mechanism for the client to agree to be bound by the Core Provisions and the Mandatory CCP Provisions. Therefore, pursuant to the Addendum, both the client and the CM agree to be bound by both the Core Provisions and the Mandatory CCP Provisions, each as amended from time to time.[34]

As discussed further below, the Addendum also creates different netting sets to facilitate close-out on CM default on a CCP service-by-CCP service basis (Cleared Transaction Sets—which are distinct from the netting set for uncleared transactions entered into under the ISDA Master Agreement, if applicable).

9.2 Key Terms and Negotiating Positions

From both the client's and the CM's perspective, at the centre of many of the negotiation points is the fact that the CM acts as an intermediary and facilitates the client's access to clearing so that the client can take the benefit of the protections offered by clearing and, if applicable, satisfy its mandatory clearing obligation under EU EMIR, UK EMIR, or other relevant regulation. However, this can create a tension in the negotiation as it drives an imbalance in the terms, which, at least in the OTC derivatives market, the parties would typically expect to apply mutually. The CM will not want to be faced with obligations under the CM/CCP Transaction or the Client Transaction which are more onerous than those of the CCP or the client under the corresponding trade, as applicable. This leads the CM to want flexibility in the actions that it can take, to restrict some actions that the client can take, and to require compensation for mismatches and losses. Conversely, the client may want to restrict the CM on some of these points as the client will not want to be in a position where the client-clearing service the CM provides is no longer acceptable to the client but the client has to continue with it in order to satisfy its mandatory clearing obligation under EU EMIR, UK EMIR, or other relevant regulation.

We discuss below the key terms of the Addendum together with considerations for the parties when negotiating their terms.

9.3 Key Terms Relating to the Role of the CM as the 'Riskless Principal'

The Addendum contains a number of provisions designed to facilitate the role of the CM as a riskless principal and ensure that the CM does not face any additional liability as a result of intermediating the client's transactions and facilitating the client's access to clearing. In addition, the Addendum splits the relevant master agreement into different netting sets: one netting set in respect of each CCP service[35] and, if applicable,

---

[34] See Section 3(e) and (f) of the Addendum (n 22).
[35] As discussed in section 5 above, subject to statutory protections so any assets of the client that sit at the CCP are protected from an English law perspective.

one relating to uncleared OTC derivatives transactions. Therefore, it is important that the Client Transaction is able to track what action each CCP is taking at CM/CCP level to ensure that the risk under the CM/CCP Transaction is mirrored under the Client Transaction.

The key terms include the following.

9.3.1 Modification Events

It is vital in the client-clearing structure that the Client Transaction and the CM/CCP Transaction are identical mirror images of one another. Otherwise, a mismatch is created which leaves the CM, as intermediary, exposed to basis risk and, potentially, leaves the client with less protection than it would expect to receive in the structure. When a transaction is cleared, the Client Transaction and the CM/CCP Transaction will be identical. However, it is possible that during the life of the transactions an event occurs (a 'Modification Trigger Event'[36]) that results in a change to the CM/CCP Transaction. This is known under the Addendum as a 'Modification Event'.[37] The Addendum, therefore, provides for the Client Transaction to be the same as the CM/CCP Transaction, including following any amendment made to the CM/CCP Transaction.

The rules of the relevant CCP may provide that if the CCP makes a change to the terms of the CM/CCP Transaction, then there is an automatic change to the corresponding Client Transaction (a Modification Change Event). If that is not the case, the Addendum allows for the Client Transaction to be amended by the CM in circumstances where the corresponding CM/CCP Transaction is amended (a Modification Mismatch Event) and for the parties to pay any related gains/losses in connection with the Relevant Event (a Modification Loss Amount).

However, if it is impossible or impracticable for a CM (i) to make a modification to the terms of the Client Transaction or (ii) to maintain the Client Transaction following an automatic change as a result of an amendment to the CM/CCP Transaction, the Addendum provides that the CM is entitled to terminate the Client Transaction. Termination may be a point of negotiation in the context of Modification Events. For example, as contemplated in the Addendum, the client may want to take steps to mitigate the issue by building in a termination period[38] so that it can transfer the transaction on a pre-default porting basis or put in place an offsetting transaction. The procedure (such as notifications required) in respect of Modification Events is set out in the Addendum.

---

[36] A Modification Trigger Event may include any event (such as change in applicable law or any action taken by any governmental authority or relevant CCP pursuant to applicable law) or action taken by or in relation to a relevant CCP or any omission by a relevant CCP to take any action. However, broadly, it does not include a termination as a result of a CCP default, a CM default, or of pre-default porting as a result of any collateral Modification Event or as a result of the action or inaction of the CM (except in specific circumstances).

[37] See Section 3(c) of the Addendum (n 22).

[38] See the definition of 'Modification Termination Period', which can be included in the Addendum Annex (n 22).

9.3.2 Payment adjustment

This provision in the Addendum[39] permits the CM to make adjustments to the Client Transaction for any payment received directly by the client from the relevant CCP.

9.3.3 Limitation of liability and indemnity

It is likely that a CM will want to limit its liability[40] to a client for losses incurred by the client as a result of action or inaction taken elsewhere in the client-clearing structure, and it will want to be indemnified[41] by a client for any losses it suffers in relation to a Client Transaction or corresponding CM/CCP Transaction.

The elective limitation of liability provision in the Addendum excludes liability of the CM[42] for liability for losses of the client resulting from (i) the performance or non-performance or insolvency of a relevant CCP; (ii) any breakdown, delay, malfunction, or failure of transmission of any electronic facility, trade repository, system, or platform used by a relevant CCP or CM or any custodian, settlement system, or any other person; and (iii) actions that the CM takes, or fails to take, for the purposes of compliance with a CCP rule set or applicable law (other than as a result of fraud, wilful default, or gross negligence). Parties elect whether this provision should apply in the Addendum Annex.

The elective indemnity in the Addendum provides the CM[43] an indemnity from the client in respect of losses incurred in connection with the Client Transaction or the CM/CCP Transaction. Parties elect whether this provision should apply in the Addendum Annex.

Limitations of liability and indemnities are not typically a feature of the ISDA Master Agreement. Therefore, the extent to which limitation of liability and indemnities are a point of discussion in the negotiation may depend on the relevant master agreement. However, these provisions are relevant as a result of the CM's role as an intermediary, with the key points of negotiation focusing on their scope; that is, how wide or narrow can the limitations of liability and indemnities be and what is excluded from that scope?

9.3.4 Limited recourse

The limited recourse provision[44] in the Addendum provides that the CM's obligations to the client are expressed as being limited by, and contingent on, performance by the relevant CCP of its corresponding obligations.

---

[39] See Section 11 of the Addendum (n 22).
[40] See Section 12 of the Addendum (n 22).
[41] See Section 13 of the Addendum (n 22).
[42] For this purpose, together with its affiliates, and their respective directors, members, officers, partners, and employees.
[43] For this purpose, together with its affiliates, and their respective directors, members, officers, partners, and employees.
[44] See Section 15 of the Addendum (n 22).

9.4 Pre-default Porting/Transfer of Positions in Absence of Default

'Pre-default porting' is the mechanism by which a client can require its CM (absent a CM or CCP default) to transfer all of its rights and obligations with respect to a Client Transaction and related collateral to another CM.[45] The Addendum provides for pre-default porting provided that certain transfer conditions, including the requirement to transfer any additional collateral and any additional transfer conditions specified by the parties in the Addendum Annex, are met and subject to the relevant CCP rules and applicable law.

Given the restricted rights of termination that a client is likely to be required to accept in relation to the CM, pre-default porting is of particular importance to a client as it could be key to protecting the client in circumstances where the CM's credit is deteriorating or even in circumstances where the CM has defaulted in relation to the client but the relevant CCP has not yet declared the CM in default. It may also be useful to a client in circumstances where the CM changes the basis on which it provides the client-clearing services. For these reasons, the client is likely to appreciate a broad right to transfer.

The CM, however, will be required to consider its position and continuing collateral obligations in relation to the CM/CCP Transaction. Consequently, a CM may want to establish stricter parameters within which pre-default porting can occur such that the client is only entitled to require a transfer when conditions that protect the CM for any immediate ongoing obligations that it may have to the CCP in relation to the CM/CCP Transactions are satisfied.

Negotiations around the pre-default porting provision focus predominantly on the conditions which need to be satisfied for the client to be entitled to require the transfer. The conditions break down into two main types—conditions relating to default and commercial conditions.

9.4.1 Default conditions
Typically, the conditions to be considered are that:

(1) the relevant CCP is not in default;
(2) the relevant CCP has not declared a default in respect of the CM; and
(3) the client is not in default, nor subject to a potential event of default.

Neither the CM nor the client should want pre-default porting to be available if the relevant CCP is in default or the relevant CCP has declared a default in respect of the CM. In either case, the parties are no longer in a pre-default scenario, meaning the relevant

---

[45] See Section 5 of the Addendum (n 22).

CCP is unlikely to take any action to facilitate a request for a 'pre-default' transfer and, even if the relevant CCP would take such action, the parties would not want this to cut across any actions taken under the default rules and the protections available in those circumstances. Consequently, these conditions are unlikely to be controversial and are included as standard in the Addendum.

A condition relating to client default is likely to be more controversial. The CM will want to have the ability to close out all Client Transactions upon client default without, potentially, having some Client Transactions in transit to another CM. That is particularly the case when the relevant client default is insolvency-related as the CM will not want to facilitate a transfer of transactions in such a scenario. However, any attempt at blocking pre-default porting when only a potential event of default has occurred with respect to a client may be seen as a step too far. A client may not want to be tied in to using the clearing services of a particular CM when it is not actually in default.

9.4.2 Commercial conditions

It is often a condition to pre-default porting that the client provides the CM with collateral to (i) protect it from the risk that one or more Client Transactions to be transferred are not so transferred and (ii) satisfy any additional collateral requirements that arise (e.g. they may be imposed by the CCP) or result from the relevant transfer in respect of any Client Transactions which are not being transferred. In the latter case, this is provided as a standard transfer condition in the Addendum.

Client-clearing negotiations may also contemplate the imposition of additional transfer conditions. Negotiations revolve around these conditions and in what circumstances they should apply. For example, a client may accept that it will need to collateralize the CM's exposure when there is a transfer of some but not all Client Transactions, but the client will expect only the bare minimum of collateral related conditions to apply when it is transferring the entire set of Client Transactions to an alternative CM.

9.5 Early Termination Following Default

Broadly, the Addendum is structured to utilize the existing mechanics set out in the relevant master agreement, where possible, with the client benefiting from protections on CM and CCP default delivered by the Core Provisions operating in conjunction with the Addendum. In the context of client clearing, it is necessary to consider three broad default scenarios: (i) client default, (ii) CM default, and (iii) CCP default.[46] For an overview, refer to Table 8.1.

Taking each type of default in turn:

---

[46] See Section 8 of the Addendum (n 22).

Table 8.1 Overview of early termination provisions following default

Client default	CM default	CCP default
Master agreement applies for cleared and uncleared transactions	Master agreement applies for cleared and uncleared transactions	Only relevant to cleared transactions
Netting across cleared sets and uncleared transactions	Netting sets are separate for cleared sets and uncleared transactions	Transactions linked to relevant CCP terminated only
Termination amount calculated according to master agreement	For cleared transactions, upon the declaration of default of the CM under the relevant CCP rules:	Netting sets created for services at relevant CCP
CM to manage close-out of corresponding CM/CCP Transactions	• transactions linked to relevant CCP terminated only	Timing of termination and valuation matches those per CCP rules
	• netting sets created for services at relevant CCP	CM and client may use set-off in respect of different termination amounts
	• timing of termination and valuation matches those per CCP rules	
	• porting per CCP rules	
	Client may use set-off in respect of different termination amounts	

Source: authors.

9.5.1 Client default

As discussed above, the CM is facing the client on a principal-to-principal basis and has obligations to the client and corresponding back-to-back obligations to the CCP. If the client goes into default, the CM does not want to be in the position where it is required to keep performing under the CM/CCP Transaction even though the client may have stopped performing under the corresponding Client Transaction. Consequently, the CM will want to have the same rights to take action on client default that it would have under a non-clearing related master agreement so that it can take action quickly to neutralize its position at the relevant CCP. From the CM's perspective, therefore, the standard events of default[47] and termination events[48] that would apply to the client under a non-clearing-related master agreement should be retained and the CM should be entitled to include in the close-out calculation any costs or gains involved in neutralizing its position under the CM/CCP Transaction at the relevant CCP.

Broadly, therefore, the Addendum, provides the CM with a right to terminate on an event of default, termination event, or similar event in respect of the client based on the close-out provisions in the relevant master agreement (subject to certain amendments

---

[47] Under an ISDA Master Agreement, events of default may include failure to pay or deliver, breach of agreement/repudiation of agreement, credit support default, misrepresentation, default under a Specified Transaction, cross default, bankruptcy, and merger without assumption.

[48] Under an ISDA Master Agreement, termination events may include illegality, force majeure, tax event, tax event upon merger, and credit event upon merger.

designed to ensure that the CM can take into account the cost or gain of neutralizing the corresponding transactions at the relevant CCP when determining the termination amount).[49]

Upon client default, cleared and uncleared transactions entered into under the relevant master agreement may form part of the same netting set and close out at the same time.

9.5.2 CM default

From the client's perspective, determining what events of default and/or termination events should apply to the CM is harder. The client is looking through the CM to the CCP and will want to take the benefit of the protections against the default of the CM that the relevant CCP offers (including post-default porting or return of residual value) and that the client has chosen. The intention of clearing is that the client is always in the same position vis-à-vis the CM as the CM is vis-à-vis the CCP. On that basis, it is arguable that limited discretion is needed and the Client Transaction should only terminate once the corresponding CM/CCP Transaction is terminated or ported as a result of the relevant CCP putting the CM into default, and the valuation of the Client Transaction following termination should match the value ascribed to the corresponding CM/CCP Transaction. In other words, the close-out process in relation to the Client Transaction should mirror what is happening with the corresponding CM/CCP Transaction. The client should not be able to take any unilateral action as it would otherwise run the risk of prejudicing the protections afforded to it by the relevant CCP and lead to a mismatch between the Client Transaction and the CM/CCP Transaction.

This is a significant departure from the OTC uncleared derivatives market where parties would generally expect events of default and termination events to apply mutually. However, for the reasons set out above, there is a solid rationale for taking this position in the context of the OTC cleared derivatives market.

In addition, a client may feel that there is a residual concern that the client may face a defaulting CM in circumstances where the relevant CCP does not take action, perhaps because the CM is not yet in default at the CM/CCP level and the CCP is unaware of the default. This will involve an assessment of the concept of 'default' in relation to the CM under the relevant CCP rules. To the extent that a client does not feel adequately protected by that concept, it may seek to negotiate that certain events of default apply in relation to CM in addition to termination in circumstances where the relevant CCP puts the CM in default. Negotiations will revolve around the number and types of default event that will apply and the consequences of the client terminating as a result of one of those events occurring. For example, a CM may accept that limited events of default can apply in relation to it, but it is likely to want to keep control of the default and valuation process as it will need to manage its back-to-back position with the CCP.

---

[49] See Section 8(a) of the Addendum (n 22).

Therefore, in respect of the Addendum, for cleared transactions, the client will typically only be able to terminate cleared transactions upon the declaration (or automatic occurrence) of CM default under the relevant CCP rules (with the timing and valuation in respect of such termination mirroring those under the relevant CCP rules).[50] The Addendum creates different Cleared Transaction Sets to facilitate close-out on CM default on a CCP-service-by-CCP-service basis. Different Cleared Transaction Sets may be terminated at different times, depending on what happens at the level of each individual CCP.

For transactions under the master agreement not covered by the Addendum (such as uncleared transactions which are not impacted by the actions of the relevant CCP), the termination rights of the client in the context of CM default remain unaffected and are the same as under the master agreement. This is to ensure that the client can assess the CM's credit risk and make its own decision as to the best course of action in relation to its uncleared portfolio.

9.5.3 CCP default

In respect of a CCP default, all transactions cleared at the relevant CCP will terminate (with the timing and valuation in respect of such termination mirroring those under the relevant CCP rules).[51]

As with CM default, the Addendum creates different Cleared Transaction Sets to facilitate close-out on CCP default on a CCP-service-by-CCP-service basis. Different Cleared Transaction Sets may be terminated at different times, depending on what happens at the level of each individual CCP.

In practice, a CCP default would appear to be unlikely (although not impossible—see further Chapter 12 'Recovery and Resolution of CCPs' by Victor de Serière in this volume).

9.5.4 Hierarchy of provisions in the case of multiple defaults

In case of multiple counterparty defaults, the Addendum generally gives priority to the default that is acted upon first or, if applicable, to the order dictated in the relevant CCP rules.[52]

9.5.5 Set-off

The Addendum provides a right of set-off to the client, in the case of a CM default, and to both CM and client, in the case of a CCP default, whereby the relevant party or parties can elect to set off relevant termination amounts due in respect of the termination of each Cleared Transaction Set and transactions under the master agreement not covered by the Addendum (such as uncleared transactions).[53]

---

[50] See Section 8(b) of the Addendum (n 22).
[51] See Section 8(c) of the Addendum (n 22).
[52] See Section 8(d) of the Addendum (n 22).
[53] See Section 8(e) of the Addendum (n 22).

9.6 Early Termination in Circumstances Other than Default

When negotiating client-clearing agreements, parties often consider whether they should have an optional right to terminate the Client Transaction and, if so, within what parameters.[54] Typically, if an optional termination right is included, the provision will operate with the party that wants to terminate giving notice to the other party of its intention to terminate, followed by a period within which the client can seek to transfer the relevant Client Transaction on a pre-default porting basis or enter into offsetting transactions, followed by termination of the relevant Client Transactions that remain outstanding with the CM in control of the close-out and valuation process so that it can manage its process with the corresponding CM/CCP Transaction.

A CM is very likely to want an optional termination right to cover the eventuality that it no longer wants to provide client-clearing services generally or with respect to a particular CCP.

A client may also want an optional right to terminate. However, if its rationale for requiring an optional termination right is solely to preserve a mutual application of terms to the extent possible, it should consider carefully the consequences of using such a right. It might be preferable for the client to rely on other mechanics available to it to terminate the relationship instead (e.g. pre-default porting) rather than starting a process that could ultimately culminate in the CM being in control of a close-out and valuation process.

As explained above, there will be good reasons why a CM may want an optional termination right. In order for the CM not to end up in control of the close-out and valuation process, it will be key for the client that there is a reasonable period between notice of termination and termination itself so that it can transfer the relevant transactions to another CM and that its right to transfer is not unduly restricted.

Negotiations in relation to any optional termination right focus, therefore, on the length of time between notice of termination and termination and on the conditions that apply to pre-default porting in those circumstances. The outcome on these points may vary, depending on which party exercises the optional termination right and, if that party is the CM, its reasons for exercising the optional termination right. To the extent applicable, fair, reasonable, non-discriminatory, and transparent (FRANDT) considerations will also be relevant (see further below).

9.6.1 Early termination for illegality or impossibility
It may be that an event occurs that will make it impossible or illegal for the parties to keep performing under a Client Transaction. Whilst a client may be comfortable that they are adequately protected in relation to CM default by the rules of the relevant CCP or otherwise does not want to run the risk of prejudicing the protections afforded to

---

[54] See Section 9 of the Addendum (n 22).

it by the CCP by taking unilateral action against the CM, it seems somewhat odd to suggest that the client should remain bound by its Client Transactions with no right to terminate in circumstances where it would be illegal or impossible for it to continue performance.

Consequently, if the parties elect for this provision to apply in the Addendum Annex, the Addendum includes an optional termination provision that provides (i) both parties with the right to terminate any Client Transaction if it would be impossible, impracticable, or unlawful for the relevant party to make or receive any payment or delivery in respect of a Client Transaction; and (ii) the CM with the right to terminate any Client Transaction if it would be impossible, impracticable, or unlawful for the CM to make or receive any payment or delivery in respect of the corresponding CM/CCP Transaction.[55] However, prior to the designation of a termination date, pre-default porting may still occur. If an event could trigger this termination provision and a default-based termination provision allowing the CM to terminate, the CM may choose which termination provision to trigger.

In practice, impossibility and impracticability may be high thresholds to meet.

9.6.2 Termination of Agreed CCP Services

If the parties elect for this provision to apply in the Addendum Annex, the Addendum includes an optional termination provision that provides the CM and the client with the right to terminate all Client Transactions with any specific Agreed CCP Service, provided that notice in writing is provided to the other party (following which termination of relevant Client Transactions will be effective).[56] The applicable notice period is negotiable and should be specified in the Addendum Annex.

During this notice period, the client may exercise its right to (i) transfer the relevant Client Transactions (in accordance with the provisions relating to 'pre-default porting—see section 9.4 above) or (ii) request that the CM accepts one or more offsetting transactions in relation to the relevant Client Transactions for clearing (in accordance with the provisions relating to 'offsetting transactions'—see section 9.7 below).

It is possible to specify in the Addendum Annex that no additional transfer conditions will apply in these circumstances in the event that the client seeks to exercise its right to pre-default porting.

9.7 Offsetting Transactions

- The Addendum provides the client with a right to request that the CM enter into transactions that offset existing Client Transactions, in whole or in part, subject

---

[55] See Section 7 of the Addendum (n 22).
[56] See Section 17 of the Addendum (n 22).

to certain offsetting conditions. In effect, this provides the client with a method of closing out the position.[57]

- Offsetting conditions include (i) the absence of designation or notification of an early termination date in respect of the clearing agreement; (ii) the satisfaction of any offsetting condition agreed for this purpose in any portfolio margining agreement between the CM and the client, including any obligations relating to the provision of additional collateral; and (iii) the requirement that any offsetting transaction will not increase the aggregate exposure limits agreed between the CM and the client in the context of all Client Transactions.

This is an important provision for the client as, generally, the client's rights to early termination are disapplied.

9.8 Other Key Terms

Above, we have considered some of the key concepts underpinning the Addendum. Other important provisions include:

9.8.1 Representations
The Addendum repeats the representations given by the parties in the relevant master agreement and facilitates any additional representations included by the parties on a case-by-case basis as specified in the Addendum Annex (e.g. a client's representations as to due authorization and the relationship between the parties, any additional representations relating to tax or a representation in respect of the provision of indirect clearing services in respect of the Client Transactions—in respect of the latter as to which see section 12.1 below).[58]

9.8.2 Compression
A client may request that the CM compresses two or more CM/CCP Transactions relating to the client in accordance with the relevant CCP rule set, following which the CM will be required to take the relevant compression action.[59]

9.8.3 Payment netting
The parties may elect that payment netting applies in respect of amounts payable in the same currency on the same day in respect of certain Specified Transactions or groups of transactions.[60] Parties elect whether this provision should apply in the Addendum Annex.

---

[57] See Section 6 of the Addendum (n 22).
[58] See Section 2 of the Addendum (n 22).
[59] See Section 3(d) of the Addendum (n 22).
[60] See Section 3(h) of the Addendum (n 22).

9.8.4 Tax

Appendix 3 to the Addendum sets out applicable tax provisions. Broadly, the intention is that a CM should not suffer any additional tax burden as a result of intermediating Client Transactions.[61]

9.8.5 Disclosure of information

The Addendum includes an elective provision allowing the parties to disclose confidential information in respect of the other where such disclosure is required by law or is made to CCPs (or any system used in connection with clearing), advisors, rating agencies, or with the consent of the other party.[62] Parties elect whether this provision should apply in the Addendum Annex.

9.8.6 Increased costs

The Addendum includes an elective increased costs provision allowing the parties flexibility to negotiate any increased costs that might apply and who bears that cost.[63] Parties elect whether this provision should apply in the Addendum Annex.

10 Addendum: Collateral

10.1 Purpose of Collateral

A CCP is required to impose, call, and collect margin to limit its credit exposure to its CMs.[64] Therefore, the relevant CCP will require a CM to provide margin in respect of the CM/CCP Transaction. The CM will, consequently, request margin from the client in respect of the Client Transaction.

There are two principal types of margin aimed at covering different risks.

10.1.1 Variation margin (VM)

Variation margin (VM) covers mark-to-market exposures of all transactions in a netting set by reference to the mark-to-market valuation attributed to those transactions. This protects counterparties against exposures related to the current market value of the OTC derivatives transaction resulting from actual changes in market price and may be exchanged frequently, even multiple times per day[65]. Typically, VM is paid in cash and the amount posted will reflect the change in mark-to-market exposure since the previous margin call. The relevant CCP, CM, and client may all be required to post and receive VM, depending on the market value of the relevant transactions at a given time.

---

[61] See Section 4 of the Addendum (n 22).
[62] See Section 14 of the Addendum (n 22).
[63] See Section 16 of the Addendum (n 22).
[64] See EU EMIR and UK EMIR (n 3), Arts 41, 46.
[65] CMs may be willing to accept VM from clients on a daily basis but the client may be subject to a funding charge or additional collateral may be required to be provided to access this service.

10.1.2 Initial margin (IM)

Initial margin (IM) is margin collected to cover potential future exposure, which could stem from movements in the market value of the derivatives position occurring between the last exchange of VM and the liquidation of positions following a default of a CM. IM is effectively an additional buffer to cover current and potential future exposures. IM is usually posted at the outset, based on established collateral amounts determined by the CCP, and remains posted with the CCP until all transactions pertaining to a client in a given account are terminated. The parties may specify which collateral may be provided as IM. Typically, IM will comprise cash or highly liquid securities which meet the requirements of the relevant CCP rules. (However, other types of collateral may also be accepted.) A CCP itself will never be required to post IM, only receive it, to ensure that the CCP remains suitably robust.

A CCP may also require a variety of other different types of margin to cover other risks arising, depending on the product being cleared.

10.2 Structure of Addendum Collateral Mechanics

In the client-clearing structure, the collateral arrangements between the parties need to support the collateral calls being made by the CCP in relation to the CM/CCP Transactions that correspond to the relevant Client Transactions. To the extent that the client-clearing agreement leverages off a master agreement that already includes collateral arrangements, it may be possible to use those mechanics for the collateral arrangements in relation to the Client Transactions as well. It will depend on the type of master agreement and the collateral arrangements as to whether any amendments are required. For a high-level comparison of ISDA vs FIA collateral documentation, refer to Table 8.2.

If the client-clearing agreement is based on FIA 'futures-style' documentation, the collateral arrangements in that agreement will probably be flexible enough to support the collateral arrangements that the parties will need for Client Transactions, and existing collateral documentation can be maintained with any relevant amendments being made in the Addendum Annex. The Addendum provides (in section 10) that the parties may elect for 'Collateral Standard Terms' to apply in the Addendum Annex. Therefore, if Collateral Standard Terms apply (and the master agreement is not a form of 1992 or 2002 ISDA Master Agreement), if an FIA agreement is listed as the 'Existing Collateral Agreement' in the Addendum Annex, then collateral in respect of Client Transactions will be delivered as per the Existing Collateral Agreement as amended by the Addendum Annex, including any election made pursuant to Section 10(b) (see further below).

If the client-clearing agreement is based on a form of ISDA Master Agreement, new collateral terms for the Client Transactions will be required (and existing collateral terms disapplied for those transactions), with amendments being made to the English CSA or the New York CSA, as applicable. In this scenario, if Collateral Standard Terms are elected

Table 8.2 ISDA vs FIA collateral documentation: A comparison

FIA collateral documentation	ISDA collateral documentation
Existing collateral arrangement maintained	Existing credit support document disapplied for cleared transactions
Presumption collateral for cleared transactions provided on transfer of title basis	Collateral provided on transfer of title basis under English CSA
	Collateral provided on security interest basis with a right of reuse under New York CSA
Any other amendments agreed in addendum annex	Any amendments to form of Paragraph 11 (English law)/Paragraph 13 (New York law) agreed in addendum annex
	Separate CSA with form of Paragraph 11 (English law)/Paragraph 13 (New York law) for cleared transactions with each relevant CCP service
	Elections specified in CSA Elections Table
Value of collateral transferred taken into account on early termination	Value of collateral transferred taken into account on early termination
Collateral protection at CCP for client positions as per Core Provisions	Collateral protection at CCP for client positions as per Core Provisions

Source: authors.

to apply in the Addendum Annex (and the master agreement is a form of 1992 or 2002 ISDA Master Agreement), (i) the Existing Collateral Agreement (which may still apply to uncleared OTC derivatives transactions between the parties) will not apply to Client Transactions and (ii) unless otherwise specified in the Addendum Annex, a new English CSA or New York CSA (depending on the governing law of the ISDA Master Agreement) per CCP service will apply to Client Transactions in each Cleared Transaction Set.[66] ISDA has published a form of Paragraph 11 to the English CSA (referred to in the Addendum as the 'English Law CSA Collateral Terms') and a form of Paragraph 13 to the New York CSA (referred to in the Addendum as the 'New York Law CSA Collateral Terms') that have been modified for use with Client Transactions. In each case, the relevant form should be set out in Appendix 1 (English Law CSA Collateral Terms) or Appendix 2 (New York Law CSA Collateral Terms) to the Addendum, as applicable, with any elections specified in the CSA Elections Table in the Addendum Annex.

The starting point in each case (assuming that English law governed collateral documentation is used) is that collateral will be provided on a title transfer basis or a security interest basis with a right of reuse. This will be the case if an English CSA or a New York CSA is used. It may not be the case otherwise and so Section 10(b) allows for parties to specify in the Addendum Annex whether the CM may use the collateral provided by the client under the Client Transactions in order to allow the CM to satisfy its obligations to

---

[66] On each date that the first Clearing Eligible Trade for an Agreed CCP Service is submitted for clearing.

provide collateral under the CM/CCP Transactions, so overriding any provision to the contrary in an Existing Collateral Agreement.[67] If this election is specified as applying, then the client will be entitled to equivalent used collateral in return, that is, collateral of the same type and value but not exactly the same collateral as posted. When considering whether this election should apply, clients should consider any relevant impacts under any relevant client asset protection regime that may otherwise be applicable. Additionally, if the collateral is to be delivered under a collateral agreement, which does not provide for collateral to be transferred either on a title transfer basis or by way of security with a right of reuse, the parties should consider whether further amendments are required.

10.3 Elections and Negotiating Points

Set out below are some points for consideration when negotiating/reflecting the commercial agreement of certain elections in the English CSA in a client cleared context.

10.3.1 VM matching
If the parties specify 'VM matching' in the CSA election table in the Addendum Annex as applicable, then VM will be called separately in respect of each currency in respect of which the Client Transactions are denominated or, if denominated in more than one currency, the currency in respect of which the relevant CCP calls for margin. This reflects the practice of CCPs in relation to VM. If it is not specified to be applicable, then VM will be called collectively in the base currency in respect of all Client Transactions. Where VM matching is not applicable, the CM may impose a fee on the client to reflect that fact that the CM will not be provided with the VM in the currency that it needs to provide to the CCP and so will have to source the VM in the correct currency itself.

10.3.2 Additional Collateral Amount
CMs may require an Additional Collateral Amount to be provided by their clients. This is an amount in excess of the IM amount which the CM must provide to the CCP on the corresponding CCP transactions. In other words, this amount is an add-on to the CCP's IM requirements in relation to the CM/CCP Transactions. To the extent that the parties agree that an Additional Collateral Amount will be provided, it will be specified in the CSA Elections Table in the Addendum Annex.

Amongst other things, an Additional Collateral Amount can be used as a means of ensuring that the CM does not need to pre-fund the collateral to the CCP. If such an amount is specified, CMs will likely want some flexibility as to when they can increase it. Conversely, a client will want to define the parameters within which the amount can be changed.

---

[67] See Section 10(b) of the Addendum (n 22).

CMs are obliged under EU EMIR and UK EMIR to pass any Additional Collateral Amounts agreed with clients which have an individually segregated account to the relevant CCP.[68]

10.3.3 Matching elections

There are a number of elections in the CSA Elections Table that will need to be made when agreeing to the terms of the collateral arrangements, including those around timing of demands for collateral, of valuations and of transfers, and the method of valuation. A key consideration when making those elections is to what extent the collateral arrangements under the Client Transactions should match and facilitate the CM's obligation to post collateral under the corresponding CM/CCP Transactions.

10.3.4 Transit risk

At any point where the CM is holding the client's collateral (and has not yet passed it on to the relevant CCP), there is a risk that, should the CM become insolvent at that particular time, the collateral may form part of the CM's insolvency estate. The extent of the risk depends on the length of time the collateral is held by the CM and the relevant insolvency law in the jurisdiction of that CM.

11 Legal Opinions

11.1 ISDA Netting and Collateral Opinions

A key question underpinning the client-clearing structure is whether, and how, the client-clearing agreement is valid and enforceable upon the insolvency of one of the counterparties in the various jurisdictions of relevance to the particular client-clearing relationship. ISDA has published two supplemental opinions (for each jurisdiction) to the existing industry standard ISDA netting and collateral opinions (which relate to the validity and enforceability of close-out netting and collateral arrangements upon the insolvency of the collateral provider) to support the client-clearing relationship as set out in the Addendum.[69] The parties will need to assess the extent to which such opinions are available for them to rely on.[70] These opinions are also important in ensuring relevant counterparties can benefit from more beneficial regulatory capital treatment in the EU and the United Kingdom.

---

[68] See EU EMIR and UK EMIR (n 3), Art. 39(6).
[69] The opinions can be accessed at https://www.isda.org/category/opinions (accessed 23 March 2023) (member access only).
[70] Generally, only ISDA members may rely on ISDA opinions.

11.2 CM Reliance Opinion

The CM reliance opinion principally concerns the enforceability of certain close-out, set-off, and default provisions of the Addendum against a client located in the relevant jurisdiction. The English law governed opinion is largely a drawdown of the standard ISDA netting and collateral opinions, although it additionally covers the enforceability of the limited recourse provisions set out in the Addendum (as to which, see section. 9.3 above).

11.3 Client Reliance Opinion

The client reliance opinion principally concerns the enforceability of certain close-out, set-off, and default provisions of the Addendum against a CM located in the relevant jurisdiction. The English law governed opinion cross-refers to, and draws down, the standard ISDA netting and collateral opinions but additionally contains new analysis relating to CCP default, the hierarchy of events, set-off, and limited recourse provisions each as set out in the Addendum (as to which, see sections 9.3 and 9.5 above), the impact on CCP rule sets, and certain CM default amendments as set out in the Annex to the opinion. The client reliance opinion does not cover an analysis of the Core Provisions or the Mandatory CCP Provisions.

12 Recent Developments and Other Considerations

This area continues to evolve and a number of documentation developments also warrant consideration, although this cannot be regarded as a definitive list).

12.1 MiFID II and MiFIR Model Provisions for the Addendum

CMs subject to EU MiFID II[71] and EU MiFIR should consider whether compliance with certain provisions of EU MiFID II and EU MiFIR is required. In 2017, ISDA published the MiFID II and MiFIR Model Provisions for the Addendum,[72] which is intended to assist CMs with compliance by providing model provisions some or all of which may form part of the Addendum (or another client-clearing agreement). In

---

[71] Directive 2014/65/EU of the European Parliament and of the Council of 15 May 2014 on markets in financial instruments and amending Directive 2002/92/EC and Directive 2011/61/EU, [2014] OJ L173/349 (12 June 2014) (EU MIFID II).

[72] The MiFID II and MiFIR Model Provisions for the Addendum can be accessed at https://www.isda.org/2017/10/18/mifid-ii-and-mifir-model-provisions (accessed 23 March 2023).

the same year, the FIA published the regulatory patch which also includes provisions aimed to facilitate compliance with certain provisions of EU MiFID II and EU MiFIR, amongst other regulatory requirements.

The ISDA model provisions relate to:

(1) Art. 25 of EU RTS 6,[73] which requires a CM to make an initial assessment of a prospective client, taking into account the nature, scale, and complexity of the prospective client's business against certain criteria and to review annually the on-going performance of its clearing clients against such criteria. The binding written agreement referred to in EU MiFID II, Art. 17(6)[74] is required to contain those criteria and set out the frequency at which the CM shall review its clients' performance against those criteria, where this review is to be conducted more than once a year. The binding written agreement shall set out the consequences for clients that do not comply with those criteria;

(2) EU RTS 6, Art. 26, which requires a CM to (i) set out and communicate to its clients appropriate trading and position limits to mitigate and manage its own counterparty, liquidity, operational, and other risks; (ii) monitor its clients' positions against such limits as close to real time as possible and have appropriate pre-trade and post-trade procedures for managing the risk of breaches of the position limits by way of appropriate margining practice and other appropriate means; and (iii) document in writing such procedures and record whether the clients comply with those procedures;

(3) EU RTS 26, Art. 4(1), which sets out the time frames for the transfer of information for cleared derivatives transactions on a bilateral basis (as to which see also section 7 above in respect of the CDEA);

(4) the EU EMIR Indirect Clearing RTS[75] and the EU MiFIR Indirect Clearing RTS,[76] which set out the requirements for the provision of indirect clearing services. In the latter case, the model provisions include a representation by the client that it is not, and will not, provide indirect clearing services in connection with the Client Transactions.

---

[73] Commission Delegated Regulation (EU) No. 2017/589 of 19 July 2016 supplementing Directive 2014/65/EU of the European Parliament and of the Council with regard to regulatory technical standards specifying the organisational requirements of investment firms engaged in algorithmic trading, [2017] OJ L87/417 (31 March 2017) (EU RTS 6).

[74] EU MiFID II (n 71), Art. 17(6) provides that:

An investment firm that acts as a general clearing member for other persons shall have in place effective systems and controls to ensure clearing services are only applied to persons who are suitable and meet clear criteria and that appropriate requirements are imposed on those persons to reduce risks to the investment firm and to the market. The investment firm shall ensure that there is a binding written agreement between the investment firm and the person regarding the essential rights and obligations arising from the provision of that service.

[75] Commission Delegated Regulation (EU) No. 2017/2155 of 22 September 2017 amending Delegated Regulation (EU) No. 149/2013 with regard to regulatory technical standards on indirect clearing arrangements, [2017] OJ L304/13 (21 November 2017) (EU EMIR Indirect Clearing RTS).

[76] Commission Delegated Regulation (EU) No. 2017/2154 of 22 September 2017 supplementing Regulation (EU) No. 600/2014 of the European Parliament and of the Council with regard to regulatory technical standards on indirect clearing arrangements, [2017] OJ L304/6 (21 November 2017) (EU MiFIR Indirect Clearing RTS).

CMs subject to the equivalent UK onshored provisions may also wish to consider making any relevant corresponding changes to the Addendum (or other relevant client-clearing agreement).

12.2   FRANDT

12.2.1 EU position

Under EU EMIR, without being obliged to contract, CMs and clients, which provide clearing services, whether directly or indirectly, are required to provide those services under fair, reasonable, non-discriminatory and transparent (FRANDT) commercial terms. Such CMs and clients are required to take all reasonable measures to identify, prevent, manage, and monitor conflicts of interest, in particular between the trading unit and the clearing unit, that may adversely affect the FRANDT provision of clearing services. Such measures shall also be taken where trading and clearing services are pro-vided by different legal entities belonging to the same group. CMs and clients shall be permitted to control the risks related to the clearing services offered.[77] The FRANDT RTS[78] specify the conditions under which the commercial terms for clearing services for OTC derivatives are to be considered to be FRANDT.[79] The conditions cover (i) the transparency of the on-boarding process, (ii) the form for a request for proposal, (iii) disclosure of commercial terms, (iv) risk control assessment, (v) requirements for the commercial terms for the provision of clearing services, (vi) fees and pass-on costs, and (vii) refusal of clearing orders, suspension, liquidation, or close-out of client positions and notice periods.

CMs (and, if relevant, clients) subject to EU EMIR should consider how they in-tend to comply with the requirements of the FRANDT RTS, including (i) ensuring that contractual provisions in the Addendum support the relevant aspects of the FRANDT RTS and/or (ii) putting sufficient internal policies and procedures in place to ensure any exercise of the contractual agreement happens in accordance with the FRANDT RTS. In determining the approach, a number of factors should be considered, including (i) the significance of point 5.1 of the Annex to the FRANDT RTS, which requires the commercial terms for the provision of clearing services to be laid down in writing, be clear and complete, and cover all essential terms and conditions for the provision of clearing services; (ii) overarching policy objectives of FRANDT in increasing ac-cess to clearing;[80] and (iii) the specific contractual term in question. Either of the two

---

[77] See EU EMIR (n 3), Art. 4(3a).

[78] Commission Delegated Regulation (EU) No. 2021/1456 of 2 June 2021 supplementing Regulation (EU) No. 648/2012 of the European Parliament and of the Council by specifying the conditions under which the commer-cial terms for clearing services for OTC derivatives are to be considered to be fair, reasonable, non-discriminatory and transparent, [2021] OJ L317/1 (8 September 2021) (FRANDT RTS).

[79] The FRANDT RTS (n 78) entered into force on 9 September 2021 and applied from 9 March 2022 (other than in respect of commercial terms for clearing services agreed before 9 September 2021, for which the relevant appli-cation date is 9 September 2022).

[80] See, e.g. the discussions which arose in the context of the FRANDT consultation procedure.

approaches described above, but in particular the internal policies and procedures approach, could, in addition, be supplemented by the provision of a separate disclosure document to the relevant client. Such a disclosure document could contain a range of information, including, but not limited to, the following: (i) a factual overview of, and background to, the FRANDT RTS; (ii) an overview of how the CM is proposing to comply with the FRANDT RTS; and (iii) other pertinent information which the CM believes is of relevance to the client.

In addition to the above, in the context of the refusal of clearing orders, suspension, liquidation, or close-out of client positions and notice periods, CMs will also need to form their own view as to the meaning of 'reasonable and duly justified'. CMs should note (without limitation): (i) Recitals (6) and (7) of the FRANDT RTS; (ii) the guidance provided in the 'Contractual terms' section of the Explanatory Memorandum published by the European Commission on 2 June 2021 in conjunction with its adopted delegated regulation specifying the conditions under which the commercial terms for clearing services for OTC derivatives are to be considered to be fair, reasonable, non-discriminatory, and transparent; and (iii) the fact that having reference to other applicable regulatory obligations or objective criteria is likely to be helpful in this regard.

12.2.2 UK position

In the United Kingdom, Section 40 of the Financial Services Act 2021 (the FSA 2021) amends UK EMIR to include broadly equivalent provisions on FRANDT to those set out in EU EMIR. The UK provisions entered into force on 1 July 2021. In addition, under the FSA 2021, the FCA is empowered to make rules specifying the conditions under which the commercial terms are FRANDT, that is, the equivalent of the FRANDT RTS in the EU). However, the FCA is not currently expected to publish any such rules.

CMs (and, if relevant, clients) subject to UK EMIR should consider how they intend to comply with the requirements of the UK FRANDT regime absent any detailed rules, including whether they wish to offer a consistent offering to UK and EU clients (if applicable).

12.3 Monitoring CCP Rules: Collateralized to Market vs Settled to Market

As discussed in section 6 above, CMs and clients should ensure that they monitor the relevant CCP rules to ensure they are aware of any relevant updates and their impacts.[81]

For example, in recent years, certain CCPs (including the Chicago Merchant Exchange (CME) and LCH Limited) have made certain amendments to their rules

---

[81] See also Chapter 10 'Segregation and Portability of Cleared OTC Derivatives in Europe' by Bas Zebregs in this volume.

that have resulted in certain cleared derivatives transactions, including a settled-to-market (STM) mechanic in addition to, or instead of, a collateralized-to-market (CTM) mechanic.[82]

12.3.1 CTM mechanic

In very broad commercial terms, a collateralized derivative is one in respect of which the parties thereto are periodically obliged to transfer to the other (or grant a security interest in) certain collateral assets with a value equal to the value of that other party's mark-to-market exposure under that derivative contract. In practice, there may be various inputs into the determination of a party's mark-to-market exposure, but the overriding theme is that the exposure of a party on a given day will reflect the estimated cost (if any) which that party would have to incur if it were to enter into an identical derivative transaction in the applicable market on such day.

It is important to note that a party's exposure to its counterparty on a given day under a CTM derivative is not reset, diminished, or extinguished during the life of the derivative by operation of the collateral mechanism. Instead, such exposure remains in existence, but it is collateralized by the transfer of collateral by the other party and governed by appropriate netting arrangements.

12.3.2 STM mechanic

The common feature of STM derivatives is that they are structured so that on a periodic basis, (i) the applicable party (or a third party) determines the current value of, and the resultant exposure of, either party (if any) under, the derivative and (ii) upon this determination, the contingent profit accruing to one of the parties as a result of the movement in the market value of the derivative since the immediately prior determination is crystallized so that such profit becomes due and payable by the applicable party, with the terms of the contract being reset to reflect this settlement of accrued profits and losses at such point so that the resulting value (as determined by the applicable party or a third party) of the derivative is adjusted accordingly.

A key feature of an STM derivative is that a party's mark-to-market exposure to its counterparty under that contract (representing accrued profit owed to it by its counterparty) is settled and thereby extinguished by the payment of the profit and loss that crystallizes following the determination of the current value and the resultant exposure. The parties (or a third party such as an external valuation agent or exchange)

---

[82] It is understood that there is a difference between derivatives that are structured and documented as CTM derivatives and derivatives that are structured and documented as STM derivatives (although neither the term CTM nor the term STM has been given a particular meaning in English law by the English courts, nor has either term been given any particular meaning under the applicable laws of the EU). These are commercial terms that are used to differentiate between two classes of derivative contract that use different means to achieve the same basic purpose, which is to mitigate or settle counterparty credit risk arising from movements in the market value of a derivative in favour of one party or the other which would otherwise constitute an uncovered exposure to the owing counterparty. However, the means of achieving that purpose, and the nature of the rights and obligations between the parties, differs between the two types of arrangement.

then record the current value of the derivative at the price at which it was previously settled and reset. This is in contrast to the position under a CTM derivative, as discussed above.

Under both arrangements the exposure that is settled or collateralized (as applicable) is the exposure arising from the movement in the market value of the derivative. Therefore, the profit or loss amount that is crystallized following the determination of the current value under an STM derivative should, in practice, be economically equivalent to the amount of exposure that must be collateralized following a revaluation of a CTM derivative.

These rule changes necessitate market participants assessing the contractual effect of the changes (including whether the changes impacted the characterization of the relevant derivatives transactions) as well as other consequences such as accounting and regulatory capital impacts.

13 Final Remarks

Whilst industry-standard OTC clearing documentation is now firmly established, this area continues to evolve to comply with new regulatory developments and to reflect market practice. With the EU focused on increasing the attractiveness of clearing in Europe, the upcoming EU EMIR review, new CCP recovery and resolution legislation, and the United Kingdom indicating that it will be reviewing UK laws derived from the EU, attention is likely to remain on clearing for some time to come. Whilst the impact of these developments on OTC clearing documentation is, as yet, uncertain, market participants should be actively monitoring regulatory and market changes and engaging with industry working groups to ensure that they are live to any necessary contractual amendments.

9

Capital Requirements for Bank Exposures to CCPs

Marc Peters[*]

1 Introduction

The Basel Framework[1] ('Basel') defines the counterparty credit risk[2] (CCR) as the risk that the counterparty to a transaction could default before the final settlement of the transaction's cash flows. In this case, Basel explains that an economic loss would occur if the transactions or portfolio of transactions with the counterparty has a positive economic value at the time of default. Unlike a firm's exposure to credit risk through a loan, where the exposure to credit risk is unilateral and only the lending bank faces the risk of loss, CCR creates a bilateral risk of loss: the market value of the transaction can be positive or negative to either counterparty to the transaction. Basel stresses the fact that the market value is uncertain and can vary over time with the movement of underlying market factors. CCR lies at the crossroad of credit and market risk. It has been particularly well illustrated during the global financial crisis of 2008 (GFC) and resulted in a fundamental paradigm change for the clearing of over-the-counter (OTC) derivatives.

---

[*] The sole responsibility of this chapter, and of any views expressed therein, lie with the author. The European Commission cannot be held responsible for its content or the use that might be made of it.

[1] See https://www.bis.org/basel_framework/index.htm (accessed 23 March 2023) (Basel Framework).

[2] See the Basel Framework (n 1), para. 50.1.

In the markets concerned, the GFC showed how central clearing counterparties (CCPs) helped to contain the contagion effects of the Lehman Brothers' default on the global financial system. Authorities and rule-makers realized that CCPs could offer a solution to ensure a greater market stability and contribute to the overall reduction of CCR in the market. Therefore, in the context of the adoption of a set of policies, regulations, and reforms to address the causes of the GFC, the G20 leaders decided, during the Pittsburgh Summit in September 2009,[3] that all standardized OTC deriva-tive contracts should be traded on exchanges or electronic trading platforms, where appropriate, and cleared through central counterparties by end-2012 at the latest. By contrast, non-centrally cleared contracts should be subject to higher capital require-ments and specific margin requirements.[4]

The implementation of this policy decision triggered actions from authorities and regulators across the world to encourage the use of CCPs and mandate the central clearing of a wide range of OTC derivatives. However, the situation varies across juris-dictions. According to the Financial Stability Board (FSB), seventeen member jurisdic-tions out of twenty-four had comprehensive standards for mandatory central clearing in force at the end of 2021, which is unchanged since the 2020 progress report. By con-trast, almost all member jurisdictions (twenty-three out of twenty-four) implemented higher bank capital requirements for non-centrally cleared derivatives at the same date. The stricter margin requirements for non-centrally cleared derivatives are in force in sixteen member jurisdictions.[5] This last result should be considered in the light of the comment made by the BCBS and IOSCO in their September 2013 standards on margin requirements,[6] according to which the effectiveness of such requirements could be undermined if they were not consistent internationally, potentially leading to regula-tory arbitrage and an unlevel playing field.

In parallel, as CCPs became central nodes for the financial system, a series of meas-ures were introduced to enhance their resilience. At the same time, considering the function of a CCP, becoming a buyer to every seller and a seller to every buyer in the cleared market through a process called 'novation', a differential regime for capital re-quirements associated to CCR was introduced between bilaterally cleared derivatives and centrally cleared derivatives. This latter differentiation was further reinforced by the introduction of more stringent margining requirements for non-centrally cleared derivatives.

---

[3] G20, 'Leaders' Statement', the Pittsburgh Summit (24–25 September 2009), https://www.fsb.org/wp-content/uploads/g20_leaders_declaration_pittsburgh_2009.pdf (accessed 23 March 2023).

[4] See Basel Committee on Banking Supervision–Board of the International Organization of Securities Commissions (BCBS–IOSCO), 'Margin Requirements for Non-Centrally Cleared Derivatives' (April 2020), https://www.bis.org/bcbs/publ/d499.pdf (accessed 23 March 2023) (BCBS–IOSCO, 'Margin Requirements for Non-Centrally Cleared Derivatives' (April 2020).

[5] See Financial Stability Board, 'OTC Derivatives Market Reforms, Implementation Progress in 2021' (December 2021), https://www.fsb.org/wp-content/uploads/P031221.pdf (accessed 23 March 2023).

[6] See BCBS–IOSCO, 'Margin Requirements for Non-Centrally Cleared Derivatives' (September 2013), https://www.iosco.org/library/pubdocs/pdf/IOSCOPD423.pdf (accessed 23 March 2023) (BCBS–IOSCO, 'Margin Requirements for Non-Centrally Cleared Derivatives' (September 2013).

Nowadays, an increasing share of derivatives' transactions is cleared centrally. Of course, the success of central clearing is partly explained by the incentives created through more favourable capital and margin requirements. It brings additional benefits to many market participants, such as the simplification of the CCR management or a more efficient and lean management of collateral and liquidity through the possibilities of multilateral netting that are inherent to the clearing process.

This, however, assumes that CCPs have the capability and the capacity to manage this centralization of risks, including during extreme circumstances. While CCPs contribute to the overall reduction of CCR in the financial system and optimize the use of collateral resources, they also create new risks. These risks are mostly associated with the loss allocation mechanisms CCPs have put in place to protect themselves from insolvency, in compliance with international standards. Central clearing represents a trade-off between loss frequency and loss severity, turning the low-probability, medium-severity risk of loss from bilateral counterparty default into the lower probability but much higher severity risk of loss from CCP stress.[7] In this perspective, although recent history has been rather benign in terms of CCP failures, the inherent cross-border and international nature of their activities, their level of interconnectedness with other financial institutions, and their growing importance following the G20 commitments on OTC derivatives stress the importance of a sound recovery and resolution framework for CCPs (see Chapter 12 'Recovery and Resolution of CCPs' by Victor de Serière in this volume)[8] as well as the maintenance of minimum requirements to ensure that banks exposed to CCPs adequately capitalize their remaining risks. The purpose of this chapter is to shed light on these prudential requirements. It first explains the treatment of exposures towards CCPs. It then continues with the treatment of exposures in the context of uncleared transactions. It further provides an overview of the other areas of the prudential framework for banks that have been influenced by the central clearing mandate. It concludes with some considerations on the future central clearing landscape.

2 Overview of the Treatment of Exposures towards CCPs

The prudential treatment of derivative exposures towards CCPs acknowledges the market structure, the clearing value chain, and how CCPs are usually accessed by market participants, including banks.

In practice, market participants have two broad possibilities to access CCPs and clear their derivatives transactions centrally: either they meet eligibility criteria imposed by

---

[7] David Murphy, 'Risks in OTC Derivatives Central Clearing', in *OTC Derivatives: Bilateral Trading & Central Clearing* (London: Palgrave Macmillan, 2013), pp. 209–230.

[8] For further insight about the EU framework, see Hannes Huhtaniemi and Marc Peters, 'Central Counterparty Recovery and Resolution: The European Perspective' (2017) 6(1) Journal of Financial Market Infrastructures 79–106; Marc Peters and Heinrich Wollny, 'Central Clearing Counterparties' Recovery and Resolution: Where Do We Stand in the European Union?' (2019) 11(2) Journal of Securities Operations and Custody 1–14.

CCPs and become direct clearing members at those CCPs or they become a client of a (general) clearing member that will offer them clearing services and indirect access to CCPs. While the latter is often the only possible option for many corporates subject to the clearing obligation, in the case of banks, both possibilities exist and will determine the resulting capital requirements for CCR. As such, the Basel Framework thus also applies to multi-level client structures where clearing services are provided by one client, which is not a direct clearing member, to another. It requires both the 'higher-level client' (the institution providing clearing services) and the 'lower-level client' (the institution clearing through that client) to capitalize that transaction as an OTC derivative.

The Basel Framework also relies on the compliance of CCPs with the 'Principles for Financial Market Infrastructures' (PFMIs)[9] that were published in 2012 by the CPMI and IOSCO) to enhance the resilience of CCPs and other critical market infrastructures.[10]

In particular, Basel defines a 'qualifying central counterparty' (QCCP) as an entity that is licensed to operate as a CCP and that is based and prudentially supervised in a jurisdiction where the relevant authority has established, and publicly indicated, that it applies to the CCP on an ongoing basis, domestic rules and regulations that are consistent with the PFMIs.[11]

Basel, however, offers a certain degree of flexibility to determine the QCCP status. Where the CCP is in a jurisdiction that does not have an authority applying the PFMIs to the CCP, then the banking supervisor may determine whether the CCP meets this definition. In addition, for a CCP to be considered a QCCP, sufficient information needs to be made available to market participants to allow each clearing member bank to calculate its capital requirement.

Considering the greater resilience of CCPs complying with the PFMIs,[12] Basel allows a preferential capital treatment for CCR exposures towards QCCPs, distinguishing between trade exposures—relating to the current and potential future exposures associated to the transactions in (OTC) derivatives—and default fund exposures—relating to the funded and unfunded contributions to the CCPs' mutualized loss allocation mechanisms. The capital requirements that apply to exposures to QCCPs are, however, capped at the requirements that would otherwise be applicable to a non-qualifying CCP (NQCCP).[13] Also, within a grace period of three months of a CCP ending to qualify as a QCCP, unless a bank's national supervisor requires otherwise, the trades with a former

[9] See Committee on Payments and Market Infrastructures (CPMI)–IOSCO, 'Principles for Financial Market Infrastructures' (April 2012), https://www.bis.org/cpmi/publ/d101a.pdf (accessed 23 March 2023).
[10] See Chapter 3 ('Development of the Regulatory Regime for OTC Derivatives Clearing' by Patrick Pearson) in this volume.
[11] According to Regulation (EU) No. 575/2013 of the European Parliament and of the Council of 26 June 2013, Art. 4, point (88) (the 'Capital Requirements Regulation' or 'CRR'), a 'qualifying central counterparty' or 'QCCP' means a central counterparty that has been either authorized in accordance with Regulation (EU) No. 648/2012 of the European Parliament and of the Council of 4 July 2012 on OTC derivatives, central counterparties and trade repositories, [2012] OJ L201/1 (27 July 2012), Art. 14 (EMIR, or recognized in accordance with Art. 25 of that Regulation.
[12] The European framework is considered more strict as it refers to an authorization under EMIR (n 11) or, in the case of a third-country CCP, a recognition by the European Securities Markets Authority (ESMA).
[13] A similar approach is applied under the CRR (n 11), Art. 303(2).

QCCP may continue to be capitalized as if they still were with a QCCP. After that time, the bank's exposures with such a CCP must be capitalized according to the rules applying to an NQCCP.[14]

To calculate the trade exposures from derivative transactions, banks having approval to use internal models are allowed to use the internal models methodology (IMM), in addition to the standardized approach for counterparty credit risk (SA–CCR). However, for the determination of the hypothetical capital requirement of a CCP (K_{CCP}) that is required for the calculation of the capital requirement of the bank exposed to the CCP, derivative exposures have to be calculated using SA–CCR only.

Despite basing the classification on compliance with the PFMIs, Basel stresses that a bank always retains the responsibility to ensure that it maintains adequate capital for its exposures. Therefore, Basel considers that, under the supervisory review process (SRP) standard, a bank should consider whether it might need to hold capital in excess of the minimum capital requirements. This could be the case if, for example, (i) a bank's dealings with a CCP give rise to more risky exposures; (ii) where, given the context of that bank's dealings, it is unclear whether the CCP meets the definition of a QCCP; or (iii) an external assessment such as an International Monetary Fund Financial Sector Assessment Program has found material shortcomings in the CCP or the regulation of CCPs, and the CCP and/or the CCP regulator have not since publicly addressed the issues identified.[15]

Where the bank acts as a clearing member, Basel expects the bank to assess, through appropriate scenario analysis and stress testing, whether the level of capital held against exposures to a CCP adequately addresses the inherent risks of those transactions. This assessment includes potential future or contingent exposures resulting from future drawings on default fund commitments and/or from secondary commitments to take over or replace offsetting transactions from clients of another clearing member in case of this clearing member defaulting or becoming insolvent.

In terms of reporting requirements, Basel sets out that a bank must monitor and report to its senior management and Board all its exposures to CCPs on a regular basis.

Looking at the evolution of the international capital regime for banks, these elements were introduced by the BCBS in 2014,[16] building on interim rules published by the Basel Committee on Banking Supervision in July 2012.[17] Further changes were introduced more recently to update certain cross references to take account of the revised credit risk standards that come into effect with the implementation of the December 2017 Basel III rules.

The 2014 version of the requirements, that took effect on 1 January 2017, differs from the interim version by (i) including a single approach for calculating capital

---

[14] See the CRR (n 11), Art. 311 in conjunction with Art. 497.

[15] See the Basel Framework (n 1) para. CRE54.3.

[16] See Basel Committee on Banking Supervision (BCBS), 'Capital Requirements for Bank Exposures to Central Counterparties' (April 2014), https://www.bis.org/publ/bcbs282.htm (accessed 23 March 2023).

[17] See BCBS, 'Capital Requirements for Bank Exposures to Central Counterparties' (July 2012), https://www.bis.org/publ/bcbs227.pdf (accessed 23 March 2023).

requirements for a bank's exposure that arises from its contributions to the mutualized default fund of a qualifying CCP (QCCP), (ii) employing the SA–CCR to measure the hypothetical capital requirement in relation to a CCP, (iii) including an explicit cap on the capital charges applicable to a bank's exposures to a QCCP, (iv) specifying how to treat multi-level client structures whereby an institution clears its trades through intermediaries linked to a CCP, and (v) incorporating responses to frequently asked questions posed to the BCBS in the course of its work on the final standard.

In terms of scope, the capital treatment determined by Basel is applicable to all exposures to CCPs such as OTC derivatives, exchange-traded derivatives, security financing transactions (SFTs) and long settlement transactions. Exchange-traded derivative transactions conducted between clearing members and clients under a bilateral agreement would require both parties to capitalize the transaction as an OTC derivative.

It is noted in this context that the clearing member will always capitalize its exposure to clients as bilateral trades, irrespective of whether the clearing member guarantees the trade or acts as an intermediary between the client and the CCP. However, to recognize the shorter close-out period for cleared transactions, clearing members can capitalize the exposure to their clients applying a margin period of risk of at least five days in IMM or SA–CCR, including for the credit valuation adjustment risk.[18]

By contrast, exposures arising from the settlement of cash transactions (equities, fixed income, spot foreign exchange, and spot commodities) are not subject to this capital treatment. For contributions to prepaid default funds covering settlement-risk-only products, the applicable risk weight is therefore 0%.

3 On the Treatment of Exposures to Qualifying CCPs

3.1 Trade Exposures

Trade exposures include the current and potential future exposure of a clearing member or a client to a CCP arising from OTC derivatives, exchange traded derivatives transactions, or securities financing transactions, as well as initial margin.[19] The current exposure of a clearing member also includes the variation margin due to the clearing member but not yet received.[20]

3.1.1 Clearing member exposures to CCPs
The basic requirement under the Basel Framework is that any trade exposure from a bank to a QCCP attracts a risk weight of 2%.[21] Where the bank acts as a general clearing

---

[18] In the EU context, see the CRR (n 11), Art. 304.
[19] See the Basel Framework (n 1) para. CRE54 and the CRR (n 11), Section 9, Chapter 6, Title II, Part 3.
[20] See the Basel Framework (n 1), para. CRE50.9.
[21] See the CRR (n 11), Art. 306(1), point (a).

member and offers clearing services to clients, the 2% risk weight also applies to the clearing member's trade exposure to the CCP that arises when the clearing member is obligated to reimburse the client for any losses suffered due to changes in the value of its transactions if the CCP defaults.

The exposure amount to which the risk weight will be applied is calculated using the methods set out in the CCR chapters of the Basel Framework. Concretely, banks having internal model approval for measuring CCR exposures will use the IMM approach while banks without that approval will calculate their exposure amounts using the standardized approach (SA–CCR) or the comprehensive approach for SFTs within the standardized approach to credit risk.

In this context, the margin period of risk (MPOR) is the following:

- a minimum of twenty days if there are disputed trades or the netting set contain illiquid collateral or exotic trades;
- a minimum of ten days in all cases for the calculation of trade exposures to CCPs for OTC derivatives;
- the lesser of one year and the remaining maturity of the transaction, with a floor of ten business days, where CCPs retain variation margin and the clearing member's collateral is not protected against the insolvency of the CCP.

Basel introduces some conditions to the methods for calculating CCR exposures to permit netting. In particular, Basel allows the total replacement cost of all contracts relevant to the trade exposure determination to be calculated as a net replacement cost if:

(1) the settlement is legally enforceable on a net basis in an event of default and regardless of whether the counterparty is insolvent or bankrupt and
(2) the applicable close-out netting sets meet the requirements set out in:
  i. the on-balance sheet netting section and, where relevant, the guarantees and credit derivatives section of the standardized approaches for the recognition of credit risk mitigation;[22]
  ii. the SA–CCR in the case of derivative transactions;[23]
  iii. the IMM in the case of cross-product netting.[24]

If the bank cannot demonstrate that netting agreements meet these requirements, each single transaction is regarded as a netting set, resulting in an absence of recognition of any netting benefit at portfolio level.

---

[22] See the Basel Framework (n 1), paras CRE22.62 and, where applicable, CRE22.63 in the case of repo-style transactions.
[23] See the Basel Framework (n 1), paras CRE52.7 and 52.8.
[24] See the Basel Framework (n 1), paras CRE53.61 and 53.71.

3.1.2 Clearing member exposures to clients

To maintain an incentive structure that facilitates central clearing also in the context of indirect clearing, Basel developed a rule that recognizes the risk-reducing element of central clearing on the close-out period in case of a client default.

Whether clearing members guarantee the trade or act as an intermediary between the client and the CCP, they are always required to capitalize their exposures (including potential credit valuation adjustment (CVA) risk exposures) to any clients as bilateral trades. However, a reduced MPOR of at least five days is used to acknowledge a likely shorter close-out period in the case of cleared client transactions.[25]

In addition, the collateral posted by the clients to the clearing members and passed on to CCPs can be used to mitigate exposures for both sides of the transaction, that is, towards the CCP and towards the client. This means that any initial margin posted by clients to their clearing member mitigates its exposure against these clients. The same treatment applies in the case of a multi-level client structure.

The objective is to replicate the benefits of central clearing along the entire clearing chain.

3.1.3 Client exposures

Similarly, the preferential treatment considered for centrally cleared transactions extends to an indirect clearing model, and a risk weight of 2% applies to any exposure resulting from transactions where a bank is either:

- a client of the clearing member, acting as a pure financial intermediary (i.e. pure back-to-back transactions with a CCP);
- a client of the clearing member, guaranteeing the performance of its client vis-à-vis the CCP; or
- a lower-level client in a multi-level client structure.

The exposure amount is calculated using one of the methods described above and the following conditions need to be met:

(1) The offsetting transactions are identified by the CCP as client transactions and supporting collateral is held by the CCP and/or the clearing member, as applicable, under a framework that prevents any losses to the client due to the default or insolvency of clearing member, the default or insolvency of any other client of the clearing member, and the joint default or insolvency of both.

(2) In the case of the default or insolvency of the clearing member, the prevailing legal arrangements ensure that the offsetting transactions are highly likely to continue to be indirectly transacted through the CCP or by the CCP.

---

[25] See the Basel Framework (n 1), para. CRE54.12.

In such a case, the client positions and corresponding collateral are transferred at market value unless the client requests to close out the position at market value. Basel takes account of the market practice and specifies in this regard that if there is a clear precedent for transactions being ported at a CCP and industry intent for this practice to continue, then these factors must be considered when assessing whether trades are highly likely to be ported. However, Basel considers that the fact that the CCP documentation does not prohibit client trades from being ported (or is silent about this possibility) is not sufficient to say that they are highly likely to be ported.

Basel also further specifies the condition set out in point (1). It considers that, upon the insolvency of the clearing member, there must be no legal impediment (other than the possible need to obtain a court order) to the transfer of the collateral belonging to clients of a defaulting clearing member to the CCP, to one or more other surviving clearing members, or to the client or the client's nominee. In addition, the client must have conducted a sufficiently grounded legal analysis (and update it regularly) to ensure the legal certainty of the framework mentioned above.

A higher risk weight of 4% is applicable if the client is not protected against the joint default of a clearing member and any other of its clients but all other conditions are met.[26]

If the conditions are not met, the assimilation to the treatment of centrally cleared transactions cannot be concluded and the bank has to capitalize its exposure (including potential CVA risk exposure) to the clearing member as a bilateral trade.

3.2 Treatment of Posted Collateral

The risk weights for any collateral posted by the bank are those that would otherwise apply to such assets under the capital adequacy framework, even though such assets have been posted as collateral. In addition, the posted collateral is subject to the CCR requirements (which would increase by the application of haircuts to the collateral) in so far as the collateral is held by the CCP or the clearing member in a non-bankruptcy remote manner. In this case, the credit risk based on the creditworthiness of the entity holding such collateral should be recognized.

Where the collateral corresponds to the definition of a trade exposure and is held by the CCP, a risk weight of 2% is applicable for banks that are clearing members and banks that are clients when the conditions specified under section 3.1.3 are met. Otherwise, the relevant risk weight of the CCP applies. There is no capital requirement for CCR exposure (i.e. the related risk weight or exposure at default is equal to zero) if the collateral is held by a custodian and is bankruptcy-remote from the CCP.

---

[26] In the EU context, these conditions are set out under the CRR (n 11), Art. 305. The application of the 4% risk weight is notably foreseen under the CRR (n 11), Art. 305(3).

Regarding the calculation of the exposure, or exposure at default (EAD), where banks use the SA–CCR to calculate exposures, collateral posted that is not held on a bankruptcy-remote basis must be accounted for in the net independent collateral amount (NICA) term. For banks using IMM models, the alpha multiplier[27]– aiming to a conservative estimate of the exposure—must be applied to the exposure on posted collateral.[28]

If the client's collateral is held at the CCP on a non-bankruptcy-remote basis and the client is not protected against the joint default of its clearing member and of any other clients of its clearing member but the rest of the conditions under section 3.1.3. are met, the applicable risk weight is 4%.

3.3 Treatment of Default Fund Exposures

Basel defines default funds contributions (or clearing deposits or guaranty fund contri-butions) as clearing members' funded or unfunded[29] contributions towards, or under-writing of, a CCP's mutualized loss-sharing arrangements. To adapt to any business model and limit possible circumventing constructions, Basel specifies that the descrip-tion given by a CCP to its mutualized loss-sharing arrangements is not determinative of their status as a default fund; rather, the substance of such arrangements govern their status.

Acknowledging the different structures that have been implemented by CCPs, the Basel Framework distinguishes the treatment of default fund exposures based on the segregation of the fund by clearing segment or not. It also takes account of the CCPs' own resources engaged in the loss allocation mechanism.

Where a default fund is common to different clearing segments or products, all con-tributions receive the corresponding risk weight without apportioning to different clearing segments or products. For segregated default funds (i.e. the clearing members' contributions are collected by product types and only accessible for specific product types), the capital requirements for those related exposures are calculated for each spe-cific product giving rise to CCR.

In case the CCP's prefunded own resources are shared among product types, the CCP has to allocate those funds to each of the calculations in proportion to the re-spective product-specific EAD.

---

[27] Under the credit counterparty risk framework, the exposure amount, or exposure at default (EAD) is cal-culated as the product of the alpha multiplier, set by default by the Basel Committee to 1.4, and the effective ex-pected positive exposure (or 'effective EPE'). The latter represents an average over time of the expected exposures. Depending on the risk profile of the portfolio, supervisory authorities have the discretion to request a higher multiplier. Examples mentioned by the Basel Framework (n 1) include: a low granularity of counterparties, high correlation of market values across counterparties, etc. Subject to supervisory approval, banks can compute in-ternal estimates of the alpha multiplier with a floor of 1.2.

[28] See the Basel Framework (n 1), para. CRE54.23.

[29] In accordance with the CRR (n 11), Art. 310, a 0% risk weight is applied to unfunded contributions to the de-fault fund of a QCCP.

In order to determine their capital requirements for their exposures arising from default fund contributions to a QCCP, clearing members apply a risk weight determined according to a risk-sensitive formula that considers:

(1) the size and quality of a QCCP's financial resources;
(2) the CCR exposures of such QCCP; and
(3) the application of such financial resources via the QCCP's loss allocation waterfall, in the case of one or more clearing member defaults.

The corresponding capital requirement (K_{CM_i}) is calculated on the basis of the hypothetical capital requirement of the CCP (K_{CCP}) due to its CCR exposures to all of its clearing members and their clients. The latter is calculated on a consistent basis for the sole purpose of determining the capitalization of clearing members' default fund contributions. It does not represent the actual capital requirements for a CCP.

K_{CCP} is calculated using the following formula, the sum applying to all of a clearing member's accounts:[30]

$$K_{CCP} = \sum_{CM_i} EAD_i \times RW \times CapitalRatio,$$

where:
(1) *RW* is set at 20%; this is a minimum requirement that can be increased by supervisors, for instance considering the credit standing of the population of clearing members or its concentration;
(2) *capital ratio* is set at 8%;
(3) CM_i represents clearing member 'i';
(4) EAD_i represents the exposure amount of the CCP towards clearing member 'i', relating to the end-of-day valuation before the last margin call of that day is exchanged. The exposure includes both the clearing member's own transactions and client transactions guaranteed by the clearing member and all values of collateral held by the CCP (including the clearing member's prefunded default fund contribution) against those transactions.

Where clearing members provide client-clearing services and clients have segregated accounts (whether omnibus accounts or individual accounts), each client segregated account should enter the sum above separately; that is, the member EAD in the formula above is then the sum of the EADs associated to each client segregated account and the EAD of any proprietary account. This is to ensure that client's collateral cannot be used to offset the CCP's exposures to clearing members' proprietary activity in the calculation of K_{CCP}. Absent separated default fund contributions for client and proprietary

---

[30] In an EU context, see EMIR (n 11), Chapter 4, Title IV.

accounts, the contributions of the clearing members are allocated according to the respective fraction of initial margin these accounts have in relation to the total initial margin posted by or for the account of the clearing member.

In terms of product handling, if any of these segregated accounts contains both derivatives and SFTs, the EAD of that segregated account is the sum of the EAD associated with derivatives and the EAD associated with SFTs. The corresponding collateral is allocated on a pro rata basis of the product-specific EADs.

For derivatives, the EAD parameter is calculated as the bilateral trade exposure the CCP has against the clearing member using the SA–CCR with an MPOR of ten business days and an offsetting of the CCP's exposure with all the collateral held by the CCP for which it has a legal claim in the event of the default of the clearing member or client.

For SFTs, the EAD parameter is equal to, $max\left(EBRM_i - IM_i - DF_i; 0\right)$ where:

(1) $EBRM_i$ is the exposure value to clearing member 'i' before risk mitigation;
(2) IM_i is the initial margin posted by the clearing member with the CCP;
(3) DF_i is the prefunded default fund contribution of the clearing member that will be required upon such clearing member's default to reduce the CCP loss, either along with or immediately following the use of its initial margin.

Once K_{CCP} is obtained, the second step in calculating the clearing member's capital requirement for its default fund contribution (K_{CM_i}) is to apply the following formula:[31]

$$K_{CM_i} = max\left(K_{CCP} \times \left(\frac{DF_i^{pref}}{DF_{CCP} + DF_{CM}^{pref}} \right); 8\% \times 2\% \times DF_i^{pref} \right)$$

where:

(1) K_{CM_i} is the capital requirement on the default fund contribution for clearing member 'i';
(2) DF_{CM}^{pref} is the total prefunded default fund contributions available from all clearing members;
(3) DF_{CCP} is the CCP's prefunded own resources (e.g. contributed capital, skin in the game, etc.), which are contributed to the default waterfall, where these resources are junior or *pari passu* to prefunded contributions by clearing members;
(4) DF_i^{pref} is the prefunded default fund contributions provided by clearing member 'i'.

Based on the formulae above, Basel effectively sets a floor to the risk weight on the default fund exposures of 2%.

---

[31] See also the CRR (n 11), Art. 308.

K_{CCP} and K_{CM_i} must be calculated at least on a quarterly basis or where there are material changes to the number or exposure of cleared transactions (also, for instance, when a CCP is clearing new products) or material changes to the financial resources of the CCP.

The resulting total capital requirement is always capped at the level of the one applying to exposures to NQCCPs.

4 On the Treatment of Exposures to Non-qualifying CCPs

A distinction is to be made between the treatment of trade exposures and the treatment of default fund exposures.[32]

4.1 Treatment of Trade Exposures

The standardized approach for credit risk is used to estimate the corresponding CCR capital requirements.

4.2 Treatment of Default Fund Exposures

A risk weight of 1,250% is applicable to these exposures, which include both funded and unfunded contributions which are liable to be paid if the CCP so requires.[33]

Where a commitment is created as a result of unfunded contributions, Basel allows a national discretion whereby national supervisors have to determine, through their supervisory review processes, the amount of unfunded commitments to which a 1,250% risk weight would apply.

5 On the Treatment of Bilaterally Cleared Transactions

To complement the programme of reforms adopted in 2009, the G20 agreed, in 2011, on margin requirements on non-centrally cleared derivatives and required the BCBS and IOSCO to develop consistent global standards for these requirements.[34] In July 2012, an initial proposal was released for consultation. In February 2013, the BCBS and IOSCO released a second consultative document. The final framework was published in September 2013 and subsequently revised in 2015, 2019, and 2020. The main modifications introduced by these reviews related to the introduction of a phase-in period for the requirement to exchange variation margin and the postponement of the phase-in periods.

---

[32] See the Basel Framework (n 1), paras CRE54.41 and 54.42. See also the CRR (n 11), Art. 306(1), point (b).
[33] See also the CRR (n 11), Art. 309.
[34] See BCBS–IOSCO, 'Margin Requirements for Non-Centrally Cleared Derivatives' (April 2020) (n 4).

Although an increasing portion of OTC derivatives is centrally cleared, bespoke and non-standardized products will likely continue to be subject to bilateral counterparty risk management and capital requirements. Based on the latest statistics published by the Bank for International Settlements (BIS), as of June 2021, around 63% of foreign exchange, interest rate, and equity-linked derivative contracts (percentage in terms of notional amounts) and about 64% of credit default swaps (percentage in terms of notional amounts) were centrally cleared.[35]

The implementation of specific margin requirements for non-centrally cleared derivatives have two main benefits:[36]

(1) The *reduction of systemic risk*—specific requirements should ensure that collateral is available to offset losses caused by the default of a derivatives counterparty, thereby contributing to mitigate systemic contagion and spillover risks. Margin requirements can also have broader macroprudential benefits by reducing the financial system's vulnerability to potentially destabilizing procyclicality and limiting the build-up of uncollateralized exposures within the financial system.

(2) The *promotion of central clearing*—margin requirements on non-centrally cleared derivatives, by reflecting the generally higher risk associated with these derivatives, will promote central clearing, making the G20's 2009 reform programme more effective.

As recognized by BCBS–IOSCO, the potential benefits of margin requirements must be weighed against the liquidity impact that would result from derivatives counterparties' need to provide liquid, high-quality collateral to meet those requirements, including potential changes to market functioning as result of increased overall demand for such collateral. Financial institutions may need to obtain and deploy additional liquidity resources to meet margin requirements over and above current levels. Moreover, the liquidity impact of margin requirements cannot be considered in isolation. Rather, it is important to recognize that other regulatory initiatives also have significant liquidity impacts. This is notably the case for the Basel liquidity standards and the clearing obligation for standardized OTC derivatives.[37]

The objective of the margin framework is to ensure that appropriate margining practices are in place for all derivatives transactions that are not cleared by a CCP (except for physically settled foreign exchange (FX)-forward and swaps). Interestingly, BCBS–IOSCO note that national supervisors could consider altering margin requirements to achieve macroprudential outcomes, such as limiting the build-up of leverage and the expansion of balance sheets. Further consideration will continue to be given by the two international standard setters to the possibility of a macroprudential 'add-on' or buffer and to the coordination issues that may arise in this respect.

---

[35] See BIS, 'Statistical Release: OTC Derivatives Statistics at end-June 2021' (November 2021), https://www.bis.org/publ/otc_hy2111.htm (accessed 23 March 2023).

[36] See BCBS–IOSCO, 'Margin Requirements for Non-Centrally Cleared Derivatives' (September 2013) (n 6).

[37] See Chapter 6 ('OTC Derivatives Clearing and Collateral Management' by Manmohan Singh) in this volume for a focused discussion on this issue.

In terms of proportionality, BCBS–IOSCO considered that non-systemic non-financial firms should not be subject to the margin requirements as this would be disproportionate to the risk they pose to the financial system, also noting that, under most national regimes, the related transactions would be exempted from central clearing mandates.

Because of the impact of the margin requirements on liquidity, particularly in the case of initial margin that requires the immobilization of collateral over the entire lifetime of a derivative transaction, BCBS–IOSCO introduced (and revised) a transitional period allowing for a gradual implementation of the requirements. By the end of that period, a minimum level of non-centrally cleared OTC derivatives activity (i.e. EUR 8 billion in gross notional outstanding amounts) will be necessary for a covered entity to be subject to the initial margin requirements.

In the same vein, BCBS–IOSCO considered an initial margin threshold under which covered entities would not be obliged to collect initial margin.

5.1 Scope

All covered entities (i.e. financial firms and systemically important non-financial entities) that engage in non-centrally cleared derivatives must exchange initial and variation margin, as appropriate, to the counterparty risks posed by such transactions. The international standards, however, allow a national discretion to determine the appropriate margin requirements for transactions between a firm and its affiliates in a way that is consistent with each jurisdiction's legal and regulatory framework.

5.2 Key Elements

The margin framework requires that all covered entities exchange, on a bilateral basis, the full amount of variation margin (i.e. no threshold) on a regular basis (e.g. daily) and initial margin with a threshold of maximum EUR 50 million. A minimum transfer amount not exceeding EUR 500,000 is allowed.

As an anti-circumvention rule, the threshold is applied at the level of the consolidated group to which the threshold is being extended and is based on all non-centrally cleared derivatives between the two consolidated groups.

The methodologies for calculating initial and variation margin that serve as the baseline for margin collected from a counterparty should be consistent across entities covered by the requirements, reflect the potential future exposure (initial margin) and current exposure (variation margin) associated with the portfolio of non-centrally cleared derivatives, and ensure that all counterparty risk exposures are covered fully with a high degree of confidence.

Initial margin should be collected at the outset of a transaction and thereafter on a consistent basis upon changes in measured potential future exposure. To mitigate procyclicality impacts, large, discrete calls for (additional) initial margin due to 'cliff-edge' triggers should be discouraged. A gradual approach should be preferred to allow counterparties to manage their liquidity needs more efficiently over time.

To account for the risk associated with the provision of initial margin in the case where one of the counterparties would default, BCBS–IOSCO came to the consensus that initial margin should be exchanged on a gross basis and held in a way that protects the posting counterparty. The international bodies therefore encouraged jurisdictions to review the relevant local laws to ensure that collateral can be sufficiently protected in the event of bankruptcy. The margin framework provides further conditions to the re-hypothecation, re-pledge or reuse of collateral. While generally allowed in the case of variation margins, such practice is strictly framed in the context of initial margins and subject to a review clause by BCBS–IOSCO.

5.3 Methodology

Like the methodology for determining the stressed value-at-risk under the market risk requirements that prevailed under the Basel Framework before the Fundamental Review of the Trading Book, the determination of the initial margin is based on a one-tailed 99% confidence interval over a ten-day horizon, based on historical data incorporating a period of significant stress. The use of a stressed period should ensure that the level of margin will be sufficiently conservative and limit its procyclicality.

Covered entities have the choice between the use of a margining model and the use of a standardized margin calculation. As for capital requirements, the use of models is subject to several conditions to ensure their robustness. These conditions are intended to ensure that the use of models does not lead to a lowering of margin standards. In particular, initial margin models should be approved by the relevant competent authority and framed by an adequate internal governance process that will notably ensure the validation of the model and the back-testing of its outcomes. Models can be used at the level of a portfolio in so far as prior approval has been obtained for the products concerned and the portfolio is covered by a single legally enforceable netting agreement. Importantly, subject to supervisory approval, initial margin models may account for diversification, hedging, and risk offsets within well-defined asset classes such as currency/rates, equity, credit, or commodities, but not across such asset classes and provided these instruments are covered by the same legally enforceable netting agreement.

Where model approval cannot be obtained or the covered entities opt for a simpler (but admittedly less risk-sensitive) approach, a standardized calculation may be used. This approach is based on (i) standardized margin rates and (ii) a regulatory formula.

As a first step, the standard rates provided in Table 9.1 below is multiplied by the gross notional size of a derivative contract to obtain the gross standardized initial margin amount. This calculation is repeated for each contract within the portfolio, with limited netting possibilities and, if any, subject to supervisory approval.

As a second step, the gross standardized initial margin (GSIM) amount is adjusted by the ratio of the net current replacement cost to gross current replacement cost

Table 9.1 Standardized initial margin requirements

Standardized initial margin schedule

Asset class	Initial margin requirement (% of notional exposure)
Credit: 0–2 year duration	2
Credit: 2–5 year duration	5
Credit 5+ year duration	10
Commodity	15
Equity	15
Foreign exchange	6
Interest rate: 0–2 year duration	1
Interest rate: 2–5 year duration	2
Interest rate 5+ year duration	4
Other	15

Source: https://www.bis.org/bcbs/publ/d499.pdf (accessed 23 March 2023).

('net-to-gross ratio', NGR) for derivative transactions subject to legally enforceable netting agreements in accordance with the following formula. The result determines the net standardized initial margin requirement (NSIM).

$$NSIM = 0.4 \times GSIM + 0.6 \times NGR \times GSIM$$

While a combination of approaches is allowed for different derivative products, the choice between a model-based approach and the standardized approach should be consistent over time.

As regards variation margin, the full amount that is needed to fully collateralize the mark-to-market exposure should be exchanged on a sufficiently frequent basis per netting set. This reflects the evolution of the profit and loss (P&L) of the concerned derivatives portfolio and allows for adequate counterparty risk management.

In both cases, counterparties are expected to have effective dispute resolution processes in place to minimize the intervals between the required exchange of margins. In practice, the specific method and parameters that will be used by each counterparty to determine the exchange of margins will be agreed and recorded at the onset of the transaction to reduce potential disputes.

5.4 Eligible Collateral

Despite the exchange of margins, counterparties may continue to be exposed to loss, depending on the nature of the collateral. The latter should be of sufficient quality to ensure its liquidation at full value, including during periods of financial stress. The margin framework therefore considers the eligibility of collateral and the application of appropriate haircuts to its valuation (thereby reflecting the risks borne by the collateral, e.g. FX).

In particular, the margin framework insists that the value of the collateral should not have a significant correlation with the creditworthiness of the counterparty or the underlying non-centrally cleared derivatives portfolio in such a way that would undermine the effectiveness of the protection offered by the margin collected, that is, 'wrong-way risk'. In addition, the accepted collateral should also be reasonably diversified.

While leaving discretion to national authorities to develop the list of acceptable assets, the margin framework provides, as an illustrative guidance, the following list: cash, high-quality government and central banks securities, high-quality corporate bonds, high-quality covered bonds, equities included in major stock indices, and gold. However, the implementation of this discretion, inevitably led to differences in the treatment of eligible collateral across jurisdictions, notably in relation to the applicable haircuts.[38] Transparency in this context, translated in the simple possibility to compare the set of eligible collateral rules across jurisdictions, seems to remain an additional issue.[39]

As for initial margin, the value of the eligible collateral can be determined by a model-based approach or a standardized approach. In the latter case, standardized regulatory haircuts are defined in the margin framework, see Table 9.2 below. Overall, the same conditions as those exposed above apply in case a model-based approach is preferred. In particular, the calibration should reflect the underlying risks that affect the value of eligible collateral, such as market price volatility, liquidity, credit risk, and FX volatility, during both normal and stressed market conditions. It is expected that, despite the use of models, haircuts are set conservatively to avoid procyclicality.

It is noted that, depending on the respective liquidity needs of counterparties and the duration of their transactions, alternative collateral may need to be substituted. In such a case, the alternative collateral is expected to meet the same requirements as the replaced one and be sufficient to meet the margin requirements after the application of appropriate haircuts.

5.5 Transition Periods

Currently, all covered entities are required to exchange variation margin to new contracts.

A longer transition period has been envisaged for initial margin as this requirement was not reflecting a current practice, required significant operational enhancements, and impacted liquidity needs.

---

[38] See, for instance, the comparison made by the International Swaps and Derivatives Association (ISDA) as of 7 May 2021 of the applicable haircuts by type of assets between various jurisdictions: https://www.isda.org/a/QWzTE/Eligible-Collateral-Comparison-5.7.21.pdf (accessed 25 June 2022).

[39] See Paul Cluley, 'Making Eligible Collateral Intelligible', Allen & Overy (31 January 2020), https://www.aima.org/article/making-eligible-collateral-intelligible.html (accessed 25 June 2022).

Table 9.2 Standardized haircuts

Asset class	Haircut (% of market value)
Cash in same currency	0
High-quality government and central bank securities: residual maturity less than one year	0.5
High-quality government and central bank securities: residual maturity between one and five years	2
High-quality government and central bank securities: residual maturity greater than five years	4
High-quality corporate\covered bonds: residual maturity less than one year	1
High-quality corporate\covered bonds: residual maturity greater than one year and less than five years	4
High-quality corporate\covered bonds: residual maturity greater than five years	8
Equities included in major stock indices	15
Gold	15
Additional (additive) haircut on asset in which the currency of the derivatives obligation differs from that of the collateral asset	8

Source: https://www.bis.org/bcbs/publ/d499.pdf (accessed 23 March 2023)

The phases for the exchange of two-way initial margin with a threshold of EUR 50 million are as follows:

- from 1 September 2016 to 31 August 2017—EUR 3 trillion;
- from 1 September 2017 to 31 August 2018—EUR 2.25 trillion;
- from 1 September 2018 to 31 August 2019—EUR 1.5 trillion;
- from 1 September 2019 to 31 August 2021—EUR 0.75 trillion;
- from 1 September 2021 to 31 August 2022—EUR 50 billion;
- from 1 September 2022 onwards—EUR 8 billion.

It applies to the aggregate month-end average notional amount of non-centrally cleared derivatives for March, April, and May of the year under consideration. Initial margin requirements apply to all new contracts entered during the periods described above.

Progressively, smaller counterparties are affected, thereby increasing the incentives for central clearing. However, access criteria to CCPs are usually strict to control their own CCR. A direct consequence of this policy, facing the increasing demand from clients that are not eligible for a fully fledged clearing membership, is that certain CCPs developed specific 'direct client access' models.[40] However, these models remain limited and the concentration of clients to certain (general) clearing members

---

[40] See Chapter 4 ('CCP Access Structures' by Christina Sell) in this volume for a discussion of different access models.

continues to grow. In turn, these could become central nodes in financial markets, if this is not already the case. In this context, one could wonder whether a revision of the prudential framework for these specific activities would not be warranted as it was the case for CCPs in 2012 when central clearing was introduced.

6 Other Areas of the Basel Framework Influenced by Central Clearing

6.1 Credit Valuation Adjustment (CVA)

CVA stands for 'credit valuation adjustment' specified at a counterparty level. It is a concept, borrowed from the accounting framework, that has been introduced into the prudential framework in the aftermath of the GFC because of the counterparty credit losses incurred by banks due to the revaluation of their derivatives transactions as their counterparties were less likely to meet their obligations while not yet being in default.

CVA relates to the adjustment of the prices of derivatives and securities financing transactions (SFTs) that is needed to reflect the deterioration in the credit quality of a counterparty in respect to an OTC derivative transaction. It could also be seen as the market value of CCR. The risk associated with the CVA therefore relates to losses arising from changing CVA values in response to changes in counterparty credit spreads and market risk factors that drive prices of derivative transactions and SFTs.

Regulatory CVA[41] usually differs from accounting CVA in two dimensions: (i) regulatory CVA excludes the effect of the bank's own default and (ii) several constraints reflecting best practice in accounting CVA are imposed on calculations of regulatory CVA.

The capital requirement for CVA risk must be calculated by all banks involved in covered transactions. Covered transactions include all derivatives *except* those transacted directly with a QCCP (or meeting the conditions for client exposures described under section 3.1.3).[42] Bilateral transactions and transactions with NQCCPs are therefore subject to capital requirements for CVA risk.

In a nutshell, two approaches are available for calculating the capital requirements for CVA risk: a standardized approach (SA–CVA) and a basic approach (BA–CVA). Banks must use the BA–CVA unless they receive approval from their relevant supervisory authority to use the SA–CVA.

6.2 Leverage Ratio

As a response to the GFC, and prior to any consideration for an output floor to model-based capital requirements, in January 2014, the Basel Framework introduced a simple

---

[41] See the Basel Framework (n 1), s. MAR50 and the CRR (n 11), Title VI, Part 3.
[42] See also the CRR (n 11), Art. 382(3).

and basic non-risk-based ratio to act as a credible supplementary measure to the risk-based capital requirements.[43]

The intention of the BCBS was to (i) restrict the build-up of leverage in the banking sector to avoid destabilizing deleveraging processes that can damage the broader financial system and the economy and (ii) reinforce the risk-based requirements with a simple, non-risk-based 'backstop' measure.

The leverage ratio is defined as a capital measure divided by an exposure measure, with this ratio expressed as a percentage. The capital measure used for the leverage ratio at any particular point in time is the tier 1 capital (being defined as the sum of common equity tier 1 and additional tier 1).

Banks must meet a minimum leverage ratio requirement of 3% at all times. In addition, global systemically important banks should meet an additional leverage ratio buffer requirement.

The exposure measure is the sum of (i) on-balance sheet exposures (excluding on-balance sheet derivative and securities financing transaction exposures), (ii) derivative exposures, (iii) SFT exposures, and (iv) off-balance sheet items.

One of the key principle of the leverage ratio measurement is that, unless specified otherwise under the Basel Framework, banks should not take account of physical or financial collateral, guarantees, or other credit risk mitigation techniques to reduce the exposure measure, nor may banks net assets and liabilities. This led, however, to some discussions in the context of central clearing and the recognition of collateral for client-cleared derivatives.

As regards central clearing, adding up exposures without allowing for netting out exposures that offset each other would require banks to hold more capital for centrally cleared transactions than for non-centrally cleared transactions. This would go against the agreed G20 reforms. The January 2014 version of the leverage ratio standard therefore allows clearing members' trade exposures to QCCPs associated with client-cleared derivatives transactions to be excluded from the exposure measure if the clearing member does not guarantee the performance of a QCCP to its clients.[44]

As regards the recognition of collateral for client-cleared derivatives, the BCBS consulted in October 2018 on the treatment of derivative exposures under the leverage ratio, in particular for those derivative transactions that a bank centrally clears on behalf of its clients.[45] Notably, it took into account the joint evaluation of the effects of the G20 financial regulatory reforms on incentives to centrally clear OTC derivatives.[46]

---

[43] See the Basel Framework (n 1), s. LEV as well as the CRR (n 11), Part 7, Arts 429 and 429(a).

[44] See BCBS, ' Basel III Leverage Ratio Framework and Disclosure Requirements, paras 27 and 28 (January 2014), https://www.bis.org/publ/bcbs270.pdf (accessed 23 March 2023).

[45] See BCBS, 'Leverage Ratio Treatment of Client Cleared Derivatives', Consultative Document (October 2018), https://www.bis.org/bcbs/publ/d451.pdf (accessed 23 March 2023).

[46] See BCBS, CPMI, FSB, and IOSCO, 'Incentives to Centrally Clear Over-the-Counter (OTC) Derivatives: A Post-Implementation Evaluation of the Effects of the G20 Financial Regulatory Reforms' (August 2018), https://www.fsb.org/wp-content/uploads/P070818.pdf (accessed 23 March 2023).

Two options were considered at the time:

(1) amend the treatment of client-cleared derivatives to allow amounts of cash and non-cash initial margin that are received from the client to offset the potential future exposure of derivatives centrally cleared on the client's behalf;

(2) amend the treatment of client-cleared derivatives to align it with the measurement determined under the SA–CCR. This option would permit both cash and non-cash forms of initial margin and variation margin received from the client to offset replacement cost and potential future exposure for client-cleared derivatives.

In June 2019, the BCBS published a revised version of the leverage ratio standards to introduce a targeted revision implementing the second option.[47] To be eligible for offset, initial margin that a bank has received from a client should be subject to appropriate segregation by the bank as defined in the relevant jurisdiction, reflecting diverging approaches to insolvency across jurisdictions.

7 Last Considerations

Following the implementation of the G20 reforms in the field of OTC derivatives, CCPs have become critical nodes for the financial system. This evolution has been reinforced by the various regulatory measures that have been reviewed in this chapter and that supported the use of central clearing beyond the clearing obligation.

As CCPs interpose themselves between market participants and guarantee each side of their trades, they enhance exposure management by providing multilateral netting of cleared trades and impose margin discipline. Through their role, CCPs have removed substantial amounts of CCR from the financial system and contribute to its soundness. However, those risks have not simply disappeared, they have just been moved elsewhere (or to someone else). While CCPs are experts in risk-managing exposures and have strong default management procedures in place to deal with clearing member defaults, CCPs also have the potential to redistribute risks to the financial system in extreme circumstances. As market participants are 'forced' into central clearing, these risks need to be adequately considered by authorities and regulators. Notably, this has been the case through prudential initiatives, launched under the auspices of the FSB, around the recovery and resolution of CCPs. However, the implementation of these varies across jurisdictions and is a matter for further follow-up and monitoring at international level.

To ensure the soundness of their risk management processes and mitigate their own CCR, CCPs impose strict access criteria to their applicant members that cannot necessarily be met by a vast majority of market participants. Some CCPs started to offer

---

[47] See BCBS, 'Leverage Ratio Treatment of Client Cleared Derivatives' (June 2019), https://www.bis.org/bcbs/publ/d467.pdf (accessed 23 March 2023).

complementary services that aim to provide some form of direct access to clients under certain conditions, but (the use of) these facilities remain(s) limited for the time being. Central clearing is, to some extent, the victim of its own success and therefore poses new challenges in terms of access.

One of these challenges will be to adequately address—and reflect in the prudential framework—the potential risks associated with the increasing role of (general) clearing members as critical intermediaries in indirect access models and the further evolution of the central clearing landscape.

III
DEFAULT MANAGEMENT

10

Segregation and Portability of Cleared OTC Derivatives in Europe

*Bas Zebregs**

1 Introduction

This chapter deals with the segregation and portability requirements for over-the-counter (OTC) derivatives clearing in Europe under the European Market Infrastructure Regulation (EMIR).[1] EMIR prescribes that client positions and assets should be held and recorded at the level of the central counterparty (CCP) separately from the assets of the clearing member (CM). The segregation and portability regime aims to ensure that upon a CM default, these assets do not become part of the bankruptcy estate of the CM but can be transferred (i.e. porting of positions and assets) to another CM or (following liquidation of client positions) returned to the client.

Following this introduction, section 2 will discuss the policy objectives as envisaged by the rule-making bodies. Section 3 will then describe the various types of collateral

* This chapter reflects only the author's personal views. I would like to thank Bridget Austad, David Horner, Jane Kuschel-Danz, Max Meulenhoff, David Murphy, Victor de Serière, and Owen Taylor for providing valuable feedback on the content.
[1] Regulation (EU) No. 648/2012 of the European Parliament and of the Council of 4 July 2012 on OTC derivatives, central counterparties and trade repositories, [2012] OJ L201/1 (27 July 2012) (EMIR).

and whether these are subject to the segregation requirements under EMIR. Section 4 proceeds with giving an overview of the various segregation models that are prescribed by EMIR as well as the models that are offered in practice. Subsequently, section 5 discusses the portability of client positions and assets or the return of any remaining collateral following the liquidation of client positions if porting cannot be achieved.[2]

This chapter does not deal with the fact that CMs or CCPs may be located outside of the European Union; it also does not deal with the possibility that not the CM but the CCP, the CCPs' custodian, or the CCPs' settlement bank defaults.[3] With respect to CCPs and CMs that are located in the United Kingdom, it should be noted that EMIR is to a large extent incorporated into English law, which means that—at least for the time being—the applicable rules with respect to segregation and portability are similar, if not (still) identical.[4]

2 Policy Objective

As early as 2009, the European Commission committed to proposing legislation with respect to strengthening the use of CCPs for OTC derivatives whereby ensuring legal protection for client positions and assets was defined as one of the key requirements.[5] In its Impact Assessment accompanying the EMIR proposal in 2010, the European Commission stated that investor protection should be increased by providing additional safeguards which enhance the portability of client positions and associated collateral.[6] From a client perspective, the segregation and portability arrangements under EMIR may be regarded as a counterbalance for the fact that designated OTC derivatives have to be mandatorily cleared. Segregation and portability also facilitate an orderly default management process by CCPs, which is beneficial to the market as a whole.[7]

---

[2] This chapter builds and elaborates on earlier works, including Bas Zebregs, 'Guaranteed Portability under EMIR?' (2011) 26(5) Journal of International Banking and Financial Law 276–278; Tariq Rasheed and Bas Zebregs, 'Can a House Divided between Itself Stand? Segregation in Derivatives Clearing' (2012) 27(5) Journal of International Banking and Financial Law 293–300 (Rasheed and Zebregs, 'Can a House Divided between Itself Stand?'); Bas Zebregs and Victor de Serière, 'Securities and Derivatives Central Counterparties in the EU: Regulatory Framework, Segregation and Portability', in Jens-Hinrich Binder and Paolo Saguato (eds), *Financial Market Infrastructures: Law and Regulation* (Oxford: Oxford University Press, 2021), pp. 221–268 (Zebregs and de Serière, 'Securities and Derivatives Central Counterparties in the EU).

[3] For a detailed analysis, see Chapters 12 ('Recovery and Resolution of CCPs' by Victor de Serière) and 15 ('Cross-Border Clearing' by Ulrich Karl) in this volume.

[4] EMIR (n 1) forms part of 'retained EU law' from 1 January 2021 as defined in the European Union (Withdrawal) Act 2018. Most CMs offering services to non-UK clients have relocated to an EU subsidiary while UK CCPs benefit from a temporary equivalence until 30 June 2025. See Chapter 16 ('Brexit: Equivalence; Location Policy' by Dermot Turing) in this volume.

[5] Communication from the Commission, 'Ensuring Efficient, Safe and Sound Derivatives Markets: Future Policy Actions' (20 October 2009), COM(2009) 563, pp. 5 and 10, https://www.eur-lex.europa.eu (accessed 23 March 2023). See EMIR (n 1), Recitals (1)–(2).

[6] Communication from the Commission, 'Impact Assessment, Accompanying EMIR', COM (2010) 484, pp. 71–72, https://www.eur-lex.europa.eu (accessed 23 March 2023) ('EMIR Impact Assessment').

[7] For a detailed analysis of CCP default management, see Chapter 11 ('Default Management' by David Horner) in this volume.

The EMIR proposal builds upon international standards.[8] In April 2012, the Committee on Payments and Market Infrastructures–International Organization of Securities Commissions (CPMI–IOSCO) issued the Principles for Financial Market Infrastructures (FMI Principles[9]), which, among other things, prescribes that CCPs should have effective and clearly defined rules and procedures to manage a CM default, including an appropriate segregation and portability regime. This regime should, at least to some extent, contribute to retaining customers' confidence in their CMs and reduce the need for closing-out positions in a period of market stress, which could cause market disruption or potentially reduce access to central clearing. The FMI Principles also stipulate that these objectives are more pertinent when the use of CCPs is mandatory.[10] Therefore, the policy objectives of the FMI Principles relate to increasing client protection, on the one hand, and reducing systemic risk on the other.

Within the European Union, which at the time included the United Kingdom, these segregation and portability requirements were implemented in EMIR, Arts 39 and 48. The explanatory notes of EMIR itself only mention that clients of CMs 'should be granted a high level of protection', without explicit reference to the positive impact a sound segregation and portability regime could have from a systemic risk point of view.[11]

2.1 Segregation and Portability: A Package Deal

Many clients provide collateral on a title transfer basis to their CM, who, in turn, provides collateral to the CCP via a title transfer or security interest.[12] This means that legal ownership resides with the CM or the CCP in order to protect the CM and/or the CCP, respectively, in case a client or CM defaults. EMIR, Art. 39 does not prescribe that non-defaulting clients retain legal ownership or provide clients with *in rem* entitlements, nor does it prohibit clients from providing collateral via a title transfer when a CM defaults.[13] This means that segregation in accordance with EMIR, Art. 39 in itself results in administrative segregation only.

---

[8] EMIR (n 1), Recital (90), which also clarifies that the European Securities Markets Authority (ESMA) should consider these standards, including future developments, when drafting regulatory technical standards under EMIR.

[9] CPMI, previously known as the Committee on Payments and Settlement Systems (CPSS) and the Technical Committee of IOSCO, 'Principles for Financial Market Infrastructures' (April 2012), Principle 13, pp. 78–81, https://www.iosco.org (accessed 23 March 2023) (FMI Principles). See also Chapter 3 ('Development of the Regulatory Regime for OTC Derivatives Clearing' by Patrick Pearson) in this volume.

[10] FMI Principles (n 9), pp. 10–11, 82–83.

[11] EMIR (n 1), Recital (64). Peter Norman, *The Risk Controllers, Central Counterparty Clearing in Globalised Financial Markets* (Chichester: Wiley, 2011), p. 343 (Norman, *The Risk Controllers*) described the proposals as 'strongly pro-client, giving CCPs considerable powers to transfer assets and positions of clients without the consent of clearing members'.

[12] More sophisticated clients with a low-risk appetite may opt for an alternative structure (see section 4.3.4 below).

[13] See Zebregs and de Serière, 'Securities and Derivatives Central Counterparties in the EU' (n 2), p. 243.

An analogy can be made with the segregation requirements in the Central Securities Depositaries Regulation (CSDR) prescribing segregation at the level of a Central Securities Depositary (CSD), Art. 38.[14] These requirements are almost identical to EMIR, Art. 39 and aim to enhance the protection of CSD participants and their clients. However, the CSDR does not provide any additional legal protection to these segregated assets and is administrative in nature. Whether the clients can derive additional legal protection from the segregation depends on applicable local legislation.[15]

EMIR, Art. 39 mandates that client positions and assets are recorded in separate accounts at the level of the CCP.[16] As mentioned above, this only results in administrative segregation of client positions and assets. However, the requirement to segregate client positions and assets is only satisfied if the netting of positions in different segregated accounts is prevented and the assets covering the positions are recorded in a segregated account which is not exposed to losses connected to positions recorded in another account.[17] To ensure that the segregation of assets also offers additional legal protection, EMIR, Art. 48(7) stipulates that client assets segregated in a client account 'shall be used exclusively to cover the positions held for their account'. EMIR also provides for a portability arrangement enabling the clients, under certain conditions, to transfer segregated positions and assets to another CM, if their CM defaults, without the consent of the defaulting CM or its administrator (see section 5 below). If such transfer of positions is not possible and positions are liquidated, the remaining collateral shall, if possible, be readily returned to the clients directly.[18] Furthermore, EMIR provides that the national insolvency laws of the European Union (EU) Member States shall not prevent the transfer of positions and/or the return of assets directly to the client in case a client defaults (see section 5.8 below).[19]

It can therefore be concluded that although the segregation of client positions and assets in EMIR, Art. 39 does not provide additional legal protection in itself, the combined arrangements under EMIR, Arts 39 and 48 intend to create a legal framework that achieves a segregation that is de facto equal to a full legal segregation whereby client positions and assets held at CCP level do not become part of the bankruptcy estate of the CM. In that sense, the segregation and portability arrangements are deeply interconnected and should be considered as a bespoke form of legal protection for clients of a CM.

---

[14] Regulation (EU) No. 909/2014 of the European Parliament and of the Council of 23 July 2014 on improving securities settlement in the European Union and on central securities depositories and amending Directives 98/26/EU and 2014/65/EU and Regulation (EU) No. 236/2012, [2014] OJ L257/1 (28 August 2014) (CSDR).

[15] CSDR (n 14), Recital (42) states that 'This Regulation should not interfere with the national law of the Member States regulating the holding of securities and arrangements maintaining the integrity of securities issues.' See, e.g. Randy Priem, 'Asset Segregation at CSDs: Protecting Investors with a Level Playing Field' (2020) 31(5) European Business Law Review 917–946.

[16] EMIR (n 1), Art. 39(2–5).

[17] EMIR (n 1), Art. 39(9).

[18] EMIR (n 1), Art. 48(5–7). See also section 5.6 below.

[19] EMIR (n 1), Art. 39(11).

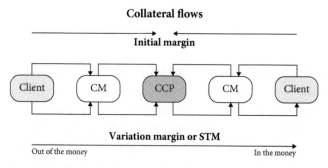

Figure 10.1 Collateral flows
Source: author.

3 Client Assets under EMIR

CCPs generally collect two types of collateral, that is, initial margin (IM) and variation margin (VM). Apart from that, clients may post additional margin on top of what is required by the CCP ('excess margin'). EMIR itself does not make a clear distinction between these types of margin.[20] I will briefly discuss these margins and the collateral flow below. In practice, the CCP (and CM) may combine margin calls which are related to multiple client accounts or different types of margin. This is allowed as long as such margin is recorded and segregated in accordance with EMIR.[21]

The segregation and portability regime under EMIR only applies to positions and assets held at the level of the CCP. This means that positions between the CM and the client, as well as assets which are held at the level of the CM, are out of scope, although it should be noted that the Markets in Financial Instruments Directive (MiFID) and/or local insolvency laws may provide for additional protection.[22] In a principal-to-principal model, positions are usually referred to as 'back-to-back' and a close-out or transfer of positions between the CM and the CCP should normally result in a close-out or 'transfer' of positions between the client and the CM as well.[23]

This section proceeds with describing the main types of collateral and whether these assets are subject to the segregation requirements under EMIR. The main collateral flows are illustrated in Figure 10.1.

---

[20] EMIR (n 1) contains some isolated references to VM and IM in Recitals (26) and (65) and Arts 53(2), 85(2), and 89(2).

[21] ESMA, 'Questions & Answers, Implementation of the Regulation (EU) No. 648/2012 on OTC Derivatives, Central Counterparties and Trade Repositories (EMIR)' (19 November 2021), ESMA70-1861941480-52, CCP Question 8(e)(2), pp. 57–58, https://www.esma.europa.eu (accessed 23 March 2023) ('ESMA Q&A').

[22] See Zebregs and de Serière, 'Securities and Derivatives Central Counterparties in the EU' (n 2), pp. 239–244 on whether MiFID (especially Art. 16(8)) prescribes additional client protection at CM level.

[23] Dermot Turing, *Clearing and Settlement* (London: Bloomsbury Professional 2021), pp. 566–568 points out that although this is the general idea, there may be mismatches. However, most client-clearing agreements contain clauses that aim to ensure that no such mismatches occur by giving the CM the right to amend transactions in order to correct any mismatches.

3.1 Variation Margin/Settlement to Market

The CCP will collect or pay out profits and losses that are accrued on cleared open OTC derivatives positions at least on a daily basis ('marking to market'), thus preventing exposures from building up over time.[24] This results in VM payments from CMs holding positions that suffered a loss ('out of the money') to the CCP. The CCP will, on the other hand, make VM payments to CMs holding positions that made a profit ('in the money').[25] The CMs will, in turn, exchange (i.e. collect or pay out) VM with their clients based on the transactions these clients clear via the CM. In practice, CCPs and CMs act as 'pass-through entities'. This is the main reason why it is market practice that VM payments are required to be made in the form of cash. Note, however, that the fact that VM is collected and paid out by the CCP at least once a day does not mean that VM obligations are insignificant compared to IM obligations. Especially in case of market stress, which is likely to occur when a bigger CM defaults, market fluctuations may result in a dramatic increase of VM payments.[26]

There was initially a lack of clarity about whether VM falls under the definition of 'assets' in EMIR, Art. 39(10), which refers to 'collateral held to cover positions'.[27] EMIR itself does not contain a definition of collateral, nor does it make any distinction between IM and VM. However, CDR EU/153/2013, Art. 1(4) mentions that margins as referred to in EMIR, Art. 41 may include both IM and VM and that all margins should be recorded by the CCP in segregated accounts held by the CM at CCP level.[28] Therefore, it can be concluded that VM should be qualified as assets as defined in EMIR, Art. 39(10) and is subject to the segregation and portability requirements under EMIR. This is relevant because although CCPs (and CMs) act as 'pass-through entities', a client is exposed to transit risk when the CM defaults (see section 4.3.4 below).

3.1.1 Settlement to market
Traditionally, the exchange of VM for cleared OTC derivatives has legally been structured as a transfer of collateral: usually referred to as 'collateralized to market' (CTM).

---

[24] Usually by comparing the closing prices at the end of the current and the previous business day. CCPs often call for intra-day margins from their CMs. See Froukelien Wendt, 'Intraday Margin of Central Counterparties: EU Practice and a Theoretical Evaluation of Benefits and Costs' (10 March 2006), pp. 1–18, https://www.ecb.europa.eu (accessed 23 March 2023).

[25] Accrued profits may be used to offset IM requirements or other payment obligations to the CCP.

[26] Basel Committee on Banking Supervision (BCBS), CPMI, and the Board of IOSCO, 'Consultative Report, Review of Margining Practices' (October 2021), p. 11, https://www.bis.org (accessed 23 March 2023) describes that during the COVID pandemic, daily CCP VM calls increased from around $25 billion in February to a peak of $140 billion on 9 March 2020 (>460%).

[27] ESMA, 'EMIR Segregation Review Report No. 3, Review on the Segregation and Portability Requirements' (13 August 2015), ESMA/2015/1253, https://www.esma.europa.eu (accessed 23 March 2023) ('ESMA Segregation Report'), issued by ESMA, p. 7 mentions that it was unclear whether VM is covered by the definition of 'assets'.

[28] Commission Delegated Regulation (EU) No. 153/2013 of 19 December 2012 supplementing Regulation No. 648/2012 of the European Parliament and of the Council with regard to regulatory technical standards on requirements for central counterparties, [2013] OJ L52/41 (23 February 2013), Arts 1(4–6) and 14(3) clarify that 'margins' in EMIR (n 1), Art. 41 may include IM and VM and contain definitions of VM and IM. See also ESMA Q&A (n 21), CCP Question 8(e)(2), pp. 57–58.

Settlement to market (STM) is a fairly recent innovation in OTC derivatives clearing whereby CMs characterize these payments as settlements rather than as a transfer of collateral. STM results in a situation whereby the market value of the derivatives is reset to zero on a daily basis, and the CMs subsequently hold less open positions on their books. This may result in lower capital requirements for the CMs and potentially lower fees for their clients.[29]

It could be argued that because daily STM payments do not legally qualify as collateral, these payments do not qualify as assets under EMIR, Art. 39(10) either. The same applies to other settlement payments, in particular the final payments at the end of the life cycle of the relevant OTC derivative transaction. Obviously, there is no reason why STM payments, as well as other settlements related to client transactions, should not benefit from the same protection as is applicable to VM. But as the term 'collateral' is not defined, it leaves room for interpretation. Alternatively, it could be argued that STM payments, as well as other settlements, are part of the 'positions' and should therefore be segregated. It would be helpful if this were to be clarified in an ESMA Q&A or, even better, in EMIR itself, also because STM payments have become increasingly common.[30]

3.2 Initial Margin

Whereas VM is looking at realized profits and losses (i.e. current exposures), IM is forward-looking, and is collected by a CCP to cover potential future exposure to CMs. A CCP is only allowed to accept highly liquid currencies and financial instruments with minimal credit and market risk as IM.[31] A CM will call for IM from its clients and may accept less liquid currencies and financial instruments: these may have to be transformed by the CM in order to be eligible for the CCP.

Whereas the CCP effectively acts as a pass-through entity for VM payments, IM will be held at the level of the CCP. IM can be posted via a double title transfer, that is, from the client to the CM and subsequently from the CM to the CCP. This means that the assets are ultimately transferred to the CCP, who then takes full ownership of these assets. It is also common that clients post collateral to the CM via a title transfer but that the CM provides collateral to the CCP on a security interest basis. In this situation, the ownership of the collateral sits with the CM, although the CCP will typically require the assets to be posted in a blocked securities account with a designated custodian or (international) central securities depository ((I)CSD). Securities will normally be located in a securities account in the name of the CCP held with a CSD or custodian.[32]

---

[29] This is particularly relevant for the leverage ratio. See Chapter 9 ('Capital Requirements for Bank Exposures to CCPs' by Marc Peters) in this volume.

[30] ESMA Q&A (n 21), CCP Question 8(e)(2), pp. 57–58 seems to refer to other payments as well but was last updated in 2015 when CCPs for OTC derivatives did not offer STM.

[31] EMIR (n 1), Art. 46(1).

[32] EMIR (n 1), Art. 47(3) mandates CCPs to hold margin securities with a CSD where available or a highly secure arrangement. See Louise Gullifer, 'Compulsory Central Clearing of OTC Derivatives: The Changing Face of

When the CCP receives cash, the CCP will, if possible, keep this cash in an account at a central bank, which implies that 'ownership' of the cash is transferred to the central bank whereby the CCP has a claim on the central bank (see also section 4.1 below).[33]

What is possible in practice largely depends on what is allowed by (or agreed with) the relevant CM and CCP. For cash, CCPs typically require a title transfer in all cases.[34] For non-cash collateral, CCPs often require CMs to provide IM via a security interest.[35] CMs, on the other hand, often require clients to post all types of collateral via a title transfer.[36] Alternative structures may be available as well (see section 4.3.4 below).

3.3 Excess Margin

Apart from IM and VM obligations imposed by the CCP, the client may post additional margin on top of the margin requested by the relevant CCP ('excess margin'). A CM may require excess margin from clients with a weaker creditworthiness. It is also common that the CM requires the client, or the client voluntarily offers, to post excess margin in order to reduce the number of settlements and to avoid prefunding (operational buffer) or in anticipation of new transactions they intend to clear via the CM.[37] Excess margin can also result from the netting of client positions at the CM level, market fluctuations, or the expiration of contracts.

Excess margin may be held at the CM level or the CCP level. For individually segregated accounts (ISAs), it is mandatory to hold excess margin at the level of the CCP, whereas for omnibus client accounts (OSAs), this is subject to what is contractually agreed between the client and the CM.[38] If excess margin is retained at the CM level, and the CM becomes the owner of the collateral assets concerned, these assets are likely to be caught up in the CM's bankrupt estate if the CM would become insolvent, unless local insolvency laws provide additional protection (see n 78). A client may provide excess margin via a title transfer but also by means of a security interest, in which case, the client remains the owner of the collateral assets. This may be beneficial if the CM defaults, but a CM may negotiate a right of reuse whereby it is able to use collateral held

---

the Provision of Collateral', in Louise Gullifer and Stefan Vogenauer (eds), *English and European Perspectives on Contract and Commercial Law* (Oxford: Hart Publishing 2014), para. 4.1.

[33] EMIR (n 1), Art. 50(1) mandates the use of central banks in order to mitigate settlement bank risk. If using a central bank is not possible, other risk-remote arrangements may be allowed as well.

[34] Eurex Clearing, 'Client Asset Protection' (brochure) (2 March 2022), p. 6, https://www.eurex.com (accessed 23 March 2023).

[35] For example, Eurex and SwapClear require CMs to provide non-cash collateral via a security interest, although for ISA accounts (see section 4.3.4 below), Eurex provides the option to provide non-cash IM via a title transfer as well.

[36] Technically it is also possible that the client provides collateral to the CM by way of a security interest and that the CM subsequently provides collateral to the CCP via a security interest (re-pledge) as well. In that situation, the ownership of the collateral sits with the client until the CM enforces its security interest. However, it is common practice that the CM first appropriates the assets and subsequently posts the assets to the CCP.

[37] Most clients post margin to their CM once per business day, whereas the CM is likely to receive intra-day margin calls as well (see EMIR (n 1), Art. 41(3)), which the CM may need to prefund if no excess margin is available.

[38] EMIR (n 1), Art. 39(6).

at the CM level for its own proprietary business as if the collateral were owned by the CM. This implies that the client will no longer be able to exercise its ownership rights with respect to the relevant assets and should carefully consider whether this risk is acceptable to it.

3.3.1 Does excess margin qualify as an 'asset'?

EMIR, Art. 39(6) stipulates that when a client opts for an ISA, any excess margin shall be posted at the level of the CCP.[39] Excess margin is described as 'any margin in excess of the client's requirement' without providing any additional clarification or definition. It may be assumed, though, that the client requirement refers to margin obligations imposed by a CCP to cover the positions cleared at this CCP. This is confirmed by ESMA in their Q&A, where they state that the obligation imposed by EMIR, Art. 39(6) refers to 'any margin called from a client, which is over and above the amount called by the CCP to cover the positions of that client'.[40] However, it could be argued that excess margin does not fall under the definition of 'assets' because the definition of 'assets' in EMIR refers to 'collateral held to cover positions'.[41] Furthermore, excess margin may be provided for a variety of other reasons. This could mean that excess margin may not be subject to the segregation and portability protections under EMIR. The definition of 'assets' is clearly not intended to exclude excess margin as envisaged under EMIR, Art. 39(6). ESMA has previously advocated amending the EMIR definition of 'assets' in order to reflect this, but this has unfortunately not been done.[42] Therefore residual uncertainty remains.

3.4 Equivalent Assets and Proceeds

The definition of 'assets' in EMIR includes 'assets equivalent to that collateral' or, in case of liquidation, 'the proceeds of the realisation of any collateral'.[43] The general idea is that clients post collateral to the CM, which is then passed on to the CCP in order to be segregated in client accounts. That does not mean, in all cases, that there is a straight pass-through of assets that the CM receives to the CCP (or vice versa). Depending on the contractual agreements between the clients and the CM, clients may not have (full) control over which assets are actually passed on to the CCP level and subsequently benefit from the segregation and portability arrangements under EMIR. First of all, a CM may negotiate a general right to transfer other assets than the assets it received from the clients to the CCP. Second, the CM may not pass on

---

[39] Section 4.3.3 below describes certain exemptions to EMIR (n 1), Art. 39(6).

[40] EMIR (n 1), Art. 39(6) and the ESMA Q&A (n 21) do not refer to excess margin with respect to omnibus segregated accounts (OSAs). This means that this excess margin may be held at CM level and that it can even be argued that excess margin held at CCP level in OSAs does not qualify as 'assets' as defined in EMIR, Art. 39(10).

[41] EMIR (n 1), Art. 39(10).

[42] ESMA Segregation Report (n 27), p. 10.

[43] ESMA Q&A (n 21), CCP Question 3(a) clarifies that EMIR (n 1), Art. 39(10) also includes the proceeds of the realization of any collateral.

all of the assets it receives, as is typically the case for OSA net accounts (section 4.3.9 below). If the CM retains certain assets, the CM will typically have discretion to decide which assets are posted to the CCP and which assets are not.[44] Third, it is possible that clients post collateral to the CM that is not eligible to be posted as margin with the CCP.[45] CMs may accept this collateral and provide transformation services so that these assets are 'transformed' into eligible assets acceptable to the CCP. A similar situation can occur the other way around as the clients do not necessarily receive back the same collateral as the collateral they initially posted with the CM. CMs may negotiate a general right to return other equivalent assets. Apart from that, CCPs tend to have discretionary powers to return equivalent assets or proceeds to clients, in particular in a default situation.

4 Segregation Models

EMIR prescribes that a CCP is subject to segregation requirements and needs to offer at least five types of accounts which can be divided into three groups:

(1) A CCP has to segregate the proprietary positions and assets of each CM and the CCP itself in separate accounts ('house accounts'). This will be discussed in section 4.2 below.

(2) A CCP has to enable each CM to segregate positions and assets of their clients in individually segregated ISA accounts or commingled omnibus segregated OSA accounts, whereby each CM shall offer their clients a choice between an ISA and an OSA account. This will be discussed in section 4.3 below.

(3) A CCP has the obligation to offer indirect clearing accounts, enabling each CM to segregate the positions and assets of indirect clients in specific omnibus net or omnibus gross accounts. This will be discussed in section 4.4 below.

Figure 10.2 illustrates the minimum segregation requirements under EMIR at CCP level.

Given the fact that segregation and portability arrangements are crucial for clients, it is important that clients obtain sufficient information to enable them to make an adequate risk assessment. EMIR, Art. 39(7) tries to facilitate this by prescribing that CMs and CCPs publicly disclose the protection levels associated with the various segregation models, including the main legal implications, as well as information on the relevant applicable insolvency laws, which should include the jurisdictions applicable to the relevant CM as well as the CCP. EMIR, however, does not prescribe to what extent

---

[44] This is relevant in particular in case of OSA net accounts, as well as OSAs where excess margin is (partially) maintained at the level of the CM (see section 4.3.9 below).

[45] The CM may contractually impose other, usually stricter, margin requirements on their clients. Unless contractually agreed with the client, the CM has no obligation to provide transformation services.

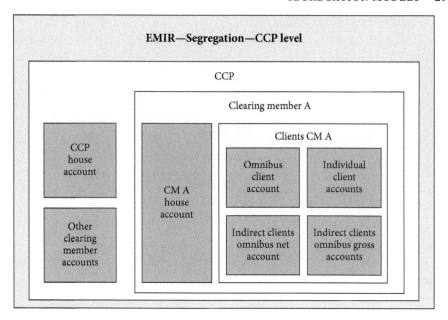

Figure 10.2 EMIR segregation—CCP level
Source: author.

information needs to be provided.[46] CMs and CCPs therefore tend to provide fairly generic information on a non-reliance basis. Some clients primarily focus on the costs, which—from a systemic risk point of view—raises the question whether the usage of more risk-remote options should not be (further) incentivized.[47]

4.1 Segregation at Custodial Level

It is important to note that segregation at the CCP level does not automatically extend to other levels of the intermediation chain. A CCP will use third parties (i.e. a CSD, national central bank (NCB), or other highly secure arrangement with authorized

---

[46] EMIR (n 1), Art. 39(7) refers to the protections offered by the various segregation levels without specifically mentioning portability risks. See CPMI and IOSCO, 'Client Clearing: Access and Portability' (September 2022), p. 23, https://www.iosco.org (accessed 23 March 2023) (CPMI–IOSCO Report), where clients expressed the view that they are not fully aware about the applicable portability processes, which prompted CPMI-IOSCO to suggest improving client disclosures.

[47] Regulation (EU) No. 575/2013 of the European Parliament and of the Council of 26 June 2013 on prudential requirements for credit institutions and investment firms and amending Regulation (EU) No. 648/2012, [2013] OJ L 176/1 (27 June 2013), Art. 305 (CRR) contains some capital incentives for using an ISA. EMIR (n 1), Art. 39(7) also prescribes disclosure of the costs of segregation models, which can be regarded as a *lex specialis* of EMIR, Arts 4(a) and 38(1) jo.; Commission Delegated Regulation (EU) No. 2021/1456, supplementing Regulation (EU) No. 648/2012 of the European Parliament and of the Council by specifying the conditions under which the commercial terms for clearing services for OTC derivatives are to be considered to be fair, reasonable, non-discriminatory and transparent (2 June 2021), Annex Art. 3.1(a)(ii) (FRANDT). See also Chapters 8 ('OTC Derivatives Clearing Documentation' by Emma Dwyer and Emma Lancelott) and 9 ('Capital Requirements for Bank Exposures to CCPs' by Marc Peters) in this volume.

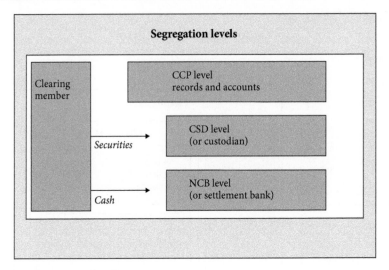

Figure 10.3 Segregation levels
Source: author.

financial institutions to hold the collateral assets it receives.[48] This can be visualized in Figure 10.3.

EMIR imposes an obligation on CCPs and CMs to segregate client positions and assets in their records and accounts, but it does not stipulate whether these segregation requirements should also be extended to the level of the above third parties. ESMA has clarified that the segregation requirements do not need to be reflected at the level of the NCB or CSD.[49] That makes sense because EMIR, Art. 47(5) stipulates that a CCP has to ensure that when it holds assets as a third party, these assets are 'identifiable separately from the assets belonging to the CCP and from assets belonging to that third party'.[50] In order to exclude any uncertainty, ESMA advocated that EMIR should be amended and make explicit that any reference to 'accounts' in EMIR, Art. 39 excludes third parties.[51] Although EMIR has not been amended accordingly, the above highlights the fact that while EMIR may provide a certain level of protection against a CM default, this does not apply to a default at the CSD or NCB level.

---

[48] EMIR (n 1), Art. 47(3–4). See ESMA Q&A (n 21), pp. 49–50.

[49] ESMA Q&A (n 21, p. 56, CCP Question 8(e)(1), which also refers to EMIR (n 1), Art. 47(5).

[50] The reference to 'identifiable separately' implies that this segregation is just administrative in nature. This can be done by means of differently titled accounts or equivalent measures. For CMs, MiFID contains similar requirements. See Commission Delegated Regulation (EU) No. EU/2017/593 of 7 April 2016 supplementing Directive 2014/65/EU of the European Parliament and of the Council with regard to safeguarding of financial instruments and funds belonging to clients, product governance obligations, and the rules applicable to the provision or reception of fees, commissions, or any monetary or non-monetary benefits, [2017] OJ L87/500 (31 March 2017), Arts 2(1)(d) and 3. In so far as the investment firm holds client assets with a CSD, the CSDR (n 14) segregation requirements apply.

[51] ESMA Segregation Report (n 27), pp. 8, 10.

This section now proceeds with describing the various types of segregated accounts at CCP level.

4.2 House Accounts

CCPs must segregate in separate records and accounts the positions and collateral received from the various CMs.[52] This means that separate proprietary accounts are maintained for each CM and for the CCP itself.[53] Although house accounts do not contain any client assets, the way the CCP, as well as EMIR, treat these house accounts may indirectly impact the protection level offered to clients.

4.2.1 Excess margin in case of default
The CM guarantees the performance of client obligations towards the CCP. In case the CM defaults, CCP rule books typically allow the CCP to use excess margin (posted by the CM) held in the house account to cover not only any losses of the CM itself but also losses related to client positions of the CM.[54] This could be regarded as a breach of the segregation requirements because EMIR stipulates that assets segregated in one account (i.e. the CM's house account) cannot be used to cover losses connected to positions recorded in another segregated account, that is, the CM's client accounts.[55] ESMA has provided clarification that this practice is allowed because this is beneficial to the clients of the defaulting CM and because the objective of the segregation requirements is to provide clients with a high level of protection in case of a CM default.[56] Furthermore, EMIR provides that a CCP shall use the margin posted by the defaulting CM prior to using any other financial resources.[57] Although these arguments make sense, it would be welcome to clarify this in EMIR itself.[58]

4.2.2 Prefunding to cover client obligations
It is common practice for CMs to offer clients the possibility to prefund their margin obligations, thus allowing clients to enter into new transactions and/or to provide clients with more time to meet their margin obligations towards the CM. This is usually done by a transfer of excess margin held in the house account of the CM to the relevant client account.[59] However, whether the margin is prefunded by the CM or not, these assets become client assets as soon as these assets are recorded in the relevant client

---

[52] EMIR (n 1), Art. 39(1). Usually, each CM has only one house account, although EMIR prescribes that a CCP should allow CMs to open multiple house accounts on request, see EMIR, Art. 39(3).

[53] CCPs are normally not expected to have derivatives positions unless they do this as part of their default management process, see Chapter 11 ('Default Management' by David Horner) in this volume.

[54] This is particularly relevant in a double default scenario (see section 4.3.6 below).

[55] EMIR (n 1), Art. 39(9)(c).

[56] ESMA Q&A (n 21), CCP Question 8(f)(1), where ESMA also refers to Recital (64). If this practice is not allowed, this would require the CCP to return the excess margin to the house account of the bankrupt CM.

[57] EMIR (n 1), Art. 45(1).

[58] See ESMA Segregation Report (n 27), p. 11.

[59] This can be done by the CM itself or by the CCP based on a power of attorney.

accounts. That implies that these assets are no longer available for the CCP to cover losses when the CM (rather than the client) defaults.[60] Therefore, the ringfencing principle of the segregated client account is maintained.

4.2.3 Appropriation of client positions and margin

It is not uncommon that clients and CMs contractually agree that, upon a client default, the CM may instruct the CCP to transfer assets from the account of the defaulting client(s) to its house account in order to handle the default appropriately, which may include liquidating assets or entering into hedging transactions. ESMA has clarified that a strict segregation of house and client positions should not prevent this practice as it is a useful tool to contain risk and avoid contagion.[61] Furthermore, ESMA stated that it is up to the CM to inform the CCP to which account positions as well as associated assets have to be allocated so that the CCP should be allowed to transfer assets upon request of the CM, if this is in accordance with the relevant clearing rule book, the CM is not in default itself, and the risks are clearly disclosed to the relevant clients.[62]

4.2.4 Guarantee fund contributions

EMIR contains an explicit carve-out from the segregation obligation for contributions paid by the CMs into the guarantee fund of the CCP.[63] Segregating these contributions would be illogical because the guarantee fund is intended to absorb losses of other CMs and is thereby, by definition, intended to cover losses connected to positions in other accounts. The contributions are therefore kept separately from the balances of the CMs in a segregated account.

4.2.5 CM affiliates

EMIR prescribes that the positions and assets of the CM have to be segregated in a house account. It should be noted, however, that many CMs have affiliates which may be active in the OTC derivatives markets as well.[64] It is possible that an affiliate becomes a CM itself and clears its proprietary transactions on its own house account, but this option may be costly and burdensome. Alternatively, a CCP may allow a CM to clear transactions of an affiliate belonging to the same legal group in the proprietary house account of the CM. In that situation, the affiliate will not be treated as a regular client, and the positions and assets of the affiliate will be ringfenced from the other clients of the CM.

In other cases, the affiliate will become a client of a CM, which will then typically be the CM belonging to the same legal group.[65] In that case, the affiliate is treated as a

---

[60] ESMA Q&A (n 21), CCP Question 8(f)(2), where ESMA refers to EMIR (n 1), Arts. 39(4) and 39(9)(a).
[61] ESMA Segregation Report (n 27), pp. 8–9, 11.
[62] ESMA Q&A (n 21), CCP Question 8(l), p. 59.
[63] EMIR (n 1), Arts 39(10) and 42.
[64] The affiliate can be the main trading entity within the group and may offer client-clearing services as well.
[65] See, e.g. Goldman Sachs International, 'Clearing Member Risk Disclosure, Direct and Indirect Clearing' (February 2021), p. 18, https://www.goldmansachs.com (accessed 23 March 2023), stating: 'we treat our affiliates in the same way as clients […], An affiliate may be part of the same omnibus account as other clients.'

regular client, which implies that they are entitled to EMIR segregation and portability arrangements just like any other client. In so far as the affiliate opts for an ISA account (see section 4.3.1 above), the positions and assets of the affiliate are ringfenced from those of the CMs other clients. However, if an affiliate opts for an OSA account, they will be part of the same OSA account as the other clients. In that case, clients in the same OSA may, in some circumstances, be exposed to losses incurred by the affiliate of the CM (see section 4.2.2 above). Whether it is allowed for an affiliate to participate in an OSA account depends on the laws of the relevant jurisdiction.[66] It could be argued that if an affiliate uses a CM within their own legal group, they should have an obligation to opt for an ISA account.[67]

4.3 Client Accounts

A CCP has to offer CMs at least the option between one OSA and one ISA account. In turn, each CM shall offer its clients a choice between at least one OSA and one ISA account. The abovementioned FMI Principles contain an obligation to segregate clients' collateral from the proprietary assets of the CM, but they do not contain an obligation to offer an ISA account.[68] It can therefore be concluded that the client segregation arrangements as mandated by EMIR go beyond what is prescribed in the FMI Principles.[69]

Unlike the United States, where local law prescribes a mandatory segregation model for (most) cleared OTC derivatives, the EU has chosen for more optionality.[70] Apart from the fact that clients should be offered at least one OSA and one ISA account, EMIR provides the market with a lot of flexibility to develop a wide variety of segregation models. For clients, this has resulted in an array of choices, making it difficult to understand the differences between the various models. On the other hand, clients are in a position to choose a segregation model that fits their needs. For CMs, it may be challenging to offer all of the available CCP models to their clients. In practice, they generally provide their clients only with a subset of these models, which is allowed as long as they offer at least one ISA and one OSA model.

---

[66] Turing, *Clearing and Settlement* (n 23), p. 569 points out that there appears to be no harmonized European view on this. See also FMI Principles (n 9), p. 85.

[67] See ESMA Segregation Report (n 27), p. 11, where ESMA suggested this.

[68] See FMI Principles (n 9), Principle 14, pp. 82–87.

[69] See ESMA Segregation Report (n 27), p. 11, where ESMA suggested making the use of ISAs mandatory in case clients exceed a certain predefined threshold. See EMIR Impact Assessment (n 6), pp. 74, 80, where the European Commission considered a number of other segregation options and referred to industry initiatives at the time. See the 'Report to the Supervisors of the Major OTC Derivatives Dealers on the Proposals of Centralized CDS Clearing Solutions for the Segregation and Portability of Customer CDS Positions and Related Margin' (30 June 2009), https://www.isda.org/a/FiiDE/full-report-on-cds-ccps.pdf (accessed 23 March 2023).

[70] The Commodity Futures Trading Commission (CFTC) mandates usage of the 'legally segregated operationally commingled model' (LSOC) with some optionality including posting and segregating excess margin at CCP level (LSOC with Excess). For more information, see e.g. Christian Chamorro-Courtland, 'The Legal Aspects of Portfolio Margining: A Move toward the LSOC Model' (2016) 10(1) Journal of Business Entrepreneurship & the Law 25–44. See Rasheed and Zebregs, 'Can a House Divided between Itself Stand?' (n 2) for a brief description of other models that have been considered.

This section now proceeds with describing the various segregation models offered in practice.

4.3.1 Individual client segregation

An ISA account requires a CCP to segregate both client positions, as well as the associated assets posted as collateral, in individually segregated client accounts.[71] This means that the positions, as well as the assets in the ISA account, should be segregated from the positions and assets of the other clients of the CM as well as those of the CM itself (house account). Subsequently, clients opting for an ISA account are not exposed to fellow customer risk (see section 4.3.6 below): this is the main advantage of an ISA account.

Another benefit of the ISA model is that the likelihood of a successful porting may be significantly bigger than for clients opting for an OSA model. This likelihood can be further increased if the client posts excess margin. Furthermore, the ISA model is relatively straightforward because both positions and collateral are segregated in individual accounts. It should therefore be relatively easy for the CCP to identify which positions and assets belong to which individual client upon a CM default, which facilitates a successful porting.

Managing an ISA account is operationally more burdensome and involves more settlements and transaction costs. Apart from that, the CM has no possibility of using excess margin for its own proprietary business, as it can with an OSA net model (see section 4.3.9 below). This means that an ISA account is less efficient and more costly than an OSA account: that is the main downside of an ISA account.

4.3.2 Excess margin

EMIR prescribes that, for clients opting for an ISA account, all excess margin should be held with the CCP.[72] This means that such excess margin cannot be retained by the CM, whereas this is still allowed for OSA accounts. Because CMs often require clients to post excess margin, especially in periods of market stress, this offers ISA clients significant additional protection. This may be particularly relevant for smaller or less attractive clients, who would otherwise not have been able to negotiate this with the CM. Furthermore, because this obligation is hardwired in EMIR, there is—in principle—no possibility for the CM and the client to contractually deviate from this obligation. If the client holds positions at multiple CCPs via the same CM, the CM and the client have to agree contractually on the allocation of the excess margin to the different CCPs.[73]

4.3.3 Exceptions to Art. 39(6)

Although this does not become apparent from EMIR itself, there are a few exceptions to the general rule that excess margin for ISA clients should be held at CCP level.

---

[71] EMIR (n 1), Art. 39(3) requires both position and asset segregation, that is, no value segregation (see section 4.3.7 below).

[72] EMIR (n 1), Art. 39(6). See also section 3.3 above.

[73] ESMA Q&A (n 21), CCP Question 8(a), pp. 55–56.

First of all, the definition of excess margin in Art. 39(6) does not include collateral assets which are not directly related to the clearing activities at the CCP.[74] ESMA has clarified, in its Q&A, that excess margin which is not directly related to clearing activities at the CCP does not have to be posted to the CCP if it is clearly documented that the CM and the client have contractually agreed to this in advance and the assets are not dedicated to cover current positions with the CCP and are clearly identified as such.[75] Second, ESMA has clarified that if a client posts excess margin in the form of a bank guarantee, there is no obligation for the CM to post an equal amount to the CCP.[76] This obviously makes sense because the client does not need the protection under EMIR as long as the bank guarantee is not enforced. Based on this rationale, it seems logical that this exception applies to similar situations as well, in particular where excess margin is held by the client and provided to the CM by means of a security interest (e.g. of a securities account) or a parental guarantee. Third, it is possible that the CM accepts excess margin in the form of assets which are not eligible to be posted as margin with the relevant CCP. The CM is not obliged to transform these assets into eligible assets unless this is contractually agreed, but the CM is obliged to post the excess margin to the CCP in so far as the CCP is operationally capable of holding the relevant assets.[77] The exceptions mentioned above make sense but are based on ESMA Q&As only. Again, it would be better to hardwire this in EMIR or lower regulations.

4.3.4 Premium protections

Clients opting for an ISA account tend to be more risk-averse, but, even with an ISA account, they are still exposed to certain risks. Some of these risks can be mitigated to some extent. Below are some premium options that may be offered to ISA clients.

Clients, including those who opted for ISA accounts, are generally exposed to some form of transit risk if their CM defaults. This is the risk that the client posts margin to its CM and the CM defaults before posting and segregating the margin at the level of the CCP or vice versa. In that situation, there is the risk that the collateral becomes part of the bankruptcy estate of the CM because the protections offered by EMIR only apply to assets which are segregated at the level of the CCP, although applicable local law or contractual documentation may provide the client with certain additional protections.[78] Transit risk can be mitigated to some extent if the CM prefunds margin to the CCP, but the CM may not be willing to do this, especially in stressed market situations, and this

---

[74] Collateral may be posted for specific services unrelated to clearing or the entire client relationship as a whole, which may include clearing, custody, collateral, and reporting services. In that situation, it is difficult to allocate margins to a specific service. This may give some leeway to circumvent Art. 39(6).

[75] ESMA Q&A (n 21), CCP Question 8(a), pp. 55–57.

[76] ESMA Q&A (n 21), CCP Question 8(k), p. 59.

[77] ESMA Q&A (n 21), CCP Question 8(k), p. 59, where ESMA also emphasizes that when the CCP accepts ineligible margin, these assets cannot be used to meet CCP margin calls.

[78] Some national regimes provide clients with additional protection. For example, in the United Kingdom, the client money rules provide clients with additional protection, whereas in the Netherlands, the Securities Book-Entry Transfer Act (Wet giraal effectenverkeer) (Art. 49f et seq) provides that derivatives positions between the client and the CM, including the associated collateral held at the level of the CM, is protected against a CM default.

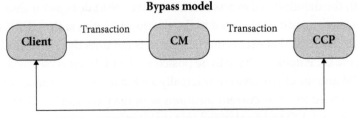

Collateral is exchanged between the client and the CCP
via a title transfer or security interest arrangement, thus
operationally bypassing the CM. Legally, this still qualifies
as a principal-to-principal model.

Figure 10.4 Bypass model
Source: author.

will trigger additional charges for the client.[79] Transit risk can also be mitigated if the CCP provides the client with the option to post collateral directly to the CCP on behalf of the CM, thus operationally bypassing the CM.[80] This can be visualized in Figure 10.4.

The CCP may offer the possibility to open separate client accounts at the level of the CSD. These are accounts in the name of the CCP but tagged to a specific client.[81] This should provide clients with more assurance that upon a CM default, assets can be identified more quickly at CSD level, which potentially increases the likelihood of a successful transfer of positions and assets to another CM ('back-up CM').[82]

On top of that, the CCP could allow clients to hold the collateral in a (blocked) custody account in their own name with an (I)CSD or custodian selected or approved by the CCP. In this structure, the client is able to provide non-cash collateral to the CCP via a security interest. Because the client retains legal title to the collateral, this structure not only mitigates the transit risk but also potentially protects the client against the risk of a CCP insolvency and may enable the client to keep on exchanging collateral with the CCP if the CM defaults.[83]

The CCP can also provide clients that opted for ISA accounts with more time to port their positions, although this will generally not be guaranteed up front (see section 5.3 below). This may also depend on the amount of excess margin held in the relevant client account or the possibility that the client has to post margins to the CCP directly following a CM default.

---

[79] In practice, CMs usually call their clients for collateral once a day. The CCPs may call for margin multiple times per day. Therefore, prefunding is quite common unless the clients post excess margin (see section 3.4 above).

[80] CPMI–IOSCO Report (n 46), pp. 19–20, states that direct payments may also increase the likelihood of porting. See also Jo Braithwaite, 'The Dilemma of Client Clearing in the OTC Derivatives Markets' (2016) 17(3) European Business Organization Law Review 371.

[81] See also section 4.1, which clarifies that this is not required.

[82] Also 'replacement clearing member' (Eurex Clearing) or 'transferee clearing member' (ICE Clearing).

[83] SwapClear has offered a CustodialSeg model since 2017 (see https://www.lch.com) (accessed 23 March 2023) whereby clients provide collateral to the CCP directly via a security interest, but market appetite appears to be limited. See also Turing, *Clearing and Settlement* (n 23), p. 571, who points out that, usually, the CM will take a second-ranking interest, which could potentially trigger a deprivation argument being made in case of porting or a leapfrog payment.

Apart from that, the CCP may provide reporting services. Even though EMIR obliges CMs to segregate client positions and assets at the level of the CCP, this segregation is not achieved automatically. In the past, there have been examples of defaulting CMs failing to segregate client assets, although they were legally obliged to do so (e.g. MF Global[84]), which is likely to deprive clients of their protection. If the CCP knows the identities of the underlying clients, as is typically the case for an ISA account, this also paves the way for CCPs to offer certain reporting services directly to such clients. Such services may be important to clients who heavily rely on their CMs to actually segregate their positions and assets. That may give clients at least some possibility to monitor if and which assets (or equivalent assets) are actually segregated in their ISA account.

4.3.5 Omnibus client segregation

When using an OSA account, the positions and/or assets of multiple clients of a particular CM are held in a commingled client account. The assets held in this account for a client are segregated from the own assets of the CM (house account) as well as the assets of other CMs, but not from the assets of other clients of the same CM within that OSA account, thus exposing each client to fellow customer risk (see section 4.3.6 below). Another disadvantage of an OSA account is that it may significantly decrease the likelihood of portability, which adds an additional layer of risk (see section 5.4 below). On the other hand omnibus segregated accounts can be more efficient and cheaper (see sections 4.3.9 and 4.3.10 below).

4.3.6 Fellow customer risk

Although in practice a wide variety of OSA account structures are offered, clients participating within the same OSA account will all be exposed to some degree of fellow customer risk.[85] Fellow customer risk can be described as the risk that collateral posted by a non-defaulting client can be used to cover losses of other (defaulting) clients within the same OSA account. If one or more clients of the CM default, that does not automatically expose the non-defaulting clients to fellow customer risk because, in principle, the CM guarantees the performance of client obligations towards the CCP. But if the default of one or more clients causes the CM to default as well ('double default scenario'), the CCP will take recourse on the aggregated client collateral pool of the OSA account, which also contains margins posted by non-defaulting clients. As a consequence, the clients in the OSA account are exposed to suffer losses on a pro rata basis.

It is important to note that fellow customer risk can occur on two levels, that is, on the position level or the collateral level. This will be briefly described below

---

[84] MF Global was accused by US authorities of mixing customer funds with its proprietary funds in order to cover liquidity shortfalls shortly before going bankrupt. See Reuters, 'MF Global Holdings to Pay $100 Million Fine in CFTC Settlement', https://www.reuters.com (accessed 23 March 2023).

[85] Consequently, an OSA structure has certain similarities with the CCP guarantee fund, which also works on the basis of a loss mutualization mechanism, see EMIR (n 1), Art. 42. In a guarantee fund, the surviving CMs may suffer a loss because of a defaulting CM, whereas in an OSA, the surviving clients may suffer a loss caused by other defaulting clients. This loss mutualization does not exist in the bilateral derivatives market.

Fellow customer risk resulting from the pooling of positions
The pooling of positions means that if the positions of a certain client decrease in value (thus triggering additional margin requirements) and this client, as well as the CM, default, the CCP can take recourse to the collateral posted by all the clients in the relevant OSA account, thus exposing the other clients to fellow customer risk because of the pooling of their positions (see section 4.3.7 below).

Fellow customer risk resulting from the pooling of collateral
Apart from that, clients are also exposed to the risk resulting from the fact that the collateral assets posted by the clients in the OSA account are pooled into a commingled collateral account. This is often referred to as 'valuation mutualization risk' or 'collateral mutualization risk'.[86] Collateral mutualization risk can be regarded as a subset of fellow customer risk as it also exposes clients to losses of other clients who post their margins in the same collateral account. Collateral mutualization risk can be explained with the example below, based on the following assumptions:

- There are two clients in the OSA account. Based on their positions, Client A has the obligation to post EUR 3 million and Client B must post EUR 1 million of IM.
- Client A provides the CM with 300 government bonds and Client B provides the CM with 100 shares. The CM passes these securities on to the CCP.
- The government bonds and the shares have an identical value of EUR 10.000 each.
- The CM as well as Client B go bankrupt and, at that moment, the value of the shares has decreased to EUR 5.000 each, whereas the bonds still have a value of EUR 10.000 each.
- The collateral account will then hold securities with a total value of EUR 3.5 million.
- Assuming the positions still require the same amount of IM, that would mean that there is a deficit of EUR 500.000.

This example shows that although Client A posted sufficient collateral to cover its own positions, Client A still suffers a loss because the collateral posted by Client B decreased in value.

4.3.7 Omnibus models in practice
EMIR only prescribes that CCPs and CMs should offer at least one OSA model, without differentiating between the different types of models. In reality, CCPs may offer a wide range of OSA models while using different terminology for similar or essentially the same characteristics, which creates another layer of complexity when it comes to

---

[86] International Swaps and Derivatives Association (ISDA), 'FIA ISDA Clearing Member Disclosure Document' (5 January 2016), p. 18, https://www.isda.org (accessed 23 March 2023) ('FIA ISDA Disclosure Document') describes this risk as 'Whether the value of the assets that relate to CCP Transactions could be reduced or not increase by as much as you expect because the assets posted in relation to other clients' CCP Transactions have decreased in value'.

understanding and comparing these models. Some of the most common features will be described in the subparagraphs below.

Position level: A generic or private position account

In so far as clients of a CM do not know the identities of the other clients, it is not possible for the client to make a proper assessment of the fellow customer risk to which it is exposed.[87] Clients and asset managers should therefore assess whether accepting fellow customer risk is in accordance with their fiduciary duties or whether opting for an ISA account is more appropriate.

It is important to recognize that the fellow customer risk is limited to the other clients participating within the same OSA account. For that reason, CCPs usually offer the possibility of opening separate OSA accounts whereby clients can select with whom they are commingled within the same OSA account. This allows clients to choose with whom they are exposed to fellow customer risk. Some clients may, for example, opt for an OSA account whereby their positions and assets are only commingled with clients belonging to the same legal group, that is, affiliates. It is also quite common that a fund manager opens an OSA account for its clients. This allows the fund manager and (potentially) the clients to control which clients can participate in the relevant OSA account and to assess the credit quality of these clients. Such 'private omnibus models' can significantly limit the fellow customer risk, while (potentially) retaining some operational and netting benefits. It is also possible to have an OSA where client positions are individually segregated but collateral is commingled (see section 4.3.8 below). In practice, these private OSA models are widely used in the OTC derivatives clearing markets. This also means that CMs may operate quite a number of OSA accounts.[88]

The fact that the client has chosen for a certain type of segregation at the position level does not automatically mean that the same type of segregation applies with respect to the collateral assets. This will be described below.

Collateral level: Asset segregation or value segregation

EMIR prescribes segregation requirements for client positions as well as the assets that cover these positions. With respect to assets, it is important to note that there is a difference between the segregation of the actual assets themselves (asset segregation) and the segregation of assets by virtue of their collateral value only (value segregation).

In case of an asset segregation model, the CCP segregates the assets posted with respect to the relevant client position account in a dedicated collateral account. The CCP can therefore identify which specific assets can be associated with the relevant segregated client position account. This means that, upon a CM default, it may be possible to port those specific assets to a back-up CM.[89]

---

[87] FMI Principles (n 9), p. 85 states that: 'Fellow customer risk is of particular concern because customers have limited, if any, ability to monitor or to manage the risk of their fellow customers.' CMs will typically not share information about other clients for confidentiality and data protection reasons.

[88] EMIR (n 1), Art. 39(3) prescribes that a CCP should facilitate the opening of multiple omnibus accounts.

[89] See section 5 below.

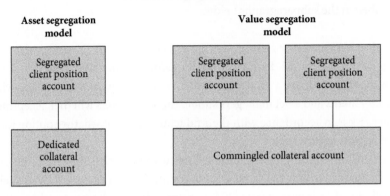

Figure 10.5 Collateral segregation models
Source: author.

Segregation and Portability of OTC Derivatives case of a value segregation model, the CCP segregates the assets as well but cannot identify which specific assets belong to which client position account. Subsequently, clients do not have an entitlement to any specific assets in the relevant commingled collateral account. Instead, they have a pro-rata entitlement to the value of the collateral corresponding with their positions. This exposes clients to additional collateral mutualization risk. Although clients in an asset-segregated account are exposed to collateral mutualization risk as well (see section 4.3.6 above), this is limited to other clients within their segregated position account. However, in case of value segregation, clients are also exposed to collateral mutualization risk with respect to clients in other segregated position accounts who commingle their collateral in the same collateral account. This is visualized in Figure 10.5.

4.3.8 Individually segregated positions with value segregation
Value segregation models are commonly used for omnibus position accounts but may also be offered for individually segregated position accounts. This means that the positions are segregated for an individual client and not commingled with those of other clients. This is the same as for an ISA account. However, unlike an ISA, the assets provided as collateral are commingled into an omnibus account together with the assets provided by other clients ('individual value segregation'). These models are widely used in the cleared OTC derivatives markets.[90] It has been advocated that individual value segregation should be regarded as an ISA as envisaged under EMIR, Art. 39(3).[91]

---

[90] London Clearing House (LCH) SwapClear offers such a model called 'Value SEG', https://www.lch.com (accessed 23 March 2023). The gross omnibus client segregation (GOSA) model of Eurex is also based on individual position segregation while commingling collateral assets with others, https://www.eurex.com (accessed 23 March 2023).

[91] See, e.g. ISDA, 'ISDA Letter to the Bank of England and Financial Conduct Authority about Individual Segregation and Default Fund Sizing', 29 May 2013, https://www.ISDA-letter-to-BoEFCA—FINAL-29-05-13F (accessed 23 March 2023).

Table 10.1 Segregation of positions vs assets

	Segregation positions per individual client	Segregation positions per group of clients
Dedicated collateral account (asset segregation)	ISA EMIR, Art. 39.3	Omnibus EMIR, Art. 39.2
Commingled collateral account with other (groups of) clients (value segregation)	Omnibus EMIR, Art. 39.2	Omnibus EMIR, Art. 39.2

Source: author

Some industry organizations supported this approach because value-based segregation models are cheaper and better aligned with the United States, where a value-based model is prescribed.[92]

EMIR states that both positions and assets held for the account of a client should be segregated at CCP level in order to qualify as an ISA under EMIR. However, EMIR does not specify whether it is required to record the specific assets (asset segregation) or whether it is sufficient to record the nominal value of the relevant assets (value segregation).[93] Because client positions are individually segregated, the client is not exposed to fellow customer risk on the position level. However, clients opting for individual value segregation are still exposed to collateral mutualization risk because the collateral is held in a commingled collateral account.

ESMA has clarified that because individual value segregation exposes the client to losses connected to collateral assets posted by other clients (i.e. collateral mutualization risk), such an account structure does not qualify as an ISA under EMIR, even though the positions themselves are individually segregated (see Table 10.1).[94] This means that all value segregation models, including those whereby positions are individually segregated, qualify as OSA models under EMIR. Thus, CMs and CCPs may offer such models, but they will still have an obligation to offer an ISA model as envisaged under EMIR, Art. 39(3).

Margin models: Omnibus net or omnibus gross
Apart from OSA models offering a variety of segregation structures on the position and/or the collateral level, there is also optionality in the amount of margin that is called by the CCP. Strictly speaking, these are not segregation models in themselves, but they can have a major impact on the amount of assets segregated at CCP level. With respect to these margin models, a distinction can be made between omnibus net and omnibus gross models. These models will be described in pars. 4.3.9 and 4.3.10.

[92] See n 70.
[93] See EMIR (n 1), Arts 39(3), 39(10), and 48(6) and ESMA Segregation Report (n 27), pp. 7, 10.
[94] ESMA Q&A (n 21), CCP Question 8(d), p. 57, which refers to EMIR (n 1), Art. 39(9)(c).

4.3.9 Omnibus net model

Before EMIR came into force, the OSA net model was the prevailing account structure for cleared OTC derivatives as well as other financial instruments.[95] In an OSA net
model, the CCP calculates margin over the netted client positions of the CM as a whole
and effectively regards the entire client portfolio of the CM in the relevant OSA account
as one single client position. The CM, on the other hand, will collect margin based on
each individual client's portfolio.

This model is cost-effective because opposite client positions are netted by the CCP
so that the amount of margin required by the CCP is lower. A limited number of accounts is also easier to manage from an operational point of view. An OSA net model
offers the CM the option of requesting lower margins or giving fee discounts to clients. However, in most cases, CMs will contractually negotiate that they can use the
difference between the gross and net margins as financing for their own commercial
activities, for example, by reinvesting the collateral (re-hypothecation). In an OSA net
model, a part of the margins is typically retained by the CM. If the CM goes bankrupt,
a client has to reclaim collateral from both the CCP and the CM. Because EMIR's segregation and portability arrangements do not apply to assets held at the CM level, such
assets are likely to become part of the bankruptcy estate unless local applicable law provides for additional protection.[96]

OSA net models complicate portability because there is a much greater chance that
there will be a shortage of collateral: any excess margin is typically held with the CM
and is thus not available for porting. In a traditional OSA net account, the CCP is typically not aware of the identity of the clients of the CM.[97]

4.3.10 Omnibus gross model

In practice, CCPs that clear OTC derivatives offer an alternative model as well, whereby
the CCP calls margin on a gross basis for each individual client position in the relevant
OSA position account. In order to do that, the CCP needs to be aware of the individual
client positions.[98] This is similar to the situation for clients who opted for individual
client segregation. However, clients in an OSA gross model are still exposed to fellow
customer risk (see section 4.3.6 above) because the gross margin collected by the CCP
is held in a commingled omnibus collateral account, which can be used by the CCP to
cover losses on the aggregate client positions in the relevant OSA position accounts.
Therefore, although the CCP is aware of individual client positions and calls for gross
margin, the clients do not benefit from the protections of an ISA account as long as there
are multiple clients in the OSA position account. That is why clients often prefer individual value segregation or a private omnibus position account (see section 4.3.7 above).

---

[95] Traditionally it was common for CMs to have only one generic OSA net account for all their clients.
[96] See n 78.
[97] In practice, the CCP will upon a CM default return the assets to the bankruptcy administrator of the CM,
EMIR (n 1), Art. 48(7). Alternatively the CCP could—in theory—try to establish the identities of the clients. It is
also possible, albeit less common, that a CCP offers an omnibus net account whereby client identity is disclosed.
[98] The CCP will typically know the identity of the clients for OSA gross accounts.

Opting for an OSA gross model is operationally less efficient as opposite positions relating to different client positions cannot be netted, as is the case in an OSA net model. Because the CCP calls for margin on a gross basis, the CM does not retain the excess margin, which means that the CM can no longer use the excess margin for its proprietary business. OSA gross models will therefore be more expensive than OSA net models. The main benefit of an OSA gross model is that, because the CCP calls for margin on a gross basis, all margin is retained at the level of the CCP. Because EMIR's segregation and portability arrangements do not apply to assets held at the CM level, this should protect these margins, to a large extent, from being caught up in the CM's bankruptcy estate.[99] Because there is more margin available when the CM defaults to cover losses in the OSA account, this increases the likelihood of porting compared to an OSA net model, although porting may still be challenging (see section 5 below).

The fact that a client opted for an OSA gross model does not automatically mean that all margin is held at the level of the CCP. This is true for the margin that results from the difference between the gross margin and the net margin amount, but if clients post excess margin on top of the gross margin amounts collected by the CCP, then it is still possible that this excess margin remains at the level of the CM because Art. 39(6) does not apply to OSA accounts.

4.3.11 Example

The difference between an OSA net and an OSA gross model can be visualized with the simplified example below as illustrated in Figure 10.6, whereby two clients of the same CM (i.e. Client X and Client Y) both enter into a number of fixed-for-floating interest rate swaps[100] with the following assumptions:

- Client X has a fixed-rate payer position with a notional of EUR 12 mio (+12).
- Client Y has an opposite fixed-rate receiver position with a notional of EUR 10 mio (-10).[101]
- The CCP issues a (simplified and fixed) IM call of EUR 100.000 per million notional.
- The CM uses exactly the same margin methodology and issues corresponding margin calls (resulting in margin calls by the CM to Clients X and Y of EUR 1.2 and 1 mio, respectively.[102]
- In the OSA net model, the CM retains all excess margin resulting from position netting.
- The CM does not call for excess margin on top of the margin requested by the CCP.

---

[99] The client is still exposed to transit risk. See also 3.3.1.

[100] For instance, a fixed for floating swap whereby one party swaps the interest cash flow of a fixed rate with the cash flow of a floating rate based on an agreed benchmark (fixed rate-payer/floating-rate receiver or vice versa).

[101] In practice, netting does not necessarily require perfectly matching positions.

[102] In practice, CMs may apply their own IM calculation models for margin calls they issue towards their clients.

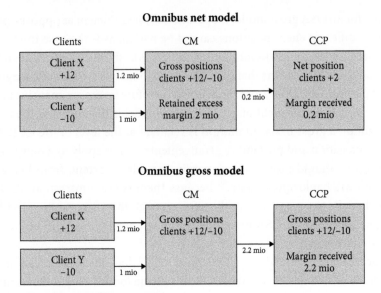

Figure 10.6 Omnibus net/gross models
Source: author.

4.4 Indirect Client Accounts

Clients of CMs ('direct clients') may also offer clearing services to their clients ('indirect clients').[103] Based on a principal-to-principal model, indirect clearing will result in at least three principal-to-principal transactions, that is (i) a transaction between the CCP and the CM, (ii) a transaction between the CM and its direct client, and (iii) a transaction between the direct client and its indirect client.[104] However, it should be noted that although indirect clearing of OTC derivatives was envisaged when EMIR was adopted, there is hardly any market demand (or CM product offering) for indirect clearing in the OTC derivatives markets at the moment.[105] Therefore, indirect client clearing is only briefly discussed below and focusses on the segregation at CCP level.

The segregation and portability requirements as laid down in EMIR do not directly apply to indirect clearing arrangements. However, EMIR states that indirect clearing arrangements should 'not increase counterparty risk and [...] benefit from protection with equivalent effect to that referred to in Articles 39 and 48' and left it up to ESMA

---

[103] In order not to deteriorate the position of indirect clients, CMs and clients offering indirect clearing should qualify as 'participants' as defined in Directive 98/26/EC of the European Parliament and of the Council of 19 May 1998 on settlement finality in payment and securities settlement systems, [1998] OJ L166/45 (11 June 1998) (SFD).

[104] Commission Delegated Regulation (EU) No. EU/149/2013 of 19 December 2012 supplementing Regulation (EU) No. 648/2012 of the European Parliament and of the Council with regard to regulatory technical standards on indirect clearing arrangements, the clearing obligation, the public register, access to a trading venue, non-financial counterparties, and risk mitigation techniques for OTC derivatives contracts not cleared by a CCP with EEA relevance, [2013] L52/11 (23 February 2013) ('Indirect Clearing CDR') envisages two additional layers, that is, a chain of five transactions in total.

[105] In the listed derivatives markets, indirect clearing arrangements are common.

to create regulatory technical standards defining which indirect clearing arrangements meet these criteria.[106] For that reason, a specific segregation regime has been developed for indirect clearing arrangements, as outlined in the Indirect Clearing CDR.[107] The segregation regime for indirect clearing is more complex because of the higher degree of intermediation. It tries to strike a balance between providing indirect clients with sufficient protection and making sure that these arrangements are manageable in practice.[108] Instead of offering indirect clients the possibility to choose between individual and omnibus client segregation at CCP level, the Indirect Clearing CRD prescribes that indirect clients should have a choice between two specific types of omnibus indirect client segregation models. In both models, the positions and assets of the indirect clients are not commingled with the positions and assets of direct clients.[109] This is important because when it comes to indirect clearing, the main concern is the default of the direct client whereby the CM performs a function similar to that of a CCP when a CM defaults.

The first model is omnibus net (also basic omnibus indirect client account), whereby the CCP records all positions and assets of the indirect clients opting for omnibus net accounts of all of the direct clients of the CM. Margin is collected on a net basis.[110] In this model, the CCP is not aware of the individual positions of each individual indirect client. Because all indirect client positions and assets are commingled into one single omnibus net account per CM, in case of a CM default the indirect clients are exposed to fellow customer risk. This relates to positions and assets of other indirect clients that opted for an omnibus net account of the same direct client as well as those of other direct clients.[111] However, the positions of indirect clients are not commingled with positions and assets of any direct clients themselves or indirect clients that have opted for an omnibus gross model. At CM level, the positions of indirect clients opting for an omnibus net account are segregated for each of its direct clients separately.

The second model is omnibus gross, whereby the CCP records all positions and assets of the indirect clients of a specific direct client of the CM that opted for an omnibus gross account.[112] That means that the CM has to open an omnibus gross indirect client account at CCP level for each of its direct clients offering indirect clearing services. At CM level, an omnibus account will be opened for all indirect clients of a specific direct client whereby EMIR prescribes that positions of each indirect client within the

---

[106] EMIR (n 1), Art. 4(3) and 4(4).

[107] EMIR (n 1), Art. 4(4) and Indirect Clearing CDR (n 104), Arts 2–5.

[108] See ESMA, 'Consultation Paper, Draft Technical Standards for the Regulation on OTC Derivatives, CCPs and Trade Repositories' (25 June 2012), ESMA/2012/379, pp. 178–180, https://www.esma.europa.eu (accessed 23 March 2023).

[109] If the CM has a client with an ISA, its indirect clients would be segregated in an OSA which is not part of the ISA holding the positions and assets of the direct client.

[110] Indirect Clearing CDR (n 104), Arts 3(1), 4(2)(a), 4(4)(a).

[111] ESMA, 'Final Report, Draft Regulatory Technical Standards on Indirect Clearing Arrangements under EMIR and MiFIR' (26 May 2016), ESMA/2016/725, p. 11, https://www.esma.europe.eu (accessed 23 March 2023) ('ESMA Final IC Report') states that positions of indirect clients opting for an omnibus gross model should not be commingled with positions of indirect clients of other clients of the CM because these indirect clients are deemed more risk-averse.

[112] Indirect Clearing CDR (n 104), Arts 3(1), 4(2)(b), 4.3, 4(4)(b).

omnibus gross account may not be used to cover positions of another indirect client. When the direct client defaults this offers similar protection as individual client segregation although the indirect clients are still exposed to collateral mutualization risk. In an omnibus gross model, the CCP will be provided with information about the positions of each individual indirect client, thus enabling the CCP to call the CM for gross margin.[113] The fact that the CCP is aware of individual positions and calls for gross margin does not prevent indirect clients from still being exposed to a degree of fellow customer risk if the CM defaults.[114] This is because their positions and assets are still commingled with the positions and assets of the other indirect clients (of the same direct client) within the same omnibus gross account.[115]

Given the above it is questionable whether this protection is equivalent to the segregation options offered to direct clients, as mandated by EMIR, Art. 4(3).[116] Apart from that, it should also be noted that, for indirect clearing, there is no equivalent of EMIR, Art. 39(11) stating that the segregation and portability regime as outlined in the Indirect Clearing CDR prevails over local insolvency laws. It would make sense to amend EMIR, Art. 4(3) by stating that indirect clearing adds an additional layer of risk instead of making a potentially false promise of equivalent protection.

5 Portability

This section describes the portability framework as envisaged under EMIR as well as the many hurdles that may prevent a successful porting of client positions and assets.

5.1 The Bilateral Situation

Traditionally, OTC derivatives have been executed bilaterally with multiple counterparties directly. For OTC derivatives classes that have not been mandated to be cleared, such as foreign exchange derivatives (FX), this is usually still the case. If a bilateral counterparty goes bankrupt, this will normally result in a close-out of all outstanding positions under the relevant derivatives master agreement: porting positions is not an option. Following such close-out, there can be lengthy discussions and legal proceedings about the value of positions in order to establish what final payment(s)

---

[113] Indirect Clearing CDR (n 104), Arts 3(2) and 5(4) jo. 4(2)(b).

[114] Commission Delegated Regulation (EU) No. EU/2017/2155 of 22 September 2017 amending Delegated Regulation (EU) No. 149/2013 with regard to regulatory technical standards on indirect clearing arrangements, [2017] OJ L304/13 (21 November 2017), Recital (6) acknowledges this.

[115] See ESMA Q&A (n 21), OTC Question 18b, pp. 39–40 clarifying that if a CM opened multiple omnibus gross accounts for the same direct client, although this is not mandated by the Indirect Clearing CDR, indirect clients should not be exposed to losses relating to another omnibus account.

[116] See ESMA Final IC Report (n 111), p. 11, where ESMAs' approach is based on 'a slide down of responsibilities' whereby the CM is in charge when a direct client defaults so that omnibus segregation at CCP level is acceptable as long as there is appropriate segregation at the CM level.

is required.[117] This means that if a counterparty defaults, this may expose the non-defaulting party to a significant replacement risk as well as a long period of uncertainty and legal proceedings.

If OTC derivatives transactions are centrally cleared, it may be possible to port client positions and assets to a back-up CM. If the CCP is unable to transfer positions within the porting window (see section 5.3), the CCP may liquidate the corresponding client positions (CM–CCP) and collateral, thus exposing the client to the costs of closing out positions and replacing them (and their supporting collateral) in stressed market situations. Although this may appear similar to a bilateral close-out of positions, clients may be exposed to additional risks.

First, it should be noted that most clients use only one or a limited number of CMs, whereas, when transacting bilaterally, they would typically hold exposures to a larger number of OTC derivatives counterparties. This results in a concentration risk. If a client has only one CM, this could mean that their entire cleared OTC derivatives portfolio is being terminated.[118] Second, the client may be confronted with a liquidation of IM. Many clients do not face this risk in the bilateral situation because they either do not post IM or they provide IM to each other via a security interest whereby the collateral is held by an external third party custodian while the client retains legal title.[119] Third, the client may be confronted with additional risks related to clearing, including fellow customer risk (see section 4.3.6 above), the risk that the CCP defaults, the risk that, following a close-out, the remaining balance will be returned to the administrator of the defaulting CM instead of to the clients themselves (see section 5.6 below), and the fact that the costs of the default management will be deducted from the assets that will be returned to the clients. Some of these risks can be mitigated to some extent, but this comes at a cost.[120]

Based on the above, it can be concluded that if porting is not successful and client positions and assets are liquidated, the client could very well be worse off than in a bilateral situation. Therefore, for the portability arrangements to serve as an incentive to clear, it is essential that the positions and assets of clients can actually be ported if a CM defaults. If porting is achievable, this can be regarded as a major benefit of clearing OTC

---

[117] Many bilateral OTC derivatives transactions in Europe are governed by an ISDA Master Agreement under English law, https://www.isda.org (accessed 23 March 2023). The 2002 version of this agreement prescribes that the non-defaulting party can elect what is called an early termination date. On this date, all outstanding transactions will be terminated and per transaction a termination value (Close-out Amount) must be determined. The sum of the Close-out Amounts and any outstanding unpaid amounts will then result in a final payment obligation (early termination amount).

[118] FSB, 'Incentives to Centrally Clear Over-the-Counter (OTC) Derivatives, A Post-Implementation Evaluation of the Effects of the G20 Financial Regulatory Reforms', Derivatives Assessment Team (7 August 2018), p. 20 (Figure C.8), https://www.fsb.org (accessed 23 March 2023) ('FSB DAT Report'). It shows that about 50% of the clients indicated that they have only one CM, mainly because having multiple CMs is not economically viable.

[119] Bigger counterparties are required to exchange IM bilaterally, see Commission Delegated Regulation (EU) No. EU/2016/2251 of 4 October 2016 supplementing Regulation (EU) No. 648/2012 of the European Parliament and of the Council on OTC derivatives, central counterparties and trade repositories with regard to regulatory technical standards for risk-mitigation techniques for OTC derivative contracts not cleared by a central counterparty, [2016] OJ L340/9 (15 December 2016).

[120] Clients also face other risks in a cleared environment, including liquidity risk, the risk that the CM terminates the relationship or uses a contractual right to refuse clearing of new transactions.

derivatives because clients can maintain their OTC derivatives portfolio and trade continuity is assured.

The portability arrangements under EMIR, Art. 48 may, at first glance, give the impression that porting can be guaranteed, but, as will be described below, the reality is that no such guarantee exists, and clients can—at best—increase their chances of porting their portfolio.

5.2 Porting Mechanism

EMIR, Art. 48 indicates that the initiative for porting positions, when it comes to making the necessary preparations, resides with the relevant client(s). In reality, it is more likely to be a joint effort of the client, the back-up CM, and the CCP. The CCP itself has an interest in porting positions and assets as it makes it easier to re-establish a matched book. Furthermore, regulators will expect a CCP to take the initiative in order to mitigate the risks for clients and the market as a whole.[121] The provision of EMIR, Art. 48(5–6) stating that the CCP is only obliged to 'at least […] trigger the procedures for the transfer' does not impose on the CCP a clear obligation to reach a specific result. This raises the question to what extent a CCP could be held liable if the porting of positions fails for reasons attributable to the CCP.[122] EMIR, Art. 48 does not clearly specify the extent of the CCP's obligations in respect of porting, and this increases the risk of CCPs being exposed to litigation, particularly if positions need to be wound down at considerable costs if porting cannot be realized.

In order for the CCP to successfully process a transfer of positions and assets, (at least) the following needs to be done:

1. The CCP needs to establish the identity of the relevant client(s) in the relevant client(s) position account.
2. The CCP needs to establish which positions can be allocated to the relevant client(s) position account.
3. The CCP needs to establish whether sufficient collateral is available and which collateral, or collateral value, as the case may be, can be allocated to the relevant client(s) position account.
4. The client(s) need to have or appoint a back-up CM (see section 5.5 below).
5. The CCP needs to receive a request for porting from the relevant client(s) in the relevant client position account (see section 5.4 below).

---

[121] See EMIR (n 1), Arts 36 and 48(2) obliging CCPs to have default procedures that include taking prompt action to contain losses following a CM default and a general obligation to act in the best interest of clients and CMs.
[122] ESMA Segregation Report (n 27), p. 10, where ESMA suggests modifying EMIR (n 1) 'to impose an obligation on the CCP to port positions and collateral depending on the chosen account structure, in the case there is a pre-existing back-up clearing member arrangement'. See also Client Clearing Annex, 'LCH Limited Default Rules' (June 2021), Art. 9, Schedule 1, https://www.lch.com (accessed 23 March 2023) ('LCH Default Rules') stating that the CCP will 'seek to port'.

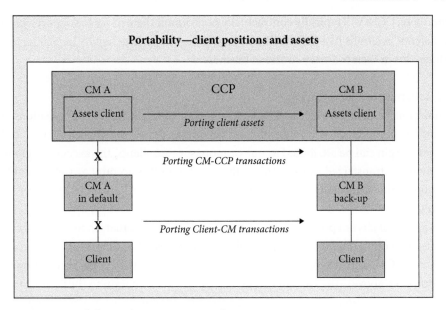

Figure 10.7 Portability—client positions and assets
Source: author.

6. The back-up CM needs to accept the transfer of the designated positions and assets within the relevant porting window (see section 5.3 below).

Porting can be done via an actual transfer of positions and assets but is normally effected by closing out the positions and re-establishing identical positions between the
back-up CM and the CCP as well as the back-up CM and the client. Ideally, the client
assets associated with the relevant client positions which are held at CCP level are then
moved simultaneously to a client account operated by the back-up CM.[123] This porting
mechanism can be visualized in Figure 10.7.

5.2.1 Partial porting
In theory, it is possible for the CCP to facilitate the transfer of not all but a part of the
clients' positions and assets to a back-up CM. Because a partial transfer breaks up the
relevant netting set, this may result in additional margin requirements. In any case,
a partial transfer of positions and assets requires additional calculations and work in
a potentially stressful period. Furthermore, porting a part of the positions, whereas
another part of the positions remains with the CM, may be challenged in court.[124]

---

[123] The back-up CM may require the client to prefund IM prior to porting, which could be problematic for the
client. It is possible that a client uses different account types, e.g. an ISA with CM A and an OSA with CM B. If CM
B defaults and all clients in the OSA agree to port to CM A, a new OSA needs to be opened in their name.
[124] Turing, *Clearing and Settlement* (n 23), p. 576 points out that cherry-picking is normally something the
defaulting party would do whereas, in this situation, the client would take that decision and that a close-out of
positions is likely to be contractually only allowed when all transactions are closed out.

Therefore, CCPs will typically contractually not commit themselves to support a partial transfer of positions in a default situation, whereas they will generally be willing to facilitate this in their ordinary course of business.[125]

5.2.2 Porting of excess margin

If one or more clients are able to find a back-up CM willing to accept their positions, the clients' positions and associated collateral can be transferred to the back-up CM. If the excess margin can be attributed to one or more specific clients, the excess margin will normally be transferred as well. This is the case for an ISA account as well as an OSA account with a dedicated collateral account (see sections 4.3.1 and 4.3.8 above on asset segregation).

However, if it is not possible for the CCP to attribute excess margin to a specific client position account, the excess margin is likely to be returned to the administrator of the defaulting CM. This is typically the case for OSA accounts with value segregation (see section 4.3.7 above). The CCP may then return the excess margin to the administrator because only the (defaulting) CM can determine which margins are posted by which clients. However, by returning the excess margin to the administrator, these assets may become part of the bankruptcy estate of the defaulting CM, unless local insolvency law provides additional protection.

5.2.3 Which assets are ported?

If it is possible to port positions and assets to a back-up CM, then it has to be established which assets are subject to porting. In the case of an ISA account, or an OSA account under an asset segregation model (i.e. a dedicated collateral account), this is obvious as the CCP can allocate precisely which collateral assets have to be transferred. In the case of an OSA account with a value segregation model (i.e. a commingled collateral account (see section 4.3.7 above), clients are only entitled to a certain collateral value based on their derivatives positions. That means that the CCP must divide the collateral over the various client position accounts. This can be done by liquidating all the assets first, but it may be possible to preserve some of the collateral, and avoid a fire sale, by allocating assets to clients via an allocation tool.[126] Clients may therefore not know beforehand which assets will be allocated to them.[127]

5.3 Porting Window Hurdle

A distinction can be made between porting in the ordinary course of business (business-as-usual porting or 'BAU porting') and portability in case the CM actually defaults. In

---

[125] See, e.g. 'LCH Default Rules' (n 122), Arts 6, 6.1, 8, 8.1, Schedule 1.

[126] Eurex uses a predefined algorithm to allocate specific margin assets (cash and securities) to specific segregated position accounts so that they can be ported together with the positions in these accounts.

[127] This may trigger litigation.

case of BAU porting, the client, its CM, and the back-up CM should normally have sufficient time to prepare for the transfer of positions, while ensuring the preservation of positions and the associated assets posted as collateral.

If a CM defaults, this is very different. Porting has to take place within a short period of time in order to ensure trade continuity as well as to allow the CCP to perform its default management process. If porting does not take place within a predefined transfer period specified in its operating procedures (the 'porting window'), the CCP is no longer obliged to port positions.[128] ESMA stated that the porting window should be 'of sufficient length to enable the client(s) to make a request for porting, and for the CCP to trigger the porting'.[129] In order to protect itself, the CCP will usually commit to a relatively short porting window. This can be as short as twenty-four hours. But even then, the porting window may not to be guaranteed if the operating procedures provide the CCP with discretion to shorten the porting window for specific clients or in specific situations.[130] On the other hand, the operating procedures of the CCP will also provide the CCP with the option to extend the porting window at its sole discretion, which may prove to be essential because it is questionable whether a porting window of twenty-four hours is sufficient to handle all porting requests when a large CM defaults.

The CCP may establish multiple porting windows for different clients. This may be connected to the type of segregated account, whereby ISA and OSA gross accounts could have a longer porting window. Other factors could be the amount of excess margin available or whether the client has an infrastructure in place in order to exchange margin directly with the CCP (see section 4.3.4 above on the bypass model).

After expiry of the porting window, the CCP may still—on a best-efforts basis—facilitate the porting of client positions, but it is entitled to perform its default management process, which may include hedging or replacing positions as well as liquidating client positions and collateral.[131]

5.4 Client Consent Hurdle

In order to initiate the transfer of positions and assets, the relevant client(s) have to file a request to the CCP. EMIR stipulates that, for ISA accounts, this has to be done by the relevant client. With respect to OSA accounts, all the clients in the relevant client position account must file such a request. The latter means that all clients have to unanimously agree on the porting of positions and assets to another back-up CM.[132] This can

---

[128] See EMIR (n 1), Art. 48(5) and 48(6).

[129] ESMA Q&A (n 21), CCP Question 3b, p. 47.

[130] See, e.g. LCH Default Rules (n 122), Art. 4.1, Schedule 1, mentioning a porting window of 'at least 24 hours', which can be shortened to twelve hours if more than 50% of the total collateral value of the clients of the defaulting CM is held in the relevant client account.

[131] EMIR (n 1), Art. 48(5) and 48(6). See also ESMA Q&A (n 21), CCP Questions 3b and 3d, pp. 47–48, which also clarifies that a CCP may execute hedging transactions or liquidate assets that relate to multiple accounts as long as the costs or gains can be allocated to specific client accounts.

[132] In case of individual value segregation (see section 4.3.8 above), a client can take the porting decision on its own because, on a position level, the client positions are individually segregated.

be a major or even insurmountable hurdle, especially if there are many clients involved. To make porting work, it would be a huge benefit if a client, or a small group of related clients in a private OSA account (see section 4.3.7 above), could file a porting request by itself.

Although EMIR, Art. 48(5) does not make a distinction between the segregation of positions and collateral, this is important when it comes to porting. A porting request can be made for each segregated client position account. In case of value segregation (see section 4.3.7 above), the collateral of multiple segregated-position accounts may be commingled in one omnibus collateral account. This means that the CCP will calculate a collateral value that can be associated with the relevant position account so that the clients in the position account can request to port their positions together with the attributed collateral value or assets that have been assigned to them by the CCP.[133]

However, if the relevant omnibus position account commingles the positions of a large number of clients, as is often the case for OSA net accounts, figuring out who these clients are and receiving client consent within a short time frame is often unrealistic. In most cases, this will result in a liquidation of positions and collateral. CPMI–IOSCO therefore suggested that the likelihood for bulk porting can be significantly increased if explicit client consent can be avoided, for example, by giving contractual consent in advance or in a simplified way, which could potentially include a negative (or advance) consent process.[134] It is also interesting to know that the United States does not require client consent but provides for the appointment of a trustee who is responsible, subject to court approval, for the transfer and/or liquidation of client positions and assets.[135] In so far as I know, such a solution has not been considered in Europe, although it may significantly increase the likelihood of porting.[136]

5.5 Back-Up CM Consent Hurdle

Apart from opting for an ISA account, the best option for a client seeking more porting assurance, is to—at least—ensure that they have an active relationship with a number of CMs. In reality, many smaller market participants have only one live CM relation and are subsequently likely to face a close-out of their positions if their CM defaults.[137] Technically speaking, it is possible, and the CCP should allow clients, to appoint a back-up CM after the moment a CM defaults, but the legal and operational onboarding of a new CM tends to be time-consuming.[138] CPMI–IOSCO has identified a number

---

[133] The allocation of collateral (value) may be challenged in court, especially if it is not clearly agreed up front how the allocation process of the relevant CCP works.

[134] CPMI–IOSCO Report (n 46), p. 22.

[135] US Bankruptcy Code, Chapter 7, Subchapter IV and CFTC Bankruptcy Regulations, Part 190.

[136] In practice, this solution may be tricky as well because the receiving CM then effectively acts as an interim back-up CM, which raises the question what this means for the business of this CM and how long it takes for clients to transfer their positions to other back-up CMs.

[137] See FSB DAT Report (n 118).

[138] ESMA Q&A (n 21), CCP Question 3b and 3c, pp. 46–47.

of regulatory impediments that may prevent a quick onboarding of new clients.[139] CPMI–IOSCO proposed to provide for temporary waivers from certain regulatory requirements in the porting phase, in particular requirements relating to know-your-customer rules, anti-money-laundering rules, position limits, and capital requirements. Although this can be helpful, it still seems unlikely that this will allow clients to set up relationships with new back-up CMs within the porting window unless this window is sufficiently extended.

5.5.1 Contractual porting limitations

If the client has live relationships with multiple CMs, this will significantly increase the likelihood of porting. But having multiple relationships does not necessarily mean that these CMs are willing to enter into a portability contract.[140] In practice, the majority of clients do not have a portability contract, so they must hope that another CM will voluntarily accept the porting of positions in the case of a CM default.[141]

Even if the client has active relationships with multiple CMs and a CM is willing to enter into a portability contract, it is highly likely that the contract contains a number of restrictive porting conditions.[142] A back-up CM is likely to put a cap on the size of the portfolio it is willing to accept, and therefore the portability contract will typically contain a porting limit. This may be fixed or linked to the amount of unutilized clearing limits.[143] But even then, these limits may not be guaranteed because CMs tend to negotiate clauses, giving them the possibility to unilaterally amend clearing and/or porting limits at notice or with a (short) notice period. In practice, the discretionary ability of a CM to reduce limits may therefore be a significant threat to the likelihood of porting.

Apart from that, a portability contract may contain a wide variety of other porting restrictions, which may include (i) the client and/or the back-up CM being below a certain credit rating; (ii) obliging the client to prefund margin with the back-up CM before porting takes place, which effectively means that the client has to be able to post margin twice; (iii) the client having to provide a significant amount of excess margin; (iv) legal or regulatory restrictions;[144] (v) extreme circumstances or market turmoil;[145] (vi) operational limitations; (vii) limitations on the types of OTC derivatives,[146] etc. Based

---

[139] CPMI–IOSCO Report (n 46), pp. 22–23.
[140] It may be hard for a back-up CM to offer a reasonable price for the service of being just a back-up CM (effectively allocating unutilized limits and clearing capacity to the client).
[141] An agreement that a CM 'will endeavour to facilitate porting' has little value from a legal perspective.
[142] Portability contracts often have a bespoke nature, which means that if a CM defaults, the relevant back-up CMs need to examine the clauses in the portability contracts within the porting window (see section 5.3 above), which may be challenging.
[143] A client will agree on clearing limits with its CM. These limits may be linked to the amount of IM or the amount of dollar duration (DV01) related to the relevant positions. Suppose that the client agreed on a clearing limit of 100 million of IM and based on its current cleared positions posted 60 million of IM (utilized limits), then the porting limit (i.e. the possibility to transfer positions and assets from another defaulting CM) would be 40 million of IM (unutilized limits). Linking the porting limit to the unutilized clearing limits makes sense assuming it makes no difference to the CM whether new positions are cleared because the client enters into new transactions or transfers existing positions to the CM.
[144] These restrictions may be formulated in a vague way, leaving a lot of room for the back-up CM to refuse portability. Restrictions can be related to additional capital charges, (perceived) objections from regulators, etc.
[145] The default of a (large) CM is likely to trigger market turmoil.
[146] This can be problematic as partial porting is usually not an option in a default scenario (see section 5.2 above).

on the above, it can be concluded that portability contracts can be helpful but will—in many cases—not be enforceable if the back-up CM is unwilling to cooperate.

5.6 Undisclosed Clients Hurdle

If the CCP is unaware of the identity of the clients in a segregated client account, the CCP does not know which positions and assets belong to which client.[147] Therefore, the CCP cannot allocate these positions and assets to one or several clients, and it will be unable to process a client porting request.

Assuming that portability is not possible, this also means that the CCP, following a close-out of positions and collateral, cannot return the final balance to the clients. Instead, if the clients are unknown to the CCP, or the CCP does not know which assets belong to which client, the remaining assets will be returned 'to the clearing member for the account of its clients' in accordance with EMIR, Art. 48(7). Although EMIR stipulates that the CM should return the assets to its clients, EMIR does not create a proprietary interest or insolvency carve-out, thus potentially leaving the clients with an unsecured claim.[148] Unfortunately, this problem has not been addressed in the latest EMIR revisions.

The CCP may, upon a CM default, actively seek to determine the identities of undisclosed clients in the relevant segregated account.[149] The most reliable way to obtain this information would be for the defaulting CM to provide the CCP with the identities of their clients. However, the bankruptcy administrator may be reluctant to provide this information to the CCP because disclosing the identities would allow a leapfrog payment directly to the clients, which would not be beneficial for the bankruptcy estate or in violation of confidentiality and/or privacy rules. This option therefore appears to be fairly theoretical unless local law provides for a legal obligation to provide this information.

Given the fact that the protections offered to clients are likely to be materially deteriorated if the CCP is not aware of (or cannot establish) the identities of the client, it could be argued that the policy objective of offering clients a 'high level of protection' cannot be achieved for undisclosed clients.[150]

However, EMIR does not make any reference to account structures which either do or do not disclose the clients' identities to the CCP, nor does it preclude a CCP from offering client accounts for undisclosed clients only.[151] Given the importance of identification, it would be advisable to reconsider this. One possibility is to mandate the CCP

---

[147] In practice, the CCP usually knows the identity of the clients for ISA and OSA gross accounts. For OSA net accounts, this is usually not the case.

[148] Turing, *Clearing and Settlement* (n 23), p. 570. Local insolvency law may provide protection though (see also n 78 above).

[149] LCH Default Rules (n 122), Art. 4.3, Schedule 1, p. 28.

[150] EMIR (n 1), Recital (64).

[151] FIA ISDA Disclosure Document (n 86), p. 5.

to offer accounts for identified clients.[152] Another option could be to include a clause in EMIR mandating the bankruptcy administrator to provide the CCP with the identity and banking details of the relevant clients in case of a CM default.

5.7 Guaranteed Porting versus Clearing Access

As mentioned before, the reality is that the vast majority of clients are unable to find a back-up CM that is willing to agree on a portability contract which provides them (up front) with sufficient guarantee that porting can actually be enforced when a CM defaults. This also reinforces the idea that the issues surrounding getting access to clearing in general are deeply interconnected with the likelihood of porting as many market participants do not have live agreements with multiple CMs.[153] If a client actively uses multiple CMs, this means that the client has access already, but the issue of access to clearing may reappear because there is (usually) no guarantee that another CM is actually willing to accept (i.e. port in) new positions in a potentially stressed market when the client really needs it. And, even if this willingness exists, the question emerges whether there is sufficient porting capacity available if one or more major CMs default because of the concentration of OTC derivatives clearing services with a limited number of CMs.[154]

5.7.1 Sponsored access
In recent years, a number of CCPs have developed new 'direct' or 'sponsored-access' models which provide clients with some form of direct membership while outsourcing certain functions and responsibilities to a 'sponsor' or 'clearing agent', which typically include default fund contributions and auction participation.[155] These models are burdensome to implement and may therefore mainly attract bigger clients.[156] Because the client has a direct relationship with the CCP, there is no need to segregate the positions

---

[152] ESMA Segregation Report (n 27), p. 11, where ESMA suggested amending EMIR (n 1) so that, at least for clients opting for an ISA, the clients' identity (as well as their banking details) should be known to the CCP.

[153] FSB DAT Report (n 118).

[154] FSB DAT Report (n 118), pp. 19–20, 51–52. It should also be noted that a high-risk concentration with one or two larger CMs may have an impact on the size of the CCP default fund and CCP capital resources. It is not unlikely that a CM default will impact multiple CCPs at the same time, who will then simultaneously run their respective default processes. CCPs may share information about a CM default with other CCPs, in so far as allowed under applicable law, and coordinate the porting process so that they know which CM has porting capacity available. See CPMI–IOSCO Report (n 46), pp. 24–25 that highlights the need of coordination by CCPs including the possibility of establishing ex ante information sharing agreements with other CCPs and known clients.

[155] Notable examples in the OTC derivatives clearing markets are the ISA direct model from Eurex and the sponsored principal model from ICE Europe, see https://www.eurex.com (accessed 23 March 2023) and https://www.theice.com (accessed 23 March 2023). See Chapter 4 ('CCP Access Structures' by Christina Sell) in this volume.

[156] David Murphy, 'Too Much, Too Young: Improving the Clearing Mandate' (2020) 8(3) Journal of Financial Market Infrastructures 45 (Murphy, 'Too Much, Too Young') mentions that even if only a few bigger, riskier clients use a sponsored model, this could potentially free up porting capacity for other smaller market participants. See also CPMI–IOSCO Report (n 46), pp. 12–13, which states that there is limited uptake in the OTC derivatives clearing markets.

and assets in a client segregated account.[157] Apart from that, these models can potentially provide for a mechanism whereby client positions and assets do not need to be ported because the client already has a direct relationship with the CCP. But because the CCP requires the client to find a new sponsor within a time frame designated by the CCP, the client is still exposed to the risk of liquidation.[158] This time frame tends to be fairly short as well, but may—similar to the porting window—be extended if the client is able to make direct payments to the CCP in the interim period, which also provides for more time to port if no new sponsor can be found.

Another option is for a CCP to set up some sort of special-purpose back-up CM, which could act as a safe haven in case one or more CMs default, although it is hard to see how such a 'sleeping special-purpose CM' could be able to clear a vast amount of OTC derivatives transactions overnight.[159]

5.8 Insolvency Challenge Risk

In section 2.1, it was already mentioned that the segregation and portability arrangements under EMIR are of a bespoke nature, whereby the clients' positions and assets are effectively ringfenced from the bankruptcy estate of the defaulting CM, regardless of whether the CM was the contractual counterparty of the CM–CCP positions or the legal owner of these assets. If the client posted collateral to the CM on a title transfer basis, and the CM subsequently provided the CCP with collateral via a security interest, then the CM remains the legal owner. However, in case of the CM defaulting, these assets would be transferable to a back-up CM or returned directly to the (disclosed) client. The administrator of the defaulting CM generally has the obligation to ensure that the bankruptcy estate is protected but, under EMIR, has to allow a transfer of positions and assets or a leapfrog payment by the CCP to the client directly. In order to make this work, it is essential that such a transfer or return of assets cannot be prevented or delayed because this would be in violation of applicable insolvency law.[160]

Apart from the fact that it is intended that EMIR prevails over national insolvency laws, it does not contain an obligation for Member States to ensure that their insolvency regimes are fully aligned with EMIR and that incompatible rules should be amended or removed.[161] Although several Member States have amended their insolvency laws

---

[157] EMIR (n 1), Arts 39 and 48 are not applicable. This, for example, means that if the sponsor asks for excess margin, the client does not benefit from the protection under EMIR (n 1), Art. 39(6).

[158] See, e.g. Eurex Clearing Conditions, Chapter I, Part 6, Art. 11.2.1, p. 293, https://www.eurex.com (accessed 23 March 2023), stating that a new clearing agent needs to be appointed before 13:00 Central European time (CET) on the next business day.

[159] Murphy, 'Too Much, Too Young' (n 158). As with all back-up CMs, the likelihood of porting heavily depends on having the operational and legal infrastructure in place before a default actually occurs.

[160] Jo Braithwaite and David Murphy, 'Got to be Certain: The Legal Framework for CCP Default Management Processes', Bank of England, Financial Stability Paper No. 37 (May 2016), https://www.bankofengland.co.uk (accessed 23 March 2023).

[161] In this respect see EMIR (n 1), Art. 87 obliging Member States to amend their insolvency laws in order to comply with SFD (n 103), Art. 9(1). Harmonization of EU insolvency laws has been on the agenda for a long time but still has a long way to go. See, e.g. Emilie Ghio, Gert-Jan Boon, David Ehmke, Jennifer Gant, Line Langkjaer,

in order to achieve this, it would be beneficial if this would be imposed by EMIR itself. The mere fact that there are discrepancies or ambiguity regarding the scope of EMIR, Arts 39 and 48 could already be detrimental to the client protection as envisaged under EMIR. Even if it is finally decided that EMIR prevails, this could lead to delays which may frustrate the process and cause uncertainty for market participants.[162]

Initially, the general thinking has been that because EMIR is an EU regulation, which is binding and directly applicable in the EU, it was sufficient to mention in a recital that the segregation and portability arrangements under EMIR 'prevail over any conflicting laws, regulations and administrative provisions of the Member States'.[163] However, legal uncertainty remained, for example, with respect to the question of how to deal with jurisdictions where the administrator needs to consent with leapfrog payments and how the porting arrangements under EMIR, which seem to rely on no more than a contractual commitment by the relevant CCP to trigger the portability procedures, can prevail over insolvency law.[164]

In December 2019, EMIR was finally amended and a new Art. 39(11) was inserted which hardwires in EMIR itself that national insolvency laws shall not prevent a CCP from porting positions and assets or returning assets directly to clients.[165] This is an important amendment, although some residual uncertainties remain because, unlike Recital (64), Art. 39(11) only refers to prevalence over national insolvency laws but not to other laws that may be applicable.[166] Furthermore, EMIR still does not explicitly state that the administrator has no involvement in the process at all. Although EMIR now clearly states that local insolvency laws shall not prevent the transfer or return of client assets or positions, the administrator could claim that some involvement is required without actually or immediately preventing the CCP from performing its default procedures. Unfortunately, Art. 39(11) is the only amendment dealing with segregation and portability, whereas ESMA concluded in 2015, in its Segregation Report, that much more is needed:

> While setting the principles and the rationale for client protection and the corresponding segregation and portability regime, EMIR lacks the granular details and

---

and Egenio Vaccari, 'Harmonising Insolvency Law in the EU: New Thoughts on Old Ideas in the Wake of the COVID-19 Pandemic' (2021) 30(3) International Insolvency Review 427–451.

[162] See Norman, *The Risk Controllers* (n 11), pp. 28–32, who gives a lively description of the handling of the Lehman default where the administrators were initially unwilling to cooperate and refused access to the CCPs' default management group, although they were obliged to in accordance with applicable English law at that time. This also underlines the fact that the administrator needs to have sufficient knowledge about the applicable regulations. In the Netherlands, the Securities Book-Entry Transfer Act (Wet giraal effectenverkeer) (Art. 49h(1)) requires the administrator to appoint a derivatives expert, approved by the regulator, to deal with portability aspects.

[163] Treaty on the Functioning of the European Union (TFEU), Art. 288 and EMIR (n 1), Recital (64). In draft versions of EMIR, the wording in Recital (64) was part of EMIR itself. It did not appear in the final 2012 text though.

[164] EMIR (n 1), Art. 48(5) and 48(6) state that 'the CCP shall, at least, contractually commit itself to trigger the procedures for the transfer of the assets and positions'. See ESMA Segregation Report (n 27), p. 12.

[165] EMIR (n 1), Art. 48(5–7).

[166] Turing, *Clearing and Settlement* (n 23), p. 572 notes that it could be argued that the EU has no authority to interfere with substantive insolvency laws, that it is questionable whether Art. 39(11) offers adequate protection if the CM is located outside of the EU, and that EMIR (n 1), Art. 39(11) and SFD (n 103), Art. 8 may direct to different jurisdictions.

328   SEGREGATION AND PORTABILITY OF OTC DERIVATIVES

would need significant improvements to reach the aims that the legislator contemplated at the time of its drafting.[167]

ESMA noted that a lot of these 'granular details', which are now often, to some extent, dealt with in its non-binding Q&As, should be included in regulatory technical standards or EMIR itself.[168] Because EMIR does not contain or foresee such amendments, an administrator could, for example, take the view that excess margin segregated for an individual client should not be ported because it does not fall under the definition of 'assets' under EMIR (see section 3.3 above). Given the importance of the segregation and portability arrangements, it would be advisable to amend EMIR to clear out any residual (potential) issues.

6 Conclusion

The segregation and portability arrangements under EMIR aim to provide clients with important protections in case their CM defaults. Although EMIR only requires that CCPs offer a small number of segregation models, in practice, clients and their CMs are confronted with a much wider range of models. This provides clients with more choice to cater to their specific needs, but the complexity of understanding and maintaining these models, the impact of the various applicable (generally untested) insolvency regimes, and striking the delicate balance between their costs and risks should not be underestimated. In the United States, a standard LSOC-model is prescribed for cleared OTC derivatives. This means that clients have limited choice but benefit from a more standardized approach.

A robust portability arrangement could serve as an important incentive to clear OTC derivatives. However, the reality is that many market participants do not have live agreements with multiple CMs, let alone hard contractual porting commitments from back-up CMs. This effectively means that clients may be able to increase the likelihood of porting but, in the end, are still at the mercy of third parties, which reinforces the idea that the issues surrounding getting access to clearing in general are deeply interconnected with the likelihood of porting.

The fact that EMIR tries to create a level playing field when it comes to segregation and portability is a good thing, but it has to be borne in mind that the disapplication of local insolvency regimes is a major infringement on the autonomy of the Member States. Given the importance of segregation and portability, and given the fact that, particularly in systemic financial crisis scenarios, where one or more CMs could default, there will be little time for discussion and resolving complex operational issues, it is of great importance that there are no doubts whatsoever when it comes to questions

---

[167] ESMA Segregation Report (n 27), p. 13.
[168] ESMA Segregation Report (n 27), p. 10.

about what assets can be ported without involvement of the administrator and that any insolvency challenge with respect to porting has no chance of holding up in court. The insertion of a new Art. 39(11) into EMIR is helpful but insufficient as there are several legal questions and interpretations that need to be definitively addressed by the EU legislators; at present, the answers and interpretations are effectively only given through non-binding ESMA Q&As.

11

Default Management

David Horner

1 Introduction

1.1 Purpose of Clearing

A clearing house aims to minimize (if not eliminate) any disturbance to a market resulting from a participant defaulting on its commitments. Most importantly, as the central counterparty (CCP), it must mitigate the impact on a defaulting participant's trading partners, who would otherwise experience broken contracts and potential trading losses. By performing this service, the CCP also protects all other market participants from the shocks that would reverberate from a disorderly default in their market.

Participants in a cleared market will know with confidence that their contracts will be honoured and will continue to perform to maturity as originally specified, irrespective of whether the original counterparty continues to perform. This arrangement offers tremendous benefits to the clearing house members and their clients. By providing multilateral netting and centralized risk management, the CCP collapses each member's bilateral risks to a single position with a very high-quality counterparty—the

CCP. This framework offers almost complete mitigation for what would otherwise be a significant and complex set of risks, requiring active monitoring and management and more capital to be set aside.

Although a CCP makes the management of counterparty risks much more efficient, it does not eliminate them. On the contrary, the risks must be managed centrally by the CCP. Like the duck floating serenely on a pond, above water, the CCP projects calm to the marketplace and its members, while underwater, its legs are paddling furiously to ensure that this vision can be sustained.

Before describing the logistical elements of default management itself, this chapter will first explain the essential risk management activities that CCPs undertake to ensure that their default management process is set up to succeed—such as having appropriate margining policies and a default fund sized to ensure that sufficient financial resources are in place to deal with all plausible scenarios. Robust margining practices will help to determine success (or otherwise) in the case of a member default. However, successful execution of default management protocols will be a function of good planning and strong logistical capabilities honed through regular, thoughtful fire drill exercises.

A CCP's membership standards should be defined such that events of default are comparatively rare. However, they absolutely should be expected. Although every scenario is different, a CCP should strive to ensure that it has a complete default management toolkit in place to cover all imaginable outcomes.

1.2 Historical Context

The modern CCP operates to much higher risk management standards than prevailed in previous decades. The single biggest catalyst for change has been the commitment to central clearing signed at the G20 in Pittsburgh in 2009, which led to the European Market Infrastructure Regulation (EMIR)[1] legislation. This framework, together with the upgraded PART 39 Derivatives Clearing Organization (DCO) rules[2] in the United States and other equivalents globally, were brought in as part of the sweeping market reforms which followed the financial crisis of 2008, an episode which clearly demonstrated the importance of resilient clearing houses to the future market landscape. Though standards for financial market infrastructures had previously existed,[3] this was the first time that detailed global standards had been codified and made legally binding.

EMIR, and the technical standards that support it, codified best practice for CCPs at a level which, at the time of its implementation, required many CCPs to improve their

---

[1] Regulation (EU) No. 648/2012 of the European Parliament and of the Council of 4 July 2012 on OTC derivatives, central counterparties and trade repositories, [2012] OJ L201/1 (27 July 2012), commonly referred to as the European Market Infrastructure Regulation (EMIR).

[2] Dodd–Frank Wall Street Reform and Consumer Protection Act 2010, Part 39—Derivatives Clearing Organizations.

[3] Most notably, the recommendations for CCPs put forward by the Committee on Payment and Settlement Systems (CPSS) and the Technical Committee of IOSCO (CPSS–IOSCO) in 2004.

risk management practices rapidly to ensure that they would meet the prescriptions of the new regime.[4] They also brought in major enhancements to the way CCPs would be supervised, giving national competent authorities a more direct role in overseeing CCP risk management practices than had previously been the case.

The modern financial risk manager also benefits from *much* tighter bank capital standards than prevailed in previous decades. Successive waves of regulation (much of it inspired by the same 2008 crisis) have increased the minimum capital ratios for banks via higher thresholds and the imposition of countercyclical buffers, with further capital required for any institutions assessed as systemically important. Methodologies applied to the calculations of risk-weighted assets (RWAs) have become more conservative, increasing the quantum of RWA against which the minimum capital ratios are measured. Taking all this into account, the amount of bank capital required to support the same portfolio of risky assets[5] increased dramatically during the post-crisis years.

A final, important consideration is the regulation governing bank recovery and resolution, another major focus of the post-crisis years. Banks are now required to have formal, detailed, recovery plans in place, which are regularly reviewed and agreed with their regulator. National resolution authorities have, ex ante, specified a toolkit of measures they might prescribe to ensure that a failing bank can be saved or, at least, wound down in an orderly manner. This means that a disorderly default of the kind experienced by Lehman Brothers in 2008 is extremely unlikely to happen in the modern financial landscape.[6]

1.3 Lessons of Lehman Brothers

Among a litany of individual disasters,[7] the default of Lehman Brothers on 15 September 2008 was, by common consensus, the nadir. The 158-year-old brokerage was deeply intertwined in the fabric of the financial markets. Its spectacular failure was a shock that reverberated throughout the financial system. However, from a CCP

---

[4] At the time EMIR (n 1) was implemented, all EU CCPs were required to re-apply for authorization under the new rules. This included a detailed, line-by-line assessment of each CCP's risk management practices against the new standards and prompt remediation of any areas not meeting the new standards.

[5] Though a common response to the post-crisis changes described was for banks to divest a large percentage of the risky assets they had previously held.

[6] Although Lehman Brothers in the United States at the time of its default was not technically a bank, in the legal sense (it was a broker-dealer), it is likely that firms undertaking the same kind of activities today on a similar scale would register as banks (as Goldman Sachs did on 21 September 2008). Having bank status provides the entity with access to central bank liquidity, a potentially crucial source of funding in an emergency (though it also imposes higher capital costs and regulatory requirements).

[7] Other notable failures of the 2008 financial crisis included: the collapse and forced sale of Bear Stearns and Merrill Lynch; the US Federal takeover of American International Group (AIG), Fannie Mae and Freddie Mac; the bankruptcy of Washington Mutual; the nationalization of Royal Bank of Scotland in the United Kingdom; the collapse of Icelandic banks Kaupthing, Landsbanki, and Glitnir; and the forced recapitalization of many other large banks around the world. Against this backdrop, the default of Lehman Brothers represented the lowest point.

clearing perspective, the Lehman Brothers default was the most striking demonstration of the benefits of clearing, in stark contrast to the events that unfolded in bilateral markets.

The London Clearing House (LCH) used only 35%[8] of the initial margin held (out of a total USD 2 billion) to complete the close-out of Lehman Brothers' cleared portfolio. No mutualized resources were required: the entire cost of the close-out was borne by the defaulter, with no impact on the other clearing members. Furthermore, LCH's clearing services remained open and operational throughout the period. All member contracts, including those that had originated with Lehman Brothers as counterparty, continued to perform: coupons were paid; securities were delivered; variation margin continued to be called and paid. The Chicago Mercantile Exchange (CME), Eurex, and the Depository Trust & Clearing Corporation (DTCC) reported similarly successful close-out processes.[9]

In bilateral markets, Lehman Brothers' trading counterparties were forced to scramble to re-establish the positions they had lost in trading conditions that were some of the worst ever seen. In the absence of their contracts with Lehman Brothers, traders suddenly found themselves with large, open-risk positions. Trading desks made and lost millions of dollars as the value of these open positions reacted violently to the unfolding market chaos.

At the end of this momentous trading day, many bank trading desks booked a net receivable from the Lehman Brothers estate, representing the last reliable mark-to-market valuation of their defaulted bilateral contracts, plus an estimate of the costs incurred re-establishing the positions. This information was passed to the banks' legal departments, who would soon begin the task of preparing their firm's claim against the Lehman Brothers' estate. It would take six years to settle all these claims, although, for the most part, they were eventually paid in full.[10] Meanwhile, for holders of cleared contracts, it was business as usual: variation margin was paid and received, securities were delivered, and contracts continued to perform as they had on any other trading day.

These contrasting experiences were a major catalyst for the waves of regulation that followed, mandating central clearing for most users of many standardized contracts and imposing higher capital charges for bilateral contracts. At the same time, the regulatory community took a hard look at risk management standards in clearing houses. If they were going to push many more contracts into clearing, they had better make sure the clearing houses were as safe as possible.

---

[8] For further detail, see Peter Norman, *The Risk Controllers, Central Counterparty Clearing in Globalised Financial Markets* (London: Wiley, 2011) (Norman, *The Risk Controllers*).

[9] The only notable exception was the Hong Kong Securities Clearing Company, which did have need to draw on its guarantee fund during its close-out of Lehman Brothers Securities Asia's portfolio.

[10] According to Erin Denison, Michael J. Fleming, and Asani Sarkar, 'Creditor Recovery in Lehman's Bankruptcy' *Liberty Street Economics* (14 January 2019), https://libertystreeteconomics.newyorkfed.org/2019/01/creditor-recovery-in-lehmans-bankruptcy.html (accessed 16 April 2023), the recovery rate for OTC claims was 100%. Holders of Lehman's corporate debt were not so fortunate; the recovery rate on their unsecured bonds was closer to 30%.

2 CCP Risk Management

2.1 Building Robust Defences

To execute on its central risk management mandate, a well-managed CCP seeks to ensure that:

(1) frequency of member defaults is kept low (by setting and maintaining high credit standards for direct members);
(2) cleared portfolios are frequently marked to market (by calling variation margin against any loss-making portfolio);
(3) sufficient financial resources are available to close out any defaulting portfolio (by setting initial margin requirements to cover all potential market risks to a high confidence level);
(4) sufficient liquidity resources are available to cover any defaulting member's obligations at the time they fall due;
(5) unforeseen scenarios are provided for with a deep 'waterfall' of mutualized resources that can be called upon if required; and
(6) client account structures and procedures are designed in such a way as to make the defaulter's client's positions and collateral reasonably portable.

This strategy should be underpinned by well-defined, tested operational processes which ensure that the CCP is ready and able to manage the logistical elements of any default that may occur.

2.2 Membership Standards

The very first layer of defence is usually to apply high credit standards to the membership via rigorous admission criteria. By maintaining a good-quality membership base, the CCP ensures that the likelihood of a member default occurring in the first place is low. Disruption or losses stemming from a default can only happen once a default has occurred!

The CPSS–IOSCO Principles for Financial Markets Infrastructures (PFMIs)[11] state that 'An FMI should have objective, risk-based, and publicly disclosed criteria for participation, which permit fair and open access.' Admission requirements are, therefore, disclosed in CCP rule books and tend to comprise objective, verifiable criteria such as minimum capitalization, financial strength indicators, operational capabilities, and regulatory oversight. Members are monitored and reviewed to ensure that they meet

---

[11] CPSS–IOSCO, 'Principles for Financial Markets Infrastructures', Principle 18 (Access and Participation Requirements), 18 April 2012.

standards on an ongoing basis, and additional margins are required from any members who migrate down the credit spectrum.

To broaden access to central clearing beyond the large banks, CCPs have developed *client-clearing* models to allow indirect access for non-members. In a client-clearing model, a *clearing broker* intermediates between the CCP and the end-user client. As part of this intermediation, the clearing broker effectively underwrites[12] the client's transactions and will be responsible for liquidating the client's portfolio should the client go into default. The clearing broker must be a direct member of the clearing house and meet all the usual membership standards, allowing the CCP to minimize its counterparty risk. This approach has been very successful in over-the-counter (OTC) and listed derivatives (futures and options), ensuring much wider access to clearing than would otherwise be possible.

Client accounts do not enjoy the full benefits of direct membership: by facing the clearing broker, they are exposed to a higher-risk counterparty than if they faced the CCP directly, albeit this risk is mitigated by the availability of porting mechanisms, should the clearing broker default. On the other hand, a client account does not carry the same obligations as membership: in general, they do not contribute to the default fund and are not required to participate in default management groups or auctions.

2.3 Variation Margin

When a member defaults, the CCP steps into all their contractual obligations. The CCP, therefore, needs to know at all times what these contracts are worth and ensure that it has adequate mitigation for any changes in value.[13] Variation margin is a regular 'true-up', which ensures that members cover their losses promptly.[14] This ensures that the CCP has a good starting point[15] from which to begin its default management procedures, should they be required. For this purpose, it is important that a CCP has reliable sources of market data and up-to-date valuation models to ensure that it can accurately recalculate the value of every member's portfolio on an ongoing basis. It is up to the CCP to determine the frequency of variation margin calls, balancing the benefit of maintaining a fully covered cleared portfolio against the potential liquidity management costs (for the CCP and its members) of doing so.

Many clearing members 'pre-fund' their margin calls by posting additional, voluntary margin contributions into their clearing account. This 'margin excess' provides a buffer against unforeseen margin calls, which helps to reduce the level of active

[12] The precise legal mechanism may differ depending on jurisdiction and the clearing model employed.
[13] For derivatives, the net present value of the forecast future cash flows associated with the contracts.
[14] In Europe, variation margin payments are usually considered to be a form of collateral. Under the US regulatory framework, variation margin payments are made in the form of settlement.
[15] Given the inherent latency involved in margin calculations and payments processing, variation margin will inevitably operate on a somewhat lagged basis, with a few hours gap between risk calculations commencing and the required funds being received by the CCP. The high confidence intervals (and, in the case of OTC clearing, margin period of risk) used for initial margin calculations provide some mitigation for this issue.

liquidity management required. In a default, most CCPs would consider margin excess to be part of the defaulter's resources and would block the withdrawal of excess, should the member fail to make good on another obligation to the CCP. Although these excess balances can be substantial, they can be withdrawn at any time (up to default), so the CCP certainly should not rely on them as a default management resource.

2.4 Initial Margin

A CCP calls initial margin[16] to cover the potential cost of liquidating a defaulted member's portfolio. This typically includes any bid-offer spreads, any mark-to-market losses incurred by the portfolio during the close-out exercise, and any losses on sale of positions via auction.[17] The scope of the initial margin model must include all material risk factors to which the member's portfolio is exposed, adequately captured to a high degree of statistical confidence.

EMIR prescribes certain minimum standards for confidence intervals, holding periods, completeness of historical data, and eligibility of products for portfolio margining. This leaves many important elements of model design in the hands of the CCP.[18] Given their importance and complexity, the monitoring and maintenance of its initial margin models are among a CCP's most time-consuming risk management activities. Analysing model performance, refreshing model parameters, and refining and improving these models requires major investment of time and effort on an ongoing basis.

Most margin models will be somewhat dynamic in nature, meaning that the *margin per unit risk* for a given contract adjusts in response to changing market conditions.[19] This change can be effected either by regularly updating margin parameters (e.g. the scenario shock sizes in a SPAN[20] model) or automatically by design, as in the case of many historic simulation[21] Value at Risk (VaR) models).

The dynamic nature of initial margin allows CCPs to refine constantly the amount of resources they hold in response to market conditions, ensuring that they always have enough, but not too much, to cover the range of plausible outcomes at any time. This makes margining more efficient as resources can be transferred back to members when they are not needed. It also gives rise to a risk, that a rapid increase in CCP margining

---

[16] Initial margin is sometimes referred to as 'performance bond'.

[17] These elements may be hard to separate and may not be straightforward to quantify individually.

[18] In practice, any material changes a CCP may wish to make to its margin models would be subject to a review and 'non-objection' by their national competent authority, who will generally also determine what counts as 'material'.

[19] The riskiness of the contract itself may also change, especially for non-linear products such as options. This is an additional effect.

[20] Standard portfolio analysis of risk, a model based on calculating and combining position-level profit-and-loss (P&L) over a discrete set of defined scenarios to infer a portfolio-level maximum loss to a given statistical confidence. SPAN is a trademark of Chicago Mercantile Exchange Inc.

[21] In historic simulation, the introduction of new, volatile scenarios will tend to increase the calculated initial margin numbers. Some models also have a volatility scaling feature which responds to current conditions, providing a further reaction function.

levels in response to a crisis situation may put further stress on its members, thereby exacerbating the crisis itself. This 'procyclicality' risk must be carefully assessed and monitored by the CCP. Like the porridge in 'Goldilocks', the margin model's reaction function must be 'not too hot' and 'not too cold'. The CCP risk managers should aim for it to be 'just right'.

During the early months of 2020, financial markets began to digest the likely severity and potential impact of the impending COVID-19 pandemic. Trading was disrupted as banks invoked their crisis management plans, splitting up trading desks into a combination of office, disaster recovery sites, and home working.[22] As new information emerged, many financial markets experienced shocks that were, depending on the asset class, the biggest since 1987, 2008, or, in some cases, all recorded history. The challenging conditions were exacerbated by the thin market liquidity resulting from the logistical challenges the banks were facing.

These events were a serious test to CCP margin practices, which are designed to react to changing circumstances but in a proportionate way. In general, OTC products (which have more conservative margining prescribed by regulation[23]) fared better than listed derivatives, for which the reaction function in some cleared markets was considered 'too hot' by many. For a much more detailed analysis of this issue, the reader may wish to refer to the reports published by CPMI–IOSCO[24] and the Commodities Future Trading Commission (CFTC)[25] in 2021.

2.5 Covering Large, Concentrated Positions

When managing a member default, the CCP will face a much stiffer challenge in situations where the defaulter's positions are large (or, worse, very large) relative to the overall size of the market. A CCP's margining practices need to take this into account. The basic initial margin model is used to calculate the worst loss a portfolio might sustain in response to adverse market moves to some defined statistical confidence. This 'core initial margin' is generally agnostic to position size, with the margin requirement scaling up linearly with the size of positions. CCPs normally prescribe additional 'market liquidity' or 'concentration' margins for positions which are large relative to normal market liquidity. These additional margins can be a significant component[26]

---

[22] During the early months of 2020, banks focused on mitigating the risk of co-locating an entire trading team to ensure that the team did not all catch the virus at the same time, leaving the desk unable to operate. Often, this was achieved by rotating the location of two or more sub-teams (often called something like the 'red team' and the 'blue team'). This was before a fully disaggregated team, with everyone working from home, became the norm. The constantly shifting operating environment was extremely disruptive to the normal rhythm of trading activity, reducing the capability of banks to act as liquidity providers for their customers.

[23] Article 24 requires a minimum confidence interval of 99.5% for OTC products (compared with 99% for non-OTC products). Article 26 requires a minimum holding period of five days for OTC derivatives, compared with two days for non-OTC products.

[24] CPMI–IOSCO consultative report published in October 2021 on 'Review of Margining Practices' includes a section on 'Evaluating the responsiveness of centrally cleared initial margin models to market stresses, with a focus on impacts and implications for CCP resources and the wider financial system'.

[25] CFTC, 'Interim Staff Report on Cleared Derivatives Markets: March–April 2020'.

[26] For very large positions, the concentration margin can be bigger than the core initial margin.

of the CCP's financial resources and receive a correspondingly high degree of focus within CCP risk management functions. The additional margin should result in incremental costs *per unit risk*, meaning that total margin requirement should grow superlinearly beyond a certain position size. CCPs usually model this additional risk by either estimating the close-out cost for large positions directly or by applying a longer holding period to their core initial margin calculations.[27]

The pure market moves that drive the core initial margin model generally have reliable and comprehensive data sets stretching back years. However, the data on trade volumes and execution pricing is much harder to find in sufficient quality and quantity to be meaningful. CCP risk managers also need to make difficult decisions about how to group similar contracts—at what point do close substitutes become fully fungible for the purposes of these calculations?[28] This conundrum applies to the aggregation of pricing and volume data *and* to the initial margin calculations themselves, which are often at a portfolio level, though a portfolio will likely contain a variety of large and small positions. Depending on the product, a CCP may often 'crowd-source' the model parameters by asking its members to fill in a 'liquidity survey'—choosing to rely on an aggregation of expert judgements rather than numerical calculation from patchy data. CCPs need to ensure that members are sufficiently incentivized to complete what can be a lengthy survey and put sufficient controls in place to ensure that the results are complete and free from bias.

Large, concentrated positions make regular appearances in post mortem examinations of CCP default management disasters. In the case of French CCP Caisse de Liquidation des Affaires en Marchandises (CLAM, 1974) one broker, Nataf, held 56% of the long open position in sugar contracts.[29] The defaulter's positions sustained such heavy losses that the financial resources of the CCP were quickly exhausted, ultimately resulting in CLAM being put into resolution by the authorities. That event took place in a different era, before minimum standards for margin coverage and default funds (CLAM had no default fund at all). A more relevant modern example was Norwegian power trader Einar Aas, who, in 2018, amassed a highly concentrated spread position in power futures (long German power, short Nordic power), the unwinding of which exceeded the initial margin posted by Aas. Operating to modern standards, National Association of Securities Dealers Automated Quotations (NASDAQ) Clearing had a cover-2-sized default fund which was more than sufficient to cover the resulting shortfall.[30]

---

[27] Evangelos Benos, Pedro Gurrola-Perez, and Michael Wood provide a comparison of these approaches in their paper 'Managing Market Liquidity Risk in Central Counterparties' (June 2017).

[28] By its nature, such modelling decisions are somewhat 'all or nothing'—contracts are either fungible (in which case, they are fully netted in the calculations) or they aren't (in which case, they are treated as completely separate and distinct). Trying to account for partial fungibility tends to introduce levels of complexity into the calculations that quickly become unmanageable.

[29] Vincent Bignon and Guillaume Vuillemey, 'The Failure of a Clearinghouse: Empirical Evidence' (2020) 24(1) Review of Finance 99–128 (Bignon and Vuillemey, 'The Failure of a Clearinghouse').

[30] Sarah Bell and Henry Holden, 'Two Defaults at CCPs, 10 Years Apart' (December 2018) BIS Quarterly Review 75.

2.6 The CCP Default 'Waterfall'

A CCP, through its rule book, will establish several layers of financial resources that may be used to cover any losses incurred by a defaulter's portfolio during the course of close-out. This recipe for loss allocation ensures that the CCP can draw on sufficient resources to cover any imaginable[31] scenario and provides appropriate incentives to the CCP's executive management and the broader clearing community, while ascribing losses as much as possible to the defaulter.[32]

Although structures may vary, the typical CCP waterfall will include some or all of the following layers, with default management losses allocated in a defined order (any recoveries from the defaulter's estate are usually repatriated to the providers of each layer of the waterfall in the reverse order to which they were originally used up):

(1) defaulter's initial margin contribution;
(2) defaulter's default fund contribution (along with initial margin, the 'defaulter's resources');
(3) CCP 'skin in the game'—capital contributed by the CCP itself;
(4) the default fund (also known as the 'guarantee fund');
(5) assessments (legal powers to call more resources from members);
(6) insurance and/or parental guarantees;
(7) further recovery tools, should these be insufficient, for example *variation margin gains haircutting*.

Layers (1)–(4) of the waterfall are the *funded* resources, usually kept in highly liquid instruments and available to the CCP at a moment's notice. Layers (5)–(7) are *unfunded* and must be called in from elsewhere (members, parent, or insurers) as and when needed. I will refer to these unfunded resources as the *deep waterfall*.

The waterfall of the modern CCP is expected to be fully comprehensive.[33] This means that the tools at its disposal should be sufficient to cover any imaginable scenario and that, should the unimaginable happen, the CCP has procedures and resources in place to close itself down in an orderly manner so as to minimize the disruption to the markets it serves. Contrast this with previous eras, when CCPs had much more flexibility to define their own default management tools and relatively limited oversight compared with today. A cover 2 default fund might have prevented the failure of CLAM in France in 1974, or indeed of the International Commodities Clearing House (ICCH) in New

---

[31] EMIR (n 1) requires that the default fund be sized to cover a broad range of 'extreme but plausible' scenarios. By this definition, the further layers of the waterfall are intended to cover even more extreme scenarios.

[32] Often referred to as the 'defaulter pays' principle.

[33] CPSS–IOSC, 'Principles of Financial Markets Infrastructure', Principle 4, key consideration 7, states that: 'An FMI should establish explicit rules and procedures that address fully any credit losses it may face as a result of any individual or combined default among its participants with respect to any of their obligations to the FMI.'

Zealand in 1989. Beyond the defaulter's margin, both CCPs were reliant on their own modest capital as their only funded resources, which proved insufficient in both cases.[34]

2.7 Skin in the Game

The CCP skin in the game is not designed to be a meaningful loss-absorbing layer. Its function is to align the incentives of the CCP and its management[35] with those of its members. This provides a hard economic reason for the CCP to ensure that its margin models and default management close-out arrangements are adequate and comprehensive. At the time of writing, the CCP Recovery and Resolution Regulation Level 1 text[36] has recently been adopted, including a prescription for a second layer of skin in the game after the funded default fund but before the unfunded mutualized resources. ESMA has also brought forward a consultation paper[37] to determine the methodology for calculating the required amount. The addition of a second layer at this level will further align the incentives of CCP management with those of their members with respect to the methodology and calibration of scenarios used to size the default fund.

2.8 Default Fund

The 'cover 2' standard prescribed by EMIR means that the fund must contain sufficient resources to cover any losses over and above the initial margin held in respect of the CCP's two largest member portfolios. To calculate the required amount, the CCP must evaluate a broad range of 'extreme but plausible' market scenarios. Like the margin model parameters, this suite of scenario definitions is of critical importance to the CCP's risk managers and will be subject to constant analysis and refinement. The default fund (often referred to as the 'guarantee fund'), properly calibrated, is the resource layer that really provides a high level of confidence to market participants that the CCP is not going to fail. Given that the risk positions of the two largest members are likely to be many times the size of a small member, this construct renders it virtually impossible for a modern CCP to run out of financial resources during the default of a small

---

[34] Like CLAM, ICCH did not have a default fund to fall back on. It *did* have an insurance policy, which failed to come to the rescue in a timely manner: Edwin Budding, Robert T. Cox, and David Murphy, 'Central Counterparties in Crisis: International Commodities Clearing House, New Zealand Futures and Options Exchange and the Stephen Francis Affair' (2016) 4(3) Journal of Financial Market Infrastructures 65–92 (Budding et al., *Central Counterparties in Crisis*).

[35] Executive compensation, especially for senior risk management roles, is often deferred for several years, with payment conditional on the skin in the game being preserved.

[36] Regulation (EU) No. 2021/23 of the European Parliament and of the Council of 16 December 2020 on a framework for the recovery and resolution of central counterparties, [2021] OJ L22/1 (22 January 2021) ('CCP Recovery and Resolution').

[37] In July 2021, the European Securities and Markets Authority (ESMA) published a consultation entitled 'ESMA70-151-3244 Consultation Paper on Draft RTS on the Methodology for Calculation and Maintenance of the Additional Amount of Pre-funded Dedicated Own Resources (Article 9(15) of CCPRRR)'.

member and very unlikely that funded resources would not cover a medium-sized or even a large member default.

Once the size of the fund is determined, the CCP will need to calculate the individual contributions required from each member, which must (according to EMIR) be proportionate to the risk that each member has in their cleared portfolio. CCPs which clear for more than one market must determine whether, and how, to segregate their default funds. Many CCPs run separate funds for each asset class or achieve a similar outcome by partitioning a single fund. This construct has the distinct advantage of giving members choice over which asset classes they are comfortable taking a degree of mutualized risk and which asset classes they prefer to remain remote from. As clearing expands to cover more esoteric asset classes (such as cryptocurrency-related contracts), this distinction becomes more important.[38]

Unlike the non-defaulting members' initial margin contributions, which are segregated outside of the default waterfall, the non-defaulting members' default fund contributions are 'at risk' of being used to cover default losses elsewhere in the service. Banks must hold a defined amount of capital to mitigate against precisely this scenario.

2.9 Liquidity Risk

Although the depth of CCP waterfalls make it highly unlikely that a CCP would fail due to running out of loss-allocating capacity, a CCP must also be mindful to ensure they have the ability to pay or settle their defaulting member's obligations *at all times* and in all conditions. A CCP risk management function will also devote considerable time and effort to develop a monitoring and limit framework to ensure that this happens. The 'cover 2' concept also applies to liquidity: the regulatory standards require that a CCP should be able to withstand a liquidity draw-down occasioned by the demise of its two largest members (i.e. to cover these members' settlement obligations as they fall due) during *extreme but plausible* adverse market conditions.

2.10 The Deep Waterfall

By construction, the initial margin and the default fund should be more than sufficient to deal with one or two defaults in any 'extreme but plausible' scenario. If the defaulter's positions sustain such heavy losses that the default fund is completely used up, something quite unexpected has occurred or something has gone seriously wrong.

---

[38] The disadvantage of these approaches is that, by construction, the overall mutualized pot needs to be bigger to cover the same extreme but plausible scenarios. A very large, fully mutualized default fund is a more efficient construct, requiring fewer total resources to cover the same range of extreme but plausible scenarios. However, a CCP running such a default fund would need to carefully define and articulate the assumptions it makes around cross-asset class correlation in a default scenario, which would determine the level of benefit provided by this kind of mutualization.

Nevertheless, the modern CCP is expected to be able to cope with such an outcome, and although the default fund is the CCP's last *funded* resource, it is far from being the last line of defence.

The first 'deep waterfall' layer is generally *powers of assessment*—broadly speaking, the ability to call in additional mutualized resources from the membership to cover any losses over and above those covered by the default fund, the defaulter's initial margin, and the CCP skin in the game. Often, the extent of these powers will scale with the size of the default fund. For example, LCH's clearing services have powers of assessment equal to the size of each default fund, effectively doubling the resources available to cover incremental losses if needed, with provisions for further rounds of assessments in scenarios where the CCP is facing multiple defaults. If the need arises, assessment contributions will be mandatory across the membership. However, provided the clearing house has a reasonably diversified membership, this measure can be quite an effective way to spread the burden. Relatively modest assessments on a per-member basis can generate large amounts of resources for the CCP at the overall level, providing reassurance and stability without imposing an undue liquidity or capital burden on the members.

Once assessment powers have been exhausted, some CCPs have mechanisms to absorb further losses, for example, by applying haircuts to the variation margin payments in a process called variation margin gains haircutting (VMGH). A VMGH process allocates further losses on the defaulter's portfolio (which otherwise cannot be covered by any remaining resources) to member accounts on an ongoing basis, in proportion to the cumulative gains on their cleared positions. The economics of this process mimic a default recovery process, effectively haircutting any post-default member receivables by a fixed percentage, consistently applied across the whole clearing service. Generally, VMGH powers will be subject to limitations in terms of either the cumulative value of haircuts and/or the amount of time such a process can run, potentially with member ballots required to ratify ongoing support for the process beyond certain checkpoints.

Some CCPs also take out insurance policies to cover certain elements of default management failure, among other things. Such policies are usually subject to restrictions on the scope of events covered and a cap on the amount that can be claimed. Capital injections from the CCP's corporate parent (if applicable) may also play a part.

2.11 Last-Resort Survival Tactics

At the very bottom of the waterfall sits *service closure*—an orderly wind-down of the CCP's activities. In this scenario, which takes place only when the CCP has exhausted all avenues for allocating losses, a final variation margin run cash-settles the present value of all remaining contracts. This is effectively a tear-up of all cleared contracts, an extremely troubling outcome for members of the CCP. If any consolation, initial margin amounts should be returned to the non-defaulting members in full, having been safely segregated from the loss-absorbing resources. At times, initial margin haircutting has been mooted as a potential deep waterfall tool for CCPs undergoing a near-death experience; however, it has, rightly, been resisted.[39]

Just before getting to service closure, a slightly less draconian measure known as *partial tear-up* may be available. Some CCPs have codified a capability, in extremis, to cash-settle (or 'tear-up') a *class of contracts* while allowing the remainder of the service to continue to operate. Depending on the market, a *class of contracts* might refer to a specific currency or grouping of similar securities, for example, bonds issued by the same obligor. This tool might prove useful if the defaulter has sustained extremely heavy losses in one particular product, the market for which has become highly dysfunctional, although the remainder of the defaulter's positions (and the CCP's other activities) remain within manageable parameters. Such an outcome is clearly quite perturbing for members experiencing cancellation of their cleared contracts but has to be much better than the alternative: a full shut-down of the CCP. From the clearing house's perspective, the experience is akin to an injured soldier submitting to the amputation of a damaged limb to prevent infection spreading to the rest of the body. The CCP has sustained some hefty damage (not least to its reputation for competent risk management) and would be much diminished by this episode, but lives to fight another day.

Although it is hard to imagine such tools ever being necessary in a modern, well-run CCP, deep waterfall measures *have* been deployed historically. For example,[40] in 1989, the ICCH resorted to 'invoicing back' the positions of a defaulted member (Stephen Francis) after exhausting the defaulter's resources, effectively a cash-settlement or 'tear-up' of the positions. Deploying a partial tear-up effectively voids any gains made by holders of the other side of the contracts. Such an outcome (non-performance of a cleared contract) is contrary to the entire purpose of the CCP.[41] It should, therefore, only be contemplated if the survival of the CCP itself is in question, as was the case during ICCH's crisis, where the partial tear-up allowed the CCP to live to fight another day.

2.12 Legal Basis

The CCP must be certain that its risk management (and default management) procedures are enforceable and will not be challenged as and when they are needed. The CCP rule book, which legally binds all members, is the mechanism through which the CCP achieves this. When entering into a new jurisdiction, the CCP will want to review local

---

[39] Making initial margin available to the CCP for default management, even *in extremis*, would undermine a fundamental principle of clearing, that margin posted to cover a member's own positions can never be touched unless that member is itself in default. It might also lead to increased capital requirements for members if initial margin at a CCP starts to attract a higher risk weighting.

[40] As described in Budding et al., *Central Counterparties in Crisis* (n 34).

[41] For this reason, any such provisions must be carefully structured in the CCP's rules to ensure that the existence of partial tear-up measures as a possibility does not undermine the accounting, netting, and/or capital treatment of the cleared trades in question.

laws to see that its activities are protected and ensure that its default management operations, and the outcomes thereof, will not be impeded by a local court.

For example, in the United Kingdom, Part VII of the Companies Act 1989 includes a
provision that normal insolvency rules do not apply in situations where a CCP invokes
its default management activities (the CCP's rule book taking precedence). Part VII
also requires that the remaining management of the defaulter or their successors (e.g.
the bankruptcy administrator) must provide the CCP with whatever assistance or information they require to perform their duties.[42] Outside of the United Kingdom, some
jurisdictions have adopted similar rules whereby CCP default management activities
are specifically codified in legislation. Other jurisdictions operate a model based on
their existing bilateral insolvency protections, sometimes with refinements to ensure
that CCP considerations are fully addressed.

Despite this framework, there have been historic cases where CCPs have not received
the full cooperation they would expect. According to *The Risk Controllers*,[43] the LCH
team responsible for managing the Lehman Brothers default were denied access to
client records until 7 p.m. on Tuesday 16 September 2008, the holding company having
originally filed for bankruptcy protection at 7 a.m. on Monday 15 September. The delays did not prevent an eventual successful outcome but, at the time, would have made a
difficult situation even more challenging.

3 Client Account Structures

3.1 Indirect Participation

Before describing the actual mechanics of default management in detail, we should first
pause to contemplate the position of *indirect participants* (i.e. a clearing member's clients) in a clearing service. In a default, the treatment of the defaulting member's client
positions is very different to their own proprietary 'house' positions. While the CCP
has, from the point the default is declared, a clear objective to close out the house positions as quickly as possible, for the client positions, the primary objective is to ensure
continuity of the contracts by porting them (and the clients' collateral) to a surviving
member.

In recent years, indirect participation in clearing via client-clearing models has
become much more prevalent as clearing mandates have expanded to include large
and, later, medium-sized buy-side participants. In OTC swaps clearing, at the time of
writing, client positions have surpassed house accounts in terms of the total margin
collected by the major CCPs. Depending on the defaulting member's business mix,

---

[42] The UK Companies Act 1989, Part VI, para. 160 states that 'any person who has or had control of any assets of
a defaulter, and any person who has or had control of any documents of or relating to a defaulter, must give such
assistance [to the CCP] as it may reasonably require for the purposes of its default proceedings.'
[43] Norman, *The Risk Controllers* (n 8).

their client positions could be a much more material concern for the CCP than the member's own positions.

The CPMI–IOSCO PFMIs[44] state that 'a CCP should structure its portability arrangements in a way that makes it highly likely that the positions and collateral of a defaulting participant's customers will be transferred to one or more other participants'. This means that the overarching purpose of the clearing house—to minimize the impact of a default on market participants—extends to indirect participants as well as direct members. The clearing house must, therefore, set up account structures and procedures that allow for client positions and collateral to be ported to one or more of the surviving members.

Any client positions that fail to port must be closed out in the same way as the defaulted member house positions, with the clients' posted margin liquidated and used to cover the cost of the close-out. Any remaining client collateral would be returned to the relevant owners. Any losses over and above the margin resources would be absorbed by the various layers of the default waterfall in the same priority order as losses on the house side.

3.2 Account Structures and Portability

Most clearing services offer more than one potential account structure to their clients—in fact, EMIR mandates that clients are at least offered some degree of choice in the level of segregation. In selecting the right account type, there is a trade-off between, on the one hand, *cost* considerations (primarily margin efficiency and the level of fees payable to the relevant clearing members) and, on the other hand, *risk* considerations, the degree of segregation enjoyed by the client and the number of back-up relationships. Although the CCP will attempt to secure a good outcome for all clients in the case of a default, its job will be made easier or harder depending on the account structure decisions made by each client. As EMIR[45] puts it:

> Clients of clearing members that clear their OTC derivative contracts with CCPs should be granted a high level of protection. The actual level of protection depends on the level of segregation that those clients choose.

The clients' first decision will be whether to hold its positions in an individually segregated account (ISA) or an omnibus segregated account (OSA). An OSA will entail some comingling of positions and/or collateral with other clients, resulting in greater margin efficiency but a weaker level of segregation. In normal times, this would not be a material concern, but in a default situation, such details are brought into sharp focus as they can mean the difference between successfully porting to a back-up clearer and

---

[44] CPSS–IOSCO, 'Principles for Financial Markets Infrastructures', Principle 14—Segregation and Portability.
[45] EMIR (n 1), Level 1 Recital, para. 64.

being liquidated. A client using an OSA account structure is unlikely to enjoy decision-making autonomy in a default as decisions on porting for OSAs tend to require unanimous agreement on behalf of all clients with positions in the account. A client in an OSA structure may not be able to port to its preferred back-up member (or, worse, to port at all) unless all other OSA participants are able to agree to the same outcome and provide positive affirmation to the CCP.

The second important decision for clients is the number of separate clearing broker relationships to maintain or, more precisely, the number of live clearing accounts they would keep open with different clearing brokers. Maintaining more than one clearing broker relationship means that a client is much more likely to have a willing recipient for its positions and collateral in case one of its brokers defaults. However, each account will have an associated running cost. Conversely, if a client has only one clearing broker relationship, it is much more exposed if that clearing broker defaults as it is logistically much more challenging to find another clearing broker willing and able to take on the positions of a client with which it has no pre-existing relationship. In such cases, the CCP may have no option but to close out its positions and liquidate its collateral, where necessary, to cover any market value erosion and/or cost of close-out.

Beyond these basic distinctions, many CCPs offer clients further choices, such as different methodologies for segregating the client's assets ('value segregation' or 'asset segregation'). For a more detailed exposition of the different client account structures available, please see Chapter 10 ('Segregation and Portability of Cleared OTC Derivatives in Europe' by Bas Zebregs) in this volume.

3.3 Client Defaults

From the CCP's perspective, a client account presents a very different risk profile to a direct clearing member as the CCP does not face the client directly and all the client's margin payments are, effectively, underwritten by the relevant clearing broker. For this reason, CCPs do not generally apply minimum credit standards to clients of their clearing members. An OTC client default is a fairly routine operational process for the CCP. Once the clearing broker confirms that they have put the client into default, the CCP will transfer the defaulting client's positions into the clearing broker's house account. From there, it is the clearing broker's responsibility to complete all the remaining steps necessary to close down the account. The CCP is not required to participate in the process any further.

Although a clearing house would not normally review the creditworthiness of individual clients, the CCP certainly *would* perform regular due diligence on its clearing member's risk management procedures. The CCP might request information on how the member manages the credit risk on its client accounts and examine the overall risk profile of its client base. Although an individual client default is unlikely to trouble the CCP, if a clearing broker was put at risk by poor risk management practices resulting in a large accumulation of defaulting clients, that certainly would be concerning for the CCP.

4 Default Management: The CCP Toolkit for Successful Close-Out

Having put in place robust margining practises and a comprehensive default waterfall, the CCP will be well positioned to manage a default successfully. However, an end-to-end default management process, especially for a large counterparty, is a very substantial undertaking. An international banking group may have several memberships of distinct clearing services within the same CCP and potentially hundreds of individual client accounts. Any work-out on this scale requires careful, detailed choreography on many fronts: financial resources alone will not be sufficient. Furthermore, decisions made during a default will inevitably be interrogated after the event by regulators, lawyers, and journalists so a CCP would be well advised to ensure that it has comprehensive, tested procedures in place and that it follows them to the letter.

4.1 Default Decision

The decision to put a clearing member into default marks the transition between 'peace time' and 'war time' for the CCP. All regular, 'business-as-usual' activities become secondary to the mission of closing out the defaulted portfolio. Such decisions must be taken quickly but calmly, having considered all the relevant facts, at the right level of seniority within the firm[46] and, most importantly, in accordance with the clearing house's published rules and procedures. Delays to a decision risk erosion of precious initial margin as markets move against the defaulter's positions, increasing the chances that the defaulter's resources will, ultimately, prove insufficient and that mutualized resources will eventually be required. In extremis, prolonged inaction can put the survival of the CCP itself at risk.[47]

The CCP's rule book provides detailed criteria under which the CCP can, and will, put a member into default. The most compelling reason is likely to be a failure to make payment on an obligation due to the clearing house, such as a call for margin. Other causes for a CCP to take action might include situations where a member has filed for bankruptcy, is under receivership, has been subjected to economic sanctions, or has

---

[46] Such decisions would generally involve the chief executive officer (CEO) and chief risk officer (CRO) of the CCP.

[47] During the default of Nataf in 1974, the clearing house Caisse de Liquidation des Affaires en Marchandises (CLAM) allowed unpaid margin calls to perpetuate for several days before finally taking the decision to put Nataf into default. According to Bignon and Vuillemey, 'The Failure of a Clearinghouse' (n 29), 'The decision to delay the declaration of default was misguided since, on the day default was declared, there was no more initial margin left to bear the cost associated with the liquidation of Nataf's position.' CLAM did not have sufficient resources to manage the default and was eventually put into resolution.

had its membership revoked by another clearing house. Such events could trigger a CCP's default management procedures even if the member in question has not missed a margin call, the rationale being that the member's failure is an inevitability at this point and that early, decisive action is the best way to protect the interests of the non-defaulting members.[48]

4.2 The Importance of Variation Margin

It is worth pausing to appreciate why maintaining variation margin is so important to the CCP and why, therefore, it must act when variation margin (VM) is not received from a prospective defaulter. VM is the lifeblood of a clearing service. In *peace time*, a clearing service is a complete, closed network containing both sides of every cleared contract. On a periodic basis (usually at the end of each day), the CCP revalues all contracts, calls VM in from members whose portfolios have lost money, and pays VM out to members who have made money. Because of the closed nature of the network, the total gains must equal the total losses: the pay-outs are match-funded by the pay-ins. However, if a member defaults on its payment in, the system quickly breaks down: the CCP has a shortfall in the available funding to pay its other members the VM they are owed and would expect to receive. It cannot continue to meet its obligations to the non-defaulting members.

The resources set aside to cover this scenario are, of course, the defaulting member's initial margin. However, the CCP cannot access these resources unless and until the member is formally put into default. If it does not act promptly against non-payment of VM, the CCP cannot fund the payments to its other members and the system grinds to a halt.

4.3 Regulatory Considerations

Default decisions are almost certain to involve communication with the relevant regulatory bodies. Indeed, EMIR[49] requires that 'where a CCP considers that the clearing member will not be able to meet its future obligations, it shall promptly inform the competent authority [the CCP's own national regulator] before the default procedure is declared or triggered'. Part 39 of Dodd–Frank contains a similar rule.

Many CCPs serve an international customer base and are supervised in multiple jurisdictions, so these interactions may involve more than one regulator. In this situation, EMIR requires the CCP's home regulator to communicate with their peers: 'The

---

[48] Many CCPs have a general power allowing them to act pre-emptively, for example, the Clearing Rules of NASDAQ Derivatives Markets state that NASDAQ Clearing may declare a member in default if 'In the judgment of Nasdaq Clearing, there is a substantial risk that the clearing member or customer will breach these rules and regulations'. LCH's rule book contains a similar provision.

[49] EMIR (n 1), Level 1 text, Art. 48 (Default Procedures). The underlining is the author's emphasis.

competent authority shall promptly communicate that information [...] to the authority responsible for the supervision of the defaulting clearing member.' In practice, the CCP would also expect to be in direct communication with the defaulting member's supervisor.

It is conceivable that the defaulter's supervisor may want to influence the decision-making process, especially if the defaulting member is of systemic importance to their jurisdiction. They may therefore ask the CCP to delay its decision until they, the supervisor, have had sufficient time to consider all the facts (they may be privy to some critical information of which the CCP is unaware). This type of intervention would be troubling for the CCP's management if it results in a prolonged delay to decision-making as any delay increases the risk that the mutualized resources of non-defaulting members will need to be used.

Since the global financial crisis of 2008, the international community has made concerted efforts to enhance the tools available to recover or resolve a failing bank. New regulation has provided much more transparency around these tools and the circumstances under which they may be used. The regulations have also mandated that banks produce much more detailed plans, approved at the most senior (generally board) level, describing how they would respond to such a scenario. In combination, these factors make it much more likely that a failing bank, with suitable intervention from its resolution authority, would be able to recover. It is imperative that the CCP default management process does not override this good work. To this end, the bank resolution legislation specifically forbids a CCP from defaulting one of its members solely because they have entered resolution. However, to allow the CCP to stay a default decision, the rescue plan *must* involve a mechanism for the failing bank to continue making margin payments as and when required. The resolution legislation *does not* prevent a CCP from putting an in-resolution member into default if the in-resolution member fails to meet any of its obligations to the CCP. The failing bank needs to be effectively 'back-stopped' by another commercial bank or its central bank, who would take on the task of making good on these obligations on an ongoing basis. This type of arrangement would allow the CCP to desist from putting its member into default while continuing to run its service and fulfil its commitments to the non-defaulting members.

4.4 Communicating the Decision

Once the national competent authority has been notified, the next task is to notify the defaulter themselves. Given the gravity of this event, the notification would normally be done by presenting a hard-copy signed letter to the offices of the defaulter[50] in person as well as electronically via email. Although this type of notification represents the formal start of default management proceedings, it is near certain that the defaulting member's senior management would already be heavily engaged in the matter, including in

---

[50] Or their appointed agent.

discussions with their opposite numbers at the CCP. A clearing service will retain the contact details of the relevant responsible people at each of its members for just such an eventuality.

CCPs are also required to communicate such occurrences quite widely, usually by posting a default notice on their website and via an email circular to members notifying them of the exact legal entity (or entities) in default and the clearing service memberships they held. Upon completion of all default management steps, the CCP would post a follow-up notice to reassure its members that their default fund contributions are no longer at risk.

4.5 Hedging

Once the default has been declared, the most critical work—closing out the defaulter's portfolio—can begin.[51] The CCP will start by assembling its default management group (DMG[52]), which will determine the overall strategy. Depending on the portfolio composition, the DMG's plan may include entering into hedges to reduce the market risk to a manageable level, then auctioning the remaining positions, which, by this point, should be relatively neutral from a market risk perspective. In some markets, it may expedient to proceed directly to an auction without pausing to de-risk the portfolio first. This might be the case for a simple portfolio of highly liquid positions. For a more complex portfolio, the DMG may decide to split the defaulter's positions into a number of sub-portfolios (e.g. separating by currency) and apply a combination of hedging and auction, depending on which is most appropriate for each sub-portfolio.

The timing of the initial hedge transactions is crucially important. Completing this quickly will minimize any value erosion caused by the effect of market moves on the defaulter's portfolio and substantially reduces the possibility that the non-defaulting members' resources will be needed later on in the process. It is, therefore, imperative that the default management team is able to assemble, agree an approved strategy, and begin execution as quickly as possible.

Once hedging begins, large, outright directional positions are likely to be the first order of business. Addressing spread risks such as long and short positions in similar underlying reference assets or mismatches in maturity profiles would be a secondary concern. For a multi-region portfolio, market opening hours will also be a consideration, with the DMG prioritizing any markets that are nearing the end of their normal trading day.

The DMG will need to be in contact with market-makers (generally, the CCP's own members) who provide liquidity in the relevant contracts. The CCP must have established communication channels with the outside world and a means of sourcing,

---

[51] The other urgent priority at the beginning of the process will be to determine a plan for porting or closing out any client positions. I will pause before discussing this piece to cover hedging and auctions in detail.
[52] A group of experienced CCP risk managers, which may include external secondees in the form of traders from member firms—see below.

executing, and confirming trades. Whereas a bank trading desk may execute dozens of trades every day, a CCP will only execute trades in a default situation, an event which (hopefully) occurs very infrequently. This means establishing lines of communication to trading venues and affirmation platforms that may lie dormant for years at a time and therefore must be regularly tested to ensure that they are still functional on both sides. Otherwise, lack of connectivity has the potential to be a critical point of failure for the whole exercise.

During the hedging process, the DMG must keep track of its progress towards de-risking the defaulter's portfolio by entering the details of all executed hedge trades into the CCP's risk system and refreshing the risk profile of the partially hedged portfolio. At the same time, the DMG will be monitoring the costs incurred through hedging and market moves and determining if and when more of the defaulter's collateral needs to be liquidated[53] to cover the escalating cost of the exercise.

This process continues until the DMG concludes that the hedging has sufficiently de-risked the defaulter's portfolio to a point where the risk of further margin erosion is small.

In OTC clearing, an auction is likely to be required to fully close out any meaningful portfolio. This is due to the difficulty and expense of precisely matching what could be thousands of individual line items through separate transactions. For listed portfolios, the choice may not be so obvious. In some cases, it may be more expedient to unwind the entire book line-by-line without the need for an auction. On the other hand, a complex, multi-currency portfolio may require several auctions to liquidate the various sub-portfolios individually.

4.6 Auctions

The organizational logistics of an auction should not be underestimated. Initially, the CCP must contact the relevant members and let them know when the auction is happening. Next, the CCP will need to provide details of the portfolio being offered. For complex OTC portfolios, this would generally be using an electronic file written in financial products markup language (FpML)[54] via the CCP's secure file transfer platform. Auction participants will want to know, ex ante, detailed rules for the auction: When, and for how long, is the auction bidding window open? Can a member cancel or amend a bid and, if so, how? What happens in the case of tied bids? The CCP must ensure that all these important questions have been considered and provide its members, the auction participants, with the answers they require. Once the auction bids are in, the CCP will need a reliable mechanism for quickly evaluating the results, communicating the outcomes, and transferring the relevant positions to the winning bidders.

---

[53] Collateral haircuts will mitigate the risk of erosion in the value of collateral.

[54] FpML, commonly used by financial markets participants to share information on OTC trade portfolios in a variety of circumstances. By using this format, the CCPs have reduced the burden on members that would otherwise result from adapting to multiple, bespoke CCP formats for default management.

A *hedged book* should be relatively unresponsive to changes in market prices and therefore its overall value should be fairly constant over time periods of several hours or even a few days. This means that, once the initial hedges have been completed, the CCP has time on its side to complete the remaining steps.

In a *risky book* auction, the value of the portfolio can very easily fluctuate, depending on the underlying market, therefore the CCP must proceed with more urgency. If the directional position is very large, information leakage must be tightly controlled. The CCP might delay releasing details of the auction portfolio until the last possible moment to reduce the possibility of information leaking in a way that might adversely affect the result.

Auction participants will also want to know whether they can bid for a portion of the risk or whether they must bid for the whole portfolio. Some CCP auction processes will accommodate bids for a defined tranche of risk. This introduces more complexity but, for large positions especially, may reduce the chance of a failed auction and potentially result in a better outcome. LCH and CME used this type of approach in October 2019 when they auctioned off the portfolio of opted-out Fed Funds—secured overnight financing rate (SOFR) basis swaps resulting from the conversion of USD discounting from Federal funds to SOFR. The LCH process allowed bidders to submit prices for as little as 10% of each swap, with the winner(s) determined by whichever combination of bids yielded the best overall price. Although not strictly a default management activity, this event leveraged many of the processes and systems used for default management and is the only occasion where live risk positions have been closed out by the SwapClear service outside the Lehman Brothers default.

4.7 Auction Incentives

In designing their auction processes, CCP risk managers aim to maximize the chance of obtaining a good price for the defaulter's portfolio by encouraging broad participation and incentivizing competitive bidding.

CCP rule books often prescribe auction participation as a necessary condition of membership and have disciplinary procedures to ensure members comply.[55] On top of that, many CCPs will provide hard economic incentives for tight bidding, for example, by juniorizing low or absent bidders at the expense of strong bidders when it comes to paying for the defaulter's losses out of the non-defaulting members' default fund contributions. The formulae to determine exactly how this incentive scheme works can be exceedingly complicated, especially for multi-currency portfolios requiring several staged auctions. Furthermore, such an incentive is only relevant if there are uncovered[56] losses to allocate. If the CCP has done a reasonable job calibrating its margin

---

[55] The economic impact of falling on the wrong side of these disciplinary procedures may be the lesser cost compared with the reputational cost of failing to provide support for the market, albeit these are likely to be ex post outcomes some weeks after the event itself.

[56] Uncovered losses would be losses that exceed the defaulter's initial margin, default contribution, and the CCP skin in the game, that is, those which require the use of non-defaulting member default fund contributions. Even

models and executing on its default management procedures, there should be no un-covered losses to allocate, which rather undermines the power and usefulness of such a construct.

It should also be acknowledged that any financial auction is a *profit opportunity* which, on its own, provides an incentive. Bidders in an auction, acting in an econom-ically rational manner, are offering to buy a set of contracts for less than they think they are worth. For directional risk, the auction bidder would seek to factor in a risk premium associated with closing out or warehousing the risk until they can sell it. They may have a pre-existing off-setting position that they are seeking to hedge cheaply, in which case, they would be able to bid more competitively. If the portfolio is primarily risk-flat but consists of many individual contracts (which, in aggregate, have high com-plexity and notional value but do not amount to much in risk terms), the auction par-ticipants will still expect to be paid for the potential regulatory capital implications (in the form of increased leveraged balance sheet requirements) and the operational costs of taking on the portfolio.

A final, important incentive is the 'franchise value' associated with giving support to the overall market. In the author's experience, the tabloid caricature of financial market traders as greedy, transactional people is inaccurate. Many trading desk heads *are* greedy, but, for the most part, their priority is *long-term profitability*, which relies on their bank's standing as a dependable partner to the markets it serves. A clearing member default is a great opportunity for bank trading desks to demonstrate these qualities!

CCP rule book requirements for auction participation generally do not extend to hedge providers. However, the profit motive and franchise value incentives are equally applicable to this activity. Some CCPs have also developed economic incentives to en-courage members to provide cost-effective hedges to their DMG.

4.8 Client Participation

One final consideration for CCPs when designing their auction procedures is whether to open up their default auctions to non-members, including to buy-side institutions. For a CCP serving a market where most of the material risk-taking activity is under-taken by client accounts with relatively limited member house account activity, they may conclude that client participation is desirable, or even necessary, to ensure a fa-vourable outcome. For other CCPs, with broad-based membership, they may prefer to limit participation to just their direct members.[57] This is especially likely to be the

---

if there are uncovered losses to allocate, the amounts involved (once the defaulter's margin is taken into account and the costs are shared across a broad membership) may not be sufficient to strongly influence a member bank's bidding behaviour.

[57] For some clearing services, this could already mean more than fifty auction participants. In such cases, the CCP might reasonably conclude that inviting any more auction participants into the process would become very complex and increase the chances of a logistical issue.

case where the CCP's process envisages hedging the portfolio before taking it to auction, in which case, the risk-taking capacity of auction participants is not a material consideration.

Whatever it concludes, a CCP must take steps to ensure that all auction participants have the necessary expertise to undertake the activity reliably and to meet expected standards of conduct during the process. This should be validated through regular, mandatory, testing. It is imperative that each default auction runs smoothly—a more important consideration than simply maximizing the number of bidders. In particular, the CCP must try to ensure that no participants seek to manipulate the outcome or use the information gleaned from auction participation improperly to serve their own agenda.

4.9 Client Porting

Aside from executing hedges against the biggest house positions, the most urgent task facing the CCP's risk managers once a default has been declared is determining which client accounts can be ported to alternate clearing brokers and completing these portfolio transfers. Most CCPs operate a 'porting window' construct to frame this decision. The window provides a stay during which the CCP cannot close out client positions. This allows some time for the required components to fall into place for a successful port. Once the porting window is over, the CCP may decide to close out client positions en masse[58] or on a case-by-case basis. In a close-out situation, the CCP follows the same process it uses for the member's own house positions (i.e. a combination of hedging and auctions) and the same considerations apply. For a defaulting bank with significant house *and* client positions, it is quite possible that the DMG may need to effect house and client close-outs simultaneously.

A porting window can be anything from four hours (e.g. LMEClear, EuroCCP) to twenty-four hours (e.g. LCH SwapClear, NASDAQ Clearing) depending on the product, with some CCPs having the ability to reduce the window in cases where the account has suffered material margin erosion. Beyond this initial window, CCPs have the right (though, importantly, *not* the obligation) to close out the clients' positions and liquidate their collateral. For client accounts that have not ported within the defined window, determining when to trigger a liquidation is one of the most difficult decisions facing the CCP's management. The decision balances the desire to provide continuity of contracts for clients (and preserve their collateral) with the need to protect the non-defaulting members (and the CCP itself) from losses sustained by the defaulter's client accounts during a prolonged period of inaction.

---

[58] Combining multiple client accounts into the same default management portfolio may provide a risk-offset benefit and lead to a lower overall cost of close-out. In this circumstance, the CCP will need an allocation key (defined ex ante, preferably!) to ensure that the overall costs are fairly apportioned to each account.

In the European model, to port a client's positions and collateral, a CCP requires written consent from both the client and the receiving clearing broker. In a default of a large clearing broker, this will require collection and validation of dozens (conceivably hundreds for a very large broker) of consent forms. For a client with an individually segregated account, with one or more live back-up accounts, this procedure is relatively tractable. For clients in an omnibus structure and/or without live back-ups, it is likely to be much more difficult.[59]

A client with no live back-ups must find a clearing broker willing to take on its account at extremely short notice, at a time when the clearing broker may be very busy supporting its established clients. Bank internal processes and controls (not to mention regulation) make the setting up of new client accounts a time-consuming process. Anti-money-laundering 'know-your-customer' checks need to be completed. Accounts need to be created, switched on, and funded in the clearing broker's systems and at the CCP. These processes would normally take several weeks—it is difficult to envisage short-cutting them to twenty-four hours (or less) without encountering blockages somewhere in the approval chain. If the client has affiliates with established relationships at another clearing broker, this may provide some hope that the clearing broker would be willing to act as a back-up, but otherwise it is likely to prove very difficult.

An omnibus account structure adds a further challenge to the scenario as the porting decision needs to be agreed among all clients whose positions are comingled in the relevant account. Depending on the CCP's rules, it may require this to be a unanimous decision. Any lack of unanimity on whether and where to port will result in the CCP closing out the positions and liquidating all the collateral by default. On a positive note, this is one area where OTC clearing has a systematic advantage over listed derivatives. In listed derivatives clearing, at the time of writing, it is still the case that individual clients (especially those in omnibus structures) are generally not visible to the CCP. Sub-accounts may have just a numerical identifier, which can only be translated into the relevant details with access to the defaulter's records.[60]

The 'futures commission merchant' (FCM) clearing model used for client clearing in the United States addresses some of these challenges by placing the decision-making powers into the hands of the CFTC, the bankruptcy court, and the CCP. This makes it much more likely that a mass port will be arranged to one or more 'white-knight' banks willing to take on a significant chunk (or, possibly, all) of the stricken clearing broker's franchise.

It should be noted that client porting decisions are not binding for all time. The transfer provides the clients with a stable 'port in a storm', allowing them to continue to make margin payments through to the CCP, removing the impetus for close-out and

---

[59] One should not assume that continuity of positions is of paramount importance to all clients. Some may be focused more on cost and efficiency considerations, willing to accept the risk of counterparty default as a cost of doing business, and happy to contract out the portfolio close-out to an authorized CCP. Such clients would effectively forgo some of the risk management benefits that clearing offers but would still benefit from the access to liquidity and potential balance sheet or capital savings that clearing provides.

[60] Something that, in the United Kingdom, Part VII of the Companies Act would entitle them to do but which may be a time-consuming step that takes things outside the porting window.

keeping their positions and accounts alive. Once the storm has passed, and with the luxury of more time, the clients may decide whether to keep their positions at the new clearing broker, transfer to a third broker, or close out the positions themselves in a less time-constrained manner. The temporary nature of the move may also help to relieve any concerns the potential 'white-knight' broker may have regarding the amount of capital or balance sheet its new clients would consume, with a shorter-term surge in usage being more palatable than a permanent increase.

4.10 External Participation in the Default Management Group

Depending on the product, a CCP may rely on seconding external traders into its team to assist in this process. This is often the case in OTC markets (e.g. swaps) but is less common in exchange-traded markets.[61] This construct ensures that the CCP has access to sufficient expertise and human resources when undertaking default management to make a successful outcome more likely. Such arrangements do bring with them complications. Member banks must be willing to give up experienced trading staff at a time when markets are likely to be volatile and they could use the expertise to help manage their own positions and provide execution services for valued customers. The seconded traders must remain disconnected from their employer's trading desk to minimize the possibility of information leakage or the appearance of conflicts of interest. It is crucial to ensure that any external DMG members arrive promptly so that hedging can begin as soon as possible. In general, these risks can be managed and do not undermine the substantial benefits an external DMG provides to this critical activity. However, for relatively simple products or portfolios, the CCP should be able to proceed (more quickly and easily) without the need for external participation in its DMG.

CCPs relying on external support will generally make it a rule book requirement[62] for members to provide a DMG trader on request and for that trader to present themselves at the CCP's offices in the event of default within a tightly defined time frame. In practice, CCPs will tend to seek out enthusiastic, committed member traders rather than unwilling conscripts!

It is important to note that, though external DMG participants provide valuable advice to the CCP's management team and equally valuable assistance in the form of trade execution, the ultimate responsibility for trading decisions made during the course of default management remains with the CCP's management team.

The COVID-19 pandemic demonstrated that modern technology has made remote trading possible, and compliance techniques have evolved to ensure that it can be done safely. However, it is still the case that a trading team undertaking complex,

---

[61] Close-out processes for exchange-traded products have less scope for complexity because of the restricted universe of contracts, which are much less bespoke compared with an OTC trade portfolio. That is not to say that an exchange-traded portfolio will not present its own challenges.

[62] CCP rule books also contain details of potential sanctions the CCP can bring against a member for failing to meet one of its membership obligations, up to and including their membership being withdrawn.

high-risk, highly time-sensitive activities will be more effective if all individuals are in the same room, allowing for zero-latency, *line-of-sight* communication among all members of the team. A CCP, therefore, will still require its DMG members to attend in person unless they are absolutely prevented from doing so, for example, by a future legal restriction on movement. Although a well-managed CCP might design and test procedures for convening the DMG remotely, should it ever be needed, for the time being, this would only be as a fallback *in extremis*, with in-person attendance firmly expected.

5 The Importance of 'Fire Drill' Exercises

RIPLEY:	'How many drops is this for you, Lieutenant?'
LIEUTENANT GORMAN:	'Thirty-eight [...] simulated.'
VASQUEZ:	'How many combat drops?'
GORMAN:	'Two [...] including this one.'

Aliens (James Cameron, 1986)

CCP member defaults are mercifully rare occurrences. A multi-asset class CCP might expect to see a member default once every few years. Some clearing services have never experienced a member default. Just as an army officer will rarely see active combat, many CCP executives have limited experience of default management outside of simulated exercises, often referred to as 'fire drills'. These exercises are the means through which the CCP management team gains experience of operating its default management procedures in a safe environment and are, therefore, invested with the utmost importance. As the old adage goes: 'Fail to plan; plan to fail'.

EMIR requires that a CCP test its default management procedures at least once a year. Most CCPs will supplement their annual comprehensive test with targeted exercises on individual components spread throughout the year. A CCP's testing programme will cover all the steps outlined in this chapter: default decision-making, hedging, auctions, client porting, and using the default waterfall. All aspects are tested: communication, reports, systems, processes, and controls. A CCP's detailed default management procedures will run to hundreds of pages across teams from risk, operations, legal, technology, and so on. It goes without saying that these documents should be accurate, comprehensive, and up to date at all times, but there will be no time for a leisurely read-through in a default situation. Regular fire drills keep the procedures *front of mind* for all the CCP's staff so that their responsibilities become second nature in a real default.

Most fire drill exercises will require active participation from the CCP's members. The CCP will test its ability to contact the individuals at member banks, who will conduct the auction bidding for their institution and ensure that those individuals are familiar with all the logistics. They will also test the ability of member firms to consume the auction portfolio description in the format provided by the CCP and the CCP's ability to transfer portfolios to the winning bidder(s). Clients may also be involved in some exercises, ensuring that they are familiar with the protocols for decision-making in a default.

Fire drill exercises are often accompanied by 'lessons learned' sessions to ensure that any residual areas of uncertainty or potential process improvements are followed up. Culturally, it is important that such exercises provide a safe space for any uncertainties to be aired. Management may be invested in the idea that a 'successful' fire drill exercise proves that their default management capabilities are in good standing. However, an exercise where some elements were found wanting is a more valuable learning experience—much better if things go wrong in a safe environment than in a live default situation.

Finally, it is also important to consider scenarios beyond 'just' a member default. Although it may seem like the default of a large clearing bank would be a sufficiently unpleasant event to provide a stern test of a CCP's capabilities, it is important to consider other events that might impair a CCP's capability to act. For example, a technology failure either internally or at a third-party infrastructure provider at the same time as a default is something that CCPs should consider in their plans.

6 Conclusions

The successful close-out of Lehman Brothers' cleared OTC positions provided a convincing demonstration that clearing house default management is capable of delivering much better outcomes for market participants than they might experience in an uncleared market. For advocates of clearing, this was a comprehensive vindication. However, with a sample size of one, it would be a stretch to conclude that CCP default management will always work best in all situations.[63]

A further limitation of the Lehman Brothers example is that it predates the widespread adoption of client clearing for OTC swaps. The clearing community has never had to deal with an OTC clearing broker default or the large-scale client-porting exercise that would result. Regular, coordinated, fire drill exercises are the key way to prepare for such an event. For a large default, there is complexity that will involve multiple CCPs, multiple regulators, members, and clients. All of these actors need to know the part they are expected to play in advance and have a good idea how the others will behave in this situation. It is therefore imperative that the entire community participate in these important exercises.

History contains several examples where CCP default management has not worked well. However, these CCP failures date from the relative *dark ages* of clearing. With the dramatic increase in risk management standards brought in by EMIR and Dodd–Frank,

---

[63] At the time of writing, Lehman Brothers is the only large-scale multi-CCP default in OTC swaps clearing. All other clearing member defaults have concerned smaller, niche markets, small counterparties, and/or exchange-traded products.

it is inconceivable to think that a modern CCP could be brought to its knees by the kind of simple failures in default management that felled CLAM and ICCH. However, the financial landscape continues to evolve, and market shocks appear with what seems like increasing regularity. It is imperative that the CCPs continuously test and improve their practises to ensure that they, and their members, remain ready and prepared for the next default.

12

Recovery and Resolution of CCPs

*Victor de Serière**

1 Introduction

This chapter deals with the European rules on recovery and resolution of central counterparties (CCPs), as set out in Regulation (EU) No. 2021/23 (16 December 2020) (the Regulation). The Regulation, of which a first proposal was published by the European Commission in 2016, entered into force on 12 August 2022. Although the European Market Infrastructure Regulation (EMIR) contributed significantly to the resilience of central counterparties (CCPs), it does not provide a framework for dealing with CCP failures. Since allowing CCPs to be subject to 'normal' insolvency proceedings may jeopardize the continuity of the critical functions CCPs provide as an essential part of the financial markets infrastructure (FMI), the European Commission concluded that a special recovery and resolution framework was necessary. The objective was, in particular, to safeguard the continuity of clearing and to

* The author is grateful to his co-editors, Bas Zebregs and Patrick Pearson, for reviewing this chapter. He is also grateful to Mirik van Rijn, currently working as counsel with the Dutch Central Bank, who reviewed section 11 on remedies. The author remains fully accountable for any omissions, inconsistencies, and mistakes.

preserve, to the extent practicable, the stability of the financial sector—all of this to the maximum extent possible without using taxpayers' money. Important groundwork leading to the adoption of the Regulation was done by the Bank for International Settlements (BIS), the International Organization of Securities Commissions (IOSCO), and the Financial Stability Board (FSB). The FSB Key Attributes of 2011 and 2014 recommended that 'Financial Markets Infrastructures should be subject to resolution regimes that apply the objective and provisions of the Key Attributes in a manner appropriate to FMIs and their critical role in financial markets.' This effectively constituted confirmation that the systemic importance of FMI entities was finally considered on (at least) an equal footing with that of systemic banks and other financial institutions. The Regulation leans heavily on the principles these organizations formulated in their various reports on financial market infrastructures.[1] For further historical background on the promulgation of the Regulation, please refer to Chapter 3 ('Development of the Regulatory Regime for OTC Derivatives Clearing' by Patrick Pearson) in this volume.[2]

After some general introductory comments (section 2), this chapter deals with successively recovery planning (section 3), resolution planning (section 4), resolvability (section 5), early intervention measures (section 6), resolution and resolution tools (sections 7 and 8), the no-creditor-worse-off (NCWO) principle (section 8), powers of the National Resolution Authority (NRA) (section 9), non-applicability of the Bank Recovery and Resolution Directive (BRRD) (section 10), and finally remedies (section 11). A brief conclusion will finally be proffered in section 12.

It is noted at the outset that while this book, in principle, only covers the clearing of over-the-counter (OTC) derivatives in Europe, this chapter deals with the recovery and resolution regime applicable to European CCPs more generally. Accordingly, no distinction is made in this chapter between OTC derivatives, on the one hand, and other types of financial instruments for which CCPs may provide clearing services on the other hand.

2 A Few Initial General Comments

In this section, some more general observations in random sequence are made on the recovery and resolution regime as envisaged by the Regulation.

---

[1] See, among others, CPSS–IOSCO, 'Principles for Financial Markets Infrastructures' (April 2012); the Financial Service Board's (FSB's) 'Key Attributes of Effective Resolution Regimes for Financial Institutions' (November 2011); the FSB's 'Guidance on Central Counterparty Resolution and Resolution Planning' (February 2017) and its 'Essential Aspects of CCP Resolution Planning' of the same date.

[2] For a comprehensive list of literature on the problems relating to the recovery and resolution of CCPs, see Jens-Hinrich Binder, 'Central Counterparties' Insolvency and Resolution', in Jens-Hinrich Binder and Paolo Saguato (eds), *Financial Market Infrastructures Law and Regulation* (Oxford: Oxford University Press, 2022), p. 295ff, fn. 2 (Binder, 'Central Counterparties' Insolvency and Resolution'); also Ron Berndsen, 'Five Fundamental Questions on Central Counterparties', CentER Discussion Paper; Vol. 2020-028 (CentER, Center for Economic Research, Tilburg University), p. 35ff.

2.1 Inspiration from the BRRD: Uncertainties about Practical Workability

The Regulation to a significant extent reflects the structure of the Bank Recovery and Resolution Directive (BRRD).[3] The sequential treatment in the BRRD of recovery, resolvability, early intervention, and resolution is largely replicated in the Regulation. The use in the Regulation of basic principles such as the NCWO principle, as set out in the BRRD, could neatly be replicated without the need for fundamental discussion. The resolution tools provided for in the Regulation are also, to a certain extent, comparable to those envisaged in the BRRD, for example, the sale-of-business tool and the bridge CCP tool. However, the so-called 'position and loss-allocation tools' are uniquely specific to CCP resolution (see section 8 below). And the Regulation's treatment of equity is substantially different, logically so given the fundamentally different function of equity in CCPs to that of the equity held in banks (see section 8.2 below). In amongst these different approaches, the Regulation attempts to address the impact and consequences of the very different business models, balance sheet compositions, and risk exposures of CCPs as compared with those of banks.

Having said this, the inspiration that the European lawmakers have derived from the BRRD is cause for concern, if only for the reason that this bank recovery and resolution regime has not yet been tested on its practical effectiveness in case of a bank failure.[4] In other words, there is a level of uncertainty as to whether the approaches taken by the bank resolution regime will prove to be practically workable. The 'translation' of the general provisions of the bank resolution regime into effective decision-making by NRAs in the form of procedural playbooks is currently being undertaken with respect to larger banks in the eurozone. The practical difficulties, as revealed in these playbook exercises, are proving to be rather challenging. In addition, despite the Single Resolution Board's (SRB's) efforts in this respect and the BRRD regime's uniformity goals, there are inevitably significant national divergences as to how NRAs implement this regime.

In this context, it is worth noting that the two regimes are unique in that they *precede* and try to *anticipate* on situations of financial crisis rather than provide an ex post facto *reaction* to previous financial crises, as lawmakers and regulators will normally be engaged in. In addition, the fact that most CCPs are directly or indirectly 'owned' by clearing members (CMs) and/or other institutions with a banking licence ensures, to a certain degree, the use of common approaches by the (prudential and conduct)

---

[3] Directive 2014/59/EU of the European Parliament and of the Council of 15 May 2014 establishing a framework for the recovery and resolution of credit institutions and investment firms and amending Council Directive 82/891/EEC, and Directives 2001/24/EC, 2002/47/EC, 2004/25/EC, 2005/56/EC, 2007/36/EC, 2011/35/EU, 2012/30/EU, and 2013/36/EU, and Regulations (EU) No 1093/2010 and (EU) No 648/2012 of the European Parliament and of the Council Text with EEA relevance, OJ L173 (12 June 2014), pp. 190–348 (subsequently amended) (BRRD).

[4] The failures of banks such as Banco Popular Espanyol cannot really be considered as testing the efficacy of the BRRD/SRMR regime.

regulators that are somewhat more predictable and easier to deal with by CCPs and their stakeholders.

Without doubt, the Regulation will yield comparable uncertainties and practical complexities as compared to those that are currently under scrutiny with the SRB and the NRAs. Finally on this point, it is noted that Singh and Turing have stated that:

> Many of the tools proposed for resolving CCPs might prove to be unusable in a crisis or even worsen the crisis. Additional tools are needed; some of those would demand that regulators accept that the existing policy belief—in particular, that mandatory clearing must carry on under all circumstances, may not hold valid in a crisis.[5]

The Union legislators did not exactly heed this warning.[6] Abandoning the 'existing policy belief' was probably a bridge too far for Union legislators, but the warning underscores this writer's conviction that continuity of clearing in a financial crisis scenario is unlikely to be successful without drastic financial government intervention (see section 2.7 below). Continuity of clearing would probably, in any event, need to entail a drastic restructuring of the failing CCP, under new ownership and governance, possibly with a more limited operational mandate.

2.2 Differing Circumstances in Which a CCP May Fail as Compared to Those in Which a Bank May Fail

The uncertainty identified in section 2.1 is exacerbated by the (possibly fundamentally different) circumstances in which CCPs may fail as compared to those in which systemic banks may fail. Generally, whilst EMIR's prudential requirements designed to make CCPs financially robust should bear out that insolvency of CCPs is really only imaginable in 'certain extreme circumstances',[7] this is not necessarily true in respect of the prudential regimes applicable to banks. The principal risk that CCPs are exposed to emanates from the failures of one or more large CMs.[8] Larger CMs are, more often than not, companies belonging to large financial groups. Their failure to honour contractual

---

[5] Singh and Turing, 'Central Counterparties Resolution—an Unresolved Problem', IMF Working Paper No. WP/18/65 (March 2018), p. 20 (Singh and Turing 'Central Counterparties Resolution'). Also published in (8 February 2018) 6(2/3) Journal of Financial Market Infrastructures 187–206.

[6] Although it must be recognized that the EMIR Refit Regulation (Regulation (EU) 2019/834 of the European Parliament and of the Council of 20 May 2019 amending Regulation (EU) No 648/2012 as regards the clearing obligation, the suspension of the clearing obligation, the reporting requirements, the risk-mitigation techniques for OTC derivative contracts not cleared by a central counterparty, the registration and supervision of trade repositories, and the requirements for trade repositories, OJ L141 (28 May 2019), pp. 42–63) provides what may be considered an 'additional recovery and resolution tool' in that the clearing obligation may be suspended in order to ensure financial stability and avoid market disruption; see, among others, EMIR Refit, Recital (13).

[7] CPSS–IOSCO, 'Principles for Financial Market Infrastructures' (April 2012), para. 1.24.

[8] See Singh and Turing, 'Central Counterparties Resolution' (n 5), p. 6. They contend that other mishaps that might befall CCPs, including operational failures, mismanagement, and erosion of business volumes, should be dealt with using the capital buffer of the CCP concerned and would be unlikely to lead to a CCP's insolvency. See also Chapter 3 ('Development of the Regulatory Regime for OTC Derivatives Clearing' by Patrick Pearson) in this volume for a description of risks to which a CCP is generally exposed.

commitments to 'their' CCPs will probably occur in an environment where these financial groups themselves are struggling. This scenario suggests a severe (arguably more likely than not systemic) financial crisis, the impact of which on the financial health of financial institutions (including specialized enterprises that are active in the FMI sector) and on asset prices (in particular collateral values) defies the imagination. Such a crisis would 'likely not just affect the CMs and "their" CCP concerned, but also other CCPs with which the CMs contract (larger CMs tend to spread their favours), other CMs,[9] and, by way of contagion, other financial institutions.

Since the Regulation's regime with respect to recovery and resolution generally relies rather heavily on the availability of support by other FMI enterprises in such a systemic financial crisis scenario, one may well query the effectiveness of the resolution tools envisaged by the Regulation. In such a scenario, would it be realistic to rely on other CCPs, on other CMs, and/or their clients to take over activities and client positions;[10] to find third parties who might be willing to step in; to expect auctions to be successful; or to rely on CMs to answer cash calls? Admittedly, legally binding commitments of CMs to provide financial support to a CCP as agreed in advance in such a CCP's rule book may help, but whether these commitments can then be relied upon (and enforced effectively and in a timely manner) is a different matter. Hopefully, we will never find out. But the circumstances in which a systemic bank might be threatened with insolvency may well be rather more benevolent in terms of available workable resolution mechanisms.

2.2 The Impact of Recovery and Resolution on Clients of CMs

Another general feature of the CCP recovery and resolution regime worth noting has to do with the fact that the Regulation necessarily limits its coverage to, in particular, the legal relationships between a CCP and 'its' CMs. This is logical for the simple reason that CCPs would not necessarily know who the clients of the CMs are, and the CMs would also not necessarily know who the clients of their clients are. The contractual arrangements are likely to differ in the various transaction levels concerned. The Regulation accordingly only in a 'stepmotherly' way addresses the effects of the use of recovery and resolution tools on the (more or less corresponding) legal relationships

---

[9] See, inter alia, Turing and Singh, 'The Morning After—the Impact on Collateral Supply after a Major Default', IMF Working Paper No. WP/18/228 (October 2018), pp. 12ff (Turing and Singh, 'The Morning After'). It is also noted that the larger CMs at London Clearing House (LCH) Clearnet will generally also be CMs at Eurex and vice versa, thus increasing the contagion risk.

[10] In Recital (42) of the Regulation, it is optimistically stated that 'a CCP or specific clearing service should also be able to be sold to or merged with a solvent third-party CCP that is able to conduct and manage the transferred clearing activities'. The sale of clearing positions to another CCP is fraught with complexities. Issues such as client acceptance policies, collateral acceptance policies, and IT compatibility are but a few examples of complexities. In this writer's opinion, the porting of positions of a failing CCP in a (near-) insolvency situation may well prove to be rather more difficult than it already undoubtedly is in the context of porting under Regulation (EU) No. 648/ 2012 of the European Parliament and of the Council of 4 July 2012 on OTC derivatives, central counterparties and trade repositories, [2012] OJ L201/1 (27 July 2012) (EMIR) in case of a CM default. See Chapter 10 ('Segregation and Portability of Cleared OTC Derivatives in Europe' by Bas Zebregs) in this volume. See also section 8 below in respect of the sale of business tools.

between CMs and their clients.[11] Admittedly, EMIR and the Markets in Financial Instruments Directive II (MiFID II) contain certain provisions in this respect protecting the interests of clients, but these are far from comprehensive and provide little legislative guidance to CMs and their clients on how to deal with the knock-on effect of these intrusions into the legal relationships between CCPs and CMs.[12]

The Regulation envisages recovery tools (and perhaps also resolution tools[13]) such as varying or suspending contracts, rematching the CCPs book by tearing up contracts, exercising variation margin gains haircutting (VMGH), to name but a few of the tools that might be employed. To the extent that these measures negatively affect CMs, these effects are likely to be passed on by CMs to their clients.[14] If, for instance, a CCP in resolution obtains access to liquidity by applying VMGH, the CM might thus be deprived of funds enabling it to comply with its corresponding obligation to give its clients the corresponding benefit of the gains concerned. This means that, to a certain extent, the price of recovery and resolution is not shared on a mutualization basis between the CCP and its CMs but borne by the CMs' clients themselves. Clients interests, one could argue, are, to that extent, subordinated to the greater good of the continuity of a CCP's critical services.

2.4 Is a Correct Loss-Allocation Balance Reached?

Whilst section 2.3 refers to just one aspect of the allocation of losses suffered by a CCP in distress, the wider issue remains whether the regime established by EMIR and the Regulation has achieved the right balance when allocating losses among the various stakeholders of a CCP. The time elapsed since the first publication of a draft regulation in 2016 and the promulgation of the Regulation in November 2020 is indicative of the difficulties the Union lawmakers had in attempting to achieve this balance. As described in Chapters 7 ('What Kind of Thing Is a Central Counterparty? The Role of Clearing Houses as a Source of Policy Controversy' by Rebecca Lewis and David Murphy) and 8

---

[11] Article 7 sub. (iii) of the Regulation requires competent authorities and ESMA resolution authorities to take into account 'the structure, nature and diversity of […] its clearing member network of clients and indirect clients'.

[12] On this topic, see, among others, Bas Zebregs and Victor de Serière, 'Derivatives Central Counterparties: Regulatory Framework, Segregation and Portability', in Paolo Saguato and Jens-Hinrich Binder (eds), *Financial Markets Infrastructures, Law and Regulation* (Oxford: Oxford University Press 2022), pp. 239ff (Zebregs and de Serière, 'Derivatives Central Counterparties').

[13] As Singh and Turing correctly point out, the approach of the Regulation makes the distinction between these phases somewhat obscure. See Singh and Turing, 'Central Counterparties Resolution' (n 5), p. 9. They submit that a clear distinction is to be made between 'recovery', on the one hand, and 'end of life' or 'a second round of recovery' on the other hand.

[14] This is recognized in Art. 63(1) of the Regulation: 'Contractual arrangements allowing clearing members to pass on to their clients the negative consequences of the resolution tools'. The Regulation does not regulate to what extent such passing on is permitted. It does, however, give a certain amount of protection to clients of CMs in that compensation a CM may receive on the basis of Art. 27(6) will have to be passed on to clients on an equivalent and proportionate basis. Article 27(6) provides that NRAs may require that, subject to certain conditions, the non-defaulting CMs are to receive compensation by the CCP concerned for losses stemming from the application of the loss-allocation tools applied by the NRA. On 12 May 2022, ESMA issued draft regulatory technical standards (RTS) on how Art. 63 is to be implemented. See its Final Report, reference: ESMA91-372-2065. At the time of writing this chapter, the RTS concerned have not yet been formalized in a Commission Delegated Regulation. See also Turing and Singh, 'The Morning After' (n 9), p. 8.

('OTC Derivatives Clearing Documentation' by Emma Dwyer and Emma Lancelott) in this volume, the allocation of losses is, in principle, in first instance determined along the lines of the various stages of the 'default waterfall'[15] and then, when the bottom of the waterfall is reached or likely to be reached without a successful outcome, in second instance according to the seniority rungs of the insolvency ladder.[16] Criticisms as expressed by CMs have over the past years focused on perceived insufficiency of *skin-in-the-game* (SITG) exposures for CCPs themselves as well as on arguably too lenient capitalization levels imposed on CCPs and accordingly limited bail-in possibilities.[17] There are obviously clearly conflicting interests at work in these discussions, which this chapter will not address; see Chapter 7 ('What Kind of Thing Is a Central Counterparty? The Role of Clearing Houses as a Source of Policy Controversy' by Rebecca Lewis and David Murphy) in this volume.

2.5 Resolution Colleges

A distinct feature of the Regulation is the function of the so-called resolution colleges. Whilst EMIR requires the establishment of 'supervisory colleges',[18] the Regulation provides for separate 'resolution colleges' to operate next to such supervisory colleges. This results in an intricate consultation and decision-making process between the NRA, the supervisory college, the resolution college, and the CCP itself, with, in addition, the involvement of the European Securities Markets Authority (ESMA) if such processes are stalled. This complex process is clearly the product of political compromise. The effectiveness of this process can, unfortunately, be properly gauged only after having been applied in practice.

The resolution colleges have a rather wider (one may argue even unwieldy) composition[19] than the supervisory colleges. The establishment of resolution colleges with broad representation of interests involved is thought to be necessary, given the cross-border nature of clearing services that many CCPs provide and the significant cross-border impact that a CCP failure is likely to have. In the drafting phase of the Regulation, the notion that a national resolution college could take measures and inform other 'involved' Member States only after the fact was, in the end, firmly rejected. These colleges will need to address situations where recovery and resolution of a CCP

---

[15] EMIR (n 10), Art. 45.

[16] Article 23 of the Regulation.

[17] See Zebregs and De Serière, 'Derivatives Central Counterparties' (n 12), p. 227. Regarding SITG, see EMIR (n 10), Art. 45(4).

[18] See Commission Delegated Regulation (EU) No. 876/2013 of 28 May 2013 supplementing Regulation (EU) No. 648/2012 of the European Parliament and of the Council with regard to regulatory technical standards on colleges for central counterparties, [2013] OJ L244/19 (13 September 2013). On the functioning of these colleges, see ESMA, 'Final Report: EMIR RTS on colleges for central counterparties', ESMA 70-151-2919 (30 March 2020).

[19] Article 4(2) of the Regulation. The composition of resolution colleges is broader than that of the so-called crisis management groups (CMGs) that the FSB has proposed. Also, the FSB recommended that these colleges would be installed for CCPs that are systematically important in more than one jurisdiction; that recommendation was not taken up by the EU legislator.

in one Member State can, and probably will, have wide repercussions in other Member States (and third countries), whose interests would not necessarily be aligned to those of the home Member State.[20] Whether the broad composition of the resolution college entails that the NRA would appropriately take into account the interests of supervisory authorities in other Member States remains to be seen in practice; certainly, the decision-making process in these resolution colleges does not as such safeguard these interests.[21]

The resolution colleges are given a more substantive remit than the supervisory colleges: they are inter alia to provide frameworks for the drawing up of resolution plans by the NRAs, for carrying out assessments of the resolvability of CCPs, and for the co-ordination of public communications about resolution plans and strategies. The colleges have to be involved in deciding how perceived resolvability impediments are to be removed. Resolution plans are to be jointly agreed in the resolution college, giving the latter an authoritative say in the resolution process itself. This follows from the requirement that resolution actions by the NRA in respect of a CCP should, in principle, be taken in accordance with the resolution plan applicable to that CCP unless the NRA would determine that actions deviating from the plan would be more effective.[22] Any such deviation must be explained by the NRA to the resolution college.[23]

2.6 Resolution of CCPs Part of a Group

Does the Regulation effectively deal with the complications arising from a CCP being a group company within a (presumably financial) conglomerate? This important question is difficult to answer. Recital (12) of the Regulation states categorically that 'CCPs are stand alone entities that are required to fulfil all requirements under this regulation and under [EMIR], independently from their parent undertaking or other group entities. The group of which the CCP forms part does not therefore need to be subject to this Regulation.' This observation is the result of discussions held in the context of drafting the Regulation on the perceived need to be able to extend the recovery and resolution regime also to parent companies and/or other relevant group entities. In the end, it was determined that such extension was politically a bridge too far.[24] Admittedly, if parent companies would fall within the gambit of the Regulation, this could cause a convergence of supervisory and resolution regimes (with the likelihood of competing interests) that would be rather difficult to manage. Nevertheless, it is debatable whether the Union legislators have wisely opted for this stand-alone approach. In any event, this

---

[20] Recital (16) of the Regulation.
[21] Differences of opinion in resolution colleges are to be resolved by way of binding ESMA mediation; see Recital (30) of the Regulation.
[22] Recitals (28) and (44) of the Regulation; Art. 14 of the Regulation.
[23] Article 72 of the Regulation.
[24] This debate was heavily influenced by the factual position of Eurex, a German CCP owned by Deutsche Börse. See Chapter 3 ('Development of the Regulatory Regime for OTC Derivatives Clearing' by Patrick Pearson) in this volume.

means that the elaborate provisions of the BRRD and Single Resolution Mechanism Regulation (SRMR) on group recovery planning, resolution planning, and inclusion of financial institutions and holding companies in the resolution process have not been mirrored in the Regulation (apart from Art. 23 of the Regulation, see below). Of course, the NRA would be in a position to ensure that recovery and resolution planning for CCPs at least takes into proper account the possible effects on group structures. See Chapter 3 ('Development of the Regulatory Regime for OTC Derivatives Clearing' by Patrick Pearson) in this volume.

Recital (12) appears to assume that a CCP's rights and obligations and risk exposures are fully ringfenced and independent from those of other entities belonging to the same group. It is, however, questionable whether EMIR fully achieves this. This chapter will not discuss this issue. In any event, the recital observes that 'the group dimension, including, inter alia, the operational, personal and financial relations of a CCP with group entities should however be taken into account in the CCP's recovery and resolution planning'.

Recital (29) and Art. 16 of the Regulation address the issue of resolvability. Resolution authorities have the power to require legal changes to the existing structure of a CCP if resolvability requirements demand this, including changes that might affect the structure of the group itself. The Union legislator, however, takes a somewhat defensive stance: according to Recital (29), the NRA, when assessing how to remove such impediments to resolution, 'should be able to suggest a different set of resolvability measures than requiring changes to the legal or operational structures of the group, if the use of such alternative measures would remove the impediments to resolvability in an equivalent way'. As is apparent from Recital (29), the EU legislators fear that enforcing such changes 'could lead to issues of legal challenge or issues of enforceability'. This is remarkable. The recital text seems to suggest that the interests of ensuring resolvability should not jeopardize other interests that prevail within the group, such as the resolvability of banks or insurance companies within the same group.[25]

According to Art. 23(1)(i) of the Regulation, resolution authorities must take into account the impact of resolution measures 'on other group entities, in particular where such group comprises other FMIs, and on the group as a whole'.[26] The BRRD and the proposed Insurance Recovery and Resolution Directive (IRRD)[27] do not contain reciprocal provisions. Efforts to ensure that a CCP in resolution is not hindered by interdependencies within a group, such as personnel sharing arrangements, intra-group outsourcing, IT platform sharing facilities, etc.,[28] may—at least, in theory—be complicated by this admonition to exercise restraint when interfering with group structures.

---

[25] See also Art. 7 sub. (a)(i) of the Regulation.
[26] The difference in language of Recital (29) as compared to that of Art. 23 of the Regulation is to be noted, begging the question what legal relevance deviating provisions of a Regulation's recitals may be considered to have.
[27] On 22 September 2021, the European Commission adopted a proposal for an Insurance Recovery and Resolution Directive.
[28] See also Victor de Serière, 'Recovery and Resolution Plans in the Context of the BRRD and the SRM: Some Fundamental Issues', in Danny Busch et al. (eds), *European Banking Union*, 2nd edition (Oxford: Oxford University Press, 2020), chapter 12.

Another example of this 'restraint' can by the way be found in Recital (40) of the Regulation, stating cryptically, 'the application of [resolution tools and powers] should not impinge on the effective resolution of cross-border groups'.

Intra-group dependencies may obviously include financial support to be given to an ailing CCP by its parent or by other group companies. According to Art. 9(13) of the Regulation,[29] recovery plans must include scenarios where any financial support commitment would not be honoured. This is obviously especially relevant where the CCP falters as a consequence of a systemic crisis also affecting other group companies. Article 12(7) sub. (j) of the Regulation requires resolution plans to describe how interdependencies would be dealt with, but Art. 12 does not (or at least not specifically) require resolution plans to assume non-availability of group support. This raises the complex question as to whether, and if so how, parental guarantees (such as the *Patronatserklärungen* in use in Germany) may be taken into account. On this issue, see also Chapter 3 ('Development of the Regulatory Regime for OTC Derivatives Clearing' by Patrick Pearson) in this volume.

All in all, one may conclude that complications arising from interdependencies of CCPs that operate as part of a financial conglomerate are recognized but not comprehensively addressed by the Regulation. Its approach is thus fundamentally different from that adopted in the BRRD. Essentially, it is up to competent authorities to ensure that the relevant EMIR provisions are adequately adhered to; if, and to the extent that, EMIR provisions do not specifically address ringfencing issues, the general provisions of EMIR relating to risk management will anyhow provide a suitable basis for the supervisory authorities, where necessary, to require further protective measures ensuring the CCP's independence from a risk perspective.

2.7 Government Stabilization Measures

The following paragraphs discuss the provision of government financial support to CCPs. A distinction is made between such support as given prior to a CCP being subject to resolution and support being given once the CCP is in resolution mode. This topic is discussed here for the reason that, in this writer's opinion, it is highly unlikely that efforts to safeguard the continuity of critical functions of a CCP in a (systemic) crisis situation could be successful without such support. The 16 November 2020 Final Report of the FSB containing 'Guidance on Financial Resources to Support CCP Resolution and on the Treatment of CCP Equity in Resolution' provides an analysis of potential resolution costs and the available resources for meeting such costs and for addressing any shortfalls in such resources. That report recognizes the many problematical and uncertain aspects of funding resolution processes but pointedly does not discuss the possibility of government support to cover shortfalls.

---

[29] See also Annex A of the Regulation, further elaborating the requirements for recovery plans.

2.8 Government Stabilization Measures Prior to Resolution

The Regulation does not deal (or rather, does not deal directly) with precautionary government support of solvent CCPs. This means that solvent CCPs may receive such support provided the EU Commission's state aid rules are complied with. In addition, though, governments will have to take into account the conditions imposed by the provisions of Art. 22(4) of the Regulation. These provisions indicate that such support should meet the conditions that (i) such support is provided in the form of a state guarantee, either to back a central bank's liquidity facilities or liabilities to third parties,[30] (ii) it is required to remedy a serious disturbance in the economy of a Member State and preserve financial stability, (iii) it is of a temporary and precautionary nature, (iv) it is proportionate, and (v) it is not used to offset previous or likely future losses of the CCP. If a CCP 'requires'[31] such support and the same is provided in circumstances where these conditions are *not* met, the CCP is deemed to be failing or likely to fail,[32] and this would constitute a resolution trigger as set out in Art. 22(3) of the Regulation. But allowing a resolution trigger to occur does not necessarily mean that such a trigger will actually be pulled.

2.9 Government Stabilization Measures for CCPs in Resolution Mode

The Regulation contains stringent provisions on the ability of governments to provide financial support to CCPs in resolution mode. The principles are laid down in Recitals (53) and (66) and Art. 27(2) of the Regulation, and the method of support to be applied is set out in Arts 45–47 of the Regulation. The basic premise is that government financial support may only be provided (i) if there is systemic crisis, (ii) as a last resort, (iii) subject to approval under the Union state aid rules, and (iv) if credible arrangements for the recovery of funds are provided for.

The term 'systemic crisis' is not defined in the Regulation.[33] Article 45(3) of the Regulation provides that whether a systemic crisis exists is a matter to be determined

---

[30] This requirement seems to imply that government support to a solvent CCP may not take the form of a direct equity capital injection or a direct government credit facility. It is not quite clear why this restriction appears to be imposed.

[31] Article 22(3)(e) of the Regulation. One may query what the consequences would be if government support is provided to a CCP if and when this is not 'required'. Presumably, this would not constitute a resolution trigger.

[32] See section 7 below for a discussion on resolution triggers.

[33] You would probably recognize one immediately if and when it occurs. An attempt at a description can be found in International Monetary Fund (IMF) e-library paper, 'Managing Systemic Banking Crises', to be found at https://www.elibrary.imf.org (accessed 23 March 2023):

> A systemic crisis emerges when problems in one or more banks are serious enough to have a significant adverse impact on the real economy. This impact is most often felt through the payment system, reductions in credit flows, or the destruction of asset values. A systemic crisis often is characterized by runs of creditors, including depositors, from both solvent and insolvent banks, thus threatening the stability of the entire banking system. The run is fueled by fears that the means of payment will be unobtainable at any price, and in a fractional reserve banking system this leads to a scramble for high-powered money and a withdrawal of external credit lines.

internally within the home Member State of the CCP concerned. But this raises the question of whether a European agency check (e.g. by the European Central Bank (ECB) or the ESRB) should not have been superimposed. However, that must have been politically a bridge too far, given the prevailing sovereign character of such determination. European oversight, if imposed, could only have been 'light', perhaps only on a consultative basis. But the approach taken by the European legislators carries the risk of possible differentiation in government intervention across the Member States: there is no level playing field in this respect. Perhaps this is unavoidable; imposing a check would require developing a set of common standards to determine whether a crisis is systemic, and such common standards might prove to be too rigid to be workable under all possible future crisis circumstances.

The condition under (ii) above ('as a last resort') signifies that government financial support should not be given prior to the exhaustion of resolution tools. However, Art. 45(3) of the Regulation provides some flexibility, in particular allowing support to be given when it is determined that the exhaustion of resolution tools is thought anyhow to be inadequate. The use of the term 'remaining resolution tools' in Art. 45(3) of the Regulation indicates that resolution tools, in any event, should have partly been applied before government intervention may take place. The determination as to the timing of government intervention will again be made on a national level and, again, without involvement of any Union agency.

In so far as state aid restrictions mentioned under (iii) above are concerned, it is noted that the European Commission has yet to determine whether its current state aid policies sufficiently take into account the idiosyncracies of a CCP's business and its functioning in the FMI realm. The consequence of this is that there is, as yet, a certain amount of uncertainty as to how state aid rules will be applied if a CCP succumbs in the context of a (threatening) systemic financial crisis.

The condition under (iv) above that repayment by the CCP of state support should be realistic would, practically speaking, be incapable of being fulfilled were it not for the mitigating provisions of Art. 27(10) of the Regulation, which lists the limited and uncertain resources from which this refunding would have to be sourced. These resources include realization of preferred claims against defaulting CMs as well as proceeds from the sale of assets of the CCP (whether or not via a bridge CCP); these are, of course, all highly uncertain sources of funding, particularly if resolution takes place in a systemic financial crisis scenario. But these uncertainties should not be considered an impediment to meeting this condition.[34]

This description obviously focuses on the banking sector. It is, however, not inconceivable that a systemic crisis occurs predominantly in the realm of financial market infrastructure (FMI). The monitoring and assessment of systemic risks that may occur in Europe is entrusted to the European Systemic Risk Board (ESRB). This institution would seem to be the logical choice for Union involvement in the determination of whether a systemic crisis occurs.

[34] See also Recital (66) of the Regulation, where it is stated that recoupment possibilities must not be considered as 'constituting an obstacle to applying government stabilisation tools'.

In addition to the above-mentioned conditionalities, Art. 27(7) of the Regulation provides that equity, debt instruments, and unsecured debt must be written down and converted into equity 'before or together with' the application of the government stabilization tool.[35] Obviously, write-down and conversion will not free up liquidity, and liquidity is what an ailing CCP most of all needs. But the write-down and conversion will absorb losses and provide a stronger post-resolution capital base for the surviving CCP; whether conversion would be sufficient to reach required prudential levels going forward would, however, be uncertain.[36]

The write-down and conversion of instruments of ownership and debt instruments will be effected by way of a constitutive decision of the NRA, that is, the decision by virtue of which the CCP in question is placed in resolution mode. This means that the government needs to coordinate with the NRA as to the timing of the financial support. It is not clear what the consequences would be if the write-down and conversion is not effected in conjunction with the government stabilization tool; surely, the validity of government's financial support would not be affected?

The methodology of government stabilization measures is given in Arts 46 (the public equity support tool) and 47 (the temporary public ownership tool) of the Regulation. Public equity support entails an equity injection by (an agency of) the home state of the CCP concerned. The temporary public ownership tool, on the other hand, entails the transfer of the existing equity to a nominee of the home state or a state-owned company. Application of each of these two tools is subject to the condition that the equity concerned will be sold to a private purchaser 'as soon as commercial and financial circumstances allow'. In each of these two tools, the government must ensure that the CCP continues to be managed on a commercial and professional basis. Given the complexity of the business, this might be a tall order if the existing senior management would no longer be available for this. The state aid framework will, in addition, ensure that the temporary state capital injection or public ownership will not provide an unfair competitive advantage to the failing CCP concerned and will presumably impose conditionalities as to the temporary nature of the government support concerned and as to the return on investment as compensation for the government intervention concerned.[37] It is noted that the Regulation does not provide for the use of other stabilization tools than those just mentioned; the extent to which variations are permissible remains unclear.

It is noted on the topic of government financial intervention that the Regulation prohibits recovery and resolution plans to assume the availability of extraordinary

---

[35] The way in which this write-down and conversion should be realized is summarily dealt with in Arts 32–34 of the Regulation. Note that Art. 33(7) sub. (a) requires that the issue of equity resulting from debt conversion must take place prior to equity injections by, or on behalf of, the state concerned.

[36] On 16 November 16 2020, the FSB issued a final report providing 'Guidance on Financial Resources to Support CCP Resolution and on the Treatment of CCP Equity in Resolution', https://www.fsb.org/2020/11/guidance-on-financial-resources-to-support-ccp-resolution-and-on-the-treatment-of-ccp-equity-in-resolution(accessed 23 March 2023).

[37] For these possible conditionalities, see Marije Louisse-Read, *Public Funding of Failing Banks in the European Union* (Deventer: Wolters Kluwer, 2020), pp. 91ff.

public financial support, central bank emergency liquidity assistance (ELA) or, more generally, central bank liquidity assistance other than as routinely provided by the national central bank concerned on its standard commercial terms.[38] Clearly, even without these express prohibitions, the inclusion of reliance on state support in these plans would be unacceptably presumptuous.

In this connection, it is noted that according to Art. 44 of the Regulation, the NRA may itself borrow funds 'where necessary to meet temporary liquidity needs in order to ensure the effective application of the resolution tools'. These can be obtained from third-party lenders (including the central bank concerned) but also from prefunded resources available in non-depleted default funds in the CCP under resolution. Presumably, these liquidity funds are to be used to cover costs incurred by the resolution authority itself rather than to supplement shortfalls at the CCP level.

A final comment on this topic is that the Regulation, whilst covering burden sharing between the home Member State of the CCP, the CCP itself, and the CCP's stakeholders,[39] does not contemplate burden sharing between Member States in case government stabilization tools are applied. There are some relatively 'loose' provisions on cooperation between resolution authorities in third countries and on recognition of third-country resolution proceedings; see Arts 76 and following of the Regulation. These provisions, however, form no basis for burden sharing. In the drafting phases of the Regulation, it proved not possible for the Member States to find a generally acceptable basis for burden sharing. This presumably means that in case of a failing CCP which does substantial business clearing transactions for counterparties in other Member States than the home Member State of the CCP, or indeed for counterparties in countries outside the European Union (EU), there is no legal basis to discuss sharing losses in situations where such other Member States or third countries have a substantive stake in keeping the CCP alive and functioning. This is particularly poignant in view of the fact that London-based CCPs London Clearing House (LCH) and ICE Clear Europe enjoy commanding oligopolistic positions in the highly concentrated markets for central clearing.[40] For the sake of completeness, it is noted that a very limited form of burden sharing is achieved through an understanding between the ECB and the Bank of England (BoE) whereby the BoE may use the EUR–GBP swap line to allow UK CCPs to obtain access to EUR-denominated liquidity under certain circumstances.[41]

---

[38] Articles 9(11) and 12(4) of the Regulation. Access to central bank liquidity is the subject of a longstanding debate: CCPs with a banking licence have access to overnight liquidity which non-bank CCPs would not necessarily enjoy. See also Chapter 3 ('Development of the Regulatory Regime for OTC Derivatives Clearing' by Patrick Pearson) in this volume.

[39] Article 27(7) of the Regulation.

[40] See Chapter 16 ('Brexit: Equivalence; Location Policy' by Dermot Turing) in this volume. Interestingly, on 30 June 2022, ICE Clear Europe announced that it would discontinue clearing credit default swaps. See https://www.theice.com/publicdocs/clear_europe/circulars/C22076.pdf (accessed 23 March 2023).

[41] See Chapter 16 ('Brexit: Equivalence; Location Policy' by Dermot Turing) in this volume.

2.10 Brexit Consequences

It is, in a sense, ironic that the Regulation is not applicable if a London-based CCP should fail. As a result of Brexit, CCPs established in the UK (LCH Ltd, ICE Clear Europe Ltd, and London Metal Exchange (LME) Ltd) are subject to the UK CCP resolution regime whilst EU-27 based CMs continue to use their clearing services. At the time of writing this chapter, it is unclear, in the long run, what will be the fate of the current temporary equivalence arrangements. Temporary reprieve is given to London-based clearing of transactions until 2025. Clearing capacity insufficiencies currently prevailing in the EU-27 are the main drivers here.[42] The reprieve appears to be given on the assumption that the UK CCP resolution regime is, and will continue to be, deemed satisfactory in comparison to the regime of the Regulation.[43] The future of access to the London-based CCPs will be the result of an intricate, mostly political rather than legal, regulatory process. This chapter will not further discuss Brexit and equivalence issues as they affect the regime of the Regulation; reference is made to Chapters 3 ('Development of the Regulatory Regime for OTC Derivatives Clearing' by Patrick Pearson) and 16 ('Brexit: Equivalence; Location Policy' by Dermot Turing) in this volume. The long and the short of it is that European and Member State regulators have no say in the process of recovery and resolution of UK-based CCPs.

3 Recovery Planning

Article 9 of the Regulation states that the mandatory recovery plan must be made up by the CCP itself.[44] The drafting and finalization of recovery plans will, however, be a matter of close collaboration between the CCP, its supervisory college, its competent authority, and its NRA. There is also detailed technical involvement of ESMA, which will set technical standards for a number of substantive issues to be addressed in recovery planning.[45] The assessment and approval of resolution plans involves a complex

---

[42] At the same time, relocation to the eurozone will, for London-based CCPs, be fraught with all but insurmountable legal and operational difficulties. See Chapter 16 ('Brexit: Equivalence; Location Policy' by Dermot Turing) in this volume.

[43] An ESMA assessment report of 16 December 2021 states (p. 41):

> Under the current regime for CCP recovery and resolution in the UK, the limited scope of (recovery and) resolution tools available to the BoE in principle seems to reduce the ex-ante possibility of misalignment of interests with non-UK authorities. However, the UK is reviewing its regime. Recent public consultations proposed a framework which seems to be similar to the one adopted in EU in many respects. New resolution tools could add discretionary powers to the BoE and potentially increase the possibility of a misalignment of interests with regards to the financial stability of the Union or one of its Member States. However, the review of the regime is still under discussion.

[44] Section A of the Annex to the Regulation sets out the detailed requirements which a recovery plan must in any event fulfil. These requirements indicate that the recovery planning process will be a major, rather complex, and time-consuming exercise for any CCP and its supervisory authorities.

[45] Articles 9(15) and 10(12) of the Regulation. On 31 January 2022, ESMA 2022 published seven final reports on the EU recovery regime, and these reports have been submitted to the EU Commission to consider. This will eventually lead to implementing Commission delegated regulations, as well as ESMA guidances. See https://

procedural process, which, if no consensus is reached, will be subject to mandatory arbitrage by ESMA.[46] Clearly, the intention of the Union's lawmakers is to ensure that these plans are comprehensive; meeting the elaborate and detailed requirements of Art. 9 and following (and section A of the Annex to the Regulation) entails a complex and time-consuming exercise. Given that there are many 'known unknowns' and 'unknown unknowns' in possible crisis scenarios, there is a distinct risk that these plans will largely prove to be paper exercises. However, in any event, the considerable benefit of these exercises will be that CCPs are forced to identify and analyse the risks to which they are possibly exposed and to map the available remedies should these risks materialize. Weaknesses will thus hopefully be exposed and will then have to be addressed; see section 4.

It is, of course, possible that the recovery planning process will expose flaws in the recoverability of the CCP concerned. In that case, the Regulation foresees an elaborate process whereby the NRA may make recommendations to the competent authority on how to address such flaws. The competent authority may disagree and not follow through on these recommendations, but it will have to justify this to the NRA. If the competent authority agrees, it may solicit the views of the CCP on the subject matter and require the CCP to submit a revised recovery plan, demonstrating how the weaknesses in question are addressed. This revised plan will again be assessed in the same manner in which the original plan was assessed. If, in the end, the perceived weaknesses are not properly addressed, the competent authority may require the CCP to take action in order to achieve certain objectives outlined in Art. 10(10) of the Regulation. These objectives are very broadly phrased, and this means that the competent authority has broad powers to impose far-reaching changes to the structure and the business of the CCP concerned. For instance, the competent authority may require the CCP to reduce its risk profile, to review its strategy and structure, to change its governance, or to make changes to its loss-allocation arrangements in order to enhance the CCP's resilience. It is unclear whether the powers of the competent authority in this context include the ability to require measures to be taken that will affect existing contractual rights of the CCP's counterparties; given that such power is not specifically granted in the Regulation, it has to be assumed that this is beyond the remit of the competent authority,[47] obviously except in so far as such measures are already covered in the contractual arrangements between the CCP and its CMs.[48]

Although the provisions discussed here address recoverability of the CCP, there is ample overlap between these provisions and those relating to resolvability as set out in

www.esma.europa.eu/press-news/esma-news/esma-publishes-final-reports-ccp-recovery-regime (accessed 23 March 2023).

[46] Article 11 of the Regulation.
[47] See also Jens-Hinrich Binder, 'Central Counterparties' Insolvency and Resolution' (n 2), p. 305 ff. Although such powers are not directly available to the NRA, it is to be noted that the NRA does have the power to direct CCPs to include contractual arrangements to that effect in their contracts with CMs.
[48] Such contractual arrangements would include the ability for the CCP to make cash calls, to cover unmatched positions, to organize voluntary auctions, and to terminate ('tear up') contracts.

Art. 15 of the Regulation. The distinction between the concepts of 'recoverable' and 're-solvable' is, in any event, not clear cut.

The risk that a CCP would be subjected to possibly fundamental requirements to address weaknesses as described in section 3 is, of course, remote; one may assume that any possible flaws would already have been addressed by the CCP in consultation with the NRA in the preparatory phase of recovery planning.

4 Resolution Planning

Resolution plans are to be made by the NRA after consultation with the competent authority and in consultation with the resolution college. The requirements that such plans must fulfil are broadly phrased in Art. 12 of the Regulation, requiring such plans to be comprehensive and detailed. The plans must, for instance, specify the circumstances and different scenarios for applying the resolution tools to be used, distinguishing between different causes underlying a CCP's failure.[49] These causes may be a default event, a non-default event, or a combination of both. A default events relates to the circumstance that the default of CMs cause the CCP to fail. A non-default event may be an operational failure (e.g. as a result of an external cyberattack or fraud or of non-performance by a party to whom a CCP has outsourced important functions) or the CCP's own management failure.[50] Also, the plans must take into consideration the impact that implementation thereof would have on 'their' CMs and, to the extent relevant information is available, on the direct and indirect clients of their CMs as well as on any linked FMIs[51] and more generally on the financial markets. This is a tall order.

The resolution college is to develop a framework for resolution plans.[52] On 12 May 2022, ESMA published its 'Final Report Containing Draft Regulatory Technical Standards (RTS) on the Contents of Resolution Plans'.[53] At the time of writing this chapter, these RTS have not yet been adopted in a Commission delegated regulation.

5 Resolvability

According to Art. 15(2) of the Regulation, 'a CCP shall be resolvable where the resolution authority considers it feasible and credible to either liquidate it under normal insolvency proceedings or to resolve it applying the resolution tools and exercising the resolution powers while ensuring the CCP's critical functions', avoiding to the maximum extent possible 'any significant adverse effect on the financial system and the

---

[49] Article 12(7) of the Regulation.

[50] Singh and Turing take the view that such non-default events should be readily managed through the capital buffers that CCPs are obliged to maintain; 'Central Counterparties Resolution' (n 5), p. 6.

[51] It is noted in this connection that interoperability of OTC derivatives clearing is at present not provided for in EMIR; see EMIR (n 10), Art. 1(3).

[52] Article 4(1) of the Regulation.

[53] ESMA91-372-2068.

potential for undue disadvantage to affected stakeholders'. The resolvability assessment is to be made by the NRA in coordination with the resolution college, and this will be done simultaneously with the drawing up and finalization of the resolution plan. If the assessment bears out that there are 'material impediments' to resolvability, Art. 16 of the Regulation provides for an elaborate procedure for the removal of such impediments. First, the CCP will be given the opportunity to propose measures to address or to remove such impediments. If such proposal is deemed by the NRA, in coordination with the resolution college, to be inadequate, the NRA is to devise alternative measures which will then be jointly decided upon by it and the resolution college. Where appropriate in view of the broader impact such measures may have, the macro-financial authorities of the Member State concerned will need to be consulted.

What the above-mentioned alternative measures could amount to is not clarified in the Regulation. Here again, the issue arises whether the powers of the resolution college encompass measures that intervene in existing contractual relationships between CCPs and CMs; again, it is submitted that in the absence of express authorization by virtue of the Regulation, such powers should not be deemed given.

All in all, a reasonably fair balance seems to have been struck in which a CCP confronted with resolvability issues is given ample opportunity to address the concerns that the NRA and/or the resolution college may have.

6 Early Intervention

Article 18 of the Regulation enables a competent authority to take certain intervention measures in situations where a CCP is (or threatens to be) no longer in compliance with applicable capital and prudential requirements[54] or poses a risk to the financial stability in the Union or a particular Member State. The competent authority may also do this if it determines that there are other signs of an emerging crisis affecting the ability of a CCP to continue its clearing services. The purpose of early intervention is to allow competent authorities to try and take remedial action to prevent a CCP from deteriorating further into a situation where resolution is inevitable.

ESMA has now issued guidelines to promote the consistent use of the said early-intervention triggers by competent authorities in the Member States.[55] If a competent authority decides to use its early-intervention powers, it must notify ESMA and the NRA and consult the supervisory college. There is no requirement for consultation of the NRA, and given that early intervention measures may affect the application of resolution tools, this seems odd. The resolution college is not in the picture in this process,

---

[54] The prudential requirements imposed on CCPs are set out in EMIR (n 10), Arts 40–50. See Chapter 8 ('OTC Derivatives Clearing Documentation' by Emma Dwyer and Emma Lancelott) in this volume; Zebregs and de Serière, 'Derivatives Central Counterparties' (n 12), p. 227.

[55] On 31 January 2022, ESMA published its Final Report ('Guidelines on the Consistent Application of the Triggers for the Use of Early Intervention Measures (Article 18(8) of the CCPRRR'); see https://www.esma.eur opa.eu/sites/default/files/library/esma91-372-1700_final_guidelines_on_eim_article_188.pdf (accessed 23 March 2023).

and one may query, given the potentially broad scope of early intervention, whether this would not have been appropriate; early intervention may, however, have to be initiated at very short notice, and consultation of the resolution college may then well be too time-consuming.

The authority of the competent authority to take early intervention measures is wide-ranging, and exercise of that authority may well substantially interfere with the business of the CCP concerned.[56] Removal of board members[57] or members of senior management unfit to perform their duties may be ordained by the competent authority. Changes to the business strategy may be required, as may changes to the legal or operational structures of the CCP. The competent authority may also impose an obligation to replenish the CCP's financial resources. The implementation of recovery measures may also be required but only if this is in the public interest and necessary to preserve financial stability, the continuity of critical functions, and/or to maintain or restore the financial resilience of the CCP.

Where Art. 18(1)(d) of the Regulation allows the competent authority to require one or more board members or senior management to be removed if they are unfit, Art. 19 provides that the competent authority may remove all or part of the board of management and senior management in case 'there is a significant deterioration in the financial situation of a CCP or the CCP infringes its legal requirements and other measures taken in accordance with Article 18 are not sufficient to reverse this situation'. While there is a subtle (somewhat obscure) difference in the 'trigger' for this removal power as compared with the triggers set out in Art. 18(1) of the Regulation, the main difference is that removals under Art. 19 may be effected regardless of whether the persons concerned are fit or not. Replacements are subject to the approval of the competent authority, which may also appoint temporary administrators if it considers any such replacement insufficient.

Finally on early intervention, Art. 20 of the Regulation provides that if a CCP in recovery caused by a non-default event[58] has applied measures whereby 'gains' that are due to the CM are not being paid to such CMs (in other words, VMGH was applied) and, as a result, the CCP concerned does not enter into resolution, compensation should be paid by the CCP to such CMs for losses thus suffered beyond the losses that were contractually committed to by the CMs concerned. Compensation could be in the form of cash, if available, or in the form of debt instruments. ESMA has developed draft technical standards for this purpose (see section 2.2 above). If these losses suffered by the CMs were passed on to their clients, compensation received for such losses should also be passed on to these clients. This is a rare instance where the Regulation concerns itself with the position of CMs' clients.

---

[56] Article 18(1) of the Regulation lists the measures that may be taken.
[57] Article 2(23) of the Regulation clarifies that the term 'board' refers to both the board of managing directors and the supervisory board.
[58] For the meaning of a non-default event, see section 4 *in fine* of this chapter.

7 Resolution

A CCP will be subjected to resolution when it is failing or likely to fail (FOLTF) (see Art. 22(1) of the Regulation). This will be the case if so determined by the competent authority after consulting the NRA or by the NRA after consulting the competent authority (in the latter case, provided that the NRA has the necessary tools to recognize a FOLTF situation). As stated earlier, the NRA and the competent authority will, in many cases, reside under the same roof, that is, that of the national central bank of the CCP's home Member State.[59] Conditions are that these authorities come to the conclusion that (i) there is no reasonable prospect that any alternative private measures, including the CCP's recovery plan or other contractual arrangements, or supervisory action, including early intervention measures taken, would prevent the failure of the CCP in question within a reasonable time frame and (ii) that resolution action is necessary in the public interest (see below). In practice, there is bound to be intensive prior consultation with the CCP's management. A conflict situation could possibly arise where a competent authority and the NRA express to have no faith in further recovery action whilst the management of the CCP concerned still believes that its failure can be averted by such action. In such a case, the views of the said authorities will, of course, prevail, subject always to remedies as set out in section 11 below.

The condition under (i) effectively means that all measures that could possibly have been taken in respect of a failing CCP on a voluntary basis, or as imposed by the competent authority in the recovery phase, have not been capable of preventing the CCP's eventual failure. It assumes that the entire default waterfall has been used and all contractual rights have been exhausted by the CCP, but to insufficient avail, or that there is no prospect that such measures and exercise of contractual rights would prevent the failure of the CCP.

Resolution of a CCP must be in the public interest, as must be determined by either the competent authority or the NRA (each after consulting the other).[60] The public interest criterion reads as follows: 'if it is necessary for and is proportionate to the achievement of the resolution objectives, and winding up of the institution under normal insolvency proceedings would not meet those resolution objectives to the same extent'. See BRRD, Art. 22(1)(c), mirrored on Art. 32(5). As stated above, if it is determined that there is no public interest, normal insolvency proceedings would have to be followed.[61] This is perhaps conceivable in the case of a relatively small, locally operating

---

[59] Although under one roof, these authorities should operate independently of one another and may have differences of opinion, for instance on whether resolution triggers have occurred. In such cases, internal central bank rules would provide for an escalation mechanism.

[60] The resolution college is not involved in this process.

[61] See Art. 75 of the Regulation: normal insolvency proceedings must be commenced by the NRA or with its consent by 'the authorities responsible for normal insolvency proceedings'. According to this provision, normal insolvency proceedings cannot be initiated by creditors of the CCP concerned.

CCP but rather difficult to imagine in the case of larger, internationally operative CCPs such as Eurex in Germany.[62]

The possible circumstances to be considered in determining whether or not a CCP can be considered to be FOLTF are set out in Art. 22(3) of the Regulation. Some of these circumstances are objectively factual, such as the need for extraordinary public support[63] (which would most likely be borne out by a CCP's request for support or by an urgent government offer of support that cannot, practically speaking, be refused) or the infringement of its authorization requirements to such an extent that this would justify licence withdrawal.[64] Others are more subjective circumstances (requiring authorities to exercise judgement), for example, in which a CCP is *likely* unable to provide a critical function, is *likely* unable to restore its viability, or is *likely* unable to pay its debts and other liabilities as they fall due.

The Regulation requires ESMA to develop guidelines to promote the convergence of supervisory and resolution practices regarding the determination of FOLTF. The Regulation states, in Art. 22(6) *in fine*, that these guidelines are to take into account the corresponding guidelines of the European Banking Agency (EBA) applicable to banks as contemplated by BRRD, Art. 36(2).[65] On 12 May 2022, ESMA published its 'Final Report Containing Detailed Guidelines on the Application of the Circumstances under Which a CCP is Deemed to Be Failing or Likely to Fail'.[66] These Guidelines are not, strictly speaking, binding on the competent authorities and the NRAs, but non-compliance will have to be reported to ESMA, stating the reasons for non-compliance.

The general resolution principles are basically set out in Art. 23 of the Regulation. To a large extent, these mirror the corresponding provisions of BRRD, Art. 34. As in the BRRD, shareholders and creditors are, in principle, to first bear the losses in the inverse sequence of the 'normal' insolvency ladder. As stated earlier, this may serve to absorb losses and to rebuild the failing CCP's post-resolution balance sheet and regulatory capital, but this does not in any way alleviate the immediate liquidity problems a failing CCP is likely to suffer.

The general resolution principles are subject to the NCWO principle. Shareholders, CMs, and creditors should in the end be no worse off than they would have been if normal insolvency proceedings were commenced at the time the resolution decision is taken by the competent authority. Article 60 of the Regulation faithfully follows the text of BRRD, Art. 34(1).[67] However, in addition, it provides that the comparison of the

---

[62] Singh and Turing make the argument that liquidation of a CCP should be a realistic option: 'Central Counterparties Resolution' (n 5), pp. 15, 16.

[63] Article 22(4) of the Regulation, modelled after BRRD (n 3), Art. 32(4)(d), states that a certain form of public support to a solvent CCP would be permissible, if necessary, 'to remedy a serious disturbance in the economy of a Member State and preserve financial stability'; see section 2.6 above. As submitted there, it appears more likely than not that substantive government support will be required in such a scenario.

[64] These authorization requirements are EMIR (n 10) licence requirements and ongoing prudential requirements; see Chapter 7 ('What Kind of Thing Is a Central Counterparty? The Role of Clearing Houses as a Source of Public Controversy' by Rebecca Lewis and David Murphy) in this volume.

[65] EBA/GL/2015/07 dated 6 August 2015.

[66] ESMA91-372-2070.

[67] See, inter alia, Christos Gortsos, 'Considerations on the Application of the NCWO Principle under the SRM Regulation', EBI Working Paper Series 2021—No. 88.

losses these stakeholders would have incurred under normal insolvency proceedings should be made 'following the full application of the applicable contractual obligations and other arrangements in its operating rules'. This addition to the NCWO principle appears to be superfluous since normal insolvency proceedings would anyhow entail that the bankruptcy trustee will, to the extent practically possible, exercise any and all contractual and regulatory rights the CCP might have. As is the case under the BRRD, the NCWO principle is to be applied on the basis of a separate valuation of the assets and liabilities of a CCP. On 12 May 2022, ESMA issued draft RTS specifying the methodology for this valuation.[68]

It goes without saying that the application of the NCWO principle is already fiendishly complicated enough with regard to banks but perhaps even more so in the case of CCPs. One only has to imagine how a bankruptcy trustee would struggle over time to realize the assets of a CCP (the value of which might widely fluctuate) and to discharge its liabilities with the proceeds thereof. The porting or unwinding of CM positions (including the foreclosure and unwinding of collateral positions not only of defaulting CMs but also of non-defaulting CMs) is, under more normal circumstances, a complex task, but in an insolvency context (likely to occur also in a broader systemic crisis environment), this becomes even more daunting. Continuity of critical functions of a failing CCP will normally require swift, confident, and expertly undertaken action, not something a bankruptcy trustee would generally be well equipped to undertake.[69] This means that, in any event, the outcome of insolvency proceedings is extremely difficult to predict.

To arrive at a realistic and fair NCWO is a extraordinarily difficult (if not altogether impossible) task; if ever a CCP would fail and be subject to resolution under the Regulation, this circumstance is unfortunately bound to trigger extensive litigation.[70]

8 Resolution Tools

Article 27(1) of the Regulation mentions four resolution tools: (i) the position and loss-allocation tools, (ii) the write-down and conversion tool, (iii) the sale-of-business tool, and finally (iv) the bridge CCP tool. The tools under (ii) through (iv) are comparable to the corresponding tools under the BRRD,[71] but the position and loss-allocation tools are 'new', specific to the resolution of CCPs. The various tools will briefly be dealt with below.

---

[68] ESMA Final Report of 12 May 2022, reference: ESMA91-372-2066, to be found on the ESMA website: https://www.esma.europa.eu/document/final-report-draft-rts-valuation-and-independent-valuer.

[69] A legal requirement for bankruptcy trustees in these circumstances to obtain the operational assistance of an industry expert would certainly help and is hereby recommended. (See, for instance, Giro Transfer Act, Art. 49h, *Wet giraal effectenverkeer*.)

[70] The FSB's 'Guidance on Central Counterparty Resolution and Resolution Planning' (1 February 2017) states, on p. 11: 'The counterfactual underlying the NCWO safeguard should be clear and transparent for both default and non-default loss scenarios.' Clarity on NCWO estimates and calculations is perhaps even more elusive for CCP resolution, as it is already proving to be for bank resolution.

[71] BRRD (n 3), Arts 38–39, 40–41, 59–61,

8.1 The Position and Loss-Allocation Tools

The position tool and loss-allocation tool are dealt with in Arts 29 and 30 of the Regulation, respectively. As Binder has rightly pointed out,[72] these tools are actually already available also in the recovery phase. Moreover, in any event, the Regulation requires these tools to be incorporated into the contractual arrangements between the CCP and its CMs.[73] Accordingly, it becomes somewhat unclear where the demarcation line between recovery and resolution lies. As, indeed, is also the case in the recovery phase, as commented on earlier, these tools, particularly in a systemic risk scenario, would be capable of significantly affecting the financial position of non-defaulting CMs, their clients, and third parties.[74] Thus, application of these tools may well have an undesirable (and probably unintended) procyclical effect in the context of a systemic crisis.[75] For this reason, Art. 21(1)(c) of the Regulation requires resolution authorities to adhere to the resolution objective that significant adverse effects on the financial system in the Union or in one or more Member States are to be avoided.[76] The NRA will need to find a fine balance between this objective and the objective to ensure the continuity of critical functions. Article 21(1) of the Regulation states that these resolution objectives are 'of equal significance' and the resolution authority is to 'balance them as appropriate to the nature and circumstances of each case'. This is an unavoidably formidable task. Although this contagion risk (that might conceivably lead to cascading CM defaults) is thus addressed in the Regulation, it is by no means eliminated.

The position tool comprises the right of the NRA to terminate contracts with defaulting CMs, to terminate contracts of the affected clearing service or asset class, or to terminate other contracts of the failing CCP.[77] Most likely, these termination rights are already catered for in the contractual termination provisions a CCP will have stipulated, but the NRA will arguably not be bound by limitations or timing requirements provided for in contracts between the failing CCP and 'its' CMs. Termination of contracts must always be preceded by a valuation thereof[78] and updating of the account

---

[72] Binder, 'Central Counterparties' Insolvency and Resolution' (n 2), p. 315.

[73] To the extent use of these tools is embedded in contractual arrangements, the NRA may disregard such arrangements if they form an impediment to the use of these tools. See, among others, Randy Priem, 'CCP Recovery and Resolution: Preventing a Financial Catastrophy' (2018) 26(3) Journal of Financial Regulation and Compliance 359 (Priem, 'CCP Recovery and Resolution'). These tools are obviously also available to the NRA if they are not, or only partially, included in contractual arrangements.

[74] See, as an example, the powers given to the NRA in Art. 29(5) of the Regulation

[75] For instance, the June 2021 'Report of the Task Force on Financial Stability', instituted by the Brookings Institution and the University of Chicago Booth School of Business, states (p. 95) that such actions 'create the potential for a highly unpredictable, unexpected and uncapped impact on both clearing members and end users': https://www.brookings.edu/wp-content/uploads/2021/06/financial-stability_report.pdf (accessed 23 March 2023). The views and recommendations of the task force are particular to the US regulatory climate for CCPs but nevertheless have relevance in the European context. See also Angela Armakolla and Jean-Paul Laurent, 'CCP Resilience and Clearing Membership' (December 2015), a research paper to be found on the Researchgate website: https://www.researchgate.net/search/publication?q=CCP+Resilience+and+Clearing+Membership.

[76] See also Art. 27(4) of the Regulation.

[77] Discontinuation of the CCP's clearing of the affected asset class or the termination of other contracts could presumably also be carried through with respect to positions of non-defaulting CMs.

[78] On 12 May 2022, ESMA issued its 'Final Report Containing Guidelines for the Methodology to Value Each Contract Prior to Termination'. The Final Report is to be found on the ESMA website: https://www.esma.europa.

balances of each CM. This exercise provides the basis for the calculation of the amounts payable by the CM to the failing CCP or vice versa. In case resolution occurs in the context of a wider financial crisis where collateral values may wildly gyrate, the timing of these valuations and calculations would, of course, be critical. Termination (also referred to as 'tearing up') of contracts, part of the position tool, is potentially disruptive to financial markets. CMs' positions may become unhedged.[79]

The loss-allocation tool is dealt with in Arts 30 (VMGH) and 31 (resolution cash calls). VMGH may briefly be explained as follows.[80] Due to market fluctuations, contracts cleared by a CCP may, from day to day, generate losses or gains. VMGH entails that while losses will continue to be collected by the CCP from the 'losing' counterparty, the (corresponding) gains are not (or only in a reduced amount) paid out by the CCP to the 'winning' counterparty. This generates cash that the CCP can apply to stem losses. VMGH may be applied across the board with regard to both positions of defaulting CMs and of non-defaulting CMs. The VMGH tool had traditionally already been included in most CCP's rule books, and Art. 30 builds on this pre-existing practice. There are downsides to using the VMGH tool. One possibly negative aspect[81] concerns its potentially procyclical effects (particularly if the time frame within which this tool may be used is open ended and if there are no caps). Another possible negative aspect is that the VMGH tool may encourage moral hazard at the level of the CCP: since the tool creates funds to stem losses, a CCP might be discouraged from timely addressing loss-making situations because of the availability of this funding source. However, the prevailing positive argument is that the tool is effective and efficient as it distributes losses, and therefore risk, widely and creates the right incentives for CMs to counter their potential risk exposure.[82] Article 30 of the Regulation states that applied haircut amounts are not refundable. Suggestions made to the FSB by the CM representatives that non-defaulting CMs should be given a post-resolution refund claim in case the failing CCP survives and becomes solvent again[83] was not convincing for the EU legislators. There is a level of unfairness in this approach, both from the CMs' and their clients' point of view.

Cash calls may be made of non-defaulting CMs to a maximum amount of twice the amount of the contribution of the CM concerned to the default fund of the failing

---

eu/sites/default/files/library/esma91-372-2067_final_report_draft_guidelines_on_valuation_prior_to_terminat ion.pdf. The Guidelines are given to NRAs on a 'comply-or-explain' basis.

[79] Priem, 'CCP Recovery and Resolution' (n 73), p. 360; see also CPMI–IOSCO, 'Recovery of Financial Market Infrastructures' (October 2014), https://www.iosco.org/library/pubdocs/pdf/IOSCOPD455.pdf (accessed 23 March 2023).

[80] See also Singh and Turing, 'Central Counterparties Resolution' (n 5), p. 14.

[81] See also Chapter 6 ('OTC Derivatives Clearing and Collateral Management' by Manmohan Singh) in this volume. It is noted that initial margin gains haircuts are not permissible under the Regulation. The question of how to deal with excess margin that has to be posted with the CCP under EMIR (n 10), Art. 39(6) is not addressed in the Regulation. This is probably a theoretical issue.

[82] See, inter alia, FSB, 'Essential Aspects of CCP Resolution Planning—Overview of Responses to the Discussion Note' (1 February 2017), p. 3 (FSB, 'Essential Aspects of CCP Resolution Planning'). See also Singh and Turing, 'Central Counterparties Resolution' (n 5), p. 17.

[83] See, inter alia, FSB, 'Essential Aspects of CCP Resolution Planning' (n 82), p. 3. See also Singh and Turing, 'Central Counterparties Resolution' (n 5), p. 17.

CCP.[84] Further requirements to be observed are set out in Art. 31 of the Regulation. Calls may be made multiple times (subject to the overall maximum), regardless whether contractual obligations of non-defaulting CMs have been exhausted. CCPs are required to provide for these cash calls to be included in their rule books. As with other resolution tools, cash calls may subject CMs to liquidity squeezes in times where the availability of liquidity may be scarce. For this reason, Art. 31(1) provides that cash calls over and above default fund contributions may only be made 'after assessing the impact of this tool on non-defaulting clearing members and the financial stability of Member States'. If a CM does not comply with a cash call, it may be put in default, meaning that its initial margin and default fund contributions may be used by the NRA as set out in EMIR, Art. 45 (default waterfall) to address the deficit.

8.2 The Write-Down and Conversion Tool

This tool is very much based on, and largely equivalent to, the corresponding tool for banks in resolution. The various practical difficulties in implementing this tool in the banking sector are only now beginning to emerge in Member States as resolution authorities in conjunction with the SRB and the banks concerned try to nail down the details and develop procedures in so-called 'playbooks', which would describe, step by step, the procedures that culminate in the write-down of equity and the debt-to-equity conversion. The experience vis-à-vis banks in resolution is bound to be a rather useful inspiration and guidance for the process that will need to be developed for CCPs in resolution. A handicap may well be that, in the case of CCPs, there is no SRB which, from a centralized platform, could smooth out (and perhaps to an extent harmonize) the different approaches that NRAs may wish to follow. The provisions of Arts 32–35 of the Regulation are broadly phrased and rather rule-based, and they will therefore grant a measure of flexibility to national authorities. These provisions do not contemplate implementing rules or technical standards by way of Commission delegated regulations (CDRs), but ESMA may be expected to provide further guidance.

The write-down and conversion serves to absorb losses, recapitalize the failing CCP (or a bridge CCP) to the required regulatory levels (if possible), or support the application of the sale-of-business tool (see below). The tool is to be applied based on a valuation to be conducted after the failing CCP has been placed in resolution. This is a 'second' valuation, to be carried out separately from the 'first' valuation, that is a prerequisite to any resolution action to be undertaken by the NRA, but the principles to be applied in these valuations are the same.[85] The valuation is to form the basis for the calculation of the extent of the required write-off of equity-and-debt instruments, and of the conversion factor to be applied in case of conversion of debt instruments. The tool

---

[84] See Chapter 11 ('Default Management' by David Horner) in this volume for a description of the default fund and its replenishment.
[85] Article 24 of the Regulation.

is to ensure full write-down of the equity (assuming the amounts of the losses incurred require this) and write-down combined, where necessary, with conversion of debt in accordance with the insolvency 'ladder' applicable in the home Member State of the failing CCP.

The tool will be applied differently, depending on the net asset value of the CCP as at the time when placed in resolution. If the CCP is deemed to have negative net asset value, the equity will need to be written down and cancelled or passed on to creditors whose debt claims have been converted. In case the CCP retains net positive asset value, the equity will need to be either written down or severely diluted by the conversion of debt. The conversion of liabilities into debt will ensure that the CCP will be capitalized post resolution (but whether that capitalization is sufficient to meet prudential capitalization rules is then uncertain) and the balance sheet will obviously be strengthened. The Regulation is principle- rather than rule-based in so far as write-down and conversion is concerned and does not contemplate that CDRs will give further rules as to how this is to be accomplished.[86] This should not prevent ESMA from providing useful clarifications and guidances, which may well eventually bear out the need for more detailed EU legislation. Clearly, the rules and guidances published with respect to bail-in under the BRRD will provide some useful precedents and inspiration.

Doubts have been expressed in literature on the efficacy of this tool. It has correctly been pointed out that discussions on the 'ideal' funding model for CCPs (which will have a profound effect on the waterfall) are still ongoing (focusing, inter alia, on the level of bail-inable debt a CCP should have on its books) and that conversion resulting in a change of ownership of the failing CCP may adversely affect the CCP's post-resolution operations.[87] In any event, given the different historical backgrounds of the larger CCPs and, for that reason, their varying funding structures, for Union law to impose an 'ideal' funding model on CCPs would seem to be impossible to achieve.

The write-down and conversion tool must be accompanied by a business reorganization plan, to be prepared and submitted by the failing CCP to the NRA within a period of a month (extendable to two months). The business reorganization plan is subject to review by the competent authority and the resolution college.

8.3 The Sale-of-Business Tool

This tool is provided for in Arts 40–41 of the Regulation. The sale can comprise the equity of a failing CCP or all or certain of its assets and liabilities. A purchaser can be a white-knight CCP or a third party, including possibly a CM. In the latter case,

---

[86] But since Recital (81) and Art. 12(9) contemplate that ESMA will develop technical standards for the contents of resolution plans, ESMA will be able to ensure that resolution plans clarify the process to be followed. On 12 May 2022, ESMA issued its Final Report, containing 'RTS on the Content of CCP Resolution Plans', reference: ESMSA91-372-2068, which can be found on the ESMA website: https://www.esma.europa.eu/sites/default/files/library/esma91-372-2068_final_report_draft_rts_on_the_content_of_resolution_plans.pdf. These draft RTS concerned have, at the time of writing this chapter, not yet been formalized in a CDR.

[87] See, among others, Binder, 'Central Counterparties Insolvency and Resolution' (n 2), p. 316.

the third party will have to demonstrate that it has sufficient expertise to manage the transferred business. The Regulation generously deals with company law and regulatory requirements, thus easing the ability of interested parties to realize a purchase. But state aid rules, if applicable, need to be complied with. The same, in principle, applies to the need to obtain a declaration of no objections (DNO) if a purchaser acquires a 'qualifying holding',[88] although a purchase may go ahead if a DNO is not obtained in a timely manner. The NRA employing this tool must aim to maximize, as far as possible, the purchase price. It is, however, not required to organize an auction; purchasers may be approached individually.[89] The proceeds of a sale would basically be applied towards the losses occurred according to the waterfall, in inverse order.[90]

The sale-of-business tool is largely comparable to that for banks under the BRRD. But the practicalities of the use of this tool in the case of failing CCPs are rather different. The complexities of a CCP's business are such that a sale of that business to a third party not being a CCP remains a largely theoretical possibility. A sale of that business to another CCP is also unlikely. Other than maybe in the case of banks, there are not that many candidates that might conceivably be interested (a CCP's business is generally monopolistic or oligopolistic in nature). The organizational, governance, and risk models and the policies of CCPs vary greatly. Accordingly, it would probably be a rather complex and time-consuming exercise to effectively absorb the business of a failing CCP in to another, healthy CCP, and that complexity might cause unwanted operational weaknesses. Porting contractual positions together with collateral posted in accordance with EMIR requirements is already in itself a complicated process, and complications will only be further exacerbated in case of a failing CCP, particularly if the cause of failure consists of the default of large CMs. The underlying reasons for the failure of the CCP may also be a strong disincentive for a purchaser: given all the safeguards that EMIR imposes on CCPs, something must have gone dramatically wrong. The circumstance of a systemic crisis would only exacerbate the difficulties touched upon above, making the use of the tool generally not a very realistic option. One final comment: CCPs will often be part of a larger financial concern, and this means that the NRA, when using the sale-of-the business tool, will have to examine (and perhaps deal with) the possible consequences thereof for the larger concern from which the clearing business is extracted.[91]

8.4 The Bridge CCP Tool

The equity or the whole or part of the assets and liabilities of a failing CCP may be transferred to a bridge CCP, which is specifically set up for that purpose and which is

---

[88] See EMIR (n 10), Arts 30 and 31.

[89] Article 41(2) of the Regulation.

[90] Article 41(4) of the Regulation.

[91] If there is proper ringfencing of the CCP within the group, this should not be much of an issue. In practice, however, there may well be significant inter-dependencies.

government-owned and controlled by the NRA. Regulatory requirements that would otherwise burden a bridge CCP are largely lifted, as the bridge CCP is deemed to be the continuation of the failing CCP.[92]

The tool is a variation on the sale-of-business tool and shares many of that tool's complexities. In case of a CCP failure (especially in case of a systemic risk environment), its use may have the significant advantage of buying time, hopefully in order to be able to divest the assets concerned later when sailing in calmer waters. But the requirement of the NRA maintaining control and ensuring continuity of critical functions does appear to put a heavy organizational burden on that authority. Transfer of the equity ownership to a government-owned bridge CCP may have the advantage that the CCP (hopefully retaining the essential operational clearing expertise[93]) could remain intact as an operational unit and could regain the confidence of its CMs and underlying clients, but the NRA must be able to remedy any existing management and/ or operational deficiencies, to cause the CCP to rematch its books, and to re-establish a suitable risk management framework—by no means an easy task. The bridge tool does not in itself deal with the causes of the CCP's failure (likely to be attributable to failing risk management), and this means that the deficiencies concerned will also move over to the bridge CCP and will have to be tackled by the latter. In addition, it is hard to imagine that the bridge CCP would not, at some point in time, require additional government liquidity funding (tax payer money!) to keep its critical functions going at a commercially viable level.

9 Powers of the Resolution Authority

By virtue of Arts 48 and 49 of the Regulation, the NRA is given broadly worded (and therefore sweeping) powers, to be exercised individually or in combination. Effectively, these powers allow the NRA to take measures without being bound by otherwise applicable regulatory, corporate law, or contractual constraints. These powers include the following. For instance, the terms of debt instruments issued by the CCP and other liabilities of the CCP may be unilaterally amended (as regards maturities, interest rates, interest payment dates and the imposition of grace periods). Debt instruments issued by the CCP may, moreover, be written down or cancelled. The board and senior management may be removed or replaced. Financial contracts may be closed out and terminated. Noticeably, Arts 48 and 49 contain no provisions on compensation to alleviate losses to contractual counterparties of the CCP in resolution as a result of the exercise of these powers.

In so far as the resolution objectives are concerned, it is noted that some of these are in contradiction with the application of certain resolution tools. For example, the objective of timely settlement of the CCP's obligations to CMs and their clients is hard to

---

[92] Article 42 of the Regulation.
[93] Otherwise, not easily to be found …

align with the powers to close out and terminate contracts or to apply VMGH. It seems unlikely, however, given the explicit powers to apply these tools, that such contradiction would have a limiting effect or could serve as a basis for a claim asserting unauthorized use of such tools. As for the general principles, use of the resolution tools in accordance with at least two of these principles are bound to give NRAs headaches. The first is the principle of NCWO. This is discussed above in the final paragraphs of section 7. The second is the principle that where a failing CCP is part of a group (which many CCPs, in any event, are), the impact of resolution tools 'on other group entities, in particular where such group comprises other FMIs, and on the group as a whole' must be taken into account. How far could the application of this principle limit the application of resolution tools? Would it be fair for an NRA to determine that ensuring the continuation of the clearing functions of a CCP is so crucial to preserve financial stability in the Member State concerned that any possible negative effects on the group or other group entities should be deemed acceptable or inevitable? Conversely, would it be possible for a CCP or any of its stakeholders to contend that non-alignment with these principles could result in the nullity of actions undertaken by the NRA and/or constitute grounds for a damages claim? See also section 2 above, where the complexities of CCPs being part of a group are further discussed.

In addition to the powers granted by virtue of Arts 48 and 49 of the Regulation, Arts 50–59 of the Regulation contain further provisions granting specific powers to the NRA. Under Art. 50, the NRA may appoint one or more special managers replacing existing management.[94] The special managers will have all powers of the management board, the supervisory board, and shareholders, subject always to the control of the NRA. These provisions are basically the same as those for the special management of banks in resolution set out in BRRD, Art. 35. Pursuant to Art. 51 of the Regulation, the NRAs may requisition services and facilities from companies belonging to the same group as the failing CCP. These services and facilities are to be provided on the same commercial terms as applied pre-resolution and otherwise on 'reasonable' commercial terms. These requisition powers are obviously of great practical importance for the continuity of the clearing services.

Article 52 contains provisions that ensure that use of resolution tools, in particular in relation to transfers of instruments of ownership, assets, and liabilities by the NRA of the CCP's home Member State, will be effective in other Member States. Affected parties, such as shareholders and creditors, cannot challenge such transfers under the laws of such other Member States. If they wish to challenge the application of resolution tools by the NRA of the home Member State,[95] they can only do so under the laws of that home Member State.

---

[94] The removal or displacement of management may already take place in the recovery phase, see Arts 18(1)(d) and 19 of the Regulation. The parallel adds to the blurring of the distinction between recovery and resolution, although the 'triggers' for these measures are different.
[95] Resulting in a reduction of amounts payable, a conversion of debt, or restructuring of the failing CCP; see Art. 52(4).

Article 53 of the Regulation deals with the situation where the laws of a third country are involved. In such a case, Art. 53(1)(a) optimistically provides that the failing CCP and the transferee of instruments of ownership or assets and liabilities will 'take all necessary steps to ensure that the action becomes effective'. More importantly, para. (2) of that Article provides that CCPs must ensure that contracts with CMs and holders of instruments of ownership and debt instruments located in or governed by the laws of a third country must be made to contain a clause by which the CCP's counterparties agree to be bound by actions taken by the NRA with respect thereto. The NRA may also require a CCP to include such a clause in contracts with holders of other liabilities located in or governed by a third-country law. The NRA may require the submission of legal opinions confirming the efficacy of these provisions. Article 53 is inspired by BRRD, Art. 55 (but it does not reflect the elaborate changes to that clause effected by BRRD II[96]).

The NRA is given certain suspension rights in Arts 55–57 of the Regulation. In Art. 55, the NRA is given the right to suspend the performance of payment or delivery obligations of both the CCP and its counterparties. This breathing space is given for a period of one day, ending at midnight (in the home Member State of the resolution authority) on the day following the day of notification of the resolution in accordance with Art. 72 of the Regulation. During that same short period, the right of secured creditors[97] of the CCP to enforce their security rights may be suspended under Art. 56. Termination rights that the CCP's counterparties may have under Art. 57 may also be suspended for the duration of that same short period, provided that the CCP's obligations for payment, delivery, and collateral obligations continue to be performed. Article 57(3), however, permits termination of contracts that are stated in the resolution notice not to be subjected to the resolution tools comprising write-down, conversion, or allocation of positions or losses.

It is noted that, according to Art. 54 of the Regulation (inspired by the provisions of BRRD, Art. 68, which are, by necessity, more elaborate), default acceleration rights of creditors of the failing CCP are restricted. Recovery measures and the application of resolution tools 'or any event directly linked to the application of that action' may not be considered insolvency proceedings,[98] an enforcement event, or event of default, provided that the substantive obligations under the contracts concerned continue to be performed by the CCP. If the excluded acceleration events coincide with non-excluded acceleration events, the latter may be invoked by the CCP's counterparty; in actual practice, the distinction may not always be clear cut. Interestingly, the Regulation has

---

[96] Directive (EU) No. 2019/879 of the European Parliament and of the Council of 20 May 2019 amending Directive 2014/59/EU as regards the loss-absorbing and recapitalization capacity of credit institutions and investment firms and Directive 98/26/EC, OJ L150 (7 June 2019), pp. 296–344.

[97] But this does not apply to (operators of) clearing and settlement systems under the Finality Directive (Directive 98/26/EC of the European Parliament and of the Council of 19 May 1998 on settlement finality in payment and securities settlement systems, OJ L166 (11 June 1998), pp. 45–50).

[98] As this term is defined in the Finality Directive, the Collateral Directive, and the Capital Requirements Regulation (CRR, Regulation (EU) No 575/2013 of the European Parliament and of the Council of 26 June 2013 on prudential requirements for credit institutions and investment firms and amending Regulation (EU) No 648/2012, OJ L176 (27 June 2013), pp. 1–337, as subsequently amended).

not taken over the BRRD provision (Art. 68(6)) confirming that these provisions are 'overriding mandatory provisions' under the 'Rome I' Regulation.[99]

Obviously, the exercise of powers by the NRA is subject to adherence to the resolution objectives (Art. 21 of the Regulation) and the general principles regarding resolution (Art. 23 of the Regulation). In addition, generally accepted general principles of Union law (among which the most important will be the principle of proportionality, the principle of legal certainty, and the protection of legitimate expectations) would apply.[100] Of course, the correct application of these principles would, in the future, where a CCP fails, be judged in the context of liability claims against the NRA by parties suffering damage from imposition of the resolution regime; the current exposure of the SRB to litigation following its SRMR resolution measures gives a troubling warning of what the future might have in store in this regard.

10 Non-applicability of the BRRD

Article 93 of the Regulation amends the BRRD so that the BRRD is effectively disapplied to CCPs. As stated earlier, a number of European CCPs (such as Eurex in Frankfurt and LCH SA in Paris) are also licensed credit institutions. One advantage of operating under a banking licence is that this allows access to ECB liquidity facilities. CCPs are subject to licence requirements under EMIR. An EMIR licence restricts the permitted activities of CCPs to 'activities linked to clearing'; commercial banking (or other) activities not necessary for or inducive to the clearing business are prohibited.[101] Thus, the disapplication of the BRRD should have no negative consequences for clients (basically only CMs) of CCPs. It does mean that the regulatory capital requirements for banks are not applicable and that only the (rather less developed and less sophisticated) EMIR capitalization requirements for CCPs apply, as further expanded on in Commission Delegated Regulation (EU) No. 152/2013. There is an ongoing debate on whether the required capitalization of CCPs effectively, under all circumstances, ensures their resilience.[102]

It is worth noting, in connection with the disapplication of the BRRD, that according to the resolution objectives, the NRA must, in the context of ensuring the continuity of a CCP's critical functions, permit 'continuous access of CMs and (where applicable) their clients to securities or cash accounts provided by the CCP and collateral in the

---

[99] Regulation (EC) No 593/2008 of the European Parliament and of the Council of 17 June 2008 on the law applicable to contractual obligations, OJ L177 (4 July 2008), pp. 6–16.

[100] For these general principles, see, inter alia, Herwig Hofmann, 'General Principles of EU Law and EU Administrative Law', in Catherine Barnard and Steve Peers (eds), *European Union Law* (Oxford: Oxford University Press, 2020); Koen Lenaerts and Jose Gutiérrez-Fons, CMLR 2010/47, 1629–1669; also Takis Tridimas, *The General Principles of EU Law*, 2nd edn (Oxford: Oxford University Press, 2006); Xavier Groussot, *General Principles of Community Law* (Zutphen: Europa Law Publishing, 2006); Ulf Bernitz, Joakim Nergelius, and Cecilia Cardner (eds), *General Principles of EC Law in a Process of Development*, European Monograph 62 (Deventer: Wolters Kluwer, 2008).

[101] EMIR (n 10), Art. 14(3).

[102] See, inter alia, Zebregs and de Serière, 'Derivatives Central Counterparties' (n 12), p. 227.

form of financial assets held by the CCP'.[103] The need to align to this objective indicates that the resolution of CCPs may not involve the write-down of debt claims of CMs that might, for whatever reason, maintain credit balances with 'their' CCP[104] and that collateral held by the CCP (as 'owner' or pledgee and presumably including collateral that the CCP has 'parked' with a CSD[105]) may not be applied towards resolution but must continue to be held and applied exclusively in the context of clearing transactions performed for the CMs concerned in accordance with the contractual arrangements between the CCP and the CMs.[106]

11 Remedies

The basic principle on remedies is set out in Recital (72) of the Regulation, stating: 'In accordance with Article 47 of the Charter, the parties concerned have the right to due process and to an effective remedy against the measures affecting them. The decisions taken by the resolution authorities should therefore be subject to the right of appeal.' Recitals (71)–(75) and Art. 74 of the Regulation provide further details with regard to available remedies.

Recital (71) (elaborated on in Art. 74(1) of the Regulation) allows for national procedural laws to subject crisis management measures[107] to ex ante judicial approval. The fact that national procedural laws are granted this possibility means that the level of judicial protection of parties affected by crisis management measures may differ from Member State to Member State; accordingly, there is no level playing field in this regard. Crisis prevention measures are defined in Art. 2(48) of the Regulation as being those measures that aim to remedy deficiencies in recovery plans or to remove obstacles to resolvability. Permitting prior judicial approval is, in itself, remarkable (although this is in line with the provisions of BRRD, Art. 85(1)) and is likely to have been the result of a political compromise borne by pressure to uphold the mechanics of national judicial systems. Although the approach taken by the Regulation is actually in accordance with the notion of national procedural autonomy in the absence of overriding Union law, it would, of course, have been more efficient not to permit such prior approval requirement or at least to ensure fuller harmonization of the national procedures concerned. These procedures would appear unnecessarily to restrict the ability of competent authorities and resolution authorities to act swiftly when crisis management measures need to be taken, even if such ex ante approval process must be 'expeditious'. According to Recital (71), 'expeditious' means within twenty-four hours, and

---

[103] Art. 21(1)(a)(ii) of the Regulation.

[104] Of course, cash deposited by CMs as contributions to a default fund would not fall under this resolution objective.

[105] EMIR (n 10), Art. 47(3).

[106] But, of course, this does not restrict the ability of the NRA to apply the position and loss-allocation tool (including VMGH) as described above.

[107] The terminology used in the Regulation is inconsistent: the recitals refer to crisis management measures, whilst Art. 74 refers to crisis prevention measures. No difference appears to be intended.

the relevant authority must be able to act forthwith after the court has issued its judgment. If the NRA decides upon crisis management measures, such decision could, in any event, be contested in appeal proceedings, and interested parties may request a stay of such crisis management measures 'for a limited period'. These rather opaque provisions of Recital (71) are, however, not fully reflected in Art. 74, raising the question what exactly the legal status is of statements in recitals if not commensurately reflected in the substantive provisions of a regulation.[108]

Recital (72) as reiterated in Art. 74(2) and (3) of the Regulation confirms that all persons affected by a decision (i) to take a crisis prevention measure, (ii) to exercise a power other than a resolution action, or (iii) to take a resolution action have the right of appeal. What is the meaning of the term 'all persons affected'? The Regulation itself provides no guidance. The interpretation of this term is a matter of Union law, and whilst the EU courts enjoy exclusive jurisdiction to interpret Union law, it is to be applied by the competent national courts. A person who is denied standing because a national court deems that person not to be affected could try and persuade that court (or a higher appellate court) to submit the issue to the EU Court of Justice for an interpretation of the term 'all persons affected'. Such person would, however, not have direct access to the EU courts. It is suggested that a failing CCP's CMs and clients of those CMs suffering negative effects of a resolution action would, in any event, have standing. However, there may be doubt in case of persons indirectly suffering such negative effects, for example, holders of equity or debt issued by the relevant CCP or its CMs or other CMs to whom positions are ported, etc., etc.[109]

In case of an appeal against a resolution decision, Art. 74(4)(a) of the Regulation provides that there shall be no automatic stay if an appeal is lodged and that the decision concerned is immediately enforceable.[110] However, Art. 74(4)(b) establishes a 'rebuttable presumption that a suspension of its enforcement would be against the public interest', inferring that a national court may conceivably order a stay if it is convinced that a decision to grant a stay does not run contrary to the public interest.

Regarding the standard of review, Recital (73) of the Regulation states that resolution authorities should be granted a significant measure of discretion in determining which course of action to take. Courts are admonished (as it were) to accept the economic assessments made by the relevant authorities, but, at the same time, they may examine whether 'the evidence relied on by the resolution authority is factually accurate, reliable and consistent, whether that evidence contains all relevant information which

---

[108] In its *Deutsches Milch/Kontor* decision (case C-136/04, para. 32), the European Court of Justice ruled that the preamble to a Community act has no binding legal force and cannot be relied upon either as a ground for derogating from the actual provisions of the act in question or for interpreting those provisions in a manner clearly contrary to their wording.

[109] In the *Trasta* decision of the European Court of Justice (ECLI:EU:C:2019:923), it was ruled that for access to an appeal on the basis of Art. 263 of the Treaty, the criterion is whether an applicant's *legal* position has been affected by the act in question; non-legal economic effects of such a decision would not be relevant. However, this interpretation is given in the context of a different procedural remedy, and the European Court might be less restrictive in interpreting the term 'all persons affected'.

[110] The provisions discussed in this paragraph relate to remedies against resolution decisions but do not apply in case of appeals against crisis management measures as defined.

should be taken into account in order to assess a complex situation and whether it is capable of substantiating the conclusions drawn therefrom'. The subtle language of the Recital[111] is not repeated in Art. 74 of the Regulation, which, in sub-section (5), gives a curt, straightforward instruction: 'The court shall use the economic assessments of the facts carried out by the resolution authority as a basis for its own assessment.' This language taken by itself would not grant the courts much leeway in assessing the facts underlying a resolution decision.

Finally, Art. 74(6) of the Regulation contains a provision aiming to ensure the finality of post-resolution transactions involving equity or debt or other assets of the failing CCP. If, for instance, a debt-to-equity conversion would take place in the context of a CCP's resolution, post-resolution trades in resulting equity instruments on the capital markets would not be affected if a court would nullify the conversion concerned. National law provisions[112] ensuring finality of capital markets trades will likely already prevent disruption of capital markets trades caused by defects in prior transactions, but this provision reinforces the notion that trading continuity is to be preserved.

The foregoing sums up the Regulation's sparse provisions on remedies.

Appeals must be lodged with the competent court in the Member State concerned (being the Member State whose NRA issued the decision that is being appealed against). This may be an administrative court or a civil court, depending on the structure of the national judicial system.[113] Possibly, an action to annul a resolution decision should be brought before the national administrative courts, whilst actions for damages would have to be brought before the civil courts. In any event, there is no level playing field in so far as remedial court action is concerned. Admittedly, the national courts would generally have to apply Union law in resolving the dispute concerned since the appeal concerns the implementation of the Regulation; applicability of Union law (with the 'safeguard' of pre-judicial rulings) at least imposes a certain level of harmonization. Because Art. 59 of the Regulation requires national administrative procedures to be observed, it is, however, also possible that resolution decisions are contested on national administrative procedural grounds. In any event, national legal systems show considerable divergence as far as remedial court proceedings are concerned, with the consequence that the level of effective judicial protection may differ significantly, depending on which Member State's NRA is involved. And, of course, remedies against resolution decisions by the United Kingdom's resolution authorities concerning UK-based CCPs will need to be sought before the competent courts in the United Kingdom; Union law would then not be applicable.[114]

---

[111] Which actually expresses the standard of review the European Court of Justice applies in cases where the national authorities are granted wide discretion when deciding on complex issues; see, among others, case C-12/03 P, *Commission v Tetra Laval* (ECLI:EU:C:2005:87), para. 39 and case T-712/15, *Crédit Mutuel Arkéa v ECB* (ECLI:EU:T:2017:15), para. 179.
[112] In conjunction with the Finality Directive (Directive 98/26/EC of 19 May 1998).
[113] Article 59 of the Regulation provides that resolution authorities are to take resolution actions 'through executive orders in accordance with national administrative competences and procedures'.
[114] A 2021 UK HM Treasury survey made the following observations in this regard: the United Kingdom was one of the first jurisdictions to legislate to establish a CCP Recovery and Resolution Regulation (CCPR&R) regime, and consequently, the UK regime as contained in the Financial Services Act 2012 predates the FSB guidance and

12   Conclusion

The overview of the Regulation's recovery and resolution regime this chapter has attempted to provide, reveals a number of uncertainties as to its practical workability. These uncertainties could jeopardize an NRA's effective dealing with a CCP's (impending) failure, should such scenario materialize. Literature has been deservedly critical of the Regulation's approach. See, for instance, Singh and Turing's concluding remarks in their paper referenced in section 2.1, and Binder's conclusions in his paper referenced in section 3. In particular, the premise that the FMI community should be able to weather a CCP insolvency without the use of taxpayer money in case of a systemic or severe non-systemic financial crisis, as foreseen by the Regulation, is debatable. The efficacy of the resolution tools that the Regulation permits to be used, to a certain extent modelled on the BRRD/SRMR, is subject to doubt. It is this writer's view that dealing with the failure of one of the larger CCPs in a crisis scenario is, in any event, likely to require substantive government financial intervention in one form or another, and that if such intervention should, for any reason, not be available, the demise of that failing CCP concerned will have to be considered a realistic possibility.

But it has to be recognized that this Regulation aims to deal with an unpredictable future scenario without the benefit of experience with past CCP failures (there have been none in Europe, bar one small CCP a long time ago). The uncertainties revealed are probably, for the time being, inevitable, and as time progresses (and further bank failures will perhaps help better the regulators' understanding of the issues to be resolved), this Regulation will undoubtedly be further refined and improved upon. Hopefully, the effectiveness of the Regulation itself will not ever be tested in practice.

the European CCPR&R regime. The United Kingdom was a key influencer in the development of the EU file and was supportive of the way the final version of the Regulation—implemented the FSB standards. The UK also has an ongoing commitment to implementing global standards. Therefore, HM Treasury extended the special resolution regime contained in the Banking Act 2009 to apply to CCPs. This sets out the stabilization options and powers available to the Bank of England for CCPs and the conditions for their use. The UK HM Treasury, along with the Bank, is working with stakeholders to consider further development of the UK regime to bring it in line with international standards. As a result, apart from few technical areas, the EU regime is not significantly different from the proposed UK regime. See HM Treasury, 'Expanded Resolution Regime: Central Counterparties' (February 2021), https://assets.publishing.service.gov.uk/government/uploads/system/uploads/attachment_data/file/962168/Expanded_Resolution_Regime_for_Central_Counterparties_-_Consultation__002_.pdf (accessed 23 March 2023). See also n 43. For the development of the UK legislation as compared to the Regulation, see also Chapter 16 ('Brexit: Equivalence; Location Policy' by Dermot Turing) in this volume.

IV

THE TRANSACTION CHAIN

13

Clearing and Trading and Settlement

Apostolos Thomadakis and Karel Lannoo*

1 Introduction

Derivatives markets have grown significantly over the past two decades. The global aggregate size of the over-the-counter (OTC) and exchange-traded derivatives (ETD) markets grew from €78 trillion to €528 trillion between 1998 and 2020 in terms of notional amounts outstanding. The OTC segment accounts for 90% of that, of which interest rate derivatives (IRD) make up the vast majority (80%). Central clearing in derivatives markets has advanced enormously since the global financial crisis (GFC) and the G20 commitments, in particular, the requirement that all standardized OTC derivatives should be centrally cleared. From 2008 to 2020, the share of derivatives contracts that were centrally cleared rose from 50% to 83%, while for certain asset classes like IRD, it reached 91%.

In a European Union (EU) context, the largest derivatives central counterparty (CCPs) clearing houses developed in the City of London, a leading global central clearing hub of OTC derivatives of all asset classes and currencies. Currently, three London-based CCPs dominate the (European) market for swaps and futures clearing. More than €3.2 trillion notional outstanding of interest rate swaps (IRS) are cleared in the City of London per day across all currencies, and about 94% of all euro-denominated IRS are traded globally. On the other hand, EU-based CCPs account for 6% of the global euro-denominated IRS market.

Since the departure of the United Kingdom from the EU, European policymakers have encouraged EU clearing members and market participants to reduce their exposure to systemically important (SI) UK CCPs. In order to reduce exposure to

---

* This chapter is based on Apostolos Thomadakis and Karel Lannoo, 'Setting EU CCP Policy—Much More Than meets the Eye' (2021) CEPS–ECMI Study (28 October). It also builds and elaborates on earlier works by the authors.

third-country CCPs, EU policymakers have also encouraged the further development of EU derivatives clearing capabilities. Potential benefits of increased use of EU CCPs could include cross-product netting with listed derivatives, which could promote trading within the EU. This could also stimulate the creation of legal, economic, and operational expertise that could spur the development of EU financial centres.

In September 2020, the European Commission (EC) enacted a time-limited equivalence decision for UK CCPs running until 30 June 2022 to offset potential risks to financial stability. In doing so, market participants in the EU have been encouraged to reduce their exposures to UK-based CCPs. However, the significant reliance of the EU financial system on services delivered by UK CCPs cannot be reduced from one day to another. Thus, and in order to avoid any cliff-edge effects, on 8 February 2022, Commissioner Mairead McGuinness announced an extension of the equivalence for UK CCPs until 30 June 2025.

The extension means that EU clearing members will be able to continue clearing through recognized UK CCPs until 30 June 2025. This will give the EU time to find ways to (i) expand central clearing activities in the EU; (ii) improve the attractiveness of EU CCPs in order to reduce the over-reliance on systemic third-country CCPs; (iii) introduce measures to further strengthen risk management standards at EU CCPs and supervisory oversight of CCP activities within the EU, and (iv) amend, wherever necessary, pieces of EU legislation (e.g. the Markets in Financial Instruments Directive (MiFID), the Capital Requirements Regulation (CRR)) in order to ensure clarity around their interaction with the European Market Infrastructure Regulation (EMIR).

Any EU policy to localize and further develop central clearing in the EU should be part of a clear long-term strategy and addressed under the broader scope of strategic autonomy that the EU wants to achieve. We should not forget that the current concentration of derivatives clearing in the United Kingdom has developed over a long period and as part of the single market. Moreover, central clearing is integrally connected with other building blocks of a large financial centre, such as the presence of intermediaries and end users, widespread subject matter expertise, a suitably adapted legal framework, and strong underlying infrastructures.

Section 2 sets the stage by introducing the reader to what clearing is, the value added of CCP clearing, its advantages, and potential concerns. Section 3 analyses the evolution of the derivatives market and the trading activity over the years. Section 4 describes the settlement process and the settlement service providers. Section 5 sets a long-term vision for the future of the European clearing market, taking financial stability, efficiency, and the development of Europe's financial markets into account. Finally, section 6 summarizes the main findings and concludes.

2 What Is Clearing?

Clearing denotes all activities from the time a commitment for a transaction is made until it is ready to be settled. In other words, it is a post-trade, pre-settlement

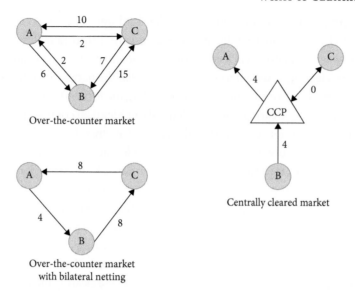

Figure 13.1 Payment obligations in an OTC market and a centrally cleared market

Source: Paul Glasserman, Ciamac Moallemi, and Kai Yuan, 'Hidden Illiquidity with Multiple Central Counterparties' (2016) 64 Operations Research 1143.

process containing various procedures such as trade capture, matching and con-firmation, position netting, and obligation calculation for trade counterparties. Clearing in this context is the process of guaranteeing the payment and exchange of assets (i.e. settlement) for derivatives transactions between the counterparties of the transaction.[1]

Clearing is performed by CCP clearing houses. A CCP is an organization that serves the transacting institutions, meaning that it interposes itself between the buyer and seller, acting as a seller to the buyer and a buyer to the seller. As an illustration using a simple example, imagine that financial institutions (e.g. dealers) A, B, and C wish to buy and sell derivatives contracts (e.g. a commodity forward) from each other (Figure 13.1).

The first option is for the financial institutions to trade bilaterally in the OTC market, which means that they initiate trades directly with each other, and each pair manages payments on its respective contract. The numbers in Figure 13.1 il-lustrate hypothetical payments due between dealers. For example, the payment for dealers A and B is eight, while the total payment between all dealers is forty-two. In the second option, and assuming that the counterparties have a payment netting agreement, this amount can be further reduced between pairs of counterparties. As a result, the payment between dealers A and B is now four, while the total payment between all dealers is twenty.

---

[1] Technically, clearing is the process of establishing positions—including the calculation of net obligations—and ensuring that financial instruments, cash, or both are available to secure the exposures arising from those positions.

By introducing a CCP into the transaction, the third option, dealers A, B, and C are now going to be facing the CCP instead of each other.[2] This means that each bilateral contract between dealers is replaced by two mirror-image contracts running though the CCP.[3] The clearing house interposes itself between the parties, serving as the counterparty to each. So in this example, instead of selling the forward contract to the buyer, the seller sells it to the clearing house, which sells an identical contract to the buyer. In this way, the clearing house is—within the circle of its members—the seller to every buyer and the buyer to every seller.[4] In essence, the clearing house steps into the middle of an OTC derivatives trade and creates two new transactions through a legal process known as novation.[5] In doing so, central clearing achieves maximal netting in our example, thus reducing the total payments due between all dealers to eight.[6]

An important distinction should be made here with regard to central clearing in terms of direct (house) and indirect (client) clearing. Direct clearing occurs when a clearing member clears its own 'house' trades (pure own-account activities) through the CCP. On the other hand, client clearing is the service provided by the clearing member to its client, under which said clearing member agrees to clear that client's trades through a CCP. The latter is significant in terms of net exposures and dominates the IRD market.

Client clearing affects the systemic risk exposure of CCPs (and thus the rank ordering of the systemic importance of institutions), even though these are not directly linked.[7] For example, given that almost all insurance companies in the EU clear their derivatives contracts indirectly via a clearing member, focusing only on direct clearing would result in underestimating the systemic risk of CCPs.[8] Thus, taking into account client clearing is crucial for understanding financial stability and contagion effects within the financial system. We will first discuss the benefits of central clearing and then examine the drawbacks.

2.1 Benefits of Central Clearing

Clearing OTC derivatives transactions through CCPs has clear advantages. Apart from the payment netting process described above (i.e. multilateral netting), one very

---

[2] For example, if all dealers are members of the same exchange (e.g. the Chicago Mercantile Exchange, CME), they will contract through the clearing house that backs that exchange (CME Clearing).

[3] Only clearing members of a CCP can trade through the CCP. Most, or all, major derivatives dealers are clearing members of the relevant CCP. An end user can trade through such dealers unless the end user is itself allowed to become a clearing member and is willing to devote the necessary resources to membership.

[4] Bank for International Settlements, 'Recommendations for Central Counterparties', Consultative Report (March 2004).

[5] Novation is the process by which a bilateral derivatives contract between two market participants is replaced by two bilateral contracts between each of the market participants and a CCP. The implication of this is that each counterparty is only exposed to the CCP's credit risk.

[6] Theoretically, the CCP always has a net risk of zero in the sense that the total payments it needs to make are equal to the total payments it is owed.

[7] See Ribleh Ali, Nick Vause, and Filip Zikes, 'Systemic Risk in Derivatives Markets: A Pilot Study Using CDS Data' (8 July 2016) Bank of England Financial Stability Paper 48.

[8] See Pawer Fiedor, Sarah Lapschies, and Lucia Orszaghova, 'Networks of Counterparties in the Centrally Cleared EU-Wide Interest Rate Derivatives Market' European Systemic Risk Board Working Paper No. 54 (September 2017) (Fiedor et al., 'Networks of Counterparties in the Centrally Cleared EU-Wide Interest Rate Derivatives Market').

important benefit relates to the fact that the CCP guarantees all future exchanges of payments between the market participants. This limiting of financial institutions' exposures to one another by replacing them with exposures to CCPs reduces counterparty credit risk, liquidity risk, and systemic risk, thus providing more stability to markets.[9] The outcome of this counterparty substitution process is that each original counterparty (i.e. buyer and seller) is now only directly exposed to the counterparty credit risk of the clearing house. However, netting benefits largely depend upon a clearing house's scale (i.e. how much of the market it clears) and scope, that is, the number of market products it clears.[10] For example, the more (comparable) contracts a CCP clears, the more its costs can decrease,[11] and consequently, the more efficient it is.[12]

The use of a CCP can substantially reduce (but not eliminate) the systemic risk posed by OTC derivatives.[13] Given the fact that a CCP interposes itself between both counterparties, the failure of any one of the clearing members does not directly affect other members, who will continue to receive and make payments on their contracts.

A CCP facilitates the transfer of a defaulted clearing member's client positions and collateral to another.[14] The portability of positions enables client positions to be transferred to non-defaulted clearing members rather than being closed out, thus affecting clients' vulnerability to losses (arising from the member's default). In doing so, portability reduces transaction costs, prevents adverse pricing impacts associated with a large default, decreases the possibility of runs on a clearing member,[15] shields clients' positions and collateral from the default of their clearing member, and promotes market and price stability. As a result, the risk of contagion decreases (at least temporarily).[16]

---

[9] See Michael Greenberger, 'Diversifying Clearinghouse Ownership in Order to Safeguard Free and Open Access to the Derivatives Clearing Market' (2013) 18 Fordham Journal of Corporate & Financial Law 245; Viral Acharya and Alberto Bisin, 'Counterparty Risk Externality: Centralized Versus Over-the-Counter Markets' (2014) 149 Journal of Economic Theory 153; Ivana Ruffini, 'Central Clearing: Risks and Customer Protections' (2015) 39 Economic Perspectives 90; Hester Peirce, 'Derivatives Clearinghouses: Clearing the Way to Failure' (2016) 64 Cleveland State Law Review 589; Asaf Bernstein, Eric Hughson, and Marc Weidenmier, 'Counterparty Risk and the Establishment of the New York Stock Exchange Clearinghouse' (2019) 127 Journal of Political Economy 689.

[10] See Colleen Baker, 'Clearinghouses for Over-the-Counter Derivatives', Volcker Alliance Working Paper (November 2016).

[11] These are cost decreases both in terms of allocation of fixed cost across more transactions and better netting and margin efficiencies.

[12] However, this may raise questions in terms of CCPs' competition. Negative effects arising from monopoly should not be ignored. We discuss these issues in more detail in Chapter 7 ('What Kind of Thing Is a Central Counterparty? The Role of Clearing Houses as a Source of Policy Controversy' by Rebecca Lewis and David Murphy) in this volume.

[13] Along the lines of Alan Greenspan (1996), who argued that the optimal number of bank failures is not zero; a CCP's function is to manage risk and not to eliminate it. See Alan Greenspan, 'Bank Supervision, Regulation, and Risk', speech, Annual Convention of the American Bankers Association (Honolulu, 5 October 1996), https://www. federalreserve.gov/boarddocs/speeches/1996/19961005.htm (accessed 12 November 2021).

[14] See Rena Miller, 'Conflicts of Interest in Derivatives Clearing', Congressional Research Service Report for Congress (22 March 2011).

[15] As Pirrong (2011) explained, if a client is confident that portability will provide protection against the default of its clearing member, there is less incentive to 'run' when the financial condition of its clearing member falls under suspicion. See Craig Pirrong, 'The Economics of Central Clearing: Theory and Practice', International Swaps and Derivatives Association Discussion Paper 1 (May 2011).

[16] Moreover, CCPs may replace defaulted contracts by buying/selling replacement contracts in an auction to the market, using the so-called initial margin (IM) to offset any costs. Such auction might be more liquid and promote market and price stability compared to an uncoordinated replacement of positions during periods of pronounced uncertainty.

Furthermore, central clearing facilitates clearing members' ability to exit positions by entering offsetting trades,[17] introduces margin uniformity and discipline, mutualizes losses, and limits the need for market participants to monitor one another.[18] With regard to operational efficiency and liquidity partitioning, CCPs expedite payments to a subset of a failed clearing member's creditors without slowing payments to others.[19] This is done by reserving a portion of the member's liquid assets and a matching amount of its short-term debts and using the first towards immediate repayment of the second. The clearing house's surviving members then receive prompt cash pay-outs instead of delayed bankruptcy pay-outs.

From a regulatory perspective, central clearing enhances transparency in several ways. Clearing houses increase regulators' ability to understand position concentrations (while introducing a new quality of concentration in the market) and counterparty credit risk exposures so that they are more easily able to quantify the positions taken and carry out stress tests. CCPs increase the transparency of position valuations and related margin requirements, thus limiting potential disputes on collateral valuation.[20] A CCP's ability to monitor participants' positions is a potentially large benefit to financial stability. In some cases, a CCP may be in a better position than supervisory authorities.[21] Moreover, if clearing members bear a clear and unambiguous shared liability for any losses incurred in the market, their incentive to ensure that each member's positions are effectively monitored is correspondingly strong.

Another important advantage of clearing and CCPs is that they reduce the chance that any unsubstantiated rumours will lead to the default of a dealer. When a dealer is thought to be experiencing difficulties, other dealers may stop posting collateral or refuse to trade with that dealer or enter into trades that are designed to reduce their exposure to the dealer. This may cause cash flow problems for the dealer and accelerate its potential default. However, such an event is less likely to occur when trades are cleared through a CCP. This is due to the risk management tools and transparency rules that require CCPs to closely monitor the performance of a member and the positions they hold. Initial margin (IM) plays a key role in this.

Related to this is the fact that a CCP provides protection against indirect forms of market contagion during a crisis or when a major clearing member defaults.[22] A CCP is in a good position to monitor counterparty risk effectively and thus reduce the level

---

[17] See Robert Bliss and Robert Steigerwald, 'Derivatives Clearing and Settlement: A Comparison of Central Counterparties and Alternative Structures' (2006) 30(4) Economic Perspectives 22.

[18] See Janet Yellen, 'Interconnectedness and Systemic Risk: Lessons from the Financial Crisis and Policy Implications', speech, American Economic Association/American Finance Association Joint Luncheon (San Diego, CA, 4 January 2013), https://www.federalreserve.gov/newsevents/speech/yellen20130104a.htm (accessed 5 December 2021) (Yellen, 'Interconnectedness and Systemic Risk').

[19] See Richard Squire, 'Clearinghouses as Liquidity Partitioning' (2014) 99 Cornell Law Review 857.

[20] See Christopher Culp, 'OTC-Cleared Derivatives: Benefits, Costs, and Implications of the "Dodd–Frank Wall Street Reform and Consumer Protection Act"' (2010) 20(2) Journal of Applied Finance 1.

[21] See Ian Davison, 'The Operation and Regulation of the Hong Kong Securities Industry', Hong Kong Securities and Futures Commission Report of the Securities Review Committee (27 May 1988).

[22] See Bob Hills, David Rule, Sarah Parkinson, and Chris Young, 'Central Counterparty Clearing Houses and Financial Stability' (June 1999) Bank of England Financial Stability Review 122.

of asymmetric information in the market.[23] CCP clearing makes securities information insensitive and, as a consequence, prevents markets drying up, as observed in OTC markets during the GFC. As a consequence, a liquidity crisis is less likely to occur.[24] With a well-managed and well-regulated CCP, market participants know that losses may be mutualized, and thus it is less likely that another participant is exposed disproportionately.[25] In this way, a CCP may contribute to much needed market liquidity in a crisis situation.

2.2 Concerns about Central Clearing

Regulatory reforms and the introduction of CCPs for certain OTC derivatives contracts have greatly lowered counterparty risk through compression of trades, better collateralization, and more efficient risk sharing. However, given the centralization of risk in CCPs following the GFC, the impact of a CCP failure would now be more significant. Thus, and apart from the several advantages of central clearing, CCPs have also brought concerns stemming from the concentration of credit risk, the impact of a member's default, cross-border clearing activities, netting efficiency losses, high costs, and interoperability arrangements.[26]

A CCP depends on the performance of each clearing house member to assist in the completion of its own obligations. The default of a significantly large clearing house member, or the default of multiple clearing members, could result in the CCP failing to perform its obligations and experiencing liquidity or solvency issues. However, the risks on these issues are significantly reduced if the variation margin (VM) is posted in a timely manner or if the IM is enough to cover any potential losses.

Other sources of CCP stress could include the default of an investment counterparty, the default of a payment bank, the risk of an extended operational disruption, or simply business risk. The European sovereign crisis, for example, highlighted and heightened

---

[23] However, this also depends on how the IM has been calculated. If, for example, the IM calculation for the portfolio that is being cleared is done conservatively, then the probability that the CCP will lose money if a member defaults can be reduced to zero. In other words, if the IM is the right one and the VM is exchanged in a timely way, then the probability of any losses due to a member's default (or the default of several members) can be close to zero. See Francesca Carapella and David Mills, 'Information Insensitive Securities: The Benefits of Central Counterparties', Conference in Honor of Warren Weber (Federal Reserve Bank of Chicago, 2014).

[24] Although asymmetric information has certainly been a key source of the financial disruptions seen, it is not a necessary condition for a market breakdown.

[25] This is only valid, however, if the CCP does not allow outsized concentrated positions. See, for example, what happened in September 2018, when a Norwegian trader failed to pay a margin call to the commodities arm of National Association of Securities Dealers Automated Quotations (NASDAQ) Clearing AB in Sweden. The CCP sold the trader's portfolio and generated a loss that exceeded both his posted margin and his default fund contribution. The balance of remaining loss was absorbed by the mutualized default fund contributions of the nondefaulting members and the 'skin-in-the-game' contribution of capital from the CCP. See, for example, Futures Industry Association, 'Central Clearing Recommendations for CCP Risk Management' (November 2018); Sarah Bell and Henry Holden, 'Two Defaults at CCPs, 10 Years Apart' (16 December 2018) Bank for International Settlements Quarterly Review.

[26] See Paul Glasserman, Ciamac Moallemi, and Kai Yuan, 'Hidden Illiquidity with Multiple Central Counterparties' (2016) 64 Operations Research 1143; Samin Ghamami and Paul Glasserman, 'Does OTC Derivatives Reform Incentivize Central Clearing?' (2017) 32 Journal of Financial Intermediation 76.

many CCPs' exposures to several of these risks.[27] In addition, many CCP members are too-big-to-fail financial institutions and banks, whose distress would be transmitted and cause systemic shocks in the banking system.[28] A recovery and resolution regulation for CCPs now exists, which should allow for organized resolution or liquidation of a CCP and to address financial stability problems that will occur.[29]

Nevertheless, CCPs' structure embeds multi-tiered layers of risk management that mutualize default risk among clearing members. This risk-sharing feature means that clearing members are mutually responsible for their own risk-taking activities for those of their clients as well as of other clearing members. Such shared financial responsibility creates important incentives for robust mutual monitoring, which also makes a clearing member default less likely.

Cross-border clearing activities of CCPs have been a concern in terms of regulation and oversight.[30] As derivatives markets are global and have become more concentrated, especially since the GFC, the vast majority of derivatives products are now cleared through a few large CCPs. These CCPs have become systemically important for multiple jurisdictions besides the one in which they are headquartered. Global CCPs also mean that a large part of the transactions they clear are submitted by financial institutions incorporated outside the CCP's country/territory. Thus, risks and losses can be channelled through CCPs and, in extreme cases, spread across borders, with potentially destabilizing effects for financial markets and financial stability across the globe.[31]

In order to address such risks, regimes for registering or recognizing third-country CCPs—as well as enhanced regulatory and supervisory cooperation and coordination between EU and third-country regulatory authorities, supervisors, and central banks—have been established. The Principles for Financial Market Infrastructures (PFMIs), a set of international standards, were vital in ensuring harmonized risk management requirements across the globe. To this end, on 2 January 2020, EMIR 2.2 entered into force, revisiting supervisory arrangements for EU and third-country CCPs in light of the growing size and cross-border dimension of clearing in the EU. EMIR 2.2 ((EU) 2019/2099) allocates the supervisory responsibilities and enhances the role of the European Securities and Markets Authority (ESMA) for both authorized EU CCPs

---

[27] See Bank of England, 'Financial Stability Report' (December 2011), p. 30.

[28] See Bern Bernanke, 'Clearinghouses, Financial Stability, and Financial Reform', speech, Financial Markets Conference (Stone Mountain, GA, 4 April 2011), https://www.bis.org/review/r110405b.pdf (accessed 11 May 2022).

[29] See Regulation (EU) No. 2021/23 of the European Parliament and of the Council of 16 December 2020 on a framework for the recovery and resolution of central counterparties, [2021] OJ L22/1 (22 January 2021).

[30] See Basel Committee on Banking Supervision–Committee on Payments and Market Infrastructure–Financial Stability Board–International Organization of Securities Commissions (BCBS–CPMI–FSB–IOSCO), 'Analysis of Central Clearing Interdependencies' (9 August 2018) (BCBS–CPMI–FSBIOSCO, 'Analysis of Central Clearing Interdependencies').

[31] Because central clearing promotes the creation of new, systemically important institutions and eliminates some opportunities for cross-product bilateral netting while only partially reducing the interconnectedness of the market, systemic risk may actually increase, rather than decrease, under mandatory central clearing. See, for example, Paul McBride, 'The Dodd–Frank Act and OTC Derivatives: The Impact of Mandatory Central Clearing on the Global OTC Derivatives Market' (2010) 44 International Law 1077; Christoph Henkel, 'Using Central Counterparties to Limit Global Financial Crises' (January 2020) 88 University of Cincinnati Law Review 397.

and recognized third-country CCPs.[32] For the former, although the home-country supervisor is the responsible competent authority of the CCP, ESMA's role has been reinforced in order to promote a convergent approach towards European CCPs and to homogenize the application of EMIR across the EU. For the latter, ESMA (through the CCP SC) is responsible for classifying third-country CCPs depending on the level of systemic risk they pose for the Union and supervising recognized CCPs that are determined to be SI tier 2 CCPs.[33]

With regard to losses in netting efficiency, it has been shown that clearing heterogeneous asset classes in separate CCPs removes the benefits of netting, thereby increasing counterparty exposures (and the probability of counterparty default) as well as collateral demands.[34] However, the loss of netting efficiency due to multiple CCPs can be offset when a single CCP clears multiple classes of derivatives or when portfolio compression takes place across CCPs.[35] Enabling netting among multiple CCPs might help to reduce the impact of large exposures and the sudden surge in liquidity needs.[36] Based on these papers, two important factors impact the efficiency of central clearing: (i) the number of CCPs and (ii) the proportion of OTC derivatives that are cleared.

While offsetting could be possible in a single CCP clearing multiple asset classes, netting efficiency disruptions could also occur due to the global fragmentation in the clearing house landscape. In a world of fragmented netting, the only trades available to a clearing house to offset losses from a dealer's default are positions cleared by that particular clearing house, a subset of all open positions with the defaulting dealer.[37] Fewer open positions mean greater residual loss for the clearing house to absorb. This is a problem that will be arise in each clearing house in which the defaulting member participates.

Although the post-GFC regulatory requirements have increased transparency and reduced risk, they have also raised the costs associated with derivatives clearing. Margin requirements and capital charges for exposures, as well as compliance and

[32] Through the creation of the CCP Supervisory Committee (CCP SC), an internal ESMA committee composed of a Chair, two independent members, and the competent authorities of Member States with an authorized CCP.

[33] In addition, ESMA's powers include the ability to conduct investigations and on-site inspections and to impose fines. See speech by Klaus Löber, Chair of the CCP SC at ESMA, on 'CCPs: Evolving Risks and Supervisory Responses', at the Derivatives Forum (Frankfurt, 23 March 2021).

[34] For example, Duffie and Zhu (2011) found that clearing a moderately large fraction of all classes of derivatives in the same CCP reduces average estimated exposures by 37%, though this might depend on the correlation between the different asset classes. If the same asset class is cleared in two different CCPs, then this will require the posting of more (or, at best, the same) IM and VM than required if clearing was taking place in only one CCP. However, if two CCPs clear different assets and are not correlated, then the IM will be the same as if clearing was taking place in one CCP. While the VM might have some netting effects, it is unlikely that the risk of default will increase. Darrell Duffie and Haoxiang Zhu, 'Does A Central Clearing Counterparty Reduce Counterparty Risk?' (2011) 1 Review of Asset Pricing Studies 74.

[35] See Marco D'Errico and Tarik Roukny, 'Compressing Over-the-Counter Markets' (2021) 69 Operations Research 1651.

[36] See Hitoshi Hayakawa, 'Does a Central Clearing Counterparty Reduce Liquidity Needs?' (2018) 13(9) Journal of Economic Interaction and Coordination 1357.

[37] When a clearing members defaults, the CCP typically liquidates or auctions the defaulting member's positions to the remaining clearing members. Since the clearing member has paid VM up to the time of default, the only exposure of the CCP is to the portfolio loss between the default time and the liquidation, that is, the liquidation cost. See Sean Griffith, 'Clearinghouse Hope or Hype? Why Mandatory Clearing May Fail to Contain Systemic Risk' (17 April 2013) 3 Harvard Business Law Review 160; Rama Cont, 'Central Clearing and Risk Transformation', Norges Bank Working Paper No. 3 (2017).

reporting costs, all have implications for market participants.[38] According to Deloitte (2014), the estimated annual added cost is approximately €15.5 billion, with margin requirements—including clearing fees, capital charges for trade exposures, and contributions to the CCP default fund—being the main driver.[39] Furthermore, costly collateral requirements may reduce potential investment, with a corresponding loss of return for clearing members,[40] and lead to cross-jurisdictional regulatory arbitrage.[41]

Another concern arises from interoperability arrangements—the links between two or more CCPs involving a cross-system execution of transactions.[42] Such arrangements increase opportunities for netting, lower outstanding gross exposures in the system,[43] and reduce complexity for clearing members.[44] However, at the same time, interconnection (links) between CCPs introduces a channel for shocks and risks to be transmitted (either directly or indirectly) from one CCP to another. This is because interconnection introduces credit exposure between linked CCPs.[45] Although the probability of a CCP default is relatively small, such an event could threaten the solvency of any surviving linked CCPs if the number of trades cleared across the link and the potential adverse movement of prices are significant enough.[46]

[38] Participating in a CCP imposes direct costs on both clearing members and clients. Clearing members incur membership fees and operational costs, including significant investments in infrastructure, as well as costs associated with requirements to post highly liquid assets at short notice, including intra-day (pursuant to CCP rules), which can create collateral funding and liquidity risks. Clients also face clearing fees and operational and collateral costs. These costs may be so high that they do not compensate for the private benefits of central clearing. Finally, in addition to counterparty risks, CCPs face business, operational, and liquidity risks, and managing these can involve placing additional requirements on their clearing members.

[39] See Deloitte, 'OTC Derivatives: The New Cost of Trading' (2014).

[40] See Ciryl Monnet and Thomas Nellen, 'The Collateral Costs of Clearing' (2021) 53 Journal of Money, Credit and Banking 939.

[41] Gandré et al. (2021) find that following the early implementation of the G20's global OTC derivatives market reform in the United States, the five largest derivatives traders in the United States (Bank of America, Citigroup, Goldman Sachs, J.P. Morgan. and Morgan Stanley) shifted up to 70% of their OTC derivatives activity abroad towards less regulated jurisdictions. The main driver of this shift was the promotion of central clearing and the fact that US banks did not want to become swap dealers and not primarily related to clearing. Pauline Gandré, Mile Mariathasan, Ouarda Merrouche, and Steve Ongena, 'Unintended Consequences of the Global Derivatives Market Reform', University of Paris Nanterre EconomiX Working Paper No. 2021-36 (2021).

[42] Interoperability allows clearing members of one CCP to centrally clear trades carried out with members of another CCP without needing to be a member of the second CCP. In doing so, clearing members can hold their positions with one CCP instead of dividing them across different CCPs, thus reducing the costs of maintaining multiple CCP memberships. See, e.g. European Systemic Risk Board, 'ESRB Report to the European Commission on the Systemic Risk Implications of CCP Interoperability Arrangements' (January 2016); European Post Trade Forum, 'EPTF Report—Annex 3: Detailed Analysis of the European Post Trade Landscape' (15 May 2017). It has been argued that having a single CCP with an adequate multicurrency central bank liquidity backstop, which is regulated and supervised and spans the broadest range of derivatives, is the ideal solution. See, e.g. International Monetary Fund, 'Meeting New Challenges to Stability and Building a Safer System', Global Financial Stability Report (April 2010); Manmohan Singh, 'Making OTC Derivatives Safe—a Fresh Look' International Monetary Fund Working Paper No. WP/11/66 (2011) (Singh, 'Making OTC Derivatives Safe'). Moreover, from a regulatory point of view, it might be easier to oversee one or a few large CCPs rather than many small ones.

[43] As the collateral in the system declines with the level of exposure, the size of intra-day margin calls also decreases and therefore so does the liquidity risk. See, e.g. Jürg Mägerle and Thomas Nellen, 'Interoperability between Central Counterparties', Swiss National Bank Working Paper No. 12 (2011); Nathanael Cox, Nicholas Garvin, and Gerard Kelly, 'Central Counterparty Links and Clearing System Exposures', Reserve Bank of Australia Research Discussion Paper No. 12 (2013) (Cox et al., 'Central Counterparty Links').

[44] Under interoperability, clearing members would not have to manage collateral calls from additional CCPs and transfers of collateral across CCPs. See John McPartland and Rebecca Lewis, 'The Challenges of Derivatives Central Counterparty Interoperability Arrangements' (2016) 4 Journal of Financial Market Infrastructures 41.

[45] All linked positions in a defaulting CCP are taken on by linked CCPs, potentially leading to very large losses.

[46] See Cox et al. 'Central Counterparty Links' (n 43).

For this reason, academics suggest that CCPs have combined stress tests that take into account the actions of other CCPs as compared to current stress tests that treat CCPs in isolation.[47]

3 What Is Settlement?

The settlement cycle is the period between execution of a trade and final settlement. Settlement is the process that refers to the exchange of cash and securities on the contractual settlement date.[48] In other words, it involves the transfer of the securities from the seller to the buyer and the transfer of funds from the buyer to the seller.[49]

A central securities depository (CSD) is either the physical entity or the system (referred to as the securities settlement system or SSS) that facilitates the settlement and safekeeping of securities and ensures the reconciliation of participant accounts. Securities can be safekept in immobilized or dematerialized form, while settlement generally occurs in book entry form. While many CSDs handle the securities for a single domestic market, others serve multiple markets.[50] International central securities depositories (ICSDs) emerged as depositories settling trades in international securities; the best known are Euroclear and Clearstream. The eurobond market developed in part in response to operational and regulatory inefficiencies in domestic bond markets and settled in the ICSDs.

The settlement landscape of the EU and Europe has not changed substantially over the past ten years. For the eurozone, the European Central Bank's (ECB) TARGET2-Securities (T2S) now acts as the ultimate platform for securities settlement, but it has not yet reached the objective of reducing the cost of settlement in the EU or further integrating back offices in Europe. The EU's Central Securities Depositaries Regulation

---

[47] To date, calls for interoperability of derivatives CCPs have not extensively materialized, in part because of the thorny risk management issues such linkages produce. The European regulatory framework covers interoperability arrangements related to transferable securities and money market instruments. ESMA has recommended extending the scope to include ETDs but not OTC derivatives: ESMA, 'Final Report: The Extension of the Scope of Interoperability Arrangements' (1 July 2015). This is due to the additional complexities involved in interoperability arrangements between CCPs clearing OTC derivatives contracts: Regulation (EU) No. 648/2012 of the European Parliament and of the Council of 4 July 2012 on OTC derivatives, central counterparties and trade repositories, [2012] OJ L201/1 (27 July 2012), Recital (73) (EMIR). Potential credit exposures are greater for OTC derivatives, while the cost of assessing risk and making risk management models compatible are much higher. Currently, there are five interoperability arrangements in Europe: three authorized CCPs located in the EU (EuroCCP in the Netherlands, CC&G in Italy, and the London Clearing House (LCH) SA in France) and two recognized third-country CCPs (LCH Ltd in the United Kingdom and Swiss SIX x-clear in Switzerland, including its Norwegian branch SIX x-clear NO). The links, which have been approved since the implementation of EMIR, mostly cover the clearing of cash equities and government bonds, with one link covering the clearing of ETDs: ESRB, 'CCP Interoperability Arrangements' (January 2019) (ESRB, 'CCP Interoperability Arrangements').

[48] The settlement date can be agreed upon at trade execution or can be prescribed by local trading conventions. Settlement may be processed on a provisional or a final basis.

[49] Most securities are settled under a rolling cycle, which means that trades are executed on day T and settled at a later date, usually between one and three days later (T + 1, T + 2, or T + 3).

[50] In some cases, this has been accomplished by links between domestic securities depositories (achieved by each depository opening an account with the other and acting as custodian for their respective members) or, in some cases, by the merge of CSDs.

(CSDR), now under review, introduced the single passport for CSDs on the basis of harmonized settlement regime, which includes cash penalties for failing transactions. But settlement markets in Europe remain highly dispersed and are an important factor in the remaining fragmentation of its capital markets.

The T2S was created with the ambition to overcome the fragmentation of settlement systems in the EU. It was launched in 2006, with the start of operations in June 2015. Today, nineteen European CSDs participate (upon thirty-nine), including the Swiss SIX SIS, with the Croatian CSD expected to join in 2023, following its accession to the eurozone, and the Finnish CSD in September of the same year. Overall, the process to create T2S took much longer than expected as well as the integration of CSDs. The costs to build the system were much higher, and the expected revenues fell with the dramatic decline in the number of settled transactions, leading to price increases. Prices per transaction at EUR 0.80 (flat rate) or decreasing from EUR 0.60 (volume-based), according to the TARGET Services Pricing Guide, are on the higher end of the 2008 ECB's business case for T2S, with substantially higher expenses for the operation of the system.[51] In addition, technological progress means that T2S would have been built using different techniques today, such as blockchain, at a possible lower cost.[52]

The creation of T2S gave a push towards harmonized rules for securities settlement and a single licence in the CSDR in 2014. Before that, CSDs in Europe functioned under national rules and a voluntary code to advance interoperability. Given the multiplicity of CSDs in Europe, and the diversity in settlement regimes, the CSDR ended up being a complex piece of regulation. CSDR is made up of seventy-six articles that aim to enhance the consistency, safety, and efficiency of security settlements. With an emphasis on cross-border settlement in Europe, it introduces standards and requirements for CSDs and harmonizes the disparate national regulations surrounding securities settlement standards of the CSDs in the EU. The 2021 Review found the passporting requirements burdensome and the compliance costs disproportionate, above all for cross-border business, which are addressed in the targeted review proposed by the EU Commission in March 2022.

As long as CSDs in the EU are not more integrated, CCPs will also be affected in their day-to-day operations, even more since the United Kingdom's departure. Creating strong local CCP facilities in the EU will also require a more integrated CSD landscape, which seems not to be advancing particularly. The latest CSD review proposals may contribute to further integration, but more will be needed, a form of 'big bang' to overcome the current fragmentation.

---

[51] See Karel Lannoo and Diego Valiante, 'Prospects and Challenges of a Pan-European Post-Trade Infrastructure', European Capital Markets Institute Policy Brief No. 20 (2012).

[52] See Jesus Bonito, 'The European Post-Trade Infrastructures after Brexit: A Central Securities Depository Perspective' (2019) 12 Journal of Securities Operations and Custody 6.

4 Current Landscape and Evolution of the Derivatives Market

Over the past twenty years, global derivatives markets have grown dramatically. Most of this growth has been in the OTC segment of the market, which has caught up with and surpassed (by many measures, including gross notional volume) the ETD market. OTC derivatives are privately negotiated contracts, which may be easily customized (although they range from highly bespoke to relatively standardized contracts) and are traded either on trading platforms or bilaterally. ETDs are standardized contracts that are traded on organized exchanges.

4.1 Development of the Market

The aggregate size of the OTC and ETD markets combined, in terms of notional amounts outstanding, grew from €78 trillion to €587 trillion between 1998 and 2021 (Figure 13.2). However, the predominance of the OTC segment of the market over ETD—measured in gross notional volume—is evident. OTC derivatives activity constitutes approximately 87% of total derivatives activity (as measured by gross notional volume), with the remaining 13% made up of ETDs. At June 2021, the size of ETD markets was €74 trillion compared to €513 trillion for OTC markets.

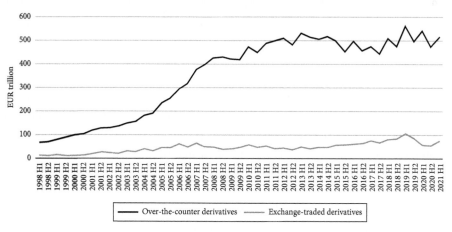

Figure 13.2 Global derivatives markets, notional amounts outstanding, EUR trillion, 1998–2021

Notes: The difference between ETD and OTC should be interpreted cautiously as it depends on compression efficiency. The notional amount of outstanding OTC derivatives contracts determines contractual payments and is an indicator of activity in OTC derivatives markets. The BIS reports data in US dollars at end June and end December of each year. For the conversion into euros, the bilateral exchange rate EUR/USD at the end of each quarter has been used.

Sources: authors' calculations based on data from the Bank for International Settlements (BIS) and Eurostat.

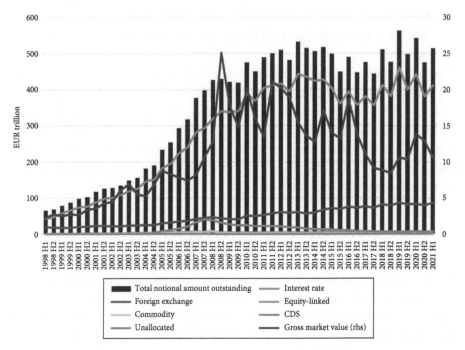

Figure 13.3 Notional amounts outstanding of global OTC derivatives market, EUR trillion, 1998–2021

Notes: The notional amount of outstanding OTC derivatives contracts determines contractual payments and is an indicator of activity in OTC derivatives markets. The gross market value represents the maximum loss that market participants would incur if all counterparties failed to meet their contractual payments and the contracts could be replaced at current market prices. The category 'Other' includes equity-linked derivatives, commodity derivatives, credit default swaps (CDS), and unallocated derivatives, that is, those of non-reporting institutions. BIS reports data in US dollars at end June and end December of each year. For the conversion into euros, the bilateral exchange rate EUR/USD at the end of each quarter has been used.

Sources: authors' calculations based on data from the BIS and Eurostat.

OTC derivatives represent a sizable fraction of financial transactions worldwide, encompassing a wide variety of contracts and asset classes. The total nominal amounts outstanding of OTC derivatives contracts, which determine contractual payments and are an indicator of activity (not risk), increased significantly from €66 trillion in June 1998 to a peak of €562 trillion in June 2019, before reaching €513 trillion in June 2021 (Figure 13.3).

While notional amounts provide a measure of the size of the market, they do not provide a measure of risk. For this reason, the gross market value, which calculates the cost of replacing all outstanding contracts at market prices, offers a better indication of the market and counterparty risk in derivatives markets.[53] Gross market value reached its all-time high of €25 trillion at the peak of the GFC at the end of 2008. Since then, and largely because of the implementation of the G20 commitments, the gross market value of outstanding contracts declined to €11 trillion in June 2021. The gross market value of

---

[53] Although the gross market value does not take into account the effect of netting for each pair of counterparties.

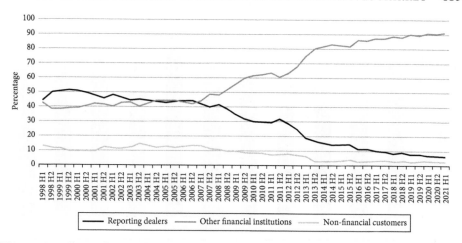

Figure 13.4 Share of notional amounts outstanding of IRD by counterparty, percentage, 1998–2021

Notes: 'Reporting dealers' mainly include commercial and investment banks and securities houses. 'Other financial institutions' include financial institutions not classified as 'reporting dealers', for example, banks, CCPs, and funds and non-bank financial institutions which may be considered as financial end users such as mutual funds, pension funds, hedge funds, currency funds, money market funds, building societies, leasing companies, insurance companies, and central banks. 'Non-financial customers' include any counterparty other than those described above, that is, mainly non-financial end users such as corporations, high net worth individuals, and non-financial government entities. The BIS reports data in US dollars at end June and end December of each year. For the conversion into euros, the bilateral exchange rate EUR/USD at the end of each quarter has been used.

Sources: authors' calculations based on data from the BIS and Eurostat.

OTC derivatives accounted for about 2% of the notional outstanding at the end of 2020, compared to its highest level of 6% at the end of 2008.

The great majority of OTC derivatives contracts are IRD. This exchange of payment, which allows one party to sell off the risk of increasing variable interest rates to a willing counterparty, stood at €411 trillion, or 80% of the entire OTC derivative market, in June 2021. Moreover, there has been a shift in the interest rate market away from bilateral settlement towards clearing houses (Figure 13.4). The notional amount of interest rate contracts between derivatives dealers has been falling steadily since 2008.[54] From December 2008 to June 2021, the notional amount of contracts bilaterally cleared between derivatives dealers dropped from €131 trillion (39%) to €30 trillion (6%). At the same time, all contracts handled by other financial institutions—mostly clearing houses—rose from €176 trillion (52%) to €445 trillion (91%).

An important factor that has contributed to and enhanced the role of CCPs in OTC derivatives markets since the GFC is trade compression. This is the practice of eliminating or reducing the size of OTC derivative positions by terminating offsetting trades or replacing them with a smaller set of netted trades. Trade compression, which can be applied to both bilateral and centrally cleared trades, leaves each counterparty's market risk exposure unchanged (or within a pre-defined range). In particular for IRD contracts, compression has increased rapidly over the past few

[54] A major factor fuelling this trend has been trade compression and the elimination of redundant contracts.

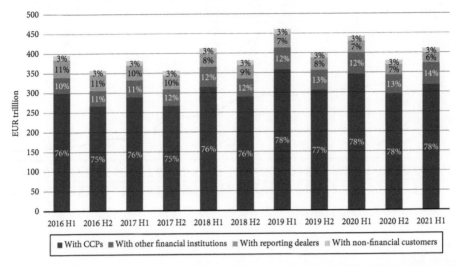

Figure 13.5 Notional amounts outstanding of IRD by counterparty, EUR trillion, 2016–2021

Notes: 'Reporting dealers' mainly include commercial and investment banks and securities houses. 'Other financial institutions' include financial institutions not classified as 'reporting dealers', for example, banks, CCPs, and funds and non-bank financial institutions which may be considered as financial end users such as mutual funds, pension funds, hedge funds, currency funds, money market funds, building societies, leasing companies, insurance companies, and central banks. 'Non-financial customers' include any counterparty other than those described above, that is, mainly non-financial end users such as corporations, high net worth individuals, and non-financial government entities. The BIS reports data in US dollars at end June and end December of each year. For the conversion into euros, the bilateral exchange rate EUR/USD at the end of each quarter has been used.

Sources: authors' calculations based on data from the BIS and Eurostat.

years. Market participants have a direct incentive to engage in trade compression as it reduces the number of individual trades to be managed, and consequently it lowers both costs and operational risk.[55]

Zooming into the category 'Other financial institutions', which includes central counterparties, the share of notional amount of IRD contracts cleared by CCPs was at 78% in June 2021 (Figure 13.5). Although CCP clearing rates seem to have plateaued over the past few years, they rose rapidly from 2008 (from about 40%) following the G20 mandate for greater clearing of standardized products.[56] Similar is the trend for credit default swaps (CDS), for which the share of contracts cleared by CCPs rose from about 10% to 64% between 2008 and 2021. However, and given the fact that

---

[55] Other factors have also contributed to the increase in compression activity. In 2015, for example, IOSCO released risk mitigation standards for non-centrally cleared OTC derivatives that encouraged trade compression. These standards required entities to implement policies and procedures to engage in portfolio compression when appropriate. Furthermore, reforms to counterparty credit risk capital requirements provide an incentive for banks to compress non-centrally cleared trades by introducing higher capital requirements for such contracts.

[56] However, there is a difference between the EU and the United States. In 2019, the clearing rate for new IRS was 69% in the EU (62% in 2017) compared to 93% in the United States (87% in 2017). Having said that, the clearing rates in the EU and the United States may not be entirely comparable since the clearing obligation in the United States came into effect before it did in the EU and does not cover the same entity base. See, e.g. FSB, 'Review of OTC Derivatives Market Reforms: Effectiveness and Broader Effects of the Reforms' (29 June 2017); Commodity Futures Trading Commission, 'Weekly Swaps Report' (27 December 2019); ESMA, 'EU Derivatives Markets: ESMA Annual Statistical Report 2020' (16 November 2020).

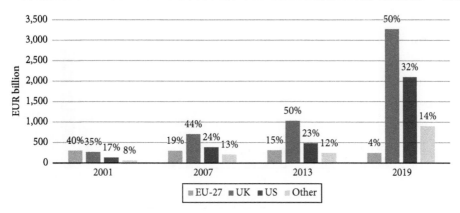

Figure 13.6 Daily average turnover of OTC IRD by country, EUR billion, 2001–2019

Notes: Figures refer to 'net-gross' basis, April 2001–2019, adjusted for local inter-dealer counting. For the conversion into euros, the bilateral exchange rate EUR/USD at the end of April of each year has been used.

Sources: authors' calculations based on data from the BIS Triennial Central Bank Survey and Eurostat.

clearing obligations apply to specific classes of interest rate and credit OTC derivatives,[57] clearing rates could further increase if more products become subject to the clearing obligation,[58] for example, cross-currency swaps and transactions denominated in non-clearable currencies.[59]

4.2 Derivatives Trading Activity

Trading of OTC IRD has grown rapidly over the past twenty years. From €762 billion in 2001, trading surged to €6.5 trillion in 2019 (Figure 13.6). Only in the past few years, between 2016 and 2019, average daily OTC turnover increased by 143%. Structural and regulatory changes that took place in OTC markets, the expansion in terms of the amount of non-price-forming trades (i.e. back-to-back and compression trades), the proliferation of electronic trading platforms, and the global uncertainty around policy rates were among the main drivers of this development.

[57] For example, under the EMIR clearing obligation (n 47), in 2019, the IRD classes subject to the obligation were basis swaps, fixed-to-float IRS, forward rate agreements (FRAs), and overnight index swaps (OIS). For credit derivatives, certain European untranched index CDS classes were subject to the obligation. See ESMA, 'Review of the Clearing Thresholds under EMIR' (22 November 2021).

[58] However, not all products that can be cleared should be subject to mandatory clearing, in principle. Furthermore, some products are cleared on a voluntary basis. Dealers have largely embraced central clearing on a voluntary basis, in particular in the IRD and credit derivatives asset classes, where they see clear capital and risk management benefits. See BCBS–CPMI–FSB–IOSCO, 'Incentives to Centrally Clear Over-The-Counter (OTC) Derivatives: A Post-Implementation Evaluation of the Effects of the G20 Financial Regulatory Reforms—Final Report' (19 November 2018).

[59] In order for clearing rates to increase further, two developments are necessary: (i) the expansion of product coverage from global clearing organizations and (ii) increased recognition by local clearing houses of other currencies. Nevertheless, given the need for historical comparison in order to establish margins, it is hard to envision exotic, illiquid, or highly structured OTC derivatives being centrally cleared in the near future or even ever.

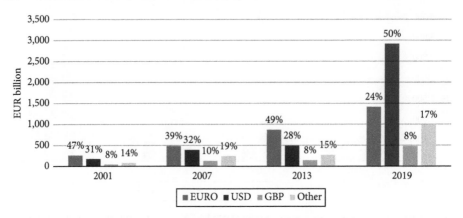

Figure 13.7 Daily average turnover of OTC IRD by currency, EUR billion, 2001–2019

Notes: Figures refer to 'net-gross' basis, April 2001–2019, adjusted for local inter-dealer counting. For the conversion into euros, the bilateral exchange rate EUR/USD at the end of April of each year has been used.

Sources: authors' calculations based on data from the BIS Triennial Central Bank Survey and Eurostat.

London is historically the prevailing dominant location for OTC IRD trading. In 2019, the global share of OTC IRD traded in the United Kingdom was 50%, compared to 35% in 2001. The United Kingdom is followed by the United States, which accounted for 32% in 2019. As for the EU-27, in absolute terms, the daily average turnover decreased to €250 billion in 2019 from its peak of €318 billion in 2013. But also in relative terms, the EU's share in the global market declined from 40% in 2001 to just 4% in 2019. The European market is highly concentrated, with French and German sales desks recording approximately 43% and 20% of that turnover in 2019, respectively.

With regard to the currency composition of the globally traded OTC IRD, euro-denominated contracts have historically been the most actively traded segment, representing, on average, 44% of global turnover up until 2013 (Figure 13.7). However, since then, and despite the significant increase in turnover of euro-denominated contracts (from €867 billion in 2013 to €1.4 trillion in 2019), their share in the global market dropped to 24%. Over the same period, US dollar-denominated contracts became the most actively traded OTC IRD, representing around 50% of the global market with a daily average turnover of €3 trillion.

This relative increase in US dollar-denominated contracts was due to increased activity in short-term maturity instruments (e.g. overnight index swaps, OIS), while the turnover of euro-denominated contracts declined for all maturities. This contrasting development can largely be explained by the two continents' different stances on monetary policy. In anticipation of policy rate rises in the United States, activity in the OIS market (which is linked to policy rates) increased.[60] In contrast, euro area market

---

[60] See Torsten Ehlers and Egemen Eren, 'The Changing Shape of Interest Rate Derivatives Markets' (11 December 2016) Bank for International Settlements Quarterly Review.

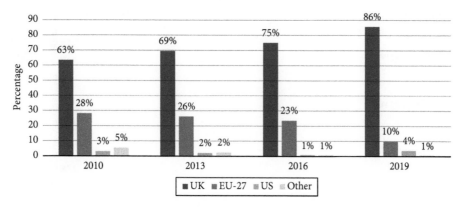

Figure 13.8 Share of euro-denominated OTC IRD by country, percentage of global euro turnover, 2010–2019

Notes: Figures refer to 'net-gross' basis, April 2001–2019, adjusted for local inter-dealer counting. For the conversion into euros, the bilateral exchange rate EUR/USD at the end of April of each year has been used.

Sources: authors' calculations based on data from the BIS Triennial Central Bank Survey and Eurostat.

participants' expectations for unchanged rates resulted in declined trading for both short- and long-maturity euro-denominated contracts.

Focusing on EUR IRD, 86% of global turnover in 2019 was via UK sales desks, up from 63% in 2010 (Figure 13.8). On the other hand, the share of euro-denominated contracts traded through sales desks in continental Europe dropped from 28% in 2010 to just 10% in 2019. France, which is the largest EU trading centre, saw its share in global EUR IRD turnover decrease from 15% to 5% over the same period.

Looking at interest rate swaps (IRS), which represent the great majority of IRD contracts, Figure 13.9 shows the flow of trades from the location of the trading venue to the location of clearing. To start with, euro IRS-traded notional executed on venue—such as swap execution facilities (SEFs), multilateral trading facilities (MTFs), organized trading facilities (OTFs)—represented 49% of total EUR IRS-traded notional globally at Q2 2021, while the remaining 51% was executed off venue. Of the 49% executed on venue, 45% is cleared in UK CCPs. More interestingly, 17% of the EUR IRS executed through an EU trading venue is cleared in the United Kingdom and only 3% in the EU. This, on the one hand, implies the important role of UK CCPs in euro-denominated derivatives but, on the other hand, highlights the very small fraction of EUR IRS that are executed on an EU trading venue and cleared within the EU by an EU CCP.

4.3 Authorized and Recognized CCPs in the EU

Due to market and regulatory fragmentation, CCPs have historically been organized in terms of national or regional borders, allowing them to adapt to the needs of local markets. However, given their clearing members and the trading venues for which they

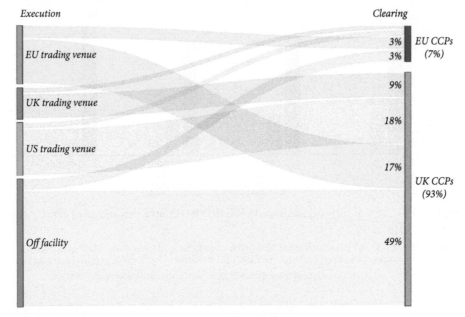

Execution   *Clearing*

Figure 13.9 Execution and clearing of EUR-denominated OTC IRS, percentage of globally cleared IRD measured in terms of notional traded, Q2 2021

Notes: The figure refers to new transactions aggregate notional traded. The products considered are all new, cleared, single-currency swaps meaning fixed-for-fixed, fixed-for-floating, and floating-for-floating (i.e. basis) but no cross currency options (i.e. swaptions) or FRAs. Data include all new, cleared IRS trades executed globally in a given month, including on venue (e.g. SEF, MTF, and OTF) and those executed off venue (i.e. off-facility) that are cleared via MarkitSERV's CCP connectivity service or where MarkitSERV receives a copy of the trade.

Source: Apostolos Thomadakis and Karel Lannoo, 'Setting EU CCP Policy—Much More Than Meets the Eye' (2021) CEPS—ECMI Study (28 October).

provide clearing services, CCPs are highly interconnected with international financial institutions and global markets.[61] Because CCPs are so large, interconnected, and integral to the operation of the financial markets, academics have identified them as too-big-to-fail entities[62] or even as very systemically important financial institutions (V-SIFIs).[63]

In the EU-27, there are currently thirteen CCPs authorized by ESMA—headquartered in eleven EU member states—to offer clearing services and activities in the EU (Table 13.1). There are nine EU countries with a single CCP, while Germany and the Netherlands each have two CCPs. In terms of products that CCPs are authorized to clear, there is significant variation. Although the majority of them may clear

---

[61] CCPs are deeply interconnected as they have direct relationships with clearing members and settlement banks and indirect relationships with clearing members' customers but also with other CCPs. Almost every big financial institution is connected to all big CCPs, and the vast majority of their derivatives trades go through clearing houses. See Colleen Baker, 'The Federal Reserve's Supporting Role behind Dodd–Frank's Clearinghouse Reforms' (2013) 3 Harvard Business Law Review 177.

[62] See Julia Lees Allen, 'Derivatives Clearinghouses and Systemic Risk: A Bankruptcy and Dodd–Frank Analysis' (2012) 64(4) Stanford Law Review 1079.

[63] See Singh, 'Making OTC Derivatives Safe' (n 42).

Table 13.1 List of European CCPs authorized to offer services and activities in the EU

Name of CCP	Country of establishment	Clearing of IRD	Place of execution	IRD class	Settlement currency
Nasdaq OMX Clearing AB	Sweden	Yes	OTC and ETD	Fixed-to-float, FRA, OIS	EUR, DKK, NOK, SEK
European Central Counterparty N.V.	Netherlands	–	–	–	–
KDPW_CCP	Poland	Yes	OTC and ETD	Basis Swap, Fixed-to-float, FRA, OIS	EUR, PLN
Eurex Clearing AG	Germany	Yes	OTC and ETD	Basis Swap, Fixed-to-float, FRA, OIS	EUR, GBP, JPY, USD
Cassa di Compensazione e Garanzia S.p.A (CCG)	Italy	–	–	–	–
London Clearing House (LCH) SA	France	–	–	–	–
European Commodity Clearing	Germany	–	–	–	–
Keler CCP	Hungary	Yes	ETD	–	–
CCP Austria Abwicklungsstelle für Börsengeschäfte GmbH (CCP.A)	Austria	–	–	–	–
BME Clearing	Spain	Yes	OTC	Basis Swap, Fixed-to-float, FRA, OIS	EUR
OMIClear—C.C., SA	Portugal	–	–	–	–
Intercontinental Exchange (ICE) Clear Netherlands B.V.	Netherlands	–	–	–	–
Athens Exchange Clearing House (Athex Clear)	Greece	–	–	–	–

Note: The CCPs listed here have been authorized to offer services and activities in the EU in accordance with Regulation (EU) No. 648/2012 on OTC derivatives, central counterparties, and trade repositories (EMIR).

Source: authors' calculations based on data from the ESMA.

derivative transactions, differences exist in terms of the asset classes for which they are authorized.[64]

With regard to IRD, out of the thirteen European CCPs, five are authorized to clear this asset class and one of them offers execution on a regulated market (the Hungarian Keler CCP). The remaining four—National Association of Securities Dealers Automated Quotations (NASDAQ) OMX Clearing, KDPW_CCP, Eurex Clearing, and BME Clearing—clear almost all OTC IRD classes, such as basis swap, fixed-to-float, FRA, and OIS. With regard to IRD products, all four CCPs clear derivatives denominated in euros and only Eurex Clearing clears IRD in international currencies such as GBP, USD, and JPY.

[64] For the list of classes of financial instruments covered by the CCP's authorization, see https://www.esma.eur opa.eu/sites/default/files/library/ccps_authorised_under_emir.pdf (accessed 29 January 2022).

Table 13.2 List of third-country CCPs recognized to clear IRD in the EU

Name of CCP	Country of establishment	Clearing of IRD	Place of execution	IRD class	Settlement currency
Chicago Mercantile Exchange (CME)	US	Yes	OTC and ETD	Basis Swap, Fixed-to-float IRS, FRA, OIS	EUR, GBP, JPY, USD, NOK, PLN, SEK
Japan Securities Clearing Corporation (JSCC)	Japan	Yes	OTC	Basis Swap, Fixed-to-float IRS	EUR, JPY, USD
OTC Clearing HK	Hong Kong	Yes	OTC	Basis Swap, Fixed-to-float IRS	EUR, USD
LCH Ltd	UK	Yes	OTC and ETD	Basis Swap, Fixed-to-float, FRA, OIS	EUR, GBP, JPY, USD, NOK, PLN, SEK

Note: The CCPs listed here have been recognized to offer services and activities in the EU in accordance with Regulation (EU) No. 648/2012 on OTC derivatives, central counterparties, and trade repositories (EMIR).

Source: authors' calculations based on data from the ESMA.

With regard to third-country CCPs, ESMA has recognized thirty-eight international CCPs as providers of clearing services and activities in the EU, subject to the existence of an equivalence agreement between the EU and the respective country.[65] Over the years, the number of recognized third-country CCPs has increased significantly from eleven in 2015 to thirty-two in 2017 and thirty-eight since the beginning of 2021. As for geographical coverage, most of these CCPs are located in Asia and Northern America. However, only four of them are recognized and active in the European OTC derivatives market covered by a clearing obligation (Table 13.2).

4.4 The CCP's Clearing Members

The offsetting of matched positions that a CCP performs is characterized both by economies of scale (i.e. the marginal costs of clearing are close to zero) and by network effects; that is, the greater the number of participants in a CCP, the more efficient it is. This network effect results in a natural tendency towards large-scale concentration.[66] One of the main reasons is that marginal costs decrease when the CCP grows due to its ability to perform two significant trading functions: netting and compression.[67]

---

[65] The list with all recognized third-country CCPs is available at https://www.esma.europa.eu/sites/default/files/library/third-country_ccps_recognised_under_emir.pdf (accessed 29 July 2022).

[66] See Tina Hasenpusch, *Clearing Services for Global Markets* (Cambridge: Cambridge University Press 2009); Ruben Lee, *Running the World's Markets: The Governance of Financial Infrastructure* (Princeton, NJ: Princeton University Press 2011); Dermot Turing, *Clearing and Settlement* (London: Bloomsbury Professional, 2012); Felix Chang, 'Second-Generation Monopolization: Parallel Exclusion in Derivatives Markets' (2016)3 Columbia Business Law Review 658.

[67] Compression allows the combining and offsetting of trades with compatible economic characteristics, resulting in a reduction in notional outstanding amount. This technique results in the reduction of the number of individual positions in the portfolio (resulting in lower capital charges and trading costs), while maintaining the same risk profile.

Table 13.3 Number of participants in CCPs

	Name of CCP	2014	2015	2016	2017	2018	2019	2020
EA	EUREX Clearing	183	186	195	190	209	218	222
	Athens Exchange Clearing House (Athex Clear)	27	25	24	19	19	19	17
	BME Clearing	58	60	65	65	64	68	67
	LCH.Clearnet SA	110	110	100	99	125	119	130
	CC&G	81	82	87	86	84	91	93
	European Central Counterparty N.V.	48	45	43	44	42	44	45
	ICE Clear Netherlands	2	3	4	–	–	–	–
	CCP Austria	57	53	50	49	51	51	48
	OMIClear—C.C., SA	–	–	–	14	14	11	9
	Total EA	566	564	568	566	608	621	631
Non-EA	KDPW_CCP	38	39	38	37	35	33	32
	KELER CCP	29	25	21	21	21	18	18
	Nasdaq OMX DM	97	92	92	88	88	97	87
	Total non-EA	164	156	151	146	144	148	137
UK	LCH.Clearnet Ltd	161	154	158	157	161	162	180
	ICE Clear Europe	80	73	78	80	81	88	87
	CME Clearing Europe Ltd	–	19	17	–	–	–	–
	LME Clear Ltd	42	42	44	46	46	45	46
	Total UK	283	288	297	283	288	295	313

Notes: The number of clearing members refers to the last day of the year. Since May 2017, ICE Clear Netherlands no longer provides clearing services for the Dutch market. CME Clearing Europe (CME CE) received authorization as a CCP under the European Market Infrastructure Regulation (EMIR) on 4 August 2014 and was closed on 12 October 2017.

Sources: Authors' calculations based on data from the European Central Bank (ECB) and individual CCPs.

For example, in terms of number of participants, at the end of 2020, the 3 UK CCPs had a total of 313 participants: LCH.Clearnet Ltd (180), ICE Clear Europe (87), and LME Clear Ltd (46). The German EUREX Clearing and the French LCH Clearnet SA had 222 and 130 participants, respectively (Table 13.3).

CCPs are increasingly interconnected with one another either indirectly via their clearing members and/or directly via interoperability arrangements.[68] Thus, in addition to the size of the member base, it is important to consider the identity of these clearing members as well as the number of CCPs in which a single member participates.

---

[68] See ESMA, 'Final Report: Possible Systemic Risk and Cost Implications of Interoperability Arrangements' (1 March 2016) (ESMA, 'Final Report: Possible Systemic Risk and Cost Implications of Interoperability Arrangements'); Angela Armakolla and Benedetta Bianchi, 'The European Central Counterparty (CCP) Ecosystem', Data Needs and Statistics Compilation for Macroprudential Analysis (Brussels, May 2017); Emanuel Alfranseder, Pawer Fiedor, Sarah Lapschies, Lucia Orszaghova, and Pawel Sobolewski, 'Indicators for the Monitoring of Central Counterparties in the EU', ESRB Occasional Paper No. 14 (March 2018).

This will allow us to better understand the impact that the default of an interconnected member could have on multiple CCPs simultaneously.

The top part of Table 13.4 shows the list of the top thirty global systemically important banks (G-SIBs) that are clearing members of the four EU and four third-country CCPs authorized and recognized to clear IRD in the EU. LCH Ltd comes first with twenty-four G-SIB members, followed by CME with nineteen and Eurex Clearing with seventeen.[69] Some institutions, such as Bank of America, Barclays, Citigroup, Deutsche Bank, J.P. Morgan Chase, and Société Générale, are members of six of the CCPs considered, while BNP Paribas is a member of seven CCPs. Similar is the view when looking at the bottom part of Table 13.4, which shows the participation of European other systemically important banks (O-SIBs) at CCPs.

G-SIBs, which are the principal clearing members in all major CCPs, are also the principal dealers in derivatives. The dealer market is characterized by a high degree of concentration among a handful of large banks. For example, according to latest data for the United States, the four large US commercial banks held 88.7% of the €143.9 trillion total notional amount of IRD held in the first quarter of 2021 (Figure 13.10). This large stake confers to the top dealers a great share of the IRD derivatives trading revenues, which can reach €2.5–3.5 billion per quarter.[70] However, it is important to highlight that a major part of the gross notional volume traded between CCPs and their largest clearing members (in particular, the top dealers) does not create significant net risk exposure.[71] This is because these large institutions (i.e. dealers) operate as intermediaries between end customers,[72] generally seeking to take largely offsetting positions despite maintaining large gross portfolios. Having said that, they do have large exposures to each other, accounting for about 70% of the total notional traded in the market,[73] and are therefore an important source of counterparty risk.[74]

The growing interconnection between CCPs and clearing members raises concerns with regard to financial stability and systemic risk.[75] A recent analysis found that at least sixteen of the twenty-six CCPs considered could be impacted by the default of any of the eleven largest clearing members.[76] This suggests a high degree of

---

[69] In 2016, Eurex Clearing had twenty-four G-SIBs as clearing members. See European Commission, 'Impact Assessment Accompanying the Document: Proposal for a Regulation of the European Parliament and of the Council Amending Regulation (EU) No. 1095/2010 Establishing a European Supervisory Authority (European Securities and Markets Authority) and Amending Regulation (EU) No. 648/2012 as regards the Procedures and Authorities Involved for the Authorisation of CCPs and the Requirements for the Recognition of Third-Country CCPs' COM (2017) 331 final.

[70] Trading revenues have comprised, on average, 12–15% of the gross revenues of the top four banks. For J.P. Morgan, a bank with a long history of trading, revenues have reached as high as 31% of gross revenues (Q2, 2020).

[71] See, e.g. Fiedor et al., 'Networks of Counterparties in the Centrally Cleared EU-Wide Interest Rate Derivatives Market' (n 8); Marco D'Errico, Stefano Battiston, Tuomas Peltonen, and Martin Scheicher, 'How Does Risk Flow in the Credit Default Swap Market?' (2018) 35 Journal of Financial Stability 53; Marco D'Errico and Tarik Roukny, 'Compressing Over-the-Counter Markets' (2021) 69 Operations Research 1651.

[72] See Franklin Allen and Anthony Santomero, 'The Theory of Financial Intermediation' (1997) 21(11–12) Journal of Banking and Finance 1461.

[73] See Evangelos Benos, Anne Wetherilt, and Filip Zikes, 'The Structure and Dynamics of the UK Credit Default Swap Market', Bank of England Financial Stability Paper No. 25 (8 November 2013).

[74] See ECB, 'Credit Default Swaps and Counterparty Risk' (August 2009).

[75] Yellen, 'Interconnectedness and Systemic Risk' (n 18).

[76] See BCBS–CPMI–FSB–IOSCO, 'Analysis of Central Clearing Interdependencies' (n 30).

Table 13.4 Membership/participation of SIBs in CCPs authorized/recognized to clear IRD in the EU

SIBs		LCH Ltd	CME	Eurex Clearing	JSCC	OTC Clearing Hong Kong	BME Clearing	KDPW_CCP	Nasdaq Clearing
Top thirty G-SIBs	Agricultural Bank of China					X			
	Bank of America	X	X	X	X	X	X		
	Bank of China	X				X			
	Bank of New York Mellon	X							
	Barclays	X	X	X	X	X	X		
	BNP Paribas	X	X	X	X	X	X	X	
	China Construction Bank					X			
	Citigroup	X	X	X	X	X	X		
	Credit Suisse	X	X	X	X		X		
	Deutsche Bank	X	X	X	X	X	X		
	Goldman Sachs	X	X	X	X		X		
	Groupe BPCE								
	Groupe Crédit Agricole	X	X	X	X	X			
	HSBC	X	X	X	X				
	Industrial & Commercial Bank of China					X			
	ING Bank	X						X	
	JP Morgan Chase	X	X	X	X	X	X		
	Mitsubishi UFJ FG	X			X				
	Mizuho FG	X	X	X	X				
	Morgan Stanley	X	X	X	X		X		
	Royal Bank of Canada	X	X	X	X				
	Santander	X	X	X	X		X		
	Société Générale	X	X	X	X	X	X		

(continued)

Table 13.4 Continued

	SIBs	LCH Ltd	CME	Eurex Clearing	JSCC	OTC Clearing Hong Kong	BME Clearing	KDPW_CCP	Nasdaq Clearing
	Standard Chartered	X				X			
	State Street	X	X						
	Sumitomo Mitsui FG				X				
	Toronto Dominion	X	X						
	UBS	X	X	X	X		X		
	UniCredit	X		X		X			
	Wells Fargo	X	X						
	Total	24	19	17	16	14	12	2	0
O-SIBs	ABN Amro Clearing Bank	X	X	X			X	X	
	Banco Bilbao Vizcaya	X	X	X			X	X	
	Banco Santander	X		X			X	X	
	CaixaBank	X		X			X		
	Commerzbank	X		X					
	Crédit Agricole	X	X	X		X			
	Danske Bank	X							X
	Deutsche Bank	X		X	X	X	X		
	DZ Bank	X		X					
	ING	X		X				X	
	Intesa Sanpaolo	X		X					
	Landesbank Baden–Württemberg	X		X					
	Nordea	X		X					X
	Skandinaviska Enskilda Banken	X		X					X
	Swedbank	X							X
	Total	15	3	13	1	2	5	3	4

Notes: Consolidated at G-SIB and O-SIB group level, based on CCPs' public websites, June 2021. The list of thirty G-SIBs was obtained by FSB (2020). The CCPs considered are the ones authorized/recognized by ESMA to offer clearing services and activities in OTC IRD.

Sources: authors' calculations based on data from CCPs' public websites, ESMA, and Financial Stability Board, '2020 List of Global Systemically Important Banks (G-SIBs)' (11 November 2020).

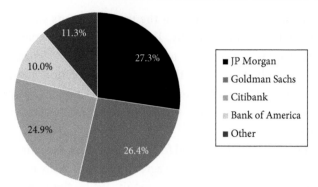

Figure 13.10 Top four US dealers in OTC IRD, percentage of notional amount, Q1 2021

Notes: These figures are based on bank derivatives activities provided by all insured US commercial banks and saving accounts associations. They refer to the global trading activity of US dealers and thus do not account for the US trading activity of dealers domiciled outside the United States.

Sources: authors' calculations based on data from the Office of the Comptroller of the Currency, 'Quarterly Report on Bank Trading and Derivatives Activities—First Quarter 2021' (June 2021) and Eurostat.

interconnectedness and dependence among the central clearing system's largest and most significant clearing members. However, such a default might be unlikely (but not impossible) because a large clearing member would most probably be resolved following the rules on recovery and resolution (adopted after the Lehman collapse) and the CCP's own buffers (described above) before it defaults at an SI CCP.

5 A Long-Term European Clearing Policy

In setting a CCP clearing policy for the EU, European policymakers need to strike a balance between financial stability and competitiveness considerations. Derivatives markets and the related institutions are global, and the markets have evolved considerably since the GFC. CCP clearing has become much more important and so have the rules affecting clearing houses. Market transparency has increased and CCP prudential rules have been implemented and have already withstood their first tests.

Since the start of the single market and in the Financial Services Action Plan (FSAP), the EU's ambition has been to strengthen the competitiveness of its financial sector and to create global players. The United Kingdom, and the City of London in particular, has benefited largely from this objective by becoming the bridgehead of Europe's financial industry, in all its dimensions, but also by attracting ever more important activities of international banks. The EU has thereby managed to remain an open market, also for third-country operators.

With the departure of the United Kingdom from the EU, the EU and the United Kingdom concluded a Withdrawal Agreement (WA) and a new Trade and Cooperation Agreement (TCA) ensuring a framework for an orderly transition to—and management of—their new relationship. Appropriate safeguards are in place to ensure orderly competition on both sides, including a dispute settlement system.

The frictions are so far most evident on the trade-in-goods side, but on the services side, business has adapted rapidly. The scale, size, and expertise that London has in financial services will continue to be important for the EU, and a new modus operandi will have to be found. On the EU side, the creation of a Banking Union (BU), and even more a Capital Markets Union (CMU), remains a work in progress. Europe's banks need to consolidate further, and capital markets need to become more integrated.

The EU has also recognized this need for openness with other third countries. It has concluded a large number of equivalence agreements with many jurisdictions around the world, agreements that are constantly monitored by the European Supervisory Authorities (ESAs). The highest number of agreements are in place for the closest trading partners such as the United States and Japan, but even with jurisdictions such as Brazil or China, several agreements are in place. Specifically on the clearing side, an equivalence agreement for CCP supervision under EMIR is in place with fourteen different jurisdictions.

Following the United Kingdom's departure from the EU, a clear EU policy is yet to emerge on the financial markets side. Although some steps have been taken, much more needs to be done. When setting a long-term strategy for the future of the EU clearing services, European authorities should consider and evaluate the potential effects of the available options in terms of financial stability, efficiency, and future development of European financial/capital markets. These three factors are highly interrelated on many levels and also requested as part of EMIR 2.2.

Efficient markets are important both for promoting a resilient and robust financial system and for developing European financial markets and infrastructures. The nature of OTC derivatives markets plays an important role in this framework. This is because transactions in OTC derivatives frequently involve counterparties in different jurisdictions, while market participants regularly trade in several currencies and across various types of OTC derivatives.

5.1 Financial Stability

CCPs concentrate counterparty risk and are critical to the functioning of cleared markets. This risk concentration in CCPs is a deliberate and inherent outcome of the policy drive towards central clearing.[77] It is a feature of CCPs' function that should be tackled in the most appropriate way. Indeed, it is precisely in recognition of the associated systemic risk implications that the international regulatory bodies, the CPMI and IOSCO, introduced the PFMIs in 2012.[78]

---

[77] See Fernando Cerezetti, Jorge Cruz Lopez, Mark Manning, and David Murphy, 'Who Pays? Who Gains? Central Counterparty Resource Provision in the Post-Pittsburgh World' (2019) 7(3) Journal of Financial Market Infrastructures 21.

[78] See Committee on Payment and Settlement Systems (CPSS)–IOSCO, 'Principles for Financial Market Infrastructures (16 April 2012) (CPSS–IOSCO, 'Principles for Financial Market Infrastructures').

If CCPs incorporate appropriate risk controls, they can enhance financial stability; otherwise, they can be a source of financial stress. European regulators have considered the extent to which instability at a third-country CCP could affect European markets and participants. Critical elements of this analysis are (i) the capacity of European authorities to oversee the CCP's activities during the normal course of business and to intervene to mitigate shocks during a crisis, if necessary, and (ii) how the structure of both the CCP and the cleared market affects the CCP's ability to mitigate financial shocks.

5.1.1 Oversight of third-country CCPs

European regulators (National Competent Authorities (NCAs), the EC, ECB, and ESMA) have coordination and oversight responsibilities for European and third-country CCPs and are particularly interested in the euro activities of third-country CCPs as well as the risks to European participants through their use of such CCPs. The main oversight objective is to ensure that risk is appropriately controlled. This means, among other things, that CCPs meet the applicable risk management standards (i.e. PFMIs) developed by the Committee on Payment and Settlement Systems (CPSS) and the Technical Committee of the IOSCO.

Supervising a CCP located in the EU is more straightforward than overseeing a CCP located in a third country. European authorities have direct powers in regulating EU CCPs and have a full set of legal mechanisms for enforcing their requirements. However, the oversight benefits would accrue only to the portion of the market being served by an EU CCP. It is more complicated for European authorities to oversee a third-country CCP since they would not be the primary regulator and would generally have less direct influence. In particular, for CCPs deemed more systemically important to the EU and designated as tier 2, ESMA has extensive direct supervisory powers.

A forum that can promote cross-border cooperation and coordination among authorities, as well as enhance preparedness for the failure of a CCP—and facilitate the resolution of the CCP in this event—is the crisis management group (CMG). CMGs have been established with the aim of enabling CCPs and regulatory and supervisory authorities to cooperate, share information, and coordinate, both during business-as-usual periods and in times of crisis, with a view to facilitating recovery or, as necessary, an orderly CCP resolution. The CMG focuses on the resolution planning and actions in relation to the CCP, opposite to those crisis management aspects relating to recovery or early intervention, which are dealt with by the EMIR College (EMIR, Art. 18) and by each authority.[79] Although CMGs play a vital role in having close and continuous cross-border regulatory cooperation and providing assurance in a crisis situation, it is important to highlight that the ultimate decision-making should reside with the resolution authority of the jurisdiction in which the CCP is established.

---

[79] In the United Kingdom, for example, CMGs are organized and chaired by the Bank of England (BoE), with CMG members including all relevant EU supervisory/resolution authorities, the ECB, and ESMA.

5.1.2 Ability to mitigate financial shocks

Having clear and robust processes in place to manage member defaults in an orderly fashion, CCPs promote financial stability. In the event of a default, the CCP takes on the obligations of the defaulting member's portfolio and manages this risk with the help of other members. This means that effective management of a default requires a strong membership base and access to liquid and efficient markets. CCP participants play an important role in that respect. Although CCPs meet harmonized risk management standards,[80] differences in their ability to manage severe shocks may occur, such as the simultaneous default of multiple clearing members.

A large CCP may be better placed and have a greater capacity to manage member defaults than a smaller EU CCP. This has to do not only with the size of the CCP but also with the diversity of its market participants from many different jurisdictions and the larger pool of surviving members to help hedge and replace the defaulted portfolio. In addition, such a CCP would also be able to have greater financial capacity to absorb losses in the event of a default.

Participating in a third-country CCP could expose EU firms to shocks arising from the default of participants based in other jurisdictions since stress might be transmitted to markets in Europe through the default management mechanism of that CCP. On the one hand, requiring European participants to clear their euro derivatives at an EU CCP might protect European markets from shocks occurring in non-EU countries. However, this benefit may be limited since European dealers will probably need to be members of third-country CCPs in order to clear non-euro derivatives products (given that, currently, the EU is missing a large centralized clearing services provider). On top of that, non-EU dealers would probably be members of CCPs located in Europe. One way or another, the interconnection and global nature of the derivatives market unavoidably exposes European participants to potential financial losses stemming from the default of CCP members based in other jurisdictions. Thus, enhancing supervisory and regulatory cooperation between the EU and third-countries should be prioritized.[81]

5.2 Efficiency

Consideration should be given to European market participants, particularly in terms of costs and liquidity. A requirement to clear euro-denominated derivatives within the EU in an EU-based CCP would induce higher costs for European market participants and would adversely affect market efficiency. This is because users of EU CCPs would be required to split their cleared portfolios between EU and non-EU CCPs. As a result, costs and the need for collateral (due to lower netting opportunities) would increase.

---

[80] See CPSS–IOSCO, 'Principles for Financial Market Infrastructures (n 78).
[81] See Apostolos Thomadakis, 'Over-the-Counter Interest Rate Derivatives: The Clock is Ticking for the UK and the EU', European Capital Markets Institute Research Report No. 13 (March 2018).

5.2.1 Costs

Costs would increase in six ways. First, users would need to pay membership and clearing fees to two CCPs. If they are already members of a third-country CCP, they would have to become members of an EU CCP (if they are not already members), thus paying additional fees. Second, users would be required to contribute to two default funds, one of the EU CCP and another of the third-country CCP. Third, they would be required to increase collateral as they would benefit from less cross-currency diversification and netting of risk exposures in their cleared portfolios.

Fourth, users would have to post margin at two different CCPs. This would further increase costs not only because margin needs to be funded by tapping capital markets but also because of debt overhang.[82] Fifth, regulatory capital costs would increase, given the reduced netting of risk exposures and the additional contributions to the default fund.[83] Sixth, dealers may recover the cost of not being able to net positions across CCPs by charging their clients. Although the price difference charged between net buyers and net sellers (known as 'CCP basis') may seem small, if multiplied by daily volume, the cost may be significant.[84]

5.2.2 Fragmentation and liquidity

Fragmentation associated with using EU CCPs would likely lead to higher costs and decreased market liquidity in euro OTC derivatives. Market participants not obliged to clear in the EU would have an incentive to concentrate their clearing through a third-country CCP. Since trading can occur only when both counterparties clear through the same CCP, European market participants would consequently have fewer trading opportunities and would face decreased market liquidity. This would consequently raise costs of clearing and trading for European market participants.

In a far-fetched scenario, increased costs associated with clearing locally could potentially result in reduced use of standardized and clearable derivatives products and thus decelerate the adoption of central clearing. Furthermore, higher costs could discourage the use of derivatives as a risk management tool and might put European market participants at a competitive disadvantage relative to their international counterparts. But, more importantly from a financial stability point of view, reduced liquidity in a fragmented market could reduce the ability of EU CCPs to effectively manage risk and handle clearing members' defaults. Opposite to that, a third-country CCP with access to a large pool of liquidity can quickly replace defaulted portfolios, thus minimizing the impact on surviving members and protecting the stability of the financial system.

Interoperability arrangements—links between two or more CCPs which involve the cross-system execution of transactions—could reduce costs related to the fragmentation

---

[82] See Leif Andersen, Darrell Duffie, and Yang Song, 'Funding Value Adjustments' (2019) 74(1) Journal of Finance 145.

[83] Capital costs would also be increased if there was no extension of equivalence, which would imply that UK CCPs are non-qualifying CCPs, that is, not recognized in accordance with EMIR (n 47).

[84] See Evangelos Benos, Wenqian Huang, Albert Menkveld, and Michalis Vasios, 'The Cost of Clearing Fragmentation' (22 April 2021), https://papers.ssrn.com/sol3/papers.cfm?abstract_id=3397065 (accessed 29 June 2021).

of clearing.[85] Currently, there are no such arrangements in place between CCPs for OTC derivatives.[86] The benefit of having links between CCPs is that it allows each counterparty to a trade to clear at a different CCP (with an inter-CCP contract arising to offset the exposures). It also allows clearing members to have access to more netting and diversification opportunities without seeking membership of multiple CCPs as well as benefiting from having a portfolio cleared at a single CCP. While interoperability is an unlikely solution for OTC derivatives, it is a tried-and-tested model for equities.

5.3 Development

A long-term vision should also take into account the future development of European financial services in the context of 'strategic autonomy'.

The development of European capital markets might be affected—either positively or negatively—by the requirement to clear euro-denominated derivatives in an EU-based CCP. On the positive side, a location policy for euro-denominated derivatives could be beneficial for the development of market infrastructures in Europe. A requirement to use an EU CCP might facilitate cross-product netting with other financial instruments or listed derivatives—but only where this product offering is available in the EU.[87] This could promote local trading,[88] while also stimulating the creation of legal, economic, and operational expertise, which might facilitate further the development of European financial centres.

Although such potential benefits are important, in absolute terms they might prove to be small or insignificant. There is a need to assess them carefully and to measure and weigh them against the disadvantages of imposing a location policy. Some of these are financial stability risks, higher costs, restricted liquidity and efficiency, greater vulnerability to financial shocks, implementation risks (associated with the development of EU CCPs to clear particular classes of trades in OTC derivatives), competitive disadvantage of European investors compared to international ones, the (un)attractiveness of EU capital markets, and the declining role of the euro as an international currency.

6 Conclusion

Derivatives markets allow local economic exposures to be shared globally, thus efficiently transferring risk. Since the GFC, central clearing has been at the forefront of the

---

[85] See ESMA, 'Final Report: Possible Systemic Risk and Cost Implications of Interoperability Arrangements' (n 68); ESRB, 'CCP Interoperability Arrangements' (n 47).

[86] Expanding interoperability arrangements for OTC derivatives would be challenging to configure as CCPs, their members, and supervisors would need to evaluate such arrangements carefully against the risk of contagion in times of market stress.

[87] Such cross-product netting is used to reduce derivative exposure. It can take the form of either derivative to derivative or financial instrument to derivative. For example, a common way to reduce derivative exposure is to have the cash equity or bond as part of a portfolio that combines cash instruments (already settled) with derivatives—with the condition that both cash instruments and derivatives are part of a portfolio within a CCP.

[88] This may be the case for EUR instruments. However, for non-EUR instruments the non-EU counterparties would still be needed to assure deep liquidity and efficient price formation.

financial regulatory agenda. One of the G20 commitments was the introduction and use of mandatory clearing, which has been the catalyst for the trend observed over the past few years where market participants clear financial trades through CCPs. Central clearing of OTC derivatives has increased transparency and reduced risks, while, at the same time, CCPs' risk management strategies have been strengthened with the introduction of the PFMIs. Nevertheless, finding the right balance between the global nature of CCPs, on the one hand, and financial stability within each individual jurisdiction, on the other, is a significant challenge.

A few global financial centres have specialized, and these centres clear the lion's share of global trades. London, for example, is a leading clearing hub for OTC derivatives. In interest rate swaps, UK CCPs have a central role and clear over 90% of the global market in currencies such as euros and dollars. Concern about the concentration of risk in third-country CCPs and foreign currency exposure has been an issue among EU policymakers and supervisors for the past two decades. Specifically in the EU, given its multijurisdictional nature, supervisors have progressed with greater European-wide supervision of CCPs, which has been sharpened with the United Kingdom's withdrawal from the EU.

In this context, ensuring that financial stability risks are adequately managed and that EU financial institutions that participate in third-country CCPs are sufficiently protected is the EC's primary task. As such, EMIR 2.2 was introduced as a means to enhance the EU framework for the supervision of third-country CCPs. The direct application of EMIR standards to systemically important CCPs and the direct involvement of ESMA (and EU central banks) in monitoring and supervising recognized third-country CCPs resolves some of the policy issues raised by the heavy reliance of the EU financial system on services provided by third-country CCPs.

In February 2022, the EC extended the equivalence decision (which was ending in June 2022) granting access to UK CCPs until June 2025. This gives the EC time to come up with measures that will make the EU CCPs more attractive, competitive, and cost-efficient to market participants as well as to strengthen the supervisory framework for EU CCPs.[89] The migration of euro-denominated positions from CCPs established in third countries to CCPs established in the EU will reduce exposures in such products to third-country CCPs and will also help to further develop the European infrastructure to clear OTC derivatives markets. In addition, the use of EU CCPs might facilitate cross-product netting with listed derivatives, which could promote trading within the EU. It will also stimulate the creation of legal, economic, and operational expertise, which will spur the development of EU financial centres.

However, such migration might be counterproductive, and instead of mitigating financial stability risk within a jurisdiction, may actually contribute to it. Not taking into account the global nature of derivatives markets and restricting access to clearing and

[89] See the Commission's decision, 'Capital Markets Union: Commission Extends Time-Limited Equivalence for UK Central Counterparties and Launches Consultation to Expand Central Clearing Activities in the EU' (8 February 2022), https://ec.europa.eu/info/publications/220208-equivalence-central-counterparties-uk_en (accessed 10 March 2022).

markets for which there is a clearing mandate runs against the G20 commitments and their justification.

Moreover, it may harm liquidity, increase costs for market participants, create distinct marketplaces for EU and non-EU firms, and reduce their efficiency to participate and compete in the global derivatives market. In addition, it would also disadvantage EU banks compared to their non-EU counterparts, as EU banks would not be able to be direct clearing members of third-country CCPs, thus impacting their client-clearing and market-making activities with non-EU clients and counterparties not subject to the requirement to clear euro-denominated products within the EU. Meanwhile, non-EU banks would preserve their ability to offer these services to non-EU clients and counterparties.

Moving forward, and in order to avoid the risk of regulatory divergence and the loss of EU supervisory oversight, systemically important third-country CCPs are required by EMIR 2.2 to continue to comply with the European standards (i.e. prudential, governance, and operational), while EU authorities continue to maintain the same degree of oversight of such CCPs. Importantly, the best way to manage any financial stability risk is to have appropriate supervisory and regulatory cooperation, working together, jointly supervising and making sure that regulators have access to the information they need to carry out their responsibilities. In that respect, the EMIR 2.2 regulatory framework seems to allow for such outcome to be achieved. The new supervisory structure should be given time to develop and evolve over the coming years before introducing any radical or unnecessary changes with unintended consequences for EU firms.

Nevertheless, it is equally important for EU market participants to be able to retain the flexibility to continue to clear their transactions through the CCP of their choice or the choice of their clients and counterparties. This allows them to continue their market-making and client-clearing activities and have access to global pools of liquidity, especially when a third-country CCP has an equivalent regulatory and supervisory regime to the European one. Enabling market participants to determine the optimal market structure based on their trading needs and objectives will allow for a more organic and customer-driven development of the European derivatives market structure. Overall, any measures should aim to develop EU capital markets and infrastructures, apply on a voluntary basis, be market driven, and be given the appropriate time.

14

Open Access for OTC Derivatives

Concept and Implications

Corentine Poilvet-Clediere and Julien Jardelot

1 Definition of Open Access

1.1 Legal Acceptance

The concept of open access can refer to a wide range of access rights and connections. Its legal acceptance has, however, a specific meaning, with the European Market Infrastructure Regulation (EMIR) and the Markets in Financial Instruments Regulation (MIFIR) both clarifying what open access is and what it is not. In this book, we will focus on the concept of open access for over-the-counter (OTC) derivatives as opposed to exchange-traded derivatives, equities, or other asset classes. The distinction between OTC derivatives and exchange-traded derivatives is developed in Chapter 1 ('After the Dust Has Settled: Clearing OTC Derivatives in Europe after a Decade of Regulation' by Bas Zebregs, Victor de Serière, Patrick Pearson, and Rezah Stegeman) in this volume.

Open access is a right, established in EU regulation, for financial markets infrastructures that are part of a wide chain to access other financial markets infrastructures (trading venues and central counterparties, CCPs). Open access provides a trading venue the right for non-discriminatory access to a CCP and vice versa. It applies to distinct parts of the financial markets chain.

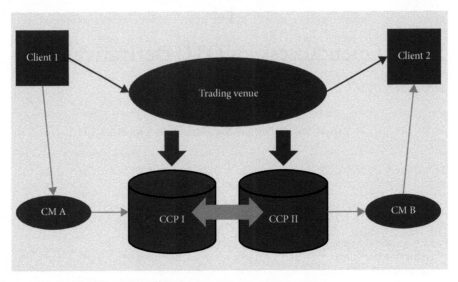

Figure 14.1 Stylized example of clearing via interoperable CCPs
Source: ESRB CCP interoperability arrangements report from January 2019.

1.2 Distinction with Other Arrangements

Open access is not to be confused with interoperability arrangements, which is not a 'right' per se but a contractual arrangement negotiated between two CCPs (i.e. same parts of the chain as opposed to different levels), allowing members of CCP 1 to interact with members of CCP 2 without having to clear in the same CCP.

There are no interoperability agreements in the OTC derivatives space for instance, notably because of the complexities it implies from a risk management perspective and the specificities of each OTC derivative contract clear by each individual CCP: the products are not identical, so interoperability is not really feasible beyond the risk aspect, which is a core element. Besides, EMIR, Recital (73) indicates that interoperability arrangements should be limited to transferable securities and money market instruments, 'given the additional complexities involved in an interoperability arrangement between CCPs clearing OTC derivative contracts'.

This was confirmed in 2015 by the European Securities Markets Authority (ESMA) in its report on extending the scope of the EMIR requirements relating to interoperability arrangements to cover transactions in classes of financial instruments other than transferable securities and money market instruments.

1.3 Origin and Evolution

As early as February 2001, the final report from the 'committee of wise men on the regulation of European securities markets', also known as the Lamfalussy Report, identified 'the excessive costs of cross-border clearing and settlement in the EU compared to the US' as a major obstacle to consolidation.[1] Among the elements highlighted, it found 'competition issues such as open and non-discriminatory access'. The first Giovannini Report, published in November 2001, also referred to the 'concerns around vertical silo structure', noting that 'such restrictions constitute a barrier by requiring investors, who engage in cross-border securities transactions on multiple stock exchanges, to use multiple post-trading systems'.[2] In 2011, the Expert Group on Market Infrastructures (EGMI) highlighted the need for 'availability of interoperable CCP services in all markets for adequately liquid cash securities, enabled by non-discriminatory access to trading venues and CSDs' as a key one for the upcoming European Union (EU) reforms.

The private sector tried to tackle this issue on its own through a Code of Conduct on Clearing and Settlement.[3] In November 2006, European securities exchanges, CCPs, and central securities depositories (CSDs), represented by trade associations the Federation of European Securities Exchanges (FESE), the European Association of Clearing Houses (EACH), and the European Central Securities Depositories Association (ECSDA), agreed to enhance transparency and increase competition in the post-trading sector. While progress was made in price transparency and service unbundling, the voluntary nature of the code did not allow delivering on what is essentially a competition.

2 Objectives of Open Access

The concept of open access applied to financial markets aims to break barriers to execution posed by financial markets infrastructures operating in silos, that is, where a market participant is obliged to use the CCPs of a financial market infrastructure group to trade on a venue operated by the same group. As some products are exclusively available on certain venues, market participants can effectively be 'forced' to use a wide range of services from a particular financial market infrastructure group if they want to trade on specific products.

The overall aim of open access is to ensure more competition in the financial market infrastructure space and that the place where a market participant trades does not determine where it clears and, in some cases, settles its transactions. This issue is particularly prominent in some exchange-traded derivatives, as explained in the European Commission impact assessment.[4]

---

[1] Final Report of the Committee of Wise Men on the Regulation of European Securities Markets, Brussels 2001, www.esma.europa.eu/sites/default/files/library/2015/11/lamfalussy_report.pdf

2 Cross-border clearing and settlement arrangements in the European Union - Giovaninni Group, Brussels 2001, https://finance.ec.europa.eu/system/files/2016-12/first_giovannini_report_en.pdf

[3] Code of Conduct: http://ec.europa.eu/internal_market/financial-markets/clearing/communication_en.htm#code. See also Chapter 3.2.5

[4] Code of Conduct: http://ec.europa.eu/internal_market/financial-markets/clearing/communication_en.htm#code. See also Chapter 3.2.5

2.1 Non-discriminatory Access to Financial Market Infrastructures

Whilst non-discriminatory access provisions were introduced by the Markets in Financial Instruments Directive MiFID,[5] it tackled investment firms' access to CCP, clearing, and settlement facilities and right to designate a settlement system, allowing operators of CCP, clearing, or securities settlement systems to refuse, on legitimate commercial grounds, to make the requested services available.[6]

In the preparation to what would be the Markets in Financial Instruments Directive II (MIFID II), a Commission staff working paper impact assessment in October 2011 identified six issues, a seventh appearing in the executive summary of 'obstacles to competition in clearing infrastructures'. While acknowledging that vertically integrated trading and clearing platforms have 'merits and relative strengths', it was identified as detrimental to effective cross-border competition. Open access is therefore a way to increase competition for clearing of financial instruments to lower investment and borrowing costs, eliminate inefficiencies, and foster innovation in European markets.[7]

In October 2011, the European Commission proposed a more robust regulatory framework to further strengthen investor protection and address the development of new trading platforms and activities and the shortcomings exposed in the wake of the financial crisis. These came in the form of a directive (MiFID II), and a regulation (MiFIR). MIFIR, Recital (28) states that:

> for effective competition between trading venues for derivatives, it is essential that trading venues have non-discriminatory and transparent access to CCPs. Non-discriminatory access to a CCP should mean that a trading venue has the right to non-discriminatory treatment in terms of how contracts traded on its platform are treated in terms of collateral requirements and netting of economically equivalent contracts and cross-margining with correlated contracts cleared by the same CCP, and non-discriminatory clearing fees.

The notion was fully developed under Title VI 'Non-discriminatory clearing access for financial instruments'.

For CCPs, Art. 35 'Non-discriminatory access to a CCP' stipulated that 'a CCP shall accept to clear financial instruments on a non-discriminatory and transparent basis, including as regards collateral requirements and fees relating to access, regardless of the trading venue on which a transaction is executed'. The same applied to trading

---

[5] Directive 2004/39/EC of the European Parliament and of the Council of the European Parliament and of the Council of 21 April 2004mon markets in financial instruments amending Council Directivers 85/611/EEC and 93/6/EEC and Directive 2000/12/EECand repealing Council Directive 93/22/EEC.

[6] Directive 2004/39/EC (n 1), Art. 34(3).

[7] European Commission proposal for a regulation of the European Parliament and the COUNCIL on markets in financial instruments and amending Regulation [EMIR] on OTC derivatives, central counterparties and trade repositories, Explanatory memorandum, paragraph 3.4.9 'on-discriminatory clearing access (Title VI—Articles 28–30)'—LexUriServ.do (europa.eu) ('Explanatory Memorandum').

venues under Art. 36 'Non-discriminatory access to a trading venue', which said that 'a trading venue shall provide trade feeds on a non-discriminatory and transparent basis, including as regards fees related to access, upon request to any CCP authorised or recognised by Regulation (EU) No 648/2012 [EMiR] that wishes to clear transactions in financial instruments that are concluded on that trading venue'.

These texts were aiming to remove barriers between trading venues and providers of clearing services to ensure more competition. These frameworks are applicable to financial instruments but not OTC derivatives, which are regulated by the EMIR framework.

3 Application: Open Access in OTC Derivatives

When it comes to OTC derivatives, the EU concept of 'open access' was introduced in September 2010 with the European Commission proposal for Regulation 648/2012 on OTC derivatives, central counterparties and trade repositories, also known as EMIR. Recital (35) introduced the concept by stating that 'this Regulation should not block fair and open access between trading venues and CCPs in the internal market', later on codified under Art. 7 on 'access to a CCP', which indicates that 'a CCP that has been authorized to clear OTC derivative contracts shall accept clearing such contracts on a non-discriminatory and transparent basis, regardless of the trading venue'. Article 8 on 'access to a trading venue' introduces similar rules for trading venues.

When it comes to OTC derivatives, markets are more open and there is less of a siloed approach. EMIR therefore introduces a concept of open access in the OTC derivatives to cater for the risk of unintended competitive distortions that the introduction of clearing obligations could cause rather than to address a market failure. This is explained in EMIR, Recital (34). Indeed, to support the newly introduced clearing obligations, EMIR sought to ensure that there would be a wide range of actors providing access to clearing OTC derivatives subject to the clearing obligation and that this obligation would not lead to the erection of barriers and in order to preserve the global nature of OTC derivatives.[8] The aim of open access in OTC derivatives is primarily to ensure that CCPs and trading venues provide a wide access to their services to other parts of the chain, for example, that a 'CCP could refuse to clear transactions executed on certain trading venues because the CCP is owned by a competing trading venue' and that they accept clearing contracts on a non-discriminatory basis, regardless of the venue of execution.

3.1 Conditions

Identical requirements apply to exchange-traded derivatives, which is why these notions were specified by Commission delegated acts under MiFIR.[9] Both EMIR and

---

[8] Explanatory Memorandum (n 3), p. 7.
[9] Commission Delegated Regulation (EU) No. 2017/581 of 24 June 2016 (MiFIR).

MIFIR aim to prevent competitive distortions by requiring non-discriminatory access to CCPs offering clearing of, respectively, OTC derivatives and exchange-traded derivatives. As a CCP may clear both, the requirements on the non-discriminatory treatment of economically equivalent contracts is applicable, irrespective of where the contracts are traded.[10] However, a CCP may require that a trading venue complies with the operational and technical requirements established by the CCP, including the risk management requirements.

EMIR imposes:

- CCPs to agree to clear transactions executed in different trading venues to the extent that those trading venues comply with the operational and technical requirements established by the CCP;[11]
- trading venues to provide CCPs with trade feeds on a transparent and non-discriminatory basis, with the main limit being that this access does not lead to interoperability for derivatives clearing or create liquidity fragmentation.[12]

As noted above, interoperability arrangements are arrangements between two CCPs; it is unclear how access to a trading venue could lead to interoperability, but this reference shows the sensitivity of the open access provisions.

A CCP that has been authorized to clear OTC derivative contracts must accept clearing such contracts on a non-discriminatory and transparent basis, including as regards collateral requirements and fees related to access, regardless of the trading venue. This, in particular, must ensure that a trading venue has the right to non-discriminatory treatment in terms of how contracts traded on that trading venue are treated in terms of:

(1) collateral requirements and netting of economically equivalent contracts, where the inclusion of such contracts in the close-out and other netting procedures of a CCP based on the applicable insolvency law would not endanger the smooth and orderly functioning, the validity, or enforceability of such procedures; and
(2) cross-margining with correlated contracts cleared by the same CCP.

3.1.1 Collateral requirements and netting of economically equivalent contracts

The notion of economically equivalent contracts is defined in very broad terms: as soon as a contract traded on a trading venue to which a CCP has granted access is in a class of financial instruments covered by the CCP's existing authorization, it is considered as having similar risk characteristics to the contracts already cleared by the CCP and

---

[10] MiFIR (n 5), Recital (8).

[11] Regulation (EU) No. 648/2012 of the European Parliament and of the Council of 4 July 2012 on OTC derivatives, central counterparties and trade repositories, [2012] OJ L201/1 (27 July 2012), Art. 7 (EMIR).

[12] EMIR (n 7), Art. 8.

therefore considered as economically equivalent.[13] The initial determination is made by the CCP.[14]

The consequence of considering contracts as economically equivalent is that, as a rule, the CCP needs to apply the same margin and collateral methodologies as to other economically equivalent contracts. This includes netting procedures, provided that any netting procedure it applies is valid and enforceable in accordance with Directive 98/26/EC and applicable insolvency law.

However, this rule has exceptions:

- The CCP can adapt its risk models and parameters to mitigate the risk factors in relation to the trading venue or the contracts traded on it.
- The CCP can subject the clearing of an economically equivalent contract to the adoption of changes to its netting procedure to exclude the netting of such contract in the case the CCP considers that the legal risk or the basis risk[15] related to a netting procedure is not sufficiently mitigated.

In both cases, the changes are considered as significant changes to the CCP's models and parameters, thus ensuring that the decision is not made solely by the CCP and its competent authority but involves ESMA and the CCP supervisory college[16] to ensure a wider review of these changes. This is due to the risk of undermining non-discriminatory access with such adaptations.

3.1.2 Cross-margining of correlated contracts cleared by the same CCP

EMIR, Art. 7 refers to 'cross-margining' inaccurately and should be understood as a reference to 'portfolio margining'. The clarification is made in the Commission delegate act that refers EMIR articles on portfolio margining,[17] and directly to the notion itself in the article:[18]

- Cross margining refers to the possibility to margin products between CCPs, a mechanism often thought about but not allowed under EMIR as each CCP must individually cater for the risks of its counterparties with margins.
- Portfolio margining refers to the ability of the CCP to allow offsets or reductions in the required margin across the financial instruments that it clears if the price risk of one financial instrument or a set of financial instruments is significantly and reliably correlated, or based on equivalent statistical parameter of dependence, with the price risk of other financial instruments.[19]

---

[13] EMIR (n 7), Recital (6).

[14] EMIR (n 7), Art. 12, para. 1.

[15] 'Basis risk' is the risk arising from less than perfectly correlated movements between two or more assets or contracts cleared by the CCP.

[16] EMIR (n 7), Art. 12, para. 3.

[17] EMIR (n 7). Art. 41 and EMIR regulatory technical standards, Commission Delegated Regulation (EU) No. 153/2013 of 19 December 2012, OJ L52, Art. 27 (EMIR RTS).

[18] MiFIR (n 5), Art. 14: 'Cross-margining of correlated contracts cleared by the same CCP (portfolio margining)'.

[19] EMIR (n 7), Art. 41 and EMIR RTS (n 13), Art. 27.

To ensure an effective non-discriminatory access, contracts with a significant and reliable correlation, or an equivalent statistical parameter of dependence, must therefore benefit from the same offsets or reductions of margins. EMIR ensures that CCPs apply the possibility to portfolio margin to all relevant correlated contracts irrespective of where the contracts are traded.

3.1.3   Process to grant access

CCPs can accept or refuse a formal request for access by a trading venue within three months of such a request, any refusal having to be substantiated with 'full reasons'.

The competent authority of the trading venue and that of the CCP can also refuse access to the CCP where such access would 'threaten the smooth and orderly functioning of the markets or would adversely affect systemic risk', these concepts being quite broad and used in other asset classes not to grant access.

The procedure for access to trading venues is similar, if not identical, the main difference being that access should not require interoperability or threaten the smooth and orderly functioning of markets due to 'liquidity fragmentation' and the trading venue has put in place adequate mechanisms to prevent such fragmentation.

This notion of liquidity fragmentation is further defined by a Commission delegated act.[20] It is deemed to occur 'when the participants in a trading venue are unable to conclude a transaction with one or more other participants in that venue because of the absence of clearing arrangements to which all participants have access'. Access by a CCP to a trading venue which is already served by another CCP shall not be deemed to give rise to liquidity fragmentation within the trading venue if all participants to the trading venue can clear, directly or indirectly, through (i) a CCP in common or (ii) clearing arrangements established by the CCPs.

In case of disagreements between competent authorities on whether to grant access or not, ESMA can assist the competent authorities in reaching an agreement.[21] In case authorities fail to find a common ground, ESMA can take a decision with binding effects for the competent authorities concerned to ensure compliance with Union law. If the authority does not comply, ESMA is even allowed to adopt a decision addressed at the CCP or the trading venue refusing to provide access.[22]

4   Expected Benefits: A Market Vision

Beyond the legal concept previously laid out, the idea of open access carries itself a certain vision of choice and competition. Indeed, since the introduction of the concept

---

[20] Commission Delegated Regulation (EU) No. 149/2013 of 19 December 2012 supplementing Regulation (EU) No. 648/2012 of the European Parliament and of the Council with regard to regulatory technical standards on indirect clearing arrangements, the clearing obligation, the public register, access to a trading venue, non-financial counterparties, and risk mitigation techniques for OTC derivatives contracts not cleared by a CCP, OJ L 052 (23 February 2013).

[21] In accordance with its powers under Regulation (EU) No. 1095/2010 of the European Parliament and of the Council of 24 November 2010 establishing a European Supervisory Authority (European Securities and Markets Authority), amending Decision No. 716/2009/EC and repealing Commission Decision 2009/77/EC, Art. 19 (Regulation (EU) No. 1095/2010), i.e. settlement of disagreements between competent authorities in cross-border situations.

[22] Regulation (EU) No 1095/2010 (n 17).

of open access in the core regulations listed in our previous sections, numerous financial market infrastructures have considered the idea of open access as being more than a mere legal insurance against non-discriminatory access to trading and clearing infrastructures.

To many, open access as a principle embodies the recognition of the needs for, and benefits of, increased competition at every step of the value chain.

By providing investors with the ability to choose where to trade and clear their product, thus preventing exchanges and clearing houses from operating a closed silo model (by tying trading, clearing, and licensing of products to a specific venue), power is given back to such investors to compare and chose their providers every step of the way.

It is expected that this increased competitive pressure on exchanges and clearing houses will generate numerous positive outcomes for the wider market.

4.1 Transparency

Increased competitive pressure could increase transparency on the market: indeed, more open markets are not only expected to bring economic benefits to customers by increasing the competitive pressure on providers but also, it is believed, to increase transparency (to allow fair comparison) and safety (as a key competitive component of the commercial proposition).

Committee on Payments and Market Infrastructure–International Organization of Securities Commissions (CPMI–IOSCO) disclosures, for example, are providing a means for direct comparison between CCP volumes, financial conditions, risks associated with a CCP, and other performance statistics improving transparency for CCP participants. In addition, introducing open access, transparency, and centralized reporting has led to the creation of new analytics, data, and reporting aggregator tools in the derivates market that allow for meaningful comparisons and provide useful insight to customers.

4.2 Efficiency

Efficiency is also due to increase on the back of open access. Market participants are led to believe that lower trading prices, reduced spreads, and a generally faster and more resilient investment in safer technology can naturally result from open, constant, and easy competitive comparison and actionable choices. The principle that markets are better served by a diversity of competing suppliers is well understood and evidenced by the lower prices and improved services that open competition tends to provide in several market segments.

The development of a wide range of sophisticated tools for best execution using transaction cost analysis in the OTC markets enables them to assess the quality of historical execution and to identify opportunities for transaction cost reductions. Open access is then playing a double role by becoming the vehicle by which the market participants can chose to benefit from the identification of lower costs and also the enabler for further price and cost reductions.

4.3 Innovation

Innovation also tends to become a more burning need when facing direct competition. Indeed, direct competition often reveals that more can be done to better serve customers, if anything by giving such customers the means to directly see and expose weaknesses vis a vis the competition. While silo-operating venues might argue that they provide sufficient innovation and service levels, such a static vision is much harder to hold when customers have the means to compare and circulate.

4.4 Safety

By increasing competitive pressure and intensifying the comparison between providers, it is often considered that open access could lead to more scale and the creation of broader and deeper pool of mutualized risk. Such evolution could increase transparency and safety within an environment in which clearing houses are free to compete and risks are dispersed rather than concentrated through artificially imposed barriers.

The 2008–2009 financial crisis has taught the market many things, among which the fact that concentrated, poorly lit, and undiversified pools of risk are the genesis to financial crises. It was for this reason that the G20 decided to mandate the clearing of a wide array of financial products to shed more light on previously opaque markets. Allowing the perpetuation of closed silos operating at the heart of the European derivatives market could act against the aim to safely manage risk across the market.

4.5 Customer Choice and Real Opportunity for Newcomers

Open access carries in its very concept a rebalancing of the relationship between providers and customers. Through this, customers have the ultimate choice of where to take their business. Equally, open access creates a fairer opportunity for newcomers to embody a real option for customers. Undeniably, for new trading venues or new clearing houses to be a real alternative for the market, they must offer customers combined trading and clearing costs that are comparable to those of the existing venues.

While the trading venues set their own trading costs, the costs of clearing will depend on whether customers can consolidate their clearing business, which, in turn, requires that the trading venues have access to it. Competition between trading venues is, therefore, expected to reduce costs, improve the quality of services, and diversify sources of liquidity.

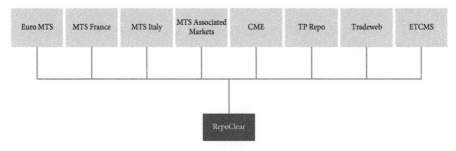

Figure 14.2 LCH RepoClear connection to trading venues
Source: authors.

CCPs' fair access to trading venues, meaning their right to access the trade feed of a venue to clear its trades, should also positively emulate competition between CCPs.

4.6 Settlement: A Path to De-fragmentation

The concept of open access also extends to fair, reasonable, and non-discriminatory connections between CSDs or between trading venues, CCPs, and CSDs.

Leveraging from open access to encourage multi-connectivity between CCPs and CSDs and among CSDs themselves is essential to de-fragment a highly siloed and complex European collateral market that currently suffers from lack of scale and velocity. In settlement too, it is widely believed that customers should lead the extension of offering, scaling up of collateral pools, and dismantling of unnecessary legal and operational barriers.

As early as November 2006, the European Code of Conduct for Clearing and Settlement created a voluntary framework to enable access between CSDs and other market infrastructures.

Under this framework, CCPs and trading venues are due to provide transaction feeds on a non-discriminatory and transparent basis to a CSD upon request by the CSD and shall charge a reasonable commercial fee for such transaction feeds to the requesting CSD. Similarly, CSDs themselves are requested to provide access to their securities settlement systems on a non-discriminatory and transparent basis to a CCP or a trading venue and may charge a reasonable commercial fee for such access.

More recently, since 2015, the Central Securities Depositaries Regulation (CSDR)[23] introduced non-discriminatory access between CSDs and to transaction feeds from CCPs and trading venues. Likewise, those market infrastructures should have access to the securities settlement systems operated by CSDs. This access may be refused only if

---

[23] Regulation (EU) No. 909/2014 of the European Parliament and of the Council of 23 July 2014 on improving securities settlement in the European Union and on central securities depositories and amending Directives 98/26/EC and 2014/65/EU and Regulation (EU) No. 236/20, Arts 50–53.

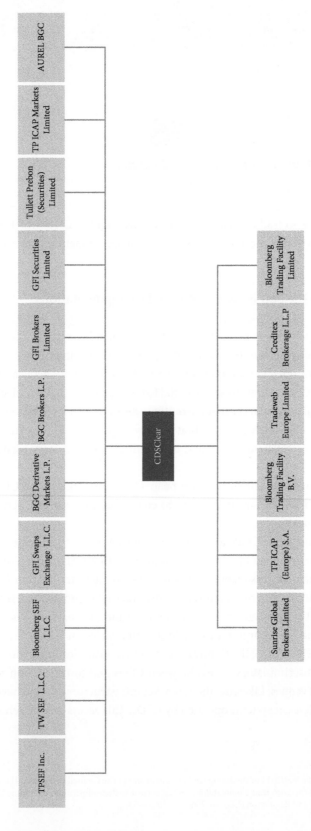

Figure 14.3 LCH CSDClear connection to trading venues
Source: authors.

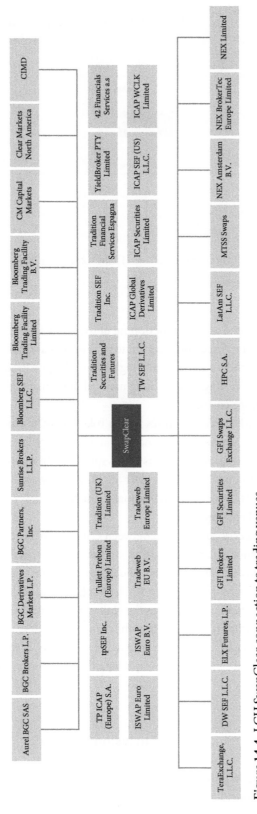

Figure 14.4 LCH SwapClear connection to trading venues

Source: authors.

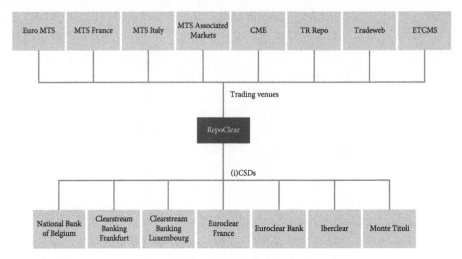

Figure 14.5 RepoClear SA trading venues and (I)CSDs connection
Source: authors.

it threatens the smooth and orderly functioning of the financial markets or causes systemic risk and may not be denied on the grounds of loss of market share.

Despite these key incentives and essential regulations, the post-trade sector, especially at settlement level, remains fragmented along national lines, making cross-border trade unnecessarily complex and costly.

Critical financial market infrastructures have a role to play in supporting customers' demand for choice, scale, and velocity by enabling and encouraging multiple connectivity across trading venues, CCPs, and CSDs. It is in this spirit that the euro-denominated fixed income clearing service of the LCH, RepoClear has built a network of links with multiple trading venues and CSDs to meet customer demand, and it remains open to further extend its offering to support client needs.

Encouraging open access downstream between CSDs and other financial market infrastructures should emulate competition in the settlement space, improve the level of service to customers, and increase the velocity of collateral—it is well recognized that the European Single Market is yet to reach simplicity and scale to really compete with other leading geographic area such as the United States or the Chinese markets (to some degree). It is commonly accepted that the competitive pressure that open access can create will, in the longer run, support the EU in taking down the remaining artificially built barriers to scale and choice—improving the overall attractiveness and competitiveness of the area.

5 Conclusion

The concept of non-discriminatory access or 'open access' is widely recognized as beneficial in the EU, considering the fragmentation of EU capital markets but also the introduction of clearing and trading obligations. Open access has proven to 'open up' barriers and enhance competition in the EU financial market infrastructure space without substantiated concerns about financial stability, quite the opposite, resulting in a diversity of trading, clearing, and settlement venues available to market participants, ensuring alternative choices and an overall increased resilience of the system.

While established in equities and OTC derivatives, the concept of open access remains controversial when it comes to exchange-traded derivatives, where it has never been applied in practice despite effectively having legally entered into force.

In the United Kingdom, while HM Treasury supports the open access regimes in equity and OTC derivatives markets, it also announced the deletion of open access for exchange traded derivatives as not suitable in a UK-only context because it was originally designed to improve cross-border capital markets in the EU.[24]

In the EU, the co-legislators twice postponed the entry into force of open access for exchange-traded derivatives, justifying their decision by referring to risks linked to the COVID-19-related market volatility and then to the exit of the United Kingdom from the EU. This was confirmed by the proposal of the European Commission to delete open access provisions to 'foster competition, innovation and development of exchange-traded derivatives in the EU on one side and building further clearing capability in the EU' in November 2021.

Despite the most recent 'cold-feet' approach observed across certain jurisdictions, it seems essential not to lose sight of the long-term fundamental objectives of open access and to revive and maintain a strong level of support for its effective application across asset classes. Real open access, upstream and downstream, is a key condition for the EU to realize a proper de-fragmented, scalable, and competitive Capital Market Union.

---

[24] See 'Open Access Regime for Exchange Traded Derivatives', https://www.gov.uk (accessed 23 March 2023).

V

CROSS-BORDER ISSUES

15

Cross-Border Clearing

Ulrich Karl

1 Introduction and General Comments

This chapter begins with a summary of the regulatory and legal frameworks of clearing, including how third-country (or foreign) central counterparties (CCPs) are treated in selected jurisdictions. After a description of the impact cross-border clearing has on capital requirements and an explanation of interoperability and bases, the chapter lays out how clearing participants (either clearing members or clients) navigate cross-border clearing. The chapter describes how these clearing participants choose which CCP to access and how to do so. After a description of operational considerations of cross-border clearing, the chapter explains risk and crisis management in a cross-border setting and particular issues when clearing in small or closed jurisdictions.

Please note that, in most cases, cross-border clearing of over-the-counter (OTC) derivatives is not different from cross-border clearing for other products, such as exchange-traded derivatives (ETDs: these are generally futures and options), repos, and cash securities. Most thoughts in this chapter will therefore be applicable to clearing in general, unless sections explicitly cover OTC derivatives.

This chapter has been written in a personal capacity and does not necessarily reflect the views of the international Swaps and Derivative Association (ISDA) and/or its members.

2 Legal and Regulatory Frameworks

2.1 Principles for Financial Markets Infrastructures

The Principles for Financial Markets Infrastructures (PFMIs)[1] form the basis for most if not all clearing regulation around the globe. These principles were published in 2012 and cover not only CCPs but also central securities depositories (CSDs), securities settlement systems (SSS), payment systems (PS), and trade registries (TRs; all together called financial markets infrastructures or FMIs). The majority (twenty-two) of the twenty-four principles, however, do affect CCPs, albeit not exclusively. These twenty-two principles cover the whole range or risk and governance of CCPs. Please note that the PFMIs are applicable to all CCPs, not just CCPs clearing OTC derivatives.

Please see Table 15.1 below for a list of the principles in the PFMIs.

Table 15.1 Principles in the PFMIs

General organization	*Credit and liquidity risk management*
• Principle 1: Legal basis	• Principle 4: Credit risk
• Principle 2: Governance	• Principle 5: Collateral
• Principle 3: Framework for the comprehensive management of risks	• Principle 6: Margin
	• Principle 7: Liquidity risk
Central securities depositories and exchange-of-value settlement systems	*Default management*
• Principle 11: Central securities depositories	• Principle 13: Participant default rules and procedures
• Principle 12: Exchange-of-value settlement systems	• Principle 14: Segregation and portability
	Access
General business and operational risk management	• Principle 18: Access and participation requirements
• Principle 15: General business risk	• Principle 19: Tiered participation arrangements
• Principle 16: Custody and investment risks	• Principle 20: FMI links
• Principle 17: Operational risk	*Transparency*
Efficiency	• Principle 23: Disclosure of rules, key procedures, and market data
• Principle 21: Efficiency and effectiveness	• Principle 24: Disclosure of market data by trade repositories
• Principle 22: Communication procedures and standards	

Source: author.

---

[1] Committee on Payment and Settlement Systems (CPSS) and Technical Committee of the International Organization of Securities Commissions (IOSCO), 'Principles for Financial Market Infrastructures' (April 2012), https://www.iosco.org, https://www.iosco.org/library/pubdocs/pdf/IOSCOPD377-PFMI.pdf (accessed 23 March 2023) (PFMIs).

The PFMIs state that 'FMIs that are determined by national authorities to be systemic-ally important are expected to observe these principles.'

While all principles are important for FMIs and could be affected by cross-border settings, the PFMIs identify principles that are especially relevant for cross-border clearing:

In principle 1 (legal risk), the PFMIs state that a CCP needs to make sure that the rules are enforceable in all jurisdictions in which the CCP has clearing members,[2] that there are no issues stemming from conflicts of laws, and that the CCP has regard to the laws applicable to the CCP, for instance, it stays if the clearing members get resolved.

Principle 2 (governance) highlights that the governance arrangements should ap-propriately identity, assess, and deal with cross-border issues. More information on governance in general can be found in Chapter 7 ('What Kind of Thing Is a Central Counterparty? The Role of Clearing Houses as a Source of Policy Controversy' by Rebecca Lewis and David Murphy) in this volume.

In principle 5 (collateral),[3] the PFMIs cover cross-border collateral and that the CCP needs to mitigate risk and to ensure that the cross-border collateral can be used in a timely manner. The principle also mentions potential operational challenges of oper-ating across borders, such as differences in time zone or operating hours of foreign CSDs or custodians. These issues affect not only the CCP but also the users of a CCP, which the chapter will consider further below (see section 8 for more details).

Principle 8 (settlement finality) requires the CCP to consider the effectiveness of cross-border recognition and protection of cross-system settlement finality. This might lead to a CCP not accepting clearing members for certain jurisdictions where the CCP does not feel it has sufficient protection of cross-system settlement finality.

Principle 17 (operational risk) covers cross-border crisis management arrangements.

Principle 20 (FMI links) does not mention cross-border issues, but such links can be helpful in a cross-border context (see section 4 below). Chapter 14 ('Open Access for OTC Derivatives: Concept and Implications' by Corentine Poilvet-Clediere and Julien Jardelot) in this volume contains more general thoughts on interoperability.

Principle 22 (communication procedures and standards) states that an 'FMI that, for example, settles a chain of transactions processed through multiple FMIs or pro-vides services to users in multiple jurisdictions should strongly consider using inter-nationally accepted communication procedures and standards to achieve efficient and effective cross-border financial communication'. This is relevant for cross-border clearing as not all CCPs in all jurisdictions use standard middleware.

The PFMIs also include responsibilities of central banks, market regulators, and other relevant authorities for financial market infrastructures which have cross-border elements but are less relevant for the subject at hand.

---

[2] See 3.1.10 of the PFMIs (n 1).
[3] Consideration 5.

2.2 The View Inside Out: The European Market Infrastructure Regulation (EMIR)

The European Market Infrastructure Regulation (EMIR)[4] forms part of the European implementation of the Pittsburgh G20 commitments[5] (clearing through CCPs and reporting to trade repositories). EMIR also covers other measures to reduce risk in OTC derivatives such as timely confirmations, compression, and uncleared margin.

While the title of EMIR suggests that the regulation covers only OTC derivatives, the rules on CCPs include all CCPs clearing OTC derivatives, ETD, repos, or cash securities.

Under EMIR, there are two ways for a CCP to provide clearing services in Europe:

- CCPs established in the EU need to be authorized.
- CCPs established in a third country need to be recognized by the European Securities and Markets Authority (ESMA).

2.2.1 Authorized CCPs
For authorized CCPs, EMIR provides a comprehensive set of rules that also implement the PFMIs in the European Union (EU). These include, for instance:

- capital requirements (Art. 16);
- senior management of the board (Art. 27);
- the Risk Committee (Art. 28);
- business continuity—general provisions (Art. 34);
- outsourcing (Art. 35);
- segregation and portability (Art. 39);
- margin requirements (Art. 41);
- a default fund (Art. 42);
- other financial resources (Art. 43);
- liquidity risk controls (Art. 44);
- the default waterfall (Art. 45);

---

[4] Regulation (EU) No. 648/2012 of the European Parliament and of the Council of 4 July 2012 on OTC derivatives, central counterparties and trade repositories, 4 July 2012, https://eur-lex.europa.eu/legal-content/EN/ALL/?uri=celex%3A32012R0648 (accessed 28 June 2022) subsequently amended. Consolidated version, https://eur-lex.europa.eu/legal-content/EN/TXT/?uri=CELEX%3A02012R0648-20210628 (accessed 23 March 2023) (EMIR).

[5] Group of Twenty (G20), 'Leader's Statement', the Pittsburg Summit (24–25 September 2009), https://www.oecd.org/g20/summits/pittsburgh/G20-Pittsburgh-Leaders-Declaration.pdf (accessed 23 March 2023). Under the section on 'improving over-the-counter derivatives markets', the Leaders' Statement of the Financial Stability Board (FSB) Pittsburgh Summit stated:

> All standardized OTC derivative contracts should be traded on exchanges or electronic trading platforms, where appropriate, and cleared through central counterparties by end 2012 at the latest. OTC derivative contracts should be reported to trade repositories. Non-centrally cleared contracts should be subject to higher capital requirements. We ask the FSB and its relevant members to assess regularly implementation and whether it is sufficient to improve transparency in the derivatives markets, mitigate systemic risk, and protect against market abuse.

- collateral requirements (Art. 46);
- investment policy (Art. 47);
- default procedures (Art. 48);
- interoperability arrangements (Art. 51).

Authorized CCPs have no bearing on cross-border clearing, at least not from a European point of view, and are not further discussed here.

2.2.2 Recognized CCPs

A third-country CCP can only be recognized if, amongst other conditions:[6]

- the EU Commission has determined that the legal and supervisory arrangements of that third country are equivalent to EMIR in relation to CCP requirements, that CCPs in this country are subject to effective supervision and enforcement, and that the third country has a regime that allows for recognition of CCPs in jurisdictions outside of this third country;
- the CCP is authorized in the third country and subject to effective supervision;
- there are cooperation arrangements between ESMA and the relevant third-country authorities;
- the third country is considered as having equivalent systems for anti-money-laundering and combating the financing of terrorism to those of the EU.

A Regulatory Technical Standard (RTS) 153/2013 defines in more detail what information the applicant CCP needs to provide to ESMA.[7] ESMA keeps a public 'List of Third-Country Central Counterparties Recognised to Offer Services and Activities in the Union'[8] (List of Recognised CCPs).

Firms established in the EU can clear as members at CCPs that are either authorized or recognized. If a third-country CCP has not been recognized, firms established in the EU can still access this CCP via subsidiaries established outside the EU but might have higher capital requirements (see section 3 below).

A clearing obligation can only be discharged at authorized or recognized CCPs: if a firm accesses a CCP that is neither authorized nor recognized via a local subsidiary, only contracts that are not subject to the clearing obligation can be cleared at this CCP. Therefore, access via a local subsidiary will mostly be used for clearing ETDs.

---

[6] See EMIR (n 4), Art. 25.

[7] Commission Delegated Regulation (EU) No. 153/2013 of 19 December 2012 supplementing Regulation (EU) No. 648/2012 of the European Parliament and of the Council with regard to regulatory technical standards on requirements for central counterparties (19 December 2012), https://eur-lex.europa.eu/legal-content/EN/TXT/HTML/?uri=CELEX:32013R0153&from=EN#d1e581-41-1 (accessed 23 March 2023).

[8] ESMA, 'List of Third-Country Central Counterparties Recognised to Offer Services and Activities in the Union' (28 March 2022), https://www.esma.europa.eu/sites/default/files/library/third-country_ccps_recognised_under_emir.pdf (accessed 21 April 2023).

2.2.3 EMIR 2.2

In 2017, the Commission proposed changes to the CCP supervision framework called EMIR 2.2.[9]

For European CCPs, EMIR 2.2 addressed concerns that in a small number of Member States CCPs are increasingly relevant for the EU financial system as a whole, whilst supervision is driven by the home country authority, and that diverging supervisory practices for CCPs across the EU could create risks of regulatory and supervisory arbitrage for CCPs and indirectly for their clearing members or clients. Also, the role of central banks—as issuers of currency—was not adequately reflected in CCP colleges.

For third-country CCPs, the Commission identified certain shortcomings in EMIR's system of equivalence and recognition, in particular regarding ongoing supervision. ESMA had encountered difficulties in accessing information from third-country CCPs, in conducting on-site inspections of third-country CCPs, and in sharing information with the relevant EU regulators, supervisors, and central banks. Other concerns were that there was the potential for misalignments between supervisory and central bank objectives within colleges in the context of third-country CCPs where non-EU authorities are involved. There was also no mechanism to ensure that the EU was informed automatically of CCP rule changes or regulation changes. And, finally, Brexit meant that a large number of euro denominated derivative contracts would be cleared outside the EU.

To address the concerns around diverging supervisory practices, EMIR 2.2 established the ESMA CCP Supervisory Committee with the role of aligning supervisory practices in the EU and to monitor recognized third-country CCPs. EMIR 2.2 also gave ESMA more direct powers for some third-country CCPs.

For third-country CCPs, EMIR 2.2 established two tiers of CCPs:

(1) tier 1 CCPs, which are not deemed systemically important for the EU or a Member State of the EU. These CCPs are treated similar to the previous recognition but have to pay fees to ESMA, and ESMA has a more active role.

(2) tier 2 CCPs, which are systemically important to the EU or a Member State. For these CCPs, there is enhanced supervision by ESMA and the central bank of issue (CBI).[10] These CCPs also have to follow certain parts of EMIR (for instance, capital requirements, requirements for internal organization management, conduct of business, margins, default fund, financial resources, liquidity, investments, stress tests, settlement, and interoperability) and must satisfy requirements from CBIs. ESMA and CBIs can request any information held by

---

[9] European Commission, 'Proposal for a Regulation of the European Parliament and of the Council amending Regulation (EU) No. 1095/2010 establishing a European Supervisory Authority (European Securities and Markets Authority) and amending Regulation (EU) No. 648/2012 as regards the procedures and authorities involved in the authorisation of CCPs and requirements for the recognition of third-country CCPs' (13 June 2017), https://eur-lex.europa.eu/legal-content/EN/TXT/?uri=CELEX:52017PC0331 (accessed 23 March 2023) (EMIR 2.2). EMIR 2.2 is one of several regulations that amended the original EMIR regulation (n 4). The following summary contains quotes from section 1.1 of the initial proposal for EMIR 2.2.

[10] A CBI is the central bank that issues the currency in which a derivative contract is denominated.

Table 15.2 Indicators for tiering of CCPs in the EU

Indicator	Threshold
Open interest (ETD) or outstanding notional (OTC) of instruments denominated in euros	EUR 1,000 billion
Margin requirement and default fund contribution (aggregated) of European clearing members	EUR 25 billion
Largest payment commitment by European entity from default of two largest clearing members	EUR 3 billion

Source: author.

CCPs and perform on-site inspections. If local requirements are comparable to EMIR, ESMA can rely on local supervision for the subset of EMIR requirements (so-called 'comparable compliance').

As a last-resort tool, ESMA, after consulting the European Stability Risk Board (ESRB) and in agreement with the CBIs, can propose for a tier 2 CCP (or certain products and services) to be de-recognized if the CCP is deemed to pose a risk to the EU or one or more Member States that cannot be mitigated by application of EMIR rules. These CCPs would only be allowed to offer clearing of these products or services if they relocated to the EU and became an authorized CCP. This is sometimes referred to as a 'location policy'. This is discussed in Chapters 3 (q'Development of the Regulatory Regime for OTC Derivatives Clearing' by Patrick Pearson) and ~@16 ('Brexit: Equivalence; location Policy' by Dermot Turing).

2.2.4 Tiering

The required analysis and criteria for tiering of recognized CCPs are documented in the Commission Delegated Regulation (EU) No. 2020/1303.[11]

To determine what tier a CCP should be in, ESMA analyses the systemic importance of the CCP for the EU or one or more Member States. ESMA has to perform a qualitative analysis and assess the following criteria:

- the nature, size and complexity of the CCP's business;
- the effect of failure of or a disruption to a CCP;
- the CCP's clearing membership structure;
- alternative clearing services provided by other CCPs;
- the CCP's relationship, interdependencies, or other interactions.

Each of these considerations includes a list of elements to take into account.

---

[11] Commission Delegated Regulation (EU) No. 2020/1303 of 14 July 2020 supplementing Regulation (EU) No. 648/2012 of the European Parliament and of the Council with regard to the criteria that ESMA should take into account to determine whether a central counterparty established in a third country is systemically important or likely to become systemically important for the financial stability of the Union or of one or more of its Member States (14 July 2020), https://eur-lex.europa.eu/legal-content/EN/TXT/?uri=uriserv:OJ.L_.2020.305.01.0007.01. ENG (accessed 23 March 2023).

ESMA may only determine, based on the criteria listed above, that a third-country CCP is a tier 2 CCP where at least one the indicators in Table 15.2 is met.

So far, two CCPs have been classified as tier 2:

- London Clearing House (LCH) Limited;
- ICE Clear Europe (ICEU).

The 'List of Recognised CCPs' identifies CCPs classified as tier 2.

ESMA conducted an analysis in the second half of 2021 to assess whether these CCPs are so systemically important that some products or services should be de-recognized. In their final report,[12] ESMA identified three services as having 'substantial systemic importance':

- LCH Ltd SwapClear for products denominated in euro and Polish Zloty;
- ICE Clear Europe for short-term interest rates (STIR) for products denominated in euros;
- ICE Clear Europe for credit default swaps (CDS) denominated in euros.

Despite the systemic importance, ESMA concluded that 'Taking into account the identified costs, benefits and consequences, it is proposed under the current circumstances, not to issue a recommendation to the Commission under Article 25(2c) with respect to LCH Ltd SwapClear, for EUR and PLN denominated products, and ICEU CDS and ICEU STIR for EUR denominated products.'[13]

ESMA, however, proposed that the reliance on these services should be reduced. At the time of writing, the EU Commission has called the market for evidence as to how such a reduction of reliance on UK CCPs could be achieved. Please refer to Chapter 16 ('Brexit: Equivalence; Location Policy' by Dermot Turing) in this volume for more details on Brexit.

2.3 Was Inside, Now Outside: CCP Supervision in the United Kingdom

The United Kingdom has retained a large body of EU law, including EMIR as amended by EMIR 2.2. Therefore, the structure of CCP supervision, both for UK CCPs and for third-country CCPs, is the same, with slight differences to account for different

---

[12] ESMA, 'Assessment Report under Article 25(2c) of EMIR—Assessment of LCH Ltd and ICE Clear Europe Ltd' (16 December 2021). A redacted report can be accessed in two parts at https://www.esma.europa.eu/sites/default/files/library/esma91-372-1945_redacted_assessment_report_under_article_252c_of_emir_ukccps_final_1of2.pdf and https://www.esma.europa.eu/sites/default/files/library/esma91-372-1945_redacted_assessment_report_under_article_252c_of_emir_ukccps_final_2of2.pdf (accessed 23 March 2023). Please see also the press release, ESMA, 'ESMA Publishes Results of Its Assessment of Systematically Important UK Central Counterparties' (17 December 2021), https://www.esma.europa.eu/press-news/esma-news/esma-publishes-results-its-assessment-systemically-important-uk-central (accessed 23 March 2023).

[13] Quoted from the Executive Summary of ESMA's final report (n 12).

Table 15.3 Quantitative thresholds used by the Bank of England for tiering of third-country CCPs

Indicator	Threshold
UK clearing member initial margin (including non-UK subsidiaries of UK headquartered firms) across all services at any point in the past five years	GBP 10 billion
UK clearing member default fund contributions (including non-UK subsidiaries of UK headquartered firms) across all services at any point in the past five years	GBP 1 billion*
Presence of an interoperability arrangement** with a UK CCP	

Notes: * Or GBP 5 billion for CCPs that hold initial margin and default fund contribution in a single fund; ** Please see under section 4 for an explanation of interoperability arrangements.
Source: author.

authorities. Responsibilities of the EU Commission are discharged under UK EMIR by His Majesty's Treasury (HMT) and responsibilities of ESMA are discharged under UK EMIR by the Bank of England.

As the United Kingdom, at the time of writing, has yet to make its own equivalent determinations and recognize CCPs that are recognized in the EU and CCPs authorized in the EU, it established a temporary recognition regime (TRR)[14] that came into effect at the end of the Brexit transitional period. Non-UK CCPs were eligible to enter the TRR if they were permitted to offer clearing services in the European Economic Area (EEA) immediately before the commencement of the TRR. This covers mostly CCPs that were recognized or authorized in the EU. CCPs that entered the TRR are treated as recognized during an initial period of three years. This gives HMT sufficient time for equivalence determinations and the Bank of England time to go through the recognition process. The Bank of England keeps a 'List of Third-Country CCPs That Are Taken to Be Eligible for Temporary Deemed Recognition in the UK by Virtue of the Temporary Recognition Regime'.[15]

End-June 2002, the Bank of England (the Bank) published its Statement of Policy,[16] which states how it will tier third-country CCPs, which, in the Statement of Policy, are called 'incoming CCPs'.

The Bank of England's approach is split into two stages: a 'triage' and an 'advanced assessment'. In triage, incoming CCPs will be assessed against quantitative thresholds (see Table 15.3). These quantitative thresholds are lower than those used by ESMA.

[14] 'The Central Counterparties (Amendment, etc., and Transitional Provision) (EU Exit) Regulations 2018' (13 November 2018), https://www.legislation.gov.uk/uksi/2018/1184/regulation/17/made (accessed 28 June 2022).

[15] Bank of England, 'List of Third-Country CCPs That Are Taken to Be Eligible for Temporary Deemed Recognition in the UK by Virtue of the Temporary Recognition Regime Established by the Central Counterparties (Amendments, etc., and Transitional Provision) (EU Exit) Regulations 2018 as Amended' (29 March 2022), https://www.bankofengland.co.uk/-/media/boe/files/financial-stability/financial-market-infrastructure-supervis ion/list-of-third-country-ccps.pdf?la=en&hash=8C96A829A5F570A235A4944912AFA278A8728399 (accessed 29 June 2022).

[16] Bank of England, 'The Bank of England's Approach to Tiering Incoming Central Counterparties under EMIR Article 25' (June 2022), https://www.bankofengland.co.uk/-/media/boe/files/paper/2022/boes-approach-to-tier ing-incoming-central-counterparties-under-emir-article-25-sop-jun-22.pdf.

If an incoming CCP does not meet any of the above criteria, it will usually be classified as tier 1.[17]

If a CCP meets one of the two quantitative criteria (initial margin or default find contribution), the Bank of England will apply the 'proportionality test': CCPs for which the UK clearing member initial margin (IM) or the UK clearing member default fund contribution (as defined in the Table 15.1 above) are less than 20% of the total IM or default fund contributions of the CCP can be still become a tier 1 CCP if the 'Level 1 informed reliance assessment'[18] establishes that the Bank of England can rely on the incoming CCP's home counties' regulation and home regulator(s)' supervision. If this is not the case, or the CCP has an interoperability arrangement with a UK CCP, the CCP will move to the advanced assessment stage.

In this stage, the Bank of England will perform a 'systemic risk assessment'. If this assessment does not identify a systemic risk to the United Kingdom, the CCP will be classified as a tier 1 CCP. If the outcome of the assessment is that the CCP poses a potential systemic risk to the United Kingdom, the Bank of England will perform a 'Level 2 informed reliance assessment' to establish whether the level of supervisory cooperation with the home regulator(s) of the CCP gives comfort to the Bank of England that it can rely on these home regulator(s)' supervision of a systemically important CCP and the level of cooperation. If this is the case, the CCP can still be a tier 1 CCP; otherwise, it will be classified as tier 2.

2.4 US Commodity Futures Trading Commission (CFTC)

As the focus of this book is on clearing in Europe, and the CFTC rules are fairly complex, this section describes the CFTC regulations related to cross-border clearing (from the US point of view) only at a very high level.[19]

The CFTC has very different approaches for CCPs clearing futures and options, on one hand, and 'swaps' (the term 'swaps' in the meaning of the US Commodities Exchange Act is roughly equal to the term OTC derivatives) on the other.

The framework for 'foreign' (non-US) CCPs clearing futures and options is defined in Part 30 of the CFTC regulations.[20] This Part stipulates who is allowed to offer a 'foreign futures contract or foreign options transaction' in the United States and does not explicitly regulate access to foreign CCPs. Part 30 provides a wide range of exemptions from registration, which, in practice, allows many foreign exchanges and their attached

---

[17] The Bank of England has a degree of discretion, for instance, if exposures to a CCP are near these thresholds.

[18] This assessment includes a review of home country regulation, the level of supervision, and the Bank of England's relationship with all relevant home authorities.

[19] I thank my colleague Ann Battle for her help with this section.

[20] Code of Federal Regulations, Title 17, Chapter I, Part 30: 'Foreign Futures and Foreign Options Transactions' (5 August 1978), https://www.ecfr.gov/current/title-17/chapter-I/part-30?toc=1 (accessed 23 March 2023).

CCPs clearing futures and options to offer their products to US entities without registering with the CFTC.[21]

On the other hand, rules for CCPs clearing swaps under CFTC regulations are very strict and extraterritorial. Please see Chapter 3 ('Developmet of the Regulatory Regime for OTC Derivatives Clearsing'by Patrick Pearson) in this volume for a discussion of the background to these differences. To offer clearing services in the United States, a CCP has to either register with the CFTC as a derivatives clearing organization or apply to be exempt from registration. To provide clearing services in the United States, a foreign CCP can follow three alternative paths:

(1) The foreign CCP can register directly with the CFTC in the same way a US CCP would do and would have to satisfy the same conditions as a US CCP would have to do. This is required if the CCP poses substantial risk to the US financial system.

(2) If the foreign CCP does not pose a substantial risk to the US financial system, the foreign CCP may apply for a registration where compliance with the CCP's home country regulatory regime would satisfy the core principles of the Commodities Exchange Act. This is called the Alternative Compliance Framework.

(3) A foreign CCP can apply for exemption from registration if the CCP is subject to comparable and comprehensive supervision by a home country regulator, which needs to have a memorandum of understanding (or similar arrangement) with the CFTC in which, amongst other things, the home regulator agrees to provide the CFTC all information deemed necessary to evaluate the eligibility of the CCP for exemption. There are other conditions, for instance, the right of inspection of the CCP's books and records. An exempt CCP can only clear for clearing members and affiliates, but not for clients in the United States.

A list of registered and exempt derivatives clearing organizations can be found on the CFTC website.[22] At the time of writing, this list does not include any derivatives clearing organizations registered under the Alternative Compliance Framework.

3 Capital Requirements in the Cross-Border Context

The capital framework for exposures to a CCP are described in detail in Chapter 9 ('Capital Requirements for Bank Exposures to CCPs' by Marc Peters) in this volume. This section summarizes the framework only as far as it is relevant for cross-border clearing.

---

[21] CFTC, 'Foreign Part 30' containing a list of 'Foreign Part 30 Exemptions' (undated), https://sirt.cftc.gov/sirt/sirt.aspx?Topic=ForeignPart30Exemptions (accessed 28 June 2022).
[22] CFTC, 'Derivatives Clearing Organizations (DCO)' (undated), https://sirt.cftc.gov/sirt/sirt.aspx?Topic=ClearingOrganizations (accessed 28 June 2022).

A dedicated framework for exposures to CCPs was introduced by the Basel 3 Framework.[23] It takes into account the risk that a CCP poses to clearing members and assigns risk weights to CCPs, both for trade exposures (exposure from transactions cleared at the CCP and margin posted to the CCP) and for default fund contributions. The Framework and its underlying quantitative models went through several iterations. The latest rules have been published by the Basel Committee in 2014[24] (bcbs282).

A key concept in the Basel III rules for exposures to CCPs is the concept of a 'qualifying CCP'. Basel rules in bcbs282 define a qualifying CCP (in summary):

- A qualifying central counterparty (QCCP) is an entity that is licensed to operate as a CCP and is permitted by the appropriate regulator/overseer to operate as such with respect to the products offered.
- The CCP is based and prudentially supervised in a jurisdiction where the relevant regulator/overseer has established, and publicly indicated that it applies to the CCP on an ongoing basis, domestic rules and regulations that are consistent with the PFMIs.
- Where the CCP is in a jurisdiction that does not have a CCP regulator applying the PFMIs to the CCP, then the banking supervisor may make the determination of whether the CCP meets this definition.

These rules have been implemented in a different fashion across jurisdictions. While in the United States, banks have to determine that a third-country (foreign) CCP is compliant with the PFMIs, in Europe, the qualifying status is linked to the recognition of a CCP on the basis that the recognition process would confirm that the CCP is compliant with the PFMIs. To cover the time it would take the European Commission to conduct equivalence determinations and for ESMA to go through the recognition process, the EU Capital Requirements Regulation (CRR)[25] includes transitional rules that allow banks to treat a CCP that has applied for recognition but where the process is still ongoing to be treated as qualifying. This transitional period has come to an end in June 2022. More details can be found in CRR, Art. 497.

The difference between a qualifying CCP and a non-qualifying CCP is significant. For a non-qualifying CCP, banks must apply the standardized approach for credit risk in the main framework, according to the category of the counterparty, to their trade exposure to a non-qualifying CCP, which will result in risk weights upwards of 50%. On the other hand, the risk weight of a qualifying CCP is 2% in contrast to that of a non-qualifying CCP.

---

[23] Basel Committee on Banking Supervision, 'Basel III: International Regulatory Framework for Banks' (undated), https://www.bis.org/bcbs/basel3.htm (accessed 28 June 2022).

[24] Basel Committee on Banking Supervision, 'Capital Requirements for Bank Exposures to Central Counterparties' (April 2014), https://www.bis.org/publ/bcbs282.pdf.

[25] 'Consolidated Text: Regulation (EU) No. 575/2013 of the European Parliament and of the Council of 26 June 2013 on prudential requirements for credit institutions and amending Regulation (EU) No. 648/2012' (initial act from 26 June 2013, latest amendments 10 April 2022), https://eur-lex.europa.eu/legal-content/EN/TXT/?uri=CELEX%3A02013R0575-20210930 (accessed 23 March 2023). The current version is called 'CRR2'.

Capital requirements for default fund contributions are based on the risk profile of a CCP (see Chapter 9 'Capital Requirements for Bank Exposures to CCPs' by Marc Peters in this volume for more detail). For an indication of the order of magnitude involved, these capital requirements are floored at an equivalent risk weight of 2%. The risk weight for default fund contributions for non-qualifying CCPs is 1,250%.

The status of a CCP depends not only on the capital rules in the CCP's home jurisdiction but also on capital rules in the jurisdiction where the clearing participant is headquartered. There are cases where a CCP is deemed to be qualifying by its local regulators, and firms located in its jurisdiction can treat the CCP as qualifying. Should some of these firms be subsidiaries of global firms and the CCP not deemed to be qualifying in the jurisdiction where the head office is located, the consolidated capital requirements will have to be calculated using the rules for non-qualifying CCPs.

Whether a CCP is qualifying or not can make a significant difference and can determine whether clearing at a certain CCP is economically viable. If a clearing member only has a small portfolio at a non-qualifying CCP, for instance, because a CCP has just been set up or the clearing member accesses a new market for the first time, the outsized capital requirements might be small on an absolute basis and in relation to the capital requirements of other business. The firm might also see these capital requirements as a cost of accessing the new CCP or the new market. Often, however, a business is measured on a risk-adjusted or capital-adjusted profit measure, which can be driven by capital requirements, or a clearing business has a certain amount of regulatory capital allocated to it. On such a basis, clearing at a non-qualifying CCP can easily become economically unfeasible.

3.1 Issues with the EU Recognition Framework

There is a logical structure to the EU framework; that is, a third-country CCP will only be recognized if the EU Commission, in their equivalence determination, and ESMA, as part of the recognition determination, have concluded that local rules in the CCP's home jurisdictions have the same outcome as the application of EMIR rules. If the outcome of the CCP rules and regulations and analysis of the CCP's rule book suggest the same broad outcome as the application of EMIR rules, the CCP can also be deemed to be following the PFMIs.

However, this framework requires a lot of work by third-country CCPs, the EU Commission and ESMA, even for smaller third-country CCPs that EU firms might only access via local subsidiaries. As of the time of writing, there are still CCPs across the globe that have not been recognized, for instance CCPs in Chile, Argentina, Indonesia, China, and Taiwan. As the amount of capital requirements for exposure to CCPs in the EU is linked to recognition status of a CCP, the backlog in recognition of third-country CCPs could mean that European firms have considerably higher capital requirements from mid-2022, when a transitionary period in CRR ends (see CRR, Art. 497).

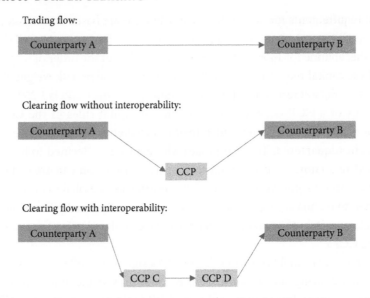

Figure 15.1 Stylized example of cleared transaction with and without interoperability
Source: author.

4 Interoperability

Interoperability arrangements allow two parties to a transaction to clear at different CCPs, as long as these CCPs have such an arrangement. As each CCP is the seller to every buyer and the buyer to every seller, these CCPs establish a transaction between themselves to make sure they are market-risk neutral. As show in the example in Figure 15.1, if counterparty A and counterparty B have traded an equity at an exchange (these counterparties might not even know who took the other side of the trade), counterparty A could clear the transaction at CCP C, while counterparty B clears its transaction at CCP D. CCP C and CCP D would establish a transaction between themselves to have a market-risk-neutral book.

At the time of writing, there are five CCPs in Europe taking part in interoperability arrangements.[26] Three of these CCPs are authorized:

- European Central Counterparty N.V. (EuroCCP) (Netherlands);
- Cassa di Compensazione e Garanzia S.p.A. (CC&G) (Italy);
- LCH SA (France).

Two CCPs are recognized by ESMA:

- LCH Ltd;
- SIX x-clear, including its Norwegian branch.

---

[26] ESRB, 'CCP Interoperability Arrangements' (January 2019), https://www.esrb.europa.eu/pub/pdf/reports/esrb.report190131_CCP_interoperability_arrangements~99908a78e7.en.pdf (accessed 23 March 2023).

These CCPs clear, under their interoperability arrangements, the following products:

- cash securities;
- ETD;
- repos.

Not all of these CCPs have interoperability links with all other CCPs or clear all of the products above under their interoperability arrangements.

Due to the complexity of such arrangements, there is no known interoperability arrangement across time zones or for OTC derivatives.[27] OTC derivatives often have longer maturities than cash products or futures, which can make risk management more complicated. Differences in legal and regulatory frameworks, risk management, and supervision of the involved CCPs could become more of an issue in interoperability arrangements for such products.

Despite not being available for OTC derivatives at the time of writing, in the context of cross-border clearing interoperability arrangements could have clear advantages: firms can, for instance, clear eligible products at their home CCP, even though the market that is being cleared or their counterparty is located abroad, if there is an interoperability arrangement for combination of products/markets, counterparties, and CCPs. A firm saves on the cost of setting up a clearing relationship with another CCP under a legal framework that this firm might not be familiar or comfortable with. The firm also needs to comply with only one set of CCPs rules, operational processes, collateral eligibility, etc. Even if a CCP that takes part in an interoperability arrangement is small, there will be sufficient market liquidity as counterparties do not have to clear at the same CCP.

There are good reasons for the interoperability arrangements listed above to be between CCPs in Europe that operate under a common set of rules. Similarly, interoperability arrangements between Indian CCPs are subject to the same regulation.

More information about interoperability can be found in Chapter 14 ('Open Access for OTC Derivatives: Concept and Implications' by Corentine Poilvet-Clediere and Julien Jardelot) in this volume.

5 Bases between CCPs

While clearing mandates around the globe follow similar rules or guidelines, there are differences between clearing mandates across jurisdictions. This is not only in terms of which products are covered but also which counterparty types are subject to mandatory clearing. For instance, in the EU, pension scheme arrangements are

---

[27] At the time of editing plans for interoperability for interest rate swaps between Hong Kong Exchange OTC Clear and the Shanghai Clearing House have been made public. This however was not public at time of writing.

temporarily exempt from clearing at time of writing,[28] while there are no similar exemptions in the United States. Often, there are hedging exemptions for corporates or smaller financial counterparties, all of which are implemented differently in different jurisdictions. Also, there could be regulatory or other restrictions that mean that not all market participants can clear at all CCPs (see section 6.2 below). Because of these differences, each CCP will have a different mix of market participants with different hedging needs and different directionality of their portfolios. If their clients have directional portfolios at a certain CCP, the portfolios of their dealers could be equally directional. This can lead to higher margin requirements for these dealers, particularly when dealers breach concentration risk thresholds at a CCP or can only find the offsetting hedging transaction cleared at a different CCP (and would have to post margin at two CCPs). The cost of the higher margin will be priced into transactions by the affected dealers. This results in these transactions being more expensive compared to the same transactions at another CCP. This price difference is called the 'basis'. The basis depends on the direction: transactions in the direction similar to the majority of clients at a CCP tend to be more expensive, while transaction in the different direction, which will reduce margin requirements for the dealer, will be cheaper. Bases can only develop where there is more than one CCP clearing the same product/contract. Bases can be volatile but usually will add costs to clearing at affected CCPs.

Bases are a cross-border clearing issue by nature of how they develop.[29] Bases cannot develop if there is no choice where to clear for a given product. Should there be a choice of clearing location, market participants will have to take existing or potential bases into account when making this choice. How a basis affects the decision depends on the nature of the basis and the direction of the portfolio in question. If there is a basis, transactions in one direction will be more expensive, but transactions in the opposite direction will be cheaper.

A basis can coincide with lower market liquidity for transactions cleared at the CCP in question, which might also affect the decision whether to clear at this CCP.

6 Choice of CCPs

Please note that the thoughts about choice and access to CCP are universal issues to consider but usually also have a cross-border angle. Most of these thoughts in this and section 7 do not exclusively apply to OTC derivatives CCPs.

In the following, a prospective clearing participant choosing a CCP is called a 'firm', 'market participant', or 'clearing participant' and all three terms mean the same in this context.

---

[28] See EMIR (n 4), Art. 89.
[29] There could theoretically be bases between two CCPs clearing the same product in one jurisdiction, but this would be very unlikely.

6.1 Product/Market Driven

Products traded at many securities and futures exchanges will be cleared by only one CCP. Therefore, for many markets and products, what CCP to use is driven by the market a firm wants to access. For instance, if a member wants to trade futures at the Chicago Mercantile Exchange (CME), the executed contracts need also to be cleared at CME. The CCP is often part of the same group (as in the CME example above), but, in other cases, a CCP clears for several exchanges, such as the US Options Clearing Corporation, which clears for sixteen exchanges, two futures markets, one alternative trading system, and OTC trade sources.[30]

An exception to the above exists if there is an interoperability arrangement, where several CCPs can clear for one market or one or more exchanges (see section 4 above).

For OTC derivatives, there is often a choice of CCP where a trade is cleared. If there is no applicable regulation that requires clearing, counterparties to an OTC derivative can even agree not to centrally clear a trade at all. If they want to clear the trade or are required to clear by regulation, the counterparties to many OTC derivative transactions can chose at which CCP to clear the transaction. Exceptions to this are, for instance, OTC derivative transactions in jurisdictions that require clearing at the local CCP.

In summary, many of these constraints can force a market participant to clear in a jurisdiction outside its own.

6.2 By Regulatory or Legal Constraints

Not all market participants are eligible to clear at all CCPs across the globe. For a market participant that wishes to access a CCP as a clearing member, there are often requirements that the CCP needs to have a certain status in the jurisdiction of the prospective clearing member: the CCP, for instance, needs to be recognized in Europe or registered or exempt under CFTC rules. Even if the CCP has the right status in the jurisdiction of the market participant, the CCP in question might not accept clearing members from the jurisdiction of the market participant, for instance, because the CCP rules might not be enforceable in this jurisdiction. This is discussed in Chapter 11 ('Default Management', by David Horner).[31] Please see under principle 1 of the PFMIs in section 2.1 above.

Usually, it is easier for a market participant to access a CCP as a client. Another possibility for the market participant to access a CCP in a jurisdiction it cannot access from the home jurisdiction is to use a local subsidiary in the jurisdiction where the CCP is located or another jurisdiction if the CCP allows members from this jurisdiction. Please see section 7 below.

---

[30] Options Clearing Corporation, 'Participant Exchanges & Futures Markets' (undated), https://www.theocc.com/Clearance-and-Settlement/Participant-Exchanges (accessed 23 March 2023).

[31] Or the CCP has not yet analysed the rules of the jurisdiction, for instance, due to a lack of demand.

6.3 Commercial and Risk Criteria

If there is a choice where to clear, market participants will have to look at several criteria when making the decision.

6.3.1 Risk
All CCPs implement local regulation and requirements from the PFMIs differently and therefore their risk management frameworks will be different. After due diligence, a market participant might decide that being a clearing member at a particular CCP is deemed to be too risky and therefore opt for an alternative CCP (if available for the product in question). Please see under section 9 below for more details.

6.3.1 Market liquidity
For nearly all market participants, it is important that there is sufficient market liquidity for transactions cleared at a CCP. It is crucial for most market participants to be able to execute a trade at the time of their choosing at a competitive price. This is important when entering a trade but even more so when a closing a trade. Market liquidity depends on many factors. The main driver is that a sufficient number of market participants find the market attractive enough to execute trades at this market. In markets where there is only one CCP (as is the case for many exchanges—see above—or closed jurisdictions), liquidity at this CCP is the same as for the overall market. If there is a choice of CCPs, the local CCP may not always offer the best market liquidity. For instance, for OTC interest rate swaps denominated in many currencies, it will often be LCH SwapClear where the best market liquidity can be found, not the CCP located in the jurisdiction where the currency in which a swap is denominated is based.

6.3.3 Operational efficiency
Another criterion is how seamless it is to clear at a CCP, from the initial onboarding to ongoing interactions to the CCP. During onboarding, the market participant will get a first impression of how complex the contracts with the CCP, the IT infrastructure, and other operational processes are and how helpful the CCP is to guide the new members through this process. In terms of ongoing interactions, it is especially important how the CCP handles requests outside of the usually well-automated core clearing operations, such as transfer of a set of transactions or a whole book to another account. This consideration has the weakest link to cross-border clearing, even though a market participant could decide on a CCP in a third-country because of advantages in efficiency provided by the third-country CCP.

6.3.4 Cost
In terms of cost, there are two aspects: the first is the direct cost of clearing at a certain CCP, that is, its clearing fees. More important, though, is the cost of funding margin, or lack thereof, if one CCP allows netting between different currencies or products,

leading to lower margin requirements. A CCP that clears a certain product in many currencies will usually net all these transactions before calculating margin requirements. This will often result in lower margin requirements than if the market participant would clear each of these transactions at a separate CCP and also saves on the cost of accessing multiple CCPs. If a CCP can net transactions of different product types, there could be a similar effect. This is not as common as cross-currency netting. There could also be issues of how these different products are treated in recovery and resolution. Please see Chapter 12 ('Recovery and Resolution of CCPs' by Victor de Serière) in this volume for more information on recovery and resolution.

6.3.5 Legal framework

A market participant might also decide to shun cross-border clearing and clear in its home jurisdiction because of familiarity with, and preference for, the local legal/regulatory framework or other concerns with cross-border clearing. The market participant needs to carefully weight other factors presented in this section, such as market liquidity, cost, and whether there is a basis and risk considerations.

7 Access to the CCP

7.1 Direct Membership vs Client Clearing

Once a market participant has selected a CCP to clear at, either by default (a given market or product can only be cleared at a certain CCP) or by a selection process using the considerations discussed in section 6 above, the market participant has to decide how to access the selected CCP. A market participant can either become a direct clearing member of the CCP, access the CCP as a client of a clearing member (a clearing member in this context is also called a client clearing service provider), or utilize a hybrid access model. Please refer to Chapter 4 ('CCP Access Structures' by Christina Sell) in this volume on access structures.

There are several considerations concerning whether to become a direct member or a client. For simplicity, and as hybrid models are fairly new, this section does not cover these hybrid access models. As these models are a hybrid between direct membership and client clearing and are different between CCPs, it is difficult to generalize considerations of when to use such models.

7.1.1 Portfolio size

Becoming a clearing member at a CCP involves fixed costs, for instance, legal documentation and the IT onboarding. Both legal onboarding and IT access can be more cumbersome and therefore more expensive for accessing the CCP as clearing members compared to access as a client. On the legal side, this includes the review of the rule book and other documentation required for onboarding. In a cross-border context, this cost can be even higher because the market participant might not be familiar with the jurisdiction in question and requires local counsel; in terms of IT onboarding, the CCP in question might use a middleware which is different from the middleware used by many global CCPs, which could make IT work linked to onboarding more expensive. This fixed cost means that a direct membership is not economic for small portfolios: the fixed cost would be carried by only a small number of transactions, which would likely make every transaction very expensive compared to competitors with more volume.

On the other hand, if the portfolio is too large and too risky, a potential client clearing service provider might not want to clear such a large portfolio, for instance, because such a portfolio would make the risk profile of the client clearing service provider more directional or very concentrated (both might result in larger margin add-ons for the client clearing service provider and/or higher default fund contributions), difficult to close out in case of a default of the prospective client, or would put too big a capital requirement on the client clearing service provider. Portfolios that are too large are not directly linked to a cross-border context; however, some of the reasons why a client clearing service provider might be reluctant to take on a client with such a large portfolio might be exacerbated if there are different jurisdictions involved.

7.1.2 Ease of access

As the 'other side of the coin' of the cost of access to a CCP as a direct clearing member, accessing a CCP as a client is usually easier to set up than a direct membership. If the market participant already has a client clearing service provider, all necessary IT connections to the client clearing service provider might already be in place and there only needs to be an additional agreement with the client clearing service provider in respect of the new CCP.

7.1.3 Legal or regulatory constraints

As mentioned in section 6.2 above, it may not be possible for the market participant to become a direct clearing member in the jurisdiction where the CCP is located because the CCP does not believe its rule book is enforceable in the home jurisdiction of the market participant, the CCP is not registered or recognized in the home jurisdiction of the market participant, or regulations in the CCP jurisdiction does not allow for clearing memberships from abroad (sometimes called remote membership). In this case, the only choice (if the market participant does not want to use another entity located elsewhere) is to access the CCP as a client of a client clearing service provider that is allowed to clear in this jurisdiction. As this likely means that the client clearing service provider is located in another jurisdiction as its prospective client, the relationship between the market participant looking to access the CCP and the client clearing service provider is likely also to be a cross- border relationship.

7.1.4 Concerns about the jurisdiction in question

The market participant might want to access a CCP in a certain jurisdiction but has concerns about this jurisdiction, for instance because the market participant is concerned about the absence of certain legal safeguards such as netting. In such a situation, it might be better to access the CCP as a client as, in most client clearing models, the client's relationship is with the client clearing service provider, which could insulate the clients from potential issues. However, access might be more expensive if the client clearing service provider might want to be compensated for the risk it takes for the client.

7.1.5 Limits

It sometimes happens that a firm is a direct clearing member at a CCP and has either a strict limit framework or is not willing to increase limits due to concerns about the jurisdictions or the CCP (see above). Should this firm wish to increase clearing at this CCP but cannot, or does not want to, change limits, another potential avenue would be to clear parts of the portfolio via a client clearing service provider.

7.2 Choice of Location

If a market participant wants to access a CCP in another jurisdiction, there are several choices of clearing location, which are also linked to how the market participants' business is organized. A market participant with several subsidiaries across the globe will likely decide on a different structure of CCP access from a market participant that does not have any subsidiaries.

The considerations below focus on clearing location. Naturally, the choice of clearing location will be affected by the choice of trading location, that is, in which jurisdiction a market participant trades and in which balance sheet the trades are booked. This is not a hard link: for instance, even if the trading jurisdiction and the clearing jurisdiction are different, branches of the entity accessing the CCP or internal client clearing relationships can be used to trade in one jurisdiction and clear in another.

7.2.1 Access to the CCP from the home jurisdiction

In this case, the market participant will access the CCP either as a remote member or via a branch in the jurisdiction of the CCP. If the market participant wishes to access the CCP as a direct member, this choice is only available if the CCP and its regulator allow remote membership and if the CCP is either registered or recognized (depending on home jurisdiction of the market participant). Access from the home jurisdiction is likely to be more cost-effective if the market participant does not have any local subsidiaries yet, or even if these are available, as there are no duplicate clearing teams or collateral pools in a central set-up. There are, however, potential time zone differences to be managed, and the market participant needs to address the potential of sourcing collateral for margin calls outside the home time zone or working hours.

7.2.2 Access to the CCP via a local subsidiary

Accessing the CCP from its home jurisdiction will likely be easier for the market participant, either as a client or a direct member. There may be fewer obstacles to become a direct clearing member as CCP and clearing members are in the same jurisdiction. Similarly, accessing the CCP as a local client of a local clearing member should avoid cross-border issues with different jurisdictions between the CCP, clearing member, and client. In both cases, onboarding, both the technology work and the negotiations of documentation with the CCP or the client clearer, can be done with local staff (if available), which could make the process more seamless and less costly. A less complex legal structure (because there are no cross-border issues) from the point of view of the CCP, might also make the onboarding process more seamless. There are also no time zone issues as staff dealing with the CCP are located in the same jurisdiction as the CCP. The downside is that the local subsidiary requires its own staff, management, governance structures, regulatory authorization, capital, liquidity, and balance sheet. Overall, the structure of the market participant as a whole will become more complex and therefore costly. Accessing a CCP this way might make most sense if the market participant already has a subsidiary in the jurisdiction of the CCP. In terms of clearing, the most obvious cost will be that the subsidiary will have to manage its own funding and liquidity pool for margin required by the CCP and potential margin calls in the future. Also, there will be some duplications in terms of staffing compared to a central team. There might also be increased capital requirements as each subsidiary has to be capitalized separately. More information related to funding and collateral can be found in Chapter 6 'OTC Derivatives Clearing and Collateral Management' by Manmohan Singh in this volume.

7.2.3 Access to a CCP from a third country

In terms of complexity and cost, this solution sits between access from the location of the market participant's head office and access from the market participant's home jurisdiction. In this solution, the market participant accesses the CCP from a jurisdiction where it is possible and advantageous to do so, both by regulation and by the CCP rules and requirements. This could be, for instance, a local hub in the region where the CCP is located, as long as the CCP has the required registration or recognition in the jurisdiction where the CCP is planned to be accessed from and the CCP allows clearing members from this jurisdiction. In terms of complexity, there could be synergies, for instance, because there is already a team that deals with CCP memberships in other countries of this region. Besides staffing, accessing several local CCPs from this hub could also provide synergies in terms of collateral sourcing and liquidity planning.

7.2.4 Indirect clearing

If the market participant wants to access the CCP as a client, there is also the possibility of becoming a client of a client clearing service provider in the home jurisdiction of the market participant. This client clearing service provider might then, in turn, be the client of a client clearing service provider in the jurisdiction of the CCP. Becoming a client of a clearing client is called 'indirect clearing' or, in the PFMIs, 'tiered participation arrangements'. Please see Chapter 4 ('CCP Access Structures' by Christina Sell) in this volume for more information about CCP access structures.

8 Operational and Commercial Considerations Linked to Cross-Border Clearing

8.1 Time Zone Differences

As cross-border clearing can involve CCPs across the globe, there are likely to be time zone differences. Section 6 above has already considered time zone difference in relation to the choice of CCPs.

Usually, on top of scheduled margin payments, such as IM and variation payments on the morning of a trading day, CCPs reserve the right to ask a clearing member for margin payments during operating hours at a short notice (called intra-day margin calls). Even if the market participant accesses the CCP as a client, depending on the client clearing agreement, the client clearing service provider might ask their clients for intra-day payments of margin calls. This means, especially for clearing members, that for the operating hours of the CCP (the time it can call for margin) staff need to be available to pay margin if required, management needs to be available to sign off these payments, and other staff, such as operations and risk management, need to be present. These are merely examples: this chapter does not go into detail on how to organize a clearing team.

While staff needs to be available even in local settings, if a firm accesses CCPs in other jurisdictions in other time zones without utilizing local or regional staff, cross-border clearing can extend the time staff need to be available.

8.2 Cross-Border Margin Payments

8.2.1 Open window of payment services and sourcing cash in other currencies late in the day

Even in a purely local setting, it can occur for a CCP to call for intra-day margin late in the day outside of the operating hours of the local payment systems. In this case, CCPs will ask for margin to be paid in other currencies where payments can still be made, for instance, dollars for a late payment in Europe. This can pose issues even in a purely local setting but will become more complicated in relation to CCPs in other time zones. Even the regular payment system for a CCP in another time zone might be outside of local business hours for the market participant. The market participant needs to have processes and systems in place to ensure that there is sufficient liquidity available in all currencies and at all payment systems that the third-country CCP uses. This is potentially easier if the market participant already has subsidiaries in these jurisdictions as liquidity management processes might already exist for other business lines. If not, the market participant needs to ensure that liquidity in all relevant currencies can be managed from its home location. On the other hand, a central treasury and central liquidity management could be more efficient as the same liquidity pool could be used for several CCPs or even other business lines.

8.2.2 Cross-border securities collateral

Many CCPs allow for a part of margin to be posted as securities collateral. Posting securities collateral is usually less flexible and takes longer than transferring cash but can have advantages in terms of credit risk, especially if the cash can be posted in a bankruptcy-remote way.[32]

At most CCPs participants can choose to pay margin exclusively in cash. Therefore, despite potential advantages of securities collateral, market participants have the choice of not using securities collateral if operational processes or sourcing the right type of securities collateral turns out to be cumbersome or costly.

Otherwise, similar considerations apply to securities collateral as to posting cash: if the market participant already has a subsidiary with the infrastructure to source and transfer securities, operational processes will be easier, but overall management of collateral stock might be less efficient than in a centralized setting. This is because every subsidiary needs to have sufficient collateral to satisfy peak demand, whereas in a centralized setting, there could be more diversification effects between the collateral requirements at different CCPs or even with other business lines.

8.2.3 Liquidity management: Intragroup loans and capital implications

The sections above discussed the relative advantages of centralized access to a third-country CCP versus access using local or regional subsidiaries. There could also be situations where the two models are mixed: a market participant might access a CCP from its head office and have processes and resources in place to satisfy usual intraday margin requirements. In case of a late margin call, for instance, driven by a spike in the market very late in the trading day, which forces the CCP to issue a margin call equally late in the day, this provision might not be sufficient. Should the market participants have subsidiaries in the relevant time zones, an obvious solution would be to ask the subsidiary to source the required liquidity to satisfy the margin call. This could, however, constitute an intragroup loan, which could result in capital charges, liquidity requirements, etc. Technically, this situation could arise even in a non-cross-border context with a local CCP, for instance, if the margin call happens outside the operating window of the local payment system and the CCP calls for margin in another currency

---

[32] Bankruptcy-remote margin is margin that will not become part of the bankruptcy estate if the CCP enters bankruptcy. For instance, this could be securities where the CCP only has a security interest, or tripartite arrangements. In any case, every arrangement requires legal review to establish whether the arrangement is indeed bankruptcy remote. Please see Chapter 9 ('Capital Requirements for Bank Exposures to CCPs' by Marc Peters) in this volume for more information on capital requirements.

in which the market participant does not have available liquidity. However, such a situation may be more likely in a cross-border context unless the cross-border situation has led the market participant to establish more fallback sources of liquidity that do not require the use of potential intragroup loans.

9 Cross-Border Risk Management Considerations

9.1 Due Diligence

While all CCPs broadly follow the PFMIs, there are differences in their risk management frameworks. As a clearing member, a market participant underwrites the counterparty risk of its fellow clearing members and therefore has an interest that the CCP has appropriate membership criteria and that it manages the risk stemming from their participation, for instance, by setting appropriate margin levels, which should not be too procyclical. Chapter 11 ('Default ManagEMENt' by Dvid Horner) dicusses this in further detail. The CCP needs sufficient mutualized resources and a credible default management process. Market participants also want to review the governance structure of a CCP and the level of influence of clearing members, for instance, whether the CCP has a risk committee where clearing members are represented. Operational resilience is as important as the liabilities of clearing members in case of the default of other member(s) or other issues at the CCP, so-called non-default losses. These are merely examples of topics that should be reviewed during a due diligence. Large banks have whole teams that review risk management frameworks at CCPs where they are members and analyse a wide range of aspects of these risk management frameworks covering most or all principles in the PFMIs. As transparency about the risk management framework, the applicable regulations, and the quality of CCP supervision can differ across countries, risk assessment of CCPs is also a cross-border issue. Large, global CCPs follow global best practice and have similar risk management processes, but there are some CCPs across the globe that have implemented the PFMIs in a different way, which their clearing members should be aware of.

In a clearing relationship, a client usually takes less risk on the CCP than clearing members. Clients do not have to bid in default auctions, do not post default fund contributions that could be at risk, and cannot be called for additional unfunded default fund contributions. Still, there are risks, for instance, if the CCP gets into extreme difficulties and has to employ loss allocation tools that spread losses across all clearing participants (for instance, variation margin gains haircutting, see Chapter 11 'Default Management' by David Horner in this volume). Depending on contractual agreements, the client clearing service provider might have the right to pass default fund losses on to their clients. Clients have to be aware of these risks. They also need to be aware of the risk to their client clearing service provider, for instance, the general credit quality or how well margin is segregated. Due to different laws and regulations being involved, the analysis of segregation will be more difficult in a cross-border context.

The client clearing service provider might not be the ultimate clearing member at the CCP in question but might use another client clearing service provider (called 'indirect clearing' or 'tiered participation arrangements', see section 7.2.4 above). For instance, a market participant might use its usual client clearing service provider in its home jurisdiction, which does not have operations in all jurisdictions. This client clearing service provider might use another, maybe more globally active client clearing service provider, which, in turn, uses its local subsidiary to access the CCP as a direct clearing member. A client needs to be aware of which firms are involved in this clearing chain to assess the counterparty credit risk.

9.2 Limit Framework

Clearing limit frameworks are generally different between firms, depending on the complexity of their operations and their general limit framework.

Limit frameworks for cleared exposures often include some or all of the following components.

9.2.1 Posted margin
This will include not only the margin required by the CCP but also any excess or over-margining, either because the CCP requires a level of additional margin or the clearing participant posts this margin for operational ease. As mentioned in section 8.2 above, especially in a cross-border context, it might be very helpful to have additional margin already posted at the CCP to reduce short-term funding pressures in case of intra-day margin calls.

The limit framework often measures the absolute amount of margin posted. Some firms, however, do not include bankruptcy-remote margin in limit monitoring as such margin is deemed to be not affected if the CCP should fail.

9.2.2 Default fund contribution
This exposure to the CCP is usually managed separately as the risk of losing the default fund is different from the risk of losing margin. The former can happen if another clearing member defaults, the latter only if the CCP itself defaults or is resolved by a resolution authority (see Chapter 11 'Default Management' by David Horner in this volume).

9.2.3 Potential future exposure
Many firms also have a potential future exposure component (i.e. an estimate of how exposure could increase over a certain time frame) in their limit framework, either based on a quantitative model or using a simplified model similar to standardized models for counterparty credit risk to calculate capital requirements (see Chapter 9 'Capital Requirements for Bank Exposures to CCPs' by Marc Peters in this volume). Other firms do not use a potential future component and use the initial margin as a proxy for potential future exposure.

9.2.4 Stressed exposure

Another potential component of a risk framework could include stressed exposures, that is, the maximum exposure to the CCP under a set of stress scenarios.

For client clearing, the limit framework must also take into account any risks to the client clearing service provider.

Setting up a limit framework is not a cross-border issue per se but will become more complex in a cross-border context. For instance, how to post margin in a bankruptcy-remote way will differ from jurisdiction to jurisdiction. In a cross-border setting with several subsidiaries accessing CCPs, it is likely that each subsidiary will monitor limits locally. It should, however, be considered whether the firms should also have an aggregated view of cleared exposures. In many larger firms, several subsidiaries will have clearing memberships at global CCPs. In this case, a consolidated view across all memberships to a CCP is extremely helpful.

10 Cross-Border Crisis Management

Fortunately, there have not been any cases where a CCP had to be recovered or resolved in the recent decades. Such a situation would involve a loss, either from one or several concurrent defaults of clearing members or a non-default loss (such as investment losses, operational errors, fraud, or cyberattacks) so large that the existing resources of a CCP are not sufficient to cover it. In such a case, most CCPs can fall back on recovery tools that could allocate part of the losses to clearing participants or a resolution authority can step in, which could also lead to loss allocation to clearing participants. Depending on the tools used, some losses will be allocated only to clearing members, for instance, via cash calls. Other losses could be allocated to all clearing participants, for instance, via tools such as variation margin gains haircutting. For more details on CCP recovery and resolution, see Chapters 11 (Default Management' by David Horner) and 12 ('Recovery and Resolution of CCPs' by Victor de Serière) in this volume.

While CCP recovery and resolution is not a cross-border issue as such, regulatory frameworks on CCP recovery and resolution vary considerably across jurisdictions. In the EU, this topic is covered by the CCP Recovery and Resolution Regulation (CCPR&R);[33] while in the UK the Bank of England has statutory powers (which are being reviewed at time of writing). While the US Dodd–Frank Act contains rules on resolution that are also applicable to CCPs, most relevant provisions for recovery and resolution are part of CCPs' rule books. Other jurisdictions, especially smaller ones, have no formal rules. A participant in a CCP, both in the home jurisdiction and outside, needs to be aware how it could be affected by these rules.

---

[33] Regulation (EU) No. 2021/23 of the European Parliament and of the Council of 16 December 2020 on a framework for the recovery and resolution of central counterparties and amending Regulations (EU) No. 1095/2010, (EU) No. 648/2012, (EU) No. 600/2014, (EU) No. 806/2014 and (EU) No. 2015/2365 and Directives 2002/47/EC, 2004/25/EC, 2007/36/EC, 2014/59/EU, and (EU) 2017/1132 (16 December 2020), https://eur-lex.europa.eu/legal-content/EN/TXT/?uri=CELEX%3A32021R0023 (CCPR&R) (accessed 23 March 2023).

A particular cross-border issue is how a jurisdiction will (if there are clear rules) or is likely to (if there are no clear rules) treat foreign clearing members or clients. While some recovery and resolution regimes explicitly ban discrimination by location,[34] others are quiet on this issue. While situations that require recovery or resolution are extremely unlikely, a clearing participant should be aware which rules in such a case apply, what additional loss-allocation tools the CCP or a resolution authority can employ, how a non-local clearing member would be treated, and whether safeguards such as the no-creditor-worse-off principle[35] are available.

While not to the same extent as clearing members, clients can also suffer losses from the employment of certain loss-allocation tools. In this case, it is important to ensure that the documentation with the client clearing service provider or local laws or regulation provide for compensation to passed through from the client clearing service provider to the client.

These considerations are generally applicable, not just in a cross-border context. As with other topics, in a cross-border context it is especially important to review the local rules and identify where they differ from what the clearing participant is used to in its home market to make sure all additional risks are fully understood.

11 Clearing in Small or Closed Jurisdictions

A particular case of cross-border clearing concerns clearing in smaller or closed jurisdictions. While ISDA makes the point that smaller jurisdictions should not need to set up a local CCP before other conditions are met,[36] there are plenty of small jurisdictions that have done so. Sometimes, a market participant in these countries has to clear at the local CCP due to a clearing obligation for certain products.

Especially if the market is closed (i.e. there are exchange controls or strict regulation about which entity is allowed to do a certain business), additional obstacles have to be overcome. Other than ensuring that all required permits and authorizations are present, exchange controls will complicate funding and liquidity management. For instance, in such jurisdictions it is very unlikely that remote clearing memberships would be allowed. Access to the CCP therefore requires a local subsidiary, which has to be suitable capitalized and requires its own funding and liquidity provisions.

---

[34] See, for instance, CCPR&R (n 33), Recital (52).

[35] In a nutshell, the no-creditor-worse-off (NCWO) safeguard ensures that no creditor (which in the clearing context are mostly clearing members and their clients, plus others like liquidity providers) will be worse off in resolution compared to what would have happened if the resolution authority had not stepped in and the CCP would have become insolvent after using all rule-book provisions, which could include recovery tools. In practice, this means that the resolution authority or an independent valuer calculates the losses each creditor would have suffered in the counterfactual insolvency and a creditor is compensated if the losses in resolution would have been higher than in insolvency.

[36] ISDA, 'Clearing in Smaller or Closed Jurisdictions' (1 October 2018), https://www.isda.org/a/tsvEE/ITC-Small-Jurisdictions-final.pdf (accessed 23 March 2023).

16

Brexit

Equivalence; Location Policy

Dermot Turing

1 Introduction

On 23 June 2016, the people of the United Kingdom voted to leave the European Union (EU). This triggered a long process of reshaping the relationship between one of the larger countries of the EU and the remaining Member States. Perhaps unforeseen by the politicians or voters, one outcome of that process has been a radical overhaul of the way that clearing is regulated.

The revised regulatory package is embodied in Regulation (EU) No. 2019/2099 (EMIR 2.2), which came into force on 1 January 2020. EMIR 2.2 fits into a refreshed set of rules about clearing, brought about through Regulation (EU) No. 2019/834 (EMIR REFIT) (in force 7 June 2019).[1] The revised code of law is to be found in an updated version of Regulation (EU) No. 648/2012, commonly referred to as EMIR.[2]

EMIR 2.2 created the most significant shift for regulation of non-EU central counterparties (CCPs) since the introduction of EMIR itself. From now on, CCPs have to be graded for systemic importance, with different degrees of EU intervention according to the grade assigned. As regards the clearing of OTC derivatives, the new framework could hardly be more important.

Brexit is closely linked to the revision of the European framework. The European Commission's legislative proposal, which culminated in EMIR 2.2, was issued on 23 October 2017, some sixteen months after the Brexit vote. Although the recitals to the

---

[1] EMIR REFIT exempts smaller financial institutions from the clearing obligation applicable to interest rate swaps and credit derivatives and allows the European Securities Markets Authority (ESMA) and the European Commission to suspend the clearing obligation altogether.

[2] Regulation (EU) No. 648/2012 of the European Parliament and of the Council of 4 July 2012 on OTC derivatives, central counterparties and trade repositories, [2012] OJ L201/1, consolidated version as at 28 June 2021 available at http://data.europa.eu/eli/reg/2012/648/2021-06-28 (accessed 8 March 2022).

EMIR 2.2 Regulation—in effect, the explanation of the background to the legislation—make no reference to Brexit, they do point to the fact that the EU had sixteen authorized CCPs, compared to thirty-three recognized non-EU CCPs, and to the growing significance of clearing. It was probably not necessary to state explicitly that the risks would increase with the departure of the United Kingdom.

The European Commission stated, in 2019, that:

'the market for central clearing of OTC derivatives is highly concentrated, in particular the market for central clearing of euro-denominated OTC interest rate derivatives, of which more than 90% are cleared in one CCP established in the United Kingdom. In 2017, 97% of euro-denominated OTC interest rate derivatives were cleared in that CCP.[3]

For products where clearing is mandated by law, the increase in cleared volumes is partly due to market participants' lack of choice as to whether they clear; it is network effects that drive concentration, making apparent choice about where they clear far less real in practice. The present picture is not much different: according to Khwaja (2022),[4] LCH Limited's SwapClear division had 92.8% of the market share in clearing of euro-denominated interest rate derivatives in 2021; competition from Eurex was hardly noticeable despite its own market share increasing (3.5% in 2019, 5.8% in 2020, 7.2% in 2021).

At the time of the Brexit vote, the United Kingdom's CCPs would, after leaving the EU, be tested against EMIR, Art. 25, which allows non-EU CCPs to be 'recognized' (and thus to accept EU firms as clearing members) if the laws of the United Kingdom relating to CCP regulation were 'equivalent' to those of the EU. That should have been straightforward enough since, as a Member State, the United Kingdom's laws were exactly those of the EU. Upon the final departure date, minor adjustments to EMIR, as applied in the United Kingdom, came into effect.[5] Those adjustments are primarily concerned with the roles of authorities—to make sense in the United Kingdom of articles of EMIR which refer to responsibilities of the European Securities and Markets Authority (ESMA), the European Commission, and so forth—rather than making substantive adjustments to the law. However, following EMIR 2.2, the simple route to recognition is no longer available since the recognition process now requires, as a first step, an assessment of systemic importance in order to categorize the CCP.

This chapter attempts to trace a pathway through the new legal and regulatory environment. Along the way, various strategic landmarks stand out: the extent to which geography is relevant to the regulation of clearing of financial products which have no

---

[3] Commission Implementing Decision (EU) No. 2019/2211 of 19 December 2019 amending Implementing Decision (EU) No. 2018/2031 determining, for a limited period of time, that the regulatory framework applicable to central counterparties in the United Kingdom of Great Britain and Northern Ireland is equivalent, in accordance with Regulation (EU) No. 648/2012 of the European Parliament and of the Council, [2019] OJ L332/157, Recital (3).

[4] Amir Khwaja, '2021 CCP Volumes and Market Share in IRD', *Clarus Financial Technology* (11 January 2022), https://www.clarusft.com/2021-ccp-volumes-and-market-share-in-ird (accessed 7 March 2022).

[5] Made under Statutory Instruments SI 2018 No. 1184, SI 2019 Nos 335 and 1416 and SI 2020 No. 646.

obvious geographical roots, the meaning of 'systemic importance' as applied to CCPs, the impact of Brexit on the industry's most important CCPs for clearing of OTC derivatives, and the policy of the EU and the European Central Bank (ECB) with regard to location of CCPs.

2 Cross-Border Regulation of CCPs

The OTC derivatives markets are international. Estimates predating the financial crisis of 2008 suggested that over 50% and perhaps as much as 75% of derivatives exposures of US banks was to foreign counterparties.[6] Since the crisis, the market for clearable OTC derivatives has grown, and there is little reason to believe it has become less international. While up-to-date statistics are difficult to obtain, and definitional questions about what constitutes a 'cross-border' transaction arise, it seems reasonably safe to conclude that—at least as far as derivatives subject to a clearing mandate are concerned—a sizeable proportion consists of transactions where at least one of the parties (the end investor or their chosen intermediary or the CCP which clears the trade) is located in a different legal jurisdiction from one or more of the others. The international nature of the transactions creates issues of regulatory jurisdiction which impinge specifically on the question of who should regulate the CCPs that clear them.

A simplistic, single-country view allows for a regulatory system under which the regulator in the CCP's country of incorporation holds the reins; the CCP's business is conducted in that country, and the users of the CCP's services—principally the clearing members of the CCP—are also based, or have the centre of their operations, there too so that the whole ecosystem is under the one regulator's oversight. For many decades, even centuries, this view of the clearing system worked well, beginning with the cleared markets of Chicago at the end of the nineteenth century and continuing well into the twentieth, even with the emergence of the cleared markets of London as a leading global force. The anchor for the regulator's jurisdiction over clearing was the exchange from which the transactions originated; the exchange was a physical place coupled to the CCP, and it would have taken an imaginative leap to dissociate that combination from a single location.

However, the beginning of clearing of OTC traded products at the LCH in the late 1990s may be taken as a starting-point for reappraisal of the single-country regulatory model. With end users and their clearing agents not being tied by an exchange, or indeed in any other meaningful way, to the country where the CCP conducted its operations, the question can more readily be posed: 'where' is a CCP actually carrying on its business? Is it necessarily the place where the CCP has its operational headquarters or where it receives margin deposits, or is it where its clearing members, or even the end

---

[6] Jan D. Lüttringhaus, 'Regulating Over-the-Counter Derivatives in the European Union—Transatlantic (Dis) Harmony after EMIR and Dodd–Frank: The Impact on (Re)Insurance Companies and Occupational Pension Funds' (2012) 18 Columbia Journal of European Law 19.

users of cleared products, are themselves located? If location is to be associated with some places other than that of the CCP's own headquarters, should other ('host state') regulators have some role in the oversight of the CCP and on what basis?

OTC derivatives are financial instruments with no obvious geographical anchors: no physical deliverable and no exchange.[7] OTC derivatives could thus be assigned to any convenient regulatory jurisdiction based on the currency of the payment or denomination of financial instruments involved, the 'location' of settlement systems, the country of incorporation (or, even more vaguely, of the 'centre of main interests') of any of the value-chain participants. On any of these grounds, it might be possible for a regulator to assert an interest in supervising a CCP which clears the transactions. Where the regulation of CCPs is concerned, and the transactions under scrutiny are wholesale market products such as clearable derivatives, it will be financial or monetary stability which is dominant in the minds of those claiming regulatory jurisdiction. The new legislative framework in Europe and the United Kingdom takes it as axiomatic that, in extreme cases, CCPs could be obliged to 'relocate' when extreme systemic threat is shown.

Nevertheless, it does not follow that the CCP's own location could be artificially changed to suit the agenda of regulators. Even in the absence of formal organized exchange, a CCP's location will usually be associated with the most liquid market. Although the CCP itself is only involved in trading activity following a default, the source of the cleared transactions will be a financial centre in which the CCP's clearing members and their clients are themselves active. There is a reason why significant CCPs are located where they are.

Evidently, the question in what circumstances, on what grounds, and how regulators should assert oversight powers over CCPs was already complex before Brexit. Kiff et al. (2022)[8] provide a useful taxonomy for home-host regulatory structures applied to CCPs. The simplest category is 'national treatment', where the host state regulator essentially ignores the home state regulation and subjects the incoming entity to its own regulatory system. At the other extreme is 'deference', where the host state regulator accepts the home state regulator's approach as sufficient and does not overlay its own rules. In practice, full deference is rarely observed, with host state regulators reserving some powers, imposing some rules, and demanding information from the home state regulator. Perhaps the most important example of deference is 'passporting', the model for host state regulation of CCPs within the EU, which allows for no host state interference. Passporting is only possible because Member States share a common regulatory framework under EMIR, overriding any contrary Member State arrangements and providing mutual confidence about regulatory standards on the vital issues.

The Kiff et al. taxonomy omits one rather significant option, which was introduced in Europe under EMIR 2.2. This is the possibility that the foreign CCP is perceived to

---

[7] OTC derivatives, by definition, are traded away from organized exchanges; the drive to insert trading of OTC derivatives into organized trading facilities is not something to do with the product but a policy response to perceived stability risk.

[8] John Kiff, Alessandro Gullo, Cory Hillier, and Panagiotis Papapaschalls, 'Applying the Central Clearing Mandate: Different Options for Different Markets', IMF Working Paper No. WP/22/14 (2022).

be so significant a risk that it should be denied access to the host state altogether unless it is 'relocated' so that it ceases to be a foreign CCP. This possibility gives legislative life to a long-standing desire expressed by the ECB that CCPs which are of systemic importance to the eurozone should be located within the eurozone and thus come under regulatory oversight of a eurozone supervisor.

In the original version of EMIR, CCPs based outside the EU ('third-country CCPs') were allowed to have EU clearing members if 'recognized'. Recognition was a form of deference, based upon a two-stage process. First, the third country's own legal and regulatory system would be scrutinized for 'equivalence' to that of EMIR; then, the way would be open for the third-country CCP to apply to ESMA to be officially recognized. The only considerations which ESMA had to take into account were:[9] whether the CCP is authorized in its home state and is subject to effective supervision ensuring full compliance with the home state's prudential requirements; feasible cooperation with the home state regulator; and whether the home state is on a money-laundering blacklist. ESMA was not empowered to superimpose any of the EMIR rules onto the CCP's EU activities. The most powerful tool given to ESMA was that of supervisory cooperation, which could allow ESMA to ask for information relating to issues perceived by ESMA to pose a threat.

This structure still exists. However, with the United Kingdom's decision to leave the EU, the recognition structure for third-country CCPs came under greater scrutiny. The fact is that two of the UK CCPs, LCH Limited and ICE Clear Europe, clear immense volumes of mandatorily clearable OTC derivatives instruments, said to amount to more than 90% or market share for euro-denominated derivatives.[10] Furthermore, clearing is a business activity which is subject to extreme network effects: if my likely trading counterparties use a particular CCP, there is a powerful incentive for me to clear at that CCP since inability to access that CCP will preclude such a trade in the absence of an 'interoperability' arrangement between that CCP and any other CCP which I may prefer.[11] So, the result is that once a CCP has built critical mass for clearing of a particular product, it will take a very potent external force to shift the clearing elsewhere. The mere fact of the United Kingdom's departure from the EU and its regulatory constructs would not, of itself, constitute such a force, especially with regard to cleared products where the geographical anchor is the existence of a liquid trading market. In so far as regulatory concerns might suggest that it is undesirable to clear OTC derivatives

---

[9] Regulation (EU) No. 648/2012 of the European Parliament and of the Council of 4 July 2012 on OTC derivatives, central counterparties and trade repositories, [2012] OJ L201/1 (27 July 2012), Art. 25(2) (EMIR).

[10] European Commission (Directorate General for Financial Stability, Financial Services and Capital), 'Call for Evidence for an Impact Assessment' (undated), https://eur-lex.europa.eu/legal-content/EN/TXT/?uri=PI_COM%3AAres%282022%291144614&qid=1646650494248 (accessed 7 March 2022).

[11] A 'network effect' exists where one market user derives additional benefits from choosing the same service provider as other users. In clearing, the network effect is driven by two main factors: first, the fact that my trade counterparty uses only CCP A makes it impossible for my side of the trade to be cleared at CCP B in the absence of an interoperability arrangement; second, margin offsets flowing from contrary market holdings (e.g. fixed and floating rate) are lost if the different positions are cleared in different CCPs. Interoperability between CCPs is difficult and, in the case of OTC derivatives, irrelevant since it applies only to clearing of transactions in transferable securities and money market instruments (EMIR (n 9), Art. 1(3)).

at a CCP located outside the EU, there was a need to reconsider the deference structure inherent in the recognition arrangements under EMIR as originally constituted.

3 The New Framework

EMIR 2.2 introduced two new levels of regulatory oversight for EU oversight of non-EU CCPs over and above the simple recognition model just described. As under the previous structure, a non-EU CCP is not allowed to have EU members unless the CCP has become recognized by ESMA. Now, there are two main options for ESMA in the recognition process: (i) for CCPs which ESMA considers not to be of systemic importance, the old regime; (ii) for 'Tier 2 CCPs', confusingly labelled since these CCPs are the ones which are systemically important, a new regime.

'Tier 2' CCPs will be granted recognition only if the CCP complies with EMIR, Art. 16 (capital) and Titles IV and V (organizational, conduct-of-business, risk management and interoperability rules).[12] Article 16 imposes the requirement for a CCP to have capital of at least EUR 7.5 million (it may be noted, in passing, that this is a minuscule sum relative to the default funds of CCPs and invisible against the initial margin deposits they take). Titles IV and V contain the organizational and business conduct rules for CCPs and the interoperability regulations (irrelevant to OTC derivatives clearing), respectively. Title IV, together with Commission Delegated Regulation 153[13] which amplifies it, ought to contain a complete regulatory code for CCP regulation in Europe, but ESMA notes[14] that there is a deficiency in that the framework for recovery and resolution of CCPs is contained in the separate Regulation for Recovery and Resolution of CCPs (the CCPR&R),[15] and the supervisory tools of the CCPR&R do not apply to third-country CCPs.

For CCPs graded as systemically important tier 2 CCPs, some degree of deference is still achievable through EMIR, Art. 25a, which allows non-EU CCPs to submit a request to ESMA to determine that complying with its home state rules satisfies compliance with EMIR, Art. 16 and Titles IV and V. This is the 'comparable compliance' regime.

The third, non-recognition, option is to be used 'as a last resort' following an assessment by ESMA (with input from EU central banks) that the 'CCP or some of its clearing services are of such substantial systemic importance that that CCP should not be recognised'. The derecognition option is sometimes known as 'tier 3'; its side effect is that if

---

[12] EMIR (n 9), Art. 25(2b).

[13] Commission Delegated Regulation (EU) No. 153/2013 of 19 December 2012 supplementing Regulation (EU) No. 648/2012 of the European Parliament and of the Council with regard to regulatory technical standards on requirements for central counterparties, [2013] OJ L52/41.

[14] See ESMA, 'ESMA Concludes Tier 2 CCP Assessment under Article 25(2c) of EMIR' (17 December 2021), ESMA91-372-1913 (ESMA, 'Tier 2 Assessment').

[15] Regulation (EU) No. 2021/23 of the European Parliament and of the Council of 16 December 2020 on a framework for the recovery and resolution of central counterparties and amending Regulations (EU) No. 1095/2010, (EU) No. 648/2012, (EU) No. 600/2014, (EU) No. 806/2014 and (EU) 2015/2365 and Directives 2002/47/EC, 2004/25/EC, 2007/36/EC, 2014/59/EU, and (EU) 2017/1132, [2021] OJ L22/1.

the CCP is not recognized, it could only continue clearing trades of the clearing members of the host state(s) concerned if it were to need to become an 'authorized' CCP, which means being incorporated and headquartered in an EU Member State; in other words, if it were to 'relocate' to the EU. Relocation is hardly straightforward. There is no tried legal mechanism for a company to remove itself from a third country to the EU; some complex reorganization would be needed, presumably involving the establishment of a new corporate entity and some multilateral agreement to transfer liabilities as well as assets.[16] Furthermore, there is no grandfathering so that any currently recognized non-EU CCP could be re-categorized or de-recognized.

Another complication for CCPs and their users which follows from Brexit is the UK legislation which adopts (or, to use British legalese, 'onshores') EU legislation as part of the continuing post-Brexit UK legal framework. The United Kingdom was obliged, until the end of the 'transitional period', to continue to apply all EU legislation which came into force before the end of 2020, which includes EMIR 2.2. The United Kingdom's version of EMIR (UK EMIR)[17] creates a kind of mirror-image of the EMIR 2.2 tiering of non-UK CCPs, which may have to be considered alongside that applicable in the EU whenever a 'cross-channel' situation arises in clearing.

The Bank of England's position on the way Brexit could alter its approach to supervision of CCPs was set out in a speech by the Deputy Governor for Financial Stability, Sir Jon Cunliffe, on 14 September 2021. He explained that equivalence assessments are 'autonomous' matters, remarking that 'the UK cannot outsource regulation and supervision of the world's leading complex financial system to another jurisdiction'. Thus, textual alignment of rules is not the objective; what is to be sought is similarity of outcomes, avoidance of disruption of cross-border financial activity, due respect to home-country regimes, and deep supervisory cooperation. The framework for most of the things on Sir Jon's shopping list ought to be found in the 'comparable compliance' arrangements introduced by EMIR 2.2 and in the versions of EMIR operating in both the EU and the United Kingdom.

4 Systemic Importance

Tiers 2 and 3 are relevant only in cases of substantial systemic importance. How 'systemic importance' is to be determined is set out in Commission Delegated Regulation (EU) No. 2020/1303 (Regulation 1303).[18] There are five criteria for ESMA to

---

[16] Since the departure of the United Kingdom from the European Union, a cross-border merger under Directive (EU) No. 2017/1132 is no longer available as a mechanism for relocation, in either direction. The United Kingdom has repealed the Companies (Cross Border Mergers) Regulations 2007, which facilitated the mechanism before Brexit.

[17] UK EMIR consists of EMIR (n 9), as it stood on 31 December 2020, modified by Statutory Instruments SI 2018 No. 1184, SI 2019 No. 335, SI 2019 No. 1416, and SI 2020 No. 646. Commission Delegated Regulation 153 is also frozen at 31 December 2020 and modified by Bank of England Technical Standards (European Market Infrastructure) (Amendment etc.) (EU Exit) (No. 1) Instrument 2019.

[18] Commission Delegated Regulation (EU) 2020/1303 of 14 July 2020 supplementing Regulation (EU) No. 648/2012 of the European Parliament and of the Council with regard to the criteria that ESMA should take into account to determine whether a central counterparty established in a third country is systemically important or likely to

consider: the nature, size, and complexity of the CCP's business; the effect of failure of, or a disruption to, a CCP; the CCP's clearing membership structure; alternative clearing services provided by other CCPs; and the CCP's relationships, interdependencies, or other interactions.

The assessment of systemic importance for the purposes of EMIR, Art. 25(2a) is spelt out in detail in Regulation 1303. Regulation 1303 is open to criticism since it is both too detailed and, at the same time, not specific enough. Each of its articles specifies a number of elements which ESMA must assess in forming its view of systemic importance. In some cases, it is a large number; for example, Art. 1 (on nature, size, and complexity of a CCP's business) lists fifteen elements, some of which have multiple points of data. Regulation 1303 thus sets out an impressively long list of quantitative data which ESMA must gather and assess, but it does not really explain where the red line is placed—which numbers, in fact, should tell ESMA that there is a systemic risk and which are fine. ESMA is left to make its own judgement, without any obvious benchmarks.

In fact, 'systemic importance' is nowhere defined—its meaning is somehow assumed, as part of the common understanding of what makes the financial world work and what puts it under threat. Traditionally, regulators used to explain it in terms of non-functioning market infrastructure. Still, there is room for argument about what jeopardizes the functioning of infrastructure and which infrastructures actually matter.

Regulation 1303 came into force at an awkward time in relation to Brexit. Its effective date was 22 September 2020, which fell after the United Kingdom had technically 'left' the EU but during the transitional period, during which all EU legislation, including new legislation with direct effect, continued to apply to the United Kingdom. Consequently, one might imagine that the approach set forth in Regulation 1303 might be part of UK law and dictate the approach of the Bank of England in determining whether a non-UK CCP is of systemic importance. Indeed, Regulation 1303 is among the EU laws frozen at the 'real' moment of the United Kingdom's departure from the EU; except that it has been disapplied by regulation 9A of the Central Counterparties (Amendment, etc., and Transitional Provision) (EU Exit) Regulations 2018,[19] which, together with other instruments, creates a modified regime for assessment of systemic importance.[20] UK EMIR keeps the EMIR 2.2 structure for recognition of non-UK CCPs, but all of the detail has been altered. Divergence has begun.

In the United Kingdom, the same list of criteria from EMIR, Art. 25(2a) applies, but it has been reshaped by Bank of England policy, as set out in a Policy Statement ('Tiering

---

become systemically important for the financial stability of the Union or of one or more of its Member States, [2020] OJ L305/7.

[19] SI 2018 No. 1184, as amended by SI 2020 No. 646.

[20] UK law in this area is hard to navigate since EMIR (n 9), Arts 25, 25a, and 25b are retained but with heavy modifications and replacements. The modifications and replacements are located in SI 2018 No. 1184 (as amended) and in the Over the Counter Derivatives, Central Counterparties and Trade Repositories (Amendment, etc., and Transitional Provision) (EU Exit) Regulations 2020, SI 2020 No. 646. Further provisions concerning systemic importance determination and comparable compliance are overlaid onto the modified version of EMIR (n 9) and are to be found in regs 13A to 13C of SI 2020 No. 1184 (as amended).

SoP').[21] The Bank of England's approach has the merit of explaining how it will apply the criteria listed in Art. 25(2a) to decide on systemic importance. The Bank of England does not have to fuss with a vast amount of data, and it has explained the principles behind its assessment. The Tiering SoP (Statement of Policy) focuses on the UK clearing members using the foreign CCP. The Bank foresees damage to UK financial stability if UK clearing members collectively contribute large amounts of initial margin[22] and default fund contributions to the CCP such that if the CCP were to fail, the ability to reclaim these amounts might be put at risk.

The Tiering SoP also explains its process for assessing systemic importance: the practice of dealing with tiering decisions. Its triage process involves a preliminary filtration of CCPs, weeding out (as tier 1 CCPs) those for which the Bank views the amount deposited with the CCP by UK clearing members as margin or default fund contributions as too small to be of concern and only then applying the EMIR, Art. 25(2a) criteria. Some further CCPs may be classified as tier 1 at this stage. Whether remaining CCPs have to be treated as tier 2 depends on the extent to which the Bank feels able to rely on the CCP's home state supervision arrangements, with more stringent reliance tests applied if 20% or more of the CCP's initial margin or default fund is contributed by UK clearing members.

Determining systemic importance, under both Regulation 1303 and the Tiering SoP, does not (unlike decision-making on resolution of failing CCPs) involve looking at the 'critical functions' of CCPs.[23] (This is to be welcomed since the discussion of what constitutes a critical function can become a rather pointless exercise in circular reasoning: a CCP carries out a critical function when its role is of systemic importance, and it is of systemic importance because its function is critical. The circularity is sometimes obscured by mentioning that OTC derivatives clearing has, since the 2008 crisis, become mandatory and by assuming that the clearing mandate somehow proves the criticality of clearing.) Nonetheless, both approaches to systemic importance for tiering purposes do prioritize the robustness of the CCP. Other factors which might be pertinent—such as the CCP's thirst for margin securities, procyclicality, the impact of default management on market liquidity, the ability of members to participate in default auctions—do not feature in the assessment of systemic importance.

It is right for regulators to be worried about CCPs' resilience. CCPs concentrate risk: one aspect of the policy drive for more clearing is the shift from a networked

---

[21] Bank of England, 'The Bank of England's Approach to Tiering Incoming Central Counterparties under EMIR Article 25', Statement of Policy (June 2022) (not to be confused with the 'Policy Statement' with the same title and date).

[22] It is not obvious why the Bank considers initial margin to be an indicator of systemic threat to the United Kingdom. Initial margin is collateral, posted to support a clearing member's positions. Whatever happens to the clearing member, its initial margin will be returned or used to offset losses on its positions; so the clearing member is no worse off even if the CCP fails (except to the extent of cash deposits and title-transfer collateral which outweigh the clearing member's positions). Perhaps initial margin is a proxy measure of significance of clearing to the UK economy. But if that is correct, the implication is that clearing must be treated as an economically critical function. Clearing is a useful risk management tool but not the only one; and while policy pronouncements assume that clearing is an essential activity, that is unproven.

[23] Critical functions are at the centre of thinking about resolution of failing CCPs: see, for example, CCP Recovery and Resolution Regulation, Regulation (EU) No. 2021/23 of 16 December 2020, OJ L 22, Art. 21.

structure, where counterparty relationships, and their associated exposures, are spread across the whole market, to a hub structure, where all risks are channelled into a single vehicle. Amplifying the concentration risk is the perception that CCPs are robust entities which weathered the 2008 financial crisis well and that the failure of a CCP is unimaginable. Any signal of weakness from a CCP could cause repercussions across markets and across borders which are a major threat to market liquidity, confidence, and the strength of an economy. Good recovery and resolution arrangements go some way to mitigating the threat.

Both EU and UK approaches thus link systemic importance to recovery and resolution. While open to some criticisms, the CCPR&R creates a modern toolkit for dealing with troubled CCPs and is probably better than any other regime anywhere;[24] but it came too late for the United Kingdom since it came into force after the end of the Brexit transitional period. The UK arrangements for CCP recovery and resolution are outdated and have a weak toolkit; this deficiency may underlie ESMA's concerns about the classification of UK CCPs in tier 2.[25]

5 Comparable Compliance

As noted, a CCP categorized as tier 2 must submit to a degree of European oversight. However, the CCP can avail itself of the 'comparable compliance' (partial-deference) regime if its home state regulatory system is similar enough to that of the EU. It might be noted that this is not dissimilar to the exercise undertaken by ESMA already in advising the European Commission on equivalence of a third country's regulatory regime, which is, of course, a precondition for recognition in the first place. However, it is possible that closer adherence to EMIR may be expected in a 'comparable-compliance' comparison than in an 'equivalence' comparison.

Detailed provisions on comparable compliance are set out in Commission Delegated Regulation (EU) No. 2020/1304 (Regulation 1304),[26] though, in practice, Regulation 1304 adds little beyond procedural rules to what can already be read in EMIR itself. It seems that the comparable-compliance assessment is done separately in relation to each of the fifty-eight non-interoperability criteria set out in Regulation 1304, allowing for a tier 2 CCP to be comparably compliant on some points but not on others. Once ESMA deems a third country's system to achieve comparable compliance, its own

[24] For review, see Randy Priem, 'CCP Recovery and Resolution: Preventing a Financial Catastrophe' (2018) 26 Journal of Financial Regulation and Compliance 351; Jens-Hinrich Binder, 'Central Counterparties Insolvency and Regulation in the EU', in Jens-Hinrich Binder and Paolo Saguato (eds), *Financial Market Infrastructures—Law and Regulation* (Oxford: Oxford University Press, 2021), p. 295; Dermot Turing, 'A Fresh Look at the Three Rs: The EU's CCP Recovery and Resolution Regulation' (2022) 37 Journal of International Banking and Financial Law 14
[25] See ESMA, 'Tier 2 Assessment' (n 14).
[26] Commission Delegated Regulation (EU) No. 2020/1304 of 14 July 2020 supplementing Regulation (EU) No 648/2012 of the European Parliament and of the Council with regard to the minimum elements to be assessed by ESMA when assessing third-country CCPs' requests for comparable compliance and the modalities and conditions of that assessment, [2020] OJ L305/13.

regulatory jurisdiction is (as with tier 1 CCPs) disapplied: it is a binary choice, like an on–off switch.

In reporting on its tier 2 assessment of UK CCPs in December 2021, ESMA called for revision of the comparable compliance framework. ESMA asked to be provided with the ability to take the degree of systemic importance of a CCP into account and for something more flexible than an on–off switch once the home state system is determined to be comparable.

At the time of writing (March 2022), no examples of comparable compliance applications or their outcomes were on the public record.

The United Kingdom has disapplied Regulation 1304, leaving the Bank of England a free hand in approaching the question of comparable compliance. The Bank's approach is set out in a second Statement of Policy,[27] affirming that it will look for equivalence of supervisory outcomes rather than an exact replica of UK EMIR. The Bank of England seems more at ease with the principle of deference than ESMA; but for ESMA, the issue is more acute because the CCPs which will presumably seek comparable compliance are the huge, systemically significant CCPs based in London, where the desire for a more tailored approach is understandable.

6 Tiering in Practice

The rules and policies have begun to be applied, starting in the EU with the UK CCPs. The European Commission has issued a formal decision that the legal and supervisory arrangements of the United Kingdom applicable to UK CCPs are equivalent to those in EMIR until 30 June 2025.[28] Among many recognized third-country CCPs, ESMA has gone on to recognize LCH Limited and ICE Clear Europe Limited as tier 2 CCPs and LME Clear Limited as a tier 1 CCP.[29]

In December 2021, ESMA completed its first assessment of the UK's tier 2 CCPs (LCH Ltd and ICE Clear Europe).[30] ESMA concluded, first, that the two UK CCPs should not be de-recognized under EMIR, Art. 25(2c), not because the two CCPs are safe enough to remain in tier 2 but because it would be too disruptive to de-recognize them: the costs of de-recognition would outweigh the benefits.[31] ESMA's commentary

---

[27] Bank of England, 'The Bank of England's Approach to Comparable Compliance under EMIR Article 25a', Statement of Policy (June 2022) (not to be confused with another 'Policy Statement' with the same title and date).

[28] Commission Implementing Decision (EU) No. 2022/174 of 8 February 2022 determining, for a limited period of time, that the regulatory framework applicable to central counterparties in the United Kingdom of Great Britain and Northern Ireland is equivalent, in accordance with Regulation (EU) No. 648/2012 of the European Parliament and of the Council, [2022] OJ L28/40.

[29] ESMA, 'List of Third-Country Central Counterparties Recognised to Offer Services and Activities in the Union' (20 August 2021 update), ESMA70-152-348.

[30] ESMA, 'Tier 2 Assessment' (n 14).

[31] The wholesale transfer of a multilaterally cleared portfolio of transactions from one CCP to another is not trivial. X's portfolio, originating from trades with A, B, C, and D, may now be complemented on the CCP's books by opposing positions with A, B, E, F, and G and in different sizes. In the absence of a cross-border legal solution allowing all rights and liabilities of the CCP to be transferred without member consent (akin to Part VII of the Financial Services and Markets Act 2000, which does the job for 'banking business' transfers domestically in the

on its assessment indicates dissatisfaction with the legal powers it enjoys as regards re-covery and resolution of CCPs, reinforcing the connection between the 'recognition' and 'resolution' concepts. ESMA's principal concern is that it enjoys no recovery and resolution powers over foreign CCPs and that the CCPR&R does not apply to them.

As for the mirror-image process in the United Kingdom, non-UK CCPs will as-sessed for their systemic importance, and labelled tier 1 or tier 2 accordingly; tier 2 CCPs must comply with most of UK EMIR and be supervised by the Bank of England, there is a comparable compliance regime, and the UK Treasury can make 'location regulations' in cases of high systemic importance so that the CCP will have to re-locate to the United Kingdom. So far, the UK Treasury has 'specified' that the legal and supervisory arrangements of the EU on CCPs—as they were on 9 November 2020—are equivalent to those of the United Kingdom's version of EMIR, Title IV and that the supervision and reciprocal recognition systems are effective. In the short term, the United Kingdom has implemented a 'temporary recognition regime' for non-UK CCPs, which lasts for three years from 1 January 2021.[32] Thus, until the end of 2023, foreign CCPs are temporarily recognized,[33] by when the Bank of England will presumably have completed its own tiering exercise under the SoP. As regards the option of complete de-recognition and requirement to relocate, the Bank of England said, in November 2021, that it 'does not envisage at present recommending the use of location regulations or "Tier 3"'.[34]

Perhaps the UK version of the EMIR framework is of limited importance, given that the most systemically significant CCPs are based in the United Kingdom; still, Eurex Clearing AG and LCH SA will certainly be affected by it. These CCPs have lost their passport into the United Kingdom so that they will be unable to have UK firms as clearing members without obtaining UK recognition; if, as seems likely, they are judged to be systemically important, they will have to comply with UK as well as EU rules, which—until the United Kingdom diverges more substantially from the EU version of EMIR—should not be a problem.

As with the EU's interim equivalence decision and recognition of UK CCPs, the United Kingdom's temporary regime feels like a stay of execution rather than a solu-tion. When time is up, there is a political danger in the mirror-image UK legislation: as far as LCH Ltd is concerned, the United Kingdom could still be threatened with the re-location option as part of the post-Brexit aftershocks. On the other side, most observers will expect that LCH Ltd and ICE Clear Europe will remain of systemic importance for the purposes of the new European regulatory framework.

United Kingdom), X would need to agree to put on countervailing trades with clearing members at both the old and new CCPs in order to effectuate the transfer.

[32] Central Counterparties (Amendment, etc., and Transitional Provision) (EU Exit) Regulations 2018, SI 2018 No. 1184.

[33] See Bank of England, 'List of Third-Country CCPs That Are Taken to Be Eligible for Temporary Deemed Recognition in the UK by Virtue of the Temporary Recognition Regime Established by the Central Counterparties (Amendments, etc., and Transitional Provision) (EU Exit) Regulations 2018 as amended' (30 April 2021 update).

[34] Bank of England, 'The Bank of England's Approach to Tiering Incoming Central Counterparties under EMIR Article 25', Consultation Paper (November 2021).

What is more difficult to predict is whether the United Kingdom's large CCPs can continue to be classified as 'tier 2' CCPs. If LCH is the largest CCP in the world, it must presumably remain a candidate for non-recognition. ESMA's existing recommendation on tiering seems to be pragmatic rather than the result of strict application of principle; but it should be noted that ESMA does not make the final call, which rests with the European Commission. Each decision will essentially be a political one.

7 Location and the ECB

The European supervisory role over systemically important tier 2 non-EU CCPs is given not to the ECB but to ESMA. This might not have been predicted before the proposal for EMIR 2.2 was published since the 'location policy' for systemically important CCPs originated from within the ECB.

In the years immediately after the financial crisis of 2008, the ECB attempted to impose a requirement for CCPs with significant business in euro-denominated instruments to be located within the eurozone. This was challenged by the United Kingdom in the European Court of Justice (ECJ) in the case *United Kingdom v European Central Bank* (the *UK v ECB* case),[35] in which it was held that the ECB had no legal power of oversight over CCPs:

> In the present case, the existence of very close links between payment systems and securities clearing systems cannot be denied, nor can the possibility that disturbances affecting securities clearing infrastructures will have repercussions for payment systems and be injurious to their smooth operation. Nevertheless, the existence of those links cannot be sufficient to justify accepting that the ECB has implicit powers to regulate securities clearing systems.

The ECJ instead suggested that the ECB could request an amendment to the European System of Central Banks (ESCB)–ECB Statute, Art. 22[36] if the power to regulate CCPs was considered necessary for the proper performance of its task of maintaining price stability. As a result, alongside the revision of EMIR, it was proposed (ECB, 2017)[37] that the jurisdiction of the ECB be expanded.

In its bid for formal legal supervisory power, the ECB asked to be able 'to require remedial action [...] in response to risks affecting the Eurosystem's primary objective' and to impose additional requirements for CCPs going beyond those set out in EMIR. This appears to have been unacceptably wide for the Council and Parliament of the EU, whose 'compromise' proposal would have limited the new power to the roles set

---

[35] *United Kingdom v European Central Bank* [2015] ECLI:EU:T:2015:133.

[36] Consolidated Version of the Treaty on European Union, [2012] OJ C326/01, Art. 127.

[37] ECB, 'Recommendation for a Decision of the European Parliament and of the Council amending Article 22 of the Statute of the European System of Central Banks and of the European Central Bank', Letter from Mario Draghi to Helena Dalli, Consilium document No. ST 10850/17 (22 June 2017) (ECB, 'Draghi–Dalli Letter').

out in the revised EMIR. In March 2019, the ECB formally withdrew its request,[38] thus preferring to continue in a state where it has no legal jurisdiction to regulate CCPs rather than have the limited additional powers which the other EU institutions were willing to grant. See also Chapter 3 ('Development of the Regulatory Regime for OTC Derivativse Clearing' by Patrick Pearson) in this volume.

The ECJ judgment was based on vires, rather than policy, grounds. The ECB is the monetary authority for the euro. More than 30% of OTC derivatives are said to be denominated in euro or other EU currencies.[39] While the currency of denomination is a palpable link to the interest of the EU regulatory and monetary authorities in clearing of such products, the denomination of a product does not necessarily prove the threat to the financial or monetary systems if the product is traded or cleared outside the jurisdiction of issue of the currency. Clearly, if a CCP is conducting activities which might threaten currency stability, it should be subject to regulation in the place where the currency is controlled, but how the location of clearing could affect currency stability is not self-evident. Two questions thus fall to be considered: what factors, in practice, determine where a CCP is actually located and what are the sources of threat emanating from clearing which are of concern to the monetary authority.

To begin with the policy issues which might argue for, or against, a CCP being located in a particular place, Van Kerckhoven and Odermatt (2021)[40] identify the following factors supporting locating a CCP in a particular country: 'promoting financial stability, tax revenue, employment, and the benefits of establishing a financial hub'; on the other side of the argument, they note that any CCP location in the EU needs to be attractive for third countries and that fragmentation of clearing among various EU centres would be damaging. The powerful network effects underpinning clearing cannot be avoided. To these considerations one might add having a large international CCP, which seems to be a matter of national pride,[41] and the magnetic allure of being able to control clearing, set against the responsibilities that come with oversight, particularly in times of stress.

Perhaps the most important factor which relates to location from a systemic perspective is the liquidity of the market for the cleared instruments. Markets, after all, are why CCPs are located in the places they are. The CCP needs to have immediate access to a deep pool of liquidity, which is available at all times, in order to complete its default management programme effectively and within the limits of the financial

---

[38] ECB, 'Withdrawal of the Recommendation of the ECB for a Decision of the European Parliament and of the Council Amending Article 22 of the Statute of the European System of Central Banks and of the European Central Bank', Letter from Mario Draghi to George Ciamba, Consilium document No. ST 7817/19 (22 March 2019) (ECB, 'Draghi–Ciambi Letter').

[39] European Commission, 'Targeted Consultation on the Review of the Central Clearing Framework in the EU', p. 5, https://finance.ec.europa.eu/system/files/2022-03/2022-central-clearing-review-consultation-document_en.pdf (accessed 28 June 2023) (European Commission, 'Targeted Consultation') citing Bank for International Settlements (BIS) data.

[40] Sven Van Kerckhoven and Jed Odermatt, 'Euro Clearing after Brexit: Shifting Locations and Oversight' (2021) 29 Journal of Financial Regulation and Compliance 187.

[41] Cf. speech by Christine Lagarde when Finance Minister of France, reported in Huw Jones, 'France Wants ECB to Lead Derivatives Clearing Push', *Reuters* (19 January 2009), https://www.reuters.com/article/eu-creditderivatives-idUKLJ16478720090119 (accessed 7 March 2022).

resources accumulated for that eventuality. The reason that CCPs managed the Lehman Brothers' default quickly and effectively is that the cleared products could be closed out easily and without serious argument about valuation—in other words, despite various mid-crisis market failures in September 2008, the markets for Lehmans' cleared portfolio remained functional. Being situated at a distance from the liquidity pool makes no sense: no amount of theory makes it easy to summon the traders from distant clearing members to explain the exigencies of a new default and get the problem resolved.

That analysis makes the legislative choice of factors as to what makes a CCP systemically important seem rather out of touch. For sure, the type of products cleared is among the leading set of factors in Regulation 1303, Art. 1(1), but the connection to default management is not spelt out. Instead, the liquidity of markets in default scenarios, as a key question, is at risk of being buried under a welter of irrelevant quantitative information. The Bank of England does not have to trouble itself with Regulation 1303, but its own approach also disregards default management practicalities in favour of a cruder test of amount of default fund (and, less convincingly, initial margin) at risk.

For its part, the ECB may have legitimate reasons for wishing to have direct powers over non-EU CCPs which clear euro-denominated instruments. These may include monetary policy, the closely allied topic of collateral, and the handling of defaults in a crisis.

As for monetary policy, the ECB considers that CCPs can pose 'risks […] to the smooth operation of payment systems and implementation of the single monetary policy, ultimately affecting the Eurosystem's primary objective of maintaining price stability'.[42] Spelling this out, 'the large payment flows between CCPs and their participants mean that inadequate financial risk management of CCPs could transmit serious financial strains to institutions that are Eurosystem monetary policy counterparties' for which the ECB is lender of last resort.[43] But this is an argument about contagion, not one pertaining to the currency of cleared transactions. Currency is evidently a connecting factor, but the connection between currency and systemic risk is not often explained. The connection may be found in the margining practices of CCPs.

Singh and Stella (2020)[44] show that collateral liquidity is as important for monetary policy as traditional money supply. Singh and Goel (2020)[45] go on to explain that there is a connection between collateral markets and monetary policy which, in recent years, means that rates are now affected by liquidity of collateral. Collateral taken by CCPs is typically denominated in the same units as the cleared instrument in order to limit basis risk; CCPs' policy with regard to collateral—including eligibility, haircuts, and the risk of dumping following a default—are all matters which could affect the stability of the currency.

[42] ECB, 'Draghi–Dalli Letter' (n 37).

[43] Fabio Panetta, 'Joining Forces—Stepping Up Coordination on Risks in Central Clearing', Speech (26 February 2020), https://www.bis.org/review/r200228c.pdf (accessed 7 March 2022).

[44] Manmohan Singh and Peter Stella, 'Money, Collateral and Safe Assets', in Manmohan Singh (ed.), *Collateral Markets and Financial Plumbing*, 3rd edn (London: Risk Books, 2020), p. 81 (Singh, *Collateral Markets*).

[45] Manmohan Singh and Rohit Goel, '"Reverse" Monetary Policy Transmission', in Singh, *Collateral Markets* (n 44), p. 99.

The linkage, and its concern to the ECB, may be amplified as follows. It seems to be standard doctrine since the financial crisis of 2008 that central banks should have looser collateral acceptability criteria for liquidity operations than might be expected in the market generally.[46] This policy is likely to lead to central banks' collateral criteria moving in the opposite direction to that of a CCP, which will wish to take a more conservative approach to risk management in times of stress, including collateral volatility or price impairment. CCPs tend to increase margin calls during times of stress.[47] There is, accordingly, a risk that a CCP might act, during a downturn, in a manner unwelcome to the monetary authority. The divergence of policy may be illustrated by reference to the divergence between haircuts required by the ECB and LCH on Italian BTPs provided as collateral.[48] Yet, despite the provable connection between currency, collateral, and default management, the assessment of systemic risk posed by CCPs seems not to delve far into these matters.

Central banks' concerns regarding stressed markets brings into the discussion the question of crisis management. Central banks may act as liquidity providers to CCPs in emergencies;[49] a concern of the ECB may be that it might be called upon to provide liquidity support to the UK CCPs. Following the *UK v ECB* case, an agreement was reached between the ECB and the Bank of England on liquidity support for UK CCPs. The ECB is willing (in principle) to allow the Bank to use the EUR–GBP swap line in place between the two central banks to allow UK CCPs to obtain access to euro liquidity where the CCPs 'are relevant for the Eurosystem from a financial stability perspective, i.e. which clear a significant volume of euro-denominated business'.[50]

Although this possibility is not expressly set out in EMIR, Art. 25(2b)(b), there are hints in EMIR 2.2, Recital (34) towards that possibility: in 'exceptional situations', central banks might be able to impose requirements on CCPs, including when there arise 'serious malfunctions of payment or settlement arrangements that impede the CCP's ability to meet its payment obligations or increase its liquidity needs'. But the principal crisis management statute, the CCPR&R, has little to say on non-EU CCPs. There is a handful of articles allowing for recognition of home state resolution proceedings and cooperation with home state authorities. There is no role for ESMA in

---

[46] See Garreth Rule, 'Collateral Management in Central Bank Balance Policy Operations', Bank of England Centre for Central Banking Studies Paper (2012); Christophe Blot and Paul Hubert, 'The Effects and Risks of ECB Collateral Framework Changes', European Parliament Paper (2018) PE 619.019 https://www.europarl.europa.eu/cmsdata/149903/OFCE_FINAL%20publication.pdf.

[47] See Bank for International Settlements Committee on the Global Financial System (BIS CGFS), 'Designing Frameworks for Central Bank Liquidity Assistance: Addressing New Challenges' CGFS Paper 58 (2010); Wenquian Huang and Előd Takáts, 'The CCP–Bank Nexus in the Time of Covid-19' (2020) 13 BIS Bulletin 2; further, EMIR (n 9), Art. 41 and Commission Delegated Regulation (EU) No. 153/2013, Art. 28 encourage CCPs to have regard to procyclicality when setting margining policy, albeit not at the cost of the CCP's soundness and financial security.

[48] See Dermot Turing, 'Clearing Away after Brexit?' (2021) 9 Journal of Financial Market Infrastructures 73.

[49] See Manmohan Singh, 'Limiting Taxpayer "Puts"—an Example from Central Counterparties' (2015) 3 Journal of Financial Market Infrastructures 1; Froukelien Wendt, 'Central Counterparties: Addressing Their Too Important to Fail Nature' (2015) 4 Journal of Financial Market Infrastructures 59; Heikki Marjosola, 'Missing Pieces in the Patchwork of EU Financial Stability Regime? The Case of Central Counterparties' (2015) 52 Common Market Law Review 1491; Deutsche Bundesbank, ECB, and Federal Reserve Bank of Chicago, 'First Joint Deutsche Bundesbank—European Central Bank—Federal Reserve Bank of Chicago Conference on CCP Risk Management, Summary of proceedings' (2019), https://www.ecb.europa.eu/paym/intro/publications/pdf/ecb.miptopical190227.en.pdf (accessed 7 March 2022).

[50] ECB, 'Draghi–Ciambi Letter' (n 38).

CCP resolution, presumably because ESMA did not have a regulatory role in respect of non-EU CCPs at the time the Regulation was originally conceived in 2016. Still less is there a role for the ECB.

8 Conclusions

The new regulatory framework for foreign CCPs gives much to think about. Some of the outcomes of the new policy are predictable enough: foreign CCPs of systemic relevance must have cross-border (dual) regulation. Policy relating to 'relocation' is perhaps cast into doubt by the tiering of LCH Limited and ICE Clear Europe; it may not ever work in practice. The new legal framework leaves the bulk of clearing of euro-denominated derivatives in London, without any incentives for market participants to change that.

In early 2022, the European Commission launched a public consultation on the future of clearing.[51] The consultation is the trailer for possible future legislation intended to correct the anomalies which have emerged from the tiering process created by EMIR 2.2. The Commission points to the fact that the clearing of euro-denominated derivatives is overwhelmingly located in the United Kingdom, which is perceived to create a source of financial instability for the EU, and to the ESMA analysis, which indicates that the cost of using the 'tier 3' relocation option makes it, in essence, an unusable tool.

What, then, might come to pass as a fresh attempt at repatriation? The consultation paper offers an array of possibilities to increase 'liquidity' in EU CCPs,[52] which is to say building up volumes in EU CCPs to the point where there is critical mass and a tipping-point is reached. The ideas include expanding the clearing obligation to more products or persons, relaxing the clearing mandate, imposing regulatory capital charges on EU entities with 'excessive' amounts of clearing elsewhere, imposing a requirement for EU firms to clear at an EU CCP, and the obligation to offer a choice of an EU clearing option to clients. Some of these suggestions may be more practical than others. Some are counter-intuitive, especially the notion that more clearing is a solution to an excess of foreign clearing.

The reduction of concentration in non-EU CCPs could be brought about by some of the suggested measures, but it does not follow that the business will have tipped over into the EU. What the Commission's plans will need to address is the awkward fact that clearing cannot be divorced from the marketplace in which the transactions originate. Two parties are involved in a trade. If my counterparty offering the product on the right terms is found in a marketplace with a high-volume CCP, which is where the counterparty wishes to clear, I will have to find a way around a rule which insists that I clear within the EU.

---

[51] European Commission, 'Targeted Consultation' (n 39).
[52] The word 'liquidity' should not be taken literally. What the Commission means to say is 'volume' or 'concentration', but those terms might allow negative inferences to be drawn.

On the responsibility for regulating CCPs, the consultation suggests a role for a supranational regulatory body (ESMA?, the ECB?) for CCPs. But the target of this regulatory suggestion is only EU CCPs; no expanded role for the ECB in oversight of non-EU CCPs is mentioned. As far as the consultation is concerned, it seems that the powers given to ESMA in respect of tier 2 CCPs may not be expanded. ESMA's plea for revision of the CCPR&R to encompass foreign CCPs may not have been heeded.

How the framework may ultimately be revised, and on what timescale, is unclear. The revised European regulatory structure for non-EU CCPs will continue to be tested in the meantime. It is perhaps unfortunate that difficult questions concerning risk management and stability will then be made harder to address owing to the highly politicized context in which they arise.

VI

THE FUTURE OF OTC DERIVATIVES CLEARING IN EUROPE

17

Potential Impact of the Distributed Ledger Technology on OTC Derivatives Markets

Randy Priem

1 Introduction

1.1 Importance of the Distributed Ledger Technology

Distributed ledger technology (DLT) has received extensive consideration over the past decade from market participants, financial market infrastructures, and regulators. DLT refers to the novel approach to record and share transactions and/or data across multiple participants in a decentralized way. A blockchain, where data is stored in blocks chained together in a chronological sequence, can then be considered as a particular kind of DLT, albeit the terms 'blockchain' and 'DLT' are often utilized interchangeably. Blockchains use algorithmic and cryptographic methods for the storage and synchronization of data in a network in an immutable manner, thereby making the possibility of fraud or manipulation more difficult.[1]

Blockchain-based DLT is initially considered as the building block of cryptocurrencies because of its use for the cryptocurrency Bitcoin. Satoshi Nakamoto, the pseudonym for the creator of Bitcoin, described this innovation for

---

[1] Harish Natarajan, Solvey Krause, and Helen Gradstein, 'Distributed Ledger Technology and Blockchain' 2017 1 World Bank Fintech Note 1 (Natarajan et al., 'Distributed Ledger Technology and Blockchain').

the first time in 2008 in its white paper as an 'electronic payment system based on cryptographic proof instead of trust, allowing any two willing parties to transact directly with each other without the need for a trusted third party'.[2]

DLT might have a variety of potential applications beyond the realm of cryptocurrencies. Proponents of DLT advocate a number of potential advantages compared to traditional centralized ledgers, such as the greater level of transparency and auditability, the increased speed with which transactions can happen, cost reductions, and potential automation (see later). The technology, in comparison with legacy systems, might thus offer a new, completely digital, and potentially more efficient way of securities trading, clearing, and settlement.[3] As per Goldman Sachs, when DLT would be applied by financial market infrastructures (i.e. trading venues, central counterparties, and central securities depositories),[4] the costs related to securities post-trading (i.e. clearing and settlement) would lessen by $11–$12 billion.[5] An examination of Banco Santander, Oliver Wyman, and Anthemis Group then shows that DLT would decrease cross-border payment and trading costs by $15–$20 billion.[6] The World Economic Forum then assessed that almost 10% of the value of the global gross domestic product (GDP) would be recorded on blockchains by 2027.[7]

---

[2] Satoshi Nakamoto, 'Bitcoin: A Peer-to-Peer Electronic Cash System', White Paper (2008), p. 1.

[3] In this chapter, trading is defined in a broad sense and captures buying and selling one or more financial instruments. This can be done on behalf of clients (i.e. the execution of orders on behalf of clients) or against proprietary capital, that is, dealing on own account. Clearing is defined as in Regulation (EU) No. 648/2012 of the European Parliament and of the Council of 4 July 2012 on OTC derivatives, central counterparties and trade repositories, [2012] OJ L201/1 (27 July 2012), Art. 2(3) (EMIR) as the process of establishing positions, including the calculation of net obligations, and ensuring that financial instruments, cash, or both, are available to secure the exposures arising from those positions. Settlement is defined in Regulation (EU) No. 909/2014 of the European Parliament and of the Council of 23 July 2014 on improving securities settlement in the European Union and on central securities depositories and amending Directives 98/26/EC and 2014/65/EU and Regulation (EU) No. 236/012, [2014] OJ L257/1 (28 August 2014), Art. 2(7) (CSDR) as the completion of a securities transaction where it is concluded with the aim of discharging the obligations of the parties to that transaction through the transfer of cash, or securities, or both.

[4] A trading venue is defined in Directive 2014/65/EU of the European Parliament and of the Council of 15 May 2014 on markets in financial instruments and amending Directive 2002/92/EC and Directive 2011/61/EU, [2014] OJ L173/349 (12 June 2014), Art. 4(24) (MiFID II) as a regulated market, a multilateral trading facility (MTF), or an organized trading facility (OTF) (see below for definitions of these types of trading venues). A central counterparty (CCP) is defined in EMIR (n 3), Art. 2(1) as a legal person that interposes itself between the counterparties to the contracts traded on one or more financial markets, becoming the buyer to every seller and the seller to every buyer. CSDR (n 3), Art. 2(1) defines a central securities depository (CSD) as a legal person that operates a securities settlement system referred to in point (3) of Section A of the Annex and provides at least one other core service listed in Section A of the Annex, meaning (i) the initial recording of securities in book-entry system and/or (ii) the provision and maintenance of securities accounts at the top-tier level.

[5] Goldman Sachs, 'Blockchain: Putting Theory in Practice' (2016), https://www.academia.edu/38946070/Goldman_Sachs_Blockchain_putting_theory_to_practice (accessed 14 April 2023) (Goldman Sachs, 'Blockchain').

[6] Banco Santander, Oliver Wyman, and Anthemis Group, 'The Fintech 2.0 Paper: Rebooting Financial Services' (2015), https://www.oliverwyman.com/our-expertise/insights/2015/jun/the-fintech-2-0-paper.html (accessed 15 November 2021).

[7] World Economic Forum, 'The Future of Financial Services: How Disruptive Innovations Are Reshaping the Way Financial Services Are Structured, Provisioned and Consumed' (2015), https://www3.weforum.org/docs/WEF_The_future__of_financial_services.pdf (accessed 15 November 2021).

1.2 DLT Pilot Cases

Because of the possible advantages and efficiency gains of DLT, financial institutions have started to experiment in recent years with proofs of concept in specific niches of the trading and post-trading ecosystem.[8] For instance, the Australian Stock Exchange (ASX) and Digital Asset started to build a DLT system for the clearing and settlement of shares, which was envisaged to be launched in 2023, but was stopped because e.g. of the technology being too slow.[9] Seaboard Corporation Common Stock (SEB) and the National Association of Securities Dealers Automated Quotations (NASDAQ) then created a DLT platform for Swedish mutual fund trading. Furthermore, the Canadian Securities Exchange is developing a DLT platform for securities clearing and settlement. This platform would allow firms to issue shares and fixed-income securities via security token offerings.[10] In 2021, Deutsche Börse, in cooperation with the Deutsche Bundesbank and Germany's Finance Agency, developed and tested an interface for electronic securities that enables payment in central bank money.[11] During the testing, the German Finance Agency issued a ten-year federal bond (Bund) in the DLT system where primary and secondary market transactions were also settled using DLT. Clearstream Banking Luxembourg, the central securities depository of the Deutsche Börse Group, is also experimenting on whether they can connect to a new DLT-enabled platform provided by Digital Asset.[12]

With respect to the OTC derivatives markets in particular, several pilot cases are being created. Fairom, a Canadian portfolio company, is developing a DLT-based tool to automate back-office operations for over-the-counter (OTC) derivatives.[13] The intention is to obtain a 30% cost decrease for financial institutions managing these financial products. The Depository Trust & Clearing Corporation (DTCC) then initiated the creation of a solution for credit derivatives processing, like credit

---

[8] See Randy Priem, 'Distributed Ledger Technology for Securities Clearing and Settlement: Benefits, Risks, and Regulatory Implications' (2020) 6(1) Financial Innovation 1 (Priem, 'Distributed Ledger Technology').

[9] Jonathan Watkins, 'ASX Says DLT Project On-Track for 2023 as Exchange Gets Ticking Off over Clearing and Settlement Issues', *The Trade* (23 September 2021), https://www.thetradenews.com/asx-says-dlt-project-on-track-for-2023-as-exchange-gets-ticking-off-over-clearing-and-settlement-issues (accessed 15 November 2021).

[10] See https://www2.thecse.com/blockchain (accessed 15 November 2021). A security token offering (STO) can be considered as a public offering in which tokenized digital securities, also called 'security tokens', are sold on security token exchanges.

[11] Deutsche Bundesbank, 'DLT-Based Securities Settlement in Central Bank Money Successfully Tested', press release (24 March 2021), https://www.bundesbank.de/en/press/press-releases/dlt-based-securities-settlement-in-central-bank-money-successfully-tested-861444 (accessed 15 November 2021).

[12] Alexander Kristofersson, 'Clearstream Prepares Shifting Its ICSD to DLT Platform', *PostTrade 360* (8 July 2021), https://posttrade360.com/news/technology/clearstream-prepares-shifting-its-icsd-to-dlt-platform (accessed 15 November 2021).

[13] Ajay Singh, 'Volatility, Settlement Risk and Distributed Ledger Technology' (28 April 2020), https://medium.com/fairom/volatility-settlement-risk-and-distributed-ledger-technology-b7f3ce6e591a (accessed 15 November 2021).

default swaps trades, on a DLT network.[14] Furthermore, the International Swaps and Derivatives Association (ISDA), in cooperation with REGnosys, developed the common domain model (CDM) to provide a global representative standard for all actions and events happening during the life of a derivative trade onto a smart contract blockchain (see par. 2.4).[15]

Despite all pilot cases, financial institutions have yet to prove that DLT is a viable and sustainable solution, and it is currently insufficiently clear from the pilot cases whether the trading and post-trading segments will become more intertwined. It is also not yet certain which DLT system in terms of operational functionality would be best suited for the trading, clearing, and settlement of securities. Because most inefficiencies are situated in the post-trading segment, one can assume that these will be addressed first before the various segments of the trade life cycle are potentially merged into one DLT solution. Also, because institutions are still in the experimental phase, the technology might still evolve considerably, and new risks and challenges might still be detected.[16]

Despite the potential benefits of the technology, there seems to be a widespread prediction that DLT will be implemented gradually. According to the German Banking Industry Committee, legacy systems and DLT will co-exist for the next few decades, with a gradual employment of the technology.[17] DLT is, indeed, still suffering from various 'barriers to entry', such as the complexity to transition from a legacy system to a DLT-based system, the negative perception of institutions linked to cryptocurrencies (which could be detrimental to the technology itself), inertia in the adoption of the technology, and regulations being unclear.

Compared to previous literature,[18] this chapter focuses in more detail on the impact of DLT on OTC derivatives markets. The chapter first explains how DLT and/or blockchains work. When the basic concepts are clear, the current trading life cycle is documented, followed by a discussion on how DLT could make the existing life cycle more efficient. The chapter will focus not only on the potential advantages of DLT but also on new risks to which this technology might give rise. In addition, the impact of DLT on OTC derivatives markets, and specifically the usage of smart contracts, will be discussed. The chapter ends with regulatory evolutions.

---

[14] DTCC, 'DTCC Enters Test Phase on Distributed Ledger Project for Credit Derivatives with Markitserv and 15 Leading Global Banks', press release (6 November 2018), https://www.dtcc.com/news/2018/november/06/dtcc-enters-test-phase-on-distributed-ledger-project-for-credit-derivatives-with-markitserv (accessed 15 November 2021).

[15] InFinite Intelligence, https://www.bobsguide.com/articles/regnosys-isdas-cdm-2-0-to-force-the-convergence-of-dlt-interoperability (accessed 15 November 2021).

[16] See Priem, 'Distributed Ledger Technology' (n 8), 1.

[17] German Banking Industry Committee, 'Response to the Consultation on the Distributed Ledger Technology Applied to Securities Markets' (2016), https://www.esma.europa.eu/press-news/consultations/consultation-distributed-ledger-technology-applied-securities-markets (accessed 14 April 2023).

[18] Priem, 'Distributed Ledger Technology' (n 8), 1 is written by the same author as this chapter and is thus the main source. See also Christian Chamorro-Courtland, 'The Future of Clearing and Settlement in Australia: Part II—Distributed Ledger Technology' (2021). 38 Company & Securities Law Journal 1.

2 Explanation of How DLT and Blockchains Function

2.1 DLT, Blockchains, and Cryptography

Although it has to be stressed that DLT is not yet a well-defined, one-size-fits-all technology, distributed ledgers and blockchains can be considered as specific type of databases where users work in a decentralized manner and data is stored in blocks that are
chained together in a chronological order. The digital assets that are traded on the distributed ledger may be created and exist exclusively (self-anchored) on the DLT itself
or may rather be digital representations of intangible or tangible assets that exist off the
ledger (anchored).[19] Crypto assets that are created and exist exclusively 'on ledger' are
called 'native tokens' or 'native assets', while crypto assets that represent intangible or
tangible assets that exist 'off ledger' are called 'non-native assets' or 'non-native tokens'.[20]
The transaction process in a DLT typically occurs via a few specific steps. First, the
usage of cryptography—and thus of public and private encryption keys—is of utmost
importance for users to be certain that their counterparties do not execute the same
transaction with another party. Hence, DLT deals with this double-spending problem
by imposing that when two clients enter into a trade, they first need to sign the deal by
using their private keys to unlock the securities and, in a second step, transfer the ownership via the public keys. In general, asymmetric key cryptography, where a public and
a private key are used, is most often applied in case of, for example, cryptocurrencies.
Both private and public keys are linked in a mathematical manner based on, for example, elliptical curve cryptography.[21] This means that the private key can decrypt the
information that is encrypted only with the corresponding public key and vice versa.
The private key is known only to the receiver (i.e. the beneficiary), while the public key
is transmitted to the sender. The public key also represents the 'address' to which the
crypto assets can be transferred. If beneficiaries lose the private key, they also lose the
right to dispose of the assets as this is equivalent to a password. Hence, it is important
for beneficiaries to properly protect their private keys.

2.2 Consensus Mechanisms

When a newly signed transaction is entered into the system, it is broadcast to a network
of peer-to-peer computers, which can be located in numerous geographical areas. The

---

[19] Financial Industry Regulatory Authority (FINRA), 'Distributed Ledger Technology: Implications of
Blockchain for the Securities Industry' (January 2017), https://www.finra.org/sites/default/files/FINRA_Blockc
hain_Report.pdf (accessed 15 November 2021) (FINRA, 'Distributed Ledger Technology').
[20] Bank for International Settlements (BIS), 'Distributed Ledger Technology in Payment, Clearing and
Settlement: An Analytical Framework' (27 February 2017), https://www.bis.org/cpmi/publ/d157.htm (accessed 15
November 2021) (BIS, 'Distributed Ledger Technology in Payment').
[21] Kariappa Bheemaiah, *The Blockchain Alternative* (Paris: A. Press, 2017) (Bheemaiah, *The Blockchain
Alternative*).

network of computers, also called nodes, will solve equations in order to validate the transaction. An example of such validation is the proof-of-work consensus mechanism, where the validators have to computationally solve intensive puzzles. Specifically for the Bitcoin blockchain, the process of generating proof-of-work (i.e. the validation process) is called 'mining'. Another type of consensus mechanism is the proof-at-stake consensus mechanism, where the creator of the next block is chosen via various combinations of random selection and wealth, that is, the stake.[22] These consensus mechanisms are applied to reach a consensus between several nodes on the validity of the underlying database.

In proof-of-work consensus mechanisms, hashing algorithms are mostly used. Hashing can be described as a computer algorithm running over a content file generating a compressed string of alphanumeric characters, that is, the hash function. These hash functions cannot be back-computed into the initial content. Every digital financial instrument could be transformed into a hash string as a private and unique identifier. This means that the hash function itself depends on the transaction data, the identities of the counterparties, and the result of previous transactions.[23] It is typically impossible to infer the values of the initial transactions and/or data from the hash function, while it is more feasible to compute the hash from the original data values. Every time a validator checks that the records are still the same and no modification has been performed, the same hash algorithm is run, leading to the same hash signature. Typically, blockchains include the hash of the previous version of the ledger, which allows for a validation of the new version of the ledger by checking whether the fixed-length output corresponds to the hash included in the updated version;[24] that is, each block encompasses a hash function reflecting the content of the previous block, which itself will have a hash function referring to the block more adjacent to the initial block.

Solving a proof-of-work puzzle is rather difficult from a computational perspective, and a single node in the network only has a small likelihood of generating the required proof-of-work without superseding a massive amount of computing resources. In the Bitcoin network, each miner that produces a valid proof-of-work receives Bitcoins as a reward, serving as a transaction fee. Because all miners execute their calculations, proof-of-work consensus mechanisms typically consume a lot of energy, raising questions on its ecological impact. This disadvantage is not present for proof-at-stake consensus mechanisms as there is less competition between validators to solve the puzzle.

These consensus mechanisms are of utmost importance in a situation where there is no centralized institution, such as a government. The reason is that one of the key goals of the validation process is to ensure that the seller is the rightful owner of the assets being sold, based on the entire transaction history recorded on the DLT system. Hashing can thus be considered as a method to make the blockchain immutable. It also helps to ensure that the seller is the rightful owner of the asset and that they have not

[22] Melanie Swan, *Blockchain Blueprint for a New Economy* (Canada: O'Reilly, 2015) (Swan, *Blockchain Blueprint for a New Economy*).
[23] Goldman Sachs, 'Blockchain' (n 5).
[24] BIS, 'Distributed Ledger Technology in Payment' (n 20).

yet sold the asset to someone else.[25] The consensus mechanisms and hashing, thereby leading to an immutable ledger, also make a cyberattack of a DLT system very difficult. Indeed, the attacker would need to take control of the majority of the validators in order to be successful (known as a 51% attack).[26]

Once confirmation in the blockchain is achieved (implying that a transaction is legitimate), it is clustered together with other transactions in a block. The blocks are then chained together, creating a history of all transactions. After this chaining, the blockchain is updated and the transaction is considered to be complete. In a distributed ledger, each node thus has a full copy in its own records of all the transactions and/or data since the ledger's inception. Furthermore, if one node has an error in its own database, it can use all the previous historical transactions as a reference point to correct itself. Because of the validation mechanisms, no computer in the network can alter the information held within the distributed ledger as the latter encompasses the history of transactions in each block, making the distributed ledger irreversible. This process of adding transactions also implies that the distributed ledger grows constantly.

2.3 Permissioned vs Unpermissioned Blockchains

While blockchains, like the ones used for the trading of Bitcoins, can be public and unpermissioned, where each computer can freely join the ledger to read and/or write, other distributed legers, such as Hyperledger Fabric, are non-public and permissioned, where only a few computers are allowed to connect. In an unpermissioned system without a central owner who controls network access and where users can join and add transactions via their relevant software, the validation mechanism plays a key role. Indeed, not every participant in such a blockchain would be a trusted party. Examples of rigorous validations could be the enrolment of numerous nodes as validators or the utilization of a stricter validation algorithm. A disadvantage then, however, is that those DLT systems would be slower.[27] In the case of Bitcoins, for instance, miners solve trillions of mathematical puzzles to calculate a hash value. This task limits the maximum quantity of transactions that can be simultaneously handled to a low number.[28]

---

[25] Rebecca Lewis, John McPartland, and Rajeev Ranjan, 'Blockchain and Financial Market Innovation' (2017) 7 Economic Perspectives 1.

[26] See Bheemaiah, *The Blockchain Alternative* (n 21). Also see Euroclear and Oliver Wyman, 'Blockchain in Capital Markets: The Price and the Journey' (February 2016), https://www.oliverwyman.com/content/dam/oliver-wyman/global/en/2016/feb/BlockChain-In-Capital-Markets.pdf (accessed 15 November 2023) (Euroclear and Wyman, 'Blockchain in Capital Markets'). See also Paul Klimos, 'The Distributed Ledger Technology: A Potential Revamp for Financial Markets?' (2018) 13(2) Capital Markets Law Journal 194–222 (Klimos, 'The Distributed Ledger Technology').

[27] Joanna Diane Caytas, 'Developing Blockchain Real-Time Clearing and Settlement in the EU, US, and Globally' (2016) Columbia Journal of European Law, http://blogs2.law.columbia.edu/cjel/preliminary-reference/2016/developing-blockchain-real-time-clearing-and-settlement-in-the-eu-u-s-and-globally-2 (accessed 15 November 2021) (Caytas, 'Developing Blockchain Real-Time Clearing and Settlement in the EU, US, and Globally').

[28] Euroclear and Slaughter and May, 'Blockchain Settlement: Regulation, Innovation and Applications' (5 February 016), https://www.euroclear.com/newsandinsights/en/Format/Whitepapers-Reports/BlockchainSettlement.html (accessed 15 November 2021) (Euroclear and Slaughter and May, 'Blockchain Settlement'). See also Goldman Sachs, 'Blockchain' (n 5).

Compared to the VISA credit card payment system, which accommodates often peak volumes of 10,000 payments per second, an unpermissioned DLT system can be inefficient in cases where large volumes need to be cleared and/or settled; for example, the Bitcoin (BTC) network only processes 4.6 transactions per second.[29]

In case of unpermissioned systems, anonymity of the users is often prevalent. For instance, in the case of Bitcoin transactions, all transactions contain a wallet address of a sender and the receiver, which can be thought of a pseudonyms.[30] The addresses linked to the transactions (i.e. the public keys) are mostly known, but the owners behind the addresses not, which is comparable to sending a message to an e-mail address that does not contain the name and family name of the recipient. This anonymity often attracts the attention of criminals as the virtual assets can then be used more easily for the financing of illegal activities.

Permissioned systems, with only authorized participants being accepted, are generally considered as more suitable for securities markets.[31] The reason is then that only participants being considered as more trustworthy would be able to join.[32] This trustworthiness then also requires a less stringent validation process. Furthermore, the risk of money laundering or other illicit activities tends to be lower when only reliable system participants are allowed to utilize the distributed ledger. Also, the need for stringent consensus mechanisms—and thus the necessity to copy all transactions and/or data to the internal databases of the nodes—would be lower when participants are considered as more trustworthy by fulfilling certain predefined access criteria. However, a permissioned system requires one (or more) institutions to act as (a) gatekeeper(s) or system administrator(s). These institutions will then need to screen potential participants before the latter can access the DLT system. These gatekeepers would grant access only to participants meeting the access criteria, which could be included in a rule book of the system.[33] The presence of a gatekeeper implies that a central institution cannot be completely ruled out in a permissioned DLT system. Such a system is thus in sharp contrast with the initially developed open Bitcoin system, where there are no access restrictions and no central institution acting as a gatekeeper.[34] Also, as there is a central institution granting access to the network, this central entity might be a potential target for cyberattacks.

---

[29] See Bheemaiah, *The Blockchain Alternative* (n 21). See also Swan, *Blockchain Blueprint for a New Economy* (n 22).

[30] Natarajan et al., 'Distributed Ledger Technology and Blockchain' (n 1).

[31] European Securities Markets Authority (ESMA), 'Distributed Ledger Technology Applied to Securities Markets' (2017), https://www.esma.europa.eu/document/report-distributed-ledger-technology-applied-securities-markets (accessed 15 November 2021) (ESMA, 'Distributed Ledger Technology Applied to Securities Markets').

[32] Michael Mainelli and Alistair Milne, 'The Impact and Potential of Blockchain on the Securities Transaction Life Cycle', Swift Institute Working Paper No. 2015-007 (2016), https://www.swiftinstitute.org/wp-content/uploads/2016/05/The-Impact-and-Potential-of-Blockchain-on-the-Securities-Transaction-Lifecycle_Mainelli-and-Milne-FINAL.pdf (accessed 15 November 2021).

[33] ESMA, 'Distributed Ledger Technology Applied to Securities Markets' (n 31).

[34] David Yermack 'Corporate Governance and Blockchains' (2017) 21(1) Review of Finance 7.

2.4 Smart Contracts and Oracles

Apart from data on transactions, distributed ledgers can also contain computer code, so-called 'smart contracts'. These contracts self-execute and can process a transaction on the ledger automatically when certain predefined conditions are met.[35] Smart contracts have become popular since the establishment of one of the most known cryptocurrency applications, Ethereum (ETH). Smart contracts are decentralized: they are not recorded in a single centralized server but are distributed amongst the system participants.[36] A smart contract has some identical features as a traditional contract: it is an agreement between two or more parties to do or not do something in exchange for something else. The difference with a traditional contract is that a smart contract is defined by code, which executes without any human intervention under precisely predefined conditions.[37] The contracts are considered to be 'self-enforcing' as they can execute automatically.[38] Some scholars even claim that a complete blockchain economy is emerging, defined as a novel type of economic system where agreed-upon transactions are enforced via rules defined in smart contracts in an autonomous manner.[39]

Smart contracts might even be executed based on information they receive external to the DLT system. So-called 'oracles' might be deployed, which can be defined as computer servers that are programmed to scour data (news) feeds in order to validate whether user-provided expressions (encompassed in the social contracts) hold true.[40] These oracles will only act as programmed, avoiding the risk of collusion with a counterparty, given the absence of a human arbitrator.[41] Oracles can use multi-signature (multisig) to incorporate outside information into the blockchain.[42] Multi-signature requires multiple keys to authorize a transaction rather than a single signature from one key. The oracle thus serves as an additional signatory that attests to information that originates from outside of a particular blockchain, thereby allowing the smart contract to execute.

---

[35] See Bheemaiah, *The Blockchain Alternative* (n 21; Swan, *Blockchain Blueprint for a New Economy* (n 22); Ryan Clements, 'Evaluating the Costs and Benefits of a Smart Contract Blockchain Framework for Credit Default Swaps' (2019) 10(2) William & Mary Business Law Review 369 (Clements, 'Evaluating the Costs and Benefits of a Smart Contract Blockchain Framework'.

[36] Swan, *Blockchain Blueprint for a New Economy* (n 22).

[37] Bheemaiah, *The Blockchain Alternative* (n 21). See also Swan, *Blockchain Blueprint for a New Economy* (n 22).

[38] ISDA and Linklaters, 'Smart Contracts and Distributed Ledger: A Legal Perspective' (3 August 2017), https://www.isda.org/2017/08/03/smart-contracts-and-distributed-ledger-a-legal-perspective (accessed 15 November 2021) (ISDA and Linklaters, 'Smart Contracts and Distributed Ledger').

[39] See Fred Niederman, Roger Clarke, Lynda Appelgate, John Leslie King, Roman Beck, and Ann Majchrzak. 'IS Research and Policy: Notes from the 2015 ICIS Senior Scholar's Forum' (2017) 40(1) Communications of the Association for Information Systems 82. See also Roman Beck, Christophe Müller-Bloch, and John Leslie King, 'Governance in the Blockchain Economy: A Framework and Research Agenda' (2018) 19(10) Journal of the Association for Information Systems 1.

[40] See Priem, 'Distributed Ledger Technology' (n 8), 1.

[41] Jerry Brito, Houman Shadab, and Andrea Castillo, 'Bitcoin Financial Regulation: Securities, Derivatives, Prediction Markets, and Gambling' (2014) 144 Columbia Science and Technology Law Review 144.

[42] Ryan Surujnath, 'Off the Chain! A Guide to Blockchain Derivatives Markets and the Implications on Systemic Risk' (2017) 22 Fordham Journal of Corporate & Financial Law 257 (Surujnath, 'Off the Chain!').

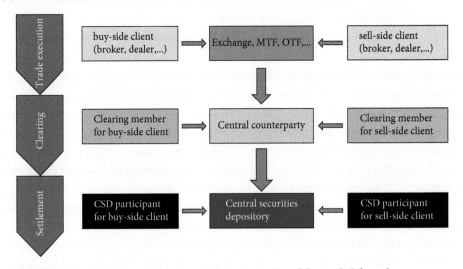

Figure 17.1 Simplified representation of the security leg of the trade life cycle

Source: Randy Priem, 'Distributed Ledger Technology for Securities Clearing and Settlement: Benefits, Risks, and Regulatory Implications' (2020) 6(1) Financial Innovation 1, available through Creative Commons Attribution 4.0 International License, http://creativecommons.org/licenses/by/4.0 (accessed 23 March 2023).

3 How DLT Could Impact the Current Trading Life Cycle

3.1 The Current Trading Life Cycle

In order to examine the influence of DLT on trading, clearing, and settlement in general, this section first presents the trade life cycle, of which clearing and settlement (i.e. post-trading) are the last two phases. Figure 17.1 is a simplified representation of the security leg of the trade life cycle.[43] Note that this representation will be different based on the type of the financial instrument (i.e. equity, fixed income, or derivative), whether the deal happens on an exchange or OTC, and whether the deal is centrally cleared via a central counterparty (CCP) or not.

Trading, clearing, and settlement currently take place in multiple sequential steps. In the trade execution phase, a buy-side and a sell-side client/investor seek to buy or sell financial instruments with each other on a trading venue, which could be a regulated exchange,[44] a multilateral trading facility (MTF),[45] or an organized trading facility

---

[43] See Priem, 'Distributed Ledger Technology' (n 8), 1.

[44] A regulated market is defined in MiFID II (n 4) as a multilateral system operated and/or managed by a market operator, which brings together, or facilitates the bringing together of, multiple third-party buying and selling interests in financial instruments—in the system and in accordance with its non-discretionary rules—in a way that results in a contract, in respect of the financial instruments admitted to trading under its rules and/or systems and which is authorized and functions regularly and in accordance with MiFID II, Title III (regulated markets).

[45] A multilateral trading facility is defined in MiFID II (n 4) as a multilateral system, operated by an investment for or a market operator, which brings together multiple third-party buying and selling interests in financial instruments—in the system and in accordance with non-discretionary rules—in a way that results in a contract in accordance with MiFID II, Title II (authorization and operating conditions for investment firms).

(OTF).[46] These investors normally act through their respective brokers. Alternatively, the trade can take place outside of an organized market and thus 'OTC'. This is often the case for derivatives (e.g. options, futures, forwards, swaps, etc.), where the European Market Infrastructures Regulation (EMIR)[47] defines them as derivatives contracts where the execution does not take place on a regulated market, as within the meaning of Directive 2004/39/EC, Art. 4(1)(21) (MiFID II),[48] or on a third-country market considered as equivalent. Hence, EMIR considers OTC derivatives contracts being traded on, for example, OTFs as OTC, but they might even be concluded in a non-systematic, ad-hoc manner between two non-financial counterparties as part of a business relationship without any brokers or dealers. In case of financial counterparties, such as credit institutions, broker-dealers commonly send their orders to their own derivatives desks or to other third-party dealers. Trading happens then bilaterally, where the terms may either resemble standardized agreements or be specific to each counterparty's requirements and needs.

When the trade is executed and the clearing phase starts, the sell instruction and buy instruction are, in case of central clearing, forwarded to the CCP. A novation then takes place whereby the CCP acts as a buyer to the seller and a seller to the buyer. The clearing members, being most likely the direct clients of the CCP acting on behalf of the buy-side and sell-side clients, post collateral (i.e. initial margin and default fund contributions)[49] to the CCP to mitigate the latter's credit and counterparty risk. Clearing members will need to post (or collect) collateral (i.e. variation margin) in function of the financial instrument's value changes until the instruments finally mature.[50]

In addition to the novation, CCPs also reduce liquidity exposures via netting, which is a type of set-off that is conducted on a multilateral basis. Netting can be defined as the process where the obligations between participants are offset against each other. This process reduces value and number of deliveries or payments that are needed to settle the set of transactions. Netting thus reduces the number of times cash has to change hands between counterparties; that is, when two counterparties have several outstanding derivatives contracts with one another, the CCP will not pay out each agreement individually but will subtract the losses from the gains and pay the net result. In case of multilateral netting, a movement consolidation among several clearing members occurs.[51] In case of bilateral clearing where no CCP is present, counterparties

---

[46] An organized trading facility is defined in MiFID II (n 4) as a multilateral system which is not a regulated market or an MTF and in which multiple third-party buying and selling interests in bonds, structured finance products, emission allowances, or derivatives are able to interact in the system in a way that results in a contract in accordance with MiFID II, Title II (authorization and operating conditions for investment firms).

[47] EMIR (n 3).

[48] MiFID II (n 4).

[49] A clearing member is a participant or client of a CCP. Initial margin is the amount of collateral that clearing members need to hold at the CCP in case of central clearing or must exchange bilaterally in order to conduct a transaction. It serves to protect against, for example, the default of the counterparty. Default fund contributions are contributions to the default fund, being the amount of collateral intended to cover losses that exceed the margin collateral and individual clearing members' default fund contributions in case of a default of a clearing member.

[50] Variation margins are the margins being paid (or received, depending on their position) by clearing members to their CCPs based on adverse price movements of the derivative contracts they hold.

[51] Surujnath, 'Off the Chain!' (n 42), 257.

often need to exchange margin without a CCP and/or perform risk mitigation techniques like portfolio reconciliation and/or compression.[52]

In a next step, the CCP—in case of central clearing—will forward the settlement instruction to the central securities depository (CSD). The CSD will operate the securities settlement system by crediting and debiting its participant's securities accounts. These participants are most likely to act on behalf of their buy-side and sell-side clients. Note, however, that in case of OTC derivatives, the settlement (being a physical or a cash settlement) mostly does not happen via central securities depositories but via a warehouse receipt or cash being transferred.

As illustrated by Figure 17.1, the current financial industry structure is dominated by centralizing institutions. The trade life cycle can be long, with numerous intermediaries having their own proprietary ledgers having overlapping information on transactions, such as volume, value, the identifiers of the counterparties, timestamps, etc. This long trade life cycle thus leads to a lot of duplication because of each market participant recording the same information internally.[53]

3.2 A Fictitious DLT System: Advantages, Risks, and the Future for Current Market Participants

Figure 17.2 represents a fictitious DLT system, being only one potential example of how a DLT system, both for currently exchange-traded or OTC instruments, could look.[54] As the system is decentralized, all clients could have a copy of the distributed ledger recording the securities, the ownership details, and the entire transaction history of each security.[55] When counterparties enter into a trade (i.e. the trading phase), they could first need to sign the transaction by applying their private keys to unlock the securities in a first step and then transfer the ownership to each other via the public key in a second step. The signed transaction could then be broadcast to the entire system in order to get validated. In order for an update of the DLT system to happen, it could require the consensus of all nodes in the DLT network.

Regarding the consensus mechanism, one possibility could be that the originator of the transaction first provides the hash value of the latest version of the ledger and validators then check whether the correct hash function was provided.[56] If this proves

---

[52] Portfolio reconciliation is a means to ensure that counterparties' books and records are synchronized and that the effects of trade events, such as novation or amendments, are accurately captured. Portfolio compression is a risk reduction technique where two or more counterparties close some or all of their derivatives and replace them with other derivative contract whose market risk as the same of the combined notional value of all the terminated derivative contracts.

[53] See Priem, 'Distributed Ledger Technology' (n 8), 1.

[54] See Priem, 'Distributed Ledger Technology' (n 8), 1.

[55] Swan, *Blockchain Blueprint for a New Economy* (n 22).

[56] See Andrea Pinna and Wiebe Ruttenberg, 'Distributed Ledger Technologies in Securities Post-Trading: Revolution or Evolution?', ECB Occasional Paper Series No. 172 (2016), https://www.ecb.europa.eu/pub/pdf/scpops/ecbop172.en.pdf (accessed 15 November 2021) (Pinna and Ruttenberg, 'Distributed Ledger Technologies in Securities Post-Trading'). See also Georgios Patsinaridis, 'Blockchain Revolution: Mitigating Systemic Risk in OTC Derivatives', SSRN Working Paper (2018), https://papers.ssrn.com/sol3/papers.cfm?abstract_id=3530443 (accessed 15 November 2021) (Patsinaridis, 'Blockchain Revolution').

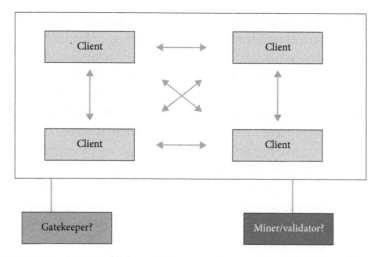

Figure 17.2 DLT system in which participants trade securities with one another

Source: Randy Priem, 'Distributed Ledger Technology for Securities Clearing and Settlement: Benefits, Risks, and Regulatory Implications' (2020) 6(1) Financial Innovation 1.

to be the case, the new transaction would then also get cryptographically hashed and permanently recorded in the distributed ledger. It would thus be difficult to add wrong transactions to the ledger without the consent of the relevant parties involved in the process.

Figure 17.2 shows that—because there could potentially be fewer intermediaries and centralizing institutions involved in the life cycle of a trade—a lot of currently re-petitive business processes could be eliminated; that is, the trade life cycle would be simplified, making the distinction between exchange-traded instruments and OTC ones even absent. The simplified trading life cycle could lead to reduced costs because manual reconciliations of potentially conflicting trade data stored in various duplicated ledgers could be eliminated.[57] The simplified trading life cycles could thus potentially lead to reduced transaction costs and settlement times. Yet, although proponents of the DLT technology believe that the technology could be applied to achieve instantaneous settlement, it is not entirely clear whether market participants would actually favour this since the ability to net transactions would disappear.[58] Netting has advantages in terms of liquidity requirements compared to real-time settlement; that is, the absence of netting would require participants to have all the required funds immediately avail-able to be able to fulfil their payment in real time.[59]

Specifically with respect to OTC derivatives, DLT can provide a multitude of advan-tages; that is, the post-trading processes of OTC derivatives currently involve a large number of manual actions, including the maintenance of records about ownership,

---

[57] See Bheemaiah, *The Blockchain Alternative* (n 21). See also ESMA, 'Distributed Ledger Technology Applied to Securities Markets' (n 31); Euroclear and Slaughter and May, 'Blockchain Settlement' (n 28).

[58] See Priem, 'Distributed Ledger Technology' (n 8), 1.

[59] See FINRA, 'Distributed Ledger Technology' (n 19). See also Caytas, 'Developing Blockchain Real-Time Clearing and Settlement in the EU, US, and Globally' (n 27).

continuous valuations, and arrangements of cross-system margin obligations. OTC derivatives trading is more costly compared to exchange trading because of the increased amount of required collateral (i.e. initial margins, variation margins, default fund contributions, etc.) that has to be exchanged with the CCP or bilaterally, depending on whether the derivative is centrally cleared or not. DLT and smart contracts could optimize the calculation and posting of margins more efficiently, thereby realizing financial cost savings for market participants. Smart contract could allow for an automatic execution and payment of margins as soon as certain criteria were met, such as the value of the underlying asset being below or above a certain threshold.[60] The main mechanisms used to mitigate risk, being delivery-versus-payment (i.e. the transfer of securities can only take place when the counterparty makes the corresponding cash payment), security or collateral exchange, netting, and multilateral clearing of exposures, can be programmed into the functionality of a DLT as smart contracts.[61]

Another advantage of having the trade life cycle on a DLT is the access of data. Since the global financial crisis of 2008, regulators require market participants to report their OTC derivative transactions to trade repositories.[62] The data in the trade repositories would then be made available to regulators in order for them to see whether the risk exposure in the market would increase. Distributed ledgers can thus be considered as useful sources of information for regulators to obtain a view on market microstructures, market expectations, and economic fundamentals. In case of a DLT for OTC derivatives, the reporting to trade repositories might not be necessary anymore. Indeed, the ledger contains all historical transactions, and giving access to a regulator would allow this party to see all transactions at once. Nowadays, there are multiple trade repositories, and market participants can choose which one they report to, so regulators now face the burden of reconciling all reported information coming from multiple sources, which would no longer be necessary in the case of a DLT system. Trade repositories utilize different trade-reporting architectures and software, thereby leading to interoperability issues between them, which hinders the surveillance functions that the trade-reporting requirements seek to achieve. The usage of DLT regarding trade reporting could also reduce data errors as market participants do not have to separately report transactions to trade repositories anymore but could simply make the distributed ledger in which trading is recorded available to their supervisors.

As highlighted before, the presented DLT system in this chapter is only a fictitious example and as the industry is still experimenting with the technology, the final market standard might be different. As an alternative, in the case of OTC derivatives, several interoperable ledgers (derivative ledgers and collateral ledgers) that use smart contracts could also exist.[63] In such an ecosystem, the parties to the derivatives transactions would submit bids and asks as usual. The matching would then take place on the

---

[60] Euroclear and Oliver Wyman, 'Blockchain in Capital Markets' (n 26).

[61] Philipp Peach, 'The Governance of Blockchain Financial Networks' (2017) 86 Modern Law Review 1073.

[62] A trade repository is defined in EMIR (n 3), Art. 2(2) as a legal person that centrally collects and maintains the records of derivatives.

[63] See Surujnath, 'Off the Chain!' (n 42), 257.

blockchain and the CCP would novate the agreements. The novation, resulting in two contracts, would then be uploaded to the derivative ledger. Throughout the lifespan of the agreement, the collateral ledger would use oracles to track price movements in the underlying assets and to automatically adjust positions. In case counterparties would need to post margins to the CCP, they would need to use an interoperable collateral and asset ledger. In case additional variation margin is required, the ledger would automatically send a payment request to the clearing member's address on the asset ledger. A DLT derivatives contract market could thus look like a system of several interoperable ledgers that use multi-signature smart contracts for effectuating transfers and oracles for collateral management and asset monitoring.

Another alternative solution is where derivative contracts are traded electronically on a private-permissioned blockchain with automatic execution functionalities.[64] Smart contracts could then be used, where the contractual terms are pre-programmed and inserted into a code to reflect the counterparties' intension. For example, in case of an option contract, the strike price, the amount of securities, and the maturity date would be included and trigger the purchase of the underlying securities using the option holder's private key. This would be followed by the nodes in the ledger verifying whether this trigger took place within the trading window. Also, for credit default swaps, the credit event determination could be contemplated in a smart contract.[65]

In case of central clearing, an alternative possibility could also be that both counterparties submit their bid and ask orders to their dealers, who would then post them on the blockchain network.[66] The CCP would match the orders and, through novation, step into the contract, thereby netting all positions. Initial and variation margin would be posted either on a digital cash account or, in case of assets, transferred onto a collateral ledger being connected with the derivatives ledger. Smart contracts would automatically calculate variation margin, thereby receiving information on price moments through oracles. At maturity or when, for example, an option holder wants to execute the derivative, the smart derivative contract would automatically calculate and close out the netted obligation and the payment would be automatically released on the cash ledger after termination of the contract. Regarding the collateral ledger, this could be a wallet where each party has the amount of collateral necessary and from which the smart contract can automatically take the collateral.[67] Clearing members would need to make sure that there are always sufficient funds in order to be able to provide margin when required. In case a clearing member posts insufficient collateral or no collateral whatsoever, the smart derivative contract could automatically terminate its account and protect counterparties from further losses.

The potential aforementioned example indicates that the trading, clearing, and settlement process of a transaction could be contemporaneous, also with the validation

---

[64] See Patsinaridis, 'Blockchain Revolution (n 56).

[65] See Clements, 'Evaluating the Costs and Benefits of a Smart Contract Blockchain Framework' (n 35), 369.

[66] See Patsinaridis, 'Blockchain Revolution' (n 56).

[67] A wallet can be defined as a device, physical medium, (cloud) service, or program to store the public and/or private keys for cryptocurrencies and/or tokens.

process whereby the new asset ownership would be reflected in the system. Post-trading (i.e. clearing and settlement) and trading could become more intertwined in a DLT environment compared to the current sequential processing of securities.[68] Some scholars even argue that as the transaction phase and clearing-and-settlement phase will occur simultaneously,[69] there will no longer be a need to distinguish between these different phases. This would imply that there is no longer a distinction between trading and post-trading, leading to a reduced role of post-trading market infrastructures.[70]

As there are many possible future DLT systems, a debate is currently ongoing whether trading venues, CCPs, and CSDs are even still necessary. According to some industry participants[71] and scholars,[72] regulated markets, MTFs, or OTFs are less likely to be directly affected as their market participants still need to find counterparties to trade with, which will not fundamentally change when DLT is applied. Alternatively, buyers and sellers could first act through brokers (i.e. trade level) and then create a transaction for the transfer of that amount of the asset, which is, in turn, transmitted to the DLT network and verified.[73] Trading venues might thus develop their own method of clearing and settlement using DLT, thereby making a CCP or CSD no longer necessary. However, there is also a possibility that market participants rather introduce the technology in a step-by-step manner, thereby first focusing on the post-trading part of the trade life cycle where most inefficiencies (i.e. manual processing, reconciliation, long custody chains, etc.) can be removed. This might be the reason why numerous exchanges are exploring the technology to apply DLT to clearing and settlement activities.

Some argue then that blockchains could make sure that financial derivatives markets do not need to rely on a single CCP anymore. In the case of cleared OTC derivatives, the risk concentration within CCPs gives rise to systemic risk concerns as these financial market infrastructures are considered too big to fail.[74] Since the 26 September 2009 summit by the G20 in Pittsburgh, the majority of OTC derivatives markets have moved from bilateral to central clearing. One of the reasons for this was that CCPs functioned as shock absorbers during the crisis and managed to close out all financial contracts with defaulted clearing members in a quick and orderly manner. For non-defaulting clearing members, CCPs guaranteed the execution of their trades and

---

[68] See Priem, 'Distributed Ledger Technology' (n 8), 1.

[69] Katya Malinova and Andreas Park, 'Market Design for Trading with Blockchain Technology', Working Paper (7 July 2016), http://blockchain.cs.ucl.ac.uk/wp-content/uploads/2016/11/Paper_18.pdf (accessed 15 November 2021).

[70] Gareth Peters and Guy Vishnia, 'Overview of Emerging Blockchain Architectures and Platforms for Electronic Trading Exchanges', SSRN Working Paper (10 November 2016), https://papers.ssrn.com/sol3/papers.cfm?abstract_id=2867344 (accessed 15 November 2021) (Peters and Vishnia, 'Overview of Emerging Blockchain Architectures').

[71] See Goldman Sachs, 'Blockchain' (n 5) and see Euroclear and Oliver Wyman, 'Blockchain in Capital Markets' (n 26).

[72] Paola Fico, 'Virtual Currencies and Blockchains: Potential Impacts on Financial Market Infrastructures and on Corporate Ownership.' SSRN Working Paper (22 February 2016), https://papers.ssrn.com/sol3/papers.cfm?abstract_id=2736035 (accessed 15 November 2021) (Fico, 'Virtual Currencies and Blockchains').

[73] Peters and Vishnia, 'Overview of Emerging Blockchain Architectures' (n 70).

[74] Emiolios Avgouleas and Aggelos Kiayias 'The Promise of Blockchain Technology for Global Securities and Derivatives Markets: The New Financial Ecosystem and the Holy Grail of Systemic Risk Containment' (2019) 20 European Business Organization Law Review 81–110.

assisted in transferring their outstanding positions to solvent clearing members. CCPs had clear benefits but nowadays have the side effect that they are too big and too important to fail.[75] Some proponents of DLT might thus claim that it could be beneficial to somewhat reduce their systemic importance by making many of their risk-mitigating activities redundant with the introduction of blockchains serving as decentralized clearing networks; that is, the blockchain itself could manage the functions usually executed by the CCP, such as the valuation of contracts, the calculation of initial and variation margin, the custody of collateral, the handling of novation and netting, and the management of the final pay-outs. Key functions of CCPs could thus be decentralized amongst nodes in the network and each node could get a specific duty. As the DLT technology could reduce counterparty risk because of the almost instantaneous settlement and pre-trade transparency due to the entire copy of the ledger in their own systems, some market players believe that CCPs, and clearing in general, are no longer necessary. CCPs can, of course, also use the technology but this can be done also by other, competing institutions.

Nevertheless, for non-cash derivatives having a maturity date, central clearing could still be useful for hedging purposes until securities and/or cash are irrevocably and finally exchanged.[76] Indeed, a distinction has to be made between transactions having a maturity and spot transactions. For spot transactions having a single clearing and settlement instruction extinguishing the obligations of each party, DLT could reduce the role of CCPs. In contrast, for derivative transactions with a (long) maturity, the outstanding rights or obligations remain throughout the entire life of the contract. Hence, the necessity to mitigate counterparty risk exists until the contract matures. For these contracts, DLT is unlikely to fully eliminate counterparty risk as there is a long time period during which counterparties incur the risk of non-performance.

Some financial institutions are then of the opinion that CSDs are not necessary anymore as the securities' issuer and the investors acquiring them can directly transact via updates of the distributed ledger. In contrast, market infrastructures could change their roles and start acting as gatekeepers or validators in case of permissioned distributed ledgers as they would face fewer competition issues and conflicts of interests compared to traders.[77] Also, CCPs and CSDs could start offering new services, such as the coordination of the evolution of the permissioned DLT protocol (e.g. modifying or updating source codes), the management and safekeeping of private keys in order to ensure network security, and the management of the introduction or cancellation of tokens on the ledger. Yet, because these services are not core clearing or settlement functions, CCPs and CSDs do not necessarily have a competitive advantage here, and other types of financial institutions could also start offering them.[78]

---

[75] Randy Priem, 'CCP Recovery and Resolution: Preventing a Financial Catastrophe' (2018) 26(3) Journal of Financial Regulation and Compliance 351–365.

[76] Priem, 'Distributed Ledger Technology' (n 8), 1. See also Pinna and Ruttenberg, 'Distributed Ledger Technologies in Securities Post-Trading' (n 56).

[77] Pinna and Ruttenberg, 'Distributed Ledger Technologies in Securities Post-Trading' (n 56).

[78] Priem, 'Distributed Ledger Technology' (n 8), 1.

As discussed above, DLT systems might bring several important advantages when applied to clearing and settlement, such as reduced counterparty risk, lower settlement fees, simplified operational processes because of fewer intermediaries, and a higher transparency level. Yet, this technology still faces challenges which first might need to be considered before the technology can be fully implemented. For instance, in order to increase transparency and trust in the DLT system, all information on the transactions in the ledgers can be observed by all system participants and copied into their own ledgers. All participants would then be aware of all the existing transactions and their details, such as the value and volume of the assets being bought. When applied to financial markets, this transparency might cause a privacy or competition issue, and thus breach applicable laws, such as the General Data Protection Regulation.[79] Certain solutions, such as advanced encryption and obfuscation techniques, are currently being explored in order to enhance participants' privacy together. Obfuscation and encryption techniques enable participants—or a central authority, depending on whether the system is permissioned or not—to validate the transactions by performing mathematical computations without having a view on the exact inputs and outputs of the computations. An example is homomorphic encryption, where the asset quantities for a transaction may be hidden to all participants except for the sender and recipient of those transactions. In such a case, all participants are, however, still able to verify the validity of the transaction. Another example is the Quorum Platform developed by J.P. Morgan. There, transactions are fully replicated across all nodes, with the database being split into a private and a public database. All the participants concur on the public database, but their private databases differ. Furthermore, the industry is currently experimenting with 'mixers', which allow users to pool a set of transactions in unpredictable combinations, thereby making the tracking of identities more difficult.[80] A potential disadvantage of these techniques is that it might make the detection of insider trading or money laundering more difficult by market regulators and compliance officers as the identity and transaction details are no longer transparent. In contrast, in the absence of proper safeguards, unethical market participants could exploit the shared and public information recorded in the system to conduct unfair market behaviour.

A second vulnerability of DLT is that, as market participants are currently developing their own niche systems, there is a risk that incompatibility issues appear between the different developed systems, leading to fragmentation.[81] When each market institution starts using its own proprietary DLT system, more operational risks would occur associated with trying to connect the various systems.[82] The lack of standardization could lead to a situation where manual post-trading validation processes are still necessary or

[79] Regulation (EU) No. 2016/679 of the European Parliament and of the Council of 27 April 2016 on the protection of natural persons with regard to the processing of personal data and on the free movement of such data, and repealing Directive 95/46/EC (GDPR). See Primavera de Filippi, 'The Interplay between Decentralization and Privacy: The Case of Blockchain Technologies' (2016) 9 Journal of Peer Production 1.

[80] Rainer Böhme, Nicolas Christin, Benjamin Edelman, and Tyler Moore, 'Bitcoin: Economics, Technology and Governance' (2015) 29(2) Journal of Economic Perspectives 213.

[81] Goldman Sachs, 'Blockchain' (n 5).

[82] Pinna and Ruttenberg, 'Distributed Ledger Technologies in Securities Post-Trading' (n 56).

become even more important, thereby hampering disintermediation.[83] Nevertheless, several market-driven initiatives are currently fostering common DLT protocols and standards. Examples are the HyperLedger Linux Foundation,[84] the R3 Consortium,[85] the Post-Trade Distributed Ledger Group,[86] and the CSD Working Group on DLT.[87] Incompatibility issues thus do not seem to be the stopping point for this technology. The establishment of an agreement on standardized DLT solutions, however, is likely to take time and could thus reduce the pace at which this DLT gets implemented. Even more, when existing market participants would want to replace their legacy system with a DLT system, both will need to be interoperable for a short-to-medium period of time.[88]

As illustrated in this section, the technological challenges of DLT systems, such as fragmentation and privacy issues, are currently being addressed by the industry. It is generally assumed that these risks will cause certain delays but will not be blocking issues. The legal challenges for this technology when applied to clearing and settlement, however, could be a hurdle when not properly addressed. Because of its importance, the rest of this chapter is addressed to these regulatory perspectives and challenges.

4 Regulatory Developments

Over the past few years, the financial industry has advocated more regulatory guidance (e.g. European CSD Association, ECSDA 2017) and/or an update of the legal framework for providers or users of DLT.[89] According to the German Banking Industry Committee (2016), DLT systems indeed function in a fundamentally different manner

---

[83] See Klimos, 'The Distributed Ledger Technology' (n 26), 194–222.

[84] The main objective of HyperLedger is to achieve cross-industry collaboration with the focus on generating improved performance of the DLT systems being developed. Among the members of the initiative are: ABN Amro, Bank of New York (BNY) Mellon, ANZ Bank, CLS Group, CME Group, DTCC, Deutsche Börse Group, J.P. Morgan, State Street, Swift, and Wells Fargo.

[85] The R3 Consortium consists of more than 200 companies, including Barclays, Banco Bilbao Vizcaya Argentaria (BBVA), Goldman Sachs, J.P. Morgan, BNY Mellon, Bank of America, Commerzbank, Deutsche Bank, HSBC, and Unicredit. The Consortium has created an open-source DLT system called Corda.

[86] The Post-Trade Distributed Ledger Group is a group of almost forty financial institutions, including financial market infrastructures, which acts as a forum to collaborate and share best practices.

[87] The CSD Working Group on DLT is a consortium comprising of Russia's National Securities Depository, Switzerland's SIX Securities Services, the Nordic subsidiary of NASDAQ, Chile's Depósito Central de Valores (DCV), South Africa's Strate, and Argentina's Caja de Valores. Together with Swift, this working group is considering the use of ISO 20022 standards for e-proxy voting in order to foster interoperability amongst DLT solutions and legacy systems.

[88] Priem, 'Distributed Ledger Technology' (n 8), 1.

[89] See ECSDA, 'ECSDA Response to the European Commission Consultation on Fintech' (2017), https://ecsda.eu/archives/5344 (accessed 15 November 2021). See also German Banking Industry Committee, 'Response to the Consultation on the Distributed Ledger Technology Applied to Securities Markets' (2016), https://www.esma.eur opa.eu/press-news/consultations/consultation-distributed-ledger-technology-applied-securities-markets (accessed 14 April 2023) (Banking Industry Committee, 'Response to the Consultation on the Distributed Ledger Technology Applied to Securities Markets'); Polish Bank Association, 'Response to the Consultation on the Distributed Ledger Technology Applied to Securities Markets' (2016), https://www.esma.europa.eu/press-news/consultations/consultation-distributed-ledger-technology-applied-securities-markets (accessed 14 April 2023); CACEIS, 'Response to the consultation on the distributed ledger technology applied to securities markets' (2016), https://www.esma.europa.eu/press-news/consultations/consultation-distributed-ledger-technology-applied-sec urities-markets (accessed 14 April 2023).

compared to legacy systems and thus a different regulatory approach could prove useful.[90] Existing regulations reflect a conceptualization of the current financial eco-system, and, at the time existing regulations were drafted, legislators could not have foreseen that DLT could become significant for financial markets.[91] However, DLT could pose some novel risks that are not yet properly mitigated by existing regula-tions.[92] For instance, as it is burdensome to correct transaction errors in a distributed ledger, new required procedures would have to be created on how to deal with possible mistakes.[93] In addition, requirements covering potential liability issues of users and rules requiring them to put compliance and risk management systems in place could become necessary.[94]

Several regulatory initiatives have been launched to examine the potential influ-ence of DLT on the (post-)trade ecosystem and to assess the necessity for new require-ments or the modification of existing rules. For instance, the European Central Bank's Target2-Securities (T2S) Harmonization Steering Group chose, in August 2016, to start a task force on DLT to assess the impact on European financial market integration.[95] In February 2017, the Bank for International Settlements (BIS) published an analyt-ical framework to examine the usage of DLT in payments, clearing, and settlement.[96] The document intends to facilitate markets authorities and central banks to detect the opportunities and risks of DLT in their conceptual, experimental, or implementation phase. Yet, the BIS framework does not include principles to which the industry should adhere.

At the same time, the European Securities Markets Authority (ESMA) published a document outlining its views on DLT in the case where it is applied to financial mar-kets.[97] The report discusses the possible risks and benefits of this technology under several scenarios and examines the potential interaction with existing European rules. At the time of the publication of the report, ESMA's view was that regulatory actions would be premature as the technology is still evolving and the existing number of prac-tical applications is low. In the case that existing clearing and settlement market infra-structures would use DLT as a technological improvement, ESMA foresaw a number of smaller regulatory challenges as the European regulatory framework does not pre-scribe the type of technology that market infrastructures have to employ and is thus

---

[90] German Banking Industry Committee, 'Response to the Consultation on the Distributed Ledger Technology Applied to Securities Markets' (n 89).

[91] Priem, 'Distributed Ledger Technology' (n 8), 1.

[92] BIS, 'Distributed Ledger Technology in Payment' (n 20).

[93] David Evans, 'Economic Aspects of Bitcoin and Other Decentralized Public-Ledger Currency Platforms', Coase-Sandor Working Paper Series in Law and Economics No. 685 (2014), https://chicagounbound.uchicago.edu/cgi/viewcontent.cgi?article=2349&context=law_and_economics (accessed 15 November 2021).

[94] Dirk A. Zetzsche, Ross P. Buckley, and Douglas W. Arner, 'The Distributed Liability of Distributed Ledgers: Legal Risks of Blockchains' (2017) University of Illinois Law Review 1361 (Zetzsche et al., 'The Distributed Liability of Distributed Ledgers').

[95] ECB Advisory Group on Market Infrastructures for Securities and Collateral, 'Paper on the Potential Impact of DLTs on Securities Post-Trading Harmonization and on the Wider EU Financial Market Integration' (September 2017), https://www.ecb.europa.eu/paym/intro/governance/shared/pdf/201709_dlt_impact_on_harmonisation_and_integration.pdf (accessed 28 June 2018).

[96] BIS, 'Distributed Ledger Technology in Payment' (n 20).

[97] ESMA, 'Distributed Ledger Technology Applied to Securities Markets' (n 31).

considered as 'technology neutral'. DLT operationally replacing the current ecosystem of market participants and market infrastructures would necessitate a different view. Permissioned DLT systems would meet two broad legal challenges: (i) existing post-trade regulations could act as a barrier to the introduction of DLT and, in a case where the technology does get implemented, (ii) DLT might introduce prudential and conduct risks that are not sufficiently addressed by the existing regulations.[98]

In July 2017, the European Commission launched an expertise hub on blockchain technology. This expertise hub started an examination of the feasibility of an EU blockchain infrastructure and investigated the conditions needed to achieve an open, trustworthy, transparent, and EU law-compliant data and transactional environment.[99] The European Commission's Directorate-General for Internal Market, Industry, Entrepreneurship, and Small and Medium Enterprises (SMEs) and its Joint Research Center also launched the #Blockchain4EU project to develop industrial-use cases for DLT and blockchain.[100]

On 24 September 2020, The European Commission proposed a DLT pilot regime for market infrastructures based on DLT.[101] The proposal is part of the digital action plan of the European Commission, which also includes legislative proposals on crypto-assets (MiCA), digital resilience (DORA), and the clarification and amendments of certain related financial services requirements, such as the definition of a financial instrument under MiFID II.[102]

The DLT pilot regime creates certain exemptions from specific requirements embedded in MiFID II and CSDR[103] to allow market infrastructures to experiment with the technology.[104] For instance, the DLT pilot regime allows an investment firm or market operator to request its national competent authority whether DLT transferable securities can be admitted to trading, even when they are not first recorded in a CSD. The CSD operating a DLT securities settlement system may then ask its competent authority to be exempted from the application of the CSDR requirements on dematerialized form, transfer orders, securities accounts, the recording of securities, the integrity of the issue, and asset segregation.

The aforementioned exemptions might be considered utile to experiment with a new technology as existing regulations—or at least certain legal interpretations of them—could be considered as a barrier to entry; that is, securities accounts as we currently

[98] Priem, 'Distributed Ledger Technology' (n 8), 1.
[99] European Commission, 'Study on Opportunity and Feasibility of a EU Blockchain Infrastructure' (2017), https://ec.europa/eu/digital-single_market/en/news/study-opportunity-and-feasibility-eu-blockchain-infrastructure (accessed 8 November 2017).
[100] Susana Nascimento, Alexandre Polvora, and Joana Sousa Lourenço, 'Blockchain for Industrial Transformations' (2018), http://publications.jrc.ec.europa.eu/repository/handle/JRC111095 (accessed 15 November 2021).
[101] European Commission, 'Proposal for a Regulation of the European Parliament and of the Council on a pilot regime for market infrastructures based on distributed ledger technology', COM/2020/594 final (2020), http://eur-lex.europa.eu/legal-content/EN/TXT/?uri=CELEX%3A52020PC0594 (accessed 15 November 2021).
[102] MiFID II (n 4).
[103] CSDR (n 3).
[104] Randy Priem, 'A European DLT Pilot Regime for Market Infrastructures: Finding a Balance between Innovation, Investor Protection, and Financial Stability', SSRN Working Paper (7 October 2021), http://papers.ssrn.com/sol3/papers.cfm?abstract_id=3919484 (accessed 15 November 2021).

know them may not exist in a DLT system but existing regulations, such as EMIR[105] and CSDR,[106] use the terminology without explicitly describing what they should look like and whether there is a legal difference between accounts, records, and/or ledgers. In this sense, these regulations are technology-neutral. Yet, securities on a DLT are not credited on traditional accounts held by a regulated entity and/or intermediary but are rather web accounts realized via electronic annotations.[107] Given the definition of a transfer order under the Settlement Finality Directive (SFD)[108] and the definition of a securities account under CSDR,[109] some Member States might be of the opinion that only double-entry (or multiple-entry) book keepings could be legally considered as accounts and that transfer orders could only happen when legacy ledgers are used. If this is indeed the case, a DLT system without double-entry accounts could potentially not be considered as a securities settlement system. As a consequence, the operator would not be able to obtain an authorization as a CSD and issuers using the DLT system would be in violation of CSDR, Art. 3.[110] Other Member States could perhaps be of the opinion that the digital address on a DLT platform to which securities are recorded (i.e. the public keys) can legally be considered as accounts. Because of the lack of clear definitions and possible divergent legal interpretation of the Member States, different views within Europe could arise, leading to a situation where DLT providers would be able to become a CSD in certain countries while not in others. Hence, even when legislators want to be technology-neutral, the interpretation of existing regulations could be such that the law at hand does become a barrier.

Alternatively, market infrastructures might have to keep the securities on securities accounts and tokenize them afterwards into the distributed ledger in order to fulfil the legal requirements, but this process could create additional operational risks. Both EMIR[111] and CSDR[112] require that CCPs and CSDs keep records and accounts that

---

[105] EMIR (n 3).

[106] CSDR (n 3).

[107] Fico, 'Virtual Currencies and Blockchains' (n 72).

[108] EC, Directive 98/26/EC of the European Parliament and of the Council of 19 May 1998 on settlement finality in payment and securities settlement systems, [1998] OJ L 166. A transfer order is defined as (i) any instruction by a participant to place at the disposal of a recipient an amount of money by means of a book entry on the accounts of a credit institution, a central bank or a settlement agent, or any instruction which results in the assumption or discharge of a payment obligation as defined by the rules of the system or (ii) an instruction by a participant to transfer the title to, or interest in, a security or securities by means of a book entry on a register or otherwise.

[109] CSDR (n 3) defines a securities account as an account on which securities may be debited or credited.

[110] CSDR (n 3), Art. 3 (book-entry form) states that any issuer established in the Union that issues, or has issued, transferable securities which are admitted to trading or traded on trading venues has to arrange for such securities to be represented in book-entry form as immobilization or subsequent to a direct issuance in dematerialized form. Where a transaction in transferable securities takes place on a trading venue, the relevant securities have to be recorded in book-entry form in a CSD on or before the intended settlement date unless they have already been so recorded. Where transferable securities are transferred following a financial collateral arrangement, those securities have to be recorded in book-entry form in a CSD on or before the intended settlement date unless they have already been so recorded.

[111] EMIR (n 3), Art. 39(1) states that a CCP has to separate records and accounts that shall enable it, at any time and without delay, to distinguish in accounts with the CCP the assets and positions held for the account of one clearing member from the assets and positions held for the account of any other clearing member and from its own assets.

[112] CSDR (n 3), Art. 38(1) mentions that for each securities settlement system it operates, a CSD shall keep records and accounts that shall enable it, at any time and without delay, to segregate in the accounts with the CSD, the securities of a participant from those of any other participant and, if applicable, from the CSD's own assets.

enable them, at any time and without delay, to segregate in their accounts the securities of their clients from those of any other client and, if applicable, from their own assets. As documented above, security accounts where a debit and/or credit is possible may be considered to be absent in a DLT environment.

The pilot regime then encompasses certain requirements in order to ensure investor protection and protect financial stability. For instance, operators need to establish a business plan including a description of critical staff, technical aspects, and how the performance of functions, services, and activities deviate from an MTF or a securities settlement system (SSS). The latter information has to be provided to the clients, participants, issuers, and/or members of the infrastructure via the infrastructure's website.

The DLT pilot regime focuses on MTFs, trading and settlement systems (TSS), and SSSs rather than on CCPs. The European Commission is of the view that DLT can allow for nearly real-time settlement, thereby making trading and settlement almost instantaneous. Central clearing is hence not considered as instantaneous trading, and settlement could make counterparty risk nearly absent. Furthermore, OTC derivatives trading is not allowed under the DLT pilot regime. The view that CCPs might still be beneficial to market liquidity, even for equity and fixed-income trading, because of their multilateral netting services is thus not taken into consideration. Yet, multilateral netting done by the CCP can be of utmost importance in stressed market circumstances, given that multilateral netting cancels multiple transactions out between multiple parties, thereby reducing the total notional value of exposure in the market.[113] Multilateral netting could happen in a DLT environment when the multi-signature technology is used; that is, multiple participants could agree on the multilateral offsetting of their claims within the market, allowing the system to automatically conduct these tasks.

Besides the fact that OTC derivatives trading is not allowed to be experimented with under the DLT pilot regime, its inclusion would also not have removed all legal barriers; that is, EMIR[114] requires standardized OTC derivative contracts to be cleared through a central counterparty. EMIR thus foresees an important role for CCPs in order to reduce counterparty credit risk, granting them a quasi-monopoly. New types of market participants, such as DLT FinTechs operating a permissioned system, may want to enter the market. If they set up a DLT system without a CCP for these types of derivatives, they would be in breach of EMIR. If CCPs would act as validators in a permissioned DLT system, it is still not clear whether the validation of trades, now often conducted by trading venues, would legally be considered as central clearing. In addition to this EMIR requirement, institutions that clear their OTC derivatives through a CCP typically have lower capital requirements. OTC derivatives trades in a DLT environment without a CCP could therefore lead to higher capital requirements for counterparties, which would make DLT systems less attractive.

In addition to the DLT pilot regime, specific new prudential and conducts risks that DLT could introduce might be looked at in the future.[115] The potential regulatory

[113] Patsinaridis, 'Blockchain Revolution' (n 56).
[114] EMIR (n 3)
[115] See Priem, 'Distributed Ledger Technology' (n 8), 1.

barriers discussed above highlight that existing financial regulations were not written with DLT in mind. Legislators were not yet aware that this technology existed—or would even be created—and could thus become important for financial markets. Even if potential regulatory barriers would be eliminated and DLT systems would be operationalized, additional requirements might have to be introduced in new or existing financial legislation in order to address prudential and/or conduct risks introduced by this technology. DLT systems might potentially be secure from a technological perspective but might spread financial risks amongst market participants that were formerly concentrated with a limited number of central institutions.[116] These new types of risk need to be formally addressed in order to protect market participants.

BIS shares the opinion that new requirements might have to be introduced, stressing that more work is needed to make sure that the legal underpinnings of DLT arrangements are sound, that their governance is robust, and that appropriate data controls are in place.[117] Indeed, DLT might be more efficient with respect to legacy systems but might also turn out to be inferior. For instance, DLTs are immutable, making it difficult to correct transaction errors. New enforceable procedures and governance requirements could be useful in order to deal with possible mistakes both from a governance and a technological perspective.[118] For this example, regulators could draft requirements to determine the correcting mechanisms that would apply and the time frame within the error needs to be solved.

In general, new rules that govern participants' interactions could be reflected upon.[119] Examples include requirements on potential liability issues of participants and rules requiring users to put compliance and risk management systems in place. With respect to the underlying software code, requirements and processes regarding changes in the code, and regarding dispute resolution, could be needed. The governance requirements could indicate rules to be followed by the parties setting up the code design, the validators, and the users of the system.[120]

Finally, more clarification is also needed on the legal status of smart contracts. Until now, only a few legislators, such as those of the state of Arizona, have given a legal status to smart contracts. Even if computer code might be too rigid to allow all contracts to be drafted in an algorithmic way,[121] regulators might start examining whether, and how, contract law should be modified for smart contracts to be valid and enforceable, given their automated and deterministic nature. Further reflection is needed on whether smart contracts can ultimately replace existing legal contracts in their entirety

---

[116] Zetzsche et al. 'The Distributed Liability of Distributed Ledgers' (n 94), 1361.
[117] BIS, 'Distributed Ledger Technology in Payment' (n 20).
[118] ESMA, 'Distributed Ledger Technology Applied to Securities Markets' (n 31).
[119] Zetzsche et al. 'The Distributed Liability of Distributed Ledgers' (n 94), 1361.
[120] Priem, 'Distributed Ledger Technology' (n 8), 1.
[121] It is often impossible to include clauses as 'in good faith' or 'commercially reasonable manner' in a smart contract. The key philosophical question is whether these clauses where discretion is possible should be eliminated via the use of smart contracts. Without them, legal uncertainty could be reduced, but, on the other hand, their absence reduces flexibility and discretion of one of the contracting parties, which might be useful in case of unforeseen circumstances. See ISDA and Linklaters, 'Smart Contracts and Distributed Ledger' (n 38).

or whether they can only be used to automate the execution of the actions that are specified in legal contracts.

5 Conclusion

DLT has received extensive consideration over the past decade from market participants, financial market infrastructures, and regulators. Because of the possible advantages and efficiency gains of DLT, financial institutions have started to experiment with several proofs of concept in particular niches of the trading and post-trading environment. Also, although not for the trading of OTC derivatives, the European Commission proposed a DLT pilot regime in order for market infrastructures to experiment with the technology.

Nevertheless, despite all pilot cases, financial institutions have yet to prove that DLT is a viable and sustainable solution, and it is currently unclear from the pilot cases whether the trading and post-trading segments will become more intertwined. Moreover, the future role of trading venues, CCPs, and CSDs in a DLT environment is still to be seen. Regarding the trading of OTC derivatives, central clearing could still be useful for hedging purposes until securities and/or cash are irrevocably and finally exchanged. CCPs could also be necessary from a multilateral netting point of view. In addition, CCPs and CSDs could start offering new services, such as the coordination of the evolution of the permissioned DLT protocol (e.g. modifying or updating source codes), the management and safekeeping of private keys in order to ensure network security, and the management of the introduction or cancellation of tokens on the ledger.

Because of the increased interest of applying DLT to securities markets and taking into account that DLT can also introduce new financial risks to the ecosystem, legislators might reflect on drafting new legislation—or adapt existing legislation—in order to mitigate these new risks as much as possible. Specific requirements governing, for example, the interaction between participants, cyber security, and error resolution in an OTC derivatives setting might be explored.

18

The Future of Centrally Cleared OTC Derivatives Markets

Evariest Callens and Klaus Löber

1 Introduction

1.1 The Present

Since the 2009 G20 Pittsburgh statement,[1] central clearing of over-the-counter (OTC) derivatives through central counterparties (CCPs) has been increasingly put forward as one of the major solutions for risk mitigation in the OTC derivatives markets. Together with an increased market demand for central clearing after the 2008 financial crisis,[2] at least three post-crisis legislative and regulatory initiatives have served as key catalysts for the increased usage of, and reliance on, CCPs for OTC derivatives. First, in line with the G20 Pittsburgh commitments, regulatory frameworks for OTC derivatives in a host of major financial market jurisdictions now contain a central clearing obligation—often referred to in the US literature as a 'clearing mandate'—for certain specified OTC derivatives and market participants.[3] Second, non-centrally cleared

---

[1] G20, 'Leaders' Statement', the Pittsburgh Summit (24–25 September 2009), recital 13, bullet 3, https://g20.org/en/g20/Documents/2009-Pittsburgh_Declaration.pdf (accessed 27 June 2022).

[2] Peter Norman, *The Risk Controllers: Central Counterparty Clearing in Globalised Financial Markets* (Chichester: Wiley 2011), pp. 298, 313 (Norman, *The Risk Controllers*). Cf. Committee on Payment Settlement Systems (CPSS), 'Market Structure Developments in the Clearing Industry: Implications for Financial Stability' (November 2010), p. 20, https://www.bis.org/cpmi/publ/d92.htm (accessed 27 June 2022) (CPSS, 'Market Structure Developments in the Clearing Industry').

[3] See Financial Stability Board (FSB), 'OTC Derivatives Market Reforms: Implementation Progress in 2021' (3 December 2021), p. 4, https://www.fsb.org/wp-content/uploads/P031221.pdf (accessed 24 March 2023). For what

OTC derivatives have been subjected to a set of regulatory risk mitigation techniques that result in making these derivatives more expensive for market participants than was the case prior to the adoption of the regulatory reforms in the aftermath of the 2008 financial crisis.[4] Third, reforms in the capital and liquidity requirements for derivatives under the Basel Framework have created a relative advantage in terms of cost of capital for centrally cleared derivatives in comparison to non-centrally cleared derivatives.[5] In recent years, some commentators have called for an even wider adoption of central clearing through CCPs.[6] The increased usage of CCPs has already produced substantial effects for the *present* structure of financial markets, for example, through reinforced netting efficiency at CCPs,[7] enhanced risk management in derivatives markets, and augmented funding liquidity risk through the (time-sensitive) encumbrance of highly liquid assets.[8]

1.2 The Future

In light of the increasingly pivotal role of CCPs in OTC derivatives markets, this concluding chapter aims to formulate conjectures about the directions in which centrally cleared OTC derivatives markets may develop in the future. Given the inherently forward-looking nature of this chapter, our analysis is necessarily limited in that it employs incomplete information about the future in an attempt to map future risks, challenges, and opportunities in centrally cleared OTC derivatives markets. Viewed from that perspective, this chapter takes a somewhat broader perspective than the previous chapters of this book.

---

regards the EU, see Regulation (EU) No. 648/2012 of the European Parliament and of the Council of 4 July 2012 on OTC derivatives, central counterparties and trade repositories, [2012] OJ L201/1 (27 July 2012), Art. 4 (EMIR). Cf. For what regards the United States, see 7 United States Code (USC) § 2(h).

[4] For what regards the EU, see EMIR (n 3), Art. 11.

[5] For what regards the EU, see the Capital Requirements Regulation: Regulation (EU) No. 575/2013 of the European Parliament and of the Council of 26 June 2013 on prudential requirements for credit institutions and investment firms and amending Regulation (EU) No. 648/2012, [2013] OJ L176/1, Art. 306(1)(a) (CRR).

[6] Ross Spence, *Collateral Transactions and Shadow Banking* (Meijers-reeks, 2021), pp. 233–236; Steven L. Schwarcz, 'Central Clearing of Financial Contracts: Theory and Regulatory Implications' (2019) 167 University of Pennsylvania Law Review 1327.

[7] Cf. on netting efficiency at CCPs: Darrell Duffie and Haoxiang Zhu, 'Does a Central Clearing Counterparty Reduce Counterparty Risk?' (2011) 1 Review of Asset Pricing Studies 74, 77–85 (Duffie and Zhu, 'Does a Central Clearing Counterparty Reduce Counterparty Risk?'). See also Rodney Garratt and Peter Zimmerman, 'Centralized Netting in Financial Networks' (2020) 112 Journal of Banking and Finance 1; Rama Cont and Thomas Kokholm, 'Central Clearing of OTC Derivatives: Bilateral vs Multilateral Netting' (2014) 31 Statistics and Risk Modeling 3.

[8] Cf. Joseph Tanega and Andrea Savi, 'Central Clearing Counterparties for OTC-Users: A Theoretical Framework' (2017) 13 New York University Journal of Law and Business 825, 848 (Tanega and Savi, 'Central Clearing Counterparties for OTC-Users'); Alexandra Heath, Gerard Kelly, Mark Manning, Sheri Markose, and Ali Rais Shaghaghi, 'CCPs and Network Stability in OTC Derivatives Markets' (2016) 27 Journal of Financial Stability 217 (Heath et al., 'CCPs and Network Stability'). See also David Marshall and Robert Steigerwald, 'The Role of Time-Critical Liquidity in Financial Markets' (2013) 37(2) Federal Reserve Bank of Chicago Economic Perspectives 30, 32; Alexandra Heath, Gerard Kelly, and Mark Manning, 'OTC Derivatives Reform: Netting and Networks', in Alexandra Heath, Matthew Lilley, and Mark Manning (eds), *Liquidity and Funding Markets: Proceedings of a Conference* (Reserve Bank of Australia, 2013), p. 33.

1.3 Overview of Contents

The remainder of this chapter is structured as follows. First, section 2 examines the potential effects for centrally cleared OTC derivatives markets of four emerging risks: cyber risk, environmental risk, new technologies, and legal risk. The assessment of these emerging risks also serves as an anchor point to discuss the potential flipside of the respective risks, that is, possible future benefits for centrally cleared OTC derivatives markets that are connected to the fields in which the risks may materialize. Second, section 3 identifies certain challenges that come with the friction between a market for centrally cleared OTC derivatives that is increasingly cross-border in nature and a regulatory and supervisory approach towards CCPs that has remained largely domestic or regional. Third, section 4 provides some reflections on potential future directions for CCP governance. Finally, section 5 will conclude.

2 Emerging Risks

2.1 Cyber Risk

As aptly articulated by the New York State Department of Financial Services, '[t]he next great financial crisis could come from a cyber attack.'[9] In the most general sense, cyber risk—which is a subtype of operational risk[10]—refers to the risk that a cyberattack or data breach will expose an entity to costs arising from financial loss, reputational damage, or disclosure of sensitive information. Cyberattacks (e.g. viruses, ransomware, distributed denial-of-service (DDoS) attacks, or web application attacks)—or, more generally, cyber risk—pose an increasingly grave threat and challenge to the financial system.[11]

2.1.1 CCPs and cyber risk
Although cyber risk threatens the financial system at large,[12] there are some factors that render CCPs particularly susceptible to cyberattacks. First, through their

---

[9] New York State Department of Financial Services (NYSDFS), 'Report on the SolarWinds Cyber Espionage Attack and Institutions' Response' (April 2021), p. 2, https://www.dfs.ny.gov/system/files/documents/2021/04/solarwinds_report_2021.pdf (accessed 27 June 2022).

[10] Operational risk is the risk that a human error, a deficiency of an (information) system, or an inadequate internal control procedure might affect expected returns. Cf. Basel Committee, 'Risk Management Guidelines for Derivatives' (1994), p. 14, http://www.bis.org/publ/bcbsc211.htm (accessed 24 March 2023); International Organization of Securities Commissions (IOSCO), 'Operational and Financial Risk Management Control Mechanisms for Over-the-Counter Derivatives Activities of Regulated Securities Firms', Report of the Technical Committee (1994), p. 3, https://www.iosco.org/publications/?subsection=public_reports (accessed 27 June 2022). See more recently, e.g. Maria Demertzis and Guntram Wolff, 'Hybrid and Cyber Security Threats and the EU's Financial System' (2020) 6 Journal of Financial Regulation 306 (Demertzis and Wolff, 'Hybrid and Cyber Security Threats').

[11] Cf. Demertzis and Wolff, 'Hybrid and Cyber Security Threats' (n 10), 306, 308–310.

[12] See, e.g. European Systemic Risk Board (ESRB), 'Systemic Cyber Risk' (February 2020), https://www.esrb.europa.eu/pub/pdf/reports/esrb.report200219_systemiccyberrisk~101a09685e.en.pdf (accessed 24 March 2023).

function as risk managers and loss absorbers, CCPs manage and transmit large volumes of cash and other valuable assets, for example, securities. This turns CCPs into plausible targets for cyberattacks that are motivated by the prospect of financial gain. Second, unlike dealers in non-centrally cleared OTC derivatives markets, who only have partial insight into the exposures of their counterparties (i.e. they only see the transactions in which they are involved), CCPs possess information on the full and accumulated exposures of all clearing members for all products cleared through the CCP.[13] The fact that CCPs hold confidential information on the transactions and positions of all clearing members means, once more, that they are plausible targets for cyberattacks. Third, the centrality of CCPs in the financial system (as counterparty in every centrally cleared transaction) means that CCPs are a likely target for cyberattacks that aim to incite financial instability or market disruption. More generally, the operational and financial connections of CCPs with clearing participants, trading venues, central banks, trade repositories, and other financial market infrastructures (FMIs) contribute to the attractiveness of CCPs as targets for cyberattacks.[14]

Furthermore, to the extent that the novel technologies discussed elsewhere in this chapter and associated automation might make further inroads into centrally cleared OTC derivatives markets, it may be expected that CCPs will become still more exposed to cyber risks.

2.1.2 Effects of cyber risk materialization at CCPs

Although it is clear that operational distress at a CCP arising from the materialization of cyber risk might—as all other forms of distress at a CCP—produce ripple effects for directly or indirectly connected entities and the financial system at large, the operational interlinkage between CCPs and the institutions mentioned also means that the materialization of cyber risk at a CCP might *directly* affect the interlinked institutions. From this perspective, cyber risk constitutes a prime example of a source of systemic risk.[15] However, different from more traditional emanations of systemic risk that depend on interconnectedness between financial market participants, cyber risk is not necessarily commensurate with the importance or size of the connected entity, meaning that small service providers to the CCP might constitute as big a threat to the CCP as the critical

---

[13] In this context, it must be recalled that CCPs may also require their clearing members to submit certain information that is not directly related to the cleared transactions, for instance, mandatory reporting of large proprietary or customer trades. See, e.g. 17 Code of Federal Regulations (CFR) § 39.13(h)(2); 7 USC § 7a-1(c)(2)(M); 17 CFR §39.22. Cf. Bob Hills, David Rule, Sarah Parkinson, and Chris Young, 'Central Counterparty Clearing Houses and Financial Stability' [1999] Financial Stability Review 122, 128.

[14] Cf. ESRB, 'Systemic Cyber Risk' (n 12).

[15] Cf. ESRB, 'Systemic Cyber Risk' (n 12), p. 39; Emanuel Kopp, Lincoln Kaffenberger, and Christopher Wilson, 'Cyber Risk, Market Failures, and Financial Stability' (2017) IMF Working Paper No. 17/185, p. 7 (Kopp et al., 'Cyber Risk, Market Failures, and Financial Stability'). The study of how risks may originate and behave within a system of interrelated nodes is not in any way restricted to the financial—or even wider, economic—system. Any type of system (e.g. an ecosystem) can be subject to emanations of systemic risk and, indeed, economic scholarship assessing systemic risk heavily draws on notions that were first developed in other sciences, for instance, network theory in biology and computer sciences. See, e.g. John Kambhu, Scott Weidman, and Neel Krishnan (eds), 'New Directions for Understanding Systemic Risk', (Report FRBNY and NAS Conference 18–19 May 2006)' (2007) 13(2) Economic Policy Review 1, 25–29.

market participants or service providers to which the CCP is connected.[16] Be that as it may, if multiple CCPs rely on the same critical third-party service provider (e.g. a cloud service provider), a single source may be the origin of systemic risk and risk propagation in the financial system. This was reflected in the 2021 CCP Stress Test executed by the European Securities and Markets Authority (ESMA), in which the operational risk component focused on events affecting third-party entities on which CCPs rely to provide their services.[17]

2.1.3 Regulatory and supervisory responses

It appears hard to comprehensively define which group of people or entities might be interested in launching cyberattacks against CCPs. This must not necessarily be problematic as adequate responses or anticipative actions in relation to cyber risks should address or anticipate these risks in a manner that proves effective independent of the source from which the cyber risk is, or might be, arising. At the same time, it should be recognized that cyberattacks are typically executed by sophisticated perpetrators and that cyber risk has a highly dynamic nature.[18] Hence, it may be exceedingly difficult to anticipate and prevent the precise ways in which CCPs may become subject to cyberattacks. Against this backdrop, existing policy and regulatory guidance on the containment of cyber risk within CCPs requires CCPs to develop a roadmap that can be used in case of cyber risk materialization but does not exhaustively prescribe the contingencies that CCPs have to anticipate or the conditions that have to be satisfied.

For instance, the Principles for Financial Market Infrastructures (PFMIs) from the Committee on Payments and Market Infrastructures (CPMI)[19] and the International Organization of Securities Commissions (IOSCO),[20] which outline high-level principles for financial market infrastructures such as CCPs, touch upon cyber risk in various principles[21] but do not spell out in detail how cyber risk to CCPs should precisely be mitigated.[22] In 2016, CPMI and IOSCO issued a document that complements

---

[16] Committee on Payments and Market Infrastructure (CPMI)–IOSCO, 'Guidance on Cyber Resilience for Financial Market Infrastructures' (June 2016), p. 4, https://www.bis.org/cpmi/publ/d146.pdf (accessed 24 March 2023) (CPMI–IOSCO, 'Guidance on Cyber Resilience').

[17] ESMA, 'Final Report: Framework for the 2021 ESMA Stress Test Exercise for Central Counterparties', ESMA91-372-1367 (7 June 2021), p. 24, https://www.esma.europa.eu/sites/default/files/library/esma91-372-1367_framework_for_the_2021_ccp_st_exercise.pdf (accessed 24 March 2023).

[18] Kopp et al., 'Cyber Risk, Market Failures, and Financial Stability' (n 15), p. 5.

[19] At the time of the adoption of the principles, the CPMI was known as the Committee on Payment and Settlement Systems (CPSS). The CPMI is an international standard setter located in Basel that articulates recommendations with respect to the regulation of payment, clearing, and settlement arrangements in global financial markets. The CPMI is administratively supported by the Bank for International Settlements (BIS), which is an international standard setter that is mainly active in the field of prudential banking regulation.

[20] IOSCO is an international standard setter located in Madrid that articulates recommendations with respect to capital markets regulation. See, for a recent contribution on the role of IOSCO, e.g.: Jean-Paul Servais, 'The International Organization of Securities Commissions (IOSCO) and the New International Financial Architecture: What Role for IOSCO in the Development and Implementation of Cross-Border Regulation and Equivalence?' (2020) 17 European Company and Financial Law Review 3.

[21] See CPSS–IOSCO, 'Principles for Financial Market Infrastructures' (April 2012), https://www.bis.org/cpmi/publ/d101a.pdf (accessed 24 March 2023) (CPSS–IOSCO, 'Principles for Financial Market Infrastructures')—see, e.g. Principle 2 (Governance), Principle 3 (Framework for the comprehensive management of risks), Principle 8 (Settlement finality), Principle 17 (Operational risk), and Principle 20 (FMI links).

[22] Cf. also the eight elements that were identified by the G7 as fundamental for the cybersecurity of the financial sector (a cybersecurity strategy and framework, a clear governance structure, a risk and control assessment,

the PFMIs with more specific guidance on cyber resilience for FMIs.[23] Although this guidance provides additional detail on how FMIs are expected to deal with cyber risk, it does not impose additional standards that go beyond the standards outlined in the PFMIs and remains rather high level.[24]

Along a similar vein, in the specific context of the European Union (EU), the European Market Infrastructure Regulation (EMIR)[25] contains a range of provisions that touch upon the resilience of IT systems and the mitigation of cyber risk.[26] However, these provisions do not adopt a highly prescriptive approach with respect to how CCPs should precisely mitigate and respond to cyber risk. In line with the internationally agreed principles touched upon above, these provisions aim to guarantee that CCPs put in place adequate roadmaps to prevent the materialization of cyber risk to the extent possible and, if needed, respond swiftly to any materialization of cyber risk.

2.1.4 DORA

In 2020, as part of the *digital finance package*,[27] the European Commission issued a proposal for a new regulation on the digital operational resilience of the financial sector, generally referred to as the Digital Operational Resilience Act (DORA).[28] DORA, which builds upon internationally recognized technical standards and industry best practices[29] and seeks to harmonize the currently fragmented legislative and

---

monitoring processes, timely responses, responsible recovery, information sharing, and continuous learning). See G7, 'Fundamental Elements of Cybersecurity for the Financial Sector' (October 2016), https://www.ecb.europa.eu/paym/pol/shared/pdf/G7_Fundamental_Elements_Oct_2016.pdf (accessed 24 March 2023).

[23] CPMI–IOSCO, 'Guidance on Cyber Resilience' (n 16).

[24] Cf. CPMI–IOSCO, Guidance on Cyber Resilience' (n 16), p. 4.

[25] EMIR (n 3).

[26] See EMIR (n 3), Arts 26 (general provisions in relation to the organizational requirements for CCPs), 34 (business continuity), and 35 (outsourcing) as well as Commission Delegated Regulation (EU) No. 153/2013 of 19 December 2012 supplementing Regulation (EU) No. 648/2012 of the European Parliament and of the Council with regard to regulatory technical standards on requirements for central counterparties, [2013] OJ L52/41, Arts 9 (information technology systems), 17 (strategy and policy), 18 (business impact analysis), 19 (disaster recovery), 20 (testing and monitoring), 21 (maintenance), 22 (crisis management), and 23 (communication) (EMIR RTS).

[27] The digital finance package was adopted by the European Commission on 24 September 2020 and, in addition to the Proposal for a Regulation of the European Parliament and of the Council on digital operational resilience for the financial sector and amending Regulations (EC) No. 1060/2009, (EU) No. 648/2012, (EU) No. 600/2014 and (EU) No. 909/2014 (24 September 2020), COM/2020/595 final (DORA), consists of the following proposals: Proposal for a Regulation of the European Parliament and of the Council on Markets in Crypto-assets, and amending Directive (EU) No. 2019/1937 (24 September 2020), COM/2020/593 final (generally referred to as MiCA); Proposal for a Regulation of the European Parliament and of the Council on a pilot regime for market infrastructures based on distributed ledger technology (24 September 2020), COM/2020/594 final (generally referred to as the DLT Pilot Regime); and Proposal for a Directive of the European Parliament and of the Council amending Directives 2006/43/EC, 2009/65/EC, 2009/138/EU, 2011/61/EU, EU/2013/36, 2014/65/EU, (EU) 2015/2366 and EU/2016/2341 (24 September 2020), COM/2020/596 final. However, MiCA and the DLT Pilot Regime are not primarily addressing the issues identified in the clearing space. See also, more generally, Proposal for a Directive of the European Parliament and of the Council on measures for a high common level of cybersecurity across the Union, repealing Directive (EU) No. 2016/1148 (16 December 2020), COM/2020/823 final (generally referred to as the NIS 2 Directive—NIS refers to network and information systems).

[28] Proposal for a Regulation of the European Parliament and of the Council on digital operational resilience for the financial sector and amending Regulations (EC) No. 1060/2009, (EU) No. 648/2012, (EU) No. 600/2014 and (EU) No. 909/2014 (24 September 2020), COM/2020/595 final.

[29] Cf. DORA Proposal (n 27).

regulatory framework for digital operational resilience and ICT security in the EU financial sector.[30] To that end, the draft regulation contains principles and rules on ICT risk management, ICT-related incidents (management, classification, and reporting), digital operational resilience testing (including requirements on threat-led penetration testing (TLPT)), management of ICT third-party risk (including an oversight framework for critical third-party service providers), and information-sharing arrangements.[31] If adopted, these rules and principles will apply to CCPs.[32]

Since DORA is a financial sector-wide legislative initiative, the question arises how the principles and rules from DORA relate to the CCP-specific framework from EMIR. Indeed, the current text of EMIR and its delegated regulations already contain provisions that directly or indirectly touch upon the resilience of IT systems and the mitigation of cyber security risk.[33] Although many DORA requirements are more granular than the ones embedded in EMIR, the DORA requirements generally do not seem to produce inconsistencies with the EMIR requirements for CCPs. In addition to material requirements, DORA also seeks to include two explicit references to DORA in the EMIR requirements for CCPs.[34] Through the inclusion of such references, tier 2, third-country CCPs will be required to comply with the DORA requirements through their obligation to comply with EMIR.[35] Problematically, however, DORA also seeks to delete the second sentence of EMIR, Art. 34(1).[36] This sentence currently reads as follows: '[the business continuity policy and disaster recovery plan] shall at least allow for the recovery of all transactions at the time of disruption to allow the CCP to continue to operate with certainty and to complete settlement on the scheduled date'.[37]

---

[30] Cf. DORA Proposal (n 27), recital 8.

[31] See DORA Proposal (n 27), chapters II–VI.

[32] See DORA Proposal (n 27), Art. 2(1)(g).

[33] See n 26.

[34] First, EMIR (n 3), Art.26, which contains the general provisions in relation to the organizational requirements for CCPs, would be amended to reflect that CCPs have to comply with the provisions of DORA and no longer with the generic adequacy requirement for CCP IT systems that currently lies embedded in EMIR, Art. 26(6) (DORA Proposal (n 27), Art. 53(1)). Second, EMIR, Art. 34, which sets out the principles on CCP business continuity, would be amended to specify that CCPs are required to adopt ICT business continuity and disaster recovery plans set up in accordance with DORA as part of their more general business continuity policy and disaster recovery plans under EMIR (DORA Proposal, Art. 53(2)).

[35] It should also be noted that the proposed amendments to EMIR (n 3) will also produce effects for the interpretation of EMIR RTS (n 26). The inclusion of explicit references to DORA (n 27) in level one appears to mean that the interpretation of the corresponding level two provisions would have to occur in accordance with DORA. However, DORA does not propose to make any amendments to Commission Delegated Regulation (EU) No. 2020/1304, which outlines the regime of so-called 'comparable compliance' for tier 2 third-country CCPs (Commission Delegated Regulation (EU) No. 2020/1304 of 14 July 2020 supplementing Regulation (EU) No. 648/2012 of the European Parliament and of the Council with regard to the minimum elements to be assessed by ESMA when assessing third-country CCPs' requests for comparable compliance and the modalities and conditions of that assessment, OJ L305/13). Currently, Commission Delegated Regulation (EU) 2020/1304, Art. 3 stipulates that ESMA shall grant comparable compliance with respect to EMIR (n 3), Art. 26(3) where the tier 2 CCP employs appropriate and proportionate systems, resources, and procedures. Since, upon adoption of DORA, the requirement in EMIR, Art. 26(3) will explicitly refer to ICT systems managed in accordance with DORA for both EU CCPs and tier 2 CCPs, the question arises whether it might be appropriate to also reflect this requirement in the context of comparable compliance for tier 2 CCPs. Along the same lines, the question arises whether the proposed explicit reference in EMIR, Art. 34 to ICT business continuity and disaster recovery plans set up in accordance with DORA warrants an amendment of the regime of comparable compliance for tier 2 CCPs.

[36] DORA Proposal (n 27), Art. 53(2).

[37] The more detailed provisions on the EMIR (n 3) business continuity policy and disaster recovery plan lie embedded in EMIR RTS (n 26), Arts 17–23.

The deletion of this sentence seems to have been proposed because a similar requirement has been included in DORA, Art. 11(3)(2), which deals with back-up policies and recovery methods for ICT systems. Although this DORA requirement will be applicable to CCPs through a proposed cross-reference in EMIR,[38] it appears that the proposed relocation of the second sentence of EMIR, Art. 34(1) from EMIR to DORA will relax the regulatory and supervisory requirements for EU and tier 2 CCPs in terms of the recovery time objective (RTO) that currently lies embedded in the second sentence of EMIR, Art. 34(1). Indeed, while the relocation of the cited provision from EMIR to DORA would mean that ICT recovery plans still have to comply with this requirement, it appears that this requirement would no longer apply to aspects of the business continuity and disaster recovery plan that are not related to ICT. Viewed from this angle, the proposed change appears to run contrary to Principle 17 of the PFMIs (operational risk), which requires, among other things, that the FMI's business continuity plan is designed to enable the FMI to complete settlement by the end of the day of the disruption, even in case of extreme circumstances.[39]

2.2 Environmental Risk

In the context of financial markets, environmental risk refers to the exposure of financial institutions or the financial sector at large 'to activities that may potentially cause or be affected by environmental degradation [...] and the loss of ecosystem services'.[40] This environmental risk may either take the form of physical risk (e.g. extreme weather events adversely affecting the CCP itself or the wider economic activity)[41] or transition risk. The latter type of risk could arise from policy initiatives trying to combat environmental degradation or the loss of ecosystem services (e.g. a ban or restriction for financial institutions to hold certain types of financial instruments) or the emergence of new technologies, such as the development and promotion of green technologies that adversely affect the value of non-green business models.[42] As such, the materialization of physical environmental risk might constitute the trigger for the materialization of transition risk, for example, through the policy responses to the materialization of physical risk. At the outset, it should also be noted that environmental risk is broader than climate risk in that it encapsulates risks that do not directly originate from climate change, for example, certain natural disasters.

[38] See n 34 and accompanying text.
[39] CPSS–IOSCO, 'Principles for Financial Market Infrastructures' (n 21), p. 94.
[40] Network for Greening the Financial System (NGFS), 'Guide for Supervisors: Integrating Climate-Related and Environmental Risks into Prudential Supervision' (May 2020), p. 9, https://www.ngfs.net/sites/default/files/medias/documents/ngfs_guide_for_supervisors.pdf (accessed 24 March 2023).
[41] Physical risk may either be acute (e.g. a flood) or chronical (e.g. global warming).
[42] Non-green business models could include CCP business models that heavily depend on the clearing of non-green asset classes, such as oil futures or gas contracts.

As outlined in the February 2022 call for evidence by ESMA on the approach to climate risk stress testing for CCPs, the impact of environmental risk for centrally cleared OTC derivatives markets might manifest itself along various lines.[43]

2.2.1 Direct implications of operational risk materialization

First, the operations of CCPs, clearing participants, and connected FMIs could be directly affected by the materialization of environmental risk that takes the form of physical risk. In other words, the operations of CCPs and the entities with which they interact should be resilient to extreme events such as climate events. Practically, this means that CCPs and connected entities should be able to activate appropriate operational back-up measures (e.g. back-up facilities) upon the materialization of this type of environmental risk.

2.2.2 Risk model implications

Second, the risk models of CCPs and clearing participants, as well as supervisory scrutiny of these risk models, should account for the potential materialization of environmental risk. Although existing CCP risk models may be expected to be resilient to environmental risk materialization that gradually moves asset prices over time (transition risk),[44] it is not self-evident that existing CCP risk models are appropriately tailored to the materialization of sudden and extreme market shocks arising from environmental risk materialization (physical risk).

Naturally, the impact of environmental risk on risk calibration will differ per type of derivative contract. It may, for instance, be expected that commodity and energy derivatives will be most directly affected. The impact that environmental risk could produce on energy derivatives was painfully illustrated by the February 2021 Texas winter storm (a so-called 'freak weather' event), which led to skyrocketing energy prices in Texas.[45] Against this background, it must be noted that the range of climate-related financial instruments submitted for central clearing to CCPs is broadening.[46] Nevertheless, it is also necessary to examine the potential risk management implications for types of derivatives and markets for which the direct link with the materialization of environmental risk is less straightforward or self-evident. For instance, credit default swaps referencing insurance companies—or, more generally, companies—could be heavily affected by the acute materialization of environmental risk, for example, a hurricane. Even more generally, the materialization of environmental risk can be expected to

---

[43] ESMA, 'Call for Evidence: An Approach to Climate Risk Stress Testing of Central Counterparties', ESMA91-372-1785 (23 February 2022), https://www.esma.europa.eu/sites/default/files/library/esma91-372-1785_call_for_evidence_on_ccp_climate_stress_tests.pdf (accessed 24 March 2023) (ESMA, 'Call for Evidence').

[44] In the long run, CCPs may, for instance, be obliged to require additional collateral from their clearing members if certain assets that are posted as collateral and are connected to 'brown' industries drop in value due to decreased market demand for these assets. Cf. ESMA, 'Call for Evidence' (n 43), p. 19.

[45] Swati Verma and Christian Schmollinger, 'Texas Power Prices Spike as Deadly Cold Wave Overwhelms Grid', *Reuters* (17 February 2021), https://www.reuters.com/business/energy/texas-power-prices-spike-deadly-cold-wave-overwhelms-grid-2021-02-17 (accessed 24 March 2023).

[46] European Association of Clearing Houses (EACH), 'Climate Risk and CCP Risk Management' (February 2021), p. 6, https://www.eachccp.eu/wp-content/uploads/2021/02/EACH-Paper-Climate-Risk-and-CCP-Risk-Management-Feb-2021.pdf (accessed 24 March 2023).

move prices in financial markets and, hence, indirectly affect the pricing of derivative contracts.

Naturally, the question arises how CCPs, clearing participants, and supervisors should incorporate environmental risk in their risk models. At the most general level, there appear to exist two potential solutions. Under the so-called single materiality approach, environmental risk is directly or indirectly factored in through traditional risk categories such as counterparty credit risk, market risk, or operational risk. Under the double materiality approach, on the other hand, environmental risk is treated as a risk category that is distinct from the traditional risk categories. The precise incorporation of environmental risk in risk models would be practically translated into, for example, initial margin calibrations, default fund contributions, and capital requirements. Regardless of the approach ultimately followed, difficulties can be expected to arise with the quantification of environmental risk because many of its emanations in the form of physical risk are connected to the occurrence of unprecedented events. This forward-looking nature creates frictions with the traditionally more backward-looking approach for risk calibration, which is largely based on historical data. Furthermore, the usage of imprecise hypothetical data could produce undesired effects through, for example, initial margin requirements.

2.2.3 Business strategy implications

Third, in addition to the risk model considerations outlined above, environmental risk may also heavily affect business strategies in the market for centrally cleared OTC derivatives, especially in the long run, for example, if transition risk (gradually) materializes. Indeed, market forces (e.g. investor behaviour) or policy interventions could lead to the phasing out of certain product lines connected to 'brown' assets and the emergence of new types of derivatives connected to 'green' assets.[47]

2.2.4 CCPs as drivers of transition?

Fourth, the question arises whether regulatory requirements or supervisory expectations addressed at CCPs should aim to incentivize or support the transition of the real economy and financial system towards a more sustainable model. In our view, it is for legislators and governments to decide what the concrete policy responses to the threats of environmental risk materialization should be. Nevertheless, financial supervisors have a well-established interest in ensuring that the markets and institutions that they supervise are resilient to (i) the materialization of environmental risk and (ii) transition in economic models, potentially instigated by policy changes from legislators and governments.[48] Additionally, courts could also play a

---

[47] ESMA, 'Call for Evidence' (n 43), p. 18.

[48] Cf. Mark Carney, 'Breaking the Tragedy of the Horizon—Climate Change and Financial Stability', speech at Lloyd's of London (29 September 2015), p. 12, https://www.bankofengland.co.uk/-/media/boe/files/speech/2015/breaking-the-tragedy-of-the-horizon-climate-change-and-financial-stability.pdf?la=en&hash=7C67E78565186 2457D99511147C7424FF5EA0C1A (accessed 24 March 2023).

role as drivers of transition within the centrally cleared OTC derivatives markets and beyond.[49]

2.3 Novel Technologies

2.3.1 Innovation

In recent years, research initiatives have increasingly focused on the implications that the adoption of distributed ledger technology (DLT)[50] and other relatively novel technologies may have for the financial sector and its regulation.[51] For a detailed analysis of the role that DLT may play for CCPs, we refer to Chapter 17 ('Potential Impact of the Distributed Ledger Technology on OTC Derivatives Markets' by Randy Priem) in this volume. In this section, we limit ourselves to the exploration of the more general implications that the adoption of novel technologies might produce for CCPs, especially regarding the technologies that leverage digitization, automation, and decentralization. At the outset, it must be noted that many of the innovations that we see in today's financial markets partially follow from the inventive reapplication of techniques that have been known for ages, such as cryptography.[52]

There are at least four ways in which the market for centrally cleared OTC derivatives could be impacted by the emergence and adoption of these novel technologies.

2.3.2 Novel assets

First, through the application of new technologies, novel variants of financial and non-financial assets are being created. These assets can take different forms, ranging from cryptocurrencies in the narrow sense of the word to digital assets in the broadest sense. Identical to traditional financial and non-financial assets, these newly created assets— or the fluctuation of their prices—can be directly or indirectly referenced in derivatives that are submitted to CCPs for central clearing. This creates challenges for both CCPs and supervisors as these assets might have risk profiles that are difficult to square with existing risk models. Furthermore, since some of the derivatives definitions in the Markets in Financial Instruments Directive II (MiFID II), Annex I refer to 'cash

---

[49] See generally, e.g. the 'Shell case': The Hague District Court 26 May 2021, C/09/571932/HA ZA 19-379, ECLI:NL:RBDHA:2021:5339, https://uitspraken.rechtspraak.nl/inziendocument?id=ECLI:NL:RBDHA:2021:5339 (accessed 24 March 2023).

[50] Although the notions of DLT and blockchain are often used interchangeably, they are not synonyms. Blockchain is a specific type of DLT. See Paul Klimos, 'The Distributed Ledger Technology: A Potential Revamp for Financial Markets?' (2018) 13 Capital Markets Law Journal 194, 196 (fn 7).

[51] See, e.g. Evariest Callens, 'Financial Instruments Entail Liabilities: Ether, Bitcoin, and Litecoin Do Not' (2021) 40 Computer Law and Security Review 1; Emilios Avgouleas and Aggelos Kiayias, 'The Promise of Blockchain Technology for Global Securities and Derivatives Markets: The New Financial Ecosystem and the 'Holy Grail' of Systemic Risk Containment' (2019) 20 European Business Organization Law Review 81 (Avgouleas and Kiayias, 'The Promise of Blockchain Technology'); Philipp Maume and Mathias Fromberger, 'Regulation of Initial Coin Offerings: Reconciling U.S. and E.U. Securities Laws' (2019) 19 Chicago Journal of International Law 548; Philipp Hacker and Chris Thomale, 'Crypto-Securities Regulation: ICOs, Token Sales and Cryptocurrencies under EU Financial Law' (2018) 15 European Company and Financial Law Review 645.

[52] Cryptography has been around for thousands of years; see, e.g. Donald Davies, 'A Brief History of Cryptography' (1997) 2(2) Information Security Technical Report 14.

settlement' and because MiFID II does not contain a definition of the notions 'cash' or 'cash settlement'[53] it is unclear whether derivatives settled in, for example, stablecoins would qualify as cash-settled derivatives. If not, these types of derivatives would escape the application of the legislative rules that employ the MiFID II derivatives notion to describe their scope of application.

2.3.3 Optimization of risk management processes

Second, new technologies hold out the potential to optimize or automate existing risk management—and potentially loss absorption—processes in centrally and non-centrally cleared OTC derivatives markets.[54] For instance, in DLT models where settlement is not instantaneous and clearing might thus play a role during the settlement cycle period, smart contracts could possibly change the way in which collateral and netting are managed. CCPs could, for example, make margin calls automatically executable in the accounts of their clearing members by encoding smart contracts in the ledger. Similarly, smart contracts could be used to execute close-out netting automatically on a 24/7 basis (also referred to as 'auto-liquidation') upon predefined events taking place, potentially leading to accelerated and simultaneous defaults across market participants and infrastructures.

Still, although the adoption of novel technologies could strengthen risk management operations at CCPs, one must probably also ask the question to what extent current inefficiencies in the provision of clearing (and settlement) services actually follow from technological constraints and whether much of the technology that would be required to improve clearing and settlement processes might not already be available. For instance, with respect to the settlement cycle of securities, it is most likely already technologically feasible to move from T + 2 (or T + 1) to T + 0. Furthermore, whilst more immediate settlement through the application of novel technologies would reduce counterparty risk (assuming sufficient liquidity on securities and cash accounts), this might have an impact on market liquidity since the benefit of netting would be lost, with possible adverse consequences on the price formation mechanism and on the ability of financial markets to absorb supply or demand shocks.

A flipside of the potential risk management efficiencies introduced by the adoption of novel technologies is that the new technologies might also introduce additional risks. For instance, the increased usage of cloud service providers (CSPs) could mean that—to the extent that CCPs or their clearing members outsource core services to a

---

[53] See Annex I Directive 2014/65/EU of the European Parliament and of the Council of 15 May 2014 on markets in financial instruments and amending Directive 2002/92/EC and Directive 2011/61/EU, [2014] OJ L 173/349 (MiFID II).

[54] See, e.g. Christian P. Fries and Peter Kohl-Landgraf, 'Smart Derivative Contracts: Detaching Transactions from Counterparty Credit Risk (Specification, Parametrisation, Valuation)', Working Paper (15 April 2018), https://papers.ssrn.com/sol3/papers.cfm?abstract_id=3163074 (accessed 24 March 2023). Cf. Dan Awrey, 'Split Derivatives: Inside the World's Most Misunderstood Contract' (2019) 36 Yale Journal on Regulation 495, 566.

single CSP—the outage at a CSP may simultaneously affect multiple CCPs and clearing members, potentially inducing, for example, failures to deliver collateral in satisfaction of initial margin calls.[55]

2.3.4 Role and position of CCPs

Third, unlike in previous rounds of innovation, the technical propositions that are currently making inroads in centrally cleared OTC derivatives markets have the potential to affect the whole value chain for the clearing of derivatives and could fundamentally change how clearing services may be provided in the future. In other words, in the long run, the role and position of CCPs in the financial market ecosystem could be profoundly affected through the adoption of novel technologies; that is, through the implementation of novel technologies, the market structure for clearing services might shift towards more modular or layered arrangements, with possibly a close, or even full, integration of trading and clearing whilst potentially segregating risk management and loss absorption functions. In any case, however, it seems that a centralized function (supported by dedicated natural persons) would remain a prerequisite to perform the type and quality of risk management services (including judgement calls, where relevant) that CCPs currently provide, although it is not self-evident that this would have to be a CCP as we currently know it.

One element that currently underpins the risk management and loss absorption functions of CCPs in OTC derivatives markets is the legal interposition of CCPs through either novation or open offer.[56] Upon CCP interposition, two mirroring legally binding contracts come into existence between the CCP and the respective entities on both sides of the transaction, either through novation or open offer. Ultimately, CCP interposition and the legally effective assumption of counterparty risk by a CCP pivotally depends on the presence of a separate (and capitalized) legal entity. The presence of a separate legal entity is also a prerequisite for the application of the current legislative and regulatory framework. Indeed, the clearing obligation under EMIR for OTC derivatives, for instance, can only be satisfied by market participants through the usage of a CCP in the sense of EMIR, and a CCP in the sense of EMIR must, under the current state of the law, necessarily be a legal person.[57] To our understanding, under the current state of the law, it is not self-evident that the functionality of a separate legal entity and, hence, CCP interposition can be delivered through automatized technologies or processes alone.[58] A DLT scheme

---

[55] Carolina Asensio, Antoine Bouveret, and Alexander Harris, 'Cloud Outsourcing and Financial Stability Risks', in ESMA (ed.), 'Report on Trends, Risks and Vulnerabilities', ESMA50-165-1842 (September 2021), p. 66, https://www.esma.europa.eu/sites/default/files/library/esma50-165-1842_trv2-2021.pdf (accessed 24 March 2023).

[56] Cf. e.g. Christian Chamorro-Courtland, 'Counterparty Substitution in Central Counterparty (CCP) Systems' (2010) 25 Banking and Finance Law Review 519.

[57] EMIR (n 3), Art. 2(1).

[58] Cf. Mark Manning, Maxwell Sutton, and Justin Zhu, 'Distributed Ledger Technology in Securities Clearing and Settlement: Some Issues' [2016] 3 Finsia Journal of Applied 30, 31. Differently, Avgouleas and Kiayias, 'The Promise of Blockchain Technology' (n 51), 81, 84 (arguing that DLT-operated liquidity and risk pools will compete with CCPs for clearing business).

geared to provide central clearing functions would need to comply with existing EU regulatory requirements, in particular the need for an authorized legal entity acting as operator as well as other requirements, for example, capital requirements; open-access rules; rules of conduct, segregation, and portability; or reporting to trade repositories. Similarly, a DLT scheme intended to be used for the bilateral clearing of OTC derivative transactions would have to be structured in such a way that it would allow parties to the trade to comply with applicable EMIR obligations such as risk mitigations techniques.

Increasingly, new market entrants may challenge some of the cornerstones of the post-2008 financial crisis clearing ecosystem, which relies on CCPs and tiered clearing arrangements differentiating between direct clearing members and their clients. Some new market entrants aim to enter the traditional clearing segment by trying to position themselves within the existing regulatory perimeter whilst challenging the existing intermediation model in central clearing, whereas others explore the boundaries of existing clearing regulation. Entities that are offering direct clearing models under a CCP licence are a good example of the first group of market actors.[59] The adoption of such models implies a move from a risk management model with two layers of loss absorption (clearing members and CCP) to a model with only one layer of loss absorption (CCP). At the other end of the spectrum, crypto-exchanges employing clearinghouse-style models to facilitate 'clearing' between their members whilst 'protecting' settlement through some form of insurance regimes constitute a prime example of the group of market participants that is exploring the boundaries of applicability of existing clearing regulation.[60]

2.3.5 Interoperability

Fourth, if different DLT models were to be applied by different clusters of market participants or FMIs, there will be issues of interoperability causing fragmentation. Adoption of a common DLT solution, or at least interoperable DLT protocols, across the financial market would solve interconnectivity issues from a purely technical perspective but may raise issues of contagion. Further, the possibility of technical interconnectivity could revive efforts towards true interoperability amongst FMIs. However, the persistence of regulatory and practical fragmentation might hamper efforts towards the development of common technical solutions. Finally, there are new service offerings suggesting more integrated trading and settlement.

---

[59] See, e.g. FTX US Derivatives, 'Permissibility and Benefits of Direct Clearing Model under the Commodity Exchange Act and CFTC Regulations', Letter to Commodities Future Trading Commission (CFTC) (8 February 2022), https://sirt.cftc.gov/sirt/sirt.aspx?Topic=CommissionOrdersandOtherActionsAD&Key=47841 (accessed 24 March 2023).

[60] See, e.g. the in-house system of 'Insurance Funds' as employed by Binance, https://www.binance.com/en/support/faq/360033525371 (accessed 24 March 2023).

2.4 Legal Risk

Legal certainty is a precondition for the orderly functioning of financial markets and FMIs. Persisting questions about scope or interpretation of existing legal regimes hamper the safety of the financial system and create uncertainties.

For instance, uncertainty pertains to the suitability of existing rules in EMIR and MiFID II to cover products and services that are based on the new technologies discussed above. One example relates to the above-mentioned usage of clearinghouse-style models in the crypto-industry to 'protect' settlement through mechanisms that resemble insurance regimes. These models appear to challenge the regulatory perimeter of EMIR because the EMIR CCP definition has not been designed to cover clearinghouses that do not legally interpose themselves between the initial counterparties.[61] In other contexts, notions such as 'clearing', 'clearing services', 'activities linked to clearing', 'cash settlement', and 'critical functions' have similarly given rise to uncertainty about the interpretation and application of the existing framework in the context of newly emerging products and services.

Another example of legal uncertainty relates to the fundamental protection of CCPs against systemic risk, which in the EU is meant to be ensured by the Settlement Finality Directive (SFD).[62] Although, arguably, the protection offered by the SFD was initially only intended for payment and securities settlement systems in the strict sense of the word, CCPs have found shelter under the protective regime of the SFD since the inception of the regime.[63] Since the adoption of an amendment in 2009, the text of the SFD also formally recognizes that clearinghouses—including CCPs—may function as system operators in the sense of the directive.[64] Moreover, EMIR now even requires that CCPs only be authorized if they have been designated as a system in the sense of the SFD.[65] However, the wording of the provisions in the SFD that seek to guarantee settlement finality has remained unchanged and thus does not cater specifically to CCPs. In practice, the application of the SFD to the clearing of transactions, which occurs prior to settlement and differs in important aspects from settlement, is ambiguous.[66] For example, it is unclear whether the clearing instructions from clearing participants to CCPs benefit from the SFD finality regime that has been tailored to transfer orders, that is, whether clearing instructions from clearing participants are irrevocable among the parties of a transaction from the moment of the entry in CCP, as determined by its

---

[61] See EMIR (n 3), Art. 2(1).

[62] Directive 98/26/EC of the European Parliament and of the Council of 19 May 1998 on settlement finality in payment and securities settlement systems, [1998] OJ L166/45 (SFD).

[63] Dermot Turing, *Clearing and Settlement in Europe* (Bloomsbury Professional 2012) 188.

[64] See SFD (n 62), Art. 2(p), as introduced by Directive 2009/44/EC of the European Parliament and of the Council of 6 May 2009 amending Directive 98/26/EC on settlement finality in payment and securities settlement systems and Directive 2002/47/EC on financial collateral arrangements as regards linked systems and credit claims, [2009] OJ L146/37.

[65] EMIR (n 3), Art. 17(4)(1).

[66] European Post Trade Forum (EPTF), 'EPTF Report' (15 May 2017), p. 93, https://ec.europa.eu/info/sites/defa ult/files/170515-eptf-report_en.pdf (accessed 24 March 2023) (EPTF, 'EPTF Report').

rules.[67] For reasons of legal certainty, a review of the SFD to address this and other issues may be warranted.[68]

3 Cross-Border Regulatory and Supervisory Approach towards CCPs

3.1 Dichotomy between Markets and Mandates

3.1.1 Global CCPs for OTC derivatives

With some notable exceptions, CCPs that clear OTC derivatives are global in nature.[69] For the following reasons, global markets with global FMIs provide significant efficiencies.

First, from an economic perspective, exposures that are connected to regional circumstances may be best hedged by trading with market participants in other jurisdictions, who are more likely to have offsetting economic exposures.[70] In order for market participants to find each other so that risks may be offset or efficiently hedged, financial markets and clearing infrastructure need to be able to connect different regional market segments. Viewed from this angle, the global character of derivatives markets thus facilitates efficient cross-border risk sharing and redistribution.[71] More generally, risk sharing through derivatives or other financial contracts is a prerequisite for capturing the economic benefits of hedging and diversification.[72]

Second, also from the perspective of the risk management tools that CCPs employ, it is useful to pool risks. That is to say, different risks might cancel out on a net basis, meaning that if they are pooled within a single CCP, risk management measures such as margin requirements and default fund requirements will be lower, reflecting the lower

---

[67] EPTF, 'EPTF Report' (n 66), p. 93. From a purely formal point of view, the SFD (n 62) does not foresee a separate category of clearing systems in the list of notified systems maintained by ESMA. This leads to different national approaches on how to notify CCPs under the SFD, either as a settlement system or under the payment system category for 'embedded payment systems', or they are denied notification all together.

[68] See, for other legal issues with the application of the SFD to CCPs, EPTF, 'EPTF Report' (n 66), p. 93.

[69] Cf. e.g. CFTC, 'Registration with Alternative Compliance for Non-U.S. Derivatives Clearing Organizations', Final rule, 85 FR 67160 (21 October 2020), p. 67189 ('Nations have borders, but markets rarely do. That is certainly the case with the global derivatives markets', reflecting a statement by former CFTC Chairman Tarbert). See, however: John Kiff, Alessandro Gullo, Cory Hillier, and Panagiotis Papapaschalis, 'Applying the Central Clearing Mandate: Different Options for Different Markets', International Monetary Fund (IMF) Working Paper No. 22/14 (28 January 2022), https://www.imf.org/en/Publications/WP/Issues/2022/01/28/Applying-the-Central-Clearing-Mandate-Different-Options-for-Different-Markets-512017 (accessed 24 March 2023) (Kiff et al., 'Applying the Central Clearing Mandate').

[70] Evangelos Benos, Wenqian Huang, Albert J. Menkveld, and Michalis Vasios, 'The Cost of Clearing Fragmentation', Working Paper (22 April 2021), p. 7, https://papers.ssrn.com/sol3/papers.cfm?abstract_id=3397065 (accessed 24 March 2023).

[71] Cf. CPSS, 'Market Structure Developments in the Clearing Industry' (n 2), p. 15.

[72] Cf. Franklin Allen, Elena Carletti, and Xian Gu, 'The Roles of Banks in Financial Systems', in Allen N. Berger, Philip Molyneux, and John O.S. Wilson (eds), *The Oxford Handbook of Banking* (Oxford: Oxford University Press, 2015), pp. 27, 31; Daniel Ladley, 'Contagion and Risk-Sharing on the Inter-Bank Market' (2013) 37 Journal of Economic Dynamics and Control 1384, 1385; Stefano Battiston, Domenico Delli Gatti, Mauro Gallegati, Bruce Greenwald, and Joseph E. Stiglitz, 'Liaisons Dangereuses: Increasing Connectivity, Risk Sharing, and Systemic Risk' (2012) 36 Journal of Economic Dynamics and Control 1121, 1122; Rustam Ibragimov, Dwight Jaffee, and Johan Walden, 'Diversification Disasters' (2011) 99 Journal of Financial Economics 333, 334.

net counterparty risk.[73] This makes the process of central clearing cheaper and, hence, more attractive to clearing participants.

Third, also in a crisis situation (i.e. in the event of one or multiple clearing member default(s)), it might be beneficial to have liquidity centralized because a sufficiently deep liquidity pool in the affected CCP can reduce the cost of the default management process at a CCP; that is, the absence of strong market liquidity for a derivative product may lead to steep discounts on (large) derivative portfolios that have to be sold off in the market, for example, in the event of a clearing member default.[74]

Fourth, within a given market segment, CCPs enjoy economies of scale,[75] that is, a decrease in the average cost of clearing correlates with an increase in the total number of derivatives that is cleared through a CCP.[76] Central clearing of a certain product type requires a substantial investment to commence business activities, but investments are largely unconnected to the number of transactions of the same product type that is channelled through the CCP.[77] Importantly, due to the fact that different types of derivatives have relatively distinct and complex dynamics in terms of market and counterparty risk calibration and management, investments in risk calibration and management can be scaled within a type of product but not necessarily across product types.[78] Therefore, different CCPs tend to exist for different market segments, for example, interest rate derivatives, credit derivatives, repos, etc.

3.1.2 Global CCPs vs local regulatory and supervisory mandates

The global OTC derivatives marketplace and the challenges that it creates for CCPs stand in sharp contrast to the largely decentralized regulatory and supervisory approach towards CCPs, which attributes a primary role to home country regulators and supervisors but might not adequately cater to the concerns of host country regulators and supervisors. More specifically, host country regulators and supervisors might have legitimate concerns about losses (and liquidity strains) being imposed through the risk mutualization mechanisms of the (offshore) CCP on clearing members and clients established in host jurisdictions.

---

[73] Cf. Tanega and Savi, 'Central Clearing Counterparties for OTC-Users' (n 8), 825, 844–845; Heath et al., 'CCPs and Network Stability' (n 8), 217, 219; Duffie and Zhu, 'Does a Central Clearing Counterparty Reduce Counterparty Risk?' (n 7), 74, 75. Cf. Felix B. Chang, 'The Systemic Risk Paradox: Banks and Clearinghouses under Regulation' [2014] Columbia Business Law Review 747, 780 (Chang, 'The Systemic Risk Paradox'); Jiabin Huang, *The Law and Regulation of Central Counterparties* (Oxford: Hart Publishing 2010), pp. 180 *et seq.* (Huang, *The Law and Regulation of Central Counterparties*);

[74] Craig Pirrong, 'The Economics of Central Clearing: Theory and Practice', ISDA Discussion Papers Series (May 2011) nn. 1, 18,https://www.isda.org/a/yiEDE/isdadiscussion-ccp-pirrong.pdf (accessed 24 March 2023); FSB, 'Implementing OTC Derivatives Market Reforms' (25 October 2010), p. 17, https://www.fsb.org/wp-content/uploads/r_101025.pdf (accessed 24 March 2023).

[75] In the most general terms, economies of scale—which are typically catalogued as supply-side scale effects—occur when the average cost per unit decreases as total output increases. See Steven A. Greenlaw and David Shapiro, *Principles of Microeconomics* (Houston: OpenStax, 2018), pp. 23, 174.

[76] Tina P. Hasenpusch, *Clearing Services for Global Markets* (Cambridge: Cambridge University Press, 2009), pp. 225–226; Craig Pirrong, 'Clearing Up Misconceptions on Clearing' (2008) 31(2) Regulation 22, 24.

[77] CPSS, 'Market Structure Developments in the Clearing Industry' (n 2), p. 12.

[78] Cf. Sean J. Griffith, 'Substituted Compliance and Systemic Risk: How to Make a Global Market in Derivatives Regulation' (2014) 98 Minnesota Law Review 1291, 1352.

Although the baseline in most jurisdictions is that CCPs are primarily regulated and supervised in the jurisdiction where they are established, home country regulation and supervision may be supplemented by host country regulation and supervision, especially for CCPs that are deemed to be of systemic or substantial systemic importance for one or more of their host countries. For instance, such approach has traditionally been taken in the United States, where the baseline is that foreign CCPs are subject to full compliance with the US rules and supervision by the CFTC,[79] albeit recently two regulatory regimes have been adopted that allow foreign CCPs to access the US market for clearing services without having to fully submit to US regulation and supervision: alternative compliance[80] and exemption from registration.[81] Similarly, in the EU, after the adoption of EMIR 2.2,[82] third-country CCPs that are deemed systemically important or likely to become systemically important for the financial stability of the EU or of one or more of its member states (tier 2 CCPs) are subject to compliance with parts of EMIR and supervision by ESMA.[83]

3.1.3 Challenges to the current regulatory and supervisory structure

The friction between, on the one hand, increasingly global OTC derivatives markets and CCPs and, on the other hand, local regulatory and supervisory mandates creates multiple present and future challenges. First, in the absence of loss mutualization through a common fiscal backstop, the jurisdiction that has the power to supervise the operations of the CCP—both during periods of relative calm and in a crisis—might not be the jurisdiction that will have to bear (part of or even the bulk of) the financial and economic consequences of financial distress at a CCP.[84] This creates the risk that part of the expenses arising from regulatory or supervisory failure may be imposed on the constituents of jurisdictions other than the CCP's home jurisdiction. Indeed, through the application of the CCP's loss distribution mechanisms, much of the economic fallout of financial distress at a CCP may fall upon the clearing members, which

---

[79] Commodity Exchange Act (CEA), § 5b, 7 USC § 7a-1. See, for the CEA: Pub. L. No. 74-675, 49 Stat. 1491 (1936).

[80] Under alternative compliance, non-systemically important foreign CCPs are allowed to register with the CFTC for the clearing of swaps yet largely 'comply' with US rules through compliance with their home country regulatory regime (17 CFR § 39.51(b)). Importantly, a CCP that obtains registration with the CFTC through alternative compliance may still only provide customer clearing services through registered futures commission merchants. In order to be eligible for alternative compliance, the foreign CCP will have to comply with any requirement that the CFTC imposes, but most importantly, the CCP must be deemed non-systemically important under a double initial margin test (17 CFR § 39.51(a) and (b)).

[81] As an alternative to registration (through alternative compliance or otherwise), the CFTC may decide to exempt a CCP from registration for the clearing of swaps if it finds that the foreign CCP is subject to comparable, comprehensive regulation and supervision by home country authorities (CEA, § 5b(h), 7 USC § 7a-1(h)). The direct implication of such exemption is that the foreign CCP must not observe US rules. Vitally, and crucially different from what is the case for registered CCPs, exempt CCPs are permitted to clear proprietary swaps of US persons and futures commission merchants but may not clear US customer positions (17 CFR, § 39.6(b)(1)).

[82] Regulation (EU) No. 2019/2099 of the European Parliament and of the Council of 23 October 2019 amending Regulation (EU) No. 648/2012 as regards the procedures and authorities involved for the authorisation of CCPs and requirements for the recognition of third-country CCPs, [2019] OJ L322/1.

[83] EMIR (n 3), Art. 25(2b).

[84] Cf. IMF, 'Euro Area Policies: Financial Sector Assessment Program. Technical Note—Supervision and Oversight of Central Counterparties and Central Securities Depositories', IMF Country Report No. 18/227 (July 2018), p. 12, http://www.astrid-online.it/static/upload/imf_/imf_ue_18-227.pdf (accessed 24 March 2023).

may not be established in the same jurisdiction as the CCP. It could even be the case that, in a crisis, the home country supervisor of the CCP will prioritize the interests of the clearing participants and other entities that are established in its jurisdiction.[85]

Second, local supervisory mandates in globalized markets may give rise to regulatory arbitrage.[86] That is to say, if regulatory and supervisory requirements differ per jurisdiction, CCPs—or, more likely, clearing participants—might find it useful to relocate their business in order to take advantage of discrepancies between regulatory and supervisory requirements in different jurisdictions.

Third, even if we were to abstract away from regulatory arbitrage (i.e. if regulatory arbitrage were not to occur), regulatory and supervisory requirements that differ per jurisdiction may distort the level playing field across the CCPs and market participants that are active in the respective jurisdictions.

Fourth, to the extent that CCPs or market participants are obliged to observe regulatory and supervisory requirements from multiple jurisdictions, they may face higher cumulative compliance cost.[87] This could, for instance, be the case if regulatory or supervisory requirements in different jurisdictions differ with respect to the calibration of initial margin or the application of large exposure limits.[88]

Fifth, the regulatory or supervisory requirements in different jurisdictions might conflict; that is, compliance with the requirements from one jurisdiction might make it impossible to simultaneously comply with the requirements from a second jurisdiction.

3.2 Present and Future Mitigation of the Dichotomy

3.2.1 International standards

At present, there are at least two elements that mitigate the dichotomy between global markets and domestic or regional mandates: international standards and CCP colleges. At the September 2013 Saint Petersburg summit, the 'Leaders' of the G20 agreed that 'jurisdictions and regulators should be able to defer to each other when it is justified by the quality of their respective regulatory and enforcement regimes, based on similar outcomes, in a non-discriminatory way, paying due respect to home country

---

[85] The prioritization of domestic interests by national authorities has been witnessed in past crises, for instance, during the banking crisis in Iceland, when domestic activities of failing banks were carved out and transferred to a 'new' bank. See Patrizia Baudino, Jon Thor Sturluson, and Jean-Philippe Svoronos, 'The Banking Crisis in Iceland', FSI Crisis Management Series No. 1 (March 2020), pp. 15 *et seq.*, https://www.bis.org/fsi/fsicms1.pdf (accessed 24 March 2023).

[86] See, for definitions of regulatory arbitrage, Tanega and Savi, 'Central Clearing Counterparties for OTC-Users' (n 8), 825, 865; Alexey Artamonov, 'Cross-Border Application of OTC Derivatives Rules: Revisiting the Substituted Compliance Approach' (2015) 1 Journal of Financial Regulation 206, 208; Frank Partnoy, 'Financial Derivatives and the Costs of Regulatory Arbitrage' (1997) 22 Journal of Corporation Law 21, 227.

[87] Cf. Yesha Yadav and Dermot Turing, 'The Extraterritorial Regulation of Clearinghouses' (2016) 2 Journal of Financial Regulation 21, 25.

[88] For instance, the US regulatory framework only prescribes a liquidation period of one day for non-OTC derivatives (e.g. futures and options), whereas the EU framework in principle requires CCPs to use a minimum liquidation period of two days for non-OTC derivatives. See 17 CFR, § 39.13(g)(2)(ii)(A)–(B); EMIR RTS (n 26), Art. 26(1)(b).

regulation regimes'.[89] In the context of centrally cleared OTC derivatives markets, the existing regulatory and supervisory regimes in major financial market jurisdictions differ in certain aspects of their implementation, yet are based on the same internationally agreed principles and pursue the same objectives. Indeed, as touched upon above, the PFMIs from the CPMI and IOSCO establish a set of high-level principles for financial market infrastructures, including CCPs.[90] These high-level international principles have served as the common baseline and benchmark for the regionally implemented legislative and regulatory frameworks for CCPs. Viewed from this perspective, this type of international standard may, to a certain extent, mitigate the effects of the dichotomy between global centrally cleared OTC derivatives markets and domestic or regional regulatory and supervisory mandates. However, the PFMIs by themselves are, by design, rather high-level in terms of the principles and key expectations. In some instances, this has led to significant differences in interpretations and applications of the PFMIs, as evidenced by the CPMI–IOSCO implementation monitoring reports[91] but also by the different degrees of procyclical performance of margin models in the COVID crisis. Consequently, there is a continuous need for further guidance on identified issues, such as cyber resilience, margin models, auction processes, or CCP recovery and resolution.

3.2.2 CCP colleges

CCP supervisory colleges offer another partial solution to the outlined tension between global markets and local regulatory and supervisory mandates. Different authorities maintain a legitimate interest in the safe and efficient functioning of CCPs, for example, CCP supervisors, market regulators, bank supervisors, central banks, and resolution authorities. This necessitates effective arrangements for the sharing of information and coordination. In many instances, bilateral cooperation arrangements may not suffice in view of the complexity and range of services offered by CCPs. It is against this background that CCP supervisory colleges have come into existence, either as voluntary arrangements organized by the lead CCP supervisor or as mandatory set-ups such as the EMIR colleges.[92] This holds true in a domestic context but even more for regionally or globally active CCPs. Indeed, in line with good international practice,[93] the lead home authorities of certain globally active CCPs have established global colleges for CCPs, which may consist of different layers of involvement depending on the degree of interest of foreign authorities. It must be noted, though, that this is not yet an accepted global best practice.

---

[89] G20, 'G20 Leaders' Declaration St Petersburg' (6 September 2013), n. 71, http://www.g20.utoronto.ca/2013/2013-0906-declaration.html (accessed 24 March 2023).

[90] CPSS–IOSCO, 'Principles for Financial Market Infrastructures' (n 21).

[91] See CPMI–IOSCO, 'Monitoring Implementation of the PFMI' (undated), https://www.bis.org/cpmi/info_mios.htm (accessed 24 March 2023).

[92] See, on EMIR colleges, EMIR (n 3), Art. 18.

[93] Cf. IOSCO, 'Lessons Learned from the Use of Global Supervisory Colleges' (January 2022), https://www.iosco.org/library/pubdocs/pdf/IOSCOPD696.pdf (accessed 24 March 2023).

Supervisory colleges—which were first established in the 1980s for the supervision of banks with cross-border activities[94] and regained traction after the 2008 financial crisis[95]—seek to unite home and host country authorities within a single collegiate body.[96] Hence, supervisory colleges allow for the combination of supervision by a home country supervisor (and possible other domestic authorities) and a more multi-jurisdictional perspective through the involvement of host country authorities in the college.[97] Naturally, since the different national authorities within a CCP college will still strive to protect the interests of the institutions and taxpayers that fall under their jurisdiction, as well as aim to safeguard financial stability in their jurisdictions, supervisory colleges cannot be a substitute for a truly international cooperative mechanism and can only offer an incomplete solution to the challenges in supervision of financial institutions, and in particular globally active FMIs such as CCPs, which are active in different jurisdictions.[98]

Similar to the cooperation amongst involved authorities through CCP supervisory colleges, lead resolution authorities may establish resolution colleges to deal with matters pertaining to CCP resolution. For example, this is required under the EU CCP Recovery and Resolution Regulation (CCPR&R).[99] For CCP resolution, due to the 2017 FSB Guidance on Central Counterparty Resolution and Resolution Planning,[100] there already exists a more robust expectation to establish cross-border crisis management groups for resolution of globally active CCPs, even if not all relevant jurisdictions have yet established relevant resolution authorities and required the establishment of crisis management groups.

3.2.3 Further reflections
In line of the challenges and current partial solutions outlined above, there appears to exist a need to further enhance (i) regulatory and supervisory convergence across CCPs and (ii) domestic and cross-border supervisory architecture. There are also

[94] Duncan E. Alford, 'Supervisory Colleges: The Global Financial Crisis and Improving International Supervisory Coordination' (2010) 24 Emory International Law Review 57, 59–61 (Alford, 'Supervisory Colleges').

[95] See, e.g. Christopher P. Buttigieg, 'Governance of Securities Regulation and Supervision: Quo Vadis Europa' (2015) 21 Columbia Journal of European Law 411, 432; IMF, 'Initial Lessons of the Crisis for the Global Architecture and the IMF' (18 February 2009), p. 9 (n 9), https://www.imf.org/external/np/pp/eng/2009/021809.pdf (accessed 24 March 2023).

[96] See also Regulation (EU) No. 1095/2010 of the European Parliament and of the Council of 24 November 2010 establishing a European Supervisory Authority (European Securities and Markets Authority), amending Decision No. 716/2009/EC and repealing Commission Decision 2009/77/EC, [2010] OJ L331/84, Art. 32 (ESMA Regulation).

[97] Eric J. Pan, 'Challenge of International Cooperation and Institutional Design in Financial Supervision: Beyond Transgovernmental Networks' (2010) 11 Chicago Journal of International Law 24, 274.

[98] Cf. Alford, 'Supervisory Colleges' (n 94), 57, 58.

[99] Regulation (EU) 2021/23 of the European Parliament and of the Council of 16 December 2020 on a framework for the recovery and resolution of central counterparties and amending Regulations (EU) No. 1095/2010, (EU) No. 648/2012, (EU) No. 600/2014, (EU) No. 806/2014 and (EU) No. 2015/2365 and Directives 2002/47/EC, 2004/25/EC, 2007/36/EC, 2014/59/EU and (EU) 2017/1132, [2021] OJ L22/1, Art. 4 (CCP Recovery and Resolution Regulation or CCPR&R).

[100] FSB, 'Guidance on Central Counterparty Resolution and Resolution Planning' (5 July 2017), p. 17 https://www.fsb.org/wp-content/uploads/P050717-1.pdf (accessed 24 March 2023).

considerations on how to enhance transparency of concentration risks across CCPs, clearing members, and clients, as could be seen in the energy markets following the Russian invasion of Ukraine. For CCPs that are systemically important in multiple jurisdictions, further reflections are needed on the most appropriate supervisory architecture. A higher degree of formality in global cooperation mechanisms, including formal powers for all involved authorities and possibly collective decision-making, could possibly be considered in this context. Steps in this direction may be found in existing global oversight arrangements such as for the Society for Worldwide Interbank Financial Telecommunications (SWIFT) or CLS Group.

4 CCP Governance

4.1 CCP Shareholder Structures

Historically, exchanges, CCPs, and other financial market infrastructures have been mutually owned by the (largest) users of the respective market infrastructure (e.g. large banks and investment firms), either directly or through mutually owned market infrastructure groups.[101] Hence, the clearing members of the CCP, who—through loss mutualization mechanisms—had, and have, most at stake if clearing members or the CCP were to fail, were also the shareholders of the CCP, allowing them to determine the overall approach towards risk management at the CCP.[102] However, in between the late 1980s and the beginning of the new millennium, market participants started to perceive their stakes in financial market infrastructure corporations or groups as static—and not sufficiently profitable—assets on their balance sheets.[103] Against this background, clearing members started to sell their participations in CCPs or market infrastructure groups, either through public offerings or private sales to corporate investors.[104] This process is often referred to as the 'demutualization' of CCPs,[105] referring to the fact that demutualized CCPs are no longer mutually owned by clearing members (losses from clearing member default are, of course, still mutualized amongst surviving clearing members in their capacity as non-shareholder clearing members).[106]

---

[101] See, e.g. Erik F. Gerding, 'Remutualization' (2020) 105 Cornell Law Review 797, 800 (Gerding, 'Remutualization'); Paolo Saguato, 'The Ownership of Clearinghouses: When 'Skin in the Game' Is Not Enough, the Remutualization of Clearinghouses' (2017) 34 Yale Journal on Regulation 601, 625 (Saguato, 'The Ownership of Clearinghouses'); Roberta S. Karmel, 'Turning Seats into Shares: Causes and Implications of Demutualization of Stock and Futures Exchanges' (2012) 53 Hastings Law Journal 367, 369.

[102] Yesha Yadav, 'The Problematic Case of Clearinghouses in Complex Markets' (2013) 101 Georgetown Law Journal 387, 414.

[103] Norman, *The Risk Controllers* (n 2), pp. 183–184.

[104] Kristin J. Johnson, 'Governing Financial Markets: Regulating Conflicts' (2013) 88 Washington Law Review 185, 204.

[105] Demutualized CCPs are sometimes referred to as 'for-profit' CCPs. The notion 'for profit' is somewhat misleading as, technically, every CCP is a privately owned for-profit company.

[106] See, e.g. Colleen M. Baker, 'Incomplete Clearinghouse Mandates' (2019) 56 American Business Law Journal 507, 548 (Baker, 'Incomplete Clearinghouse Mandates'); Saguato, 'The Ownership of Clearinghouses' (n 101), 601, 625.

Present shareholder structures of CCPs vary across a spectrum of ownership models.[107] Some CCPs are still largely owned by clearing members, whereas others have effectively demutualized and are now owned by (sometimes publicly traded) financial market infrastructure groups, financial institutions (e.g. hedge funds), or other non-clearing member investors.[108] In recent years, especially after CCP usage had gained momentum through a regulatory push for central clearing through CCPs, clearing members who sold their participations in CCPs have sought other ways to retrieve impact on CCP risk management decisions.[109] This will be discussed in section 4.2.

4.2 Remutualization?

The governance of 'demutualized' CCPs may result in policies or decisions that are not necessarily well aligned with the stakes of the users of the CCP (i.e. the clearing members) and the public.[110] That is to say, non-clearing member investors can be expected to be primarily interested in profits, which may inter alia be attained through higher revenue via less stringent risk management requirements.[111] Clearing member-shareholders, on the other hand, may be more incentivized to plead for rigorous risk management practices with a view to minimizing the (mutualized) losses of a clearing member default. The primary driver behind these diverging incentivizes between different types of investors can be traced back to the structure of the default waterfall and its loss distribution extensions in the CCP recovery and resolution stage. Whereas non-clearing member investors only share in losses arising from clearing member default through the (limited) capital contribution of the CCP to the default waterfall, clearing member-investors have much more funds on the line through the loss-sharing mechanisms in the default waterfall. Hence, an agency problem arises between the shareholders, who have limited financial resources at stake but possess the control rights—which may be used to determine risk mitigation practices at the CCP—and the clearing members, who are liable for the lion's share of the losses but have a limited say on the default waterfall and risk mitigation practices at the CCP.[112] This raises the

---

[107] CPSS, 'Market Structure Developments in the Clearing Industry' (n 2), p. 63.

[108] Saguato, 'The Ownership of Clearinghouses' (n 101), 601, 612.

[109] See, e.g. Allianz, Blackrock, Citigroup, Goldman Sachs, Societé Generale, J.P. Morgan, State Street, T. Rowe Price, and Vanguard, 'A Path Forward for CCP Resilience, Recovery, and Resolution', White Paper (24 October 2019), https://www.goldmansachs.com/media-relations/press-releases/current/multimedia/ccp-paper.pdf (accessed 24 March 2023) (Allianz et al., 'A Path Forward for CCP Resilience, Recovery, and Resolution').

[110] Baker, 'Incomplete Clearinghouse Mandates' (n 106), 507, 550.

[111] Wenqian Huang, 'Central Counterparty Capitalization and Misaligned Incentives', BIS Working Papers No. 767 (February 2019), p. 3; Stephen J. Lubben, 'Always Crashing in the Same Car—Clearinghouse Rescue in the United States under Dodd–Frank' (2017) 3 Journal of Financial Regulation 133, 147; Lemuria Carter, Jennifer Hancock, and Mark Manning, 'Ownership, Incentives and Regulation of CCP Risks', in Martin Diehl, Biliana Alexandrova-Kabadjova, Richard Heuver, Serafin Martínez-Jaramillo (eds), Analyzing the Economics of Financial Market Infrastructures (Hershey: IGI Global, 2016), pp. 272, 278; Yesha Yadav, 'Clearinghouses and Regulation by Proxy' (2014) 43 Georgia Journal of International and Comparative Law 161, 166, 173, 179; Adam J. Levitin, 'Response: The Tenuous Case for Derivatives Clearinghouses' (2013) 101 Georgetown Law Journal 445, 463–464.

[112] Saguato, 'The Ownership of Clearinghouses' (n 101), 601, 642 et seq.

question of whether current shareholder structures of CCPs are optimal from a govern-ance perspective.

According to one strand in legal scholarship, this is not the case. These authors have pleaded for the 'remutualization' of CCPs so that CCP governance rights may return to the entities that bear the greatest risk in case of losses arising from clearing member or CCP default.[113] In the same vein, clearing members have tried to reinforce their gov-ernance positions within CCPs (e.g. by proposing that clearing member voting mech-anisms be introduced)[114] and have pushed for larger skin in the game from the CCP in the default waterfall.[115]

4.3 Consolidation in the Market for Clearing Services?

Another question in relation to CCP governance pertains to the optimal number of competitors in the clearing space. As such, this question is not new,[116] but the evolu-tions outlined in this chapter may have an impact on the answer to the question. Viewed through the narrow and theoretical lens of netting efficiency, a single CCP that clears all financial products in financial markets would be most efficient.[117] On the other hand, from a more practical point of view, concentration of all risks within a single node could produce an uncontrollable risk nucleus, amounting to a single point of failure, especially if coordination across jurisdictions is less than perfect.[118] Furthermore, not every domestic market has the maturity or size to have its own CCP.[119] Complete con-solidation would also mean that competition is eliminated entirely from the market for clearing services, which could have detrimental effects, inter alia in terms of in-novation. Against this background, further consolidation in the market for clearing services may be expected. Additionally, future public-sector interventions could also contemplate consolidation, following on the Eurosystem example of Target2-Securities (T2S) for the securities settlement space or the creation of CLS as a public–private part-nership in the foreign exchange (FX) payment space.

---

[113] Gerding, 'Remutualization' (n 101); Baker, 'Incomplete Clearinghouse Mandates' (n 106); Saguato, 'The Ownership of Clearinghouses' (n 101). See, however, Sean J. Griffith, 'Governing Systemic Risk: Towards a Governance Structure for Derivatives Clearinghouses' (2012) 61 Emory Law Journal 1153, 1201 et seq.

[114] One venue through which clearing members can currently already voice their opinions on CCP risk man-agement is the CCP risk committee. See, on the CCP risk committee, EMIR (n 3), Art. 28(1).

[115] See, e.g. Allianz et al., 'A Path Forward for CCP Resilience, Recovery, and Resolution' (n 109). Cf. Saguato, 'The Ownership of Clearinghouses' (n 101), 601, 643.

[116] See, e.g. Huang, The Law and Regulation of Central Counterparties (n 73), pp. 180 et seq.

[117] Tanega and Savi, 'Central Clearing Counterparties for OTC-Users' (n 8), 825, 844–845; Heath et al. 'CCPs and Network Stability' (n 8), 217, 219; Duffie and Zhu, 'Does a Central Clearing Counterparty Reduce Counterparty Risk?' (n 7), 74, 75. Cf. Chang, 'The Systemic Risk Paradox' (n 73), 747, 780; Huang, The Law and Regulation of Central Counterparties (n 73), pp. 180 et seq. The ECB has reported that investment banks in the EU were already calling for a single CCP as early as 2001: ECB, 'The Eurosystem's Policy Line with Regard to Consolidation in Central Counterparty Clearing' (27 September 2001), p. 1, https://www.ecb.europa.eu/paym/pdf/market/secmar/centralcounterpartyclearing.pdf (accessed 24 March 2023).

[118] Centre for European Policy Studies (CEPS), 'Setting EU CCP Policy—Much More Than Meets the Eye' (28 October 2021), p. 41, https://www.ceps.eu/ceps-publications/setting-eu-ccp-policy-much-more-than-meets-the-eye (accessed 24 March 2023).

[119] Cf. Kiff et al., 'Applying the Central Clearing Mandate' (n 69), p. 15.

4.4 Clearing as a Public Service

A final governance consideration is whether the provision of central clearing to financial markets should not be seen as a public good in view of the inherent and increasing mitigation of systemic risks. Traditionally, a number of CCPs has been publicly owned, usually by central banks. In other areas, such as large value payment systems, public ownership is even more widespread. The rationale behind public ownership in these cases is that central clearing is considered to be a public utility service, which should not be driven by profit considerations because competition between private commercial actors may encourage arbitrage on margin and default fund calculations. Additionally, central bank involvement may facilitate access to central bank liquidity and collateral management services.

5 Conclusions

Financial markets are in constant flux. New players and services, often leveraging new technology, emerge and challenge the status quo. Changes in markets, regulation, the environment, and global politics affect the business and risk profiles of financial market participants. The central clearing sector is no exception to this. Moreover, with its crucial position as a bulwark against systemic instability, the central clearing sector sits at the heart of modern financial markets and is particularly exposed to the speed of the ever-evolving financial system. In view of this, complacency of CCPs, but also of CCP regulators and supervisors, is not an option. Emerging risks need to be identified, understood, and—to the fullest extent possible—mitigated. At the same time, the role and function of CCPs should be reviewed at regular intervals, to make sure that (i) they are still fulfilling their potential as sophisticated risk managers, in particular in the OTC derivatives market segment; (ii) their benefits still exceed the costs and risks; and (iii) the ecosystem supporting CCPs, including their regulatory underpinning as well as the design and architecture of CCP governance and ownership, is best suited to support both domestic and global markets. Based on recent evolutions and policy initiatives, this concluding chapter has aimed to formulate conjectures about the directions in which centrally cleared OTC derivatives markets may develop in the future. Given the inherently forward-looking nature of this exercise, our analysis has necessarily been incomplete. As the future unfolds, we will find out more about the direction of travel for centrally cleared OTC derivatives markets.

Index

For the benefit of digital users, indexed terms that span two pages (e.g., 52–53) may, on occasion, appear on only one of those pages.

Tables and figures are indicated by *t* and *f* following the page number